International Arbitration and Mediation

KLUWER LAW INTERNATIONAL

International Arbitration and Mediation

A Practical Guide

Michael McIlwrath

John Savage

Wolters Kluwer

Law & Business

AUSTIN   BOSTON   CHICAGO   NEW YORK   THE NETHERLANDS

Published by:
Kluwer Law International
PO Box 316
2400 AH Alphen aan den Rijn
The Netherlands
Website: www.kluwerlaw.com

Sold and distributed in North, Central and South America by:
Aspen Publishers, Inc.
7201 McKinney Circle
Frederick, MD 21704
United States of America
Email: customer.service@aspenpublishers.com

Sold and distributed in all other countries by:
Turpin Distribution Services Ltd.
Stratton Business Park
Pegasus Drive, Biggleswade
Bedfordshire SG18 8TQ
United Kingdom
Email: kluwerlaw@turpin-distribution.com

Printed on acid-free paper.

ISBN 978-90-411-2610-8

© 2010 Kluwer Law International BV, The Netherlands

Printed in Great Britain.

Table of Contents

Chapter Two
Negotiating an International Dispute Resolution Agreement

Chapter Three
When the Dispute Arises

Introduction

Today's business world is about risk. Those who can accept risk – and manage the **I-001** downside – will be rewarded. In international contracts, dispute resolution often is or should be the single most important consideration in deciding whether a particular risk is one to accept. The value of the contract may ultimately reside in how any disputes arising out of it will be resolved. Indeed, a contract may contain a whole package of risk mitigation devices, such as limitations of liability, warranties, and rights of termination for non-performance or recovery in the event of wrongful termination, but if there is no certainty that these provisions will be enforced, it can effectively be the same as having no contract at all.

This book is chiefly intended as a resource for those indispensable advisers – in- **I-002** house lawyers and their counterparts in private practice – who counsel businesses on questions of dispute resolution when planning and documenting international deals, and who work with the same clients to achieve a successful resolution when disputes emerge. We attempt to provide concrete answers to practical business questions, explain how to accept risks rather than avoid them, predict the likely consequences (and costs) of decisions, and suggest legal strategies that do more than pursue litigation victories at any cost. The underlying assumption is that a 'successful' result of a dispute will always be defined by how close it comes to achieving a party's commercial goals.

Another of our aims is to assist parties in the imperfect world in which business is **I-003** done, rather than provide an objective, abstract discussion of the theory of dispute resolution in its different forms. For example, we do not assume that dispute resolution clauses are 'drafted' in a vacuum in which the proposing party always has its clause accepted by the other contracting party, and we acknowledge that there are dangers in stressing one form of dispute resolution at the expense of real-world commercial needs. Take, for example, the dispute resolution clause in this valet parking ticket from a hotel in New Delhi:

Example Ia – Dispute Resolution Clause

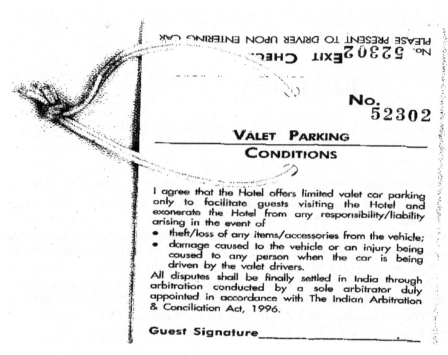

Presumably, the hotel inserted the arbitration clause in its valet parking tickets to avoid being subjected to inefficient local courts when disputes arise with customers who complain of damage or losses. Perhaps the hotel believes this clause will discourage small or frivolous claims by imposing the additional cost of an arbitrator. That may be, but the cost will also be imposed on the hotel, possibly in addition to having to litigate the matter before the courts. In fact, the courts may be called to decide in the first instance the enforceability of a dispute resolution clause contained in a stub given to customers as they walk to the hotel registration desk.

I-004 The real question, however, is whether the hotel wishes to manage its valet parking claims through an artful legal practice or by accepting the risk of inefficient courts and relying on good customer management to avoid ending up there. It is unlikely the hotel will ever be in the position of asserting claims against its valet parking customers, so the inefficiencies of the courts may even be to the hotel's advantage. At the same time, an arbitration clause in this context can create an impression that the hotel wishes to create an obstacle for customers who may have meritorious claims. Assuming this clause is enforceable (already a large assumption), is there really any commercial advantage to including it in the valet parking stub? As we discuss throughout this book, there are many instances in which arbitration will represent the better approach to resolving disputes. However, it would be wrong to assume it will be optimal for every intersection of commercial interests.

Rather, we recognise that the most important contracts for a business will almost **I-005** always be negotiated texts that require substantial compromise. Likewise, we recognise that most parties exist in a resource-constrained environment in which their willingness to subject themselves to different forms of dispute resolution will depend not only on concerns over fairness but on the costs they will incur along the way, and whether those costs are justified. Not all businesses will have the luxury (or leverage) to insist on dispute resolution in their backyard under their home country's laws, and there may be financial rewards for those who can get comfortable with and accept, the other side's preferences. Recognising this, we present international arbitration as an established means of mitigating the risk of dispute resolution away from home, as an area of legal practice that is accessible rather than esoteric. We believe arbitration can be astutely supplemented through a considered and strategic use of mediation, which, while less established than arbitration in international practice today, appears to be spreading at an even faster rate.

Our focus is on international rather than domestic disputes. Access to effective **I-006** dispute resolution is a cornerstone of a business' ability to grow outside of its home market, and the resolution of international disputes – disputes between parties from different nations – often presents a series of challenges not encountered in the domestic context. In particular, many parties in an international business relationship will desire a neutral dispute resolution forum, such as international arbitration, rather than the other party's courts. This concern should be irrelevant to two parties from the same country, as they share the same national courts and should be equally comfortable (or uncomfortable) bringing their disputes before them, with a possible exception where one party is a local subsidiary of a foreign parent. Also, enforcement of decisions across national borders can be tricky, although international arbitration often makes it easier.

We examine the whole of the international dispute resolution process, from the **I-007** outset – when parties agree in their contracts how to resolve disputes – through any disputes that emerge, and concluding with the endgame of enforcement. We emphasise the range of methods of dispute resolution and, notably, the settlement of international business disputes through negotiation that can be facilitated by mediation.

We do not advocate any particular form of dispute resolution as the preferred **I-008** option for every case, and we believe that even when one form of dispute resolution is the best option, a party would be wise to challenge the received wisdom (if it can identify one) as to how it should be conducted. A party's business objectives should set the direction, not someone else's perceptions of how to proceed. The considerations that go into the decision of whether to include arbitration in a valet parking ticket are not so different from those behind a complex international contract. Legal concepts must be connected with realistic commercial objectives, or they may do more harm than good. No sensible lawyer would recommend the same terms and conditions for all contracts. Given the range of available dispute resolution systems, and the diversity of contracts in international business, it would be similarly unwise to adopt a 'one-size-fits-all' approach to disputes clauses.

I.   ORGANISATION OF THIS BOOK

I-009 We have tried to make the book user friendly. This means using straightforward language, with a presentation style that includes checklists and panels to highlight important issues. We also share anecdotes that generally consist of our own, sometimes unhappy experiences over the years. We have assumed that a party involved in an international dispute will have practical questions such as 'how long will it take, how much will it cost, and will we be able to enforce it?' We have tried to provide practical, direct answers. We also include forms and other resources in the appendices, including sample arbitration clauses and submissions.

I-010 The book is divided into chapters that follow the life cycle of an international commercial dispute, as seen through the eyes of the parties. Chapter 1, *The Elements of an International Dispute Resolution Agreement*, does what it says by explaining the various components of a dispute resolution clause. We also try to provide some guidance to parties by evaluating which elements would work best for their different contracts, such as which institutions may be 'better' at administering an international arbitration or organising an international mediation, and the countries where the environment is most favourable to the conduct of international dispute resolution. In Chapter 2, *Negotiating an International Dispute Resolution Agreement*, we acknowledge that the dispute resolution clause of most international contracts will present an opportunity for parties to negotiate, and we suggest different risk assessment and negotiation strategies to help the parties optimise the agreed method of resolution.

I-011 With Chapters 3 and 4, we shift gears and focus on the dispute that is now under-way or about to be. In Chapter 3, *When the Dispute Arises*, we discuss how parties can improve their positions before proceedings are commenced, from taking threshold preliminary steps to preserve their rights to deciding whether and how to appoint counsel, performing an early case assessment (ECA), and calculating the likely costs of the dispute. Having estimated outcomes and costs of resorting to proceedings in Chapter 3, we suggest ways of improving on the potential results in Chapter 4, *International Settlement Negotiation and Mediation*. The premise of this chapter is that once armed with a reasonable estimate of the likely outcome and costs of achieving it, a party is well-positioned to seek a superior result through settlement.

Chapters 5 to 7, by contrast, assume that settlement efforts have failed, and we **I-012** return to the topic of international arbitration as the contractually selected means of achieving a final disposition of the parties' dispute. Chapter 5, *The Conduct of the Arbitration*, provides a step-by-step guide to the unfolding proceedings, paying special attention to the opportunities presented for parties to influence the course of the arbitration. At the end of Chapter 5, we assume that the parties will have an arbitration award in hand. Chapter 6, *After the Arbitration: Challenge, Recognition, and Enforcement of the Award*, addresses the many difficult issues related to the challenge and enforcement of that award. Chapter 7, *ICSID and Investment Treaty Arbitration*, is designed to provide guidance about the special protections that investment treaties offer parties doing business in foreign countries. We discuss how parties can enhance their access to those protections through their contracting practices and how disputes are likely to be resolved when these protections are available.

II.   INTERNATIONAL ARBITRATION

At this stage, we should specify what we mean by 'international' dispute resolution **I-013** and how it differs from domestic forms of litigation, mediation, and arbitration in the country of one of the parties.

While international arbitration may be seen as the natural alternative to litigation in **I-014** domestic courts, it also stands in contrast to 'domestic arbitration'. Domestic arbitration is in many cases just a slightly modified form of litigation as conducted before the courts of the place of arbitration, only before arbitrators and not judges. Unfortunately for many parties, the advantages of an international arbitration are easy to lose if a party does not defend its expectation of a truly international proceeding.

International arbitration defined. Arbitration is a process by which parties agree to **I-015** the binding resolution of their disputes by adjudicators, known as arbitrators, who are selected by the parties, either directly or indirectly via a mechanism chosen by the parties. The three key criteria are thus that arbitration is always a product of agreement between the disputing parties (which distinguishes it from court litigation, which need not be chosen by the parties together), the dispute is resolved by people selected by the parties (which also distinguishes arbitration from court litigation, where parties do not select their judge), and the resolution is binding (which distinguishes arbitration from non-binding processes such as mediation).

There is much discussion in the literature, as well as provisions in arbitration laws **I-016** and rules, about what an 'international' arbitration is. Strictly speaking, an international arbitration is likely to be defined as an arbitration between parties of different nationalities, or an arbitration between parties of the same nationality where there are one or more other factors that connect the arbitration to a second country. These could be the place of arbitration or perhaps the subject matter of the dispute being in that second country, or even the applicability of a foreign law.

I-017 As a practical matter, however, an arbitration meeting the above criteria can too easily lose its 'international' character in matters of procedure when it is conducted by arbitrators and counsel who come from the same country. Parties may unintentionally make counsel and arbitrator appointments that lead to such an outcome. This risk – and how to avoid it – is discussed in more detail in Chapter 3, *When the Dispute Arises*, and Chapter 5, *The Conduct of the Arbitration*.

I-018 *Increased harmonisation of international practice.* As international arbitration grows as the standard method of resolving disputes arising out of international business transactions, an increasingly harmonised practice has begun to emerge around the world. This can be seen in the convergence of modern municipal arbitration statutes, the rules of the leading arbitral institutions, the promulgation of international standards for use in arbitration, such as the International Bar Association (IBA) Rules of Evidence and the IBA Guidelines on Conflicts, and procedural practices commonly adopted in proceedings. The resulting law and practice of this form of truly transnational arbitration is a hybrid between civil-law and common-law procedures, which is considered to be suitable for the resolution of disputes between parties of different nationalities, often represented by counsel from different parts of the world, who are usually appearing before a multinational tribunal.

Not that this ever really happens	The claimant was from an eastern European country, and the respondent from southern Europe. Their dispute arose under a contract that required the claimant to build a substantial portion of the respondent's infrastructure, which the respondent refused to honour. Although the contract provided for any disputes to be decided in London, under English law, the claimant appointed an eminent Belgian lawyer as arbitrator. The respondent appointed a well-known English barrister as arbitrator. The party-appointed arbitrators selected as chair an English lawyer practicing in Paris, with considerable experience of international arbitration. The respondent appointed English counsel known for his capabilities in English domestic litigation. Despite the connections with England (place of arbitration, governing law, the nationality of two arbitrators, and one side's law firm), the respondent found itself at a net disadvantage when the arbitrators opted for an international approach to the proceedings, and the respondent's insistence on English procedural points fell on deaf ears.

I-019 *The international arbitration 'bar'.* Further evidence of harmonisation includes the emergence of an international arbitration bar, comprised of lawyers from different countries and backgrounds who are truly specialised in the area. Likewise, there is now a large community of international arbitrators, which overlaps to a certain extent with the international arbitration bar. These lawyers and arbitrators serve in arbitrations around the world, not merely in arbitrations in their home country. Their practices increasingly focus exclusively or predominantly on international arbitration, which is not conducted as an offshoot of their main domestic litigation or transactional practice. The proceedings in which these lawyers and arbitrators are involved may bear little resemblance to the procedures of the courts of the place of the arbitration, or indeed of any other courts, but will often closely resemble dozens of other arbitrations being heard at the same time in different locations around the globe.

'Local' international arbitration. Not all international arbitration meets this har- **I-020** monised, globalised, and specialised description. There is another group of international arbitrations that are perhaps more reminiscent of the local court system of the place where the arbitration is held. These 'local' international arbitrations are frequently manned by non-specialist lawyers and arbitrators, who are naturally more likely to fall back upon local court procedures with which they are familiar than to follow specialised, internationally accepted practices. For example, both authors have witnessed English barristers representing parties in international arbitrations in London arguing that obscure rules of the English courts should apply because the proceedings in question were 'London arbitrations'. In each case the arbitrators gave our learned friends' submissions short shrift, rightly observing that there is no such thing as a 'London arbitration' in an international context, and that international rules and practices applied.

Sometimes, both disputing parties will be represented by law firms from the place **I-021** of arbitration that have little experience in international arbitration. Both will treat the arbitration in the same way as a local court litigation, and their clients may not know any better. The arbitrators may know better, but faced with counsel on both sides who conduct the arbitration like local court litigation, there is a limit to how much the arbitrators can do about it. In some cases, the arbitrators will also be more familiar with the local courts than with international arbitration, and in some countries are almost invariably retired judges.

Not that this ever really happens	The claimant and the respondent (neither of whom were English) appointed well-known English barristers as co-arbitrators. Perhaps unsurprisingly, the party-appointed arbitrators selected a prominent English barrister as chair. On advice of their external law firms, both parties supplemented their representation by appointing, in addition to external counsel, prominent English barristers to help present their cases before the arbitral tribunal. Both parties found themselves quickly immersed in the idiosyncrasies of English pleading practices rather than procedures more commonly followed in international arbitration.

I-022 *The importance of the international versus local distinction.* Does this distinction between truly international arbitration and local international arbitration matter? It does, at least in that parties who choose international arbitration often do so precisely to avoid local court procedures and to bring neutrality into the proceedings. When a non-English party agrees to arbitration in England, it is unlikely to do so because it hankers after a proceeding that mimics litigation in the English courts; if that is what the non-English party wanted, it would presumably opt directly for the courts. By choosing international arbitration as their dispute resolution mechanism, parties are bargaining for something different: an effective, neutral proceeding that will be equally familiar to both parties, and one which will be adapted to resolving disputes between parties from different countries and cultures. Resolving disputes in this sort of truly international manner forms the principal subject matter of this book.

I-023 *The international enforceability of arbitration awards.* Another crucial feature of international arbitration – whether truly international or 'local' – is the enforceability across borders of international arbitral awards. This is largely the result of the New York Convention of 1958, to which over 140 states are party. It facilitates, in theory at least, the enforcement in those states of awards issued outside those states. While in practice the enforcement record of many Convention states is far from perfect, few will deny that because of the New York Convention an international arbitral award is a title far more valuable internationally than a domestic court judgment.

III.   INTERNATIONAL MEDIATION

I-024 As we discuss in subsequent chapters, mediation can provide numerous advantages to parties as a means of reducing the risk, uncertainty, and cost of international commercial disputes. The main challenge facing mediation today is that it remains virtually unknown or relatively little practiced in many countries. To encourage and increase its use as a means of settling commercial disputes, some companies have adopted a preference for mediation as a matter of contracting policy, while others have signed 'pledges' by which they agree to attempt to resolve any disputes through mediation before proceeding with binding dispute resolution. There really is no equivalent of such broad 'pledges' by which parties commit outside their contracts to resolve commercial disputes via arbitration, and it is unlikely there ever will be, given the nature of arbitration and the fact that (unlike mediation, in our view) it may not be appropriate for each contract.[1]

I-025 *How international mediation compares with domestic mediation.* The formalities and 'procedural' aspects of mediation can have little, if any, variation from one

---

1.   This is not to ignore the fact that some industries have an accepted practice of making arbitration their preferred form of dispute resolution between parties commonly trading within that industry (the reinsurance industry being a good example).

domestic practice to another or when conducted internationally. Mediation is in most respects more similar to negotiation than to litigation or arbitration, and negotiation is something that most parties are already familiar and comfortable with. Thus, a party or counsel with experience with domestic mediation in one country would likely feel comfortable mediating a dispute in another country, or in an international context more generally.

International mediation defined. The term 'international mediation' merits some **I-026** explanation. In the context of the commercial disputes discussed in this book, it is an attempt by parties to an international commercial transaction to reach settlement through the assistance of a neutral third party, and nothing more. It is an emphatically distinct form of resolving disputes and is not, contrary to one common misconception, a form of 'mini-arbitration' or 'non-binding arbitration'.

Challenge of getting to mediation. Mediation can provide parties a proven means **I-027** of avoiding disputes or simplifying the process of their resolution. But despite the suitability of mediation for resolving international commercial disputes, parties should not assume that their counterparts will be familiar with and willing to consider it when a dispute arises. This is because mediation suffers from a level of awareness among lawyers and businesses that varies significantly with geographic location. For example, the same proposal to mediate that meets with scepticism in Italy or Sweden may stand a good chance of being accepted in the United Kingdom, Norway, or North America. This does not mean that Italian and Swedish lawyers, or their clients, are not able to settle cases on positive terms for their clients. It simply means that these legal cultures have not developed an awareness of mediation in the same way as has occurred in other jurisdictions where it is regularly used as a tool to resolve commercial disputes.

Not that this ever really happens	One of the authors, the in-house counsel, first proposed mediation to a counterparty in a coastal city in the south of Italy, in a dispute with a construction supplier that had sued for alleged extra costs on a project in Russia. The offer was accompanied with a polite statement that the company was willing to find the right solution and an explanation of what the in-house counsel had read about how mediation might move the parties beyond their deadlock. Opposing counsel dismissed the offer, with a wave of the hand and scoffing: 'We already have a neutral third party to decide our dispute: the judge!' End of meeting; end of settlement discussions. This was in 1999, and as of this writing the case is still pending in the courts, on appeal. The supplier has collected nothing on its claims in the interim and is now in liquidation.

In some countries, particularly those with emerging economies in which govern- **I-028** ments participate strongly in the ownership and management of a significant portion of the nation's commercial activity, mediation (or any form of settlement) may face bureaucratic or other institutional obstacles, such as the fear that settlement may signal a manager's incompetence or even corruption. This is unfortunate, because it is often those countries where more efficient forms of dispute resolution are most needed.

Not that this ever really happens	The second time the in-house counsel among the authors offered mediation to a counterparty was in a developing country, and although it was also a failure (in terms of getting a mediation started), at least the rejection was polite. The general manager of a government-owned entity said that he appreciated the explanation of what mediation might accomplish in helping the parties avoid the arbitration that was getting underway, but he did not want the suspicion of corruption that a settlement might create. So it was better for him not to settle and let the arbitration continue. This was also in 1999, and at the time of this writing the arbitration is still pending.

IV. INTERNATIONAL MEDIATION AND ARBITRATION AS RISK MITIGATORS

I-029 The value of international mediation and arbitration as tools for doing business is thus that parties can enter into contracts globally having reduced their concerns about dispute resolution. In the best of cases, they will settle any disputes before embarking on any formal proceedings. And, when disputes are not settled at the outset, international arbitration should avoid the necessity of knowing and understanding the idiosyncrasies of local dispute resolution. But it will provide this benefit only if a party takes positive steps to preserve the international character of dispute resolution and resist the forces tugging it towards domestic procedures.

Chapter One

The Elements of an International Dispute Resolution Agreement

Parties to cross-border contracts can agree to submit disputes to a particular form of **1-001** dispute resolution both before and after those disputes arise. This dispute resolution agreement in most instances is a clause that the parties insert into a broader contact between them (usually described as the main contract). Occasionally, they may decide after a dispute arises that they prefer arbitration over the available courts and enter into a 'submission agreement', by which they agree to submit their existing dispute to arbitration even though their contract makes no provision for it. In contrast, mediation was traditionally proposed only after a dispute arose, but the cost of arbitration and litigation is increasingly leading parties to agree in advance to attempt settlement through mediation before they can proceed to arbitration or the courts. This is often through a mediation requirement in the dispute resolution clause.

Parties and commentators often refer to the 'drafting' of dispute clauses, a term that **1-002** does not nearly capture the degree of negotiation and compromise that may take place before a final text is agreed. While we discuss the negotiation of dispute clauses in Chapter 2, in this chapter we look at the elements that a dispute clause may or should contain. We consider the broad range of available options that, if clearly expressed, will ensure that disputes will be resolved as the parties expected, as well as the practical implications of a failure to develop and express an effective dispute resolution agreement.

The danger of an incomplete or unclear dispute clause. If the contract fails to set **1-003** out the most basic elements of dispute resolution, or is not clear in stating what those elements are, a variety of difficult subsidiary disputes may arise, which may weaken a party's settlement leverage and prevent the merits being decided effectively. This can happen (1) even before a settlement negotiation is initiated, for example when the lack of an effective dispute option reduces the potential claimant's negotiation leverage and expectations; (2) at the inception of legal proceedings when one party refers a dispute to a court or arbitration, while the other objects that the forum was not the one chosen by the parties; (3) during the arbitration, as for example when one party contests the tribunal's jurisdiction to decide certain of the claims before it; or (4) after the arbitration, when the losing party applies to have the award set aside, or resists enforcement, on grounds such as that the parties did not agree to submit the decided issues to arbitration. This chapter explores methods for negotiating the text of an arbitration clause in order to avoid these sorts of problems.

Not that this ever really happens: the financial impact of a defective dispute clause *before* **legal action is initiated**	Party A's representatives had scheduled a meeting at the offices of Party B in Madrid in an effort to settle Party B's refusal to pay the EUR 1.5 million that remained due to Party A under the contract. A minor technical issue was being raised to justify non-payment, but the real reason was not a secret. Party B had found itself in financial difficulties and was selectively resisting or delaying payments to as many of its suppliers as it could. In preparing for the meeting, Party A discovered that the dispute resolution clause in its contract provided for 'any disagreements under the contract to be settled by arbitration under the Spanish Institute of Arbitration, with any dispute to be submitted for binding resolution under the rules of the International Chamber of Commerce (ICC) in Paris. Acceptance of arbitration, however, shall not deprive the Court of Madrid to hear any actual disputes that may exist between the parties'. Realising that the initiation of legal proceedings would first require years of litigating the question of whether the dispute should be heard in the court or one of the mentioned arbitration institutions (one of which did not appear to exist), Party A lowered its expectations and settled for a payment of EUR 400,000. The 'cost' of a defective dispute clause, in this case, was over EUR 1 million even before litigation or arbitration was started.

I.   DIFFERENT SORTS OF INTERNATIONAL DISPUTE
           RESOLUTION CLAUSES

1-004 There are several different sorts of agreement that parties may use to provide for the resolution of an international commercial dispute. The principal ones among them are introduced in paragraphs 1-005 to 1-009 below.

Agreements to submit disputes to court. Where the parties to a contract have agreed **1-005** to refer their disputes to court, they will typically set out that agreement in a clause in their main contract, often referred to as a forum selection clause. That clause will usually designate one or more courts to which a party may or must refer any dispute that arises out of the contract, and will often specify whether or not the jurisdiction of the designated courts is exclusive or not. If the jurisdiction of a court is stated to be exclusive, the intention is that a party cannot sue the other in another court. If it is non-exclusive, the intention is that a party cannot object to the jurisdiction of that court, but can sue in another court if it wishes. If there is no forum selection clause and no arbitration agreement, a party can start legal action against its counterparty in any court that will accept jurisdiction over the dispute.

Agreements to arbitrate. Arbitration is a creature of contract. An arbitration agree- **1-006** ment, or agreement to arbitrate, is itself the contract in which parties agree to refer disputes between them to arbitration. It most often takes the form of an arbitration clause inserted in the parties' main contract, but it can also be an independent agreement entered into before, at the same time as, or after the main contract. If the arbitration agreement is concluded after the dispute arises, it is known as a sub-mission agreement (paragraph 1-009 below). Although arbitration agreements may be part of the parties' main contract, they survive the termination or breach of the main contract except in the rare cases where the parties agree otherwise. In other words, even though the contractual relations between the parties may have ended, their agreement to submit disputes to arbitration will continue. Where a party has entered into a valid arbitration agreement, it must submit disputes covered by that agreement to arbitration, and courts will enforce the arbitration agreement by declining to hear disputes covered by it and referring the parties instead to arbitration.

Agreements to mediate: in the shadow of agreements to litigate or arbitrate. **1-007** Agreements to mediate obey many of the same principles as agreements to arbi-trate and will also survive the termination or breach of the main contract. Importantly, an agreement to mediate will only complement an arbitration clause; it will not replace the need for binding dispute resolution. In fact, the presence of a credible threat of effective, binding dispute resolution will encourage parties to engage constructively in negotiation or mediation. Particular attention should therefore be paid to what is needed to construct an arbitration clause with teeth and how to include a mediation provision that may avert the need for that arbitra-tion to take place. In many jurisdictions a mediation agreement will require the parties to attempt mediation but, unlike with arbitration, does not compel them to continue with the process if it is not to their liking.

Agreements to arbitrate in investment treaties. A relatively new and unusual form **1-008** of agreement to arbitrate is that found in investment treaty arbitration, where a state party to the investment treaty makes a general offer of arbitration in the treaty to a category of investors from the other state party, and one or more members of that investor group perfects the arbitration agreement by accepting the offer of arbitration when a dispute arises.[1]

1-009 *Submission agreements.* Parties enter into a submission agreement when they are already in dispute and agree to submit that dispute to arbitration, despite the absence of an existing arbitration agreement. Although submission agreements obey the same principles as other arbitration agreements, they are less common because parties with a pending dispute seldom agree on the forum for resolving it. While there is no formal practice of 'submission agreements' with respect to mediation, mediators commonly require parties to enter into a 'mediation agreement' irrespective of whether there is a requirement to mediate in the contract.[2]

II.   THE BASIC COMPONENTS OF AN INTERNATIONAL DISPUTE RESOLUTION AGREEMENT

1-010 Dispute resolution clauses that contemplate arbitration consist of at least four sorts of components: first, the submission or reference of disputes to the chosen form of dispute resolution, which is the essence of the agreement; second, a number of important variables, such as the place, language, and rules of arbitration; third, optional 'bells and whistles'– features that are not strictly needed to ensure an effective dispute resolution agreement, but which the parties may choose to include to enhance the agreement in view of their own circumstances; and fourth, any requirement to attempt mediation before arbitration or court action may be initiated. The first three components are presented in turn below, followed by special attention to the provision for mediation.

1-011 *The benefits of simplicity and recommended institutional clauses.* Before getting to the specifics, we give a general word of advice to anyone involved in the negotiation or drafting of a dispute resolution clause: it is important to keep dispute resolution agreements as simple as possible. The more complex they are, the more scope there is for internal inconsistencies and other difficulties of interpretation, which a defending party can exploit before, during or after any proceeding (e.g., by raising objections to the jurisdiction of an arbitral tribunal, or seeking to set aside or resist enforcement of an arbitral award). The leading arbitral institutions all publish model or standard arbitration clauses that are clear, simple, and effective. They contain the submission of disputes to arbitration and explain what the variables are (the parties then have to agree on those variables). They contain few or none of the optional 'bells and whistles' that can often be redundant or counterproductive. Parties are often wise to prefer these sorts of simple, effective arbitration agreements over the long and intricate offerings often put forward by lawyers in large

---

1. The same sort of arbitration agreement is formed where a state makes, in an investment law, an offer of arbitration to investors, which an investor with a claim against the state later accepts. Chapter 7, *ICSID and Investment Treaty Arbitration*.
2. Chapter 4, *International Settlement Negotiation and Mediation*.

transactions. Even in complex transactions, simple institutional model clauses are good starting points and can easily be adapted to reflect the agreement of the parties.

The probability of negotiation and the limitations of boilerplate. While the clauses **1-012** recommended by arbitration institutions are simple, good, and in many instances will suffice even in a complex agreement, that does not mean that parties to complex and highly negotiated contracts should slavishly cut and paste arbitration agreements from institutions' websites, or from previous contracts for that matter, without giving consideration to any special needs that may arise in the course of the contract's performance. And even when a party wishes to cut and paste a boilerplate clause, this may not be possible. An arbitration clause has significant value independent of the other clauses of the contract and each party will want to enhance the protection of its own interests and to mitigate its own perceptions of risk. Thus, while it is fine to speak of how to 'draft' an international dispute resolution clause, it is better to be prepared to *negotiate* one, with consideration for the types of disputes that might arise.

Not that this ever really happens	The seller, a US company, appeared at the contract negotiations prepared to discuss price and delivery terms and assuming that the buyer would accept the seller's international terms and conditions of sale, which provided for ICC arbitration in New York, under New York law. The buyer, an Egyptian company, was prepared to discuss and be flexible on price and delivery but insisted on dispute resolution in Cairo. While both parties were happy with their negotiated price and delivery terms, they were unable to reach agreement on the form of dispute resolution to be adopted, and negotiations over what each side viewed as a profitable contract were delayed for six months while each waited for the other to move from their position on dispute resolution.

A.   THE CORE OF THE ARBITRATION AGREEMENT: SUBMISSION OF DISPUTES TO ARBITRATION

The operative sentence of an arbitration agreement identifies a group of disputes **1-013** that may arise in the future (or an existing dispute, in the rare case of a submission agreement) and stipulates that the disputes thus identified will or may be resolved by arbitration.

Identification of disputes. Looking first at the identification of the disputes to be **1-014** referred to arbitration, the usual practice is to identify as broad a group as could possibly be connected with the contract. Typical wording is 'all disputes arising out of or in connection with this contract'. Assuming the parties do want to refer all disputes arising out of their contract to arbitration, they should look no further than this simple, catch-all language. It will cover claims based on contract as well as those sounding in tort or other extra-contractual theories. It will also cover claims or defences that the contract never came into existence, as well as disputes regarding the termination of the contract. Trying to be more specific in one's identification of disputes can be hazardous: one example is where parties agree to refer 'all disputes concerning the interpretation or performance of this contract' to arbitration, intending this to cover all disputes arising out of the contract. It is arguable that such a clause would not cover claims or defences concerning the termination of the contract, or concerning the existence of the contract in the first place. If contracting parties feel the urge to be more specific in their definition of disputes to be referred to arbitration, they can begin with the catch-all language and then add the more specifically described disputes as a subset of the broader group of disputes. Appropriate language in such a case would be 'all disputes arising out of or in connection with this contract including, without limitation, disputes concerning the interpretation or performance of this contract'.

1-015 It is perhaps possible to further enhance the enforceability of an arbitration clause by expanding the category of matters that are to be referred to arbitration. For example, instead of simply referring to 'disputes', one sometimes sees broader language such as 'all disputes, disagreements, claims, or controversies',[3] which may then be given the defined term 'disputes'. How much difference this sort of wording will make is unclear, but it is unlikely to reduce the effectiveness of the arbitration clause so there is little harm in including it.

1-016 *Carve-outs for certain types of disputes.* If the parties want certain disputes to be referred to arbitration, but not others, they can draft their clause accordingly. A common example is where parties wish to submit technical matters for resolution by experts, with other disputes resolved by arbitrators. These sorts of clauses need to be carefully drafted, to minimise later disagreement over which dispute belongs in which forum. For example, if the dispute is whether equipment should be repaired or replaced during a warranty period, should it be treated as a technical matter (a problem with the equipment) or a legal or commercial matter (the application of the contractual warranty)? The answer may unfortunately be both, giving the claimant the option of choosing which forum to proceed in, and the respondent an opportunity to contest jurisdiction no matter which forum is chosen. Clauses referring disputes to expert resolution are also troublesome because of the uncertain legal status of expert determination: is it arbitration, or is it some other form of dispute resolution? Another difficult issue is the relationship between the expert

---

3. See the SCC Model Clause: 'Any dispute, controversy or claim arising out of or in connection with this contract, or the breach, termination or invalidity thereof . . .'. See also the UNCITRAL Model Clause proposed by the SIAC: 'Any dispute, controversy or claim arising out of or relating to this contract, or the breach, termination or invalidity thereof . . . .'

determination provision and the arbitration clause: are the arbitrators able to reopen matters determined by an expert and, if so, in which circumstances?

Modern presumption in favour of arbitration and (hopefully) the demise of the 'under' versus 'out of' debate	Parties to international contracts should be aware that the language of their arbitration clause may need to be tested in the courts of more than one country, and they should therefore strive for clarity (and avoid language that may lead to the unfortunate result that their dispute is held to be not covered by the arbitration agreement). Still, they may find comfort in the modern trend in which the courts of most countries will construe language with a presumption in favour of arbitration. For example, in England, the House of Lords (now the Supreme Court) recently refused to draw a distinction between a dispute 'arising under' and a dispute 'arising out of' the contract; both expressions were construed equally broadly. In its own words, the court made a 'fresh start' and departed from earlier case law that had made semantic distinctions between the phrases 'arising under', 'arising out of', 'in relation to', and 'in connection with' the contract.[4]

Jurisdiction even if there is no 'dispute'? There have been cases where parties **1-017** object to a tribunal's jurisdiction and seek judgment in the courts on the basis that there is no disputed fact or issue – notably that a debt is acknowledged and there is no arguable defence to a claim for its payment – and therefore nothing to refer to arbitration.[5] Although the English courts, in particular, have been tolerant of this sort of argument in the past, most arbitral tribunals and courts are likely to give it short shrift today. If a party considers there to be a dispute and articulates any sort of disagreement between the parties, it should be difficult for the opponent to argue that there is in fact no dispute – at a minimum there is a dispute about whether there is a dispute. Courts will generally find, in the presence of an arbitration agreement, that any disagreement as to whether a dispute exists should be resolved by duly appointed arbitrators. In practical terms, this means that a creditor will generally not have a right to sue immediately in court for payment, and it will need to first go to arbitration. Thus, if a party's only or main concern in drafting a dispute resolution clause is the ability to sue promptly for payment, it should consider whether arbitration is the optimal method of dispute resolution, or whether the courts should be the preferred forum.

---

4. *Premium Nafta Products Limited* (twentieth Defendant) *and others* (Respondents) *v. Fili Shipping Company Limited* (fourteenth Claimant) *and others* (Appellants), 17 Oct. 2007, [2007] UKHL 40.
5. See N. Blackaby & C. Partasides with A. Redfern & M. Hunter, *Redfern & Hunter on International Arbitration*, 5th edn (Oxford: Oxford University Press, 2009), para. 1-059.

B.   REFERRAL TO ARBITRATION

1-018 Once the parties have identified the group of disputes they wish to have resolved (generally being all disputes arising out of the contract), the next stage is to refer those disputes for resolution to arbitration (or other selected method of dispute resolution). This may seem straightforward, but there are at least two issues here. The first is whether the submission of those disputes to arbitration is mandatory; the second is whether the resolution is intended to be final and binding.

1-019 *Direct and unambiguous language.* Parties intending that all their disputes be resolved by arbitration should use suitably directive language, leaving no room for an argument that arbitration is merely optional. So, words such as 'shall be referred' to arbitration are better than 'may be referred', as the use of the word 'may' introduces an element of uncertainty: it could suggest that the parties are not required to submit their disputes to arbitration and are also entitled to submit them to the courts, at least until one of them resorts to arbitration.

Not that this ever really happens	The parties' contract specified that all disputes would be settled by arbitration under the rules of the ICC, except that the buyer had the option of referring any dispute to the courts of its home country at any point before the arbitrators rendered their award. When a dispute arose over non-payment of USD 2 million due under the contract, the seller hesitated to commence arbitration, fearful that it would embark on an expensive and lengthy procedure, only to have a successful decision snatched away by a late decision of the buyer to move the dispute to the local courts. Fortunately for the seller, ICC practice and local procedural law intervened (to the buyer's surprise). By having signed the 'terms of reference' as part of the ICC procedure at the outset of the arbitration,[6] the buyer was deemed to have waived its ability to revoke the jurisdiction of the arbitrators over the dispute.

1-020 *'Final and binding'.* The parties may also specify that resolution by arbitration is to be final and binding, if that is indeed the intention. (The ICC's recommended clause, for example, uses equivalent language, 'finally settled by arbitration'). It is not clear that this wording adds much, as international arbitration is inherently about the binding resolution of disputes, and an arbitral award will likely be held to be final even when those words are not present. But one can't predict the ruling of all judges in all countries on this point, and including the wording does no harm if it reflects the parties' intentions it may at least discourage an opponent from challenging the final and binding nature of an award. Inclusion will certainly make

---

6. Chapter 5, *The Conduct of the Arbitration.*

sense in a contract with different tiers of dispute resolution procedures,[7] to indicate which is the final and binding tier.

Meaning of 'final and binding'. But what does 'final and binding' mean? 'Final' **1-021** describes the arbitral award's status relative to other dispute resolution processes. It means that the dispute is finally resolved and cannot be reopened, subject only to any recourse against the award made available by the law of the arbitration (this recourse is usually an action to set the award aside on a limited number of narrow grounds).[8] 'Binding' describes the effect of the award on the parties: once issued the parties must comply with it, and if they fail to do so of their own accord, it can be enforced against them under the processes established for that purpose by the laws of the places where enforcement is sought. However, where a party commences an action before the courts of the place of arbitration to set the award aside, its binding effect may be suspended.[9]

Language on 'appeal' procedures. Thus, the words 'final and binding' in arbitra- **1-022** tion agreements refer to the determination of the merits of the dispute; they do not mean that once an award is issued all litigation will cease. We have seen that in most cases an action to set the award aside will be available in the courts of the seat of the arbitration.[10] While there will be occasions when parties may wish to include language that allows for either party to appeal a final award, this is generally inadvisable. Arbitration that is subject to some form of review on the merits, whether by a court or by another arbitral tribunal, does not fit easily within the typical legal conception of arbitration as a final and binding process (subject only to actions to set aside). Certainly an arbitration agreement providing for a review of the merits by the courts may not be valid – or at least the part of it that stipulates the review of the merits may not be valid.[11] As a practical matter, implementing an appeal before an arbitral tribunal is likely to be difficult, requiring creative drafting about the appointment of new arbitrators to constitute a separate tribunal for the review of the findings, with further procedures that provide for what would be done in the event of any findings of error in the initial award. Certainly, international arbitration subject to appeal before an arbitral tribunal is not commonly encountered, and major institutions and arbitration rules do not provide for an appeal process within the arbitration. This sort of appeal will inject legal and practical difficulties into the dispute resolution process that would make the outcome less predictable, not more so. Also, having no appeal within the arbitration helps

---

7. Paragraph 1–198 below.
8. Chapter 6, *After the Arbitration.*
9. *Ibid.*
10. Only a handful of countries allow parties to contract out of an action to set aside, and even then a number of conditions need to be fulfilled. Chapter 6, *After the Arbitration.*
11. See, e.g., the judgment of the United States Supreme Court on 25 Mar. 2008 in the *Hall Street Assocs. v. Mattel, Inc.* case, which held that the parties could not agree to expand the grounds for vacatur by the US courts beyond those exclusively listed in the Federal Arbitration Act.

expedite the process.[12] But it does require the parties to have confidence in the arbitration to which they have agreed, which is best achieved through careful drafting of the arbitration agreement and its diligent implementation – particularly when appointing the arbitral tribunal.[13]

1-023 *Summary of essential drafting concepts.* To summarise on the submission of disputes to arbitration or another dispute resolution mechanism, both parties will likely be better served if they cast the net broadly when identifying or defining the disputes to be submitted, then make it clear that those disputes 'shall' be resolved by that method of dispute resolution, and conclude by confirming that the resolution shall be final and binding.

C.   THE FOUR MAIN VARIABLES OF AN INTERNATIONAL
       ARBITRATION CLAUSE

1-024 Once the parties have agreed to submit disputes to arbitration and have expressed that intention in writing, they have the essence of the arbitration agreement. But in order to achieve an effective arbitration, more detail is needed (or highly recommended) regarding the basic characteristics of the proceeding that will take place.[14] In particular, there are four variables that we believe should be addressed in every arbitration agreement, in the following order of priority: (1) the place of arbitration, (2) the arbitral institution or the applicable ad hoc rules if there is to be no institution, (3) the number of arbitrators, and (4) the language of the arbitration.

Procedural versus Substantive Law	Some readers may have noted that we do not include the 'governing' or 'substantive' law of the contract among the important elements of a dispute resolution clause. Despite the fact that a 'governing law' provision is sometimes included in or adjacent to a contractual dispute resolution clause, it is an independent feature that relates to the main contract itself, and not to how the arbitration should be organised and conducted. The substantive or governing law of the contract and the law governing the arbitration procedure (if there is one) are often different.

---

12. Chapter 2, *Negotiating an International Dispute Resolution Agreement.*
13. Chapter 5, *The Conduct of the Arbitration.*
14. An agreement simply to submit disputes to arbitration may not be enough to ensure that an effective arbitration takes place. The clause may not work in practice because it is uncertain, given that there is no stated link between the clause and a specific country, whether the courts in any jurisdiction would agree to appoint arbitrators and thus allow the arbitration to proceed.

1. The Place (or 'Seat') of Arbitration

The importance of the place of arbitration. The most important variable in an **1-025**
international arbitration clause is the place (or 'seat') of arbitration. It is the city
to which the arbitration is legally attached. But this does not mean that any physical
activity, such as hearings or a tribunal's meetings to deliberate, need occur there
(a point discussed later in this chapter). The choice of the place of arbitration brings
with it at least three major legal consequences: (1) it determines, at least in traditional thinking, which municipal law should govern the arbitration (by 'law governing the arbitration' or 'law of the arbitration' we mean the law governing the
procedure to be followed, not the law governing the substance of the dispute);
(2) of most relevance in practice, the place of arbitration determines which courts
supervise and support – or in some cases, interfere with and obstruct – the arbitration, and this includes which courts hear an action to set aside the award; and
(3) the place of arbitration determines the 'nationality' of the award, which is
important for enforcement purposes. It is for these reasons that the choice of the
place of arbitration is so significant: if the parties choose a place of arbitration that
is not 'friendly' to arbitration, there is plenty of scope for a delinquent party to
derail any arbitration held there, or to have the courts of that place set aside a
resulting award, leading the arbitration clause to be effectively worthless.[15]

Question:	We are negotiating with an English company and prefer arbi-tration outside the UK, but they are insisting on arbitration under the rules of the London Court of International Arbitration (LCIA), in London. Is it possible to agree to LCIA arbitration, but with the place of arbitration in another country?
Answer:	Yes. In fact, this is permitted under the rules of most arbitral institutions.

Institutions decoupled from place. The place of arbitration is not the same thing as **1-026**
the arbitral institution, although the two concepts are often confused. Whereas the
place of arbitration is the city where the arbitration takes place, at least in a legal
sense, an arbitral institution is an organisation that administers arbitrations when
called upon by parties to do so in their contracts. The location of an institution in a
given city does not mean that the place of arbitration must also be in the same city,
although that is frequently the case.[16] Instead, the arbitral institution and the place
of arbitration are different and should be treated as two independent variables, each

---

15. An interesting approach to selection of the place of arbitration is commonly encountered in
    arbitration clauses negotiated by Japanese parties. In order to discourage the commencement of
    proceedings, the parties agree that the place of arbitration will be in the respondent's home city.
16. Under the rules of certain institutions, such as the LCIA and the SIAC, if the parties fail to
    choose the place of arbitration, the default position is that the place of arbitration is the city in
    which the institution is located (London and Singapore respectively).

of which needs to be separately agreed upon. So, for example, ICC arbitration in Singapore is a perfectly acceptable combination, even though the ICC is based in Paris. Likewise Singapore International Arbitration Centre (SIAC) arbitration in Geneva will work well, despite the SIAC's location in Singapore.

1-027 *Place of arbitration distinct from venue of hearings.* The venue for most international arbitration hearings will be at the place of arbitration. But this need not always be the case, unless the parties so agree, because the place of arbitration is a concept distinct from the location where the hearings actually take place. Thus, Article 14(2) of the ICC Rules permits the tribunal to hold 'hearings and meetings' wherever it considers appropriate, after consultation with the parties and provided the parties have not agreed otherwise.[17]

1-028 *Reasons for holding hearings somewhere other than place of arbitration.* There may be a number of reasons in practice for holding the hearings somewhere other the place of arbitration: there might be events in the place of arbitration that make holding a hearing there impractical or undesirable: participants may be effectively prevented from travelling to the place of arbitration;[18] anti-suit injunctions may have been issued by the courts of the place of arbitration, preventing the arbitrations from being held there;[19] or it may simply be more convenient for the participants, or a majority of them, to hold the hearing in a location other than the place of arbitration.

Not that this ever really happens: moveable hearing venues	Arbitral tribunals occasionally do use the flexibility given by arbitration rules such as those of the ICC to hold hearings in locations other than the place of arbitration. One example in which one of the authors was involved was an ICC arbitration with the seat in Hong Kong, where a hearing on jurisdiction was to take place in early 2003. At that time the SARS epidemic gripped East Asia, and particularly Hong Kong and other parts of China. The tribunal therefore suggested, and the parties agreed, that the hearing take place in Singapore, which was less affected. In a more recent ICC case where the seat of arbitration was in the United States, the hearings were held in Canada because the chair of the tribunal was barred from entry into the United States under legislation relating the United States' boycott of Cuba, as he was a director of a company that operated assets in Cuba confiscated from

---

17. See, similarly, Art. 16.2 of the LCIA Rules and Art. 18.2 of the SIAC Rules. See also, e.g., Art. 20(2) of the Model Law and Art. 1037(3) of the Netherlands Arbitration Act.
18. See box below on moveable hearing venues.
19. *Ibid.*

> American owners in 1959. And in the well-known *Himpurna v. PLN* arbitration, the tribunal moved hearings to The Hague from the seat of arbitration in Jakarta because of an anti-suit injunction issued by the Central District Court of Jakarta.

Consequences of failure to agree on place of arbitration. If the parties fail **1-029** to choose the place of arbitration, it will be determined in accordance with the institutional rules selected by the parties. Article 14(1) of the ICC Rules provides that the ICC Court will fix the place of arbitration. In LCIA and SIAC arbitration, London and Singapore, respectively, will be the place of arbitration if no place is agreed to by the parties, unless the institution decides otherwise in view of all the circumstances.[20] Article 16 of the United Nations Commission on International Trade Law (UNCITRAL) Rules leaves it to the tribunal to select the place of arbitration. In the rare situation where the parties have not selected the place of arbitration, an administering institution, or a set of arbitration rules, the place of arbitration will be determined by the arbitral tribunal.[21]

An exception: ICSID arbitration. An important exception to the present discussion **1-030** of the place of international arbitration is arbitration under the auspices of the International Centre for Settlement of Investment Disputes (ICSID). One of the peculiarities of ICSID arbitrations is that they have no 'place of arbitration' in the sense discussed here. As ICSID is a self-contained system governed by its own treaty and arbitration rules, there is no call for its arbitrations to be attached to any national legal order. There remains the practical issue of where hearings should take place in an ICSID arbitration: the ICSID Convention specifies that the 'place of proceedings' will be the seat of the World Bank in Washington, DC, unless the parties agree otherwise. In practice, hearings in ICSID arbitrations often take place at locations other than Washington, DC, including the Peace Palace in The Hague and the World Bank's offices in Paris. One factor that contributed to this was the heightened security environment in the United States after September 2001, which made it more difficult for lawyers, witnesses, and client representatives from some countries, notably Muslim nations, to travel to the United States to attend hearings there.[22]

a.   *Place of Arbitration and Procedural Law*

What is the procedural law? International arbitration does not exist in a legal **1-031** vacuum. It has a legal framework on at least three levels: the agreement to arbitrate between the parties (which often incorporates by reference institutional arbitration rules) and the law governing that agreement; the municipal law of the seat of arbitration governing the arbitration proceedings and the challenge of (or action

---

20. See Art. 16.1 of the LCIA Rules and Art. 18.1 of the SIAC Rules.
21. See, e.g., Art. 20(1) of the Model Law and Art. 176(3) of the Swiss PILA.
22. Chapter 7, *ICSID and Investment Treaty Arbitration.*

to set aside) any award; and the municipal laws and international instruments governing the recognition and enforcement of the award made in that arbitration. The second of these three, the law governing the arbitration proceedings, is sometimes referred to by the Latin phrase '*lex arbitri*'. It is not necessarily the same as the law governing the substance of the dispute, which is the law that applies to the parties' claims and defences on the merits. Usually the parties will specify in their contract the law they choose to govern that contract, and arbitrators will apply that law when resolving the parties' claims and defences on the merits, or at least to those arising in contract. Yet the parties rarely agree *explicitly* on the law of the arbitration.[23] Instead, they accept it implicitly through their agreement on the place of the arbitration. This is expressed in most municipal arbitration statutes: examples include Article 1(2) of the Model Law, section 2(1) of the English Arbitration Act, and Article 176(1) of the Swiss PILA.

1-032 *The argument for 'delocalisation' of international arbitration.* Some authors, chiefly from continental Europe, argue that the law of the arbitration is not the law of the seat, and that international arbitration is instead 'delocalised', governed only by transnational rules of international arbitration and the laws of the places where the award is enforced.[24] In practice, however, international arbitration (other than particular systems such as ICSID arbitration) is not independent of the law of the seat, in the sense that municipal arbitration laws do, to a greater or lesser extent, seek to regulate international arbitration where the place of arbitration is in their territory. On the other hand, it is certainly possible for international arbitrators to disregard the law of the seat and go on to render an enforceable award: this is because a finding by the courts of the seat invalidating the award will not necessarily bind the enforcement courts of other countries; those courts, such as those of France, will allow the enforcement of international awards that have been set aside at the seat of arbitration or are otherwise inconsistent with the law of the seat, providing the award complies with the law of the enforcement jurisdiction. Suppose, for example, the seat of arbitration is in the home country of one of the parties, that party asks its home courts to issue an anti-suit injunction against the parties to the arbitration and the arbitrators, and the courts agree. The international arbitrators can (and some might argue must) continue the arbitration and issue an award, and that award may be enforceable in countries such as France, which do not consider the setting aside of the award (or injunctions against the arbitration) by the courts of the seat to be sufficient to prevent enforcement.[25]

---

23. Party agreement on the law governing the arbitration would not, in any case, be wholly effective, as it would not override the mandatory laws of the place of arbitration. It is likely to be effective in overriding non-mandatory provisions of that law, however, in the same way as would the parties' selection of institutional arbitration rules (see, e.g., s. 4(5) of the English Arbitration Act).

24. See G. Petrochilos, *Procedural Law in International Arbitration* (Oxford: Oxford University Press, 2004), 19 et seq.

25. Chapter 6, *After the Arbitration*. See also, E. Gaillard, Aspects philosophiques du droit de l'arbitrage international, *The Pocket Books of The Hague Academy of International Law* (Leiden/Boston: Martinus Nijhoff Publ., 2008).

Again, the more traditional approach, giving greater deference to the law of the seat, still has more currency today in practice. But the clear trend is toward more delocalisation of international arbitration. This results from the combination of at least three factors: first, modern arbitration laws reduce the number of mandatory provisions regulating international arbitration in their territory, giving the parties and arbitrators significant or total autonomy over the procedure and, allowing parties to waive their right to challenge awards; second, the increasing use and harmonisation of institutional and other arbitration rules creates truly transnational procedural standards divorced from local or even regional approaches; and, third and more generally, there is growing recognition that parties electing international arbitration do so to avoid, and not to replicate, the procedures of the courts of any one jurisdiction.

Mandatory requirements of municipal law. Most municipal arbitration laws con- **1-033** tain a small number of mandatory provisions, and a larger number of provisions that are not mandatory but that will apply where the parties have not reached agreement on the issues they cover. This means in practice that where the parties agree to apply the arbitration rules of an arbitral institution or of UNCITRAL, by that agreement they will depart from and override the non-mandatory provisions of the arbitration law of the place of arbitration, leaving only its mandatory provisions to regulate the arbitration together with the agreed arbitration rules.[26] The mandatory provisions of most modern arbitration statutes are relatively few and address, for instance, the form of the arbitration agreement;[27] the competence of the tribunal to rule on its own jurisdiction;[28] and the availability of recourse against the award in the courts of the place of the arbitration.[29] The advent and widespread popularity around the world of the UNCITRAL Model Law on International Commercial Arbitration have further reduced variations between the mandatory requirements of different national laws.

Special country requirements. Still, the mandatory provisions of some jurisdictions **1-034** may require the parties to take particular steps to reduce the risk of invalidation of an arbitration clause or the challenge of an award in the local courts. China is a good example: at the time of writing, agreements providing for arbitration in mainland China must expressly refer to the arbitration taking place under the auspices of an institution and not only to the arbitration rules of the institution.[30] In Italy, arbitration clauses are one of a handful of clauses considered by the country's civil procedure code to be a 'material waiver' of statutory rights

---

26. See Art. 16.3 of the LCIA Rules. See also Art. 6 of the Internal Rules of the International Court of Arbitration of the ICC.
27. See, e.g., Art. 7(2) of the Model Law.
28. See, e.g., Art. 16 of the Model Law.
29. See, e.g., Arts 34 et seq. of the Model Law.
30. This is in order to counter the argument that the parties are providing for ad hoc arbitration in China, which is not permitted under Chinese law. Thus the ICC Model Clause for arbitration in mainland China reads: 'All disputes arising out of or in connection with the present contract shall be submitted to the International Court of Arbitration of the International Chamber of

(*clausole vessatorie*). Because of this, arbitration clauses can be invalid if contained in one party's standard terms without being specifically acknowledged in writing by the other party (even though they may be expressly referenced in the negotiated language of the agreement). For this reason, contracts requiring arbitration in Italy often contain a separate signature line for this acknowledgment, as in the example below.[31] Of course, before agreeing that a certain city will be the place of arbitration, parties should ascertain whether there are any formalities or idiosyncrasies that must be respected in order for the arbitration clause to be deemed valid. Fortunately, the examples found in Chinese and Italian laws do not appear to be common. Most 'arbitration-friendly' jurisdictions have laws that support and encourage arbitration, with no idiosyncrasies that might defeat the validity of an arbitration clause.

Example 1a – 'Express Acceptance' of Arbitration Clauses
(and Other Provisions) under Italian Procedural Law

Buyer expressly declares its acceptance of all articles in the present General Terms and Conditions for Sale and more specifically the Articles 2 (Payment), 3 (Taxes and Duties), 4 (Delivery, Title Transfer; Risk of Loss, Storage), 6 (Compliance with Laws, Codes, and Standards), 7 (Warranty), 9 (Limitation of Liability), 10 (Dispute Resolution), and 12 (General Clauses) as per Articles 1341 and 1342 of the Italian Civil Code.

Signature _____

1-035 *Non-mandatory rules of the procedural law.* The non-mandatory provisions of municipal arbitration laws deal with issues similar to those addressed by arbitration rules, which is the basic minimum of regulation needed to get the arbitration off the ground and running. The constitution of the arbitral tribunal is a key focus, because once the tribunal is constituted, arbitration laws (and arbitration rules for that matter) delegate much of the regulation of the arbitration to the parties and, failing their agreement, to the tribunal.[32]

1-036 *Impact of other local rules that may unduly restrict or inconvenience the parties or their counsel.* Laws and regulations of the place of arbitration other than those directly addressing arbitration can also have an impact in practice on any

---

Commerce and shall be finally settled under the Rules of Arbitration of the International Chamber of Commerce by one or more arbitrators appointed in accordance with the said Rules.' See the ICC website, at <www.iccwbo.org/court/arbitration/id4114/index.html>. Note, though, that it is still uncertain whether arbitration in China may validly be conducted under the auspices of non-Chinese institutions such as the ICC (para. 1–132 below).

31. This requirement of Italian law does not apply to arbitration clauses fully contained (as opposed to being incorporated by reference) in the main, or negotiated, portion of the contract.

32. See, e.g., Art. 19(2) of the Model Law.

arbitration held in that jurisdiction. For example, in some jurisdictions regulations governing the legal profession may prevent an individual not admitted to the bar of the place of arbitration serving as arbitrator or counsel in an arbitration held there. This sort of restriction is unwarranted in international arbitration – one of the attractions of which is that a party can be represented by any person of its choosing, whether or not that person is a lawyer[33] – and is the mark of a place of arbitration to be avoided.

Not that this ever really happens: arbitral protectionism?	Miami, Florida (USA) was, until 2005, a place of international arbitration commonly agreed in contracts between companies in Central and South America, on the one hand, and companies located in North America and elsewhere, on the other. In 2005, however, the state came close to adopting a rule that would have required parties to international arbitration proceedings sited in Florida to be represented by counsel admitted to practice law in the state. While perhaps conceived by its sponsors as a protectionist measure to promote the local legal profession, it would have run counter to its purpose by effectively transforming the state into a disfavoured forum for international arbitration. Indeed, although implementation of the rule was ultimately averted through a last minute effort by Florida's own international arbitration bar, it remains to be seen whether the anti-internationalist hostility reflected in the proposed rule may have damaged perceptions of the state as a suitable forum for international arbitration.[34]

b.   *Place of Arbitration and the Courts*

Place of arbitration and power of courts to intervene. Although international **1-037** arbitration is an alternative to the courts, this does not mean that courts will have no involvement in an international arbitration. They can and do become involved, because they have coercive powers and arbitrators do not, and they can use these coercive powers either in support of the arbitration or by interfering with and obstructing the proceeding. The line between supporting and interfering with arbitration is what, in practice, separates an arbitration-friendly place from an arbitration-unfriendly one, and the main reason why great care should be taken when choosing the seat of the arbitration. After all, many countries today have excellent arbitration laws, and most are party to the New York Convention, but by no means do all of them have arbitration-friendly courts that apply national arbitration legislation and international instruments according to their letter and spirit.

---

33. See, e.g., Art. 4 of the UNCITRAL Rules.
34. Similar restrictions were in force in Japan and Singapore but have been repealed.

1-038 *When one party takes the contractual dispute to court despite an arbitration clause.* The courts of the place of arbitration can become involved before, during, and after the arbitration. Before an arbitration commences, a disputing party that has argu- ably agreed to arbitration may decide to bring its dispute to a court instead. This may or may not be the courts of the place of the arbitration.

1-039 *Reasons for going to court.* Why would a party go to court despite a clause providing for arbitration? There are several possible reasons. It may truly believe that arbitration was never agreed by the parties; it may consider its chances of success on the merits to be higher than in arbitration; it may wish to avoid the costs of initiating and conducting an arbitration; or, it may simply want to put off the day of reckoning: courts in some countries can take upwards of ten years to finally decide a dispute, whereas most arbitrations produce a final decision within two years. Whatever the reason, the submission of the dispute to the court puts the opposing party – if it wishes to insist on its right to arbitration – in the position of having immediately to object to the jurisdiction of the court over the dispute.

1-040 *When one party takes a dispute to arbitration despite the absence of a valid arbi- tration agreement.* The converse of taking a dispute to court in the face of the existence of an arbitration clause is the decision to initiate arbitration even though the existence or validity of the arbitration clause is questionable, or where one or more of the claims arguably falls outside the agreement to arbitrate. Again, a party may do this because it truly believes arbitrators have jurisdiction over the claims, or for tactical reasons. And again, the opposing party, if it objects to arbitration, will need to voice its objection promptly.

1-041 *The consequences of a failure to object to jurisdiction of the courts or arbitrators.* If the counterparty does not object to the jurisdiction of the court or the arbitral tribunal, the action will continue in that forum. Depending on the case, this may be the entire dispute or just a subset of the claims advanced. For example, if a party commences a court action despite the existence of an arbitration clause, and the adversary does not object, in all probability the court will accept jurisdiction and decide the merits of the dispute. There will be no arbitration. Similarly, if a party raises in arbitration some claims that arise under the contract containing the arbi- tration clause, and others that are outside of it, and there is no objection, the arbitrators may accept jurisdiction and decide all of the claims. There will be no litigation in the courts of the claims that fall outside of the arbitration clause.

Not that this ever really happens: failure to raise a timely jurisdictional objection	The buyer of a business initiated arbitration claiming that the seller had breached several representations and warranties contained in the parties' sale of business agreement, as well as a claim that the seller had infringed local tort law by improp- erly transferring funds between the transferred entities before the sale. The seller asserted defences that the contractual rep- resentation and warranty claims were time barred by strict lim- itations contained in the parties' contract and that the tort claim

> was unfounded. At the first substantive hearing, the tribunal raised with the seller whether it had objected anywhere in its initial pleadings to jurisdiction over the tort claim. The seller had not. The tribunal's final award agreed with the seller's defences on the contractual time bars, but found against the seller on the tort claim, which the tribunal stated it had jurisdiction to decide only because the seller had not objected in time to having the claim decided in arbitration rather than in the relevant courts.

The competence-competence rule. If the arbitration agreement is well drafted and **1-042** the counterparty objects to the court's jurisdiction,[35] the courts in arbitration-friendly jurisdictions are likely to enforce the arbitration agreement and to refer the parties to arbitration. This is the consequence of Article II(3) of the New York Convention and provisions of municipal law such as Article 8 of the Model Law, which require the court to 'refer the parties to arbitration unless it finds that the [arbitration] agreement is null and void, inoperative, or incapable of being performed'. The real question here is whether a court should conduct a full enquiry into whether the arbitration clause is 'null and void, inoperative, or incapable of being performed', or only a prima facie analysis. A court in an arbitration-friendly place of arbitration can be expected to take the latter approach and to refer the case without delay to arbitrators if it finds the arbitration agreement to be valid after only a superficial review.[36] The arbitrators will have jurisdiction in the first instance to hear and decide the entirety of any jurisdictional objection, including objections based on the alleged invalidity of the arbitration clause. This is the 'positive effect' of what is known as the competence-competence rule: the arbitrators are competent to determine their own competence (jurisdiction) in the first instance; the 'negative effect' of the competence-competence rule is that the courts, except where the arbitration agreement is invalid or inoperative on its face, must send that issue to be determined in the first instance by the arbitrators.

Not that this ever really happens: consequence of failure to raise timely	In an arbitration of a complex construction dispute, a contractor commenced arbitration against the project engineer and the owner. The owner was mentioned in the engineer's contract on the basis of which the contractor had sued, but was not a party and had no direct obligations under it. The owner overlooked what could have been a complete defence and immediate exit: an objection to jurisdiction. Rather than object to its

---

35. This objection is known as a 'motion to compel arbitration' in the United States.
36. See E. Gaillard & Y. Banifatemi, 'Negative Effect of Competence-Competence: The Rule of Priority in Favour of the Arbitrators', in *Enforcement of Arbitration Agreements and International Arbitral Awards – The New York Convention in Practice*, ed. E. Gaillard & D. Di Pietro (London: Cameron May, 2008), 257 et seq.

jurisdictional objection	presence in the arbitration, the owner instead raised its own defences. The parties eventually settled, but only after the owner had expended significant legal fees mounting a vigorous defence justifying its conduct in relation to a contract it had never signed.

1-043 *Challenging unfavourable jurisdiction decision before the courts.* A party who, as a preliminary issue, unsuccessfully objects before an arbitral tribunal to that tribunal's jurisdiction may then be able to bring its objection to the courts of the place of arbitration for a final decision. In most arbitration-friendly jurisdictions, the unsuccessful party need not (and in some cases cannot) wait until the end of the arbitration and instead may (or in some cases must) apply to the courts shortly after receiving the unfavourable decision.[37] Otherwise, if the objection is a meritorious one, the objecting party will endure the whole of the arbitration only to have the court of the place of arbitration conclude that the claim should never have been subject to arbitration in the first place.[38]

1-044 *Role of courts in supporting the appointment of a tribunal.* Once an arbitration is on foot, the courts of the place of arbitration may play a significant role in helping constitute the tribunal, but only if the parties have not agreed on alternative procedures, such as those contained in the institutional or other arbitration rules discussed below. For example, under the Model Law, the state enacting the law may designate a court to appoint arbitrators and decide challenges raised against arbitrators.[39] Often, this will be the presiding judge or 'president' of the civil courts in the city designated as the place of arbitration in the parties' agreement.

1-045 *Role of courts in granting interim or emergency measures.* The parties may also apply to the courts of the place of arbitration for interim measures, such as injunctions or attachments, in support of both an ongoing arbitration and an arbitration that is yet to begin.[40] Importantly, an application to the courts for interim measures is generally compatible with the parties' arbitration agreement. There is a reason for this, which is that only the courts – not the arbitrators – have the power of the state to compel parties and non-parties to act or refrain from acting. A party does not therefore waive its right to begin or continue arbitration by asking for court intervention in this way.[41] The key here is that the parties call upon the courts of the place of the arbitration to support the arbitration by ordering interim measures that make the arbitration more effective, and do not undermine it.

---

37. See, e.g., Art. 16(3) of the Model Law.
38. Note, though, that an action to set aside an award by arbitrators declining (as opposed to retaining) jurisdiction is not available in certain jurisdictions. Germany and Singapore are two examples. There is nothing express in the Model Law regarding the availability of an action to set aside an award declining jurisdiction.
39. See Arts 6, 11(3), 11(4), 13(3) and 14 of the Model Law.
40. Chapter 5, *The Conduct of the Arbitration.*
41. *Ibid.*

Role of courts in hearing actions to set aside the award. It is perhaps after the **1-046** arbitration has ended that the courts of the place of arbitration play their most influential role: in most jurisdictions worldwide parties may challenge the award (also referred to as applying to have the award 'set aside', 'annulled', or, to use American terminology, 'vacated').[42] The grounds on which an award may be set aside are similar in most countries even if their interpretation by different courts can vary greatly.[43] The guiding principle, in arbitration-friendly jurisdictions at least, is that an action to set aside is not an appeal and is not therefore concerned with the correctness of the tribunal's decision on the merits. Instead, actions to set aside focus on whether the arbitration met certain fundamental minimum standards – relating to jurisdiction, natural justice, and public policy. In most arbitration-friendly places, the courts will interpret the grounds for setting aside narrowly and will not reopen the merits of the award. In these places, France and Switzerland being among the best-known examples, very few actions to set aside will succeed. However, in less arbitration-friendly environments, the courts will readily delve into the merits, a higher proportion of actions to set aside prosper, and the court proceedings can take many years, which is likely – even if the award is not set aside – to delay its enforcement.

Distinction between setting aside and resisting enforcement. Actions to set aside **1-047** are different from actions to resist recognition and enforcement of the award.[44] An award debtor can only bring an action to set aside in the courts of the place of arbitration,[45] while it can resist enforcement in any jurisdiction where the award creditor attempts to enforce the award.[46] The result of a successful action to set aside is that the award ceases to exist and, in mainstream thinking at least, cannot be enforced anywhere, least of all in the jurisdiction of the court that set the award aside.[47] It is back to square one, although the parties are free to start a second arbitration, as the arbitration agreement will generally be unaffected by the setting aside of the award. In contrast, the result of a successful action to resist enforcement of an award is simply to prevent recognition and enforcement in the country in which the action is taken. The award creditor remains free to seek recognition and enforcement against assets outside that country, and the award itself remains intact.

---

42. Contracting parties can waive their right to apply to seek the setting aside of an award where the place of arbitration is in countries such as Sweden (under s. 51 of the Sweden Arbitration Act), Switzerland (under Art. 192(2) of the Swiss PILA), or Tunisia (under Art. 78 of the Tunisia Arbitration Code). However, in all three jurisdictions a waiver is only possible where none of the parties is domiciled in the jurisdiction.
43. The nature of an action to set aside and the grounds for doing so are discussed in Ch. 6, *After the Arbitration*.
44. Chapter 6, *After the Arbitration*.
45. *Ibid.*
46. *Ibid.*
47. However, see Ch. 6, *After the Arbitration,* on the recognition and enforcement in certain jurisdictions, e.g., France, of awards set aside by the courts of the place of arbitration.

1-048 Whether the local courts support or obstruct arbitration is, for these reasons, a key factor – probably *the* key factor – to consider when selecting the place of arbitration.

c.   *Place of Arbitration and Enforceability of Awards*

1-049 *Impact of place of arbitration on determination of enforcement regime.* Another consequence of the choice of the place of arbitration is its impact on the regime governing the enforcement of arbitral awards.[48] For example, the New York Convention facilitates the enforcement of those awards that it characterises as 'foreign', and to be foreign an award must be 'made in the territory of a State other than the State where the recognition and enforcement' of the award is sought.[49] The territory in which an award is 'made' is the place of arbitration. Also, states that have ratified the New York Convention are entitled to make a 'reciprocity reservation', by which they elect not to apply the Convention to awards made in the territory of a State that is not a party to the Convention.[50] It is therefore a matter of common practice and common sense for contracting parties who want an arbitration that leads to an award that is enforceable in practice to locate the place of arbitration in a state that is party to the New York Convention. However, it would be quite difficult today not to do so, as over 140 countries are now party to the Convention. Since the recent accessions of Pakistan and the United Arab Emirates, there are very few countries of major commercial significance that remain outside the Convention.[51]

1-050 *Place of arbitration and refusal to enforce under New York Convention.* As discussed in Chapter 6, the place of arbitration will also be relevant to the grounds for refusal of recognition and enforcement under the New York Convention, two of which (in relation to the validity of the arbitration agreement and to the award being set aside or suspended) directly refer to the law of the country where the award was made.[52]

---

48. Chapter 6, *After the Arbitration.*
49. See Art. I of the New York Convention.
50. See Art. I(3) of the New York Convention.
51. At the time of writing, the following countries are among those that are not parties to the Convention: Angola, Benin, Chad, Congo RDC, Ethiopia, Iraq, Libya, Mozambique, Myanmar, Namibia, North Korea, Qatar, Sierra Leone, Somalia, Sudan, Turkmenistan, and Uzbekistan. The Republic of China (Taiwan) is also not party to the Convention. For a current listing of parties to the Convention, go to <www.uncitral.org/uncitral/en/uncitral_texts/arbitration/NYConvention_status.html>.
52. See Art. V(1)(a) and (e) of the New York Convention. These provisions are considered below, at Ch. 6, *After The Arbitration.*

d.   *Good and Bad Places of Arbitration*

Because the choice of the place of arbitration is so significant, parties will want to **1-051**
identify the 'good' and 'bad' places. Much will of course depend on the perspective
and interests of each of the parties negotiating the arbitration agreement at issue: a
contracting party may well have every reason to insist on arbitration in its home-
town, or as close to it as possible, and its leverage may be so great that it can
convince the other party to agree.

Good places. An objective measure of what is a 'good' place of arbitration would **1-052**
be whether an international arbitration can be fairly and effectively held in that
place, with support from the local courts, leading to an enforceable award. This is
likely to be possible if the place of arbitration enjoys a modern arbitration law
(especially if inspired by the UNCITRAL Model Law), strong, efficient, and unbiased courts to enforce that law, and membership of the New York Convention. The
strength of the courts is the most important inquiry in practice, as most countries
today have solid arbitration laws and are party to the Convention. But not all of
these countries – far from it – have courts that consistently apply the relevant laws
and the Convention in an arbitration-friendly manner.

Practical considerations. When deciding on the best place of arbitration, there may **1-053**
also be practical considerations that have little to do with whether the place is
'good' or 'bad' in terms of its friendliness towards arbitration. Often, convenience
to the parties is a driving force behind the selection of the place of arbitration. Most
significantly among these are geographical considerations. For example, there is
unlikely to be much sense in two contracting parties from Asia selecting New
York, London, or Geneva as a place of arbitration; there are perfectly acceptable
places of arbitration much closer to home. Less commonly, parties, key witnesses
and even arbitrators may be barred from entry into certain countries canvassed as
places of arbitration; in others they may face an avoidable inconvenience. For
example, parties or counsel from Cuba or Iran would find it difficult or impossible
to gain entry to the United States for an arbitration hearing. India and Russia
(among other countries) impose strict visa requirements for citizens coming
from most European and North American countries, making it logistically more
challenging to plan for an international proceeding. The inconvenience for the
foreign party may be enough to justify the choice of a different location, even if
there are other reasons to disfavour India and Russia as a place of arbitration. The
choice of a place of arbitration where travel by foreign arbitrators or counsel is
possible but not advised for security or health reasons will likely mean that the pool
of available arbitrators, and perhaps counsel, is reduced.

A practical solution? Where the place of arbitration is difficult for foreign arbi- **1-054**
trators or counsel to access, one possible solution is – as introduced earlier – to
agree in the dispute resolution clause to have the hearings held at a different
location, without affecting the legal consequences of the choice of place of
arbitration.

1-055 *ICC list of commonly chosen places of arbitration.* A fair list of objectively 'good' places of arbitration is that compiled by the ICC of the most commonly chosen places of ICC arbitration. For places of arbitration selected by contracting parties or by the ICC in arbitrations filed with the ICC in 2008, the statistics are as follows:[53]

Country	Number of Times Selected During 2008
France	87
Switzerland	83
United Kingdom	61
Germany	40
United States of America	34
Singapore	31
Austria	15
Spain	13
China[54]	12
Belgium	11
Netherlands	10
Sweden	10
Mexico	9
Brazil	8
Italy	8

1-056 *Specify the city, not the country.* Although this is a list of countries, parties must specify a city as the place of arbitration, rather than the country where it is located, as it will be the courts of that city that will have jurisdiction over the dispute. In most cases, the regime applicable to international arbitration will be the same throughout the country, but this is not always the case: for example, Hong Kong has a very different arbitration law and court system to those found in mainland China. The capital cities of the countries listed above are generally the cities that attract most of the arbitrations. Switzerland is an exception, as the places of arbitration in most international cases are Geneva and Zürich. In the United States, New York is the city most often chosen as the place of arbitration in international disputes, although Miami has also featured prominently in contracts between companies in Central and South America and elsewhere.[55]

---

53. See '2008 Statistical Report', *ICC International Court of Arbitration Bulletin*, vol. 20, no. 1, 2009, at 5.
54. Importantly, this includes Hong Kong, which accounted for the twelve cases in question.
55. But see our discussion above about efforts of the state of Florida to 'localise' international arbitration, the consequences of which may not yet have been felt (if they are to be felt) on Miami's reputation as a leading place of international arbitration.

Cities off the beaten path in arbitration-friendly countries. It is advisable for **1-057** parties to avoid locating arbitrations in small cities, and instead to select a city with an international reputation as a seat of arbitration. The courts of large cities in arbitration-friendly countries will have experience in supporting the process of arbitration. The risk presented by a smaller town – even in a country known as being arbitration-friendly – is that there are likely to be few or no judges with experience in matters of international arbitration.

Arbitration-unfriendly countries. Perhaps somewhat counterintuitively, there are **1-058** some countries that have legal systems and courts that may provide an adequate form of dispute resolution for business disputes, yet have a reputation for short-comings when it comes to supporting arbitration. In the past, the laws and courts of England and the United States have frequently (and correctly) been accused of being less friendly towards international arbitration than the courts of many other nations. However, the courts of each country have become significantly more arbitration-friendly in recent years.

Judicial corruption or lack of independence. The inhabitants of many parts of **1-059** the world live with justice systems that are exposed to considerable levels of corruption, incompetence, and lack of independence. The international watchdog organisation Transparency International surveyed judicial corruption in thirty-two countries in 2007, concluding that it can take many forms and have different causes. The most commonly identified sources of corruption in the Transparency International survey were:

- *Judicial appointments*: the failure to appoint judges on merit can lead to the selection of pliant, corruptible judges.
- *Poor salaries and insecure working conditions*: unfair processes for promotion and transfer, as well as a lack of training for judges, lead to judges and other court personnel being vulnerable to bribery.
- *Accountability and discipline*: unfair or ineffective processes for the discipline and removal of corrupt judges can often lead instead to the removal of independent judges for reasons of political expediency.
- *Lack of transparency*: opaque court processes prevent the media and civil society from monitoring court activity and exposing judicial corruption.[56]

The assessment of judicial corruption in a particular country can evolve, and may **1-060** vary widely from one country to another in a similar region. Transparency International's annual corruption index, and the organisation's report on judicial corruption, are valuable and updated resources in this area.[57]

---

56. Global Corruption Report 2007, Executive Summary: Key Judicial Corruption Problems (Transparency International, 2007).
57. This information is publicly available at the Transparency International website, <www.transparency.org>.

1-061 *Perceptions of lack of judicial efficiency.* Even where the courts are perceived to be fair or relatively free of corruption, they may be extremely slow in disposing of matters relating to arbitration. This can, in practice, be almost as harmful for an arbitration as judicial corruption, with an arbitration bogged down for many years because of a pending application within an inefficient court system. Delay in the handling of litigation of any type is likely to be indicative of the speed with which courts will resolve issues relating to an arbitration.

2.   Institutions that Administer Arbitration and Mediation and Their Rules

1-062 The second variable in an effective international arbitration agreement, after the place of arbitration, is the choice of institution, or of the rules of arbitration if no institution is chosen. This section considers arbitration when it is administered by institutions (with mediation discussed separately below), as well as the merits of different international and regional institutions providing this service. We also consider the merits of different forms of ad hoc procedures – arbitration administered by the arbitral tribunal itself rather than by an institution.

a.   *Nature and Role of Arbitral Institutions*

1-063 *The arbitral institution.* One of the most common distinctions in international arbitration is between proceedings administered by an arbitration institution (referred to here as 'institutional' or 'administered' arbitration) and those that are not administered by an institution (generally known as 'ad hoc' arbitration). Parties drafting arbitration agreements for or in international contracts should always specify whether any arbitration is to be administered by an institution, and if they decide that it is, they should select that institution by name in their agreement. Usually the rules of the administering institution selected in this way will govern the arbitration procedure. Sometimes, though, an institution will administer arbitrations governed by other rules; for example, the HKIAC, the LCIA, and the SIAC all regularly administer arbitrations under the UNCITRAL Rules.

Question:	Is there a difference in how institutional and ad hoc proceedings are started and notified?
Answer:	Yes. An institution, such as the ICC, will provide a method by which the claimant supplies its request for arbitration directly to the institution, which takes care to 'notify' the respondent of the commencement of proceedings and of the time limits for responding to the request. There is no other requirement for the claimant to initiate the proceeding, other than a filing fee, which is usually modest. By contrast, in an ad hoc proceeding,

the claimant may be required to take several steps to legally 'notify' a respondent located in a different country. With some variation depending on the local law of the respondent, these steps may include the need to translate the request for arbitration into the language used by the local courts and serve the request through international judicial channels initiated in the country of the claimant, or hiring a counsel in the country of the respondent to ensure that each notification step is conducted locally. These potentially time-consuming and expensive administrative procedures are generally avoided when the parties have agreed that an arbitration institution will administer the proceedings.

What does an arbitral institution do? It is important to distinguish the **1-064** arbitral institution from the arbitrator or arbitrators who form the arbitral tribunal. The institution does not decide the dispute; the arbitral tribunal does. Instead, the institution 'administers' the arbitration, as explained in more detail below.

The institution's arbitration rules. An institution publishes rules of arbitration, **1-065** which it revises every ten years or so. These rules govern the arbitration procedure, unless the parties agree otherwise (and if they do, they often agree to apply the UNCITRAL Rules, which are similar to most rules issued by institutions). The rules give certain powers to the institution, and it is the exercise of those powers that forms the core of an institution's responsibilities and, as a practical matter, how the institution will administer the proceedings.

The institution's role in getting an arbitration started. The institution plays a **1-066** critical role in the initial stages of the arbitration, before the arbitral tribunal has been constituted: it receives the submission from the claimant commencing the proceedings (such as the Request for Arbitration, in the case of ICC arbitration); it notifies the respondent of the commencement of the arbitration and the steps the respondent should take; it may exercise control over whether the case is manifestly outside the institution's jurisdiction and therefore should not proceed;[58] and it supervises the constitution of the tribunal (and often appoints the chair or sole arbitrator and decides the challenge and removal of any arbitrator). The institution will also provide the parties with advice and information at the outset of the proceedings, although they pledge to maintain impartiality.

Establishing the cost structure of the arbitration. Importantly, the institution also **1-067** fixes the fees payable to the arbitrators and arranges for payment. Some institutions, such as the ICDR and the LCIA, will fix the hourly rates of the arbitrators. Others, such as the ICC or the SIAC, provide for the arbitrators to be compensated through fees indexed to the amount in dispute. In either case, the parties will pay

---

58. See, e.g., Art. 6(2) of the ICC Rules and Rule 6 of ICSID's Institution Rules.

the institution either a single advance payment or a handful of instalments determined by the institution. The institution will disburse payment to the arbitrators when they perform their work. If the parties settle after having paid an advance, the institution will also arrange to refund any unpaid portion of it.

1-068 *Value added tax (VAT) and other tax implications of arbitration fees.* In many countries, whether as a result of tax requirements or company policy, a party will not be able to make a payment unless it is supported by an invoice validly issued under a legal obligation. An institution (or arbitrators acting in the absence of an institution) that demands payment of an advance on fees may not be in a position to issue an 'invoice' to the parties, as the underlying performance has not been rendered. Rather, an institution (or the arbitrators) will hold the advance in a form of escrow until performance is rendered and the payments made. Only then will it be possible for a formal invoice to be issued. If a party cannot make payment of the advance without an invoice, institutions and arbitrators will generally be willing to issue a 'pro forma' invoice that is sufficient for tax purposes if a party specifically requests one.

Not that this ever really happens: arbitral tax evasion?	The arbitrators delivered their award, which was subsequently issued by an international arbitral institution, which assessed and allocated the final amount of the fees payable by the parties as the award expressed should be done. One of the arbitrators, however, informed the party based in the same country as that arbitrator that it was also liable for his VAT on the amounts received. The party responded that in order for VAT to be paid directly to the arbitrator, he should issue an invoice showing the amount he had received, as well as a receipt for VAT payment. The arbitrator refused and embarked instead on an exchange of increasingly acrimonious letters with the party's tax advisors. They continued to explain that the governing tax law prevented the party from paying VAT without documentation showing how much the arbitrator had received from the institution. Instead of providing the requested documentation, the arbitrator sued the party for his VAT in a country where the courts are known for their efficiency (which is probably why the parties had opted out of them in favour of arbitration). The case was still pending at the time of writing.

1-069 *Transferring procedural control to the arbitral tribunal, while retaining an administrative and monitoring role.* After the appointment of the tribunal, the arbitrators take over the administration of the procedural aspects of the case, and the institution plays a supporting or background role, except when arranging payment of arbitrators' fees. Generally, the institution will have one or more case managers or administrators who will monitor all correspondence between the parties and the tribunal and ensure that the conduct of the arbitration is consistent with the institution's rules and practices. Some institutions also review or 'scrutinise' a draft of the arbitral award before it can be issued to the parties.[59] This process involves the institution exercising quality control, requiring changes of form, and suggesting changes of substance. However, the institutions are at pains to insist that they do not interfere with the arbitrators' freedom of decision. Once the award is finalised, the institution dispatches it to the parties.

Summary of institution's role. The institution's function is thus, in summary, to get **1-070** the arbitration started, with a suitable tribunal in place, to help the tribunal keep the arbitration running smoothly thereafter, and to ensure quality control. This can be a role of great significance where one or more of the parties is inexperienced or dilatory, but is of less relevance in an arbitration between experienced parties who share a common goal of achieving an effective resolution of their dispute.

b. **Which Arbitral Institution to Choose?**

Spoilt for choice? There are dozens, if not hundreds, of institutions around the **1-071** globe offering to administer international arbitrations. We would recommend only a fraction of these, but this still leaves a respectable and diverse pool from which to choose. We examine some of the leading institutions below.

i. International Chamber of Commerce (ICC)[60]

There is no denying the truly global nature of the International Court of Arbitration (the **1-072** Court) of the ICC. It was established in 1923 and is headquartered in Paris. The Court and the case management teams operate at the ICC's headquarters in Paris, with the exception of one case management team based since 2008 in Hong Kong. The ICC has administered over 15,000 arbitrations in total and currently accepts over 500 new cases per year.[61] An important feature of the ICC is the truly multinational nature of the Court, which is comprised of 126 members from 88 countries. Many of the members are well-known arbitration practitioners, as are the Chair of the Court and its Secretary General. The Court is the body that decides certain (largely procedural) matters relating to pending cases, including whether to set cases in motion (under Article 6(2) of the ICC Rules), disposing of challenges of arbitrators (under Article 11 of the ICC Rules), fixing the fees of arbitrators and effecting payment (under Article 31 of the ICC Rules), and scrutinising draft awards (under Article 27 of the ICC Rules).

The ICC Court. The ICC Court has an administrative function – it does not decide the **1-073** merits of ICC arbitrations. The members of the Court are appointed for three-year terms. The Court sits once a week and issues decisions on matters referred to it by its secretariat, which consists of a staff of case managers who interact directly with the

---

59. See, e.g., Art. 27 of the ICC Rules and Art. 27.1 of the SIAC Rules.
60. The ICC Arbitration Rules are available at <www.iccwbo.org/court/arbitration>.
61. See <www.iccwbo.org/court/arbitration/id4086/index.html>; and 2008 Statistical Report, ICC International Court of Arbitration Bulletin, vol. 20, no. 1, 2009, at 5.

parties and the arbitrators. For example, when parties (and/or the co-arbitrators they have appointed) are unable to reach agreement on the appointment or replacement of an arbitrator, it is the ICC Court that will make the appointment.[62] The appointment of arbitrators (and mediators) is done in consultation with the ICC's national committees (see below), while administrative decisions relating to the conduct of the proceeding are often made by the Court on the basis of recommendations received from the case management team within the secretariat.

1-074 *ICC national committees.* The ICC has national committees consisting of member companies and businessmen in over ninety countries around the world. The ICC Court will seek the input and recommendation of a national committee before making any appointments. Article 9(3) of the ICC Rules provides that 'Where the Court is to appoint a sole arbitrator or the chairman of an Arbitral Tribunal, it shall make the appointment upon a proposal of a National Committee of the ICC that it considers to be appropriate'. There is no requirement that the arbitration be located in the country of the national committee consulted, or of any national committee. While the ICC claims this provides a greater guarantee to parties of the quality and effectiveness of any appointments made, in practice it is not clear that the use of national committees offers this advantage. Certainly, as the ICC's process of consultation with the national committee is not something to which parties are privy, they have no way of knowing what, if any, benefit has come from it. In fact, a criticism sometimes heard about certain national committees is that they are a means of channelling appointments to the same arbitrators, with certain individuals receiving the bulk of ICC appointments for a given country. Again, because the process of consultation is not revealed to parties, it is difficult for outsiders to assess the validity of this criticism.

1-075 *ICC case managers.* The ICC's case management staff within the secretariat reports to the Secretary General of the ICC and generally comprises young lawyers from around the world with interest in and experience of international arbitration. These lawyers – called 'counsel' or 'assistant counsel' – are divided, on the basis of their background and language ability, into several teams covering different parts of the world, roughly grouped according to language, similarity of legal systems, geographic proximity, and the ICC's caseload. When a case is initiated with the ICC, it is assigned to one of the case management teams on the basis of a number of factors, including (but not exclusively) the place of arbitration, the location of the parties, and any other relevant considerations, such as the language of the arbitration. The ICC case managers do not attend arbitration hearings or serve as secretaries to arbitral tribunals (as members of ICSID's secretariat do, for example). However, they and their teams assist parties by answering queries while (in their own words) 'maintaining strict neutrality'. The case managers serve as the go-between in the relations between the parties and tribunal, on the one hand, and the ICC Court, on the other. For example, if a party challenges an arbitrator on the basis of an alleged conflict of interest with the other party, the case managers will receive and review any submissions from the parties, elicit any responses from the arbitrators, and present their recommendations to the Court for its ruling on the request.

---

62. See Arts 8 and 9 of the ICC Rules.

The terms of reference. One key, and oft-criticised, feature of ICC arbitration is the **1-076** establishment of an instrument known as the 'terms of reference'. What is it exactly? In short, it is a document signed by the parties and the arbitrators that summarises the parties' cases and the issues in dispute. As we explain in more detail below,[63] we think the terms of reference and similar requirements in other forms of institutional arbitration are helpful as, for example, they can remove uncertainties at the outset of some arbitrations (such as erratic language in the arbitration agreement that might undermine the validity or efficacy of the arbitration unless addressed at the outset). But it is important that these steps be properly managed so as not to unduly burden or delay the proceedings.

Time limits. The ICC Rules set a six-month time limit for the rendering of the **1-077** award, which runs from the date of the signature or approval of the terms of reference. In practice, this deadline is almost never respected. The ICC Court has the right to extend this six-month time limit on a reasoned request from the tribunal or its own initiative, and it routinely exercises that right. The average duration of a mid-sized ICC arbitration before a three-member tribunal, from request for arbitration until award, is in our experience more likely to be around two years. Thus, parties to an ICC arbitration should expect to receive regular correspondence from the institution noting that the time for rendering the arbitral award has been extended for a certain number of months.

Scrutiny of awards. One distinctive function of the ICC Court is, as noted earlier, to **1-078** scrutinise awards. When the arbitral tribunal is ready to deliver its award, the tribunal is required to submit it in draft form for scrutiny by the ICC Court. The Court corrects typographical errors and includes costs figures in the award. Also, the Court 'without affecting the Arbitral Tribunal's liberty of decision, may draw its attention to points of substance'.[64] For the parties, the scrutiny process provides an additional layer of quality assurance, although it can delay issuance of the award by a month or more, as drafts of the award are shuttled from the tribunal to the Court and back, often for multiple changes before final approval and issuance. It is said that upwards of 90% of the draft awards presented by tribunals receive at least one request from the Court for changes to be made.[65]

ICC cost calculations. One area where the ICC stands out, and not always in a **1-079** positive way, is its approach to calculating fees and requiring their upfront deposit into an escrow account managed by the ICC itself. The ICC calculates its own and the arbitrators' fees on the basis of the amount in dispute, with a sliding scale and a minimum and maximum fee figure (the maximum is around five times the minimum). For example, if the amount in dispute is between USD 10 million and USD 50 million, the fees at the time of writing for each member of a three-person tribunal will be between USD 28,750 plus 0.05% of the amount in dispute

---

63. Chapter 5, *The Conduct of the Arbitration.*
64. See Art. 27 of the ICC Rules.
65. International Dispute Negotiation: Audio Interview with ICC Case Manager Francesca Mazza (IDN 27, 23 May 2008); <www.cpradr.org>.

over USD 10 million and USD 145,400 plus 0.193% of the amount in dispute. If the amount in dispute is exactly USD 10 million, the arbitrators' fees will range from a minimum figure for all three arbitrators together of USD 109,410 to a maximum figure of USD 528,000 with the average being USD 318,705. The ICC's administrative costs for the same dispute will be USD 51,400. Where the final amount of fees will fall within this range depends on a number of factors, such as the diligence of the arbitrators, the time spent, the rapidity of the proceedings, and the complexity of the dispute.[66] Where there are 'exceptional circumstances', as discussed further below, the Court may fix the fees of the arbitrators at a figure higher or lower than that which would result from the application of the relevant scale.[67] Adding further to the complexity, the ICC fee schedules are in US dollars only, meaning amounts in different currencies will need to be converted, and the fees actually payable at the time of commencing and concluding the arbitration may be subject to variations in foreign exchange rates.

1-080 *ICC 'cost calculator'.* If all of this sounds difficult to follow, it is. Fortunately, the ICC simplifies matters somewhat by making a convenient 'cost calculator' available on its website for calculating the range of potential fees and the 'advance' the parties will be required to pay in order for the arbitration to proceed. Below are some examples of calculations taken directly from the ICC cost calculator, all based on a sole arbitrator and a three-member tribunal. In each case, the ICC calculates the highest and lowest amounts permitted by the ICC fee schedules and then provides the 'average', which is used to assess the initial advance on fees paid by the parties (see below). The amounts are the total that will be due for the arbitration, of which each side will initially be responsible for advancing 50% – for example, for a dispute valued at USD 10 million with three arbitrators, the claimant would be expected to advance half of USD 318,705 at the start of the proceedings:

Amount in Dispute (in USD)	ICC Administrative Fees (in USD)	Sole Arbitrator			Three Arbitrators		
		Minimum (in USD)	Average (in USD)	Maximum (in USD)	Minimum (in USD)	Average (in USD)	Maximum (in USD)
200,000	6,950	5,100	13,625	22,150	15,300	40,875	66,450
1 million	19,500	13,470	36,985	60,500	40,410	110,955	181,500
10 million	51,400	36,470	106,235	176,000	109,410	318,705	528,000
50 million	85,400	59,670	161,835	264,000	179,010	485,505	792,000
100 million	88,800	72,970	202,485	332,000	218,910	607,455	996,000

1-081 *Advantages and disadvantages of ICC ad valorem system.* The ICC's ad valorem system of calculating costs has the merit of providing parties with some certainty in advance as to their maximum exposure to arbitrators' fees. Also, it does not

---

66.   Appendix III, Art. 2(2) of the ICC Rules
67.   See Art. 31(2) of the ICC Rules.

encourage arbitrators to extend the arbitration and its hearings, as doing so will not greatly influence their remuneration. The problem is that the system may encourage arbitrators to take short cuts: they may not be paid significantly more – and may even be paid less – if they hear the parties over several weeks and issue a long and detailed award than if they conduct a hearing of less than a week and write a short-form award, which they issue rapidly.

Comparison of the ICC's ad valorem with other systems. The principal alternative **1-082** to the ICC's ad valorem remuneration system is to pay arbitrators on the basis of the time they spend on a case. Other institutions, such as ICSID, the ICDR and the LCIA, employ this approach. The advantage of a time-based system is that it rewards the arbitrators for the work they actually perform and encourages them to give appropriate attention to each case, not just to cases with large amounts in dispute. But critics of this approach argue that paying arbitrators by the hour encourages them to spend more time on a case than is warranted, in order to increase their remuneration. Interestingly, the SIAC has recently moved away from an essentially time-based system to an ad valorem system. This is one way in which the SIAC seems to be modelling itself on the ICC.

Ad valorem versus hourly compensation schemes. At the end of the day, we think **1-083** that there is not really that much to choose between the two payment systems in the abstract. Arbitrators are aware that if parties or institutions feel the arbitrators allow the way they are remunerated to improperly influence the level of attention they give a case – whether by giving too much or not enough – future appointments may be harder to come by. In our experience of both ad valorem and time-based methods, cases of dissatisfaction with the level of arbitrator attention are not confined to arbitrations where only one or other method of remuneration applies. More problematic are ad hoc arbitrations, where the parties are at the mercy of the arbitrators in the absence of an institution to keep remuneration in check.

ICC advance on costs. One area where the ICC could make improvements relating to **1-084** costs concerns timing: the ICC Rules require the parties, at least in practice, to pay the full amount of anticipated arbitrators' fees in the first months of the arbitration. This almost always means the parties will have paid many months or even years before the tribunal performs the bulk of its work (conducting the final hearing and drafting the award). If the case settles, the unused payment is refunded to the parties but, of course, once the fees have been paid in, the level of refund is out of the parties' control. In any case, there seems to be little justification for requiring the entire payment to be made up front. It seems significantly fairer for payment to be made in stages during the arbitration, as is the case with other institutions and the practice in ad hoc arbitrations. And it may also be the case that payment of such a substantial amount of the fees in advance may discourage the parties from attempting to settle in the course of the arbitration, on the view that they have already paid a significant portion of the costs to be incurred.

Effect of counterclaims on the ICC cost calculation. The ICC calculates fees on the **1-085** basis of the entire amount in dispute, claims, and counterclaims combined. Here, the ICC's cost policies also fall short, as it is not by any means certain that a counterclaim will double the amount of work required by the arbitrators. This is particularly true of counterclaims that are closely related to an affirmative claim (e.g., where the owner of a construction project that failed to complete on schedule claims liquidated damages for the delay, and the contractor counterclaims for prolongation costs). In these cases, the ICC will calculate fees not on the basis of one similarly disputed amount claimed by each side, but on twice the amount, because two parties claim that amount. We see little justification for this mechanical approach, when it is evident that the arbitrators' workload is not increased or, if it is, not by an amount that reflects the increase in fees.

1-086 *ICC discretion to increase the advance on costs.* Under Article 31(2) of the ICC Rules, the ICC Court does have discretion to fix a higher amount of fees in the event that it perceives a particularly demanding arbitration warrants such an increase (see panel). The risk in this practice is that it undermines one of the key benefits of ICC arbitration: the predictability of the costs of the arbitration.

Not that this ever really happens: the quadrupled advance on costs	The claimant's request for arbitration demanded that the respondent pay USD 2 million due for its performance on a portion of a complex construction project. The respondent counterclaimed for the same USD 2 million, on the grounds that the same portion of the contract had not been performed. The parties' arbitration clause provided for ICC arbitration, with a provision for an award to be rendered within nine months of the appointment of the chair of the arbitral tribunal. In assessing the advance on fees to be paid by the parties, the ICC ignored the overlap between the claims and counterclaims and doubled the 'amount in dispute' for the purposes of calculating fees. Having established the amount in dispute and calculating the costs that would normally be advanced for a USD 4 million dispute, the ICC *additionally* doubled the advance due on this larger amount, effectively quadrupling it on the grounds that the parties' contractual time limitation on the arbitration amounted to a 'fast-track' requirement, therefore justifying a larger advance. The parties immediately amended their dispute resolution clause to provide for ad hoc arbitration and withdrew their case from the ICC.

1-087 In conclusion, while there are some grounds for complaint with ICC arbitration (particularly in respect of the calculation and advance on costs), it remains popular for good reason: it is genuinely international; it enjoys a strong reputation worldwide, which can be important both when convincing contracting parties to agree to arbitration and before enforcement courts or courts of the seat of arbitration; and more generally, it can be relied upon for the sound administration of arbitration irrespective of the origin and nature of the parties.

ii. International Centre for Dispute Resolution (ICDR)[68]

1-088 The ICDR is the international branch of the American Arbitration Association (AAA). The AAA is the largest arbitration institution in the world, administering tens of thousands of arbitrations each year, virtually all of them in the United States. It established the ICDR specifically to promote and manage the institution's growing international caseload. The ICDR is based in Dublin although, as discussed below (paragraph 1-092), most of its operations and case management staff remain in New York. In late 2008, the ICDR announced plans to open operations in Bahrain, generally considered a leading arbitration forum in the Arab Gulf states. The ICDR also has a joint venture with the SIAC, although little publicity is given to it.

1-089 *AAA arbitrations administered by the ICDR.* Parties to an international contract who have agreed to arbitration under the rules of the AAA can be surprised after the initiation of proceedings to discover that their case is managed by the ICDR. This is because the AAA automatically refers to the ICDR any dispute involving a non-US party. The AAA and ICDR claim this is to ensure that international arbitrations receive appropriate treatment from case managers with relevant experience. In practice, the AAA is a well-regarded and experienced institution in its own right, and having the ICDR administer the case may change little except the letterhead of the manager supervising the case file (who may well be in the same office as her AAA counterpart).

1-090 *The ICDR arbitration rules.* The ICDR has its own set of international arbitration rules, which are intended to be similar to the UNCITRAL Rules, only updated.

1-091 *Decisions on arbitrator appointments and administrative matters.* Unlike the ICC and the LCIA, the ICDR does not have a 'court' to take key decisions regarding aspects of the conduct of the proceedings. Instead, the management level above the case manager – generally senior employees with substantial experience in conducting AAA arbitrations – will perform the same or similar functions, including the appointment or replacement of an arbitrator. In practice, this means that the ICDR can often reach administrative decisions more quickly than the ICC and the LCIA, for example. For the same reason, ICDR decisions on administrative matters are also less likely to have the appearance of a compromise reached in committee.

1-092 *ICDR case managers.* The ICDR's case managers operate from within the AAA's offices in New York. The ICDR has indicated that this may change, however, and that it plans to locate some case managers in Europe in the near future. The ICDR/ AAA case managers tend to have North American backgrounds, and parties to an ICDR proceeding should not expect the same degree of national and linguistic diversity they would find with the ICC case management teams. For arbitrations

---

68. The ICDR international dispute resolution procedures are available at <www.adr.org/icdr>.

conducted mainly in the English language, however, we have not seen that the relative levels of national and linguistic diversity make a meaningful difference in the ability of either institution to conduct the proceedings efficiently.

1-093 *ICDR pool of arbitrators.* Unlike the ICC, which has no list or panel of arbitrators, the ICDR has a pool of some 400 international arbitrators who are subjected to a selection process and periodic quality review by the institution in order to maintain their presence on the list. This pool appears to draw heavily on the same group of well-known international arbitrators often associated with ICC and LCIA arbitrations.

The ICDR Energy Arbitrators List	The ICDR administers an 'energy arbitrators list' for disputes involving international projects related to the energy industry (including oil and gas and plant construction disputes). This list of around 140 arbitrators was first developed at the request of parties involved in international energy-related disputes. It is maintained by the ICDR with names and resumes of arbitrators considered to have significant industry-related experience, and it is periodically updated after vetting with parties and counsel involved in these disputes. The list is publicly available, at <http://energyarbitratorslist.icdr.org>. Parties in an ICDR arbitration can either make use of the list themselves or insist that the ICDR make use of the list if the dispute is in any way related to international energy contracts or projects.

1-094 *ICDR list procedure for appointing arbitrators.* An advantage of the ICDR over other leading institutions is the use of a 'list' procedure by which the institution will appoint a chair or sole arbitrator. Typically, the ICDR case manager will elicit input from each party as to the characteristics they seek, such as experience in particular types of disputes, legal background, nationality, and so on. The case manager will then select a list of ten names from the ICDR database of potential candidates that best match the desires of both sides. If the co-arbitrators and/or parties are unable to agree on an arbitrator from the ICDR's proposed list (or another of their own choosing), the ICDR will appoint the arbitrator from among the candidates listed. This procedure, which we have seen used effectively, provides parties with a greater degree of predictability at this critical stage of the arbitration than might be on offer where the arbitrator is appointed by the institution directly.

1-095 *Emergency measures of protection.* One selling point of the ICDR Rules is the availability of emergency measures of protection, under the procedure set out at Article 37 of the Rules. If there is an agreement to refer disputes to ICDR arbitration, a party may apply to the ICDR for the appointment of an emergency arbitrator, who will consider the application for emergency measures on an expedited basis. This gives the parties the option of seeking emergency measures from a body other than a court pending the constitution of the full arbitral tribunal. In some cases, it may be preferable to apply to the courts, but in others – for example, where the courts with jurisdiction are not strong or efficient – it may be better to apply to an emergency arbitrator.

Cross selling of ICDR mediation services. Another distinctive feature of ICDR **1-096** arbitration is the institution's claim to provide 'solutions' rather than a particular service. It is not uncommon for ICDR case managers to invite the parties to attempt settlement through the institution's mediation services. The ICDR will do this even in cases in which the parties' contract is silent on the use of mediation. As parties can always decline this offer, we certainly see no downside to the approach. On the contrary, as we discuss below, given that mediation is generally a valuable tool for resolving international business disputes but remains relatively unknown in many countries, we think this is a good thing.

ICDR fees. The ICDR requires payment of an initial fee on filing the Request for **1-097** Arbitration and case service fees that are paid subsequently. Both the filing fee and case service fee are calculated according to the ICDR administrative fee schedule.[69] The fees charged by the tribunals administered by the ICDR are based on time worked, rather than the amount in dispute. The ICDR negotiates the arbitrators' fees, which the parties must accept before the appointments may be confirmed.

Lack of scrutiny of the award. Unlike the ICC, the ICDR does not scrutinise awards **1-098** drafted by arbitral tribunals before they are distributed to the parties. While this may remove one step in the process and therefore increase the speed of the delivery of an award, it means that parties will not have the benefit of a review designed to ensure that any arbitration award is free of serious flaws that may impede a party's ability to enforce it.

iii.   London Court of International Arbitration (LCIA)[70]

Despite its name and its headquarters in London, the LCIA is today an international **1-099** institution with ambitions to become a serious competitor of the ICC. The LCIA was founded in 1891 and currently receives roughly 130 cases annually – significantly less than the ICC but a respectable number nonetheless. Perhaps not surprisingly given its roots, LCIA arbitration is especially popular with parties from the United Kingdom and the United States, which together account for about 30% of the parties to LCIA arbitration. In 2008, the LCIA opened a regional hub in Dubai, in cooperation with the Dubai International Financial Centre, known as the DIFC-LCIA. In 2009, the LCIA opened an office in New Delhi, India.

Similarities of the LCIA and the ICC. In practical terms, the LCIA does not differ **1-100** substantially from the ICC in many respects. The arbitrators appointed by the LCIA are generally the same as those appointed by the ICC. The LCIA operates a court that, in the same way as the ICC, comprises leading arbitration practitioners and takes the key decisions concerning the institution's caseload. The secretariat

---

69.   The ICDR Administrative Fees Schedule is available at <www.adr.org/sp.asp?id=33994>.
70.   The LCIA Arbitration Rules are available at <www.lcia.org>.

deals with the day-to-day administration of disputes. The LCIA Court decides issues of appointment, challenge, and replacement of arbitrators.

1-101 *Expedited formation of the tribunal.* One significant advantage of the LCIA Arbitration Rules over many other arbitration rules is the provision – without the need for a specific agreement – for the expedited formation of arbitral tribunals. This allows parties to accelerate, in situations of exceptional urgency, the time-consuming process of forming the tribunal.[71] For example, a party may wish to apply to the tribunal for emergency injunctive relief, as opposed to seeking it from courts. The difficulty with this option in arbitration is that it will usually take months for the tribunal to be constituted; the possibility of having the expedited formation of a tribunal, sometimes in a matter of days, gives potential claimants an effective solution in practice to this perennial problem.

1-102 *Other arbitration services offered by the LCIA.* The LCIA also acts as appointing authority and administrator in proceedings under the UNCITRAL Rules and will act as 'fundholder' for deposits filed on account of the costs in otherwise entirely ad hoc proceedings.

1-103 *Fees in LCIA arbitrations.* The LCIA's charges, and the fees charged by the tribunals it appoints, are based on the time worked, rather than the amount in dispute. An initial registration fee (of GBP 1,500 at the time of writing) is payable on filing the Request for Arbitration. Thereafter, hourly rates are applied both by the LCIA and by its arbitrators, with part of the LCIA's charges calculated by reference to the tribunal's fees. The LCIA sets a maximum hourly rate of GBP 350 (USD 574), which is low – at least compared to the hourly rates of most or all partners in large arbitration practices, many of whom are appointed to serve as arbitrators. For an illustration of how this might compare with the ICC's ad valorem approach to fees, see the following table.

ICC v. LCIA Arbitrators' Fees: Different Methods but Similar Results?

Examples	*ICC*	*LCIA*
Example 1		
We assume the arbitration is fairly straightforward with a sole arbitrator and USD 1 million in dispute. 75 hours of the arbitrator's time for the whole case seems reasonable to us.	The average sole arbitrator's fees would be USD 36,985.	75 hours at the maximum LCIA hourly rate of USD 574 would be USD 43,050. If we take an average LCIA hourly rate of USD 400, it would be USD 30,750.

---

71.   Chapter 5, *The Conduct of the Arbitration.*

Examples	ICC	LCIA
Example 2		
We assume the case is more complex, with USD 100 million in dispute and before a tribunal of three leading arbitrators. For this, we think 1000 hours of total arbitrator time would be reasonable.	The average arbitrators' fees in an ICC case would be USD 202,485 per arbitrator = USD 607,455 for the whole tribunal.	For three top arbitrators, charging the maximum LCIA hourly fee of USD 574, 1000 hours would amount to USD 574,000.

iv. Singapore International Arbitration Centre (SIAC)[72]
In Asia there are two prominent regional institutions: the Hong Kong International **1-104** Arbitration Centre (HKIAC, discussed below) and the SIAC. The SIAC is a more traditional institution than the HKIAC, in that it actively and comprehensively administers the disputes brought before it, which are generally governed either by the SIAC's own arbitration rules or by the UNCITRAL Rules.

Rules and fee structure. The SIAC's 2007 arbitration rules and ad valorem fee **1-105** schedule are similar to the ICC's rules and fee structure, although a number of distinct features stand out. A significant amendment in the SIAC's new arbitration rules is the introduction of a requirement that the tribunal and the parties prepare a Memorandum of Issues within forty-five days following completion of the parties' submission of written statements.[73] The Memorandum of Issues defines the matters that the tribunal is to decide in its award and must be signed by the parties and the tribunal. While the SIAC's Memorandum of Issues appears similar to the drawing up of terms of reference in ICC arbitration, the major differences are that it is drawn up only after the parties have fully argued their respective cases in writing (whereas the terms of reference are established before the parties serve their main submissions) and that it focuses on the issues that the tribunal has to decide in its award (and does not require a reiteration of the parties' positions).

SIAC administering ICC arbitration. In one recent and controversial instance, the **1-106** SIAC agreed to administer an arbitration in accordance with the ICC Rules. This led to a challenge by the respondent before the Singapore courts of the tribunal's decision to retain jurisdiction over the case. In June 2009, the Singapore Court of Appeal upheld this 'hybrid' arbitration clause.[74] While the arbitrators, the SIAC and the Singapore courts found the arbitration clause to be valid in that case, we

---

72. The SIAC Rules are available at <www.siac.org.sg>.
73. See Rule 17 of the SIAC Rules.
74. See *Singapore Court of Appeal in Insigma Technology Co Ltd v. Alstom Technology Ltd* [2009] SGCA 24.

think parties should avoid these sorts of clauses: their validity is at least questionable, and they may not be upheld by tribunals, institutions or courts in other cases; certainly, they add little or no value, and are invitations to delay and disruption that could be avoided by using a traditional clause such as the model clauses of the ICC or the SIAC.

1-107 *Pool of arbitrators.* The SIAC maintains two panels of arbitrators: an international panel of about 90 arbitrators, many of whom are leading global players, and a regional panel of about 130 arbitrators, where the profile of the arbitrators is more Asia-centric.

1-108 *Scrutiny of award.* Another new requirement in the latest revision of the SIAC Arbitration Rules is that a tribunal must submit its draft award to the SIAC Registrar for scrutiny and approval on matters of form before the award may be issued.[75] The Registrar may suggest modifications as to form and may also draw the tribunal's attention to points of substance. With this new feature, which formalises the institution's previously existing practice, the SIAC exercises control over the quality of the award in the same way as the ICC.

1-109 *SIAC procedure for appointing arbitrators.* Absent agreement by the parties on the appointment of the arbitrators, they will be appointed by the Chair of the SIAC.

1-110 *Issues in the past.* In the past, the SIAC has marketed itself to arbitration users on the basis of its low costs (including the low fees it pays to arbitrators). While this may be an effective pitch to parties entering into small contracts, it is unlikely to be appropriate for larger contracts and the more significant disputes they generate. We think that institutions should ensure that their fee structure encourages all arbitrators to serve – especially the most qualified, who are often among the more expensive. If an institution is overzealous in keeping arbitrator fees low, the parties may not have a sufficiently free or wide choice of arbitrators, and may be limited in practice to those who are less qualified for a particular dispute. Worse, an arbitrator selected by a party may later decline to serve because he is unable to agree to terms with the institution. This means the appointing party will lose its first-choice arbitrator, and the substance of that party's case may also be negatively impacted.[76]

1-111 *Recent changes at the SIAC.* In 2009, the SIAC appointed new executive management and a new board of directors. The new leadership comprises arbitration specialists from around the world and reflects the SIAC's ambition to compete with long-established, truly international institutions such as the ICC, ICDR and the LCIA.[77] This change

---

75. See Rule 27.1 of the SIAC Rules.

76. One example would be where the arbitration agreement provides for other steps, such as the appointment of the other arbitrators, to follow within a certain period from the appointment of the first arbitrator. If the first arbitrator later declines to serve because he cannot come to terms with the institution on fees, those other steps may be invalidated and the arbitration delayed on the basis that the first arbitrator was never in fact appointed.

77. Declaration of interest: one of the authors serves on the new board of directors of the SIAC.

in leadership coincides with substantial growth in the number and size of the SIAC's cases.

v.   International Centre for Settlement of Investment Disputes (ICSID)

ICSID: exclusively for investor-state arbitrations. ICSID deals exclusively with **1-112** the resolution of investment disputes between investors and states, most of which arise today under investment treaties. Because of this narrow and exclusive focus, ICSID is rather different from the other institutions considered here.[78] While the substance of ICSID's specialised regime is discussed below in Chapter 7, the distinctive features of the institution are worth briefly noting here.

ICSID's defining characteristics. ICSID is an institution created by the 1965 **1-113** ICSID Convention.[79] It is an affiliate of the World Bank and is based in the World Bank's premises in Washington, DC. ICSID has a busy and efficient sec- retariat, staffed with lawyers with particular expertise or interest in international law. There is no regional emphasis, despite the seat of the institution being in the United States. ICSID arbitrations concern parties from around the world and are usually conducted in one or two of the three official languages of ICSID: English, French and Spanish. ICSID's counsel play a more active role in arbitrations than many of their counterparts at other institutions (such as the ICC). For example, the counsel assigned to a given case will serve as secretary to the tribunal and will attend hearings and issue correspondence on behalf of the tribunal. ICSID is led by a Secretary-General, who until recently was also the General Counsel of the World Bank. ICSID Secretary-General is now a position in its own right, separate from that of the General Counsel of the World Bank.

Growth in investment arbitration. The growth in the volume of foreign private **1-114** investment in developing countries in the recent years, coupled with the increase in the number of bilateral investment treaties providing for ICSID arbitration, have led to a burgeoning ICSID caseload: for example, 154 cases were administered by ICSID in 2008, including twenty-four commenced during that year; this compares with nineteen cases administered in 1997–1998. However, the number of ICSID cases commenced annually remains modest – in the region of twenty – when com- pared with other major institutions such as the ICC and the LCIA. Still, the growth of

---

78.   A small minority of ICSID cases are brought on the basis of arbitration clauses contained in contracts between investors and states where the parties agree, in the traditional way, to refer disputes to ICSID arbitration. This contrasts with arbitration agreements in investment treaty arbitration, which consist of an offer of arbitration (at ICSID or otherwise) made by a state in an investment treaty, followed by an investor's subsequent acceptance of that offer when or shortly before it commences arbitration. Similar, but much less common, are arbitration agreements formed by an offer of ICSID arbitration by a state in its investment law and a subsequent acceptance by the investor.
79.   The Convention on the Settlement of Investment Disputes between States and Nationals of Other States came into force on 14 Oct. 1966 and is available at <http://icsid.worldbank.org/ ICSID>.

investment arbitration has spurred the growth of international counsel and arbitrators specialised in this particular form of dispute resolution.

1-115 *Registration.* ICSID's practices and rules are somewhat different from those of other institutions; many of these differences result from the institution's specialisation in investor-state disputes. Of particular note is the role of the ICSID secretariat in deciding whether to register cases, which is a first threshold the claiming party must cross before the dispute is referred to a tribunal. The Secretary-General will decline to register a case that she deems is 'manifestly outside [ICSID's] jurisdiction'.[80] There is no recourse, at least within the ICSID system, against a decision not to register a case. This gatekeeper function is performed with vigour, and the Centre will investigate the claim thoroughly at this very early stage, sometimes directing multiple requests to the claiming party for further information or evidence concerning how the claim falls within the Centre's jurisdiction (which is defined in Article 25(1) of the ICSID Convention). This registration process can take many months, and claims that do not meet the applicable threshold will be denied registration.[81]

1-116 *Procedure for early dismissal of frivolous claims.* Rule 41 of the ICSID Arbitration Rules was recently amended to allow a party to make a preliminary objection that the claim is 'manifestly without legal merit'. This new procedure is essentially an expedited mechanism for resolving, and ultimately deterring, frivolous claims. The availability of the mechanism may result in making registration of ICSID claims easier and quicker, as the 'gatekeeper' function previously exercised by ICSID can now be performed by the tribunal. At the time of writing, this mechanism had been tested in practice only once.[82]

1-117 *ICSID arbitrators.* Another interesting structural feature of ICSID is its panel system for the appointment of arbitrators. ICSID maintains a non-exclusive Panel of Arbitrators. Each Contracting State to the ICSID Convention (and there are over 140 of them) may designate four individuals to that Panel. These individuals need not be nationals of the appointing States and are in some cases from fields other than the law and arbitration, although competence in the field of law is of 'particular importance'. The Chair of ICSID may also designate ten individuals to the Panel, each of different nationalities. In practice, however, the arbitrators most likely to receive ICSID appointments are those who are well known in the worlds of international law and international commercial arbitration and who are not necessarily on the ICSID Panel.

1-118 *ICSID procedure for appointing arbitrators.* Where the parties are unable to agree on the appointment of an arbitrator, the arbitrator will be appointed by ICSID's

---

80. See Rule 6 of the ICSID Institution Rules.
81. See Art. 36(2) of the ICSID Convention and Rule 6(1) of the ICSID Institution Rules.
82. See *Trans-Global Petroleum, Inc. v. Jordan* (ICSID Case No. ARB/07/25), Decision on the Respondent's Objection Under Rule 41(5) of the ICSID Arbitration Rules (12 May 2008), available at <http://ita.law.uvic.ca>.

Chair after consulting both parties as far as possible. The Chair will appoint the arbitrator from ICSID's panel of arbitrators.

Arbitrator fees. ICSID arbitrators are paid on the basis of the time they spend **1-119** working on the case in which they are appointed. At the time of writing, the rate was USD 3,000 per eight-hour day.[83]

Comparing ICSID and other arbitral institutions. The general view is that ICSID **1-120** works well and the active role played by ICSID's own counsel is valuable, especially given the difficulties that sometimes arise in arbitrations involving developing states. But while ICSID's relevance has grown because of its high profile and the recent increase in its caseload, it still operates in a confined and unique sphere. It is therefore difficult in many respects to compare ICSID meaningfully with other arbitral institutions.

vi.   Regional Institutions

Recent years have seen a growth in the reputation and number of regional and national **1-121** institutions providing arbitration services around the world, as well as efforts of the international institutions to match this trend by offering a local version of their services. For parties seeking alternatives to global institutions for efficient administered arbitration, there is an ample menu of choices, both at the level of regional institutions (although not truly global, typically handling arbitrations involving parties from multiple nearby countries) and national institutions (typically handling domestic arbitrations but with sufficient capability and experience to handle an international arbitration). A number of high-quality regional institutions across the world attract cases because they are perceived to be competent and 'neutral', in that they are not located in the country of origin of the disputing parties. For example, the HKIAC, the Arbitration Institute of the Stockholm Chamber of Commerce (SCC) and the Swiss Chambers can be considered to be both true regional players as well as international institutions that are perceived to be neutral (and which in fact administer many cases with no parties from Hong Kong, Sweden and Switzerland, respectively). This is in much the same way that Hong Kong, Sweden and Switzerland are considered neutral places of arbitration. Other institutions, such as the German Arbitration Institute (DIS) in Germany, the Milan Arbitration Chamber in Italy, and the major Chinese institutions, have a more 'national' caseload, which predominantly involves at least one party from the country where the institution is located. We look at these 'national' institutions later, but note at the outset that parties should avoid dismissing them as domestic institutions and instead consider their (often excellent) capabilities as administrators of international arbitrations.

Hong Kong International Arbitration Centre.[84] The HKIAC is a dynamic institu- **1-122** tion that is active in a number of areas, including domain name arbitrations and

---

83. See ICSID's Schedule of Arbitrators' Fees at <http://icsid.worldbank.org/ICSID>.
84. The HKIAC Administered Arbitration Rules are available at <www.hkiac.org/HKIAC/HKIAC_English/main.html>.

mediation. In September 2008, the HKIAC adopted a new set of rules, the Administered Arbitration Rules, which are based on the UNCITRAL Rules. Parties may also agree that a dispute under the rules of other arbitral institutions – such as the ICC or the LCIA – although administered by the institution whose rules apply, will be heard at the HKIAC. The HKIAC has stated that it seeks to maintain what the Centre describes as a 'light touch', by which it means a modest amount of administrative involvement by the institution. Arbitrators' fees are not set by the HKIAC but are instead the responsibility of the parties, although the HKIAC may consult with the arbitrators to assist the parties in setting their fees.[85] The HKIAC lays claim to a large number of cases (between 300 and 400 at last count).[86] However, it is our understanding from the HKIAC that only around 20% of these are actually administered by the Centre, with the balance involving the Centre in some other way (such as the hearings being held in the Centre's premises). The HKIAC maintains a panel of arbitrators containing many of the familiar names from worldwide international arbitration practice, as well as arbitrators with a more Asian emphasis.

1-123 *Stockholm Chamber of Commerce.*[87] Europe's leading regional institutions include the Arbitration Institute of the SCC and the Swiss Chambers. Each of these two institutions had over 150 cases pending in 2006–2007. The SCC attracts disputes involving parties from CIS (former Soviet) republics, as well as from China. It also hosts a significant number of investment treaty arbitrations. New SCC Arbitration Rules entered into force on 1 January 2007.

1-124 *Swiss Chambers of Commerce.*[88] The Swiss Chambers of Commerce issued unified Swiss Rules of International Arbitration in 2004, based on the UNCITRAL Rules. Apart from the provisions commonly encountered in major arbitration rules, noticeable features of the SCC and Swiss Chambers arbitration rules include the possibility of expedited arbitration proceedings[89] and the incorporation of a provision on consolidation of arbitrations.[90]

1-125 *Arbitration institutions in the Middle East.* In the Middle East, the best-known arbitral institution is the Cairo Regional Centre of International Commercial Arbitration.[91] Up and coming is the Dubai International Arbitration Centre (DIAC)[92] in the United Arab Emirates, which introduced new arbitration rules in 2007. The explosive economic growth in the Middle East, particularly in the

---

85. See Art. 3 of the HKIAC Administered Arbitration Rules.
86. See HKIAC statistics at <www.hkiac.org/HKIAC/HKIAC_English/main.html>.
87. The SCC Rules are available at <www.sccinstitute.com>.
88. The Swiss Rules of International Arbitration are available at <www.sccam.org/sa/en>.
89. See the SCC Rules for Expedited Arbitrations and Art. 4 of the Swiss Rules of International Arbitration.
90. See Art. 11 of the SCC Arbitration Rules and s. V of the Swiss Rules on International Arbitration.
91. For the CRCICA website, go to <www.crcica.org.eg>.
92. For the DIAC website, go to <www.diac.ae>.

Arab Gulf countries, has been accompanied by the introduction of new arbitration institutions in the region at both a regional and national level.[93] These institutions have not yet achieved the recognition of, say, the HKIAC or the SIAC and are handicapped to an extent by being located in jurisdictions where the courts have not always appeared favourably disposed towards international arbitration.

Regionalisation efforts of international institutions. Not ones to ignore a trend, the **1-126** leading global institutions – ICC, ICDR, and LCIA – have each embarked on initiatives designed to capitalise on the perceived preferences of some parties for a more localised approach to arbitration by opening their own regional operations:

- *DIFC-LCIA.* In February 2008, the LCIA opened offices in cooperation with the Dubai International Financial Centre, in the United Arab Emirates, as a means of promoting arbitrations sited in the region. Although the UAE has not traditionally been regarded as a jurisdiction friendly to arbitration (the country was long one of the hold-outs on the New York Convention, which it did not ratify until 2008), the opening of the DIFC-LCIA was followed in September 2008 by new UAE arbitration legislation based on the UNCITRAL Model Law. Hopes are high that the UAE may soon become a world-class international arbitration hub in the Middle East. The LCIA has also recently opened an office in India.
- *ICDR-Bahrain.* Bahrain has long been regarded as perhaps the leading jurisdiction in the Middle East in which to site arbitrations, as a result of the country's domestic arbitration law and its ratification of the New York Convention. An ICDR-Bahrain initiative, scheduled to open in late 2009, will compete directly with the DIFC-LCIA initiative, as well as with other institutions in the region.
- *ICC-Hong Kong.* In November 2008, the ICC International Court of Arbitration opened an office for the management of Asian cases from Hong Kong, while at the same time actively lobbying both the Chinese government and the Hong Kong local government to address the issue of recognition and enforcement of ICC awards with a seat in mainland China.

vii.   National Institutions

Western Europe. Europe's best-known 'national' institutions include the DIS (in **1-127** Germany),[94] the chamber of Arbitration of Milan (CAM),[95] the Paris Arbitration and Mediation Center (CMAP),[96] and the Netherlands Arbitration Institute (NAI).[97] Each of these institutions could claim to have a similar or even greater

---

93. See discussion of the DIFC-LCIA at para. 1–126 below.
94. For the DIS website, go to <www.dis-arb.de>.
95. For the CAM website, go to <www.camera-arbitrate.it>.
96. For the CMAP website, go to <www.cmap.fr>.
97. For the NAI website, go to <www.nai-nl.org/english>.

capability to handle international arbitration proceedings than many of the regional institutions listed above. There are also new and emerging institutions in Europe, such as the Arbitration Tribunal of Barcelona (TAB),[98] which was formed in 1989, and which has seen a growth in its caseload following recent reforms of Spain's arbitration law. While some of these institutions, such as the CMAP and the DIS, already have a fair degree of experience in administering arbitrations with international parties, others – such as the TAB – can presently be regarded as fair alternatives to the local courts, even if they do not yet have substantial experience in administering truly international arbitrations involving a foreign party.

Not that this ever really happens: a threat immediately defused	A non-German party represented by one of the authors was once told by its business counterpart in Stuttgart that if the parties did not settle, the (German) side would 'take the dispute to Stuttgart arbitration' as provided in the parties' contract. The non-German party, briefed by counsel before the meeting, replied that there was no such thing as 'Stuttgart arbitration' and that even though the parties' contract provided for arbitration before the 'Stuttgart Chamber of Commerce', this was no more than a post office box to initiate proceedings before the DIS in Cologne. The opposing business manager – deprived of his hometown advantage – glared angrily at his colleague, the company's internal counsel, and promptly changed the topic of discussion from the subject he had introduced.

1-128 *Russia and Eastern Europe.* One institution from Eastern Europe with a reputation for efficiently managing disputes among parties located in the region is the Court of Arbitration attached to the Hungarian Chamber of Commerce and Industry, in Budapest. In addition, the Hungarian courts are known for acting fairly and for support of arbitration proceedings. Unlike the Hungarian example, however, many Eastern European countries have yet to develop judicial systems with an international reputation for high standards of integrity, let alone the expertise and willingness to support arbitration. Consequently, it remains common practice for parties to international contracts to site their disputes in locations outside the region – with Stockholm and the SCC retaining their popularity earned before the fall of the Soviet Union.

Misleading terminology: Russian	Occasionally parties involved in negotiations in Russia will hear, or have proposed, an 'arbitration court', such as the 'Arbitration Court of Moscow'. Despite the misleading terminology, these are simply municipal courts, not a form of arbitration.

---

98.   The TAB arbitration rules are available at <www.tab.es>.

'arbitration courts'	Acceptance of them in a contractual dispute resolution clause means the parties will have agreed to resolve disputes via litigation in the Russian courts. At the time of writing, neither of the authors would advise a non-Russian party to readily accept this option.

Africa. With the exception of the Cairo Chamber (paragraph 1-125 above), the **1-129** African continent has not seen the same degree of development in international arbitration as other regions. In our experience, the leading international institutions – particularly the ICC – are well known in Africa and clauses providing for arbitration under their auspices are likely to be included in large international contracts relating to Africa.

North America. The AAA is the leading arbitration institution in the United States, **1-130** although it is its international arm – the ICDR, discussed earlier (paragraphs 1-088 to 1-098) – that administers international disputes referred to the AAA. Other prominent US institutions that administer arbitration include JAMS[99] and The International Institute for Conflict Prevention and Resolution (CPR),[100] but their offering has a domestic flavour. This can be seen in their rosters of arbitrators, which essentially comprise former judges and litigation lawyers from the United States.

Central and South America. AAA and ICDR arbitration tend to be sufficiently well **1-131** known and well regarded in many Central and South American jurisdictions to be included in large international contracts in that part of the world. The ICDR has notably opened an office in Mexico City together with the Mediation and Arbitration Commission of the Mexico City National Chamber of Commerce (CANACO). The ICDR has also administered arbitrations under the Inter-American Commercial Arbitration Commission Rules. There have also been, over the past few years, growing initiatives in several Latin American countries to develop arbitration institutions, but these currently have a domestic focus.[101]

Asia. The best-known institutions in China are the China International Economic **1-132** and Trade Arbitration Commission (CIETAC)[102] and the Beijing Arbitration Commission (BAC).[103] They are important not only because of the rise of China but also because Chinese law is currently interpreted by many as not permitting either ad hoc arbitration in China or arbitration in China administered by institutions based outside China. Therefore, if parties agree to conduct international arbitration in China, they should currently do so at a Chinese institution such as CIETAC or the BAC. These institutions have made significant

---

99. The JAMS website is at <www.jamsadr.com>.
100. The CPR website is at <www.cpradr.org>.
101. See, e.g., P.E. Mason & M. Gomm-Santos, 'New Keys to Arbitration in Latin-America', *Journal of International Arbitration* 25, no. 1 (2008): 31 et seq.
102. The CIETAC website is at <www.cietac.org.cn/english/introduction/intro_1.htm>.
103. The BAC website is at <www.bjac.org.cn/en/index.asp>.

progress through recent improvements to their rules and diversification of their panels of arbitrators. Still, they will have less experience of international arbitration than some other institutions considered here, and their fee structures – which are on the low side, at least by European standards – may deter the more established international arbitrators.[104]

1-133 *CIETAC.* The 2005 update of the CIETAC Arbitration Rules is a positive development in that CIETAC has moved away from the closed-list system and allowed greater party autonomy in the appointment of arbitrators.[105] However, certain elements of CIETAC arbitration may still strike non-Chinese parties as undesirable or at least unusual. For example, CIETAC may appoint a sole or presiding arbitrator of the same nationality as one of the parties. In practice, this means that there is a distinct possibility that the sole arbitrator or the presiding arbitrator will be a Chinese national, where the parties fail to agree on the appointment.[106] Also, under the CIETAC rules and Chinese law, provisional measures in support of arbitration may only be obtained from the Chinese courts, but not from the arbitral tribunal.[107] Additionally, Chinese will be the language of the arbitral proceedings if the parties do not agree otherwise.[108]

---

104. See, e.g., the following extract of an interview conducted by Dr Michael Moser with Vice Chairman Yu Jianlong of CIETAC: 'In 2006, foreign panelists were appointed to sit as arbitrators in about 10 percent of CIETAC's foreign-related cases. While this number is not as high as many might expect, we have witnessed a trend over the past five years where the parties are increasingly appointing non-Chinese arbitrators. And in some cases, CIETAC has made default appointments of foreign arbitrators where the parties' arbitration agreement has not identified the nationality of arbitrator(s).

   Currently, CIETAC charges a rather low arbitration fee on an ad valorem basis. The arbitration fee, which is calculated according to the Fee Schedule, includes both the administrative fee of CIETAC and the costs of the arbitrators' fees and expenses. Usually the amount CIETAC charges is adequate to cover remuneration for domestic arbitrators (which is fixed on the basis of the amount in dispute, the workload of the case and the complexity of the case). It is inadequate to cover the remuneration expected by foreign arbitrators, however, most of whom are comfortable with an hourly rate system. To overcome this difficulty, CIETAC will in practice, in accordance with Art. 69 of its Rules, collect from parties an additional "actual expense" for appointment of a non-Chinese arbitrator or tribunal chair (presiding arbitrator) so as to cover his/her remuneration and expenses. Most parties refrain from appointing foreign arbitrators because cost factors enter into the equation in their choice of arbitrators. But I remain convinced that the fee schedule of CIETAC should be adjusted to conform to international standards'. (M.J. Moser & Y. Jianlong, 'CIETAC and Its Work – An Interview with Vice Chairman Yu Jianlong', *Journal of International Arbitration* 24, no. 6 (2007): 55–564).
105. An unfortunate, relatively recent development at CIETAC was the arrest and detention, on corruption charges, of Dr Wang Sheng Chang. Dr Wang was CIETAC's well-regarded Secretary-General and perhaps the leading Chinese figure in international arbitration. See *Global Arbitration Review* 1, no. 2 (2006). Dr Wang was released in late 2009.
106. See Arts 21 and 22 of the CIETAC Arbitration Rules.
107. See Arts 17 and 18 of the CIETAC Arbitration Rules.
108. See Art. 67 of the CIETAC Arbitration Rules.

Other Asian institutions. Other reputable institutions in Asia include the Japanese **1-134** Commercial Arbitration Association (JCAA) and the Korea Commercial Arbitration Board (KCAB), although each of these currently has relatively little experience of administering international arbitrations. Each is focused on international arbitrations involving at least one party from, respectively, Japan and Korea. The Kuala Lumpur Regional Centre for Arbitration (KLRCA) also handles a small number of international arbitrations each year.

A cautionary note about some national arbitration institutions. There are some **1-135** national arbitration institutions that, despite having been around for a number of years, do not have a good reputation for administering international proceedings. Absent confirmation from reliable sources on the independence of a national institution and its experience in administering arbitrations involving international parties, non-local parties are advised to avoid them.

Not that this ever really happens: the dark side of arbitration?	Some years ago, one of the authors was involved in proceedings conducted by a little-known national arbitration institution. The experience can only be described as the dark side of arbitration. The president of the institution insisted on appointing the chair of the arbitral tribunal without consulting either of the parties or the co-arbitrators. The newly appointed chair, a partner in the law firm that had negotiated and drafted the contract in dispute, refused to recuse himself from the appointment, and the institution refused to remove him. When the respondent complained, the president of the institution lamented the challenge of his 'close personal friend'. It was only after the respondent threatened to take the conflict to court (which would have been public) that the chair recused himself, with a letter to this book's co-author intimating the possibility of a claim for defamation for having suggested that his association with the other party's law firm might undermine his impartiality.

Conducting due diligence on an institution. If a party faces pressure from its **1-136** counterparty to accept arbitration before an institution that is not among the more recognised names that we have considered above, there may not be a problem: as we said at the outset, there are probably hundreds of international arbitral institutions worldwide, of which we have discussed only a dozen or so, and many of the others will also be perfectly satisfactory. But where the proposed institution is not among the leading worldwide institutions, we recommend a careful investigation of its ability to competently handle an international dispute. Competence is not a given, and neutrality may be illusory.

Hallmarks of a leading institution	Here are some considerations to help decide whether to agree to submit disputes to an institution being proposed: (i) How many international arbitrations has the institution conducted each year and in total? An institution should track this type of information and have it at the ready. Ideally the annual number will be at least in double figures. (ii) What is the institution's reputation among international arbitration practitioners, including those based in and outside the place where the institution is situated? (iii) Does the institution have access to quality arbitrators (which includes paying them adequate remuneration)? (iv) Does the institution have international, high-quality governance and management? (v) How are arbitrators appointed or replaced, in the absence of agreement of the parties or their nominated co-arbitrators? Preferably, this will be carried out in consultation with a court or committee of professionals engaged in the practice of arbitration, not made by a single individual in the organisation (often the case in smaller institutions that conduct few proceedings each year). (vi) Do the institution's arbitration rules provide for international proceedings? One key way of identifying this is to check whether the rules for the appointment of arbitrators provide for the chair of a three-member arbitral tribunal to be from a country other than that of either of the parties.

1-137 *Conclusion regarding arbitral institutions.* There are many good options among the leading global, regional, and national institutions. Their rules and practices are similar, by and large, although the fees they charge are often calculated in different ways. Parties opting for international arbitration should select one of the leading institutions to administer any disputes that arise out of their contract. Which institution will likely depend on the centre of gravity of the dispute: for example, if both parties are from Asia, an Asian institution or one of the global institutions would make more sense than, say, the SCC or the DIS. If the parties are from different parts of the world, leverage may allow one party to insist on an institution nearer to home; if not, one of the global institutions is likely to be an acceptable choice to all parties.

Checklist 1a – Arbitral Institutions

Name of Institution/ Location	Characteristics	Fee Basis	Comments
ICC	Truly global and multinational. Decades of experience administering arbitrations	Ad valorem	Currently the most well-established international institution
ICDR	Branch of the AAA	Initial registration fee and hourly rate for arbitrators agreed by institution	More of a focus on the Americas
LCIA	Historically influenced by UK; more international recently. Procedure for expedited formation of tribunal	Initial registration fee, then on basis of hourly rates	Especially popular with parties from UK and US. Regional hub in Dubai in cooperation with DIFC
ICSID	Exclusively for resolution of investment disputes between investors and states	Registration fee of USD 25,000 administrative charge of USD 20,000 following constitution of tribunal, and on annual basis thereafter. Arbitrators paid on basis of time worked, USD 3,000 per eight-hour day	Huge growth over the past few years, as a result of boom in investment treaty arbitration

Name of Institution/ Location	Characteristics	Fee Basis	Comments
HKIAC	Procedures based on UNCITRAL Rules	Administrative fees ad valorem, with a sliding scale, or by agreement between the parties and the arbitrators	One of Asia's two most prominent international arbitration institutions
SIAC	Rules similar to ICC rules	Ad valorem	One of Asia's two most prominent international arbitration institutions
CIETAC	Rules still have a few undesirable aspects for non-Chinese parties (e.g., regarding appointment of arbitrators)	Ad valorem, may collect an extra fee from parties, in excess of fee determined under fee schedule	Restrictions in China regarding ad hoc arbitrations and arbitrations administered by institutions outside China. If arbitration in China, advisable to choose CIETAC (or BAC) Fee levels on the low side may not be attractive to established international arbitrators

3.   Ad Hoc Arbitration

1-138 Where arbitration is the preferred form of international dispute resolution, should contracting parties agree to have a third party, an arbitral institution, administer any proceedings? Or is it better to cut out the institution and instead have an 'ad hoc' arbitration, administered by the parties and the tribunal? We believe, for the reasons we explain below, that institutional arbitration should be favoured in most instances, but a properly drafted ad hoc arbitration clause will also lead to perfectly workable dispute resolution.

UNCITRAL Arbitration Rules. The most popular form of ad hoc international **1-139** arbitration adopted by parties who do not wish to have an institution administer the proceedings is arbitration under the UNCITRAL Arbitration Rules. These rules are a little dated (they go back to 1976) but were, at the time of writing, in the process of being revised. They are, in many ways, similar to institutional rules. However, one distinctive feature is that if the parties do not specify the 'appointing authority' – who will appoint and replace the arbitrators if the parties cannot agree among themselves – the Permanent Court of Arbitration in The Hague will designate the appointing authority, which then appoints the relevant arbitrator or arbitrators. As this two-step default procedure makes the arbitration longer, the parties should instead agree if possible in their contracts on an appointing authority (such as one of the prominent international arbitration institutions).[109]

Other forms of non-administered arbitration. There are two other commonly **1-140** adopted forms of ad hoc procedures: rules made available by institutions, such as CPR, that do not administer the proceedings, and arbitrations conducted with no involvement of an institution at all, which are instead regulated only by the parties' agreement and the arbitration law of the place of arbitration.

Claimed advantages of ad hoc arbitration. Proponents of ad hoc arbitration gen- **1-141** erally cite its supposed flexibility as an advantage, in that the arbitration is not constrained by institutional rules. This claim does not hold up to scrutiny. In practice, institutional rules already leave parties and arbitrators considerable room for agreement or direction, respectively, as to how the proceedings are run. Also, if the parties want more flexibility, they can incorporate that into their arbitration clause without having to go as far as dispensing with an arbitral institution entirely, although they should be careful that any amendments they craft do not result in ambiguity when read together with the institutional rules.

Cost of ad hoc arbitration. Although there is certainly a perception that institu- **1-142** tional arbitration is expensive, the truth is that the administrative costs added by the institution are modest. It is likely that any complaint is not really about the fees charged by the institutions, but that parties do not perceive that institutions add value or do enough to move the arbitration along to justify those fees. But for a party who understands how to tap the potential of an institution, it can be valuable in ensuring the smooth conduct of proceedings, which is something that will not be available in an ad hoc proceeding.[110] As for the costs of the arbitration, the different approaches of institutions to arbitrators' fees are set out above, and they are not usually significant when compared with the other costs of the dispute (principally the fees of the parties' lawyers). In fact, because an ad hoc tribunal will not have the administrative support of an institution, it may impose on the parties the additional charge of a secretary (an administrative assistant) that may go some

---

109. See our suggested clause at Appendix 5.
110. Chapter 5 contains suggestions of ways parties can 'leverage' the role of the institution.

way to offsetting any cost saving ad hoc arbitration might otherwise have achieved over institutional arbitration.[111] At the end of the day, parties must ask themselves whether they are happy to sign up for a procedure that allows the arbitrators to set their own levels of compensation while at the same time giving them control over the process that will be generating their fees.[112]

1-143 *Timing of ad hoc arbitration.* Some advocates of ad hoc arbitration argue that ad hoc arbitration is quicker than its institutional cousin. There is some truth to this, but not because of any differences in the applicable arbitration rules or arbitrators (in fact, the rules and the population of arbitrators are likely to be similar in both cases). Rather, some arbitrators will defer to the institution for time management and rely on the institution to extend any time limits, whereas in ad hoc cases they may be required to seek and even obtain the consent of the parties themselves before extending the time for issuance of an award. Under the ad hoc procedural rules in many countries, Spain and Italy being examples, the tribunal must render an award within six months of being constituted, unless the tribunal appoints its own expert to provide a report on certain technical issues, in which case it may have an additional six months to render the award. The only way of extending this period is with the consent of both parties. Where ad hoc arbitrators are bound by such time limitations (and at least one of the parties is reluctant to grant generous extensions), the proceedings can move and conclude more quickly than an institutional arbitration. But where no such time limitations exist, an ad hoc proceeding may take longer than an institutional arbitration, notably because the institution is not available to move the proceedings forward expeditiously.

1-144 *Confidentiality of ad hoc arbitration.* Ad hoc arbitration may appear more confidential than institutional arbitration, in that no institution needs be informed even of the existence of the arbitration. However, we do not consider the risk of a reputable institution disclosing confidential information to be significant. And in the absence of an institution a party may ask for the assistance of the courts – in the appointment of arbitrators, for instance – which may compromise the supposedly enhanced confidentiality if the issue is heard in open court or if the judgment is published. Moreover, confidentiality in international arbitration is often

---

111. As discussed in Ch. 5, *The Conduct of the Arbitration*, a tribunal's use of a secretary may have other repercussions on the quality of the proceedings by involving a 'fourth arbitrator' who may, without any legitimacy, influence the course of the proceedings.

112. One example of ad hoc arbitrators going too far can be seen in the case of *Sea Containers Ltd v. ICT Pty Ltd* [2002] NSWCA 84, where the three arbitrators were removed for misconduct in an arbitration held under the New South Wales Commercial Arbitration Act. The arbitrators in that case had threatened not to make further orders in the proceedings unless the parties agreed to pay a cancellation fee, which was not part of the original terms of their remuneration. The court held that the arbitrators' behaviour passed beyond the realms of unseemliness into misconduct – and misconduct of a very high order. See also G. Griffith & R. Pintos Lopez, 'Renegotiating Arbitrators' Terms of Remuneration', *Journal of International Arbitration* 19, no. 6 (2002): 581–659.

illusory, and a party can never safely assume that it will exist, regardless of whether the proceeding is institutional or ad hoc.[113]

Institutional versus ad hoc? There is rarely any downside in having a reputable **1-145** institution administer an arbitration, provided that the institution is selected judiciously (as discussed above). There can be serious disadvantages with ad hoc arbitration in certain circumstances, notably where there is a risk that a contractual counterparty may not participate in any arbitration in good faith or at all, or where the seat of the arbitration is in a jurisdiction that is not recognised as being 'pro-arbitration'. In either of these cases, and especially where the two combine, the involvement of a competent administering institution offers the parties some security, as it will be alert to prevent or mitigate disruption by a party or the courts of the seat. For example, at least one of the arbitrators (the chair or sole arbitrator) is likely to be appointed by the institution, and if the institution is reputable, that choice will not be influenced by the parties or the courts of the seat. If there were no institution involved, and assuming that the parties had not agreed upon a satisfactory authority to appoint the arbitrators (either in their arbitration clause directly or indirectly by choosing appropriate arbitration rules, such as those of UNCITRAL), it is likely that the courts of the place of arbitration would make the appointment by default. This may lead to difficulties in countries not known for favouring international arbitration. Likewise, the institution will usually decide challenges of arbitrators expeditiously and fairly, which the courts of the seat – which would ordinarily decide challenges in the absence of an institution – may be less well equipped to do than the institution. However, what neither an institution nor an ad hoc tribunal can do is prevent a party from challenging the resulting award in the courts of the seat. This is the Achilles heel of international arbitration held in arbitration-unfriendly jurisdictions.[114] However, an institution can, through procedures such as the careful appointment of arbitrators and the scrutiny of draft awards, help reduce the likelihood of an award being set aside.

| **Not that this ever really happens: dangers of arbitrator fee caps** | Having an institution administer an UNCITRAL Rules arbitration is not always a guarantee of efficiency. In an UNCITRAL rules case in which one of the authors was involved, the arbitrator nominated by the claimant would not agree to the fee cap imposed by the administering institution and declined to serve. By that time, the two other members of the tribunal had been appointed by the institution (as the respondent declined to nominate an arbitrator), following deadlines running from the first arbitrator's appointment. The first arbitrator's subsequent decision not to serve led the respondent, rather ingeniously, to challenge the appointment and jurisdiction of the remaining |

---

113. Chapter 5, *The Conduct of the Arbitration.*
114. Chapter 6, *After the Arbitration.*

> members of the tribunal. The respondent's grounds were that the appointment of the first arbitrator had not yet taken place, as he had decided not to serve, so that there was no trigger for the appointment of the second and third arbitrators, who had therefore been invalidly appointed by the institution. The challenge was ultimately rejected by the tribunal, on the ground that the first arbitrator had been validly appointed beforehand, and his later withdrawal effectively amounted to a resignation, which did not revive the respondent's right to appoint its own arbitrator as that had elapsed. However, this outcome was not reached before significant time and expense had been spent by both parties in written and oral argument.

1-146 *Other advantages of institutional over ad hoc arbitration.* Institutional arbitration offers other forms of comfort that ad hoc arbitration cannot provide. Reputable institutions will give administrative support and advice to arbitrators, they keep the proceedings moving along, and in some cases (such as the ICC and the SIAC) they 'scrutinise' the award to ensure it meets the institution's quality standards (which can be of substantial value, especially to a party that must enforce an award). The institutions also fix the arbitrators' fees and organise their payment. This means parties will not need to engage in the occasionally unsavoury process of negotiating fees with their own judges, some of whom, experience suggests, can demand fees in ad hoc arbitration that are substantially higher than those they would receive in an equivalent institutional case. There is, after all, no institution in an ad hoc arbitration to keep the arbitrators' fees in check, and there are no institutional fee scales applicable in ad hoc arbitration to give parties guidance as to the fees they can expect to pay. Also, a party to an administered arbitration need not address vexed issues such as whether to pay directly the fees of the arbitrator it appoints (with or without disclosure of the amount to the other party or arbitrators, and without any requirement that all or any arbitrators receive the same remuneration).

> **Not that this ever really happens: unusual fee practices in ad hoc arbitration**
>
> The ad hoc arbitration had nearly concluded when one of the party-appointed arbitrators suddenly resigned for health reasons. Due to the advanced state of the proceedings, the party that had appointed him promptly appointed a replacement arbitrator with a greater amount of experience in international arbitration and rates substantially higher than his predecessor and the other arbitrators. There being no institution to determine arbitrators' fees, the next two months were dedicated to discussion among the three arbitrators about how to account for the fact that one arbitrator had substantially higher rates than the other two. Finally, a solution was agreed by the tribunal. It provided that thenceforth *all three* arbitrators would be compensated at the higher rate of its newest member, 'in the interest

> of the parties' in avoiding any appearance of inequality among them. At these higher rates, the newly constituted tribunal then proceeded to re-hear the entirety of the evidence previously presented during the course of the arbitration.

In short, for parties drafting international contracts it is generally preferable to **1-147** select institutional arbitration over ad hoc arbitration, especially as there is today a relatively broad choice of competent arbitral institutions operating regionally and worldwide. There may be some exceptional cases where ad hoc arbitration is preferable to institutional arbitration, but even then the desirable features can usually be incorporated into an institutional arbitration, either through careful drafting of the arbitration clause or party management of the institution's involvement.

Checklist 1b – Relative Advantages and Disadvantages of Institutional versus Ad Hoc Arbitration

Features of Institutional Arbitration	Features of Ad Hoc Arbitration
Institution's rules apply.	Ad hoc rules, if chosen, will apply. If not chosen, law of place of arbitration will apply.
Institutions help move the arbitration along.	It is easier for a recalcitrant party to delay ad hoc proceedings.
An institutional arbitration and resulting award may be regarded by some courts with greater respect and confidence than an ad hoc arbitration and resulting award.	Outside the country of the place of arbitration. Ad hoc arbitration and award may not enjoy the same degree of respect as institutional arbitrations.
Institutions levy administrative charges (although usually modest).	There are no administrative charges, but tribunal is more likely to appoint a 'secretary' to handle administrative aspects, whose charges may equal or exceed those of an institution.
Institution takes care of arbitrator remuneration.	Parties are required to negotiate remuneration with arbitrators.
Arbitrators' fees are more predictable than in ad hoc arbitration.	Arbitrators' fees are not subject to limitations set by institution.
Institutions may be less flexible than ad hoc arbitration, as parties are bound by institutional arbitral rules.	Ad hoc arbitration likely to be more flexible than institutional arbitration, as there are no institutional rules to bind parties.

4.   Number of Arbitrators

1-148 The third main variable upon which parties should agree when negotiating and drafting arbitration clauses is the number of arbitrators who will form the tribunal. Nowadays the choice is almost always between a tribunal of either one arbitrator (known as the 'sole arbitrator', but also referred to as the 'tribunal') or three arbitrators. A sole arbitrator is usually appointed by agreement of the parties or, failing that, by the arbitral institution or other appointing authority. A three-member tribunal will usually comprise two co-arbitrators, one appointed by each disputing party, and a chair appointed either by agreement of the parties or the co-arbitrators or, failing that, again by the arbitral institution or other appointing authority.

1-149 *Advantages of sole arbitrator.* The obvious advantages of having one arbitrator are speed and cost of decision. The sole arbitrator will have only her diary to consult when fixing hearing dates, and there will be no need for deliberation meetings. She can therefore act, decide, and draft the award more quickly than if she needed to work with two busy co-arbitrators. A quicker arbitration is generally a cheaper arbitration, and paying for one arbitrator rather than three also saves the parties money. Further advantages are that there will be no temptation to reach a compromise solution with other members of the tribunal, no risk of dissenting opinions that might undermine a majority award, and no risk of an arbitrator appointed by a delinquent defendant disrupting the arbitration by, for example, resigning at an inopportune moment.

1-150 *Disadvantages of sole arbitrator.* There are potential disadvantages to agreeing to have a dispute heard by a sole arbitrator. For one thing, the parties will not have the assistance usually provided by the co-arbitrators in identifying and agreeing upon a suitable chair. Thus, it is more likely that a sole arbitrator will need to be appointed by means of the default mechanism provided in the arbitration rules or law. But perhaps most significantly, by agreeing to a sole arbitrator, a party will not have the benefit of appointing a co-arbitrator who can provide some degree of assurance that due process will be followed and that issues raised will be given appropriate attention.

1-151 *Advantages of three-member tribunal.* It is always comforting for a party to have on the tribunal a person whom it has nominated, and in whom it has confidence, who will ensure that the tribunal as a whole understands and considers the arguments and evidence advanced by that party, and who will assist in the appointment of the third arbitrator. The presence of party-appointed arbitrators also provides a safeguard against mistakes or misconduct by the tribunal. In addition, the party's ability to nominate an arbitrator means that party can see to it that at least one member of the tribunal will possess attributes that the party considers important to the resolution of the dispute (such as familiarity with the governing law, a given language, or a relevant technical discipline).[115] Lastly, three arbitrators may be more suited to large, complex cases than a sole arbitrator, as they can share the burden of conducting the hearing and writing the award, and they are likely to be less susceptible to reach a 'rogue' or extreme outcome.

Disadvantages of a three-member tribunal. The downside of three-member tribu- **1-152** nals is that they cost more and that it generally takes much longer for three people to coordinate their schedules and complete the arbitration. There is also a risk that any decision by the tribunal will be the fruit of compromise reached in order to have a unanimous decision.

Matching the size of the tribunal to the size of likely disputes. Our recommendation **1-153** is that contracting parties agree to arbitration before a sole arbitrator in situations that are likely to give rise to day-to-day disputes of a smaller size, and that they should prefer a three-member tribunal in situations where the size and complexity will merit the additional time and cost, such as larger, more controversial, or more strategically significant contracts. There are three ways to achieve this. The first is by making the determination before entering into the contract as to whether the tribunal will be composed of one or three members. The second is to draft the arbitration clause so as to specify that the number of arbitrators will depend on the size of the dispute. The third is to leave the question to be resolved by the arbitral institution administering the arbitration.

Difficulties with arbitration clauses with a varying number of arbitrators. Clauses **1-154** specifying that the number of arbitrators will be one or three according to the amount at stake are rare. This is probably because it is often difficult to tell, at the outset of an arbitration when the tribunal is being constituted, what the true amount at stake is. For example, the value of the claims may be unspecified or uncertain, and the full list of claims and counterclaims may not be known. We think the best approach, at least in institutional arbitration, is to avoid these sorts of issues either by agreeing in the arbitration clause on a fixed number of arbitrators, or by leaving the determination of the number of arbitrators to the institution.

Allowing the institution to choose the number of arbitrators. Leaving the decision **1-155** on the number of the arbitrators to an institution can be accomplished by referring specifically to the institution's rules on the issue or, more commonly, through the parties' silence in their arbitration agreement on the number of arbitrators: if the parties do not agree on the number of arbitrators, the arbitral institution selected by the parties will make that determination. Most institutions provide that a sole arbitrator will hear the dispute, unless a tribunal of three arbitrators is warranted in the circumstances. For example, Article 8(2) of the ICC Rules states that the ICC Court will appoint a sole arbitrator 'except where it appears to the Court that the dispute is

---

115. A party can also achieve this by stipulating in the arbitration clause itself that all arbitrators, or perhaps just the chair must possess certain attributes or qualifications.

such to warrant the appointment of three arbitrators'. In practice, the rule of thumb is that the ICC Court will appoint a sole arbitrator where the amount in dispute is less than USD 1.5 million, and will seriously consider doing so where it is between USD 1.5 million and USD 5 million. Where no institution administers the arbitration, the law of the place of arbitration will resolve the issue. For example, Article 10(2) of the Model Law provides that failing a determination by the parties, 'the number of arbitrators shall be three'. Leaving the choice of the number of arbitrators to the institution makes sense provided the parties have first made themselves comfortable with what the rules say. In particular, the ICC's approach allows sufficient flexibility and avoids the problems that result from an arbitration clause that lays down hard rules based on amounts in dispute.

5.   Language of the Arbitration

1-156 The fourth and final main variable that should be addressed by parties drafting an international arbitration agreement is the language of the arbitration.[116] The parties should ideally agree upon just one language in which both will be comfortable conducting the arbitration and, equally importantly, in which a large enough pool of competent arbitrators will be comfortable conducting the arbitration. If the parties agree upon a language of arbitration that is not one of the world's major tongues, there is a risk that there will be too few experienced international arbitrators conversant in that language to allow the parties a satisfactory choice. The problem is especially acute when it comes to selecting a chain, who is typically a national of a country other than those of the disputing parties and is therefore less likely to be conversant with a relatively obscure language of arbitration.

1-157 *Specifying multiple languages.* Parties occasionally agree, as a compromise, to conduct their arbitrations in two languages (the first language of each party), although this can lead to a cumbersome process requiring the translation of documents and the need for simultaneous translation at any hearings. One unusual feature of ICSID arbitration is that ICSID Rule 22 entitles each party to select one of the three official ICSID languages (English, French and Spanish), leading many ICSID arbitrations to be conducted in two languages – typically an investor (the claimant) will commence the arbitration in English and the respondent state will exercise its right to have the arbitration conducted in one of the other official languages as well as English. Parties should avoid adopting more than one language at the drafting stage if they can, as it makes the arbitration longer, more expensive, and, in all probability, less easy overall for the parties to follow than if it had been in one language (often English) that both parties understand.

---

116. While there is little harm in extending the same language to any requirement of mediation, it is not necessary to do so. Mediation is a purely consensual process and the parties will have the opportunity to adapt the procedures, and language, to suit their needs at the time of any mediation.

Practical consequences of the choice of language. Having an arbitration conducted **1-158** in a given language will mean that the award is in that language, as well as the written and oral submissions (although they may be translated from another language). Documentary evidence will be produced in its original language, with a translation into the language of the arbitration if the two are different. Likewise, witnesses are generally free to testify in their native tongue, even if this is different from the language of the arbitration, in which case the testimony will be translated by an interpreter present at the hearing. In cases where the tribunal and counsel are familiar with the language of the evidence where it is different from the language of the arbitration, the tribunal may not require the evidence to be translated. In any event, the tribunal will usually issue specific directions on language issues during the arbitration, as the requirements of the case become clearer. It is not, as a result, normally worthwhile to address those details in the arbitration agreement, other than to agree on the language of the arbitration.

Consequences of the failure to specify language. If the parties do not agree on the **1-159** language of the arbitration in their arbitration agreement, either the institution or the tribunal will determine the language of the arbitration. In this situation, the language of the arbitration will most commonly be the language of the arbitration agreement[117] or of the contract containing or incorporating the arbitration agreement,[118] which very often will be the same. However, some institutional rules may directly determine the language of the arbitration without regard to the contract or other aspects of the dispute: The CIETAC Rules, for instance, provide that, absent an agreement by the parties on the language of the arbitration, 'the Chinese language shall be the official language to be used in the arbitration proceedings'.[119] Thus, parties specifying CIETAC as the administering institution in their dispute resolution clause, and who do not want the proceedings to be held in Chinese, must select in their clause another language in which they wish the arbitration to be conducted.

Practical advantages of specifying the language. While of no great legal signif- **1-160** icance, the language of the arbitration can be of enormous importance in practice. A party will think twice about engaging in arbitration of a dispute in a language with which it is unfamiliar, as not only will the party not readily understand what is going on, its choice of counsel and arbitrator may be restricted and its costs increased – often dramatically – because of the need for translation of the evidence and, in some cases, the submissions. It is therefore imperative that contracting parties ensure that the arbitration will be conducted in a language with which they are familiar.

---

117. See, e.g., Art. 17.1 of the LCIA Rules.
118. See, e.g., Art. 16 of the ICC Rules.
119. See Art. 67 of the CIETAC Rules.

D.   'Bells and Whistles'

1-161 *List of 'bells and whistles' almost endless.* Once the parties have stated which disputes are covered by the arbitration agreement, that those disputes must be resolved by arbitration, and selected the four main variables just discussed, the arbitration agreement will be perfectly workable in most jurisdictions. This is why the leading institutional model clauses go no further than these elements. However, the parties may wish to address in their dispute resolution clauses any number of other issues that ordinarily are less vital to the effectiveness of those agreements than the points considered above, but which may be of special concern to the parties in light of their particular circumstances. There is really no limit to what the parties can and do include in the way of these 'bells and whistles', but we focus on a selection of the most common areas where parties attempt to embellish their arbitration clause, beginning with the difficult issues of joinder and consolidation, where parties attempt to address the presence of multiple parties or multiple contracts.

1-162 *A word of warning.* Because each 'bell' or 'whistle' is likely to be a step away from simplicity in the drafting of the disputes clause, parties must weigh the potential benefits of this level of detail against the costs of complexity and potential inflexibility at the time a dispute arises.[120]

'Bells', 'whistles', and unnecessary verbiage in ICC practice	In ICC practice, a request for arbitration that invokes a non-standard dispute resolution clause (and 'non-standard' is the rule more than the exception) will generate a letter from the assigned case manager at the inception of the case asking the parties to comment on its meaning and significance in the proceeding. This results from a tendency of parties to seek to enhance, improve, or (we can say here) 'overlawyer' dispute resolution clauses by encumbering them with requirements on the timing of the appointment of arbitrators, rules of joinder and consolidation, and even evidentiary and procedural matters. For example, the ICC case manager may ask the parties to comment on a clause that requires them to appoint arbitrators within a certain period and the two party-appointed arbitrators to make their appointments within another specified period. Why? Because the ICC Rules themselves, which the parties have otherwise accepted to apply, already provide time periods for these appointments. Thus, the ICC seeks confirmation from the parties as to whether and to what extent they intended to depart, in their contract, from the ICC Rules.

---

120.   The parties should always set out in their contracts their agreement on which substantive law governs the contract (which is to be distinguished from the law regulating the procedural aspects of the arbitration). The contract's governing law is conceptually independent of the parties' dispute resolution agreement and we therefore do not address it further in this chapter.

1. Joinder and Consolidation

Joinder of third parties to arbitration. One of the enduring downsides of **1-163**
international arbitration is the difficulty or impossibility for the disputing parties
to join third parties to the arbitration, even if they are involved in the underlying
project or transaction and their presence is needed for effective or at least efficient
resolution of the dispute. If a third party were joined, the traditional two-sided
arbitration would become what is referred to as 'multi-party' and even 'multi-sided'
proceedings, for which the terms 'triagonal' and even 'poliagonal' have been
applied to distinguish them from proceedings with multiple parties constituting
the two sides of a traditional dispute.

Joinder of a party	A typical example of where joinder might be desired by one party is where the owner of a construction project sues the main contractor for delay or defects for which the main contractor holds a subcontractor responsible. From the main contractor's perspective, the presence of all three parties in one arbitration would assist the efficient disposal of the dispute, as having one arbitration rather than two would mean an aggregate saving of cost and time and would avoid conflicting decisions in the two different proceedings. However, the owner and subcontractor – who are not usually parties to a contract or an arbitration agreement between each other – may not see it that way and may decline to participate with the other in the initial arbitration in order to put themselves in a stronger tactical position vis-à-vis the main contractor. In most municipal courts, the main contractor would be able to join the third party to the litigation. In arbitration, it cannot.

Absence of guidelines on joinder. Joinder is an area that many major institutions do **1-164**
not address in their rules. The ICC Rules contemplate only traditional two-sided
arbitration, for example. The LCIA Rules do allow joinder of a third party on the
application of an existing party to the arbitration, providing the third party agrees
(but the agreement of all parties to the arbitration is not needed).[121] There is very
little published information, however, on how the LCIA in practice will handle
joinder requests if one of the existing parties objects, or the impact that joinder may
have on the enforceability of any resulting arbitration awards.

Specifying a joinder requirement in an arbitration clause. Because the institutions **1-165**
do not really provide a reliable solution to the multi-party problem, parties often
consider adding specific language in their dispute resolution clause designed to
allow joinder of third parties. The proposed procedural mechanism for achieving

---

121. See Art. 22.1(h) of the LCIA Rules.

such multi-sided arbitration is usually a clause by which the parties agree to be joined to an arbitration proceeding involving similar facts or issues.

1-166 *Problems with joinder.* Although there is a superficial appeal of efficiency, multi-sided arbitration can create more problems than it seeks to fix. Among the likely problems are how the parties can be put on an equal footing when appointing arbitrators, whether proceedings are more vulnerable to delay, and how each party's contractual rights (and limitations of liability) can be separately enforced. Taking our earlier example, the subcontractor will have priced its contract according to its obligations towards the main contractor. If there is a dispute, the subcontractor will argue that it should be involved in an arbitration in respect of its obligations to the main contractor only, and it should not find itself involved in a potentially much broader (and very likely more expensive) arbitration between the main contractor and the owner. The owner, for its part, may also object to having its arbitration bogged down by the resolution of claims by or against a subcontractor with whom it did not contract. The risk is, more generally, that by giving effect to a clause providing for joinder, there will be a violation of the rights of one of the parties, giving that party an opening to challenge the validity of the arbitration agreement or any award issued in the arbitration.

1-167 *Joinder: special drafting considerations.* If parties still desire to include an effective provision for joinder in their arbitration clause, all parties should sign and clearly become party to that clause, either directly or by reference. Also, each party should be granted an equal right to appoint arbitrators, making it difficult or impossible to join a party to an arbitration after the tribunal has been appointed. More generally, the arbitration clause and the procedures it incorporates should treat all parties (and especially the 'joined' party) equally. One way of simplifying this is to have all the parties concerned enter into a 'framework' or 'umbrella' arbitration agreement that sets out the consent of all of them to be party to the same arbitration, as well as the guarantees of equal treatment just described. Still, even the most careful drafting may not save an arbitration clause with joinder provisions from eventual challenge in the courts. This is one area where it really is essential for parties to seek specialist advice. There are a handful of helpful publications that go into this level of detail,[122] although these should be used to assist the drafting of a customised solution, rather than for mechanical cutting and pasting.

1-168 *Consolidation of related arbitrations.* A similar problem to the multi-sided situation just discussed arises where two or more arbitrations are pending between the same parties under the same or similar contracts. The difference between this sort of situation and multi-sided cases is that in this case there are two or more arbitrations, not just one, and that the parties are the same in each proceeding, so there is no issue of having to include a new party to the arbitration.

---

122. See, e.g., G.B. Born, *International Arbitration and Forum Selection Agreements: Drafting and Enforcing*, 2nd edn (Netherlands: Kluwer Law International, 2006); P.D. Friedland, *Arbitration Clauses for International Contracts*, 2nd edn (New York: Juris Publishing, 2007).

Consolidation	Party A starts an arbitration against Party B under their contract, known as contract C. Party B may then countersue Party A in a different arbitration under the same contract or may bring the same or similar claims in another arbitration against Party A under contract D, a separate contract between the same parties. In each case it would be far more efficient for the two arbitrations to be consolidated and heard together, as that would save time and cost and would avoid conflicting decisions. However, one of the parties may well, for tactical reasons, be unwilling to agree to consolidate the arbitrations (although it may be challenging to justify such a decision before an institution or a tribunal where the claims and counterclaims are all asserted under the same contract).

Ability of institutions to order consolidation. Certain institutional rules do go some **1-169** way towards a solution to the problem of consolidation: for example, the ICC Rules (Article 4(6)) permit the ICC Court to order the consolidation of arbitrations concerning the same legal relationship between the same parties, prior to the signature or ICC Court approval of the terms of reference. Unfortunately, the Rules do not disclose the circumstances in which the institution will be inclined to accept or reject a request for consolidation. The uncertainty as to how a request for consolidation will be handled is compounded by the fact that the ICC does not publish its decisions in this regard.

Drafting consolidation provisions. To overcome the uncertainties left by institu- **1-170** tional rules and national law, parties themselves may wish to include specific language in their arbitration agreements that allow consolidation of parallel arbitrations. Like joinder provisions, however, consolidation clauses are difficult to draft. The parties must again take great care to ensure all of them have equal rights in the appointment of arbitrators, and that all have equal or similar opportunities to present their case, else any award is likely to be vulnerable to challenge for want of due process. These considerations make it inadvisable to attempt to use a 'boilerplate' consolidation provision – wording tailored to each contract is much better.

Informal or de facto consolidation. Solutions short of full-blown consolidation are **1-171** available to parties, either through decision-making by the arbitral institution, or through the parties' own agreement. One possible solution could involve appointing the same arbitrators in the parallel arbitrations; however, if one of the parties is unwilling to consolidate, it is likely it will also resist appointing the same tribunal in the two parallel cases. The reticent party can defeat consolidation in the case of a three-member tribunal simply by appointing a different arbitrator in each arbitration.

1-172 *Appointing the same arbitrator in parallel arbitrations.* If an arbitrator is appointed by one party, or by an institution or other third party, in related arbitrations between the same parties, he may have to disclose in each case his appointment in the other arbitration, and the reticent party may challenge the arbitrator in one or both arbitrations on the grounds that he may be prejudiced by his knowledge of the arguments and evidence gained in the other arbitration. An arbitrator is not as a matter of principle precluded from sitting in two parallel or related arbitrations between the same parties, and institutions may adopt different approaches to handling these situations. For example, the ICC apparently looks at multiple factors when deciding on a request to consolidate or a challenge to the appointment of the same arbitrator in multiple proceedings, including whether the parties, the counsel, and the issues in the parallel arbitrations are the same, as well as the stage the proceedings have reached.[123] Whether the parties have appointed the same counsel strikes us irrelevant to the question of whether a proceeding should be consolidated. Parties may wish to have the same counsel in entirely unrelated proceedings; or in related proceedings they might potentially 'game' the system by appointing different counsel only to defeat a request for consolidation. One commentator on multi-party arbitration has stated that the key to the resolution of such a challenge should be whether a decision has been reached in one of the parallel arbitrations that may generate prejudice on the part of the arbitrator in the second arbitration.[124]

Not that this ever really happens: some common arbitrator issues, different outcomes	The owner of a power plant alleged that certain equipment that had been ordered did not meet its needs, and that this was a either a breach of contract by the project engineer who had specified the plant's performance requirements or a breach of contract by the company engaged to build the equipment to the engineer's specifications. The owner started two ICC arbitrations, one against the engineer and another against the equipment supplier, each under the separate contract with each party. The owner appointed the same arbitrator in both proceedings. The equipment supplier accepted this dual appointment, but the engineer objected. The ICC, the institution chosen in each of the contractual dispute resolution clauses, upheld the engineer's objection and refused to allow the arbitrator to serve in both arbitrations, even though this increased the chances of inconsistent results over the same disputed issue. Two years later, one of the parties found itself in an identical situation, only in an arbitration administered by the ICDR.

---

123. See A.M. Whitesell & E. Silva-Romero, *Multiparty and Multicontract Arbitration: Recent ICC Experience, Complex Arbitrations* (Special Supplement to the ICC International Court of Arbitration Bulletin, 2003), 7.
124. See B. Hanotiau, *Complex Arbitrations – Multiparty, Multicontract, Multi-issue and Class Actions* (Netherlands: Kluwer Law International, 2005), 219.

> Over the objections of one of the parties, the ICDR allowed a common arbitrator to serve in both proceedings. Neither the ICC nor the ICDR provided any reasoning for its decision, although the ICC's decision appeared to defer to concerns over a party's ability to subsequently raise its objection as a ground for challenge of the award or its enforcement on the basis of the dual appointment, while the ICDR decision appeared to be grounded in the respect for a party's right to appoint an arbitrator of its choosing.

Sequencing proceedings as an alternative to consolidating. Another solution that **1-173** may minimise the harm caused by unconsolidated but related arbitrations between the same parties – and especially the risk of conflicting decisions – is for the tribunal in the later proceeding to wait until the first case concludes before proceeding with the merits of the second case. This can be achieved by party agreement or, failing that, by decision of the tribunal. A stay in these situations is probably not precluded in principle.[125] However, those objecting to a stay will argue that an arbitral tribunal should exercise its mandate and proceed to decide the dispute the parties agreed to submit to it, while proponents of a stay will invoke the fair administration of justice. If one or more arbitrators are common to the parallel proceedings, one tribunal reaching a decision before the other may create grounds for challenge in the second arbitration of the arbitrators sitting in both arbitrations, as those arbitrators will arguably no longer be impartial as they will have expressed a view on factual and legal issues to be decided in the second arbitration. But if a party has not challenged those arbitrators by that time, it may well be held to have waived its right to do so.

2. Requiring Negotiation Prior to Arbitration

Requirement to negotiate. It is common practice to include in dispute resolution **1-174** provisions a requirement that, before a dispute is referred to mediation and/or arbitration, it must be referred to some sort of structured negotiation between the parties. This may involve procedural steps such as the delivery of a notice of dispute to the opponent and the passage of a period of time during which negotiations should take place.

Value of negotiation clauses? In our experience, negotiation clauses are not help- **1-175** ful, at best. Parties seem to include such a requirement because they believe it will make the dispute clause appear more amicable to the other party during contractual negotiations, as if to say, 'we genuinely hope we can resolve any disputes without the need for arbitration'. As a practical matter, however, these clauses add little or

---

125. See International Law Association – Toronto Conference (2006) – International Commercial Arbitration, Final Report on *Lis Pendens* and Arbitration.

no value when a dispute actually arises. If senior business people wish to engage in negotiations before proceeding with more formal methods of dispute resolution, they will do so without being compelled by a 'negotiation' requirement in their contract. Similarly, if the senior business managers do not wish to negotiate, they will simply ignore the existence of the clause and proceed to the next step of formal dispute resolution. Instead, clauses requiring parties to negotiate may aggravate the dispute by creating difficult preliminary issues as to whether the requirement is binding and, if so, whether it was complied with.[126]

3.   ICC Pre-Arbitral Referee Procedure

1-176 *ICC Pre-Arbitral Referee Procedure.* Parties may usefully agree in their arbitration agreement to adopt the ICC's Pre-Arbitral Referee Procedure, for the grant of temporary urgent measures. The referee procedure is an emergency proceeding, before a referee appointed by agreement of the parties or the ICC. The proceeding is independent of and without prejudice to the subsequent litigation or arbitration of the merits of the case. The procedure allows the parties to seek urgent provisional measures before the constitution of the arbitral tribunal.[127] It is only available to the parties where they have expressly agreed to it: a reference to arbitration under the ICC Rules is not sufficient – there must be specific reference to the ICC Rules for a Pre-Arbitral Referee Procedure. Also, reference by the parties to the ICC Pre-Arbitral Referee Procedure may be combined with the choice of arbitration under the auspices of another arbitral institution or of ad hoc arbitration.

1-177 *Pre-Arbitral Referee Procedure in practice.* The ICC Pre-Arbitral Referee Procedure[128] was established in 1990 but was not used for over ten years, with the first pre-arbitral referee decision being rendered in October 2001. The first pre-arbitral referee measure ordered was that a respondent continue the performance of a contract; the second measure ordered prohibited a respondent from modifying a number of contracts related to the contract in dispute in the arbitration.[129]

1-178 *Utility of Pre-Arbitral Referee Procedure.* The possibility of recourse to the Pre-Arbitral Referee Procedure may be valuable in cases where an arbitration has not yet begun, or where it has begun but an arbitral tribunal has not yet been constituted and cannot therefore grant the urgent measures sought. The applicant could turn to a national court for interim measures in these circumstances, but for various reasons – such as the efficiency or otherwise of the relevant court, confidentiality, or the poor prospects of enforcement – a mechanism outside the courts may be desirable.

---

126. Chapter 3, *When the Dispute Arises*, at I.
127. See the Foreword to the ICC Rules for a Pre-Arbitral Referee Procedure as well as Art. 2.1 (Powers of the Referee).
128. Available at <www.iccwbo.org/court/arbitration>.
129. See, E. Gaillard & P. Pinsolle, 'The ICC Pre-Arbitral Referee: First Practical Experiences', *Arbitration International* 20, no. 1 (2004): 1 et seq.

Uncertainty as to enforceability of ICC pre-arbitral referee orders. Questions have **1-179** arisen as to whether and how a pre-arbitral referee's orders are to be enforced or challenged, and notably as to the nature of a pre-arbitral referee's order and whether it may be characterised as an arbitral award for the purposes of the New York Convention. The French courts, the only national courts called upon to decide this issue to date, have held that a pre-arbitral referee's order is not an award (and have in consequence rejected an action to set it aside); instead they found the order to be binding only as a result of the parties' agreement.[130] Available information suggests that all pre-arbitral referee orders issued to date have been complied with voluntarily.

ICDR Emergency Measures of Protection. The ICDR has a similar procedure set **1-180** out in Article 37 of its Rules, under which a party may apply to an 'emergency arbitrator' for 'emergency rules of protection'. This procedure is available in all cases where the parties consent to ICDR arbitration, unless the parties agree otherwise.

4. Arbitrator Qualifications

Provisions in arbitration clause specifying arbitrator qualifications. One of the **1-181** attractions of arbitration is that the parties can agree on qualifications that the arbitrators – their judges – should possess and other conditions that the arbitrators should fulfil. This gives the parties comfort that their disputes will be resolved by people whom they perceive to be up to the task. Provisions of this sort typically require arbitrators to have certain legal or other professional qualifications or experience, to be of certain nationalities (or more commonly, not to be of the same nationality as the contracting parties), to have previously served as a judge, to be familiar with – or even expert in – specific legal systems, to speak certain languages, to be resident in a given country, or a combination of any or all of these.

The danger with these sorts of requirements is that they may, especially when **1-182** several are used in combination, reduce the pool of available arbitrators to a dangerously low level. Also, the key qualities that parties should be looking for in an arbitrator are not always tangible matters capable of expression in an arbitration agreement, and of subsequent enforcement. It is therefore doubtful whether it is productive to narrow the pool of arbitrators by requiring them to have specific qualifications or satisfy certain conditions. The one exception to this is where the parties will have a need for very rapid dispute resolution. In these cases the parties may even wish to agree at the outset not just on the qualifications of the arbitrator, but the actual person to act in that capacity and any replacements if that person is unable to serve.

---

130. *Ibid.*

1-183 *Reassurance from a party's own nomination of 'its' arbitrator.* Instead of requiring that arbitrators demonstrate certain qualifications believed to be relevant at the time of contracting, parties with concerns as to the capability of the tribunal should simply provide for a three-member tribunal with each party having the right to nominate an arbitrator, and with the two party-appointed arbitrators selecting the chair. A party's involvement in the appointment of two of the three arbitrators gives it a good measure of control over the quality of the tribunal once the contours of the dispute are clear.

5.   Procedure and Evidence

1-184 *Provisions in arbitration clause on procedure and evidence.* Parties may want to include in their arbitration agreement specific provisions about the procedure they wish to be followed in their arbitration. These may be directions or aspirations as to the overall duration of the arbitration or as to the timing of specific procedural steps. The parties may also agree on issues of evidence: for instance, they may require the arbitrators to follow the IBA Rules of Evidence, or to use the IBA Rules as guidance; they may prefer to have more extensive discovery, including depositions, than is the norm; or they may agree to exclude all discovery.

1-185 *Pros and cons of detailed agreement on procedure and evidence.* For the most part, detailed provisions as to particular procedures and evidence – in the absence of a very specific contractual or project need – are unnecessarily cumbersome and potentially even a danger to the efficient conduct of the proceedings. Instead we would recommend referring to the IBA Rules if parties desire some certainty as to the precise nature of the procedures that a tribunal will apply. If parties insist on drawing up their own procedural provisions in their contract, we recommend they take care to ensure that any agreement on procedure and evidence is consistent with any institutional or other arbitration rules chosen. This will include stating clearly in the arbitration agreement that it takes precedence over any conflicting provision in the arbitration rules.

6.   Allocation of Costs

1-186 *Costs.* Parties sometimes specify in their arbitration agreements how to allocate between them the costs of the arbitration, which usually include the parties' legal fees as well as the fees of the arbitrators and of any arbitral institution. The rule most broadly applied in international arbitration where there is no agreement between the parties on costs is that the loser pays most or all of the costs of the winner. A contractual provision of this kind, if clearly worded, causes no real difficulty, although its utility is increasingly limited as it reflects widespread practice in international arbitration in the absence of party agreement. By the same token, if the intention of the parties is that each party should bear its own costs regardless of the outcome of the arbitration, this should be expressed in the parties' arbitration agreement because it is a departure from usual practice.

Inadvisability of 'each side shall bear its own costs' provision. There is generally **1-187** no early resolution mechanism available in international arbitration, such as summary judgment or similar means of dispensing with a weak or unfounded claim before trial. A party to an international arbitration with frivolous claims can therefore often succeed in pursuing those claims to trial. The probability that the claiming party will be required to pay the costs of the defence is one factor that may discourage the pursuit of frivolous claims, and we therefore think it is inadvisable for parties to agree otherwise in their contract.

7. Time Limits for Award

Time limits for rendering an award. Occasionally, parties will include a restriction **1-188** on the time period by which the arbitrators must issue a final award, such as 'nine months from the constitution of the arbitral tribunal or 'six months from the confirmation of the chair of the arbitral tribunal'. Some arbitration rules already contain similar limitations. For example, the ICC Rules require the arbitrators to deliver a final award within six months of the signing of the terms of reference. But the ICC Rules leave the institution with the authority to extend the time limitation at its own initiative or at the request of the arbitral tribunal, even if one of the parties objects to the extension.[131] Establishing a time limitation directly in a contractual dispute resolution clause means that the specified period may be extended only by the agreement of the parties, through what could be regarded as an amendment of their contract.

Pros and cons of putting time limits in the arbitration clause. The advantage of **1-189** incorporating in one's agreement a specific deadline for rendering the award is that it encourages the arbitral tribunal to swiftly conclude the proceedings before its term expires. One disadvantage, particularly if the period is very short, is that it may make it more difficult for the parties to find arbitrators willing to undertake to complete an arbitration within the specified period. Perhaps more importantly, there is a risk that it may not be possible in practice for the arbitrators to comply with the time limit, and that one of the parties will not agree to extend it. If that were to happen, the validity and enforceability of the award might be compromised. Our view is therefore that very short, hard time limits are best avoided; instead parties should consider some form of 'soft' or 'best efforts' obligation upon the arbitrators to issue their award by a specified date, or should adopt 'expedited' arbitration rules offered by insitutions such as CPR or DIS or SCC.

8. Baseball Arbitration

'Baseball arbitration' and similar modifications to the arbitration process. Other **1-190** creative ways in which parties can influence through additional contractual terms

---

131. Chapter 5, *The Conduct of the Arbitration.*

how an arbitration will actually be conducted include providing for 'baseball arbitration'. This draws its name from the practice by which disputes are resolved in the United States between professional players of the sport and their teams. After presenting their case in full, each side submits a 'baseball number' – signifying the relief sought – to the arbitrators, who must choose the number presented by one side or the other. The arbitrators are not at liberty, for example, to reject the parties' numbers in favour of a middle ground they believe to be fair and in accordance with the parties' rights.

1-191 *Pros and cons of baseball arbitration.* One advantage of baseball arbitration is that it should encourage settlement because the parties are unlikely to submit their most aggressive or 'best-case' numbers, because doing so would give rise to the risk of the arbitrators choosing a more moderate number submitted by the opposing party. The parties are therefore forced to accept some degree of moderation in their claims and resulting settlement negotiations. Baseball arbitration can present its own set of challenges, however, not least of which is that there is no established set of 'baseball arbitration rules'. This can leave the parties with uncertainty as to how the proceedings are likely to unfold. For example, the arbitral tribunal may need to determine how many baseball numbers the parties must submit: one number for the entire arbitration (inclusive of all claims and counterclaims), two numbers (one for the claimant's case and one for any counterclaims), or perhaps multiple numbers (one for each individual claim, and one for each counterclaim). A tribunal's decision as to how, and how many, baseball numbers are to be presented will have a substantial impact on the conduct of the arbitration and its outcome.

9.   Waiver of Sovereign Immunity

1-192 *Agreements with states or state entities: waiver of sovereign immunity.* Where one party to the arbitration agreement is a state or a state entity, the other party should seek a waiver by the state party in the parties' contract of any immunity from jurisdiction or from execution that the state party may enjoy. The real issue is immunity from execution of the award, as in most legal systems it is accepted today that a party automatically waives its immunity from jurisdiction[132] – but not generally its immunity from execution[133] – by the act of agreeing to arbitrate. In an interesting development, the French courts have held that reference in the arbitration clause to arbitration rules (such as those of the ICC) that contain an undertaking by the parties to carry out the award will amount to a waiver of immunity of execution by the state party to the arbitration.[134] Still, there is certainly no guarantee that other courts will reach the same conclusion. What is clear is that

---

132. Chapter 6, *After the Arbitration.*
133. See, e.g., Art. 55 of the ICSID Convention.
134. See *Creighton Limited v. Minister of Finance and Minister of Internal Affairs and Agriculture of the Government of the State of Qatar,* Decision of the French Court of Cassation, 6 Jul. 2000, *Yearbook Commercial Arbitration XXV* (2000), 458–460.

the absence of an express waiver in the parties' contract will place the state party in a far stronger position when resisting enforcement of an award against it, whatever the place of enforcement. A waiver should be as comprehensive and specific as possible (stipulating, for example, that the waiver covers assets used for diplomatic purposes, if that is the parties' intention), because the courts may be expected to interpret waivers of sovereign immunity restrictively.[135]

E.   CONCLUSION ON ELEMENTS OF AN ARBITRATION CLAUSE

The table below sets out, for convenience, the elements of the international arbi- **1-193** tration clause just examined.

Checklist 1c – The Elements of an International Arbitration Clause at a Glance

Essence of Clause	Identification of disputes	'All disputes arising out of or in connection with the present contract'
	Submission to mediation [if desired]	'shall be submitted by the parties for settlement by mediation. If a dispute is not settled by mediation, it'
	Submission to arbitration	'shall be referred to and finally resolved by arbitration'
Main Variables	Institution [if desired] and rules	'at [name of institution] and in accordance with the [name of institution's rules].' or, if ad hoc arbitration is preferred, 'in accordance with the UNCITRAL Arbitration Rules. The appointing authority shall be [name of appointing authority].'
	Place of arbitration	'The place of the arbitration shall be [city, country].'
	Number of arbitrators	'The number of arbitrators shall be [one or three].'
	Language of arbitration	'The language of the arbitration shall be [language].'

---

135.   Chapter 6, *After the Arbitration.*

'Bells and Whistles'	Consider adding language tailored to parties' circumstances, including on following issues:
	• Joinder • Consolidation • Requirement for formal notices and/or prior negotiations • Pre-Arbitral referee procedure • Qualifications of arbitrators • Procedure and evidence • Allocation of costs • Limitation on time for rendering award • Waiver of sovereign immunity

III.   AGREEMENTS TO MEDIATE BEFORE ARBITRATION

1-194 A timeless cliché of disputes lawyers is that a bad settlement is always better than a good litigation. As we discuss in Chapter 4, mediation has emerged as an effective means for assisting parties in reaching a resolution on their own, before a resolution is handed to them by judges or arbitrators. We think parties to any international contract should consider whether it is opportune to include in their contract a requirement of mediation before proceeding to final and binding resolution in arbitration or court litigation, in order to increase the probability of settlement.

1-195 *Requiring negotiations before arbitration.* It has been common practice in international contracts for many years to preface a dispute resolution clause with language stating that the parties 'shall attempt to resolve their dispute first by negotiation' or something similar. As considered earlier, we see little value in such clauses, as negotiation is always an option that will be known to the parties and likely attempted before they resort to other forms of dispute resolution – whether or not the parties stipulate in their agreement that they must conduct negotiations before starting binding dispute resolution. Of more value than a requirement to negotiate will be a requirement to mediate, as this is more likely to have the intended effect of leading to a settlement.

1-196 *Step clauses.* A contractual mediation clause will be contained within the contract's general dispute resolution provision and, as with an arbitration clause, will typically apply to 'any and all disputes arising under the contract'. A dispute resolution clause that contains both mediation and arbitration requirements is known as a 'step' or 'tiered' clause, because dispute resolution is sequenced, beginning with a non-binding process such as mediation and ending with a binding process such as arbitration or litigation. The sequence also stages dispute resolution so that the least burdensome procedure for the parties (the non-binding process) is attempted first.

Med-arb procedures. There is considerable debate over whether parties should vest **1-197** the powers to both mediate and arbitrate a dispute in the same third party or parties. This has led to a procedure known as 'med-arb', which in international dispute resolution practice is much more frequently discussed in learned commentary than actually used. While a clause that contemplates med-arb may appear superficially similar to a step requirement (because it contains obligations of both mediation and arbitration), it is in fact a very different creature. In our view, it will almost always be inappropriate to include a med-arb clause in an international contract, for a number of reasons. First, and most importantly, it will deny the parties one of the key distinguishing characteristics of mediation, which is that they can engage in open discussions with the mediator confident that these discussions will not be shared with the ultimate adjudicator if mediation fails. Thus, the mediation will not really be a mediation at all, but a 'pre-arbitration'. Second, a med-arb clause will unduly restrict the parties' ability to choose competent mediators and arbitrators. While many arbitrators may be quick to claim mediation competency, and vice-versa, the truth is that mediation and arbitration are very different animals, and the pool of individuals with substantial experience or training in both areas (particularly with an international dimension) is small.

Arb-med: something completely different	Michael Leathes, former head of intellectual property of British-American Tobacco and the founder of the International Mediation Institute (IMI), has advocated a form of dispute resolution that could be termed 'arb-med' (as opposed to 'med-arb'). Under this approach, the parties complete an arbitration, and the tribunal renders its award but does not disclose it to the parties. The parties then attempt to negotiate a settlement with the assistance of a mediator (not one of the arbitrators), with either of them at liberty to terminate the mediation at any time and accept the results of the arbitration. This form of dispute resolution may be advantageous in cases where the parties have significant overlapping commercial interests that they can use to engage each other constructively in order to improve their outcome versus the arbitration award.

A.   The Elements of a Mediation Step Clause

Mediation is a purely consensual process that will only succeed if both parties **1-198** desire to reach a settlement. As a result, many of the concerns about the place of dispute resolution, courts, and certain requirements or formalities that apply in the case of arbitration clauses are not present in the case of mediation. Still, a mediation clause typically sets out certain procedures to be followed before initiating arbitration, such as whether the mediation requirement is obligatory, any applicable rules of procedure, any mediation institution, and any timing limitations. Below are some model step clauses suggested by the ICC that provide for mediation ADR in ICC terminology and then arbitration under the rules of institutions that offer both mediation and arbitration services we also include model step clauses for mediation and arbitration under different mediation and arbitration institutions or rules.

Example 1b – Optional Mediation

The parties may at any time, without prejudice to any other proceedings, seek to settle any dispute arising out of or in connection with the present contract in accordance with the ICC ADR Rules.

Example 1c – Obligation to Consider Mediation

In the event of any dispute arising out of or in connection with the present contract, the parties agree in the first instance to discuss and consider submitting the matter to settlement proceedings under the ICC ADR Rules.

Example 1d – Obligation to Submit Dispute to Mediation with an Automatic Expiration Mechanism

In the event of any dispute arising out of or in connection with the present contract, the parties agree to submit the matter to settlement proceedings under the ICC ADR Rules. If the dispute has not been settled pursuant to the said Rules within forty-five days following the filing of a Request for ADR or within such other period as the parties may agree in writing, the parties shall have no further obligations under this paragraph.

Example 1e – Obligation to Submit Dispute to Mediation Followed by ICC Arbitration as Required

In the event of any dispute arising out of or in connection with the present contract, the parties agree to submit the matter to settlement proceedings under the ICC ADR Rules. If the dispute has not been settled pursuant to the said Rules within forty-five days following the filing of a Request for ADR or within such other period as the parties may agree in writing, such dispute shall be finally settled under the Rules of Arbitration of the ICC by one or more arbitrators appointed in accordance with the said Rules of Arbitration. The seat, or legal place, of the arbitration shall be [specify city]. The language to be used in the mediation and in the arbitration shall be [specify language].

Example 1f – Mediation Followed by Ad Hoc Arbitration (UNCITRAL)

Attempt at Settlement. In the event of a dispute, controversy, or claim arising out of or relating to this agreement, including any question regarding its existence, validity, breach, or termination, the parties shall first seek settlement of that dispute by mediation in accordance with the Mediation Rules of the Centre for Effective Dispute Resolution (CEDR).[136]

Arbitration. If the dispute is not settled by mediation within forty-five days of the date of notice of a request for mediation, or such further period as the parties shall agree in writing, the dispute shall be referred to and finally resolved by arbitration under the UNCITRAL Arbitration Rules as at present in force, which Rules are deemed to be incorporated by reference into this clause. The number of arbitrators shall be [specify one or three]. The seat, or legal place, of arbitration shall be [specify city]. Pursuant to Article 6 of the UNCITRAL Arbitration Rules, the functions referred to in Articles 11(3), 11(4), 13(3), 14, 16(3), and 34(2) shall be performed by [specify arbitration institution to act as appointing authority] (the 'Appointing Authority'). The language to be used in the mediation and in the arbitration shall be [specify language].

Mandatory mediation versus obligation to consider. The most critical aspect of a **1-199** mediation clause is whether it requires the parties to actually attempt mediation before initiating arbitration or going to court, or merely to consider recourse to mediation. Given the varying levels of familiarity with mediation in many parts of the world, the inclusion in a contract of a requirement only to 'consider' mediation may be easier to negotiate, but will be much less valuable in encouraging the opposing party to actually attempt settlement through mediation at the time of a dispute. We therefore recommend making mediation a requirement. Moreover, a mediation clause with teeth may also be easier for the parties to manage in the long run. In some jurisdictions, notably the United Kingdom, courts favour mediation and already take a dim view of parties who fail to make a good faith effort to settle their dispute. Thus, requiring mediation before arbitration will spare both parties any need to investigate at the time of a dispute whether an obligation merely to 'consider' mediation in fact imposes a more onerous obligation.

---

136. Parties may specify any mediation institution in connection with any form of institutional or ad hoc form of arbitration. We use CEDR here only by way of example.

1-200 *Time limits.* A mediation clause should preferably state a period by which the parties must attempt settlement through mediation, before they proceed to arbitration or court litigation. The period of time should be reasonable in light of the parties' locations and how far they may need to travel, but should not be so long as to merely delay the ultimate adjudication of the dispute in the event no settlement is reached. We think periods of forty-five, sixty, or ninety days are usually reasonable. The period should run from a fixed date, preferably from the date of notification by one party to the other of a request for mediation.

1-201 *Procedural rules and mediation.* The parties should provide in their contract a general framework for a mediation by specifying the rules under which any mediation will be conducted. When the rules are those of a mediation or arbitration institution, they will provide a mechanism for the appointment of the mediator in the absence of agreement by the parties. Beyond that, the rules themselves rarely differ in their essential elements: the obligations of the parties and mediator to treat as confidential all matters discussed, and the methods of compensating the mediator and/or the institution. But unlike arbitration, relatively little attention will be paid to any formal rules of procedure once a mediation is planned or underway. This is because mediation remains at all times an informal and consensual process that can and should be adapted as required to fit the needs of particular parties or disputes.[137]

B. MEDIATION INSTITUTIONS

1-202 There are two broad categories of institutions that provide mediation services: institutions that specialise in providing mediation services only, and institutions that provide a range of dispute resolution services, including arbitration as well as mediation. We look below at some of the differences between each category of institution and the advantages and disadvantages of each.

1-203 *Specialist mediation institutions.* The past thirty years have seen a flowering of mediation institutions around the world, most having a national or at most regional focus, rather than an international reach. Many offer training services and qualify mediators, in addition to helping parties identify and appoint mediators. Training can be a major source of income for some mediation institutions.

1-204 *Advantages of specialist mediation institutions.* Because of their specialisation, mediation institutions should by their nature offer a higher guarantee of the quality of the service offered. Mediation is what they do, and generally they will maintain a restricted pool of qualified mediators who are subject to quality review. Some

---

137. As discussed in Ch. 4, *International Settlement Negotiation and Mediation*, parties will almost always agree on the date, duration, and any procedures when initiating the mediation, either on their own initiative or at the prompting of the mediator.

institutions, such as JAMS in the United States, are companies or partnerships that are owned by their mediator members. Others, such as CPR in the United States and CEDR in the United Kingdom, are non-profit organisations that exist to promote mediation (in the case of CEDR, this is on behalf of the organisation's pool of mediators). Because mediation institutions are generally national or regional in their coverage (as opposed to being international), they will also be highly attuned to local culture or dispute practices that may be relevant to organising and conducting a mediation locally. Another significant advantage is cost: the services of mediation institutions are generally much cheaper than the same services offered by arbitration institutions.

Disadvantages of specialist mediation institutions. Because a mediation institution **1-205** will not offer binding dispute resolution services, the reference to such an institution in a contract's arbitration clause means that the mediation and arbitration institutions will be different. This may be cause difficulty because, if the other party is unfamiliar with the process of mediation, it may view the request to include an additional institution (with an unfamiliar name) as an unnecessary complication in the disputes clause. Another possible disadvantage of a mediation-only institution in an international context is that the institution's familiarity with local practice and culture is likely to come at the price of a limited ability to support an international dispute through its restricted pool of local mediators.

Mediator appointments. For commercial disputes, most mediation institutions will **1-206** attempt to facilitate agreement among the parties in the choice of a mediator by supplying a list of candidates whom they believe best match what the parties are seeking for their particular dispute. If none of the candidates are to the parties' liking, a mediation institution can be expected to supply a different list if one or both parties request one.

Arbitration institutions that offer mediation services. In just the past decade, at least **1-207** three of the leading international arbitration institutions – the ICC, ICDR, and the LCIA – have all either added a mediation capability or enhanced an existing capability to their portfolio of dispute resolution services. So have regional arbitration institutions, such as the CMAP. While an arbitration's mediation rules and capabilities are a positive factor when considering which institution to adopt, parties will want to know and consider how the institution conducts its mediations before actually going to the organisation for the appointment or management of a mediation. The pros and cons of mediation services offered by arbitration institutions are, not surprisingly, the converse of those of specialised mediation institutions.

Question:	Is it likely that an arbitration institution will take a different approach to mediation than an institution dedicated to providing mediation services?
Answer:	Yes. For example, mediation institutions may be very free with information about their mediators and even make information

> about them (and their mediation success rates) publicly available on the institution's websites. By contrast, arbitration institutions are more likely to closely guard such information, possibly out of arbitration-derived concerns of confidentiality. If the institution will not say who its mediators are and how they are appointed (and there are institutions that will not provide this information), then parties may be reluctant – rightly in our view – to rely on the institution if a dispute arises.

1-208 *Advantages of arbitration institutions that offer mediation services.* On the fair assumption that any mediation is better than no mediation, a significant advantage that arbitration institutions offer is that they allow a party to propose and have accepted a 'one-stop shop' form of dispute resolution. For example, if a party has already accepted ICC arbitration, it is not a huge step to also include an additional provision (one sentence) that any arbitration will be preceded by mediation under the ICC ADR Rules. The leading international arbitration institutions may also be able to offer practical services, such as access to facilities needed to get a mediation up and running in different countries.

1-209 *Disadvantages of arbitration institutions that offer mediation services.* The main disadvantage of selecting the mediation rules of an arbitration institution is that arbitration institutions have less experience of identifying mediators (in the event the parties are unable to do so on their own) or organising and conducting a mediation. The statistics of the ICC and the ICDR, for example, show an average number of mediations conducted per year that remains in the low double digits (and until 2005, for the ICC, in single digits). As a consequence, an arbitration institution may take an overly formalistic approach to mediation, treating it more as it would an arbitration and tolerating a substantially higher cost structure than would ordinarily be expected by parties experienced in mediation.

1-210 *Mediator appointments by arbitration institutions.* There is no consistent practice by which arbitration institutions identify and appoint mediators, and it is not a given that an arbitration institution will be as forthcoming as a mediation institution. For example, the ICC does not, as a rule, provide parties with lists of candidates. Instead, the ADR case manager will elicit input from any relevant national committees and directly appoint the mediator from among candidates that the parties will not have seen. But if a party does request a list of potential candidates, the ICC will oblige even though the practice is not contemplated by its ADR rules. By contrast, the practice of the ICDR is to supply the parties with lists of potential mediators and to facilitate their agreement on an appointment.

1-211 *Passively offering or actively selling mediation services to parties in dispute?* Some institutions play a passive role in providing mediation to parties only when they request it, while others will propose mediation at the commencement of arbitration, regardless of whether the parties have referred to it in their contracts.

We think the latter is the better practice, as it does more to help the parties reach an early resolution without the need for completing the arbitration.

Mediation with the ICDR and ICC	Both the ICDR and the ICC offer mediation as well as arbitration services, and both are similar in that neither institution has a closed 'pool' of mediators (as mediation institutions do). Instead, they use their international reach to identify an appropriate mediator at the time of a dispute. While similar in these important respects, their approach to 'marketing' their mediation services is, in practice, very different. The ICDR will promote mediation to the parties in any ICDR arbitration, regardless of whether their dispute resolution clause has specified a preference for mediation. In this, the ICDR seeks to leverage the institution's dual role of provider of both mediation and arbitration services. The ICC, by contrast, maintains its mediation and arbitration services in separate management 'silos' and will not propose mediation to parties involved in an arbitration unless the parties themselves have first agreed to do this. The assumption appears to be that mediation is not an accepted practice in many countries, and therefore the ICC does not wish to intrude on party expectations. We think there is little harm in proposing mediation to parties who have commenced arbitration; in our view, parties to an international commercial dispute are unlikely to react badly to a suggestion from the institution that they attempt settlement through mediation, and the proposal of mediation by a reputed institution may prompt parties to try a worthwhile dispute resolution option that they may not previously have considered.

Chapter Two

Negotiating an International Dispute Resolution Agreement

In Chapter 1, we surveyed the different elements that make up an international **2-001** dispute resolution agreement. In this chapter, we look at how parties should go about negotiating these agreements. In many international negotiations the parties are able to agree without difficulty many of the so-called 'standard' terms that appear consistently in different contracts, such as payment, warranties, and termination. Yet they can find themselves in a difficult process of negotiation and compromise when it comes to dispute resolution, which can go as far as one or the other side threatening to walk away from discussions. Unlike those other clauses, which are capable of being answered by yes or no or in otherwise simple terms (Shall we agree to limit the seller's liability? Will warranties last six or twelve months?), dispute clauses may present a more complex set of legal, cultural, and other issues.

We address below the difficult advice that business managers never like to hear, **2-002** which is that the other party's intractable position on dispute resolution leads the adviser to recommend abandoning negotiation of the contract. Before getting to that extreme result, however, we suggest parties treat the negotiation of the dispute clause as they would any other part of the contract: as an opportunity to reach the best possible overall deal through informed negotiating. We stress the value of international arbitration in mitigating risks associated with compromise, and the utility of a mediation requirement to further minimise the risk that disputes will ever reach the stage of an inherently imperfect method of binding resolution. Rather than encouraging a party to draw a hard line in the sand on dispute resolution, we propose negotiation strategies that treat the other party's inflexibility as a potential opportunity that can be quantified and assessed just like any other form of commercial risk. Finally, we discuss the rare occasions when, only after all else fails, the other side's insistence that its own dispute terms are a 'deal-breaker' really should break the deal.

I.   ATTEMPTING TO AVOID NEGOTIATION: 'STANDARD' DISPUTE CLAUSES

2-003 *'Company policy'*. Many companies develop – for better or worse – 'standard' dispute resolution clauses that they seek to impose in all of their international contracts. Some will claim – in what is really an attempt to avoid negotiation – that they are required by 'company policy' to include these clauses in their contracts. There can be advantages to standard clauses (and policies regarding their use), but they are likely outweighed by the disadvantages of the inflexibility they impose.

2-004 *Potential advantages of standard dispute resolution clauses*. While in general parties are wise to avoid the slavish application of the same dispute clause in all types of contracts, there will be times when it is sensible and efficient to adopt a standard dispute clause. Having a standard clause (or being able to say a particular form of dispute resolution is required by company policy) of course means employees will not have the flexibility, or the appearance of flexibility, to negotiate this contract provision. This inflexibility can make sense when a party has substantial negotiating leverage (the ability to impose contractual conditions on other parties) or negotiators who lack either the level of sophistication or the support of competent counsel to negotiate a reasonable dispute clause on their own.

Question:	Our company/client is demanding standard terms and conditions for all of our international contracts, including the place and type of dispute resolution. What is the best dispute resolution method for us to adopt?
Answer:	This question is a common source of tension coming between company managers and their lawyers. On the one hand, managers need and want clear guidance on the degree of risk they face when agreeing to a contract. On the other hand, lawyers know that the best dispute clauses are tailored on a case-by-case basis to the particularities of the contract and its parties. Still, if future contracts will be of a similar type and nature, it will often be feasible to develop a 'standard' clause that is suitable, or at least workable, for most or all of the disputes the contracts might produce.

2-005 *The price of inflexibility*. The difficulty with standard dispute resolution provisions is that the other party may try to increase its expected contract benefits in order to justify what it may perceive as increased risk. A party who intends to be inflexible, therefore, would be wise to close negotiations on price and other contract terms before announcing its inflexibility on dispute resolution. In fact, this may be why many dispute resolution clauses are the last provisions to be negotiated in a contract, with one or both parties hoping that the other agreed provisions make the transaction sufficiently attractive to accept less-than-ideal dispute resolution.

My Way versus the Highway Negotiations	Party A: Now let's discuss Article 21 of your proposed terms and conditions. It requires disputes to be resolved in the courts of your country under your country's laws. We would like to change that to ICC arbitration in Geneva.
	Party B: We are the customer, so it is fair for disputes to be resolved here in our country. Let's now move to the next article of the contract, please.
	Party A: No, this is important. We want ICC arbitration in Geneva. We can also accept ICDR arbitration in London.
	Party B: As I told you, we are the customer, the project is here, and the disputes should be resolved here, too. This is not a point we are willing to negotiate.
	Party A: If you cannot be flexible on dispute resolution, I will discuss it with upper management, and we will consider accepting your preferred clause only in the context of the entire contract.

II.　　　　　　NEGOTIATING THE DISPUTE CLAUSE ON THE BASIS OF COMMON DISPUTE RESOLUTION VALUES

A wise negotiator will not only establish her objectives before entering a negoti- **2-006** ation, she will also have a strategy to achieve those objectives when she sits down with the other party. When negotiating dispute clauses, both lawyers and commercial negotiators should come prepared to articulate the reasons for their preferences and to respond to objections. Unfortunately, many parties make the mistake of simply insisting on their position (perhaps a standard clause required by 'company policy', as discussed above) as the only fair one under the circumstances, which can lead to frustrating 'mine or yours' negotiations, and which can easily result in upsetting the overall contract negotiations or a dispute clause that is disadvantageous to one or even both sides. By contrast, a party is more likely to be successful if it starts a negotiation by understanding what the other side is seeking to accomplish, identifying any middle ground, and coming to the negotiation prepared with options that will satisfy the interests and objectives of both sides.

Negotiating based on Common Dispute Resolution Values	Party A: Article 21 of your proposed terms and conditions requires disputes to be resolved in the courts of your country under your country's laws.
	Party B: Well, we are the customer, the project is here, so we think disputes should be resolved in our courts, which are fair.
	Party A: Actually, I was not questioning your decision, just trying to understand what you are hoping to achieve. We also want to resolve disputes through a fair process, but we are not familiar with the courts here – are they efficient?
	Party B: They could be better, but are acceptable to us.
	Party A: It sounds like we share the same values, even if we do not yet agree on how to implement them. Can we discuss other options that might satisfy our mutual desire for fairness and efficiency?
	Party B: Propose something, so we can consider it.

2-007 Most parties will share fairness and efficiency of process as common values in dispute resolution, or at least they should if they are negotiating in good faith. Even when the dispute clause becomes the most hotly contested part of what is being drafted in a contract, these common values should not be in conflict.

2-008 Perhaps the best strategy for negotiating any type of contract or contractual clause is to have multiple, reasonable 'fallback' positions–alternatives that can be proposed when the party's preferred clause or position is not acceptable to the other negotiating party. We provide below some guidance on developing fallback positions for the negotiation of dispute clauses, gauged to address the type of objections raised, and consistent, in our view, with common dispute resolution values.

A.   Answering Objections to Using Arbitration (Rather Than the Courts)

2-009 While international arbitration has many advantages, enthusiasm for it is not universal, and a party should be prepared to encounter common objections to adopting it as a method of dispute resolution. We look first at what we believe to be the main advantages and disadvantages of arbitration and litigation, before suggesting some strategies for resisting objections to using arbitration.

1. Arbitration or Litigation: Which Is Better?

Checklist 2a – Considerations in Favour of Choosing International Arbitration

The following factors should influence a decision to choose international arbitration over the courts, provided that the courts being considered are available to the parties and have a reputation for fairness (independence), efficiency and competence. If the available courts do not have a reputation for fairness, efficiency or competence or, worse, if they are known to be corrupt, then we would not recommend that they be considered as a viable option. An affirmative answer to any of the following questions suggests that international arbitration should at least be considered as the method of dispute resolution for the contract in question.

Considerations in Favour of Choosing International Arbitration	*Yes/No*
Neutrality: Does a party wish to avoid the home courts of the other?	
Enforcement: Is it likely there will be a need to enforce a right of payment against assets of a party located outside the country where the court decision would be rendered?	
Efficiency: Is the time from the start of the litigation to obtaining an enforceable judgment in the available court likely to be excessive when compared with international arbitration?	
Cost: Will the cost of litigating in the courts significantly exceed the cost of international arbitration?	
Flexibility: Is it important for the parties to be able to design their own bespoke dispute resolution process for this contract?	
Competence: Is it likely that complex or technical issues will be involved that may challenge the capabilities of the court?	
Convenience: Is the dispute likely to require witnesses and documents located in different countries and involve languages that are not the same as that or those of the available court?	
Confidentiality: Is it important for the parties to keep their disputes out of the public eye?[1]	
Moderation: Is it desirable to avoid the risk of potentially extreme or unusual decisions by a court?	

---

1. Note, as we discuss in Ch. 5, that the presumption that arbitration is 'confidential' is often misplaced.

2-010 *Neutrality.* Perhaps the main advantage of international arbitration is that it is not litigation in the home courts of one of the parties. In that sense, arbitration is 'neutral': choosing international arbitration should reassure parties who are concerned that litigation in the other side's courts will favour the other side. For example, it is unlikely that a Chinese party contracting with an American party will want to subject itself to the rigours of the US court system; and it is equally unlikely that the American party will be enthusiastic about litigating in the Chinese courts. International arbitration falls somewhere between the two: it will be fair and reasonably efficient, and each party is likely to be equally comfortable or uncomfortable with the process.

2-011 *Enforcement of the outcome.* One of the clearest advantages of international arbitration is the ability, under the New York Convention and similar instruments facilitating enforcement, to enforce an award outside the country where it was rendered. Enforcing court judgments across borders is much more challenging in many parts of the world, as there is no worldwide equivalent of the New York Convention to assist with cross-border enforcement.[2] However, cross-border enforcement is only relevant if (1) the other party has any assets outside the country where the dispute would be decided, and (2) there is likely to be a need to enforce any award. The second point can be too quickly taken for granted. Many parties to international contracts will have secured ways of ensuring performance that do not depend on the contract's method of dispute resolution: for instance, a seller who is paid in full on delivery, or who obtains the benefit of an unconditional letter of credit upon signing the contract, may treat enforcement as a lower priority than the buyer who will want compensation or an equivalent remedy if the goods are defective. By contrast, if the ability to enforce an award in the country of the other contracting party is a priority, this may be a powerful argument in favour of resolving disputes in the courts of the country where the other party's assets are located. It is generally the case that a local court judgment is the quickest route to enforcing payment. Of course, this must be balanced against the fairness and efficiency of the local courts: the foreign party needs to have a fair opportunity to get a judgment to enforce, and to get it reasonably quickly. If the likely duration is five or more years, then an efficiently managed international arbitration may represent a significant short cut to a remedy.

2-012 *Efficiency: speed of resolution and enforcement.* In the courts of many countries, cases can sit dormant for years. It is worth asking, even if the cost of litigating in the courts is low, would it be a problem to have to wait for a dispute to be decided there? The passage of time may give rise to concerns other than costs, such as the impact of unresolved litigation on a company's financial statements and the unpredictability of similar contracts the company is currently performing. Perhaps the best measure of time is how long it takes to obtain a judgment that can be enforced against the

---

2.   However, there are some multilateral or bilateral agreements among states notably in Europe, which facilitate enforcement of foreign court judgments.

losing party. In Italy, for example, judgments are enforceable upon a decision of the court of first instance (trial court), even if they are subject to appeals that may take many years. In other countries, such as the United Arab Emirates, a court judgment will not be enforceable until all appeals have been exhausted. While speed is not something parties should assume or take for granted with arbitration, they can expect to have a reasonable degree of control over those parts of the process most likely to lead to a longer or shorter proceeding.

Cost: the myth that arbitration is cheaper. Cost is often a major concern of one or **2-013** even both parties negotiating an international dispute resolution clause. Chapter 3 discusses ways of estimating the total costs of resolving a dispute when one arises, but can this cost be meaningfully assessed at the time of negotiating the contract? In the case of international arbitration, the answer is that it is fair to assume that it will cost as much or more than litigating in any of the available courts. Often it will cost much more, as litigation in the courts of many countries (particularly civil law countries) is relatively inexpensive compared with more expensive locations (mainly common law countries). Therefore, for instance, an international arbitration will likely cost more than the equivalent litigation in France or Brazil, but it will probably not exceed the costs of an equivalent litigation in the United States and United Kingdom (and will cost less than a trial and a full set of appeals in those countries).

Flexibility, competence, and convenience. The flexibility of an international arbi- **2-014** tration can be a real advantage when the alternative is a distant foreign court where disputes are resolved in a foreign language. For example, while German courts are known to be impartial and reasonably efficient, that does not mean a non-German party will necessarily appreciate the requirement of having to translate all of the key documents into German, and to fly in witnesses from Asia or the Americas for hearings to be conducted with an interpreter. Nor will the party appreciate the need to have all the court submissions made in German, which may render the party's ability to provide input more difficult. Convenience is in some respects just another way of expressing costs, but it is one that is sometimes underestimated when choosing between litigation in the courts and arbitration.

Confidentiality. The notion that all arbitration proceedings are kept strictly confi- **2-015** dential is not correct. The rules of some institutions, for example, may restrict the ability of the arbitrators to make public any aspect of the proceedings, but they generally do not place the same restrictions on the parties. Even when confidentiality is imposed on parties by the arbitration rules, it is difficult in practice to ensure that confidentiality will be respected. If a party takes its dispute to the press, there is little or no immediate recourse for the other party, except perhaps to determine whether its own press statement is warranted. Claiming damages for loss is a possibility, but this may require new proceedings, and establishing loss will be problematic in many cases.[3]

---

3. Chapter 3, *When the Dispute Arises.*

2-016 The confidentiality of an arbitration will be further compromised if at any point either of the parties applies to the courts, whether in support of the arbitration (for instance, to establish the validity of the arbitration agreement or appoint arbitrators), in ancillary proceedings (to grant interim measures), or in challenge and enforcement proceedings (an arbitration award must be brought before the courts if enforcement is sought, which may allow or even require both parties to re-litigate substantive points of the claims and defences, and open up the arbitration to judicial scrutiny and, unless measures are taken in court to protect confidentiality, to the full gaze of the public).[4]

2-017 *The myth that parties always value confidentiality.* It is worth questioning whether parties to a particular transaction genuinely value confidentiality, instead of simply assuming that arbitration is advantageous because it is 'confidential'. For example, if a party is willing to subject disputes under the same type of contract to resolution in the courts of its own country, then it is fair to presume that its desire for confidentiality is a 'nice to have' but not a 'need to have'.

2-018 *Moderation in decision making.* Judges are appointed by the state rather than by disputing parties (as is the case in arbitration). As they are not appointed by the parties, some consider judges to be more willing than arbitrators to reach an outcome that is extremely favourable to one side. There is probably some truth to the perception that arbitrators are more inclined to avoid interpretations of contracts that lead to extreme results when they can reasonably be avoided. This is particularly the case with tribunals consisting of three arbitrators, in which a desire to achieve consensus may further reduce the likelihood of an extreme result.

Checklist 2b – Considerations in Favour of Choosing Court Litigation

The following considerations could lead a party to prefer litigation in an available court. Once again, however, the underlying premise is that the court has a reputation for fairness, efficiency and competence. An affirmative answer to any of the following questions would suggest that the parties should at least consider dispute resolution in the available court.

Considerations in favour of choosing court litigation	*Yes/No*
Appeals: Is it desirable to preserve the right of appeal of an adverse decision?	
Multiple parties: Is it desirable to preserve the right to join third parties in the litigation?	
Cost: Is litigating in court cheaper than international	

---

4. Chapter 6, *After the Arbitration.*

Considerations in favour of choosing court litigation	Yes/No
arbitration?	
Speed: Is the time taken until receiving an enforceable judgment reasonable compared to international arbitration?	
Clear resolution: Is it desirable to obtain a determination of a contractual provision that is a clear-cut victory for one side rather than a middle ground?	
Settlement promotion: Does the party favour or desire the inclination of courts to nudge parties towards settlement, often by providing an early indication of the likely outcome, before all the evidence is in?	

Appeals. It is probably the case that few parties to an international contract choose **2-019** to resolve their contractual disputes by arbitration because they desire to waive their right of appeal in the event of an unfavourable outcome. In any event, because a party may decide to challenge an award on largely procedural grounds, adding time and cost to the total proceedings, the waiver of appeal may be an illusory 'advantage', at least in terms of efficiency of dispute resolution. Rather than seeing the lack of a true appeal as an advantage of arbitration, it may be that some parties view the right of appeal as a guarantee of better justice that they are not so willing to give up. In such cases, the party wishing to maintain its right to an appeal on the merits would be well advised to resolve disputes in a court with an appeals system known to be fair and efficient.

Multiple parties. In some cases, in which there are many different parties contrib- **2-020** uting towards a common outcome, a party may wish to have the ability to bring multiple parties into proceedings to establish liability if and when the common outcome is not achieved as expected. An example is a complex construction project where there may be an owner, a project engineer, a construction contractor, and various subcontractors and suppliers of equipment and services. In the event of a claim against one of them, that party may want to have the ability to turn against another party, or at least obtain evidence from it. In such cases, where the most efficient outcome is likely to be best achieved by having the responsibilities of multiple parties under different contracts adjudicated together, court litigation is generally a superior method of doing so. While there have been various proposals to allow arbitrators to 'join' other parties to an arbitration, these are little tested and, absent special circumstances and careful drafting, are more of an attempt to shoehorn a court practice into arbitration, where it does not easily fit.[5]

---

5. See discussion of joinder and consolidation, Ch. 5, *The Conduct of the Arbitration*.

2-021 *Cost: the myth (or common complaint?) that arbitration is more expensive.* The most common complaint about international arbitration is that it is a cumbersome and expensive procedure compared with the efficient dispute resolution that would have been available in the courts of one of the parties. As already introduced in our discussion on reasons for preferring arbitration, it is true that arbitration can be more expensive than the courts. It just depends which courts. While the cost of arbitration might be competitive with litigation in the courts of some common law countries (such as the United Kingdom and the United States), it is generally more – or much more – expensive than litigation in the courts of other parts of the world. Importantly, the cost advantage of litigation may be reduced or eliminated if one takes account of the full appeals process, which is available in the court system but not in arbitration. In any event, the cost of arbitration is not always going to be a priority for both parties, particularly when one of them does not consider the available court options to be suitable.

2-022 *Clear resolution.* There may be instances in which a party will have a preference for a court decision that provides one party with a total victory, even if that means a decision some might characterise as extreme, rather than run the risk of an arbitration award that may be the result of compromise. We say this while also noting that with most international business contracts, it is most likely that both of the parties will prefer moderation, at least at the stage when they are contracting and unable to predict the circumstances of any future disputes. Also, we think the stereotypical portrayal of arbitration as a process of compromise and 'splitting the baby' is increasingly outdated, reducing the importance of this factor in any assessment of the appropriate dispute resolution method.

2-023 *Settlement promotion.* Judges may be willing to, or even enthusiastic about, providing an indication at an early stage of the proceedings of how the case is likely to conclude. This may be useful to the parties: an early indication that their case is weak or problematic may encourage them to settle (which is why judges give this sort of early indication). It can also be unhelpful where, for example, a party would want to develop the complexities of the case before the judge forms an opinion as to which side is in the right. Arbitrators, in contrast, will probably be unwilling to provide an early indication of their views of the dispute, at least in the absence of agreement of both parties.

2-024 *Weighing the considerations together.* A party should weigh up the different considerations examined above before deciding whether to press for arbitration or litigation in a given international contract. In our view, most parties to an international contract of any size are likely to conclude that international arbitration will be the method of dispute resolution best suited to their contract, principally on account of its neutrality and the international enforceability of arbitral awards. This is why it is fair to say that international arbitration has become the most popular method of resolution of international business disputes.

2.   Strategies to Address Resistance to Arbitration

Not all parties would necessarily agree with our view of the pros and cons of **2-025** arbitration. Some multinational companies are reluctant to accept arbitration, often on grounds that it is too expensive, with certain among them even forbidding arbitration in their contracts.[6] Companies in developing countries may reject arbitration based on the perception that it is biased towards companies based in industrialised countries. While we do not agree with such extreme positions (just as we would not endorse a proposal to include arbitration in every contract), we discuss below ways of treating the other side's concerns as legitimate and bringing mutually acceptable solutions to the table.

These solutions can range from adapting the type and place of arbitration to agree- **2-026** ing to a modified form of arbitration to address a specific concern. For example, if the contract is a letter of credit that may be drawn down only upon the satisfaction of certain conditions, the potential creditor may insist on dispute resolution in the courts in order to obtain a rapidly enforceable order in the event of a breach. An acceptable alternative could be arbitration with expedited procedures provided by a leading arbitration institution.[7] We explore these alternatives or fallback positions next.

Perhaps the most common problem encountered in negotiating a dispute clause is **2-027** one party's insistence on resolving disputes in its own country's courts, where the other party finds that unacceptable. Reasonable negotiation responses, as grounds for rejecting the option of local courts, can range from convenience (they are far away and in a language not easily accessible for the foreign party) to unfamiliarity with the proposed court system, to concerns about fairness and corruption. When the concerns are of the type for which a party will not be willing to compromise (usually corruption or manifest unfairness), international arbitration can provide many variations of middle ground that either side, if reasonable, should be willing to accept.

In addition to considering the potential consequences of accepting local courts, it is **2-028** sometimes worth questioning whether a party is sincere about rejecting international arbitration or is merely positioning itself to angle for other contractual concessions. The party will usually be keenly aware of the poor reputation of its home courts and, like the foreign party, may not wish to have its disputes decided there. A clever party, particularly one seeking to enhance its bargaining position,

---

6. Other companies have turned their back on international arbitration because they have been on the losing end of a large arbitration. This makes little sense, especially in parts of the world where the courts are unreliable, inefficient, or both, and are therefore an unworthy alternative to arbitration for cross-border disputes.
7. Chapter 1, *The Elements of an International Dispute Resolution Agreement*, and Ch. 5, *The Conduct of the Arbitration.*

may therefore insist on its own local courts only to be in a position to trade it for other concessions in negotiations.

2-029 It will therefore be valuable for the foreign party to have some knowledge of the reputation of the local justice system, as it is perceived by local interests, and the practice of local companies when it comes to dispute resolution. It will also be important to know whether one is dealing with a private entity (which will have more contracting flexibility) or a government or government-owned entity (which often will not – and its insistence on local dispute resolution may be sincere).

2-030 *Fallback position 1: acceptable forms of arbitration that satisfy the other party's concerns or desire for 'local' dispute resolution.* Parties who negotiate international contracts in good faith will usually have little excuse for insisting on one and only one type of dispute resolution. As we have outlined in Chapter 1, dispute resolution is a buyer's market, both as to the rules and place of arbitration: the major providers of international dispute resolution services – for example the ICC, ICDR/AAA, LCIA, and SIAC – compete not only with each other, but with regional and national arbitration institutions and various forms of ad hoc arbitration available in different countries. Similarly, there are many countries with a reputation for supporting arbitration, and a party can show substantial flexibility by allowing, for example, the other side to choose the place of dispute resolution from among a range of acceptable choices, for example, Geneva, London, Paris, Stockholm, New York, Hong Kong or Singapore. While not limitless, the combination of different institutions and places of dispute resolution (even within the same geographic area) makes it difficult for a party to insist reasonably that none of the proposed options is acceptable.

2-031 As noted above, it is difficult to conceive of a party in good faith insisting on one particular institution and nothing else. A reasonable party facing an objection to its proposed institution should be ready with alternatives that have a good reputation, including institutions within reasonable geographic proximity to the other party (and perhaps within the same country as the other party). For example, if the other party is in Asia, there is the SIAC or the HKIAC. In the Gulf, there is the DIFC-LCIA in Dubai and the ICDR in Bahrain. Increasingly, local chambers of commerce and bar associations – often supported by the leading international institutions – are establishing arbitration centres that allow an astute party to provide for a reasonable form of arbitration while accepting or even proposing a regional flavour.

2-032 We add a cautionary note, however, that not all regional institutions are created equal when it comes to international disputes. As discussed in Chapter 1, it is not a given that a national or regional institution will be able to competently support an international arbitration, particularly with respect to the appointment of arbitrators in the absence of party agreement. While the authors have seen a number of competent national or regional institutions (many of which are mentioned in this book), they have also encountered what appear to be local, provincial institutions that lack a true international sensitivity and capability. For example, one of the authors recently contacted a regional institution in connection with a contract negotiation, only to discover that its entire panel of arbitrators consisted of local lawyers within the city where the institution is based. While the neutrality of the institution did not seem to be in doubt, a party could not, at least in this case, presume the institution would be competent handling an international dispute.

Fallback position 2: the modified arbitration clause. Before abandoning the pos- **2-033** sibility of arbitration altogether, a party may offer to modify the dispute clause so as to address the concerns raised, for example over the time and cost of arbitration. One solution would be to agree to impose strict time limits, such as a specified number of months in which the arbitrators must render an award.[8] Another would be to adopt the 'fast-track' arbitration procedures of some arbitration institutions or simply move one's business to institutions that offer superior case management.[9]

Fallback position 3: considering viable court options. There are times when a party **2-034** may need to accept that court litigation is the best means of resolving disputes under a certain contract. For example, we have seen increasing demand in complex international projects for some type of consolidation of disputes among different parties and contracts – and/or joinder of third parties – as a means to bring all potential parties and issues into a single arbitration. Few such clauses have been tested in practice, and even the largest arbitral institutions are wary of these sorts of demands made of them in arbitration agreements.[10] Parties would therefore be well advised to tread lightly before introducing such initiatives in their own contracts. As noted above in paragraphs 2–020, if disputes are likely to involve more than two parties, court litigation may become more attractive for at least one of them, assuming jurisdiction can be had over all potential parties (this also assumes that the available courts can be regarded as fair, competent, and efficient, as we have discussed in Chapter 1). If there is a preference for the courts, but it is not possible to agree to resolve disputes in the local courts of the other party, there are competent neutral (but in some cases expensive) courts, such as the English Commercial Court and Singapore's High Court, that are geared towards resolving quickly and fairly disputes involving only parties from third countries. But before referring disputes to the courts of a third country, parties should get assurance that those courts will accept jurisdiction over their dispute, which may have little connection with the country of those courts other than the contractual forum selection.

---

8. Chapter 1, *The Elements of an International Dispute Resolution Agreement.*
9. *Ibid.*
10. *Ibid.*

B.   ANSWERING OBJECTIONS TO INSTITUTIONAL ARBITRATION

2-035 Some parties may be amenable to arbitration, but will refuse to agree to the administration of the arbitration by an institution of any type. There are many reasons parties prefer ad hoc (unadministered) arbitration over institutional arbitration, ranging from standard industry practice to suspicion (well-founded or not) over the nature and/or cost of institutions. Ad hoc arbitration is traditionally popular in contracts in certain business sectors such as insurance and shipping, where participants deal regularly with each other and feel they can trust their counterparties to 'play the game'. It is also popular in England and Commonwealth countries such as Australia, Hong Kong, and Singapore, where the courts are usually familiar with and supportive of ad hoc proceedings.[11] It is popular for the same reason in countries such as Italy, where domestic businesses have regularly used arbitration for commercial disputes, without substantial reliance on institutions. In the developing world, and particularly among state-owned enterprises, ad hoc arbitration may sometimes be preferred because it is perceived as neutral and less expensive than institutional arbitration.

2-036 As we discuss in Chapter 1, we think the concern over the cost of institutional arbitration is misplaced. The additional administrative expenses imposed by an institution are almost always low (at least compared to the other expenses incurred in an arbitration), and there is a good case for preferring arbitration administered by an institution as a way to reduce the overall cost of the proceedings. So, assuming one party has a strong preference for an institution, it may have strong arguments for persuading the other party that institutional arbitration is in fact the most cost-effective solution.

2-037 *Fallback position 1: UNCITRAL arbitration.* For parties who refuse to be persuaded as to the potential benefits of institutional arbitration, an alternative that is often acceptable is unadministered (ad hoc) arbitration in a suitable jurisdiction under the UNCITRAL Rules. However, UNCITRAL and other forms of ad hoc arbitration can present challenges, especially when held in arbitration-unfriendly countries and where one of the parties is disruptive or dilatory. Before proposing to include ad hoc arbitration in a dispute resolution clause, a party should feel confident in the ability of the courts of the place of the arbitration to support the arbitration and prevent disruption and delay.

2-038 When accepting any form of ad hoc arbitration (including UNCITRAL), parties should always try to specify a well-known arbitration institution as the 'appointing

---

11. We note, though, that ad hoc arbitration in China is not recognised by Chinese arbitration law and is not therefore recommended for arbitration in China. See, N. Darwazeh & M.J. Moser, 'Arbitration inside China', in *Managing Business Disputes in Today's China: Duelling with Dragons*, ed. M.J. Moser (Netherland: Kluwer Law International, 2007), 45 et seq.

authority', which will decide on any appointments or substitution of arbitrators in the event the parties cannot agree.[12]

Fallback position 2 with caution: 'pure ad hoc' arbitration. It is not unusual in **2-039** some parts of the world for parties to insist on ad hoc arbitration, without subjecting it to a formal set of arbitration rules. This *'pure ad hoc'* arbitration is conducted under any rules directly set out in the parties' agreement and under the procedural rules set out in the arbitration law of the place of arbitration. We think this option should only be seriously considered in places known to have a strong court system and a robust arbitration law. Recourse to the courts may be necessary in case of disagreement, for example, over the appointment or challenge of arbitrators, as the appointing authority is often, by default, the presiding judge of the courts of the city that is the place of arbitration. In the absence of a robust and pro-arbitration legal system, the risks of disruptive and dilatory behaviour by a party, and interference or absence of support from the courts of the place of the arbitration, will seriously reduce the chances of conducting an effective arbitration. Counterparties in good faith should be amenable, at the very least, to involving an institution or, at a minimum, following the UNCITRAL Rules.

C.   Answering the Insistence on Arbitration in a Country
                        Without a Reliable Court System

There are some countries where a foreign party will simply not want to resolve **2-040** disputes, whether in the courts or in arbitration. Given the number of locations that can be comfortably proposed, a reasonable 'local' party should have some degree of flexibility on the place of dispute resolution: arbitration in Paris instead of London, or Hong Kong instead of Singapore, is unlikely to materially disadvantage the more flexible party, even if the other party is located in one of those countries. But what if the less flexible party is insisting on arbitration on its home turf, which is a less arbitration-friendly place?

Fallback position 1: trading place of arbitration for governing law or other con- **2-041** *cessions in the method of dispute resolution.* If dispute resolution in the other party's country is not desirable, it may be possible to 'trade' the place of arbitration for another point being negotiated, such as the arbitral institution or even the governing law. Being able to demonstrate flexibility on the other contract points can make it acceptable and even attractive for the other party to agree to resolve disputes abroad. For example, in a contract negotiation between parties based in Germany and the Congo, the Congolese party may demand arbitration in Brazzaville under Congolese law. The German party may be reluctant to accept this, and may instead take the position that it can accept Congolese law (largely based on French law) in exchange for arbitration in Geneva, London, or another neutral location.

---

12. Chapter 1, *The Elements of an International Dispute Resolution Agreement.*

2-042 *Fallback position 2: reliance on the experience and creativity of arbitration institutions.* Parties should remember that arbitration institutions survive by being useful to contracting parties. But, it is striking that parties are not more willing to just ring them up for free advice on negotiating dispute clauses in difficult countries. Both international and regional institutions may have substantial experience in dealing with parties in a particular country and may be able to offer solutions that will not occur to a party or their outside counsel.

2-043 For example, to address concerns about the perception that Egyptian courts might interfere with arbitrations sited in Cairo, the Chamber of Arbitration of Milan and the Cairo Regional Centre for International Commercial Arbitration (CRCICA) have developed a cooperation agreement that allows parties to conduct proceedings under the auspices of *both* institutions, with hearings to take place in Cairo while the official, or legal site, of arbitration stays in Milan. The Egyptian party obtains its goal of 'Cairo arbitration' (with filing of the case, hearings and institution all in Cairo), while the foreign party obtains an international arbitration that (by having the legal seat in Milan) mitigates its concern over the possibility of interference by the Egyptian courts.

Example 2a – 'Cairo Clause' of the Chamber of Arbitration of Milan

> All disputes arising out of this contract shall be settled by arbitration under the Rules of the CRCICA in compliance with the Cooperation Agreement in the field of International Commercial Arbitration between the CRCICA and the Chamber of Arbitration of Milan dated 15 December 2003. The arbitral procedure may be initiated with the deposit of the introductory act in Milan and in such case the deposit will have the same effects, according to the above–mentioned Rules, as if made at the Cairo Centre. The Arbitral Tribunal shall consist of three arbitrators appointed pursuant to the Rules of the CRCICA. The Arbitral Tribunal shall decide in accordance with the law of Egypt. The seat of arbitration shall be Milan, however any relevant hearings may be held in Cairo. The language of the arbitration shall be English.

2-044 A party should never feel reluctant to call or e-mail a case manager or even the head of an international or regional arbitration institution to seek advice on negotiating dispute clauses with parties from a particular country. In our experience, institutions are more than happy to help when asked.

2-045 *Fallback position 3: hearing in the other party's country, but place of arbitration in a third country.* This fallback position is similar to the 'Cairo' solution discussed above, but without relying on an institution's rules to that effect. If the reason why the other side insists on arbitration in its own country is one of cost or convenience, proposing to hold hearings locally may be enough for the other party to accept to have the legal seat of arbitration be in a third country.

Example 2b – 'Hearings Elsewhere' Clause

(with UNCITRAL Rules and ICC as appointing authority)

Any dispute shall be referred to and finally resolved by arbitration under the UNCITRAL Arbitration Rules as at present in force, which Rules are deemed to be incorporated by reference into this clause. The number of arbitrators shall be three (3). The seat, or legal place, of arbitration shall be Paris, although any hearings shall be conducted in Cairo. Pursuant to Article 6 of the UNCITRAL Arbitration Rules, the functions referred to in Articles 11(3), 11(4), 13(3), 14, 16(3), and 34(2) shall be performed by the ICC International Court of Arbitration (the 'Appointing Authority'). The language to be used in the arbitration shall be English.

Fallback position 4: 'buffers' between the parties and the courts (arbitration **2-046** *institution and a requirement of mediation).* There may be situations in which the other side cannot be moved from its insistence on having a local place of arbitration. As we discuss below, there will be times when most parties will not be prepared to accept the risk of local courts playing a significant role in appointing arbitrators, substituting them, or otherwise becoming involved in the substance of the arbitration. But for parties who believe the rewards of the proposed contract may justify the risk, there are two mechanisms that can diminish the chances of the courts undermining the arbitration, either or both of which can be adopted:

- *Interposition of an international arbitration institution.* Agreeing to a major international institution (such as the ICC, ICDR, or LCIA) to administer the arbitration instead of relying on an ad hoc proceeding (UNCITRAL or otherwise) can create a valuable 'buffer' between the parties and the courts. This is because the parties will have agreed that these institutions – not the courts – are to resolve any disputes over the appointment of the arbitrators or the conduct of the proceedings. In the event that the courts nonetheless interfere in the arbitration, resulting in an adverse award, the foreign party may well have good ground on which to resist its enforcement outside the country in which it was rendered. Hence, we regard this as a defensive mechanism: it affords some protection against a renegade or manifestly unjust arbitration award. In addition, the leading international institutions (particularly the ICC and the ICDR) play active roles in working with governments in developing countries, and their local visibility and reputation may discourage a court from engaging in improper conduct.
- *Mediation before arbitration requirement.* The second buffer, which can be both an offensive and defensive mechanism, is to include in the dispute resolution clause a requirement to attempt settlement through mediation before either party can proceed to submit to arbitration. Mediation has

been consistently shown to help parties avoid litigation,[13] but at least one of the parties to an international contract may be unwilling to mediate once a dispute arises. Therefore, by increasing the likelihood of a mediation actually taking place, and of a settlement being reached as a result, a requirement of mediation can reduce the possibility of a party finding itself involved in arbitration with the risk of local court interference.

III.   MITIGATING, QUANTIFYING, AND ACCEPTING THE
                             RISKS OF DISADVANTAGEOUS OR IMPERFECT
                             DISPUTE RESOLUTION

2-047 Businesses will not enter into contracts when they perceive the risk and cost to be greater than the expected returns. Of course, this does not necessarily lead to the conclusion that a disadvantageous or imperfect disputes clause should always lead the disadvantaged party to reject the contract:

- *Disadvantageous dispute clause.* By 'disadvantageous dispute clause' we mean a dispute clause that is enforceable and will lead to a binding arbitration award or court decision, but the terms of which are favourable to one side. This may be because of convenience (e.g., the place of arbitration is geographically closer to one side) or for reasons going to the type of dispute mechanism chosen (e.g., the agreement by a US party to CIETAC arbitration in China in Chinese in a contract with a Chinese counterparty).
- *Imperfect dispute clause.* By this we mean there is some aspect of the dispute clause that creates doubts as to whether it can lead to an arbitration award or court judgment that can be effectively enforced against the assets of the opposing party.

2-048 *Whether the expected benefits of the contract justify the risk.* In some circumstances, disadvantageous or imperfect dispute clauses may lead potentially disadvantaged parties to abandon the negotiations. In practice, this will be a rare occurrence. Despite imperfections in a dispute clause, many parties will not want to forego an important contract. Rather, they will want to ensure that the other terms of the contract justify taking the dispute risk, or that they will be able mitigate the imperfections during the contract's performance. For example, if the clause leaves doubts about whether it will lead to an enforceable arbitration award, the potentially disadvantaged party may seek adjustments in price, a requirement of advance payments and/or a right of suspension of performance in the event of non-payment.

2-049 *Contracutal protections and concessions.* There are at least two ways of making an otherwise unacceptable dispute clause more palatable: contractual protections and concessions. These are means by which the contract can be modified either to

---

13. Chapter 4, *International Settlement Negotiation and Mediation.*

reduce the degree of perceived risk of the disadvantageous or imperfect dispute clause or to compensate the party for agreeing to accept it. In other words, the disadvantaged party should treat the unfavourable dispute clause as it would any other negotiating point and shift the initial cost of the risk to the party whose inflexibility has imposed it. So there is, as we have seen earlier in this chapter, a yin to its yang for the inflexible party. Refusing accommodation on dispute resolution can handicap negotiations in other areas or impose additional costs, even if no dispute ever arises under the contract.

Contractual protections	These are measures that ensure a party will receive all or at least a substantial portion of its expected benefits, even if it is unable to enforce its rights through the dispute resolution clause. For example, if the risk of non-payment is increased, then the party should try to negotiate other adequate financial guarantees, whether in the form of irrevocable letters of credit, insurance bonds, advance payments, or the right to suspend performance or withhold shipment until payment is received. Contractual protections can apply equally to buyers. A purchaser buying from a seller in a foreign location can compensate for an unfavourable or imperfect dispute clause by ensuring that payments will be made only after goods are delivered or services rendered, or that there are other protections in place that are adequate to cover the buyer's financial risk, such as letters of credit covering advance payments, without recourse to the contract's dispute clause. (This is also called an 'advance payment bond' by which a seller guarantees its future performance in return for receiving an immediate payment.)
Contractual concessions	These are simply provisions that may make the overall contract more attractive to the disadvantaged party, who may then become more willing to accept the risk of uncertain dispute resolution. For example, a party may be unwilling to accept the risk of local dispute resolution in another country when it will be putting USD 1 million of its capital at risk in return for only USD 100,000 in expected profits. But it may be willing if the amount of capital initially put at risk is less, or the expected return is substantially more.

Contractual protections and concessions are by no means perfect solutions (there **2-050** can be costs that will not be completely covered if the other party breaches its obligations). However, they can give a party sufficient comfort for it to be able to justify entering into the contract without a watertight disputes clause.

2-051 *Questioning the 'home court advantage'.* The most commonly perceived disadvantage is a dispute clause that requires arbitration or court litigation in the country of one of the parties. The foreign party will naturally feel they will be litigating against a party that possesses a 'home court advantage', which they may perceive as the significant convenience and comfort of resolving disputes at home or, more substantively, as the courts showing a bias towards the local party. There is no denying that it is often seen as an advantage to be able to resolve disputes in the courts of one's own country or city. Certainly, for the local party dispute resolution will be more predictable on account of acquired experience, and therefore may appear safer than dispute resolution in some other part of the world.

2-052 However, it is not always fair to assume that the local party will be substantively advantaged by its local status. It may even be that parties who repeatedly appear in their home courts with unreasonable (and ultimately losing) positions will not engender a positive reputation or sympathy in litigation with a foreign party. As for the potential convenience or strategic advantage to the local party of litigating at home, the foreign party can often deflate this simply by hiring local lawyers with experience in appearing in the local courts. Regarding judicial bias towards the local party, reputable judges in any country will be disinclined to favour any party, local or foreign, and are generally held to rigorous ethical requirements and constant training to ensure they remain impartial. The question, therefore, is whether notwithstanding their mandate, local judges will exercise either a conscious or hidden bias in favour of the local party. In countries where the courts are known to be relatively independent and free of corruption, we believe the answer is that they will not.[14]

2-053 Where the local courts do not have a good reputation for efficiency, quality, or ethical behaviour, reputable local companies may actually prefer dispute resolution in foreign locations. Inefficient or just plain bad justice may be less inconvenient for the local litigant, but that does not mean that the local litigant will like it any better than the foreign party.

2-054 *Investment treaty protections.* Investment treaties may provide some protection of last resort for a party that has entered into a contract that contains a disadvantageous dispute resolution provision. If there is an investment treaty between the party's home state and the state in which the dispute resolution take place, the treaty can play a role in at least two situations. This assumes that the contract is an investment covered by the treaty – and most international contracts will be investments within the meaning of investment treaties. First, if the contract is with a state or a subdivision of the state, then the treaty is likely to offer the investor

---

14. For countries where the courts are known to suffer from corruption, the assumption of local bias may also be incorrect, but for a different and dismaying reason: the judge will favour whoever is willing to pay more, which may or may not be the local party.

the opportunity to sue the state or its subdivision in an effective arbitration under the treaty rather than in the less effective dispute resolution forum stipulated in the contract. Second, if the contract is with a private party, and not with the state or a subdivision of the state, and the foreign party feels it has not received justice in the courts of the counterparty's state, then the foreign party may have an action against the state under the investment treaty based on the substandard treatment of its investment by the courts, the actions of which will be attributable to the state.[15]

However, investment treaty arbitration is arduous and expensive, with a number of **2-055** jurisdictional hurdles obstructing most claimants even where there is a treaty between the foreign party's state and the state of its counterparty. The existence of a contract with its own dispute resolution terms, albeit disadvantageous to the foreign party, will make it more difficult still for the foreign party to overcome the jurisdictional hurdles in an investment treaty arbitration. This is why we describe investment treaty arbitration in this context as a protection of last resort.

Accepting dispute resolution that will not lead to an enforceable result. While it **2-056** may seem heretical to suggest that parties should accept a dispute clause that will not lead to an enforceable result, many parties will do this where they do not place high value on enforceability. Thus, before walking away from a deal on the basis of a dispute clause of doubtful enforceability, it is important to ask whether there will ever be a need to enforce a financial judgment at all. If, for example, the contract already provides adequate protections that a seller will be paid (in advance, before shipment, or through irrevocable letters of credit), the seller may be relatively indifferent about its ability to enforce judgments against the buyer.

Similarly, even when enforcement against the other party is a concern, it is fair to **2-057** ask whether it has any assets located outside its home country. If not, then an arbitration award is likely to provide little or no enforcement advantage, as the foreign party will in any event need to avail itself of the local courts in order to reach the assets of the other party.

IV.   SPOTTING THE REAL DEAL-BREAKERS

There will be times when a dispute clause is so disadvantageous or imperfect that it **2-058** will not be in the interest of a business to accept the risk of the contract. Given the variety of dispute resolution options and mitigation devices available in international contracting practice, we expect these situations to be infrequent. But they can and do appear, and it is important to know when the bottom has been reached and the deal is not worth doing. Although businesses make money in accepting and managing risk, they also expect clear guidance on when to walk away because the risk is too great or expensive to justify any expected benefits under the contract.

---

15. Chapter 7, *ICSID and Investment Treaty Arbitration.*

2-059 *Local courts as a deal-breaker.* The most likely deal-breaker is one side's inflexible insistence on resolving disputes in its own courts when the other party may need the support of the contract's dispute resolution clause in order to enforce its rights. Even when corruption is not a concern, local justice can mean having a significant dispute heard over the course of several years in a crowded court building, case files spilling out of unlocked hallway cabinets, and courtrooms in which scores of litigants jostle to place their documents under a mound on the judge's desk, when the judges are actually present in the courthouse.[16]

2-060 The concerns that apply to the home courts of a foreign counterparty may also apply to an arbitration sited in that country, as the courts are likely to interfere with arbitrations held on their turf. In this chapter we have suggested several ways of mitigating this risk through different forms of arbitration and mediation (and we will discuss methods of mitigating risk after a dispute arises in subsequent chapters), but for any arbitration held in a country with an inadequate, corrupt, or arbitration-hostile court system, there will be residual risks after all mitigation steps are taken that a party may still find too great to allow it to enter into the contract. If the other party remains intractable in its insistence on local arbitration, and this cannot be accepted by the other party, it is better to recognise earlier rather than later that the deal is not one worth doing.

Not that this ever really happens: a real deal-breaker	In a competitive bidding in India, the customer stated that any party that did not accept its contractual terms and conditions would be disqualified. Many of the terms were relatively standard, but the dispute resolution clause provided for an ad hoc arbitration in Mumbai in which the customer – at its sole discretion – had the unilateral right to appoint a sole arbitrator. The only limitation on the customer's appointing authority was that the sole arbitrator would be 'an esteemed individual' (as determined by the customer). A colleague of one of the co-authors, the company's regional sales manager, requested a legal opinion that the clause did not pose unreasonable risk to the company. The legal department refused to provide the opinion, much to his disappointment (and despite his threats to take the matter up with the company's CEO). Some months later, the co-author met up with the sales manager and asked who had won the bid. 'No one', he said. 'None of the bidders accepted the customer's terms and conditions, so they are going to re-bid the contract with a different dispute clause.'

---

16. In more than one country we have brought witnesses from faraway places to testify at a critical hearing, only to discover through a sign posted at the entrance to the court building that the judges were all on strike that day (or worse, only during the hours scheduled for the hearing) or attending a conference in another city, and that the parties would be notified of when the hearings would be rescheduled (usually in at least six months' time).

Bet well before leaving an opportunity for a competitor. The sales manager who **2-061** will lose a deal to a competitor should also be able to appreciate the guidance that helped avoid an unacceptable risk. This will be the case if the reason for rejecting the contract is based on sound analysis and judgment drawn from informed sources or experience. The competitor may well be worse off for having accepted. Of course, only time will tell who placed the better bet.

Chapter Three

When the Dispute Arises

Commercial litigation of any type presents parties with the dual challenge of simultaneously asserting a strong legal position while attempting to evaluate and avoid the negative impacts of events that are yet to unfold. The parties will want to make a reasonable assessment of the likely outcome of the litigation and the costs of getting there, and they may also wish to consider the attractiveness of less expensive alternatives along the way. International arbitration is no different than any other type of litigation in this respect. In this chapter, we discuss (1) the preservation and optimisation of a party's position after the dispute has arisen but before an arbitration has started; (2) strategic alternatives at the beginning of arbitration, including mediation, designed to reduce costs and optimise outcome; (3) the decision whether to retain outside counsel, who to retain, how to retain them, and when to consider replacing them; and (4) conducting an early case assessment (ECA), an initial evaluation of the dispute that quantifies the range of probable outcomes and the associated costs. As we discuss in subsequent chapters, the ECA will be relevant to establishing the commercial (non-legal) objectives that the party hopes to accomplish, whether through negotiations, mediation, or completing the arbitration.

Question: Is it possible to estimate how much an international arbitration will cost?

Answer: Yes. Costs generally fall into four categories: the fees and expenses of arbitrators, institutions, counsel, and experts, which can all be estimated with rough approximation. In addition, parties can usually estimate the financial impact of allocating their own employees to supporting the arbitration, some of whom will also appear as witnesses. You are probably also interested in knowing when you are likely to incur these costs and whether the winner will be able to recover all or some of them from the loser. It should be possible to reasonably estimate all of this before an arbitration is fully underway.

I.   PRELIMINARIES ONCE LITIGATION IS PROBABLE

3-002 The moment when an existing contract is about to give rise to a dispute should not be difficult to identify. It can be when a letter arrives from the counterparty's external counsel, or from the counterparty itself (usually authored by their counsel), suggesting that proceedings will begin shortly unless certain demands are met. Regardless of whether one is on the initiating (claimant) or defending (respondent) side, the checklist below contains some of the issues that should be quickly examined once proceedings appear likely or imminent. More explanation of each item follows the checklist.

Checklist 3a – Preliminaries Once Arbitration or Litigation Is Probable

Issue	*Suggested Action*
Contractual pre-arbitration procedures	Check whether contract dispute clause (or other provision) requires steps to be taken by either side, and consider consequences of compliance and non-compliance
'Letters before action'	Determine appropriateness of sending one to opposing party if 'natural claimant'
Communications internally and externally (especially with opponent) concerning issues in dispute	Advise employees of existence of dispute (if not informed) and any restrictions on internal or external communications
Key employees and witnesses	Identify who may need to be available before and during arbitration, possibly inform supervising managers and human resources
Document retention	Determine whether a document retention notice should be sent to employees to ensure that relevant documents are retained
Insurance	Consider whether coverage may exist and provide notice to insurers under relevant policies
Media	Assess whether media coverage or press inquiries are likely and, if so, prepare appropriate statement
Management briefings	See Early Case Assessment (ECA), addressed below in section III
Informal resolution options	Explore any options for informal resolution (negotiations, mediation) before incurring significant expense and before positions become further polarised and solidified

A.   Contractual Pre-arbitration Procedures

The most obvious and immediate step once a dispute appears on the horizon is to **3-003** obtain a copy of the executed contract out of which the dispute arises. With contract in hand, it should be relatively easy to determine whether the dispute resolution clause (or any other provision) requires particular steps to be taken before arbitration (or court litigation) may be initiated. Typical steps of this sort may include the issuance by the claimant to the other party of a notice of dispute, an attempt at resolution through negotiations, mediation, or any combination of these, all of which may have deadlines for performance and longstop dates attached.[1] The overall intention is that a party cannot start arbitration until the stipulated steps have been performed, or until the longstop dates for their performance have passed. Parties should assume that any correspondence between them concerning the pre-action steps will become part of the documentary record in a subsequent arbitration, and they should take special care as a result.

Strategic considerations regarding pre-arbitration steps. Once the party has iden- **3-004** tified if there are any contractually required steps before arbitration, it will need to decide whether to take them. The potential dilemma here is that the party may consider these steps futile after having already conducted fruitless informal negotiations, and may think that complying will delay its opportunity to obtain redress for no good reason. A party may hold legitimate concerns about whether such delay can be tolerated. For example, it may allow the counterparty additional time to prepare its defence or, worse, make itself 'judgment proof'. Also, if the 'natural claimant' goes through the preliminary steps in this way, it may allow the counterparty to take the initiative by itself ignoring those steps and starting arbitration immediately, while the first party is patiently waiting for the relevant deadlines to expire. In some cases, delay may even cause a request for arbitration to become time barred (whether under contract or statute), although the pre-action notification of a claim may be sufficient to avoid the time bar.

Keeping an eye on the clock	Whether a claim is time barred will turn on the contractual terms and the law governing the contract. For example, the period for notifying a claim of a hidden non-conformity (also called latent defects) in equipment or other goods supplied under an international contract may be governed by any or all of the following: (1) an express contractual warranty period; (2) the limitation period provided in Article 39 of the United Nations Convention on the International Sale of Goods (CISG), if it applies; and (3) any other applicable limitation period provided under the governing law of the contract (although where the CISG applies, it will generally be deemed

---

1. Chapter 1, *The Elements of an International Dispute Resolution Agreement.*

> to supplant the period provided by the governing law of the contract).

3-005 *Potential consequences of non-compliance with pre-action procedures.* If it is important for the claimant to start arbitration without delay, and if it believes the preliminary steps will serve no purpose, it may consider ignoring them and commencing arbitration immediately. This strategy is not without its risks, both in the arbitration and outside it (it may, for example, have a negative impact on pending or future settlement negotiations). In the arbitration, the risk is that the respondent will object before the tribunal and the administering institution, arguing that the arbitration has been improperly commenced and should not be permitted to proceed. The impact of non-compliance with pre-action procedural steps may vary according to the arbitrators appointed, the institution, and the place of arbitration. Institutions may not take a position one way or the other and may instead defer to the arbitral tribunal. Some arbitrators will disregard non-compliance with pre-arbitration requirements and allow parties who have proceeded straight to arbitration to do so with impunity. This has been the case in investment treaty arbitration in particular, where the non-observance by claimants of 'cooling-off' or 'waiting' periods before the commencement of arbitration have, despite the respondents' objections, not led to suspension or dismissal of the arbitration. However, in at least one case the impatient claimant was required to bear the costs of the part of the arbitration held before the expiry of the waiting period.

3-006 Still, there is a risk that the institution or the tribunal will suspend the arbitration while the preliminary steps are performed or, worse, dismiss the case altogether. The respondent may also obtain the same result in the courts, whether by seeking to enjoin the proceedings or contesting a subsequent award. Even courts that generally defer to the decisions of arbitral tribunals on questions of their own jurisdiction may not be so deferential when it comes to compliance with pre-action procedures. For example, English courts have taken a harder line than investment tribunals, suspending court proceedings until the parties have complied with clear, mandatory pre-action procedures.[2]

3-007 A party should also consider the purpose for which pre-action procedural steps are intended before deciding to ignore them. A dispute resolution clause that expressly requires negotiation by senior executives before initiating arbitration may be fruitful once a dispute arises even if, the party genuinely believes such efforts will be futile and merely add costs or delay final resolution. As already noted, a mediation requirement before arbitration is likely to be even more effective in promoting an early resolution; and the efforts of preparing for a mediation, or a meeting of senior executives, is unlikely to add much to the time and costs to be incurred. In fact, even if the parties do not settle, the amount of time a party invests in attempting to

---

2. See, e.g., *Cable & Wireless Plc v. IBM United Kingdom Ltd*, [2002] 2 All ER (Comm) 1041.

assess and resolve a dispute at the outset will almost always reduce the expenditures required later in the arbitration and potentially narrow the issues. In addition, by forcing each side to take more formal steps before actually initiating arbitration and perhaps requiring the parties to put at least some of their cards on the table, compliance with pre-action procedural steps may involve different decision makers on each side or shed light that can cause an apparently intractable dispute to settle before the full costs of the arbitration are incurred.

B.   Letters Before Action and Preliminary Correspondence

In many instances it will be helpful, and in some jurisdictions required by law, for **3-008** claimants to notify the other party that proceedings will be commenced unless certain action is taken, usually the making of a payment. The letter should lay out in brief, matter-of-fact terms what the complaint is, specifically what action the complainant requires of the recipient, and what action the complainant will take if the recipient does not comply with the request, often by a certain deadline.

Example 3a – Letter Before Action

Re: Contract between ABC Company and XYZ Company, dated 15 November 2009 for certain services

Dear Sirs,
We write on behalf of ABC Company concerning the above-referenced contract. As we have previously notified you, in the months of August, September, and October, XYZ Company did not deliver services as required by Article 10 (Scope of Supply) of the parties' contract. As a consequence, and to mitigate its potential exposure, ABC Company has retained certain substitute services at substantial cost, amounting to a total of USD 600,000.

Given XYZ's continued non-compliance with the contract, this is to notify you that ABC Company hereby demands (1) payment of the USD 600,000, and (2) immediate confirmation from XYZ that it will resume performance of its contractual obligations.

In the event that XYZ fails to comply with the above requests within fifteen days of receipt of this letter, ABC will have no choice but to terminate the contract and commence arbitration for damages. We hope that XYZ will agree that it would be better to avoid such an outcome, and we look forward to your favourable response to our requests.

Sincerely,
Lawyer (or Manager) of ABC Company

3-009 Parties should carefully consider the drafting of a pre-action letter, avoiding any inflammatory language or characterisations in a communication which is almost certain to become an exhibit in the ensuing arbitration. For the same reason, once litigation is imminent or threatened, commercial managers and employees should be advised to subject correspondence to a lawyer's review before transmitting it to the other side (or have the lawyer author the correspondence in the first place). This may seem obvious to many, but more than one outcome has been substantially influenced by letters written shortly before the start of proceedings, and in the heat of the moment, that subsequently become exhibits in support of the other side's claim or defence.

Careful what you ask for: the danger of inflating claims in pre-action correspondence	While many parties will be tempted to 'ask for the sun, the moon, and the stars' in a pre-action demand letter in order to create maximum negotiation leverage, parties and counsel should consider carefully the potential downside. In an international arbitration, a claim that unrealistically demands the entire cosmos has the potential to backfire and actually reduce negotiation leverage when it cannot be maintained or will be obviously weak in an ensuing arbitration. As we discuss below in section III with respect to early evaluations of risk and estimating costs, a party that does not prevail on its claim is likely to become liable for the costs incurred by the other side in defending it, and this will often apply to a failed portion of a claim that the party has otherwise won. We have seen instances in which a side has had a victory substantially eroded by liability for costs on a failed portion, usually one that was unreasonably extreme at the outset.

3-010 *Danger of settlement offers in pre-action correspondence.* In international disputes, it is not always clear which ethical rules govern the parties' correspondence, and lawyers may wrongly believe they can freely disregard the usual ethical limitations that apply in their domestic disputes. For example, many legal cultures afford special treatment to pre-action correspondence made in furtherance of settlement efforts, and such correspondence may not be produced by the opposing party and may not be regarded as an admission of liability. This is especially true where the correspondence is marked as being 'without prejudice' or otherwise subject to settlement privilege. Despite the existence of this rule, and the possibility of sanctions for its violation, less scrupulous lawyers – or simply lawyers with a different background or training – may produce an opposing party's settlement offer in subsequent proceedings, on the grounds that the offer was an admission of liability. Thus, opposing counsel's propriety (or familiarity with these rules and customs) should never be presumed: correspondence promoting settlement should always be written with the understanding that the other party may produce it in a subsequent arbitration and should, at a minimum, be marked with words such as 'without prejudice' or 'for the purposes of settlement only'.

At the same time, we believe that most international arbitrators will frown on the **3-011** practice of producing an opposing party's settlement offer and characterising it as an admission of liability, and doing so may backfire on the producing party.

C.   PRIVILEGE AND NEW DOCUMENT CREATION

In many international arbitrations today, each party will be ordered by the tribunal **3-012** to produce certain documents in its possession at the request of the other party.[3] Parties, especially if they are from civil law countries, may not be familiar with this sort of process or the exposure associated with their continued creation of documents. After a dispute arises, and despite protections such as privilege, a party should be careful about generating documents of any sort relating to the matters in dispute.

- *Communications with the opposing party.* For a number of reasons, it may not be possible or even advisable for a party to cease its communications with the opposing side even after the onset of proceedings. Written communications may be among the party's ongoing contractual obligations, for example, or it may simply be advantageous to the party's negotiating position to maintain a friendly and amicable disposition despite the other side's act of hostility in commencing (or threatening to commence) arbitration. It is likely that these communications will be produced by one or other party as evidence in the proceedings. It is highly advisable, therefore, to ensure that the party's employees are aware of this, so that they have any communications with the opposing party authored or reviewed by counsel.
- *Internal communications.* It is only natural when a significant dispute arises for the people involved to speculate about the possible causes and potential consequences, and to do so via e-mail and other electronic means such as informal chat programs. Because these informal internal communications become electronic documents that may be produced in an arbitration (even if they would not have been subject to production in litigation in the party's own country), it is wise at the onset of formal proceedings to notify employees that they should use care or even avoid creating new documents that discuss or describe the disputed issues, and to coordinate with counsel if they have any doubts about whether to do so.
- *Communications with a party's own counsel.* It is reasonable to expect in international arbitration that the tribunal will apply rules of legal privilege and will not require parties to produce communications relating to the dispute with the lawyers who are representing them in the dispute.

---

3. Chapter 5, *The Conduct of the Arbitration*. See also, IBA Rules, Art. 3.

The tribunal is unlikely in our experience to distinguish here between communications with in-house or outside counsel.[4] It makes sense to mark as 'privileged' documents that a party believes are subject to a legal privilege. Although the presence on a document of the word 'privileged' in itself does not confer the status of privilege (and its absence will not mean that no privilege exists), it does indicate the author's view of the document's status, and it can help a party quickly identify documents that it believes are not subject to production.[5]

D.   KEY EMPLOYEES AND WITNESSES

3-013 A party preparing claims or defences in a dispute will need the input of its employees, agents, and others working with the party on the matters in dispute. These people will be able to provide the party with useful information to flesh out the documentary record, and some may be so close to the facts that the party will wish to call them to provide witness evidence in the arbitration. It would be unwise to assume that all key employees and witnesses will be readily available during the period they will be needed before and during the arbitration, which may take two or more years. Potential witnesses may no longer be with the company (or even alive). Those who do remain may feel overburdened or reluctant to become involved when asked to support the arbitration effort.

3-014 *Reassuring potential witnesses.* Thus, at the start of any significant dispute, it can be prudent to contact commercial and human resources managers to inform them of the potential need for employees as witnesses. At a minimum, they will understand the burdens that may be placed on employees in assisting the arbitration. An e-mail from managers to their employees directing them to provide support can also be helpful. It is important for employees involved in disputes to receive assurances that their managers understand the burdens placed on them, and that they will be permitted and encouraged to support the dispute through to its final resolution.

3-015 *Potential witnesses who may retire or exit the company during the dispute.* In the course of a dispute, some witnesses may retire or simply leave the company, sometimes under less than happy circumstances. There are two concerns that can be addressed on a preliminary basis. The first is ensuring the availability of the former employee as a potential witness, or at least that the employee will not improperly cooperate with or testify for the opposing party. With sufficient advance notice, supervisors and human resource managers may be able to

---

4. This is decidedly not the case in some jurisdictions and fields, such as European competition law. For example, in 2007 the European Court of Justice held that communications with in-house counsel generally will not benefit from an assertion of privilege in the event they are seized in the course of a European Commission investigation or dawn raid. See Joined Cases T-125/03 and T-253/03, *Akzo Nobel Chemicals Ltd and Akcros Chemicals Ltd. v. Commission of the European Communities*, Judgment of the Court of Justice of the European Communities (Court of First Instance), 17 Sep. 2007.
5. Chapter 5, *The Conduct of the Arbitration.*

negotiate positive departure terms that provide for continued support in any dispute. Employees who leave the company to work for a contractual counterparty can be requested to sign, or be reminded of having previously signed, confidentiality undertakings. The second concern is to secure from any departing witness (leaving under any circumstances) all her documents and records.

Not that this ever really happens: allowing witnesses to depart without securing future cooperation	The acquired company had a substantial portfolio of pending disputes at the time of its acquisition. The legal and finance teams of the new parent had based their pre-acquisition risk assessments of the disputes on the assumption that key witnesses would remain available once the acquisition was completed. Human resources, however, had different plans and shortly after the acquisition presented almost all members of senior leadership with severance packages, none of which required or requested continued cooperation in any pending or future disputes. As a result, the legal and finance teams revised their risk assessments of several of the pending disputes to take into account the likely unavailability of key witnesses. The retrospective 'lesson learned' was that it would have been advisable – and not too difficult – to obtain commitments from departing officers to assist with any future disputes relating to the acquired business. (Realistically, however, it may be difficult in practice to ensure the cooperation of departed employees, whatever their contractual commitments, especially where they depart on bad terms).

E.   DOCUMENTS

Importance of documents relating to the dispute. Perhaps the most important **3-016** source of information and evidence about a dispute is the record comprised of documents created by the parties during their relationship. At the outset of a dispute it will therefore be critical for a party to assemble, from all available sources, its documentary record. The party will also be expected to perform the same exercise if, as is increasingly common in international arbitration, it is required to produce documents in its possession, custody, or control to the opposing party.

Document retention notices. Over the past several years, many international com- **3-017** panies have adopted comprehensive document retention policies to preserve and destroy documents on a routine basis. Such policies will generally provide for the preservation of relevant documents in the event of litigation or investigations. Even those that have not adopted formal policies for preserving documents are likely to have procedures to ensure that documents are retained for statutory reasons, as required by regulatory and tax authorities in the jurisdictions in which the company operates. In any event, once an international arbitration is threatened or imminent, a party should take steps to ensure that documents that may be relevant to the dispute are preserved, so that the documentary record is available to support its case, and to ensure that it is in a position to comply with its document production obligations in the contemplated arbitration. The usual way of doing this is by e-mailing a notice to all employees who are or may be connected with the disputed project or contract, requesting them to retain documents relating to that project or contract.

Example 3b – Document Retention Notice

Confidential and Attorney-Client Privileged

Document Retention Notice

Supersedes any prior notice on this matter

As you may be aware, XYZ has initiated arbitration against ABC Company alleging breach of a contract between the companies dated 1 January 2002 (the 'Contract'). This notice is to request that you preserve all documents that relate to the Contract and/or its performance.

Why did I receive this notice? Based on your job function or position with the company, we have identified you (and other employees) as someone who could have documents that relate to the Contract and/or its performance. Your documents that relate to the Contract and/or its performance must be preserved and not altered. The inadvertent destruction or alteration of these documents could result in the inability of the company to properly investigate its claim or defences, and could also result in adverse financial consequences and even criminal and civil penalties, so any doubts should be resolved in favour of preserving any document that appears to relate to the Contract and/or its performance.

What should I do? DO NOT DELETE, DESTROY, OR ALTER ANY DOCUMENTS RELATED TO THE CONTRACT AND/OR ITS PERFOR-MANCE. In addition to your personal and electronic records, we also need you to take all necessary steps to preserve documents that might be stored in shared server databases and physical file cabinets. Do not create new documents that relate to the Contract and/or its performance (including in response to this notice) without consulting with counsel.

Do I need to provide my documents to someone? At this point, we are only seeking to preserve all documents relating to the Contract and/or its perfor-mance. If the time comes to collect these documents from you, you will be contacted with further information and instructions on how to proceed.

> *Communications.* If you believe others should receive a copy of this notice, if you need to receive this policy in different languages, or if you have any questions about this notice, please call the undersigned at the telephone number below.
>
> Thank you for your cooperation and assistance with this important matter.

Defining 'document' and relevance. Employees may need assistance in **3-018** understanding what constitutes a 'document', such as e-mails, voice mail, and digital recordings, as well as what categories of document to look for. In most disputes arising under a contract, for example, it is likely that all categories of document concerning the disputed project or contract may be relevant and should be preserved. This will include documents evidencing or addressing the contractual negotiations, the performance of the contract, and the parties' grievances. The documents to be preserved will include those exchanged with the other side (such as correspondence and meeting minutes), with third parties (perhaps correspondence with consultants, suppliers, or customers), and internal documents (such as internal e-mails, briefing notes, meeting minutes, resolutions, as well as employees' own personal notes, working papers, and *aide-mémoires*).

Metadata. In recent years, much attention has been given to the amount of hidden **3-019** information that can be embedded in electronic documents of any type and that can be easily retrieved by anyone with the tools and inclination to look for it. Commonly referred to as 'metadata', this information can include the name of the creator of the document, the date it was created, the identities of the different people who may have edited the document, as well as the dates of their edits and the changes they made. At the time a dispute starts, significant hidden information may already have been transmitted in correspondence previously exchanged by the parties. In some jurisdictions (mainly the United States), metadata can figure prominently in the electronic documentation that is required to be produced in discovery. Unfortunately, while metadata may lead to some gains in the quantity of information produced, it also adds considerable costs. There is currently no accepted practice on what should or should not be made available in the way of metadata in a truly international proceeding. Before demanding that metadata be included with documents produced, a party should consider whether material and genuinely useful information will be retrieved that will justify the substantial additional cost.[6]

---

6. Chapter 5, *The Conduct of the Arbitration.*

Example 3c – Metadata Extracted from MS Word Document
(Extraction through MS Workshare Protect)

HIGH-RISK ELEMENTS
6 Hidden track changes

- We are prepared to accept a financial settlement of 50% of our claim (Deletion by Larry Lawyer)
- Without prejudice (Insertion by Larry lawyer)
- We require your chair's personal involvement in resolving (Deletion by Larry Lawyer)
- Unless payment is immediately received, we intend to start court proceedings immediately (Insertion by Mike Manager)
- Unless payment is immediately received, we intend to start court proceedings immediately (Deletion by Larry Lawyer)
- We invite immediate payment to avoid the need for the parties to have recourse to the methods of dispute resolution provided in the contract (Insertion by Larry Lawyer)

MEDIUM-RISK ELEMENTS
4 Custom properties
- _AdHocReviewCycleID: -658751854
- _Author Email: l.lawyer@claimantcompany.com

1 Document reviewer
- l lawyer

1 Last ten authors (without unc paths)
- C:\Documents and Settings\llawyer\Desktop

LOW-RISK ELEMENTS
6 Document statistics
- Creation date: 9/18/2008 11:28:00 a.m.
- Last author: llawyer
- Last print date: 5/30/2008 2:09:00 p.m.
- Last save time: 9/18/2008 11:35:00 a.m.
- Revision number: 9
- Total editing time: 45 minutes

3-020 A party should also guard against unwittingly providing metadata to the opposing side through correspondence that may continue after litigation is imminent or threatened. There are common software programs that are used to purge metadata from documents created with Microsoft Word and other word-processing programs, and which can be useful when communicating with the opposing party, its counsel, and arbitral tribunals. Also, it is common practice today to convert letters and other electronic documents to pdf files for transmission. Converting to pdf is a simple and cost-effective way to avoid the unwitting transmission of the hidden information embedded in an electronic document.

Not that this ever really happens: inadvertent disclosure via meta data	In the course of setting up business in the United Kingdom, a government agency refused to issue certain certifications that would have authorised Seller to distribute its products in that country. In frustration, Seller turned to a well-known London law firm, which drafted a letter from Seller's manager explaining why relevant English administrative law required the certifications to be promptly issued. Seller concluded its letter by stating its desire to resolve the matter without the need to involve lawyers to interface with the government agency. The agency responded, noting at the outset that lawyers were already involved since the metadata embedded in the letter from the Seller's manager showed it had been created and edited by lawyers at a well-known London law firm.

F.   INSURANCE NOTIFICATIONS

Some types of losses may be covered in full or in part by a party's insurance **3-021** policy.[7] Many insurers require that they be notified by a potential claimant of the loss, or by a potential respondent of a claim against it concerning that loss, within a very short time period after the party becomes aware of it. Even if the party is uncertain as to whether its policy (or policies) may apply to the particular loss, it is prudent to promptly send a notification immediately upon becoming aware of the loss or claim (within one or two days). If it is later acknowledged that there is in fact no coverage, there will have been no harm in sending the notice. If, however, there is coverage (or at least an argument that there is coverage), a party should not risk forfeiting the benefit of that coverage by failing to give timely notice. It is usually sufficient to submit a short notification with available details of the event that may be covered (which will allow the insurer to assess whether coverage may exist), together with a commitment to provide a more complete report at a later time.

Example 3d – First Notice to Insurer

This is to advise you of a possible claim under our insurance policy dated 1 January 2009, XL123456. In general terms, on [date] we were notified of the commencement of an arbitration by XYZ company (the 'claimant'), seeking payment of USD 10,523,450 in damages arising from a fire that occurred

---

7. An insurance litigation colleague of one of the co-authors provides the handy rule of thumb that 'if something went boom! or burned in a fire, then there is a good chance that insurance coverage will exist somewhere'.

following an alleged failure of equipment supplied by ABC on [date]. The fire occurred at the claimant's factory in Canada. The incident occurred on 1 January 2008. According to the request for arbitration, the cause of the equipment failure was a flexible tube supplied with our equipment, and which XYZ alleges was defective.

We are investigating the allegations made by the claimant. We note that the original contract for the supply of our equipment was signed in 1988, and that we are in the process of locating any relevant technical documentation relating to the sale. We will report more fully in due course.

G.   MEDIA

3-022 Most commercial disputes, even those that provoke substantial and heated attention within the disputing parties' organisations, are unlikely to generate attention from the media. Occasionally, however, a dispute will involve broader public concerns for which it is reasonable to expect some or even considerable interest. For example, it is reasonable to expect media inquiries if the dispute is with a country over access to national resources, or concerns the construction of an important infrastructure project such as an airport or railway, or with a company with hundreds or thousands of employees whose jobs may be affected by the dispute, or other matters that involve the interests of more than just the disputing parties.

3-023 *The dangers of litigating in the media.* The tactic of attempting to litigate one's dispute in the media carries substantial risks and should not be attempted without having first given serious consideration to the potential consequences. First, taking a strong position in the press may encourage the other side to respond in kind, and the parties may find it more difficult later to accept compromise solutions if and when settlement discussions become possible. Second, arbitrators and judges are unlikely to take a favourable view of a party's attempt to air its case in the press. Third, there may be an obligation to treat the dispute as confidential, particularly if the contract or any applicable rules of arbitration contain express wording to that effect, so that disclosure to the media may represent an independent breach of the contract.

3-024 Finally, and perhaps most importantly, parties may mistakenly believe that the media will report the story as the party believes it should be reported. This assumption is almost always wrong. In our experience, it is rare for reporters in any country to be able to appreciate the complexities of an international commercial dispute, and in any event it is near certain that the reporter will not see the case the same way as the party providing the information about it. Before deciding to work with the media on an arbitration or litigation, parties should realise that they are unlikely to be able to control the message that is delivered. If a disputing party does choose to work with the media, we would advise it to retain a specialist in public relations to advise on strategy as well as to serve as the first contact for any inquiries.

Not that this ever really happens: media manipulation	One of the co-authors was once involved in an attempt to settle a significant dispute with the prime minister of a certain country, after an arbitral tribunal had ordered the country to pay a considerable award of damages for breach of an infra-structure contract. The meeting was cordial, but nothing was concluded about whether the country would pay, when, or how. The next day, however, the country's mass circulation daily (aligned with the prime minister's political party), wrote on its front page: '[the claimant] withdraws the claim, but takes other projects'. Obviously, the prime minister had used his appearance at the meeting to gain political ground within the country, without actually having conceded anything. The claimant party declined to engage in a debate in the country's domestic media, on the view that ultimately no harm was done by the misleading portrayal and correcting the false impression would only provoke unnecessary displeasure from the prime minister's office, making settlement even less likely in the future.

Media 'holding statements'. Where one disputing party has already spoken with **3-025** the media, and the media contact the other party for comment, one option is to make no comment, especially if the case is confidential (as international arbitrations may be). But 'no comment' can make the party appear evasive or weak in the eyes of the press and its readership. It may make sense in these circumstances to release a short, general statement to the press giving the party's position in response to that disclosed by the first party. The party making the responsive statement may conclude by saying that as the dispute is confidential, it does not intend to make any further substantive public comment until the dispute is resolved.

Example 3e – Media Holding Statement

ABC Company confirms that it is involved in a dispute relating to a decision by XYZ Country to terminate a contract [description of the contract]. ABC Company denies that a valid reason existed to terminate the contract. ABC Company remains committed to supporting XYZ Country and is hopeful that the parties will be able to resolve this matter amicably and fairly. If that is not possible, ABC Company will pursue its claims vigorously in the appropriate forum.   [As the dispute is confidential, ABC Company does not propose to make any further public comment about the dispute until it has been resolved.]   ABC Company is a global provider of [description of company plus name of person and contact information for media inquiries].

II. THE DECISION WHETHER TO SUBMIT OR RESPOND TO A REQUEST FOR ARBITRATION

3-026 The decision to commence arbitration (or respond to a request for arbitration) brings with it a number of strategic choices that a party must make at the outset. Better to be a claimant or respondent? Is defaulting a viable option? Also, are there problems with the parties' dispute resolution clause that could be clarified or otherwise addressed to mutual advantage at the start of the arbitration? And, finally, should some form of settlement meeting be proposed and, if so, when?

A. CLAIMANT OR RESPONDENT?

3-027 When a dispute emerges, one party is often the natural claimant (e.g., a seller of goods who is unpaid), and one the natural respondent (e.g., the buyer who has failed to pay). Either party may consider it in its interests to place itself in a different posture. Most commonly, a natural respondent may decide to take the initiative and begin arbitration for tactical reasons, such as to place the action in its preferred forum, or where it believes attack is the best form of defence on the merits, or simply by asking for declaratory relief to ensure the claim is resolved expeditiously where the natural claimant is hesitating. Conversely, but less frequently, the natural claimant may consider that there is no urgent need to assert its claims in formal action, and that it has nothing to lose by being the respondent. In that case, it may prefer to continue with its attempts to resolve the case by means other than formal action and will not be concerned if the opponent starts formal action first.

3-028 If a party decides it is in its interest to move first (by launching the arbitration), this will generally entail doing more groundwork at an early stage than the defending party. There may be some instances, however, such as the need to secure interim measures in an emergency situation, in which a party concludes that it has no alternative to moving quickly into the proceedings and developing its case thereafter.

B. ALTERNATIVES TO COMMENCING ARBITRATION, OR TO BE CARRIED OUT IN CONJUNCTION WITH STARTING ARBITRATION

3-029 Before beginning an arbitration, a party may want to consider whether alternative procedures are available that may advantage the party (or both parties) if undertaken before proceedings are underway. We discuss throughout this book the desirability of considering the use of mediation to promote the settlement of most international commercial disputes. Other procedures to explore include applying for interim measures in the courts,[8] triggering the ICC's pre-arbitral referee procedure,[9] seeking investment treaty remedies,[10] or starting litigation in the courts if there is some doubt as to the scope of validity of the arbitration clause.

Is default a viable option? Before the respondent takes any steps in an arbitration **3-030** and incurs significant costs, it may be worth asking 'what if we don't participate in the arbitration and default instead?' Deciding to default is not something a party will do lightly, but there may be instances in which a party concludes that defaulting will be more advantageous than participating – particularly where the expense and effort demanded by participation outweighs the risk of an award being made and enforced against the defaulting party.[11]

C.   AMENDING THE DISPUTE RESOLUTION CLAUSE

If the dispute resolution clause contained in the parties' contract is lacking in any **3-031** essential way, the potential deficiencies will become apparent as the parties consider the possibility of commencing arbitration. Unfortunately, dispute resolution clauses can generally be improved only by amending the contract, which would require the agreement of both parties at a time when their relationship is already strained. Still, if it is possible to agree on an improvement, it would be better to accomplish this before proceedings are underway. Before proposing this, however, a party should consider whether acknowledging any defect in the clause may prompt the other party to take advantage of the defect in the clause, which it may not have noticed or planned to invoke.

D.   CONSIDERING AND PROPOSING INFORMAL RESOLUTION OPTIONS

Disputes settle better when they settle early. This is a general rule and application **3-032** of common sense: parties can avoid substantial costs and damage to their relationship by resolving their disputes without recourse to formal proceedings. But parties and counsel in a dispute will often come to the opposite conclusion, which is that settlement discussions will be more beneficial once the other side has seen the arguments they will face in the proceedings, and as a result will be persuaded to moderate their extreme position or interpretation of the facts or law. This assumption may sometimes be correct, although it must be considered against the risk that allowing a dispute to develop further will only make settlement more difficult.

---

8. Chapter 5, *The Conduct of the Arbitration*.
9. Chapter 1, *The Elements of an International Dispute Resolution Agreement*.
10. Chapter 7, *ICSID and Investment Treaty Arbitration*.
11. Chapter 6, *After the Arbitration*.

3-033 Escalation on one side may often lead to escalation on the other, and a stronger belief in the correctness of one's own position. If it is true that many parties settle in the course of an arbitration, most often this is not due to the persuasive power of the other party or its counsel. Rather, it is because one or both sides are worn down by the proceedings (financially and otherwise). Thus, the best time to propose informal methods of resolution – such as business negotiations or mediation – is often not after proceedings are underway and substantial efforts have been expended, but *before* the other side has spent significant sums and become blind to the weaknesses of its case, and before the relationship between the parties has deteriorated after one of them has started arbitration or litigation.

3-034 *Strategic advantages to offering mediation (even if not accepted) at the outset of a dispute.* A party may be concerned that an offer of mediation made to the opposing party will be construed as a sign of weakness (and even that the receiving party may disclose the offer to the tribunal in the arbitration and will argue that the offer is an admission of liability or of certain facts). We believe these concerns are misplaced. An offer to mediate will generally convey confidence in one's own case and a willingness to be reasonable in seeking to compromise. Indeed, the *rejection* of an offer to mediate risks conveying not only unreasonableness but also a lack of comfort with one's own case. There is, in our view, rarely any downside to offering to mediate, and it may be in a party's strategic interests to propose mediation at the onset of proceedings even if it is likely that the offer will be rejected. A rejected offer will still convey confidence and reasonableness and may nonetheless promote future opportunities to settle and preserve any relationship interests that may exist between the parties. Of course, if the offer is accepted and the mediation leads to settlement, this would be a greater success.

III.   USING EARLY EVALUATION TO QUANTIFY THE ENTIRE DISPUTE RISK

3-035 In virtually every country there are entities that will pursue any small amount of money owed and will defend every claim to the last small coin. They are called 'bankruptcies'. Companies that hope to have a healthy future, however, will assess when the battle is one that is really worth the fight. As noted earlier, the essential challenge to a party when a dispute arises is identifying whether to proceed with the dispute or settle. In simple terms, any business leader is likely to expect the lawyer to be able to answer the question, 'Is the settlement we can get today better than the outcome we will get through arbitration or litigation?' Conversely, it would not be unusual or surprising after the receipt of an arbitration award, whether positive or negative in a lawyer's eyes, for some managers to look back and ask, 'Is this better than the settlement we could have had two years ago?'

A.   THE NATURE OF AN EARLY CASE ASSESSMENT
                                      (ECA): PREDICTING THE ULTIMATE OUTCOME
                                      AND THE COST OF GETTING THERE

The same work that will need to be undertaken to prepare for an arbitration can be **3-036** simultaneously and productively applied towards a quantification of probable outcomes and costs. Some companies have policies requiring their counsel to provide an ECA of significant matters and to submit a completed ECA within a set period of time (such as sixty days) whenever a dispute arises or litigation of any type is commenced. An ECA may take a variety of different forms, depending on the considerations important to the party. (An example of the information an ECA may contain is set out in Appendix 6).

At its most basic, an ECA will provide an informed estimate of the likely out- **3-037** come of the proceedings, the costs that will be incurred, and any significant legal or factual issues (such as the risk of not being able to enforce a favourable award). The purpose is to put the party in the position of being able to sensibly evaluate all possible options for the dispute, from seeing the arbitration through to conclusion to pursuing settlement through informal methods of dispute resolution (negotiations or mediation). Despite (or perhaps because of) its simplicity, the following ECA is likely to be appreciated by business leaders as being consistent with the approach they are accustomed to using for all other types of commercial risk:

Example 3f – Simple ECA Format

	Liability (in USD)	Net Costs (in USD)	Net Impact (in USD)
Best case	_____	+ _____	_____
Worst case	_____	+ _____	_____
Most likely	_____	+ _____	_____

In this example, 'liability' is used on the assumption that the party is the **3-038** respondent. It could just as easily be 'recovery' if the party is the claimant. As for costs, this is intended as the 'net costs' to the party of conducting and completing the litigation. 'Net' is a useful concept because the party will likely want to know both its recoverable and unrecoverable costs – in other words, the amounts it will spend which, it will never see again as a consequence of having conducted the litigation. For example, in a best-case situation the respondent may assume it will recover a significant portion but not all of its external costs, or even all of its external costs but not the time of its internal managers who supported the litigation.

Thus, it is unlikely, even with the availability of substantial cost recovery,[12] that a party's net costs would ever be zero.

3-039 *Cost of an ECA.* The scope and expense of an ECA should be proportionate to the amount in dispute. As will be discussed below, conducting an ECA can involve substantial time of (and be a burden to) a party's employees, not to mention the expense involved. Consequently, the scope and depth of an ECA should be reasonably calibrated to the amount and any other interests in dispute. While bet-the-company or otherwise substantial claims may merit a considerable investigation that justifies the resulting burdens and costs, this will often not be the case with smaller-sized claims. No ECA, no matter how thorough, will be able to predict the exact outcome of a litigation. While it is true that more work will generally lead to a more precise estimate of probable outcomes, proportionality and common sense should be applied to any decision of how many stones must be unturned in order to obtain a reasonable view of the likely conclusion.

3-040 *ECA as a baseline to improve a party's case.* What can be done that would change the 'most likely' case? In completing the ECA, the party and its counsel are likely to identify numerous factual and legal issues that, if further investigated or developed, may cause the assessment of a likely outcome to change materially or even dramatically. For example, if the claimant is requesting damages far in excess of a contractual limitation of liability, an issue that could impact the evaluation is whether the limitation might be invalid under the governing law of the contract or inoperative in the particular factual circumstances of the case.

3-041 The simple scheme above can be further refined in many ways, such as by adding more detail to the liability/recovery entry, detailing the cost section (for example to take into consideration costs that would be waived in a settlement), or including other items important to the party, such as the impact on a commercial relationship and the potential loss of future business as the result of the dispute. For ease of explanation, however, we have kept with the simple example above. Using a dispute in which the claimant has commenced arbitration for USD 12 million in damages, the table might be completed by the respondent, after due diligence on the claims, as follows:[13]

---

12. Chapter 5, *The Conduct of the Arbitration.*
13. The 'net costs' column should always have a number, even in arbitrations in which it may be possible to recover all costs as the prevailing party. This is for several reasons: cost recovery is never a certainty and there will almost always be costs that will not be recoverable. Also, there is often the possibility of a settlement in which each side will accept responsibility for its own costs incurred to date. Perhaps most importantly, costs are expensed by parties in the year in which they were incurred (i.e., they are not considered liabilities that can be reflected on a balance sheet in the same way that a claim for damages may need to be reflected). Thus, a party may be required to set aside financial reserves (provisions) for liability, but not for costs.

Example 3g – Simple ECA Case (USD 12 Million Disputed Amount)

	Liability (in USD)	Net Costs (in USD)	Net Impact (in USD)
Best case	0	250,000	250,000
Worst case	2,000,000	1,000,000	3,000,000
Most likely	1,000,000	500,000	1,500,000

In the above example, the 'best' and 'worst' scenarios should be treated as rea- **3-042** sonably probable, not theoretical outcomes or highly unlikely extremes. For example, if the claimant's demand is for USD 2 million in contractual damages, plus USD 10 million in other damages (USD 12 million total), but the 'other' damages are expressly excluded by the contract, then a realistic 'worst case' may be USD 2 million, not USD 12 million. Another way of looking at this is from the claimant's point of view, as its best case should be the opposite of the respondent's worst case. In this example, if the claimant believes it has a reasonable but not bulletproof claim for USD 2 million and has asserted the USD 10 million as a threat to obtain negotiation leverage, then USD 2 million is the claimant's best case, not the hypothetical USD 12 million demanded. This is not to say that extreme outcomes never occur. It is just that highly improbable outcomes cannot serve as the basis of sound planning or decision making.

Checklist 3b – Conduct of an ECA within 60 Days

What	Who	When
Scope of ECA defined	Party and outside counsel	Day 1
Document collection	All employees and witnesses having documents potentially relevant to the dispute	Within 15 days
Document review	Counsel and witnesses together	Within 30 days
Meetings with witnesses	Counsel and witnesses together	Within 45 days
Input from experts	Counsel leads, with party input on appropriate expertise	As necessary to complete case assessment
Review and assessment of issues under governing	Counsel	Immediately

What	Who	When
law		
Assessment of potential issues or defences under dispute clause, arbitration rules, and law of place of arbitration	Counsel	Immediately
Assessment of probable costs and possibility of cost recovery	Counsel	On completion of ECA
Range of probable outcomes	Counsel	On completion of ECA
Critical issues that, if developed, could substantially influence a more favourable outcome	Counsel	On completion of ECA

3-043 *Confidentiality and privilege of case assessments.* ECAs and similar assessments of the strengths and weaknesses of a party's case are intended for internal consumption only. In many cases, it will be damaging for any internal assessment, especially if detailed and truly objective, to fall into the hands of the opponent. The party preparing the ECA should therefore take special care in preserving its confidentiality by, for example, marking the document as confidential and restricting its circulation. It is also important to ensure that any assessment is covered by privilege, to prevent it being produced in any arbitration or litigation if it were to fall into the hands of the opponent. Privilege is likely to attach to a case assessment in most jurisdictions as the document is prepared in contemplation of litigation, and it may also be a communication of legal advice between lawyer and client.[14]

3-044 *The limitations of a one-sided account.* When preparing at the outset of the case (or conducting an ECA), the lawyer will have had access only to her own client's documents and information. The opposing party may possess different documents and information that may not come to light until after arbitration is underway. As the purpose of an ECA is to assess probable outcomes in the event no settlement is reached (and perhaps to recommend settlement strategies to avoid such outcomes), at least some consideration must be given to the risk of new (or previously ignored) facts coming to light as the arbitration progresses. The lawyer is wise to advise the client of these considerations even when no ECA is requested and she is merely preparing a claim or defence to a claim.

---

14. Chapter 5, *The Conduct of the Arbitration.*

Using an ECA to plan for the next stage of the dispute. Perhaps the main advantage **3-045** of an early assessment is that it provides an approximate summary of potential exposure that will be useful in the course of the dispute: immediately, if there is any chance of settlement (and to evaluate whether the outcome achievable in settlement is better than the likely outcome in arbitration); and, as the proceedings progress, to keep a party's management apprised of developments, avoid surprises, and confirm or adjust strategy during the course of the proceedings. An ECA should be a constant 'reality check' by which a party can regularly measure expectations for the dispute and, as it progresses, assess the accuracy of estimated outcomes.

B.   GATHERING EVIDENCE AND ASSESSING THE FACTS

One of the aims of an ECA is to ensure that key facts and legal issues become **3-046** known to a party when they are most useful, which is before, or early in, the proceedings. Certainly, a reliable ECA will not be possible without access to, and an assessment of, the most critical documents and witness evidence. But, by the same measure, it should be possible to perform a meaningful ECA without a full-scale preparation for the entirety of a litigation. Indeed, it may not be possible at the commencement of an international arbitration to prepare a comprehensive ECA, as the party is unlikely to know just how the arbitration will be conducted until the arbitral tribunal is in place, and it has had the benefit of, at a minimum, the other party's submissions and the documents on which it intends to rely. It is for this reason that an ECA should be treated as an ongoing project that is periodically revisited during the proceedings.

Document collection. The answer to the question of what documentation should **3-047** be provided to counsel relating to the disputed transaction or project is, simply, all of it. As noted earlier, one of the preliminary steps a party can take to preserve its position at the outset of a dispute is to send employees a document retention notice requesting that they preserve all electronic and other documentation relating to the dispute for later retrieval. If the case does not settle in its preliminary stage, it will become necessary to gather and then review all relevant documentation in preparation for the arbitration. Review of this documentation will usually provide the cornerstone of a reliable early case evaluation.

Logistical difficulties of gathering documents from sources in different countries. **3-048** Document collection and review can be especially challenging in international arbitration if, as is commonly true in larger cases, the documents are in the hands of employees and potential witnesses scattered in different locations and in different languages. Nonetheless, they should be gathered and read, both to support the party's own case and to satisfy any obligations to produce the documents to the other side.[15]

3-049 *Privacy restrictions on the ability to gather or produce documents in transnational cases.* Increasingly, privacy laws in many countries (and particularly in Europe) may limit a company's ability to retrieve and produce internal employee communications where they include personal data or information relating to the employees. Personal data and information can encompass, for example, some employee e-mails that may be relevant to the dispute. Retrieving employee documents is one privacy concern; another is transmitting these documents outside the jurisdiction in which they are located, which may present a separate issue. In our experience, however, employees covered by privacy laws do not usually object to the transmission of their documents in support of an arbitration; on the contrary, they will often actively participate in identifying and explaining the most relevant documents in their possession.

3-050 *Addressing complications in document collection.* The importance of locating and gathering all the possibly relevant documents at an early stage cannot be overstated: in many international arbitrations, tribunals give contemporaneous documents more weight than witness evidence, and only through their early location and collection will there be sufficient time to review them (and translate them if needed), enabling them to be used productively both for estimating potential risk exposure and subsequently in the proceedings. Fortunately, most of the problems relating to the collection, review, and even production of documents can be addressed through planning both before and during an arbitration. If a company has document management and retention policies in place, and they are followed, the task will be much easier when a dispute arises, as the existence, location, and ownership of the documents, and any associated privacy issues, should be apparent. If not, more detailed investigation is likely to be needed. This is one of the areas where being able to rely on in-house lawyers is most critical (supported by outside counsel if more manpower is needed). The in-house counsel should be effective in locating employees with relevant documents and persuading their custodians to make them available promptly.

3-051 *Document review.* Once documents have been gathered, they will need to be reviewed by counsel, which will usually be done together with the document custodians (who may or may not become witnesses), who can help counsel quickly understand the meaning of the documents and the context in which they were created. This review can be conducted at a distance, using documents in electronic form (especially if the documents are numerous), or at the custodian's location to allow the reviewer to interview the custodian at the same time. This can be an expensive and time-consuming exercise, but the work is vital not only for the ECA

---

15. Chapter 5, *The Conduct of the Arbitration.*

but also for the preparation of any arbitration and for any document production requested by the opponent in that arbitration.[16]

Witness interviews. Interviewing – not interrogating – those involved in the dispute **3-052** and who may later become witnesses is perhaps the most rapid means of understanding the complex background to a dispute. In many countries, however, lawyers conducting informal interviews with witnesses is not customary, and doing so may even be restricted or prohibited by ethical rules applicable to counsel in domestic litigation.[17] Reluctance to speak candidly with outside counsel can usually be avoided or at least reduced by introducing the lawyer through a manager or in-house lawyer whom the employees already know, accompanied with careful instructions that employees should speak openly about the events leading up to the dispute. In some instances, it may be necessary to underline to employees that the outside counsel is on the same side. The perennial question 'what should I tell our lawyer about this dispute?' has the same answer no matter what country the employee may be from: 'the truth'.

Witness biases: developing an objective account. It would be unusual for all the **3-053** people who have been closely connected with a dispute to remain objective about the events that gave rise to it, or to be impartial about the potential outcomes. More typically, they will have formed strong or even passionate opinions about events and the other side and will be keen to see their views vindicated through legal process. In an international dispute, counsel should be mindful of the biases that lead people from any culture or background – in good faith – to reach conclusions about events that may vary from a slight bias to severe self-deception.

The universality of self-deception. Thus, lawyers should not expect individuals **3-054** from *one* particular country or culture to present a biased view of events; they should expect individuals from *all* countries and cultures (including their own culture and themselves) to relate events with inherent (and unconscious) biases, which may vary by degree from one individual to another. In fact, in international dispute resolution, there may be far more opportunity for parties to deceive themselves about the likely outcome, given the degree of uncertain information and number of variables involved in setting up and conducting an international proceeding.

Cognitive biases influencing a party's perception of the relative strengths of its **3-055** *position*. Self-deception may be a significant – perhaps the most significant –

---

16. Chapter 5, *The Conduct of the Arbitration*.
17. See G. B. Born, International Commercial Arbitration, vol. II, 2308–2309 (The Netherlands: Kluwer Law International, 2009); and H. van Houtte, 'Counsel–Witness Relations and Professional Misconduct in Civil Law Systems', *Arbitration International* 19, no. 4 (2003): 457 et seq. See also Part VII (Conduct of Work by Practising Barristers), Section 705 (Contact with witnesses) of the Code of Conduct of the Bar of England & Wales.

aspect of human psychology that contributes to dispute generation (and erroneous predictions of their outcome), but it is not the only one. Several relevant cognitive biases are described below.

Cognitive biases that may affect interpretations of a dispute by people from any country or cultural background:

Anchoring	The tendency to rely too heavily, or 'anchor', on one trait or piece of information when making decisions. For example, litigants can misjudge a potential outcome by placing too much reliance on a particular contract clause or event that occurred, to the exclusion of other facts and the surrounding law. The anchoring effect can be particularly useful in settlement negotiations. When the range of potential outcomes is broad, a party may want to seize the opportunity to make the first settlement offer, providing an effective 'anchor' on which subsequent discussion will occur. An ECA will help a party avoid being unfairly 'anchored' by offers or demands by the opponent.
Bandwagon effect	The tendency to believe things because many other people do so too. Commonly in international commercial disputes, at least one of the parties (and usually both) will be an organisation, whether a company or a governmental entity. Multiple people within an organisation may share an interpretation of events or certain expectations giving rise to a dispute, not because the interpretation or expectations are reasonable, but simply because others in their organisation hold the same views. Again, an ECA may help determine if the collective view is reasonable.
Déformation professionnelle	The tendency to look at things according to the conventions of one's own profession, forgetting any broader point of view. This is also known as 'when you're a hammer, everything looks like a nail'. For example, when both technical and commercial portions of a contract are in dispute, technical employees may overly emphasise the technical aspects, ignoring relevant commercial and contractual points.
Selective perception	The tendency for expectations to affect perception, to give greater consideration to facts or circumstances that support one's own interests and discount or ignore negative facts or circumstances.

3-056 *Considering the possibility of self-deception and bias.* Given the tendency of witnesses, at least at the outset, to unwittingly give accounts that may be less than objective, the lawyer should evaluate with a dose of scepticism the information and opinion provided in initial interviews. The weight to be given to any one person's account will of course vary according to her credibility, which the interviewing lawyer will want to assess at the same time as the content of her testimony. In particular, cross-checking the interviewee's account with the accounts of others involved in the same events, and especially with the contemporaneous documents, is essential to form a reliable picture of events.

The power of selective perception and self-deception in international dispute negotiations	For several years and in different locations around the world, one of the authors has conducted a course for company employees on negotiations to resolve an international commercial dispute. The scenario involves the failure of oil and gas equipment. Participants on each side are given the same inconclusive technical data about possible causes of the failure, but different objectives for negotiation relating to their position of buyer or seller. No matter where the course is held, from Kuala Lumpur to Oslo to Pennsylvania, participants consistently engage in heated and highly emotional exchanges based on sincere beliefs that the technical data supports only *their* side's interpretation, often culminating in accusations of bad-faith dealings by the other side. The point of the exercise – which is supported by years of data drawn from the assessments of each side – is to illustrate that 'where you stand depends on where you sit'. A party's position on one side of the table or the other can have a substantial impact not only on their negotiating objectives, but also the emotions that drive them and beliefs about the reliability of the underlying data supporting those objectives.[18]

Although skewed or biased accounts will most often err on the side of undue **3-057** optimism, that is not always the case. On the contrary, some employees may not be on the best terms with a company, others may have in the past expressed views opposing the decisions that led to the dispute, and some may simply wish to avoid what they assume will be the substantial burden of assisting counsel throughout the course of the dispute (often not an unrealistic assumption). In such cases, they may present, even unconsciously, negative biases about the circumstances leading up to the dispute. Lawyers may therefore find themselves advising that the case may not be as bad as the client initially believed.

---

18. M. McIlwrath, 'Selective Perception and Bad-Faith Allegations in Commercial Settlement Discussions', in *Alternatives* (CPR Institute, October 2004), 151.

C.   Assessing the Legal Merits

3-058 Once the lawyer has what she believes to be a fair picture of the facts of the dispute, she will begin to develop the legal theory or theories of the case, under the relevant contracts and applicable law. This may require advice from experts or lawyers qualified in a legal system in which the arbitration lawyer is not qualified. This is a fundamental part of both the ECA and the preparation of the party's case, and lateral thinking, an open mind, brainstorming, and cooperation with the client's team are all invaluable at this crucial stage.

3-059 *Strategic considerations regarding the dispute resolution clause, the rules of arbitration, and/or the procedural law of the place of arbitration.* There may be important procedural, jurisdictional, or other similar arguments that should be thrown into the mix with the facts and the basic theory of the merits of the case. These might include whether one party can or should commence court action rather than arbitration; which parties should be sued or, if possible, joined in the arbitration; which of several contracts to sue under; whether more than one arbitration should be commenced, and if so, if they should be consolidated; whether to raise counterclaims, and if so, in which proceeding; whether to seek interim relief, and if so, where; if either party should challenge jurisdiction if arbitration is commenced; whether to sue a state under an investment treaty (if one is available), rather than the parties' contract; and the likely or possible consequences of each of these decisions.

D.   Potential Implications of an ECA on Balance Sheet
          Accounting (Financial Reserves of Disputes)

3-060 A party's determination that an unfavourable outcome is probable will often create an obligation to make a financial reserve (provision) on its balance sheet. For companies that establish their balance sheets under the Generally Accepted Accounting Principles (GAAP), the applicable standard for setting litigation risk reserves is Financial Accounting Standard 5, or FAS 5. Under FAS 5, a pending or threatened litigation must be disclosed on a company's financial statement if it is 'reasonably possible' that there will be a loss.

3-061 *What FAS 5 covers (liability) and what it does not (party's own costs).* A litigation reserve under FAS 5 relates only to liability for a loss. That means the amount that the company may be obliged to pay at the conclusion of proceedings. It does not include a party's own costs of its defence, that is, the costs of lawyers, experts, and arbitrators, as these costs are instead expensed as they are incurred. 'Expensed' means that while they may be budgeted (and changed) each year, no reserve (or provision) is set aside for them, and therefore they do not appear as an impairment on a company's balance sheet.

The consequences of setting aside a reserve. Setting a financial reserve essen- **3-062** tially freezes the amount on a company's balance sheet, making it unavailable for reporting as company profits. A reserve that appears on a balance sheet for a dispute is generally not a momentary thing. Once provided, the reserve will often remain on the balance sheet until there is a binding arbitration award, court decision, or settlement. And even then, the reserve will be released to profits only to the extent that it is greater than the binding determination or settlement amount. As a consequence, the amount is likely to be the subject of periodic review by external auditors. They will want to ascertain that it is accurate, meaning sufficiently high to cover the risk but not an overstatement of the probable outcome.

Methodology for calculating a financial reserve under GAAP accounting. FAS 5 is **3-063** a rule used to determine losses and gains, and it asks two sets of simple questions. Both must be answered affirmatively in order for a reserve to be required. Is it probable and likely that an asset is impaired or a liability has been incurred? Another way of asking this is whether the probability is greater than 50% that the company is liable for some portion of the other party's claims. If yes, then is it possible to reasonably estimate the range of possible outcomes? If so, the most probable amount among the different options presented is reserved. Where different outcomes are equally probable, the *low* end of the range is the reserve amount. There is a common misconception that companies, in exercising prudence, must always reserve the higher amount. That is only the case when the higher amount is more probable.

Not that this ever really happens: how not to advise clients on dispute reserves	Actually, this happens quite a lot. Counsel who are not experienced in GAAP accounting may take a view that clients and their auditors will want to know the *maximum* hypothetical risk from a dispute, rather than the most *probable* amount of risk. Thus, one of the authors (the in-house counsel) has occasionally had to address the letter sent by an inexperienced external counsel to auditors expressing an improbably high degree of risk from a dispute. For example, external counsel for one domestic litigation involving claims totalling over EUR 5 million informed the in-house litigation lawyer that a negative outcome was highly unlikely, given that the claims all appeared to be baseless and the requested damages significantly inflated. But the same counsel then responded to an inquiry from the company's external auditors, recommending a financial reserve of EUR 5 million, that is, the full value of the claim. This created some amount of embarrassment for the in-house legal team, which had not advised the business of a need to post such a large financial reserve. The external counsel subsequently explained

> that in their own opinion, large companies would want to reserve the maximum potential exposure for disputes, and that is what they provided. Again, when applying FAS 5, the key concepts are probability and 'estimability', not a worst-case scenario.

3-064 *Determining when to set a reserve for a dispute.* Where FAS 5 applies and a party believes that it has sufficient information to reasonably answer questions of the probability and estimability of a loss, then a reserve should be made for the dispute on the company's balance sheet. At the start of an international arbitration, however, a party may not be able to assess probability for purposes of FAS 5, at least until the arbitral tribunal is appointed and preliminary issues are addressed. For example, there may be threshold issues of whether the proceedings will continue in arbitration or court litigation and, if in arbitration, whether the appointment and orientation of the tribunal may impact the assessment of potential liability.

3-065 *Risk of reserves being held against a party.* A relatively common request for documents may seek disclosure of a respondent's financial reserve for a dispute, in the attempt to show that the respondent has itself admitted (at least internally) the likelihood that it is liable for the claim. Under the relatively restrictive rules that apply to document production in international arbitration, it may be challenging to convince a tribunal to order production of documents evidencing the amount reserved. Still, a claimant may seek the same information through a company's publicly disclosed filings or statements provided to investors, in that portion of the balance sheet relating to reserves for contingent events. Most companies disclose only a general reserve fund that is inclusive of all pending litigation, not reserves for specific disputes, although recent recommendations for accounting changes in the United States have proposed that companies disclose with specificity as to each dispute for which a reserve is established.[19] One legitimate concern about such a requirement is that claimants will cite specific litigation reserves as admissions of liability.

E.   Estimating the Total Cost of the Arbitration
          and Factors Influencing Costs

3-066 Legal fees can be a significant component of the costs of any dispute, but they are not the only one that must be considered when attempting to quantify the total cost

---

19. The Financial Accounting Standards Board published an exposure draft entitled 'Disclosure of Certain Loss Contingencies, an amendment of FASB Statements No. 5 and 141(R)' proposing amendments to the disclosure requirements for loss contingencies currently set forth in FASB Statement No. 5, Accounting for Contingencies. This amendment to FAS 5 (which has not been adopted at the time of writing) would require much more extensive disclosures in company notes to financial statements relating to pending or threatened litigation.

impact (aside from any impact of a finding on the merits). Some considerations will be reliably quantifiable at the outset of proceedings; others less reliably so, but a ballpark figure will still be achievable. These costs can be divided between a party's direct expenditures or out-of-pocket costs and its lost productivity or opportunities.

Cost scenarios according to 'civil law' or 'common law' nature of arbitration. **3-067** Below is an example of a high-level, line-item estimate of a party's total arbitration costs, without considering the possibility of cost recovery (an important factor that is discussed further below in paragraph 3–083). The example is based on a hypothetical arbitration of moderate factual complexity before three arbitrators in which the claimant seeks USD 6 million and the respondent counterclaims for USD 4 million (giving a total of USD 10 million in claims and counterclaims). In these examples, the arbitrators are compensated on an hourly basis and not by the ad valorem method based on the amount in dispute. The first estimate is for an arbitration with a predominantly civil law approach to litigation.

Example 3h – Detailed Estimate of Costs
(Predominantly Civil Law Proceeding, for example in
France, Italy, or Switzerland)

	Low (in USD)	High (in USD)	Mid-Point (in USD)
3 Arbitrators (50%)[20]	100,000	250,000	175,000
Arbitral institution (50%)	12,000	25,000	18,500
Legal fees	150,000	500,000	325,000
Tribunal's expert (50%)	10,000	50,000	30,000
Party's direct costs	5,000	10,000	7,500
TOTAL	277,000	835,000	556,000

Contrast this estimate with the same dispute conducted with arbitrators and counsel **3-068** with a preference for a common law approach to dispute resolution, emphasising the need for witness testimony given at evidentiary hearings and an extensive document production exercise.

---

20. The figure of 50% indicates that each party pays a 50% share of the item and that the amounts given are 50% of the total amount.

Example 3i – Detailed Estimate of Costs
(Predominantly Common Law Proceeding, for example in US or UK)

	Low (in USD)	High (in USD)	Mid-point (in USD)
3 Arbitrators (50%)	200,000	500,000	350,000
Arbitral institution (50%)	12,000	25,000	18,500
Legal fees	400,000	1,500,000	950,000
Party expert	30,000	180,000	95,000
Party's direct costs	10,000	20,000	15,000
TOTAL	652,000	2,225,000	1,428,500

3-069 As can be observed in the examples above, a realistic cost estimate cannot be divorced from the practicalities of how the arbitration will be conducted, much of which will be in the hands of the parties. For example, if the party is estimating costs before appointing its arbitrator, it should consider whether it desires a tribunal dominated by arbitrators with a preference for arbitration as conducted in civil law jurisdictions or in the common law tradition. In a commercial dispute of moderate size and complexity, even a party from a common law background may prefer a tribunal that favours a less costly civil law approach to dispute resolution, with less emphasis on witness testimony, lengthy evidentiary hearings, and extensive document production.

Checklist 3c – Detailing the Cost Estimate

Expenditure	Description
Arbitrators' fees and expenses	Fees to be paid to the arbitrator or arbitrators for their services during the proceedings, which may vary depending on the number of arbitrators, type of arbitration, and administering institution, and can be significantly influenced by the conduct of the parties, their counsel, and the arbitrators themselves in the course of the proceedings
Arbitral institutions' fees	The fees charged by an institution to oversee the proceedings and resolve disputes over the appointment and substitution of arbitrators. Usually a low cost relative to other expenditures

Expenditure	Description
Legal fees and expenses	The costs of all counsel who will assist or represent the party during the proceeding and through enforcement, including any ancillary proceedings in court. This item will usually form the largest portion of a party's costs
Expert fees and expenses	Cost of legal or technical experts who will testify on the party's behalf
Party's own direct costs	Cost of employees who may need to travel to another city or country to attend meetings with counsel or a hearing
Party's own indirect costs	The time and effort that employees will devote to the arbitration instead of forward-looking projects

Out-of-pocket costs. As noted, legal fees are the major component of a party's out- **3-070** of-pocket costs. The other cost items are the fees and expenses of arbitrators, an arbitral institution (if one is used), external experts, and any travel and hotel costs that a party will be required to bear for its employees to attend meetings with lawyers or hearings. All of these are quantifiable, with varying degrees of precision.

Cost of internal lawyers. Companies that employ their own in-house counsel may **3-071** have specialised internal lawyers dedicated to resolving or managing disputes. Although recovering the cost of internal lawyers may be less frequently ordered than the cost of external counsel,[21] it is certainly not unheard of and is a cost that can be reasonably estimated.

Legal fees. When estimating costs, a party should ensure that it has considered: **3-072**

- *All phases of the arbitration.* If there is a risk that an award will be challenged or a party may need to bring enforcement proceedings, then the party should estimate all costs through those final stages. For example, it may well be that one or more different law firms will be necessary in order to enforce or resist enforcement of the award in different jurisdictions around the world.

---

21. For the purposes of estimating and recovering a party's costs, we put in-house counsel on the same footing as outside counsel, if they directly represent the party in the proceedings. There is no requirement for a party to retain outside counsel to represent it in an international arbitration, and parties may justifiably expect to budget for and potentially recover the costs of their defence, regardless of whether it is conducted by in-house or external lawyers.

- *All aspects of the arbitration.* Similarly, if there are jurisdictional objections to the arbitration or a request for interim measures, there may be a need for local, in-country counsel to support that ancillary litigation during the course of the arbitration.
- *Other material expenses.* There may be numerous other expenditures that a law firm may incur on behalf of the client in the course of an arbitration, but, if they are for services provided by third parties, the firm may not take such costs into consideration when providing an estimate. For example, if the dispute is highly fact intensive and will depend on the review (and possible production) of a substantial number of documents, the firm may convert the documents into electronic files that can be quickly and efficiently reviewed. This is likely to reduce the amount of time the firm will bill, but at the additional cost of digitising the documents, which in some instances can be significant. The party should ensure that the estimate of legal fees takes into consideration this type of cost.

3-073 *Expert fees.* Even in the early stages of a dispute, and before arbitration is under-way, it should be possible to determine whether it is reasonably likely that experts will be necessary to help prove any legal or technical issues. An expert in an international arbitration will most likely be required to submit an 'expert report' stating her conclusions on the disputed item, and on the basis of which the expert will give any live testimony required at a hearing. It is easy to underestimate this task and the costs of completing it. The expert will likely charge for time spent reviewing the background information relevant to the dispute, preparing her report (including the costs of travelling to any meetings with witnesses or counsel), preparing for a hearing, attending the hearing and/or conferencing with the opposing party's expert, and providing further observations or additional reports post-hearing in response to any inquiries that may result from the testimony of either side's expert.

3-074 *Arbitrator fees and administrative fees.* The starting point for calculating the fees payable to arbitrators and any administrating institution will be the dispute resolution clause of the contract at issue and the rules under which the arbitrators are appointed. Some arbitration institutions (most notably the ICC) provide for a total range or amount of arbitrator fees on the basis of the amount in dispute. Under this ad valorem approach, payment of much or all of the fees will be due at the start of the proceedings in the form of an advance. The ICC provides on its website a convenient 'cost calculator', giving parties an easy way to calculate what they will be required to pay.[22] In the event of a settlement in the early phases of an arbitration, most institutions will refund a portion of what the party has paid in advance.[23]

---

22. Chapter 1, *The Elements of Dispute Resdution Agreement.*
23. Chapter 5, *The Conduct of the Arbitration.*

Arbitrator fees calculated on an hourly or daily basis. Arbitrators billing on an **3-075**
hourly basis should disclose their rates to the parties at the start of the proceedings.
Where an institution is administering the proceedings, it will generally be responsible for fixing the rates of the arbitrators, billing the parties as the arbitration
progresses, and compensating the arbitrators. It is not unheard of for arbitrators,
when not constrained by an institution, to charge the parties considerably more
than they would be able to charge in an institutional arbitration. At the same
time, there are many instances where arbitrators charge the parties considerably
less than the usual hourly rate they charge clients if they have a practice as counsel.
Because the parties cannot fully control arbitrator costs, when putting together an
estimate they should take the probable range of fees and settle on a middle point.

Administrative (institutional) fees. As discussed in Chapter 1, the fees that institu- **3-076**
tions themselves charge are generally a small fraction of what is paid to arbitrators,
but they can nonetheless be substantial in disputes of large size, particularly where
the ad valorem method of calculating fees is applied. For example, in an ICC
proceeding in which the amount in dispute is USD 10 million, the average fees
for a three-arbitrator tribunal will be USD 318,705 and USD 51,400 for the fees of
the institution itself. In all events, the institution itself should, at the outset of the
proceedings, be able to provide the parties with an estimate of its own fees.

Claims, counterclaims, and ad valorem fee calculations. As noted in Chapter 1, **3-077**
parties should be mindful when involved in an arbitration under a fixed or ad
valorem fee system (such as that of the ICC) that the fees will be calculated on
the basis of the total amount of claims and counterclaims, even if the claim and
counterclaim involve a dispute over the same sum of money. An example: the
claimant seeks USD 10 million in payment due under a contract, which the claimant alleges the respondent terminated without cause; the respondent submits a
counterclaim that the USD 10 million is not due on account of defects and
other losses suffered also having a value of USD 10 million. While the parties
may see the dispute as being over the same sum of money (USD 10 million, which
is either due or not due to the claimant), the institution will often mechanically
calculate the advance on the basis of USD 20 million, which is the total amount of
claims and counterclaims with no regard given to their substance.

Taxes on costs (and estimating them). VAT can add a substantial additional amount **3-078**
(in some cases 20% or more) to the fees charged by an institution, arbitrators,
external counsel, and others. Whether a party will be charged VAT and whether it
may be able to recover all or some portion of this cost can depend on a variety of
factors that may not be known to the party at the outset of an arbitration, such as the
tax rules in the location of the billing party (arbitrators and counsel, for example)
and in the location of the party itself, or whether the party will be able to offset
VAT on its books in the year in which the VAT is incurred. Unfortunately, in
almost all cases any fee estimates, whether provided by the institution, arbitrators
in an ad hoc proceeding, or directly from counsel, will *not* include assumptions
about VAT. For example, the ICC cost calculator gives no consideration to the

possible application of VAT, as the ICC has no way of knowing whether it will apply to a party or arbitrators in any given case. Thus, parties may be prudent to include in their cost estimates a reasonably conservative provision for VAT.

3-079 *Secretary to the tribunal.* As considered elsewhere,[24] it is increasingly common, especially in ad hoc proceedings, for three-arbitrator tribunals to appoint a 'secretary' to fulfil the administrative functions of an institution. Often this will be a lawyer affiliated with the office or law firm of the chair of the tribunal. Fees charged for a secretary are usually small in relative terms, but they are an additional cost for the parties. Typically, a tribunal will ask the parties to agree on the appointment of the secretary, and parties may legitimately ask for an estimate of the secretary's costs. A rough rule of thumb is that the charges for a secretary should not exceed the fees of the arbitration institution administering the case (or, in an ad hoc arbitration, the fees that a reputable institution would charge).

3-080 *Joint and several liability for arbitrators' fees and expenses.* The general rule in international arbitration is that parties are jointly and severally liable for the entirety of the costs of the arbitral tribunal. This rule is likely to apply even in cases where the contract's dispute resolution clause expressly states that each side will bear its own legal fees and share equally the cost of the tribunal. These agreements are between the parties, not conditions placed on the arbitrators. In practice, a party should anticipate – in both institutional and ad hoc arbitrations – that an advance on the arbitrators' fees will need to be paid before the case can proceed. If an adversary defaults in payment, therefore, the other party is left with the decision of whether to abandon the proceedings or pay the defaulting party's share in order to continue them.[25] In practical terms, this means that a claimant or counterclaimant who believes the opponent will default on the fees of the institution or arbitral tribunal will need to include this additional expense (the other side's share of the fees) in its estimate.

3-081 *Lost productivity and opportunities: the indirect costs of a dispute.* In addition to the external out-of-pocket costs incurred by a party conducting a litigation, there are at least two sorts of internal and indirect costs that the litigating party will bear. The first, lost productivity, is the cost of devoting employee time to supporting a litigation, which will almost certainly relate to a contract signed months or years in the past. The employer is therefore paying its employee to engage in an activity that is not forward looking; while it may be revenue protecting, it is not revenue generating. The second category of internal and indirect loss, lost opportunities, reflects the likelihood that the very existence of the dispute may cause potential commercial opportunities to be ignored (by employees immersed in the dispute rather than seeking out and negotiating new contracts) or even destroyed (through the damage to the relationship with the opposing party).

---

24. Chapter 1, *The Elements of an International Dispute Resolution* Agreement, and Ch. 5, *The Conduct of the Arbitration.*
25. Chapter 5, *The Conduct of the Arbitration.*

Quantification of the indirect costs. Some loss of productivity can be quantified. **3-082** For example, if one or more employees become fully or substantially dedicated to the arbitration, it should be possible just to include their salary for that period as an additional expense in the arbitration. If, as in many cases, multiple employees will devote the occasional day to the arbitration, rather than being involved full time, it may still be possible to collect their cumulative hours to quantify the cost of their involvement. It will be challenging, however, to quantify the impact a dispute may have on the employee's productivity in their day job outside the dispute. Similarly, it will be difficult to put a number on the opportunities that might have been pursued and transformed into new business had employees been pursuing them instead of participating in an arbitration, or had the party maintained a positive relationship with the adversary. Yet this may at times be the greatest cost of a dispute.

Calculating the chances of cost recovery. In many international arbitrations, the **3-083** losing party will be liable for some or even all of the winning party's out-of-pocket costs.[26] When estimating overall costs, a party should in theory ask how much, if any, it can reasonably expect to recover in the event it wins, and how much in addition to its own costs it will have to pay in the event of losing. In practice, while cost recovery may be relatively predictable in court litigation in some jurisdictions, there are a number of problems when attempting to estimate the potential for cost recovery in an international arbitration, at least at the onset of the proceedings. In an international arbitration, a 'victory' on the underlying claim may lead to an award recovering all, a portion, or none of the costs incurred. The recoverable amount will likely depend on the approach adopted by the arbitrators, who may not even be appointed at the time of completing an ECA, which may implicate both their personal preferences as well as the dynamics and potential compromise among the members of the tribunal. The authors have seen several instances in which a prevailing party has seen its victory somewhat muted by an award on costs or interest that is less than what should arguably have been due. We do not comment on the propriety of such awards but simply note that in practice future cost recovery is difficult to estimate until proceedings are well underway.

Litigation funding. A recent phenomenon in the international arbitration world is **3-084** litigation funding, which has recently become popular in England in particular and is known to also be developing more generally in the international arbitration field. Specialist companies, including hedge funds, purchase interests in claims at the outset of the case. Generally, the purchase involves an agreement by which the company funds the cost of pursuing the claim in arbitration and/or enforcement in return for a significant portion of any amounts eventually collected. Naturally, the funder will first want to ensure that the claim is large and solid enough, and that the debtor has sufficient assets for collection on any award.

---

26. Chapter 5, *The Conduct of the Arbitration.*

IV.   ENGAGING AND DISENGAGING COUNSEL

3-085 Parties in most international arbitrations are represented by lawyers in private practice, who work with representatives of the parties – often commercial people and in-house lawyers if the company is of sufficient size to have in-house legal capacity – to present their client's case to the arbitrators. However, there is no rule in arbitration that says parties must be represented by outside lawyers, or indeed that they must be represented by lawyers at all. Instead, the principle in international arbitration is that the parties 'may be represented or assisted by persons of their choice'.[27]

3-086 Also, just because the contract calls for dispute resolution in one place or under a given law, this does not lead to the conclusion that the parties should appoint counsel or arbitrators from the same place or legal background. The real question is whether there is reason to favour a domestic-style arbitration, a result that is virtually guaranteed if counsel and arbitrators all hail from the same country and legal background (regardless of where the parties may be from). A party may therefore choose to appoint counsel (or not) and arbitrators who will steer the proceedings away from local idiosyncrasies.

3-087 *When to involve counsel.* Lawyers are fond of admonishing parties that they should have been contacted earlier in order to avoid the dispute or protect the party's rights. There is usually truth to this, even if delivered with some amount of self-promotion by counsel and the benefit of hindsight. The decision whether to involve outside counsel, and when, is a matter of judgment based on a number of factors. These include: (1) whether the party has internal legal counsel who are competent and comfortable in handling disputes through the relevant phases; (2) whether the party will have the financial resources needed to involve outside counsel at an early stage or at all; (3) whether the dispute presents issues or problems that need special expertise that can only be obtained through external counsel; and (4) whether the dispute has developed to the point in which counsel's involvement is warranted in the light of the above circumstances.

A.   'IN-SOURCING' ARBITRATION WORK

3-088 The first question regarding the hiring of counsel should not therefore be whom to hire, but whether one even needs outside counsel at all. In other words, does the party have the ability to represent itself in the arbitration, considering demands such as legal expertise, language capability, and available manpower, as well as the interests at stake? Because of their knowledge of their own business and relevant industry practices, in-house lawyers may be capable of handling disputes of all types on equal or even better footing than outside counsel.

---

27. See Art. 4 of the UNCITRAL Rules.

Practical considerations in favour of in-sourcing arbitration work. Handling a dispute **3-089** entirely in-house will be sensible only if the party (usually a large multinational or a government) has one or more members of its legal team who not only feel comfortable doing so but who also are able to dedicate a large portion of their time to the case during its most active periods. Fortunately (at least in this respect), most international arbitrations do not move at a rapid pace, so parties that choose to conduct proceedings without relying on outside counsel may find that they have ample time to prepare submissions and arrange to attend hearings. Given the costs of outside lawyers and law firms, a decision to 'in-source' arbitration work may be the option that offers the least financial downside to a party facing an international dispute.

Checklist 3d – In-Sourcing vs. Outsourcing Legal Work

Criterion	*Issue*
Speed of the proceedings	Is the case likely to take a year or more? The pace of international arbitration may give in-house counsel ample time to keep up with the proceedings[28]
Language of the arbitration	Does the party have the language capability in house to draft submissions and argue at hearings?
Complexity of the dispute and need for resources	Is the dispute relatively straightforward and/ or of a type capable of being handled internally?
Subject-matter expertise	Is the party sufficiently comfortable with the governing law and type of dispute?
Legal fees	If outside counsel is retained, will the legal fees likely overshadow the amount in dispute?

While we do not wish to appear to endorse the lack of preparation or competence **3-090** by in-house counsel venturing for the first time into arbitration, our experience is that most tribunals will make allowances for inexperience. In fact, because tribunals are concerned to ensure due process is afforded to all parties, some arbitrators may compensate for inexperienced or absent counsel by advancing on their own initiative the arguments that counsel should have made.

---

28. Indeed, many international arbitrations are unlikely to be concluded in less than two years. Contrast this, for example, with the procedure of 'adjudication' in UK construction disputes, in which a decision must be reached within twenty-eight days of the commencement of the dispute. Such a pace would present serious challenges for a typically resource-limited in-house legal department.

B.   Retaining External Counsel

3-091 Generally speaking, parties will appoint outside counsel when they feel they lack
sufficient personnel, confidence, or expertise to conduct an international arbitration of the size or importance that confronts them. It is not always clear, however,
that external counsel can do a better job than in-house lawyers who are familiar
with the company's products, services, employees, and processes. It is therefore
advisable for parties to take special care in the appointment of specialised arbitration counsel.

Checklist 3e – Pitfalls to Avoid in Appointing External Counsel

Concern	Potential Pitfall	Potential Solution
Reactive appointments	The tendency of some parties to appoint counsel as a reaction to the appointment made by the other side or the governing law or place of dispute resolution	Appoint counsel in order to optimise the party's own interests
Retaining counsel with appropriate skills and experience	Appointing the lawyer not on the basis of the skills involved but on account of being usual counsel or the one who drafted the disputed contract	Canvassing a sufficiently broad number of candidates to evaluate experience and skills in international arbitration and suitability for the particular dispute
Mediation capability	Taking for granted that counsel will have experience in negotiating and settling international commercial disputes	Request potential counsel to provide mediation credentials (i.e., experience promoting mediation and using it as a tool to settle cases)
Geographic location	Retaining counsel who are distant from the dispute's 'centre of gravity' (location of management and witnesses), which may result in additional cost and inconvenience	Assess ability of proposed counsel to provide support at or near the dispute's centre of gravity
Language	Retaining counsel who may lack language skills to communicate effectively with the employees, witnesses, and arbitrators involved	Consider the need for language capabilities when retaining counsel

Concern	Potential Pitfall	Potential Solution
Governing law	Ignoring or placing too much reliance on familiarity with the substantive law to be applied	Consider the relation of governing law to the dispute, and whether much rides on issues of substantive law (i.e., when experience in the governing law will be more important)?

Proactive, not reactive, counsel appointments. It is perhaps too common for parties **3-092** to appoint counsel (and arbitrators for that matter) as a reaction to the place of dispute resolution, governing law, or even to the appointment made by the other side, rather than on the basis of an independent and comprehensive evaluation of the counsel most suitable for the dispute.

The objection may be that if a dispute is governed by English law, a party needs **3-093** to appoint a lawyer from that country, even though that country may be far from the party's home. The same can be said with respect to the place of arbitration. A better view is that the governing law and place of arbitration are among the criteria that a party appointing counsel should take into account, but are certainly not the only criteria, nor necessarily the most important. It is quite customary in international arbitration for counsel not to be admitted or otherwise qualified in the jurisdiction of the governing law or place of arbitration, and instead for the substantive law to be proved by expert witnesses from that jurisdiction. As we explore in more detail in the paragraphs that follow, we think the selection of counsel should be decided on the basis of a number of factors, with expertise and experience in international arbitration being at or close to the top of the list.

Identifying potential outside counsel. Which outside counsel should be hired **3-094** when the time is ripe to do so, and how should a party go about locating them? The most natural starting point for most people is to call a lawyer they already know and trust and ask for recommendations or if that lawyer can assist them. This might be the proverbial lawyer 'down the hall', which in practical terms could well be the same law firm that worked on the disputed transaction or that has traditionally represented the client in other disputes. On the one hand, the flexibility offered by international arbitration means a party should certainly consider the advantages of any existing long-term relationships with outside lawyers who have acquired a substantial knowledge of the business and its people. On the other hand, if the dispute involves the interpretation of a contract that the law firm assisted in drafting, the client may have reason to doubt whether the firm can be truly objective in its ability to provide an assessment of the potential outcomes. The party's task is always one of finding the lawyer most suited to the task, and this might or might not be the lawyer who is already known to the party.

3-095 Lawyers and law firms survive by accepting work, not turning it away, and many have an innate tendency to exaggerate their experience and accept work that would be better handled by someone else. When choosing outside counsel for an international arbitration, a party may wish to look beyond its regular litigation lawyer or law firms in order retain the best lawyer for the particular dispute. There are numerous avenues for gathering names of potential candidates. In addition to mining existing relationships with colleagues and outside lawyers for suggestions, a party may also wish to consider global legal guides.[29] While these guides can have their limitations and in some cases only list those who pay to be listed (or give more prominence to paying entries), in the absence of other sources of information they can at least be a useful departure point for further inquiries.

3-096 *Counsel selection criteria.* Having narrowed the list of candidates to a handful of law firms, it can be helpful to attempt to rank each firm on the basis of the criteria that the ideal counsel should satisfy. Experience in international arbitration is one factor a party should consider: there is today a specialist international arbitration bar around the world, consisting of teams of arbitration lawyers from large international firms as well as boutique players; other firms may have experienced litigation or corporate lawyers who successfully turn their hand to international arbitration. Other factors to consider include some degree of familiarity with the governing law of the disputed contract, although for the reasons discussed above this will generally not be necessary so long as the firm has reasonable access to and the ability to develop points of the applicable law. A firm's resources may be important if the case is expected to be particularly large or complex. As many firms now have teams of specialised lawyers, what may set a firm apart from another in a particular case are other characteristics and capabilities and how these align with the preferences of the client, including whether the firm would propose to resource the case with a large or small team (most large firms have no difficulty scaling up, but many are unable or unwilling to scale down), whether the firm has a track record of adopting technology or making use of legal support in lower-cost countries, whether it is familiar with mediation of international commercial disputes, and whether it is able to communicate in the language of the employees who will be involved in the dispute.

3-097 *Law firm culture with respect to mediation and negotiation capabilities.* Some firms have an unfortunate reputation of 'litigating at all costs'. While an irate client who feels mistreated by the opposing party may find this approach emotionally satisfactory (at least until it receives the first bill), it is unlikely to be consistent with an ability to negotiate positive outcomes. By contrast, a skill that can be identified

---

29. The various Chambers and Legal 500 directories are probably the best known. See <www.chambersandpartners.com> and <www.legal500.com>.

through careful selection is a lawyer's competence in negotiation and mediation, with a track record of success in proposing and conducting mediation, particularly in diverse cultures and where the mediations have led to settlements. In the United States and United Kingdom, some law firms have departments dedicated to commercial mediation, and there are firms in which all lawyers are required to undergo mediation and negotiation training. Yet even where mediation is a familiar form of dispute resolution, individual competence in the field can vary widely, and the international experience of practitioners may be thin. In part, this is because mediation is a profession that in most domestic settings has few generally accepted standards of practice, training, and certification, and none in the international setting.[30] Thus, the ability to convince other parties to come to the settlement table in mediation cannot be undervalued, especially in the context of international commercial disputes.

Parties may be able to overcome this handicap by taking settlement into their own **3-098** hands and proposing mediation directly to the other party, bypassing the lawyers on both sides.[31] If the party believes its outside counsel will not add value to the conduct of a negotiation or mediation, there is no requirement to have any lawyers present (mediation is a settlement negotiation procedure that the parties themselves control). Still, a counsel's willingness to propose mediation as a tool for early settlement should always be seen as positive by parties with a commercial orientation.

A lawyer's existing familiarity with the client's business. There are certainly **3-099** advantages for clients in being able to work repeatedly with the same lawyers. First and foremost is that the usual counsel will have developed his own knowledge of the client's business, which a new, specialised arbitration counsel is unlikely to have. Indeed, establishing a relationship of trust can take years, if it is to develop at all. One of the co-authors estimates that over half of first-time counsel appointments by his company do not lead to subsequent engagements with the same firm. It is true that a client's usual external counsel may be as well suited as specialised arbitration counsel to the task of assisting the client in obtaining a positive outcome in negotiations or mediation. International arbitration, however, presents a different set of challenges. The difficulty for the client is that while its usual outside counsel may be competent in domestic dispute resolution, for example, they may be blind to the opportunities and risks involved in international arbitration. We have seen many instances in which a party's usual law firm for domestic litigation has given poor client service (which the client may not have realised) by treating an international arbitration as it would a domestic proceeding. Ideally, the client's

---

30. There are, however, initiatives afoot. For example, in 2002, the European Commission issued its European ADR Code of Conduct, designed to promote common standards and ethical conduct for mediation in the Member States of the European Union. In 2008, the International Mediation Institute, a non-profit organisation in the Netherlands with the support of leading mediation professionals around the world, undertook an initiative to develop international standards in mediator qualification and practice. See <www.imimediation.com>.

31. Chapter 4, *International Settlement Negotiation and Mediation*.

'go-to' counsel for domestic litigation will also have knowledge and experience in international arbitration.

| **Not that this ever really happens: know your client, or at least its name** | Years ago one of the co-authors retained a large US law firm to assist Nuovo Pignone, his division's lead company and the seat of its headquarters in Italy. The engagement was the first for the firm and was a substantial one. The firm had multiple lawyers reviewing documents, interviewing witnesses, and engaging in considerable discussion with the internal legal team. During the two years of the engagement, however, the firm's memos and correspondence to the internal legal department and the client's Italian managers consistently referred to the company as 'Nuovo'. While 'Pignone' and 'NP' were common shorthand used within the company, the name employed by the firm's lawyers had never been among them, and for an obvious reason. 'Nuovo' simply means 'new' in Italian. The equivalent would have been to refer to General Electric as 'General'. Despite considerable hints from in-house counsel that use of the term was irritating to the in-house teams, the firm's lawyers never did correct their faux pas. And not surprisingly, the company's legal department also complained that the quality of the firm's legal advice generally suffered from a failure to appreciate the realities of the company's business. Having treated the client as a generic company with an Italian-sounding name, the firm failed to engender the respect necessary to obtain future engagements. Lawyers who are capable of performing high-quality legal work are nevertheless likely to disappoint their clients when they fail to appreciate who the client is and how it operates. |

3-100 *Geographical, linguistic, and cultural considerations.* The ability to work effectively and easily with the client's people on the ground over an extended period is mainly a function of location and language. The difference that can be made by a counsel who is 'local', at least to some degree, can too easily be taken for granted. Being near the dispute's 'centre of gravity' may not always be an essential requirement, but a party can easily become frustrated when the appointed outside counsel must travel long distances at significant cost (and delay) to attend meetings with employees with whom, to make matters worse, they lack the language skills to communicate effectively.

3-101 *Internationalism.* While considerations arising from a counsel's cultural and legal background can also be relevant in understanding the background to a transnational dispute, competent counsel from any country can generally be expected to learn and adapt to these differences. Beyond language capabilities, special cultural skills are not usually something a party will require of its counsel in an international arbitration. On the contrary, if there is a special talent in international proceedings, it is the ability to work without reference to or creating expectations based on any particular culture or legal system, including (and especially) one's own. For example, in a truly international arbitration it would be just as imprudent for an American or British lawyer to expect to obtain the broad disclosure of documents on the basis of their legal culture as it would be for a Swiss lawyer to expect there to be no disclosure at all on the basis of his.

As a result, some law firms have adopted an 'internationalist' approach, meaning **3-102** that they have an integrated practice of lawyers from different backgrounds and may be able to conduct the same arbitration out of any of their offices in the United States, Europe, Asia, or a combination of all three. Some boutique firms, particularly in Europe, have the same sort of capability with only a small handful of lawyers. In contrast, some firms may claim an international capability by counting their foreign offices or affiliations with firms in other countries. If the location and nationality of the litigation lawyers is in and from one country, however, then it is fair to assume the firm's practice is 'international' only in the sense of representing clients in domestic litigation between parties of different nationalities. While these firms may acquit themselves well in domestic litigation, they may be ill-prepared to conduct a proceeding before a truly international tribunal. What may be routine practices in a domestic litigation may be viewed as unattractive parochialism in an international proceeding.

Not that this ever really happens: parochial domestic practices	Both of the authors have seen multiple instances in which a party's usual domestic counsel has brought a parochial, domestic approach to an international arbitration, with poor effect (and negative consequences) for its client. In one example, the claimant, an insurance company, appointed the law firm that handled its routine court litigation in France, much of which consisted of personal injury cases. The lawyers acted exactly as they would in French court proceedings. In one example, a substitute and uninformed lawyer stood in for the appointed counsel at the procedural hearing when the colleague handling the case was engaged elsewhere, visibly irritating the tribunal with his inability to agree on any points of procedure. The counsel later ignored the importance of most of the evidentiary submissions, possibly assuming that the tribunal would appoint an expert to decide most substantive matters in dispute (which it did not). The insurance company (the claimant) lost the case, with a substantial cost assessment against it.

Counsel selection matrix. Below is an example of a matrix developed to distinguish **3-103** law firms on the basis of criteria developed for an international arbitration to be conducted under French law and concerning a construction project. The criteria here are used to distinguish among law firms that are all equally qualified by the party as having an adequate reputation and capability to conduct an international arbitration. Thus, 'international arbitration' is not among the criteria being rated, because the capability is assumed to exist in all.

3-104 In the example below, the party gives a relative weight (the 'multiplier') to the importance it assigns to each area being ranked, so that for Firm E, for example, a ranking of 3 in construction disputes is multiplied by 5 to give a weighted result of 15 in that category.

3-105 As always, a party should guard against the slavish application of tools of this type and use them instead as a guide to focusing on the criteria they hold most important. This approach can be useful for leveraging the strengths of law firms already known to a party and assessing new firms in order to obtain the best possible fit for a case. For example, as between the leading candidates below, Firm C and Firm E, a party may conclude on reflection that its main and immediate goal is to achieve an early settlement. Firm E has only a moderate ranking in construction, which the party deems important enough to give it the highest multiplier, but more experience in mediating international commercial disputes and/or integrating mediation into the law firm's arbitration practice, and its fees are low. By contrast, Firm B has the greater experience in construction disputes and has developed a substantial familiarity with the party through past representations. Yet it is the more expensive of the two, is relatively weak in mediation capabilities, and its lawyers are in offices that are distant from the dispute's centre of gravity. The party may therefore conclude that its immediate commercial goals, the relative cost advantage, and convenience of having the external lawyers in close proximity to its own employees make Firm E the more attractive candidate for this particular case. On that basis, the party may feel comfortable engaging a firm it has not used before, rather than relying on its usual outside counsel, confident that the higher overall score on the matrix justifies the change.

3-106 *Considerations of diversity in selecting counsel.* There are a number of other factors that clients regularly use when selecting outside counsel. These include, for example, diversity within a law firm, or the willingness of the firm to provide training or to second lawyers to the client. It is just as appropriate to apply these considerations to international arbitration as to other engagements. It should be obvious that one form of diversity – variety in languages, cultures, and legal backgrounds among the firm's lawyers – is even more important for international disputes than for domestic cases.

3-107 *Anticipating the possibility of law firm conflicts.* In disputes involving large companies and large law firms, it is increasingly commonplace for a party's preferred counsel to decline the engagement on account of an unwaivable conflict of interest involving the opposing party. In fact, this may be more the rule than the exception in complex international projects, in which there can be multiple parties and large law firms involved at different stages. For this reason, it is always useful to have one or more fallback firms in the event of a conflict that disables the party's preferred firm.

Example 3j – Use of Objective Selection Criteria to Evaluate Qualification

Firm	Subject-matter experience			Existing Familiarity with Party	Fees (1 High; 5 Low)	Mediation – Relevant Skills/Reputation	Distance/Availability	Alternative Fee Structure Possible?	TOTAL
	French Civil Code	Transportation & Maritime Law	Construction						
Multiplier	3	2	5	3	4	4	2	—	—
Firm A	2	2	3	1	1	4	1	y	50
Firm B	3	3	5	5	2	2	3	y	77
Firm C	1	3	5	5	2	5	1	y	78
Firm D	5	3	1	1	3	1	5	y	55
Firm E	5	3	3	2	4	4	4	n	82

3-108 *Formally engaging counsel for the dispute.* Having identified and selected the appropriate counsel, there are some formalities that parties should follow before, during, and immediately after the appointment. These formalities set the terms of the engagement and establish the ground rules and conditions for a successful working relationship. By doing so early, parties and counsel can also determine earlier whether there are any irreconcilable differences that can lead the party to bring in replacement counsel before significant costs have been incurred or the case has advanced to a point at which replacing counsel would be even more inconvenient or disruptive.

Checklist 3f – Appointing and Replacing External Counsel

What	*When*	*Risk if Not Done*
Non-binding fee estimate	Before appointment	Potential for conflict between party and counsel if they do not share expectations of what the proceedings are likely to cost
Alternative fee arrangements	Before appointment	Missed opportunity; difficult to put in place once appointment is made
Engagement letter	Upon appointment	Parties may disagree later on the terms of the counsel's representation
Detailed budget	Within 30–60 days of appointment	Counsel will lack guidance on party's expectations; party will have difficulty predicting what will be spent and when
Monthly, detailed billing	Always	Party will be surprised/ frustrated by large or unexpected bill. Detailed monthly bills allow parties to track work and monitor efficiency
Replacing counsel	Upon failure (or insistent or repeated failure) to provide estimate, comply with terms of engagement letter, respect budget, or comply with any other client instructions	Relationship will not improve as proceedings advance, and the party may wish it had ended the engagement earlier, when doing so would have been less disruptive to the client's position in the arbitration

Engagement letters. Some parties will insist upon their own letter outlining the **3-109** terms of the engagement for all work undertaken by external counsel. Similarly, some law firms will send the client an engagement letter at the outset of the representation. These can run from simple one-page statements of the work to be performed and agreed fee structure, to multiple pages of lengthy terms and conditions. Generally, clients can reject or ignore these longer engagement letters with impunity, as law firms are unlikely to insist they be accepted as a condition for undertaking work on an international arbitration. In fact, many firms do not propose engagement letters at all. In all events, it can be good practice for parties to ensure that the agreed terms of engagement are clearly spelled out in a letter countersigned by both the counsel and the party. This can help both sides avoid disagreement later about the nature of the representation that the lawyer or firm has undertaken.

There is no need for an engagement letter to be long and complex even if the party **3-110** may wish to include additional matters governing the relationship with outside counsel, such as the nature of certain work to be performed, the identity of the lawyers working on the arbitration, special fee arrangements, terms of billing, conflicts of interest, and so forth.

C.   ESTIMATING, BUDGETING, AND MANAGING
COSTS OF EXTERNAL COUNSEL

A lawyer may think his first and only priority is to provide high-quality legal **3-111** support. The person paying the bills, however, may take high-quality legal support for granted and have only one thought on her mind: what's this going to cost us? The old saw about the 'inherent unpredictability of litigation' finds little sympathy among people whose daily responsibility includes making and adhering to budgets. Little can be more frustrating to an in-house lawyer than an external counsel who says that it is impossible to predict the cost of an arbitration or any other form of litigation. Providing a reasonable, non-binding estimate can have its hazards but is never impossible, no matter how complex or difficult a dispute may appear. While in-house managers will generally be able to recognise and accommodate a genuinely unpredictable event, they will have little patience with a professional who declares himself incapable of estimating what his services will cost.

Non-binding fee estimates. A fee estimate is generally a non-binding prediction of **3-112** the fees that a lawyer will charge a client in the course of the representation and is distinct from a budget, which is usually more detailed and can be either binding or non-binding. While it may be too early at the stage of retaining counsel to demand a detailed budget, it should be possible shortly after appointing counsel to request a non-binding estimate of their fees. At this stage, counsel will have had the opportunity to review the contract at issue and the key points in dispute and may have formed a preliminary view of potential strategies. In fact, counsel versed in providing estimates may present cost scenarios that are tied to the different strategies the client may choose to adopt, whether as alternatives to each other or as a sequentially staged strategy. If an ECA is to be used, the cost of carrying this out should be included in the initial estimate.

Example 3k – Rough Fee Estimate
(for a reasonably large, single-issue international arbitration)

> *Phase 1*: USD ____ for completion of ECA (early case evaluation), answer to request for arbitration, appointment of tribunal, and preliminary hearing (to be incurred within six months).
> *Phase 2*: USD ____for two full submissions (to be incurred between six and eighteen months). Add USD ____ for jurisdiction objection, USD ____ for IBA Rules document production, and USD ____ for interim measures.
> *Phase 3*: USD ____ for one-week hearing and one post-hearing submission (to be incurred between twelve and twenty-four months).
> *Phase 4*: USD ____ for any challenge and enforcement work (to be incurred as from twenty-four months).

> **Question:** We asked our law firm for a cost estimate if the dispute goes to arbitration. They said the issues are complex, so an estimate is impossible to provide; they gave their hourly rates instead. How can we get a better handle on the likely cost of the arbitration?
>
> **Answer:** You may want to change your law firm. Now.

3-113 *Alternative fee arrangements.* There are as many different types of fee arrangements as are allowed by the ethical rules under which the appointed counsel may be operating. For example, while counsel in the United States or Brazil may propose to undertake to represent a client through an entire arbitration on the basis of a contingency fee (a percentage of the amount awarded or contested), counsel in France, Germany or Italy may be required by their ethical rules to decline this type of fee structure. There are a number of other types of arrangements, however, that law firms may be willing to explore with the client as alternatives to the firm's usual billing practices, some of which are presented below, with notes of caution for each.

3-114 *Contingency (success) fees and special considerations.* Where agreeing to a fee contingent upon the successful outcome of the arbitration, the party should specify that the fee (or most of it at least) will be payable only after payment on settlement or a favourable award, and not merely after the issuance of the award. When the dispute is against a state-owned entity, and persons serving as governmental employees may make settlement decisions, the party may wish to take special care to avoid any subsequent allegation of the success fee being used as a conduit for an improper payment. Parties should remember that for the purposes of many anti-corruption laws, external lawyers are third parties appointed to act on their behalf, whose actions can be attributed to the party itself, even when not expressly authorised by the party itself.

Other types of fee arrangements in international arbitration. Other alternative fee **3-115** arrangements can include:

- a fixed one-off or annual retainer plus a contingency fee, which is a common arrangement in litigation in jurisdictions such as France;
- an agreement that the lawyer receives a bonus based on a positive outcome, to write off a portion of the fees if the outcome is negative, or both together;
- fixed price arrangements under which the lawyer or firm agrees to conduct the arbitration for a set amount for the entire proceeding, or for each stage;
- a fee cap, where the lawyer applies an hourly or other rate and where the total will not exceed a given amount;
- blended rate fees, where instead of a firm's different lawyers billing at different rates, they all bill at the same rate;
- simple discounts on the lawyers' hourly rates, which may increase with the volume of work done; and
- a combination of any of the above.

Potential impact of fee shifting on alternative fee arrangements. The general rule in **3-116** international arbitration is that the losing party must reimburse part or all of the winning party's costs.[32] Thus, an arrangement where a lawyer agrees to 'zero cost in the event of losing' may really mean the party agrees to '0% of our legal fees; 100% of the other side's'. International arbitration can be expensive, and the other side's costs may be substantial, so a party should give serious thought to the risk of being held to pay them and question whether the proposal of 'no win, no fee' is as good as it initially sounds.

Budgets. In contrast to the non-binding estimate given at the start of the litigation, **3-117** budgets are developed and modified in the course of the proceedings to help parties to predict the timing and amount of their expenditures. Budgets tend to be detailed, broken down by line item, and cover the periods in which the costs will be incurred. This can be months, quarters, or the phases dictated by the procedural timetable in the arbitration.

Differences in billing practices. There is no standard international practice as to **3-118** when a lawyer should send a bill to the client, what it should contain, or when the client should pay. On the contrary, billing practices can vary dramatically among law firms, even within the same country. A party can reduce or even avoid this degree of uncertainty by fixing the terms of billing directly in the engagement letter (as discussed above in paragraphs 3–108 and 3–109).

Timing of bills. While litigation lawyers in one country may traditionally bill their **3-119** clients on a monthly basis or even on the basis of retainers (advance payments), in

---

32. Chapter 5, *The Conduct of the Arbitration.*

another they would not be expected to send the main bill until the conclusion of the proceedings. For example, a lawyer billing under the traditional Italian tariff schedule (a national schedule that establishes minimum and maximum legal fees a lawyer may charge) would not even know until the conclusion of the case how much to request for the lion's share of the fees, as the fee schedule varies dramatically based on the difficulty of the dispute and 'the result obtained'. Obviously, billing practices of this type, of which there are equivalents in other countries, can make it more difficult to predict either the amount of legal fees that will be spent in a dispute or when they will be due. Bills sent promptly at the beginning of each month help the client understand the work being done and what it is costing while there is still time to do something about it. As noted already, monthly billing is also something that can be required of external counsel in an engagement letter.

3-120 *Content of bills.* Just as the timing of a lawyer's bill can vary, so can its contents. In some countries (the United States, Canada, and the United Kingdom being good examples), it is normal for lawyers to provide a detailed statement of the work performed, and law firms may have sophisticated software that accounts for every minute of work by each member of its legal team, as well as any photocopies, telephone calls, and other sundry items that the lawyer may typically pass on to its clients. While this type of billing may be standard practice and even required by companies located in a particular country, it may come as a surprise to a client in a country in which the lawyer traditionally bills a set or fixed amount that is proportionate to the amount in dispute, and in which photocopying and telephone charges are considered part of the lawyer's overhead, not something to be charged to the client.

3-121 *Bill, draft bill, or pro forma?* In some countries, a bill may be subject to VAT or other taxes immediately upon being issued. As a result, the practice may be for lawyers to send a final 'bill' only after having agreed with the client the amount that will be paid. Similarly, tax and accounting rules can require a client to book the amount of the bill on its internal financial statements upon its issuance (before payment and even if it is contested). In practice, the existence of such tax and accounting requirements may lead lawyers either to (a) ask the client for 'permission' to send a bill for a certain amount or (b) send a pro forma or 'draft bill' to the client and issue the bill itself only after having received payment.

3-122 *When is payment due?* Although a law firm may expect that its bill will be paid promptly upon issuance, client practices and expectations can vary dramatically. For example, the lawyer may expect payment to be received within days of presentation, when the client's practice is to wait at least 120 days or longer. Variations in expectations on payment can inadvertently strain the lawyer–client relationship, compounded by the fact that there is also no standard practice on how frequently firms should remind clients of an unpaid bill. A curt and formal letter demanding payment can come as a surprise to a client that does not consider itself to be behind on payments. Less obviously, counsel should not feel that cultural differences should prevent them from soliciting payments of overdue bills. On the contrary, in many countries non-payment of bills may be due to reasons as simple as errors in the name or address of the entity billed, failure to provide VAT numbers, or other bureaucratic necessities that may not even be identified until the delay is raised.

Agreement on billing. Fortunately, counsel and parties can just as easily avoid or at **3-123** least minimise problems in the area of billing and payment by specifically agreeing at the outset how they should occur. The engagement letter, discussed in paragraphs 3–108 and 3–109 above, is the ideal place to include such agreement. Most areas are 'either/or' in that the lawyer and client will necessarily need to adopt the practice of either one or the other, such as whether the lawyer must provide a statement of the hourly work performed by lawyers or is permitted to bill for sundry items such as photocopying or telephone bills.

Detailed monthly billing. The simplest way to track and manage the costs of any **3-124** complex litigation is to require counsel to submit monthly fee statements, shortly after the month ends, for all services rendered in the previous month, and to set out in detail what those services were. This allows the client to be aware of exactly what work the lawyer has been doing and how much it has cost and to evaluate the lawyer's efficiency. Most importantly, where there is a problem, detailed monthly bills enable the client to detect it early and ask the lawyer to correct it before further costs are incurred.

Client and counsel responsibility for establishing common expectations. **3-125** Engagement letters and fee estimates are only a part of the effort to build the framework within which the lawyer and client will work productively together in an international dispute. Other components include the lawyer informing the client of any expectations that are unrealistic or otherwise unlikely to be achieved, both as to the likely costs and the potential outcome of the dispute. Indeed, the ethical rules applicable to lawyers in most countries will generally require the lawyer to do this. Although clients may not always be bound by similar ethical rules governing their relationship with outside counsel, the power to discharge a lawyer at will comes with the responsibility to fully communicate the party's expectations regarding the dispute and any concerns or constraints that may be relevant to the lawyer's ability to effectively assist the client in the course of the proceedings. For example, if the client is under severe budgetary pressure and the costs of the arbitration are likely to drive decisions on strategy, the client must make sure the lawyer understands this. Neither the lawyer nor client will be well served – particularly in an international proceeding in which the counsel and party will frequently be called to make judgment calls together – by cultivating a relationship that is lacking in candour. Put another way, a party can only increase the likelihood of being satisfied with its counsel's performance if it conveys its honest expectations at the beginning, and throughout the course, of the dispute.

D.   Disengaging and Replacing External Counsel

3-126 When a lawyer fails or refuses to provide a non-binding estimate of fees (and most often it is a refusal), adhere to an agreed budget, or to follow any other client instructions, the party should be asking itself whether it has engaged suitable counsel. Competent lawyers are professionals and capable of responding to constructive criticism and taking corrective steps. If instructions are not being followed, a warning from the client may be all that is necessary. But if the offending conduct persists and is identified early in the representation, there may be minimal cost (and likely substantial savings) in replacing counsel. Waiting until an international arbitration is well underway to replace counsel may not only be more expensive, it may also cause significant disruption that will be detrimental to the merits of the party's case.

Not that this ever really happens: firing counsel after damage is done	The lawyer overran his budget by over 100% for the initial phase of the arbitration, while identifying potential candidates for appointment as co-arbitrator and chair. The lawyer was warned and the budget revisited to make sure it was accurate and fair. The lawyer subsequently overran the revised budget by 150% in preparing the party's statement of defence, and again in preparing a reply. This was too much for the party, which then discharged the lawyer and hired new counsel. After doing so, the party discovered that its former counsel had not just overrun budgets but had also ignored the party's express request to assert a potentially winning argument (which the Tribunal ruled was now time-barred). An unfortunate lesson learned by the client was that counsel who easily ignores a client's admonitions and views on legal fees may be similarly inclined to ignore instructions about the arguments and defences to be submitted.

3-127 There are other reasons for replacing counsel in the early stage of a dispute or in a proceeding already underway that have little or nothing to do with the counsel's handling of the case or any other part of performance. For example, in the context of an acquisition of a company with pending arbitrations, the acquiring company may elect one of two strategies. The first is to continue proceedings with existing counsel, in which case the counsel may have an opportunity to create a relationship with a new client (the acquiring parent). Or the new parent may instead decide to have its traditional counsel replace the acquired company's counsel for purposes of simplicity in having all disputes consolidated with a single firm (or a similar need to integrate its affiliates) or merely out of a fear of the unfamiliar.

Notifying an adversary of the substitution of counsel. If for whatever reason a **3-128** decision is made to replace counsel, consideration should be given to whether notice to the other side is necessary. If the proceedings are at their very early stages (and the counsel has appeared only in pre-action correspondence or not at all), the party will be spared the potentially awkward need to notify the change. In the event, however, that proceedings have already commenced and counsel has officially appeared at the time of their disengagement, it will be necessary to notify the opposing party, the arbitral institution (if proceedings are administered), and arbitrators if any have been appointed. This notification can be sent by the former counsel, new counsel, or the party itself, and no reasons need be given. Often, in these situations, the less said the better.

Administrative issues relating to the disengagement of counsel. Substituting **3-129** counsel at any stage of a dispute may, in some countries, give rise to issues relating to any fees that may be due – or arguably due – to the former counsel. A formal letter of disengagement, with a demand for an immediate invoice of all amounts due, can be a prudent step. If local law at the place of arbitration is relevant and is also the place of the lawyer's engagement, local rules governing the rights and conduct of lawyers may give a former lawyer an opportunity to assert a lien on the proceedings (or any award) or to seek to prevent new counsel from accepting the engagement until the former lawyer's bills have been settled.

Chapter Four

International Settlement
Negotiation and Mediation

In the first paragraph of this book, we set out our main theme, which is that **4-001** international business is about accepting risk, not avoiding it. Throughout, we have discussed how parties to international transactions can accept the risk of disputes and enhance their positions by understanding the legal tools and strategic opportunities available at each stage of the contract negotiation and dispute resolution processes. Mediation is where this rubber hits the road, as both a legal tool and a means of improving outcomes. Although it has yet to develop into a commonly used mechanism for resolving international business disputes, it is undeniable that mediation has this potential and that recourse to it is on the rise.

Question:	What should we be willing to accept in order to settle this dispute?
Answer:	Anything as good as or better than what you can reasonably expect from arbitration or litigation, after considering all of the associated costs and likely impact on the business.

In addition to its usually cited benefits – savings of time, cost, and commercial **4-002** relationships – mediation provides a common process of dispute resolution that does not require parties to possess any special training, experience, or skills other than their negotiating abilities, and does not advantage parties from one jurisdiction or another. It can be, in other words, a means of simplifying and demystifying the process of international dispute resolution.

Against that background, this chapter explores the ways that parties can use medi- **4-003** ation to create and exploit leverage in settlement negotiations, preferably before substantial costs of arbitration have been incurred. In doing so, we make the assumption that a party will have estimated the range of probable outcomes of its dispute and the costs that will be incurred if no settlement is reached.[1] From that starting point, we discuss: (1) the risk of sub-optimal settlements of international commercial disputes, and the strategic use of mediation to enhance the range of negotiation opportunities; (2) proposing and organising a mediation of an international commercial dispute; and (3) mediation advocacy and how parties can conduct the process to enhance the outcome.

4-004 *Confusing ADR terminology.* The term 'mediation' is unfortunate in more ways than one. It does not convey much, if any, idea of the objectives of the process or what it consists of. Literal translations into other languages only compound confusion. In Italian, *'mediazione'* is the practice of brokering, and the term *'mediatore'* is more likely to conjure up an image of a stockbroker rather than a legal practitioner. To avoid this ambiguity, the Latinate term 'conciliation' is sometimes used in international practice, even though it is no better at describing the process and may even connote an inappropriate meekness. In many parts of the world, mediation travels under the equally confusing acronym 'ADR', which stands for *alternative* dispute resolution. Moreover, the term ADR, which in the United States can also encompass arbitration, simply begs the question, 'alternative to what'? (The mediation arm of the ICC avoids this question, with its 'ADR Rules' referring to *amicable* dispute resolution.)

4-005 In this chapter we use the terms 'mediation' and 'ADR' interchangeably. We note that the term 'conciliation' is sometimes used interchangeably with 'mediation', and in other cases is used to denote a particular style or dispute resolution practice that has its roots in the procedural histories of different countries. For example, in Switzerland, the term 'mediation' is used to describe a process in which a neutral third party is expected to be elicitative and non-evaluative, who refrains from making any proposals, and where the outcome should be based on subjective interests, whereas 'conciliation' is used to describe a more directive and evaluative process, in which the neutral is expected to express a non-binding opinion based on objective or legal norms and to suggest a zone of possible agreement. Both involve a process in which a neutral assists the parties in reaching a settlement, but the styles and processes can be different experiences for the parties and their lawyers. Such distinctions, to the extent they exist and may be relevant, should not pose a problem if the parties focus on the substantive process and do not become overly preoccupied with the nomenclature.

4-006 *Beyond 'win/win' and expanding pies.* While no doubt some disputes are settled on terms in which cooperation leads to a resolution that is 'win/win' or based on the idea of 'expanding the pie', we believe these cases are the exception rather than the rule. In our experience, the blunt truth about international business disputes is that each side will usually be out to increase its own slice without much regard for how much pie will be left for the other, and that parties to international business transactions generally do not need or want to be coached in identifying which

---

1. See the discussion on Early Case Assessment (ECA) in Ch. 3, s. III.

opportunities are in their best interest.[2] In this chapter and elsewhere in this book, therefore, we treat mediation simply as a form of negotiation that is sharply focused and usually assisted by a neutral third party.

We assume that in most cases the disputing parties will be engaged in a form of **4-007** 'distributive bargaining' when they attempt to resolve their conflict. This is the most basic form of negotiation in which each dollar paid in settlement will make one side that much richer and the other that much poorer. Thus, our discussion of mediation is straightforward in focusing on its effectiveness in helping parties obtain optimal outcomes for themselves based on the numbers that appear in the dispute.

Type of disputes suitable for mediation. Having attempted to address the issue of **4-008** nomenclature above, we also wish to be clear that nothing about what we are proposing is meant to suggest that parties to a dispute should adopt mediation as an 'alternative' to anything else written in this book.[3] Rather, we discuss mediation as a tool that may be suitable for *any* dispute that a party wishes to attempt to settle, even if our focus is on disputes contemplated in or arising out of international commercial contracts that are likely to have an arbitration clause. A party who excludes mediation from consideration for any type of dispute does so at the risk of missing opportunities and obtaining poorer results than what otherwise might have been available. For example, an argument can be made that claims of fraud are not appropriate for mediation, as they presumably inject principles that a party must defend through binding adjudication. But we have seen cases involving fraud claims settle during or after mediation, with no real added difficulty as compared to disputes with no claim of fraud – and with the same benefits.

---

2. The expanded pie metaphor is by now so commonplace that we have introduced it without definition here. To avoid any misunderstanding, however, we note that the concept refers to a solution in which the total amount being divided is made greater by identifying common interests or concessions that have a greater value to the receiving party than their cost to the providing party. For example, a seller may offer to settle a dispute of a USD 10 claim by giving the buyer a USD 10 discount on a product that retails for USD 100. If the buyer intends to purchase new products from the seller, it may perceive that it has received full value in settlement. For its part, the seller may both turn a profit on the sale (assuming its profit margin is over 10%) and preserve a customer relationship. In theory, the parties have used their cooperation to construct a settlement in which they are both better off than had they simply divided up the USD 10 claim in a cash settlement (or permitted a judge or arbitrator to make their decision for them with all the associated costs of reaching the decision). As noted, in this section we focus on the existing pie (i.e., finding ways to divide up the USD 10 claim) which, we believe, is in fact the more challenging task in international commercial disputes.

3. The genesis of the 'alternative' moniker (in ADR) was in the United States, where mediation and arbitration were initially proposed to parties as ways of resolving their disputes through a private process rather than the public system of court litigation. In some quarters of the United States today, the term 'ADR' continues to be used in reference to all forms of private dispute resolution (e.g., mediation and arbitration) even if the rest of the world appears to apply the term only to mediation. For international commercial transactions and the disputes that can arise under them, the term 'alternative' has little sense since, in effect, parties may legitimately consider litigation in the courts of a particular country as an 'alternative' to other resolution options, including arbitration and even litigation in the courts of another country.

4-009 So we make no attempt to define the scope of commercial disputes for which mediation may be suitable, noting only that this scope is certainly broader than that covered by arbitration. For example, whereas most arbitration rules are ill-suited to the resolution of multi-sided disputes involving different contractual relationships (or parties outside of any contractual relationship),[4] mediation faces no such restrictions. All it needs to bring multiple parties together in mediation is their desire to settle.

4-010 *When mediation is appropriate.* As noted above, mediation is merely a form of negotiation, and each dispute is likely to have different dynamics and times when negotiations are possible or their efficacy can be enhanced. Generally, a good rule of thumb is that settlement negotiations – and mediation with them – should take place at the earliest stage after the dispute arises when both parties are prepared to engage in a meaningful discussion. Depending on the parties and the particular circumstances of the dispute, this can come at any moment up to, during, and even after the arbitration. And more than one suitable moment may present itself in the same dispute. The time to propose mediation also should not depend entirely on whether the other side is inclined to engage in the process; there are moments when just *proposing* mediation may provide strategic advantage to the proposing party even when it is probable the offer to mediate will be rejected. Finally, as discussed below, there may be ways of using mediation strategically to augment the arbitration process, or of planning for mediation to occur in the course of an arbitration, to obtain the best possible outcome for the parties.

I.   OPTIMISING THE SETTLEMENT PROCESS

4-011 Parties involved in an arbitration may say they do not want to settle (or cannot), but it is rarely the case that a party will wish to pursue the arbitration to conclusion when it can obtain a more favourable resolution by agreement. This is also true of parties that can be described as difficult, or acting in bad faith. Even a scoundrel will take a good deal if he can get it (and he in fact may have provoked or maintained the arbitration in order to obtain one). One frequently mentioned example of party recalcitrance to pursue settlement is when the dispute involves a government or government-owned entity, and its managers are reluctant to accept responsibility for compromising any defences (however tenuous) to a claim for payment. But even in these cases a settlement is usually possible if the other side is willing to accept the position of the government-owned entity or something close to it. This may not be a good settlement from the other side's point of view, but it would be wrong to say that a settlement is not actually possible. Once the possibility of settlement is acknowledged to exist, the question is whether its terms can be improved so that it will be seen as being more advantageous than the alternative of litigating the dispute through to its conclusion.

---

4. For discussion of the problems of multi-party and multi-sided arbitration, see Ch. 1, *The Elements of an International Dispute Resolution Agreement,* and Ch. 5, *The Conduct of the Arbitration.*

A.   Sᴇᴛᴛʟᴇᴍᴇɴᴛ Gᴏᴀʟs ᴛʜᴀᴛ Lᴇᴠᴇʀᴀɢᴇ
                                ᴛʜᴇ Uɴᴄᴇʀᴛᴀɪɴᴛɪᴇs ᴏғ ᴀ Dɪsᴘᴜᴛᴇ

Again, parties will engage in settlement discussions if they believe they can reach **4-012** an agreement that is as good as or better than what is available through binding dispute resolution. Rather than pursue a detour on negotiation theory and settlements,[5] perhaps it is easier to think of this in the terms once expressed by a senior manager to one of the authors: 'is the deal we can get today better than the deal we can get through two years of arbitration?' For a party to understand the point at which a settlement becomes attractive, however, requires a degree of predictability of outcome and costs, and a strategy to enhance the opportunities available.

Mitigating the uncertainties of international arbitration. The famed flexibility of **4-013** international arbitration can easily be translated into a sequence of events, each of which can give rise to varying degrees of uncertainty as to the likely outcome and cost of reaching the conclusion of the proceedings. For example, as noted in the following chapter, *The Conduct of the Arbitration*, the appointment of the tribunal is critical to determining how the proceedings will be conducted: will they be in a civil law, common law, or hybrid fashion? Until the tribunal is in place, it may not be reasonably possible to predict the direction the arbitration will take, including the types and range of evidence to be presented, the duration, or the cost of the proceedings. Similarly, once the proceedings have been concluded, as explained in Chapter 6, *After the Arbitration*, there may be opportunities available to the losing party to challenge the award or defeat its enforcement. The point is that many factors may conspire to create an impression of a high degree of unpredictability at the outset of the arbitration. But within the extremes are potential ranges that parties can usefully estimate for purposes of evaluating settlement possibilities[6] and the direction that they want the arbitration to take.

Perceptions of litigation cost and risk on settlement positions. We consider else- **4-014** where ways of reasonably estimating potential costs of arbitration and key factors that influence those costs.[7] Party *perceptions* of cost, however, and how these perceptions can influence a willingness or desire to settle, are a somewhat different matter. As much as these perceptions may be grounded in reality, they are also subjective opinions that will be formed on the basis of experiences (of the party or those with whom it consults, including its counsel) in familiar jurisdictions. And while international arbitration is not generally regarded by anyone today as an

---

5. Under the commonly used negotiation lexicon, parties can be said to seek through settlement a better outcome than their 'BATNA', which stands for Best Alternative To Negotiated Agreement, popularised in the well-known book on negotiation, *Getting to Yes*, by Roger Fisher & William Ury.
6. See the discussion of Early Case Assessment (ECA) in Ch. 3, s. III.
7. Chapter 3, *When the Dispute Arises*, and Ch. 5, *The Conduct of the Arbitration*.

inexpensive means of resolving disputes, how a party perceives that cost can have a significant impact on its tolerance for continuing the arbitration.

4-015 It is useful to think of parties as coming from predominantly low-cost and high-cost (or variable-cost) dispute resolution jurisdictions. As parties everywhere tend to view the costs of litigation as being high, we use the terms 'low' and 'high' relative to each other here. For example, for a contract dispute involving a sum of USD 1 million, a party in a low-cost jurisdiction may reasonably predict it will expend USD 20,000 in legal fees, while a party from a high-cost jurisdiction may expect to spend in excess of USD 200,000 to resolve the same dispute.[8] As the cost of litigation in one jurisdiction is clearly much higher than the other in absolute terms, a party from that location may have an appetite for conflict that is considerably lower as a result. But when confronted with an international arbitration, one or both parties may simply not have a frame of reference for estimating costs unless they have had previous, similar experiences.

Not that this ever really happens: impact of cost perceptions on settlement	When the parties reached a roadblock and no further progress towards settlement seemed possible, the mediator asked each side if they had considered the probable costs of resolving their dispute through international arbitration, as contemplated by their contract's dispute resolution clause. He suggested the probable costs could exceed EUR 1 million for each side. Counsel for the claimant, perhaps hoping to impress the respondent with the threat of expensive litigation, added that the total cost to each party might even approach EUR 2 million. The respondent, having had experience with previous international arbitrations, found the estimates to be high but not altogether impossible and did not change its settlement position. The claimant's representative, however, was visibly stunned at his own lawyer's estimate, as he had clearly never considered such costs as being possible in his home (civil law) jurisdiction. Shortly after this exchange, the claimant's representative agreed to substantially lower his last demand, and the parties settled.

4-016 Party perceptions of cost and the various uncertainties of international arbitration can lead them to adopt different, and contrasting, assumptions, each of which can lead them to accept sub-optimal outcomes.[9] On the one hand, uncertainty may

---

8. Since most costs (fees) are initially borne by parties out of pocket, and a common practice in settlement is for each party to bear its own costs, we make no distinctions in this chapter for jurisdictions where prevailing parties are permitted to recover from the losers all or a portion of what they spent.

9. By 'optimal' we mean the result that would have been attained either through binding resolution, i.e., the arbitration award, or through better negotiation.

drive them to underestimate their risk and likely costs, so that they remain rooted in their positions and overlook reasonable settlement opportunities. On the other hand, uncertainty may cause a risk-averse party to overestimate the risk and cost of arbitration, thus settling for less than what they would have achieved through a final award. In either case, the effect is the same: the party has failed to obtain the optimal outcome.

A common position is for a party to say that it is willing to be reasonable, but that it **4-017** cannot settle alone and that the other side needs to be willing to acknowledge the risks that it faces and negotiate on the basis of them. Otherwise, the argument goes, any concessions made in the name of settlement will unilaterally favour the side that is unrealistically optimistic about the dispute. There is some wisdom in this argument in the context of domestic litigation between parties from similar backgrounds and with access to equal information useful for estimating likely outcomes. With the alternative to settlement being an award obtained at the conclusion of an international arbitration, however, the most common default assumption is the uncertainty discussed above. This presents an opportunity for the party that is better informed about the arbitration process to manage the uncertainties in its favour.

Use of early case assessments (ECAs) to assess and improve settlement options. **4-018** Throughout this section, we have presumed that parties will either have performed an ECA[10] or will at least have a reasonable familiarity with the range of probable outcomes and the costs of arbitration. A party that has performed an ECA will have a net advantage over a party that has not; the ECA not only arms a party with convincing arguments about its strengths and responses to its weaknesses, but may place the party in a position of identifying and seizing settlement opportunities, the value of which the adverse party may not be able to fully appreciate.

Question:	Why should I do an ECA sooner in the process, before we have fully developed the case in our pleadings?
Answer:	An ECA is not a perfect assessment, but something that can be refined in the course of the arbitration. Conducting one early (as the name implies) is important to maintaining reasonably consistent settlement expectations. Unless a party has performed a reasonably complete ECA, it may hold unrealistically high expectations (and fail to appreciate the costs) until the tribunal is constituted, pleadings submitted, and an evidentiary hearing looms on the horizon. Thus, the party may at the outset fail to recognise reasonable settlement opportunities. Once the proceedings are underway, however, the claimant may substantially lower its expectations as submissions

10. Chapter 3, *When the Dispute Arises.*

> are made and bills for the arbitration come due. At this stage, the party may be inclined to accept a lower number (and perhaps too low a number). An advantage of an early evaluation of risk and costs is that it should smooth party expectations during the course of the proceedings so that they are neither too high nor too low at any given stage. Helping a party focus and optimise its settlement position is perhaps the greatest advantage of an ECA.

B.   SELLING THE IDEA OF MEDIATION

4-019 While mediation will often provide an opportunity for parties to optimise their potential outcomes, in many instances an offer to mediate will instead trigger serious negotiations between the parties, without the involvement of a mediator. If this leads to a satisfactory settlement, then the offer will have had its intended effect even if no mediation ever takes place.

4-020 We could, without great difficulty, list the handful of jurisdictions where mediation is an accepted tool of business dispute resolution, and provide a much longer list of places where it remains largely unknown or little utilised. While the United States and the United Kingdom are the most prominent because of their large legal markets, other common law jurisdictions (Canada, Australia, New Zealand, and Singapore among them) also have relatively healthy mediation practices. India and Nigeria, by contrast, are large common law jurisdictions where mediation is occasionally discussed but appears to be little practiced in commercial disputes. Civil law countries where the development of mediation has been relatively successful include the Netherlands and Norway. For most of the rest of the world, mediation is either an unknown, niche, or newly introduced practice in the business context.

4-021 *Selling mediation internally – anticipating resistance.* One of the authors, when proposing to a senior manager the possibility of engaging in mediation in the course of an arbitration, was met with a dumbfounded look and the question 'are we settling or arbitrating?' The notion that arbitration, once initiated, precludes any possibility of settlement is more common among business managers than one might imagine. The perpetual challenge for those representing commercial parties is to appeal to desires to pursue concrete business objectives while at the same time avoiding an appearance of weakness. Fortunately, anecdotal experiences indicate that once executives participate in mediation, they tend to view the process favourably, perhaps because at its core it is not far from what they do every day: negotiation.

Not that this ever really happens: mediation sells itself once managers try it	In-house counsel suggested to the general manager of his company's Stockholm-based division that mediation might help settle a thorny intellectual property dispute with a Norwegian company. The manager complained that he did not want to appear weak and, in any event, did not see how mediation could succeed when past efforts to settle had failed miserably. Although he noted that the other side would continue to be 'typically Norwegian' in its stubborn refusal to recognise the flaws in its case, he ultimately consented to mediation being proposed. The Norwegian party accepted, and two weeks later both sides met in Oslo and settled their dispute on the day of the mediation. (The Norwegian manager complained at one point that he had wished to settle earlier, but was prevented by the 'typically Swedish' stubbornness of the other side.) A year later, the Swedish manager contacted his in-house lawyer to ask a favour. He explained that his division had a new dispute, this time with another Swedish company, and that the other side's lawyers did not understand anything about mediation. Would the lawyer call them to explain the process and convince them to try mediation?

By contrast, we have not found executives readily expressing similar approval for arbitration (or other forms of litigation, for that matter) when they are required to play a direct role in the process. While they may accept it as a necessary cost of doing business, they are not shy about expressing their impatience with either the pace or the cost of the proceedings.

Checklist 4a – Advantages of Mediation versus International Arbitration

	Mediation	Arbitration
Time	Can be organised on short notice and typically lasts no more than a day	Measured in months, if not years
Cost	Negligible or modest incremental cost	Substantial
Face-to-face meeting of decision makers	A fundamental part of the mediation process; often a requirement made by the mediator	Not required and rarely occurs

	Mediation	*Arbitration*
Confidentiality	All discussions with the other party and the mediator subject to mediation confidentiality, and may not be produced or used as evidence in arbitration or other legal proceedings	Not confidential as to admissions by either side in the course of the proceedings; proceedings confidential as to external parties (but results subject to public disclosure)
Relationship with other party	Less harmful to commercial interests with opposing party than other forms of dispute resolution. Even if parties do not settle, willingness to mediate can preserve relations	As injurious to commercial relations as any other form of litigation
Ability to structure creative solutions	Provides the opportunity to reconcile overlapping interests the parties may have failed to recognise on their own, and structure a settlement accordingly	Like judges, arbitrators can only award or reject what is claimed or counterclaimed, usually monetary sums

4-022 *Downside to trying mediation?* Perhaps the most obvious – but occasionally overlooked – selling point of mediation is that there is little downside to attempting it other than the time spent in mediation. On the contrary, even if a settlement is not reached, the work performed in preparing to mediate is generally work that would need to be done for an arbitration, and each party will understand the case better, so that a settlement may be possible later.

1.   Proposing Mediation to the Other Side(s)

4-023 Settlement, of course, will deprive the party's external lawyers of revenue they may have expected to earn by taking the dispute through arbitration or litigation. In fact, it is said that lawyers in private practice in some countries have not embraced ADR because they believe it stands for 'Alarming Drop in Revenues'. While we believe that the better lawyers everywhere will always be the ones who attempt to steer their clients towards the best possible outcomes, especially settlement, we recognise that in many places there will be lawyers who view settlement as none of their business. And there will be others, as there are in every profession, who may find ways to discourage settlement in a short-sighted view that litigation is better for their pocketbooks. Antipathy towards settlement efforts, and mediation in particular, is difficult to explain in any other way.

Proposing mediation directly to the other party or its counsel. Even where the other **4-024** side's advisors may be unfamiliar with or opposed to mediation for reasons not easily understood, parties – not their lawyers – are the ultimate decision makers. Because the obstructionist lawyer should not have the last say on matters of settlement, parties should consider the appropriateness of whether to propose mediation to the other side's counsel or directly to the other party's management. Either way, the likelihood of an offer to mediate being accepted can be enhanced if the offer is conveyed with a willingness to concede ground on the selection of the mediator, any mediation institution or rules (even if already specified in the parties' contract), and the location and timing of the mediation. The risk that the other party will select someone not skilled or suited to helping the parties settle their dispute can be mitigated in part by insisting only on certain basic requirements, such as language skills and a demonstrated competency in mediation (discussed below in paragraphs 4-053 to 4-056).

Proposing mediation through an institution. An effective but rarely utilised way of **4-025** successfully proposing mediation is not to make the offer directly, but to ask a mediation institution to approach the other side. In general, institutions that specialise in mediation services have no difficulty in freely communicating with a party's counsel and/or its representatives. Arbitration institutions that also offer mediation services may be less inclined to do so, for fear of compromising the institution's neutrality with respect to the dispute. But this may change as a arbitral institutions acquire more experience with mediation.

Not that this ever really happens: using the institution to help initiate mediation	Counsel for respondents was a partner at a well-known London law firm. Throughout the course of the M&A dispute he had rebuffed each offer by the claimant's counsel to attempt settlement through mediation, saying 'our side needs more information before it can consider settling the GBP 10 million claim'. So for eighteen months the parties had engaged in an expensive process of exchanging volumes of forensic accounting information that appeared only to make them more entrenched in their positions. In frustration, the claimant's counsel contacted a London-based mediation institution, which in turn contacted the principals of the respondents to discuss the possibility of mediation. One week later the parties' representatives met without their counsel and agreed to settle, without mediation ever having taken place (or even having been agreed to).

4-026 *The difficulty of proposing mediation to governments and government-owned entities.* Many large international disputes are between a private entity on the one side and a government or government-owned entity on the other. Mediations are not unheard of in this context, but they are the rare exception rather than the rule. This is largely because states and the companies they control are managed by employees who for the most part will see themselves as civil servants with no personal stake in a positive (or negative) outcome of a dispute. While a settlement may help their side obtain a better outcome and spend less than continuing with arbitration, they may not have authorisation to settle, particularly once a matter goes to arbitration, and seeking authorisation may expose them to internal criticism. An arbitration, by contrast, will have an outcome determined by the arbitrators. Thus, although the private party may wish to settle on very reasonable terms, it may not find it has a willing interlocutor, or even any interlocutor, on the other side.

4-027 One potential solution for these situations is to suggest that the employees of the state entity ask the supervisory authority, usually a board of directors, to authorise management to negotiate a settlement, including in mediation. The problem with this approach, is that the board will generally require a written settlement offer from the private party on the basis of which to issue the authorisation to negotiate up to that amount. Authorising negotiation on the basis of an offer the board itself has not accepted is likely to defeat the purpose of any subsequent negotiation.

Not that this ever really happens: negotiating with government employees	Counsel for the private company that had built a portion of the government-owned refinery in India proposed to its general manager that they submit their dispute to mediation rather than proceed with arbitration. Although the claim submitted to arbitration was strong, the proceedings would be long and expensive, and relations between the companies were good; the private party was willing to compromise substantially if the refinery would do the same. The general manager thanked the counsel for his explanation of mediation but said he did not want the suspicion of corruption that a settlement might create. It was safer for him if the parties just continued with the arbitration, even if that meant his side would pay more in an award and incur significant costs along the way.

4-028 *Proposing mediation for disputes involving multiple parties.* Some disputes, such as those those arising in connection with complex infrastructure projects, may be particularly difficult to settle when they involve more than two parties engaged in activities across more than one contract. Triggering an arbitration may lead to an award or settlement of one part of the dispute, only to trigger liabilities, and a related dispute, under another contract. The litigation (or arbitration) option is to embark on perhaps years of independent legal proceedings attempting to unravel responsibilities within the contractual and legal matrix. Mediation can be an effective means of getting all parties into a single room and resolving the dispute, at a mere fraction of the time and cost of traditional dispute resolution.

Not that this ever really happens: mediation of complex, multi-party disputes	The parties to the dispute were the owner of a manufacturing facility, an engineering company it had engaged to plan an extension of its plant, the supplier of industrial equipment that was part of the extension, and the civil works contractor that had carried out the construction work at the site. Operation of the plant extension was impacted when the industrial equipment failed shortly after start up, with the owner accusing the engineering company, the engineer accusing the equipment supplier, and the equipment supplier accusing the engineer and the construction contractor. Efforts to consolidate the disputes into a single proceeding were unsuccessful, in the absence of common dispute resolution provisions and a willingness of all of the parties to consolidate the dispute. Court and arbitration proceedings were already pending when all four parties (and an insurer) assembled at a mediation and settled with a joint payment to the owner and its insurer. Although the combined payment was considerable, it was substantially less than the total amount the parties would have spent on lawyers, arbitrators, and experts to resolve their dispute through the legal channels that had already been activated.

2.   Arb-Med: Combining Mediation and Arbitration

Many disputes that were once intractable become considerably more amenable to **4-029** settlement once the parties have had an opportunity to develop their case. Mediation within an arbitration, or 'arb-med', can present an attractive way of reaching settlement by combining the advantages of each form of dispute resolution. There are different forms of arb-med, but the general concept is that the parties agree that they will try mediation at an appropriate time during the course of the arbitration, or, similarly, they empower the arbitral tribunal to suggest when it believes a suitable time for mediation has been reached.

The key issue here is whether the parties will want a member of the arbitral tribunal **4-030** to act as a mediator or, as is more likely in our experience, will retain someone else specifically for this purpose. While a mediation may benefit from a tribunal's familiarity with the case, a competent arbitrator is not necessarily a competent mediator, and the arbitrators may simply not have suitable skills to help the parties reach agreement. Moreover, the parties themselves may be reluctant to state their true settlement positions to their arbitrators, for fear that it will lead the arbitrators to conclude that they would happily accept such an outcome in an award.

4-031 To illustrate the creativity that can be used to develop a suitable arb-med process, we present two examples below:

- *The sealed envelope containing the arbitration award.* International mediation advocate Michael Leathes, formerly head of intellectual property for British-American Tobacco, has pioneered a form of arb-med in which the parties actually complete an arbitration before attempting mediation.[11] The arbitrators deliver an award that is placed in a sealed envelope. The parties then negotiate to see if they can reach a settlement that is better than what they believe is in the award. This form of arb-med does not require any particular set-up or advance agreement other than a willingness to mediate the dispute during the period between when proceedings are concluded and the award is rendered. Of course, the downside to mediating at the conclusion of the arbitral proceedings is that the costs of arbitration (with the exception of enforcement proceedings) will have already been incurred. Still, where the parties have a relationship – or the possibility of a relationship – mediation at the conclusion of an arbitration may encourage them to identify opportunities that they will be unwilling to pursue once the award is rendered.

- *Including the possibility of mediation in the arbitrator's terms of engagement or an initial procedural timetable.* Mercedes Tarazón, an international mediator and arbitrator based in Barcelona, has developed her own form of arb-med. When acting as sole arbitrator, she asks the parties at the outset to empower her to suggest they try mediation if at some point in the proceedings she believes that a settlement might be possible. Generally, this comes once the parties have submitted their main pleadings and developed at least a substantial portion of their evidentiary case. She then sends them a letter, proposing several dates on which they can convene for a mediation. At the time of this writing, she reported having conducted fourteen such arb-med proceedings, with all leading to a settlement (and return appointments as arbitrator).[12] A simple variation on this technique could be, for example, to ask the arbitral tribunal to include in the procedural timetable (or provisional schedule) a provision that the parties consider mediation at specified points during the case.

---

11. The procedure described here is set out in detail in the case study co-authored by the parties to such a procedure, M. Leathes, B. Bulder, W. Kervers, & M. Schonewille, 'Einstein's Lesson in Mediation', *Managing IP* (July–August 2006).

12. This procedure is described by Ms Tarazon in episode 52 of International Dispute Negotiation, available at <www.cpradr.org>.

II.　　　　　FINDING AN INTERNATIONAL MEDIATOR
　　　　　　AND ORGANISING THE MEDIATION

Probably the most common question raised about mediation (both domestic and **4-032**
international) is how a party should go about identifying a suitable mediator. We
would rephrase that as two slightly different questions: (1) how does one go about
locating candidates for a mediator role, and (2) how does one select a mediator who
is appropriate for the dispute? We make this distinction because, as we note below,
the process of identifying candidates is one that leads to the sharing of information
about them with the other side, culminating in agreement on who should be
appointed.

As it stands today, use of mediation to resolve international commercial disputes is **4-033**
still in its incipient stages, and it remains a fair assumption that in most cases at
least one of the parties will have had no experience at all with it. As for mediators,
only a small handful today have experience outside their home jurisdictions.
Similarly, institutions that offer mediation services (including arbitration institutions) report a strikingly low number of international commercial disputes being
submitted to mediation, although the numbers appear to be growing.[13] Thus, a
party who proposes or agrees to submit an international commercial dispute to
mediation currently proceeds against a background of scant established
international practice. While this does not need to impede the efficacy of any
mediation itself, it does pose different challenges when compared with setting
up either an international arbitration or a mediation between purely domestic
parties.

A.　　　　Agreeing on When and Where

First things first: dates and location. Mediation is fundamentally different from **4-034**
arbitration in many ways, perhaps most notably in operating on a much shorter time
frame, usually measured in only a few weeks or months. Thus, parties should not
begin assembling lists of candidates or contacting potential mediators until they
have agreed on an acceptable location and possible dates, or ranges of dates, in
which the mediation can take place. In theory, the parties could contact mediators
to ask for dates of their availability, but in our experience this is a frustrating and
often unworkable approach. By the time the parties report back on whether the
dates are suitable, the mediator may say his previous dates are now filled and
propose new dates, and so on. Thus, and except for truly rare cases, it will be
better to start first with when and where the mediation is to occur and then find a
mediator who can suit the schedule rather than vice versa.

13.　For e.g., the ICC and the ICDR report the number of requests for mediation conducted under
　　　their auspices, and reported an upwards trend in requests between 2000 and 2008.

4-035 *Scheduling.* As noted below, in most circumstances parties should plan for the actual mediation to take just one day. There is no fixed or recommended rule as to how far off into the future that day should be scheduled. At a minimum, it should be as much time as the parties feel they need to adequately prepare and to ensure the attendance of someone from their side with reasonable decision-making authority. A mediation can generally be scheduled a couple of weeks off, even in the case of an international dispute with decision makers, a mediator, and parties all coming from different countries. Rarely should it take longer.

4-036 *Location.* Unlike arbitration, the place of mediation and the basic format to be followed are generally left to the parties to decide after the dispute has arisen. Only then can they begin speaking with potential candidates or institutions about scheduling the mediation. Generally, the mediation should be held at a place that is convenient to all of parties and likely mediator candidates (considering that the parties will share any travel costs of the mediator). If the parties cannot reach agreement on location, an easy rule is to adopt the place of arbitration specified in the contract. Alternatively, there is usually no downside to holding a mediation at the other party's place of business, except for the travel costs of the foreign party.

B.   Finding the Right Mediator for the Parties and the Dispute

4-037 Once parties have agreed on location and potential dates, they will proceed to what is currently the most challenging part of international mediation: identifying candidates and selecting a mediator. Obviously, they will want someone who possesses the qualities and skills they perceive would be helpful in achieving resolution of their dispute. The international character of a dispute will only magnify the difficulties parties already face in locating someone each side will trust and respect. Unfortunately for parties, the identification of suitable candidates and agreement on the appointment of mediators (and arbitrators, for that matter) will be based on imperfect information transmitted via word-of-mouth, and what can be gleaned from a curriculum vitae or an initial discussion with the candidate. Although there are some promising indications that this will change as private international dispute resolution matures, it is currently through these arguably unreliable channels that parties must generally weigh their considerations about a mediator's suitability. We discuss below certain criteria and considerations that can help parties assess the suitability of candidates.

4-038 In the case of a dispute between two domestic parties, the ease with which they are able to locate mediators will vary based on the country in which the dispute arises. In the United States, for example, there are dozens of institutions at the national and local levels that can provide parties with names of qualified candidates. By contrast, in countries where mediation is less developed, there may be few or no institutions to provide such a service. For better or for worse, international mediation is in the latter situation, with few institutions even claiming to specialise in the resolution of international commercial disputes.

Facilitative versus evaluative mediators. Most of the discussion in this chapter has **4-039** focused on the use of 'facilitative mediators', that is, mediators whose role is to help parties overcome their barriers to resolution by facilitating communication between them. There is another breed of mediator – a distinct and significant minority – called 'evaluative mediators'. Depending on the nature of the dispute and the disputants, the evaluative mediator may be what the parties require. Before considering the use of an evaluative mediator, however, parties should consider the possible consequences of an evaluation delivered at a time when one or both of the parties are not prepared to accept an adverse assessment of their case.

1.   Traditional Sources of Information about Potential Mediators

Just as there are lawyers in some countries who claim to be mediators after having **4-040** attended a conference or heard a lecture on the subject, there are arbitrators who also hold themselves out as mediators despite having no training or experience of the process. They are not mediators as the term is generally used to refer to a specific profession. However, a complaint levelled against the mediation profession in some jurisdictions is that it is not a 'profession' at all, at least as the term is generally used to refer to a certain degree of training, certification, and standards. 'Throw a stone, hit a mediator', is how one prominent US mediator has described the unregulated system in the United States (which is also true of most other countries) by which one can claim to be a mediator merely by announcing one's intentions.[14]

> **Question:** If an international arbitrator claims on their CV to be a 'mediator', can I assume they have at least been trained in mediation and have experience of the process?
>
> **Answer:** No. Unfortunately, just calling oneself a mediator is absolutely no indication of a person's qualification or skills to conduct a mediation. With the exception of the newly introduced initiative of the International Mediation Institute (discussed below), there is really no formal qualification or definition of an 'international mediator'. Even for domestic mediation, most countries do not have an authority or professional body that restricts or regulates the qualifications or competence of anyone claiming to be a 'mediator'.

---

14. J. Meyer, 'Mediators Alert: Now Certification Goes Global', *Alternatives* 26 (Mar. 2008) (CPR Institute): 57–66.

4-041 *The opposing party: sharing information about potential candidates.* The selection of a mediator is too often confused by inexperienced counsel and parties with the process of selecting an arbitrator, perhaps because there are superficial similarities in appointing a neutral third party in the context of a dispute in which trust will be lacking. But, in contrast with the adversarial process of appointing someone who will adjudicate a dispute and hopefully be favourable to one side's positions, the selection of a mediator should be a more collaborative process. Indeed, it is in a party's strategic interest to find someone that the *other* side will like and trust (since settlement is the goal). There are also tactical advantages to deferring to the other side's preferences for a mediator. A savvy party will treat the selection process not as an adversarial one, but as genuine collaboration, and use that collaboration to build trust that will be useful in the mediation. It should come as no surprise, therefore, that a meaningful number of cases are successfully resolved by the parties as a result of this dialogue and before a mediation even takes place.[15]

4-042 *Word-of-mouth.* As with the appointment of arbitrators, what parties really hope to identify in candidates are the soft qualities and skills that are not readily apparent from a curriculum vitae or public listing of the mediator's name and general qualifications. The best source for this, but by no means a perfect one, is a peer who attributes a past settlement to a particular mediator's skills. However, word-of-mouth recommendations from a domestic context may be less useful in international cases where the issues and parties are likely to vary even more substantially from one dispute to another. While a previous party's satisfaction with a certain mediator is a helpful endorsement, it should be considered no more than a starting point in the process of identification of suitable candidates.

| **Not that this ever really happens: relying on word-of-month recommend-ations** | The dispute involved parties from Asia and Europe, and each side began to make inquiries about potential mediation candidates. Ultimately, the parties relied on an institution to provide a list of names, from which the parties settled on three potential candidates. The respondent made inquiries about all three and shared with the claimant information received from its contacts with dispute resolution experience in the region. All spoke well of the reputations of the three candidates, but one person had noted that candidate 1's highly successful practice would likely impede him from accepting any appointments for at least six months. Another reported 'word on the street' that candidate 2 might be prolonging his mediations to earn a larger fee, to |

---

15. There is some empirical support for this observation in data from mediation institutions, which often report that they receive far more inquiries from parties seeking to start a mediation than those who actually continue with an appointment and mediation. It is not unreasonable to infer that some of these cases do not proceed because the parties have been able to settle after agreeing to attempt mediation.

compensate for a recent dearth of appointments. For the third candidate, the respondent had received no substantive information, other than that he was known as a mediator. Given the need to move swiftly, the parties therefore chose candidate 3, in the absence of any negative gossip/intelligence about him.

2.   Mediation and Arbitration Institutions

Although an institution may have the experience to appoint someone well qualified **4-043** for the dispute, the parties' failure to reach agreement on a mediator is not a good way for them to start the mediation process. That said, parties should feel comfortable asking institutions to provide a list of potential mediators to consider. There is no downside to this, and institutions will attempt to identify candidates who meet the selection criteria provided by the parties. Additionally, obtaining a list of names from institutions can reduce the risk of 'reactive devaluation' that a party may encounter from the other side when proposing candidates. Ironically, this psychological term is part of the toolkit used by mediators to overcome negative or mistrustful feelings that one side will associate with the other's proposals.

When drawing up a list, institutions will have one of two sources for the candidates: **4-044** a closed pool of mediators maintained by the institution, as is the case with many mediation institutions, and 'going-to-market' to find suitable candidates, an approach usually adopted by arbitration institutions that also offer mediation services.

Mediation institutions. Many mediation institutions maintain a closed pool or list **4-045** of mediators and often exist as a form of cooperative or partnership for the benefit of the mediators included in the pool. For example, this is the approach followed by the CEDR in London and JAMS in the United States, both well-known institutions. Mediation institutions, because of their desire to promote the practices of the mediators associated with them, are generally happy to assist parties by providing lists of suitable candidates, often at no charge.[16] The advantages of this approach, particularly for domestic disputes, is that the institution regulates the quality of its pool and will likely have the benefit of experiences and party feedback that it can use to help parties find the mediator most suitable for their dispute. The drawback, of course, is that the pool is likely to be limited for the most part to mediators whose only experience is with domestic disputes. In the best of cases, however, the institution's pool may include a handful of highly experienced commercial mediators with international experience, and parties can

---

16. Other mediation institutions that follow this model are the ACB in the Netherlands and the Singapore Mediation Centre (SMC).

benefit from having them on their list. Also, certain institutions offer specific subject-matter expertise for disputes where there is a belief that appointing a specialised neutral may be preferable (e.g., GAFTA for commodities and shipping disputes, and WIPO (the World Intellectual Property Organization) for intellectual property disputes).

4-046 *Arbitration institutions that provide mediation services.* Three of the leading international arbitration institutions – the ICC, ICDR, and the LCIA – now offer mediation services in addition to arbitration. This is also true of some leading regional institutions, such as the Milan Arbitration Chamber and the CMAP in Paris. Rather than maintaining their own pools of mediators, arbitration institutions take a 'go-to-market' approach in attempting to find the most suitable candidate for the parties. The ICDR, for example, will request input from the parties and then refer the matter to its regional offices to identify suitable candidates. The ICC adopts a similar approach, relying on its network of 'national committees' to identify suitable mediators. While the ICC does not in its ADR Rules state that it will provide parties with a list of candidates, it will in practice oblige either party's request for a list once an ADR proceeding has been initiated. Arbitration institutions may also be able to assist the parties with their administrative and logistical needs, such as negotiating fees with the mediator, arranging for suitable meeting and mediation facilities, and managing all aspects of invoicing and payment.

4-047 However, there are disadvantages with requesting names from an arbitration institution. The first is that, unlike mediation specialists who refer parties to their listed mediators, arbitration institutions will charge the parties a fee to conduct their search, and they will not provide a list until the parties have appointed the institution and engaged them in the process. The second is that an arbitration institution will have less experience in mediation than a dedicated mediation institution. The ICC's national committees, for example, have experience in appointing arbitrators for hundreds of arbitrations initiated each year, but as of this writing the total annual ICC caseload of mediations is less than 10% of the arbitration case load (although it is growing more rapidly).

4-048 In a nutshell, the go-to-market approach adopted by an international arbitration institution (with their experience in international commercial disputes) can compare favourably with the restricted pool of largely domestic mediators maintained by an institution that specialises in mediation.

3.   Emerging Information Sources: Certification, Directories, and Blogs

4-049 If cross-border dispute resolution is to keep pace with the growth of international business, it would be reasonable to expect that growth to be accompanied not only by an increased use of arbitration and mediation, but also the specialisation of the providers of these professional services and information about them. We discuss what may be emerging trends: certification, directories, and 'blogs'.

Mediator certification. If the practice of mediation is to grow across borders as **4-050** well as within them, it would be reasonable to expect parties to seek out information about their potential mediators and certain guarantees regarding the quality of the service they will provide. With this in mind, the International Mediation Institute (IMI) was established as a non-profit in the Netherlands in 2007 to promote international mediation standards and certify the 'minimum competency' of mediators around the world.[17] The institute worked closely with leading mediators in multiple countries to develop ethics and competency standards for the practice of mediation. IMI had adopted standards to certify leading mediators in multiple jurisdictions around the world and make information about these mediators available in the institute's web-based 'portal', at <www.IMImediation.org>.

Mediator directories. As mediation grows, publicly accessible databases are **4-051** emerging that include practical information about mediators, such as feedback from parties with their impressions of the mediator and his/her capabilities, in addition to basic biographical information. Parties can freely search these databases at no charge. As of this writing, at least two such databases have come into existence. The web-based portal of the IMI, <www.IMImediation.org>, is limited to mediators who have agreed to abide by IMI's ethical guidelines. IMI's database initially lists only those mediators who are considered at the top of the profession in different countries (and who meet IMI's threshold criteria). It aims to be, in other words, a resource for both starting the process of identifying a suitable mediator and for vetting any candidates discussed. Another mediator database providing qualitative information about mediators is the Mediate.com in the United States, <www.mediate.com>.

Blogs. The number of 'blogs' by and about mediators is an interesting source of **4-052** information that appears to be growing. There is even a 'World Directory' of mediation blogs at <www.adrblogs.com>.[18] Mediator blogs can provide information about the mediators who write and maintain them, as well as information about the writings and activities of their colleagues. Even if these professional blogs appear to be intended more for mediation peers than for parties, they can be a

---

17. Declaration of interest: one of the authors was the Chair of the IMI's Board for 2009.
18. Examples of some of the many useful blogs that are listed: Mediator Blah Blah...<www.mediatorblahblah.blogspot.com>, Mediation Channel <www.mediationchannel.com>, and Settle It Now! <www.negotiationlawblog.com>. Taking by way of example one of the blogs listed above, during a two-month period in 2008, the blog's author had attended a week-long international mediation training conducted in another country, was corresponding with mediators in different jurisdictions, and expressed strong opinions about which techniques were most effective for overcoming roadblocks to settlement.

means of identifying global trends and negotiation tips, and they can be useful for parties who wish to recommend a particular mediator as a candidate.

4.   Important Criteria for Identifying a Suitable Mediator

4-053 As should by now be apparent, parties may be required to rely on a good deal of largely imperfect information, much of it transmitted via word-of-mouth, when identifying candidates to mediate an international commercial dispute. Below, however, are some of the more objective criteria that can be gleaned either from a curriculum vitae or an initial discussion, and which can be helpful for parties in agreeing on the most suitable person. For the most part, these are considerations for which parties will be willing to make trades. For example, they may be willing to sacrifice schedule (availability on preferred dates) in order to have a mediator who meets other important criteria, such as style or domain expertise.

Checklist 4b – Considerations when Selecting Mediators

- Availability
- Competence in mediation – training and certification
- Experience as mediator
- Mediation style
- Language
- Nationality
- Cultural awareness
- Subject-matter (domain) expertise

4-054 *Investigating mediator qualifications through ex parte communications with the mediator.* In contrast with arbitration, there is no prohibition of ex parte communications when it comes to discussing any aspect of the dispute with a mediator, or with any mediator candidates. Indeed, there is a presumption that ex parte communications *will* take place, as the process is largely built on the mediator's ability to engage in candid separate discussions with each side. Thus, the best way to discover whether a mediator is suitable for a particular dispute is often just to call him and discuss his qualifications. To avoid the appearance of seeking to influence the mediator (and compromising his neutrality), parties should simply be transparent with each other that they will do this, and that they expect the other side will do the same. This is true not just of the appointment process, but also during the mediation itself.

Not that this ever really happens: a misplaced prohibition on ex parte Communications	In a mediation appointment provided by an arbitration institution, the institution's case manager, obviously more familiar with the process of appointing arbitrators, sent the parties a letter 'confirming' the mediator's appointment and instructing them not to engage in ex parte communications with him. Counsel for both parties answered that they intended to ignore that instruction, and they did.[19]

Availability. It goes without saying that a mediator must be able to attend a medi- **4-055** ation on dates and at a location convenient and acceptable to the parties. Indeed, it is probably the first item parties should investigate to avoid spending their time unproductively considering a candidate who will not be available.

Competency in mediation – training and certification. As noted above, one side **4-056** may secure a tactical advantage if the other side feels it had the greater hand in selecting the mediator, as the other side's negotiation team may as a result be more inclined to defer to the mediator when its efforts are aimed at encouraging that party to reduce its settlement expectations. But there is a limit to how much one should reasonably defer to the other side in selecting a mediator, and this limit is the minimum level of mediation capability of the person to be selected. Given that anyone can hold themselves out as a mediator, and many do (who should not), parties should be live to whether proposed candidates grasp what mediation entails. From a theoretical perspective, it is true that the downside to an ineffective mediation is simply that the parties do not settle, that is, they proceed with their dispute as before. In reality, however, an unqualified mediator can be more harmful. An ineffective mediation – in which the parties do not at least walk away with a better understanding of their disagreement – can discourage the parties from engaging in further negotiations. Or, worse still, an ill-suited or unqualified mediator can unintentionally stoke the dispute into a greater level of conflict than had the mediation never taken place.

---

19. While the arbitration institution (or its case manager) may have lacked experience in appointing mediators, the quality of the service provided did not suffer. In fact, counsel for each of the sides subsequently wrote to the institution to express their gratitude for the high level of support provided, which included: conducting a search for a mediator, negotiating a favourable fee with their selected candidate, organising a meeting facility for the mediation, and managing all aspects of invoicing and payment.

Not that this ever really happens: an unqualified 'mediator' makes things worse	The buyer, a North American company, alleged certain breaches of representations and warranties contained in its agreement to purchase a business unit from the European seller. The seller suggested the parties engage in mediation. The buyer accepted, and the parties engaged as a mediator an esteemed professor of law, also well known as an international arbitrator, from the European country whose laws governed the contract. The professor initiated the mediation by presenting to the parties a legal opinion he had written. The opinion stated that the professor had reviewed the contract, the position papers, and supporting documentation provided by the parties and had concluded that the seller's interpretation was, in fact, the correct one. He asked the parties how they now wanted to proceed. The buyer, infuriated, rejected the offer, left the mediation, and shortly thereafter commenced arbitration.

4-057 Means of establishing that proposed candidates actually possess appropriate skills as a mediator (although not necessarily cross-cultural or international mediation capabilities) include the following:

- Association with a mediation institution;
- Certification by an appropriate body;
- Participation in mediator qualification courses held under the auspices of reputable provider institutions.

4-058 *The broad range of mediation styles.* Parties should be transparent with each other about exactly what sort of process they expect to have when they search for a mediator, to avoid any later misunderstanding. For example, it is possible for parties to both agree on 'mediation' using an institution, but with different expectations as to the process and the substantive skills of the mediator. One party may desire an 'objective', facts- and law-oriented process based on specific subject-matter expertise applied to documented facts, and the other a future-looking 'subjective' process, focusing on interpersonal and relationship-based issues. If a mediator is appointed without these expectations having been identified and properly discussed, the mediator (and the mediation) may be a disappointment to one of the parties, and possibly both. Below are two key stylistic distinctions parties may wish to consider:

- *Evaluative versus facilitative?* Will it make a difference whether the parties choose an evaluative process (the mediator will tell the parties how she predicts the potential outcome) or a purely facilitative process? In some cases, it may make no difference, as the parties simply want to achieve a faster and cheaper outcome. In other cases, however, this difference may be important, such as where the possibility of probing into subjective interests and perceptions may generate a broader range of options and different outcomes, which may be better aligned with the parties' future interests (e.g., in creating or strengthening a future business relationship).

– *Different international styles*. In common law jurisdictions the parties may expect the mediator to make a greater use of caucuses (separate meetings with each party) as opposed to a practice used more widely in continental European jurisdictions with a greater emphasis on joint sessions or co-mediation (with two mediators). It is impossible to generalise and stereotype, but there can be a danger in underestimating these differences when seeking to set up a mediation process.

Question: The other side holds an unrealistic view of the potential outcome of the case. Shouldn't we prefer a good evaluative mediator to get them to change their view or perhaps educate us if we got things wrong?

Answer: Great caution should be exercised before agreeing to an evaluative form of mediation. While decision makers may say they prefer an 'evaluative' mediator who will give the parties a non-binding prediction of potential outcomes on particular issues or even the entire dispute, they may not like hearing they are wrong. An evaluation given too early in the process can upset the ability to reach settlement. By contrast, party representatives (particularly managers) may be surprised when they find themselves for the first time in a facilitative mediation with a lawyer or former judge who refuses to declare which party, in her view, has the winning position. Still, the mediator's facilitative ability – whether in shuttle diplomacy or as an intelligent sounding board – can often be effective at provoking a settlement even when one or more of the parties has adopted what appears to be an unrealistically extreme litigation position.

Mixing of styles to suit the parties and the dispute. Rather than draw hard lines **4-059** between different mediation styles, it may be more appropriate to credit experienced mediators with the discretion to identify the best approach for a particular case. For example, while there are mediators who do nothing but facilitate and others who only evaluate, most mediators will fall somewhere in between the extremes. If the parties consent, most facilitative mediators will provide an evaluation of a key point, usually how they predict a disputed issue of law or fact would be decided by a judge or arbitrator. Often, parties will request this evaluation in order to help them move past an impasse in their negotiations. How can parties learn which approach the mediator will use? The simple answer is to ask.

4-060 *Language capability, interpreters, and co-mediators.* Obviously, the mediator must be able to communicate with the parties' representatives and speak the language that will be used at the plenary session during the mediation (see below). For a mediation to be successful, we have not found it to be essential that the mediator speak the native language of both parties, or even one of them. Indeed, finding a mediator with the linguistic capabilities to converse in the native language of all participants in a complex multinational mediation may narrow the range of suitable mediators without adding appreciable value. The point is that the mediator should be conversant in a language that the parties' representatives will be able to understand. If that language is only, say, English or French, and the parties' representatives are conversant, that should be good enough.

4-061 If the parties do not speak a common language and are unable to identify or settle on a mediator who speaks their different languages well enough to move things forward, there are two potential solutions. The first is to engage the services of an interpreter. But, because the mediator is likely to spend most of her time in separate sessions with each party, an interpreter may hamper their open communications. The second approach, and one that some mediators prefer even for domestic mediation,[20] is to engage the services of a 'co-mediator' to overcome the linguistic and even possible cultural issues that may arise.

4-062 *Nationality.* The issue of nationality is often important in an arbitration context. This can also be the case in mediation, but for different reasons and in different ways. Mediation generally has no equivalent to the default rule of some arbitration institutions in which the chair may not be of the same nationality of either party, at least not without both parties' consent. Imposing such a condition may be unduly limiting. Whereas 'nationality' in an arbitration is considered to be the place of citizenship or incorporation of the formal parties to the proceeding, in a mediation the actual participants may come from a range of national and cultural backgrounds different from the place of incorporation of the legal entities to the dispute. We provide three simple guideposts to considering whether nationality should be given consideration, and what weight should be placed on it.

4-063 First, the nationality of a mediator should matter only to the extent that the parties believe it would be beneficial to helping them resolve their dispute. They may believe, for example, that someone of the same or different nationality as one or both of them would be helpful under the particular circumstances. Or they may decide that the mediator's nationality makes little or even no difference at all for their particular dispute.

---

20. See, e.g., J. Beer & E. Stief, *The Mediator's Handbook*, 3rd edn (Canada: New Society Publishers, 1998).

Not that this ever really happens: a truly international mediation	One of the authors was involved in a mediation in which on his side alone the three party representatives at the mediation came from Italy, Egypt, and the United States. The Italian was the business leader, the American her project manager who had main responsibility for managing the dispute in question, and the Egyptian was the sales manager who had signed the contract containing the disputed terms. The opposing party came from yet another country, as did the mediator, and the dispute involved a contract carried out by the parties in a sixth country.

Second, where cultural sensitivity is among the concerns, the mediator's nation- **4-064** ality may not be meaningful (e.g., the mediator may have been raised as a 'third-culture kid') or it may even be misleading, for example, assuming a person to be of an Asian culture, based on their passport, whereas they may have been raised and completely educated in an American or European culture.

Not that this ever really happens: a good mediator can transcend different nationalities	One of the authors has on two occasions appointed an Oslo-based mediator for disputes in which the author represented the Norwegian party on one occasion and was adverse to a Norwegian party on the other. Both mediations involved party representatives whose native language the mediator did not speak, and the mediation itself was conducted mainly in English. Yet both mediations led to settlements, which the author attributes to the perceptiveness and skills of the mediator in structuring the parties' negotiations, not his nationality or even linguistic abilities.

Third, and more important, it may paradoxically be an advantage in certain cases **4-065** for the mediator to be of the same nationality or culture as one party. This may help to ensure a better appreciation or any cultural issues that may be acting as an impediment to settlement, where the cultural differences are great. Allowing the other party to choose a mediator of its preference and of their nationality, or to suggest a list of three neutrals having the same nationality as the other party, can be a way of conveying confidence and trust in the process and in the other party (obviously with the proviso that it is important to agree on a mediator who is properly trained and who will not be biased).

Assessing the conflict and whether culture plays a role. When dealing with sophis- **4-066** ticated, experienced parties, placing undeserved stress on the 'culture' of one of the parties can trivialise legitimate commercial differences. In most cases what drives parties into a commercial litigation is disagreement over allocation of money, or differences of opinion over what occurred or the repercussions under the contract. One of the authors once informally surveyed international dispute resolution professionals around the world for examples of commercial disputes caused by cultural differences. Among the many anecdotes given, in none was a cultural difference the genuine source of the conflict. Rather, all were instances in which one of the parties had mistakenly stereotyped the other side or blamed a perceived cultural difference as the cause of the dispute, only to discover in the course of negotiations or litigation that the starting perception was wrong and that the two sides actually had more in common than they had initially believed. So finding a mediator with appropriate cultural knowledge of both parties does not mean that culture is among the possible causes of the conflict between them; rather, understanding their culture may improve the chances of promoting settlement of their conflict.

4-067 One final consideration about attempting to inject culture into the selection of a mediator is that a party may unintentionally consider it to be a factor that pertains only to the other side, that is, that 'their' culture is part of the problem while 'our' culture causes no issues. This is not a healthy way to view disputes, nor one conducive to settlement. As discussed below in section III on mediation advocacy, the mediation process gives parties an opportunity to disabuse themselves of stereotypes or any view that the other side's 'culture' was to blame for the dispute. To assume that cultural factors may be influencing only the other side's decision makers can lead to inappropriate conclusions about what is preventing the parties from reaching settlement.

Not that this ever really happens: unfairly blaming culture for bad behaviour	The dispute lawyer for a business unit explained to his company's general counsel that the mediation with an Eastern European customer had failed to produce a settlement. He explained that the failure was due to the deceptive tactics and obnoxious behaviour of a certain 'Josef', the customer's senior project manager, who had consistently undermined any efforts at compromise. 'Well, of course', said the general counsel, 'the problem is that Josef is from [that European country].' 'No', answered the dispute lawyer, 'the problem is that Josef is a jerk'. While culture can play an important factor in the resolution of conflict, it can also be a code for stereotypes that overlook important differences among individuals involved in their dispute.

4-068 *Experience as mediator.* The ability to identify points of disagreement and help parties reach settlement is a skill that improves with experience. The next question is what type of experience. A good starting point is experience conducting mediations of business disputes of a similar type and complexity, even if only in disputes between domestic litigants.

4-069 *Subject-matter expertise.* Parties may desire, and benefit from, a mediator they can trust to understand *their* dispute, and who can be brought up to speed quickly on points of disagreement. For example, if the contract is governed by New York law, the parties may prefer a mediator who has some degree of familiarity with that law. How much familiarity – say, the general knowledge of New York legal principles of a mediator from another common-law country or the expertise of an experienced New York lawyer or former judge – will likely depend on the importance of any legal principles in dispute.

Often even more important will be the parties' desire for someone who can appre- **4-070** ciate the factual circumstances involved in the dispute and keep them in proper perspective. For example, if the dispute arises out of a complex financial transaction, then the decision makers on each side may feel more comfortable with a mediator who shares their understanding with respect to that type of business. The same can be said of construction and infrastructure disputes, in which the decision makers may share a common engineering background, even if acquired in different countries, and may feel they would benefit from a mediator who can quickly grasp the technical challenges faced in their project and the points in dispute. Being familiar with the relevant industry or commercial background of the dispute can also help mediators avoid unintentional gaffes or counterproductive behaviour in the course of the mediation.

Not that this ever really happens: failing to grasp the basics	There are times when a party will want a mediator who is well grounded at least in the fundamentals of the subject matter of the dispute. Failure to appreciate the basics can lead to party frustration rather than resolution. For example, during a caucusing (private) session with the mediator in a highly technical engineering dispute, the respondent's representative, an engineer, explained the contract's technical specifications and how the claimant's assertions relied on incorrect mathematical calculations. The mediator thanked the engineer for his thorough explanation and said he would return after discussing it with the other party. After the mediator had left the room, the engineer appeared irritated with the mediator's failure to at least agree that the claimant's math was wrong. His lawyer explained that the mediator likely wanted to maintain his appearance of neutrality on the issue. 'If he believes anyone can just add numbers together this way, then he is clearly not "neutral"', responded the engineer.

C. MEDIATOR FEES

Conventional wisdom holds that mediator fees, whatever amount they may be, are **4-071** almost always a small fraction of the other costs in dispute. But rates can be highly volatile when looking at candidates from more than one country. Indeed, rates can vary even within the same country, as was demonstrated by a survey conducted in

2008 by *The Mediator Magazine* of the rates of thirty of the United Kingdom's most well-known mediators (many of whom would be included in any list of the world's most experienced international mediators).[21]

What mediators do charge

Billing Rates

		£100,000 Dispute	£1m Dispute	5hrs Prep	Total Bill (£1m Dispute)
1	Karl Mackie (CEDR)	£4,500.00	£5,500.00	£2,500.00	£8,000.00
2	Eileen Carroll (CEDR)	£4,500.00	£5,500.00	£2,500.00	£8,000.00
3	David Shapiro	£5,000.00	£5,000.00	£2,250.00	£7,250.00
4	Tony Willis	£5,000.00	£5,000.00	£2,000.00	£7,000.00
5	Stephen Ruttle QC	£4,500.00	£5,000.00	£2,000.00	£7,000.00
6	Bill Wood QC	£5,000.00	£5,000.00	£2,000.00	£7,000.00
7	Phillip Howell-Richardson	£4,500.00	£4,500.00	£2,000.00	£6,500.00
8	Richard Lord QC	£4,000.00	£4,000.00	£2,000.00	£6,000.00
9	Hilary Heilbron QC	£4,000.00	£4,000.00	£2,000.00	£6,000.00
10	Jane Andrewartha	£3,900.00	£3,900.00	£1,950.00	£5,850.00
11	Sir Oliver Popplewell	£3,750.00	£3,750.00	£2,000.00	£5,750.00
12	Sir Roger Buckley	£3,500.00	£3,750.00	£2,000.00	£5,750.00
13	David Cornes	£3,950.00	£3,950.00	£1,775.00	£5,725.00
14	Andrew Paton	£3,300.00	£4,125.00	£1,375.00	£5,500.00
15	Mark Jackson Stops	£3,000.00	£4,500.00	£700 (3hrs inc)	£5,200.00
16	Michel Kallipetis QC	£2,000.00	£3,000.00	£1,750.00	£4,750.00
17	Nicholas Pryor	£2,000.00	£3,000.00	£1,750.00	£4,750.00
18	Bill Marsh	£2,000.00	£3,000.00	£1,750.00	£4,750.00
19	Charles Dodson	£2,000.00	£3,000.00	£1,750.00	£4,750.00
20	David Miles	£3,100.00	£3,100.00	£1,550.00	£4,650.00
21	Jane Player	£2,500.00	£4,500.00	Inc	£4,500.00
22	Jon Lang	£4,500.00	£4,500.00	Inc	£4,500.00
23	David Richbell	£3,500.00	£4,500.00	10hrs inc	£4,500.00
24	Chris Fitton	£3,355.00	£3,930.00	£285 (4hrs inc)	£4,215.00
25	Amanda Bucklow	£3,500.00	£3,500.00	£700 (3hrs inc)	£4,200.00
26	Nick Pearson	£4,160.00	£4,160.00	5hrs inc	£4,160.00
27	Roger Tabakin	£2,500.00	£3,500.00	£600 (3hrs inc)	£4,100.00
28	Andrew Fraley	£4,020.00	£4,020.00	Inc	£4,020.00
29	James Wilson	£4,000.00	£4,000.00	Inc	£4,000.00
30	Philip Bartle QC	£1,300.00	£2,000.00	£1,500.00	£3,500.00

For this survey, *The Mediator* approached every mediator ranked in the 2007 edition of *The Legal 500*. The vast majority were forthcoming with details and, as publishers, we are grateful for the profession's candour.

Day rates mediators quoted were broadly similar when adjusted for the fact that some mediators quote on the basis of a 10-hour day and others assume an eight-hour day. Charging for additional time on the day is relatively common, although some mediators take the view that their fee is for the duration of the mediation regardless of how late it runs.

How mediators choose to bill for preparation time varies widely. The accepted wisdom is that clients are more comfortable with a fixed-fee, and some mediators offer a package which incorporates preparation time into their day rate. Mediators like Jane Player and Jon Lang incorporate all necessary preparation into their day rate; David Richbell allows for 10 hours of preparation and travel; Nick Pearson five hours; Chris Fitton, four; and Amanda Bucklow, Mark Jackson Stops and Roger Tabakin allow for three hours.

As can be seen, even within the United Kingdom, where mediation can be said to be a highly developed practice area (relative to other countries), rates are not standard or even similar. Variation exists both in the total amount that would be

---

21. M. Rushton, 'The Price Is Wrong', *Mediator Magazine* (2008), reproduced with permission.

charged for the same mediation and the method of calculating the fees (some applying an hourly rate, others a fixed rate, and others a hybrid that varies according to the amount of preparation required). And the variation is significant, with some charging more than double what others would ask to mediate the same dispute.

Parties can expect this variation to increase when they are looking at candidates **4-072** from more than one country. Moreover, parties should not confuse the rates a mediator quotes as reflecting that person's qualifications, level of experience, or suitability for a particular dispute. Rather, quoted rates may reflect nothing more than what a mediator believes the market will bear, or simply what the parties in a particular dispute might be prepared to pay. It is not unheard of (and in fact may be relatively commonplace) for an inexperienced mediator in one country to charge several times the quoted rates of a highly skilled and experienced mediator in another country.

Not that this ever really happens: fees of USD 500 to USD 60,000 for the same dispute	The parties sought a mediator who understood English law (the law of the contract) but who would also be sensitive to cultural expectations of a dispute taking place involving parties from Southeast Asia and Europe. Because the dispute involved total claims of less than USD 4 million, and the main purpose of the mediation was to avoid the costs of arbitration, the rates of proposed mediators quickly became an important consideration. The claimant initially contacted an English barrister with experience as an arbitrator and mediator in construction disputes, who proposed to conduct a three-day mediation for USD 60,000 plus his costs for first-class travel to Asia and five days in a hotel. The respondent rejected this and contacted different mediation centres in Asia and Europe, and was quoted rates from USD 500 to USD 15,000 for a single day. The claimant then contacted an international arbitration institution (not the one provided for in the contract), which conducted a search and proposed mediators based in Hong Kong and Singapore with qualifications in English law. The parties settled on one of these candidates, whose fee for a one-day mediation (after it was renegotiated by the institution at the request of the parties) was USD 10,000, inclusive of preparation time, plus travel costs.

How mediators charge and are paid. There is no standard approach, either in **4-073** domestic or international practice, as to how mediators charge. Common methods are by the hour, by the day, or via a fixed fee inclusive of any preparatory work. As for how these costs are allocated, the commonly accepted rule in mediation is that the parties share equally the costs of the mediator (as well as any mediation facilities). The exception is when one party, for whatever reason, must cancel or reschedule the mediation. In such events, the cancelling party is responsible for all charges incurred.

4-074 *Success fees*. Contingency or success fees do not appear to be commonly suggested by mediators, with some notable exceptions.[22] In all events, we suggest the caveat of 'buyer beware' when discussing rates with potential mediators, as high price does not always correlate with high quality of service. Ironically, rates that appear to be unusually high can be an indication of unfamiliarity with mediation (possibly confusing it with arbitration).

Not that this ever really happens: the inexperienced mediator would have charged	The parties, a US claimant and an Italian respondent, were looking for a mediator to help them settle the dispute over the divestiture of the Italian party's business unit, and contemplated Rome as the place of mediation. Key issues in dispute involved the interpretation of points under the contract, which was governed by Italian law. The parties sought the services of an Italian mediator, and the claimant's law firm in Milan polled potential candidates. One, a lawyer with another law firm in Milan, whose curriculum vitae showed no qualification or training in mediation, proposed to charge a fee calculated on the basis of the amount in dispute, as well as a 'success fee', which would also have been based on the amount in dispute. The resulting fees for a one-day mediation would have been either EUR 25,000 in the event of no settlement being reached, and EUR 90,000 if a settlement was agreed. The claimant rejected the proposal (and the mediator), and the parties ultimately retained a person trained by a reputable mediation institution who charged a total of EUR 3,000 inclusive of all preparation.

4-075 *Negotiating the mediator's fee*. Given the lack of standard rates charged by prominent mediators, parties will want to enquire about fees sooner rather than later in their discussions with potential candidates. Like any other providers of services, mediators can be flexible in what they charge, and the most advantageous time for parties to negotiate rates is before they have engaged the mediator and blocked a date for the mediation. Parties may also be able to negotiate the methods of payment, as well as any other considerations, such as fees to be charged in the event of cancellation or rescheduling the date of the mediation.

---

22. We have heard of one well-known mediator who serves as 'party mediation advisor' for one party and charges a flat fee plus a percentage of the difference between the offer on the table going into the mediation and any increase on that offer obtained in a settlement. He is apparently able to obtain significant success fees as a result, which parties are happy to pay.

D.   Affirming the Confidentiality of the Mediation

While in most legal systems settlement offers will be privileged or confidential in **4-076** some way – so that a party may not freely introduce them into evidence in litigation or rely upon them as admissions of liability – the extent of the privilege or confidentiality can vary widely from jurisdiction to jurisdiction. In France, for example, the privilege will exist only if the offer was made by one external lawyer to another. In other jurisdictions, such as England, an offer to settle may not be produced in the proceeding on the merits, but may in some instances be produced as part of process for allocating payment of legal fees (in the event the offer was not accepted).

In an international dispute, mediation should have the advantage of allowing **4-077** parties to convey and discuss offers directly with each other, without having to worry about different rules on settlement privilege. It is a sacrosanct principle of mediation (stated in the rules of all mediation institutions and virtually all supporting legislation in existence today) that what gets said during the course of the mediation is confidential. But because practices outside the mediation can vary from one country to another, there are some nuances that parties should heed if they have any concern about the possibility that information they share will be used in a subsequent arbitration or litigation.

Statements made to the mediator. A mediator should be protected from testifying in **4-078** a subsequent arbitration about what the parties said to him or in his presence. We believe that tribunals in international arbitration today will honour this privilege and that, even if they do not, no serious mediator will agree to give testimony with respect to any part of what transpired in a mediation. Parties should therefore be confident that they can be candid with the information they choose to share with the mediator, without fear of it subsequently being used against them in arbitration or in a court proceeding.

Statements made to, or in the presence of, the other side. Under all commercial **4-079** mediation rules with which we are familiar, statements made to the other side in the course of a mediation are also confidential, in order to facilitate candid discussion. Similarly, most agreements to mediate contain an obligation to treat all communications as confidential. Whether the communications are also 'privileged' as a matter of law – under a 'settlement' or 'without prejudice' privilege, which would prevent an arbitrator or judge from allowing the communications into evidence – is another matter and will depend on the laws of the place of the arbitration or litigation.[23] While we are reasonably confident that an international arbitral tribunal would reject any attempt by a party to introduce statements made by the other

---

23. For example, in the United States, a pro-mediation jurisdiction, legal privilege of mediation communications is contemplated by the Uniform Mediation Act, with exceptions for threats of violence or other harm. But only a minority of US states have adopted the Act to date. Most mediation agreements make confidentiality a contractual obligation, which of course can be breached.

party during the course of mediation, in practice what has been conveyed to the tribunal has been conveyed and the harm cannot easily be undone. Unfortunately, we have seen instances in which counsel have disregarded any ethical considerations and produced a prior settlement offer as an admission of liability in support of their client's case. The risk is that once the tribunal has heard the amount for which a party was once willing to settle, they may be subconsciously persuaded that the party accepts that amount as a fair outcome. Therefore, and regrettably, parties must give careful consideration to the impact of any offers conveyed directly to the other side, and they may wish to take advantage of the role of the mediator to diminish this risk (as discussed below).

4-080 *Documents.* Again, in theory, documents shared with the other party in the course of mediation should be subject to contractual confidentiality and legal privilege. If a party wants to improve the chances of the confidentiality or privilege being preserved, it should mark the document as a 'mediation document' or 'subject to mediation privilege and confidentiality'. For documents created specifically for the mediation, such as a presentation summarising the dispute, there is perhaps less danger of this being subsequently produced in arbitration (and these documents will generally be favourable to the party that created them in any event). But it will be more difficult to argue that contemporaneous documentary evidence is covered by mediation privilege and confidentiality and/or to demonstrate that the adverse party could not have obtained or learned of the document except through the mediation.[24]

4-081 *Confidentiality agreements.* Given the uncertainty surrounding the legal or ethical rules of mediation or settlement privilege that may be applicable to each side and their counsel, parties to mediation and other settlement discussions can take the additional step of entering into a settlement confidentiality document. This can be used for any settlement discussion (not just mediation) in order to facilitate the sharing of information without fear of creating documents disclosable in arbitration or litigation. Some mediation institutions – and most mediators – will require the parties to enter into an agreement to mediate, which will both explain the mediation process and ask them to reaffirm their commitment to the confidentiality of matters discussed in the mediation.

---

24. In theory, this means that a document covered by a mediation privilege (but not specifically created for the mediation) cannot be produced in a subsequent arbitration without the consent of the party that produced it in the mediation. In practice, this impediment is slight, as the opposing party, now aware of the existence of the document, can simply request that it be produced, if it is relevant to the issues in dispute. Chapter 5, *The Conduct of the Arbitration.* In contrast, a document created purely for the purposes of mediation should not be subject to subsequent production in arbitration or litigation.

E.   MEDIATION LOGISTICS

The parties will need to agree in advance of the mediation on where it will take **4-082**
place, the meeting facilities to be used, how to allocate the costs of the facilities,
and so on. While there are no set rules as to any of this, there are general practices
(and common sense) to which the parties can refer.

Location of the mediation. Given that mediation is merely a form of negotiation, **4-083**
there is little procedural value to be gained from locating the mediation in a
'neutral' country. An international mediation will therefore usually be held in
the country of one of the parties, where it will be easier and more economical
for the party from the host country to arrange for the facilities. Some parties may
desire (and the mediator may recommend) that the mediation itself take place at a
'neutral' location within the chosen country, such as the mediator's office, a hotel
conference room, or a hearing or meeting room provided by an arbitration or
mediation institution. Other parties may be indifferent to location and agree to
have the mediation conducted at the other party's place of business or the offices of
its counsel. We do not intend to prescribe any of these approaches or address their
relative merits, as each case will be different. It is important, however, for parties to
organise their mediation at a location where both sides feel comfortable and neither
feels it is disadvantaged.

Facilities costs. As for costs of the facilities, the practice is that (as with the fees of **4-084**
the mediator) each party will bear half the costs of any facilities and related
expenses (equipment rentals, meals, and so forth).

Adequacy of meeting rooms. Parties should ensure there will be an adequate **4-085**
number of rooms available so that each party will have a separate place in
which to engage in private, confidential discussions, including private sessions
with the mediator. In theory, a two-party dispute would have three rooms: a joint
meeting room (which may also be the mediator's room) and two rooms for each
party to engage in their confidential discussions. In practice, however, two rooms
are usually sufficient for a two-party dispute, with the room used for joint sessions
doubling as a party's private meeting room. Equally important is the size of the
rooms.

Not that this ever really happens: cramped quarters	One of the authors was once involved in a mediation for which no advance count had been taken of the number of people who would be present. At awkward joint meeting sessions, representatives of the multiple parties, their insurers, and counsel for each, all crammed into tiny conference rooms too small to hold them. Interestingly, however, the case settled, possibly helped by the intimacy (and occasional hilarity) created by being in close quarters with the other side.

F.   SCHEDULING CONSIDERATIONS IN DELAYING OR DEFERRING
                                  THE ARBITRATION OR OTHER BINDING DISPUTE RESOLUTION
                                  PENDING MEDIATION

4-086 As noted at the outset of this chapter, mediation is complementary to other forms of
dispute resolution, not an alternative, and a party should not feel it must postpone
an arbitration unless it is in its interest to do so. Common sense, however, dictates
an important distinction between delaying an arbitration that is in its initial stages
of organisation (or yet to be initiated) and postponing a proceeding that is already
well underway.

4-087 *Arbitration yet to be initiated or no evidentiary hearing scheduled.* Because a
settlement will allow the parties to avoid the costs of arbitration, it generally
makes sense to agree to delay the initiation or organisation of an arbitration that
is not yet fully underway, absent circumstances of particular urgency. Even where
the tribunal has been constituted and initial submissions have been made, the
parties can usually agree to suspend the proceedings while they attempt settlement,
without unduly impacting the arbitration schedule.

4-088 *Arbitration underway and evidentiary hearing scheduled.* If the arbitration is
underway and the tribunal has already scheduled hearing dates, it may not be
practical or beneficial for parties to delay the arbitration while they attempt mediation. A postponement at this stage will be disruptive to the schedule, and the need
to reorganise it by finding future dates when the arbitrators, parties, and witnesses
are all available may result in greater delays in the arbitration than the time
requested for the mediation, and greater overall costs for the parties in the event
the mediation does not lead to settlement. Fortunately, if the parties elect to mediate when the arbitration is at an advanced stage, they should already be well
prepared on the issues and require little additional time to prepare.

4-089 *Cancelling or rescheduling the mediation.* Once engaged for a particular date,
many mediators will charge a 'cancellation fee' if the mediation is cancelled.
The amount depends on the mediator but can be a substantial portion or all of
the agreed fee. The mediator may also charge to reschedule the mediation for
another date. Such charges are in principle reasonable, since the mediator cannot
accept other work on the dates scheduled by the parties. Still, parties should be able
to negotiate with the mediator at the time of engagement to apply at least a sliding
schedule so that the fee is reduced if the cancellation or rescheduling occurs well in
advance of the agreed date. In the event that both parties agree to cancel or
reschedule the mediation, the general rule is that they share these costs equally;
otherwise, the cost should fairly be borne by the cancelling party.

III.   MEDIATION ADVOCACY

4-090 Mediation is unlike arbitration in that it has no formal procedures other than what
the parties may agree in a given case, and it makes no demand that they have any

special training, skills, or even that they appear at the table with counsel. And while the language of the mediation may shift with location and the parties, the basic concept will not. Its user-friendliness is universal in that a party can comfortably attempt resolution through mediation regardless of where in the world it takes place, or of where the parties come from. It is a negotiation, and how the parties seek to exploit the process is really up to them. This flexibility, and universality, does not mean that the process is so open-ended as to give rise to uncertainty as to how the mediation will take place. On the contrary, the process is sufficiently predictable as to provide a good advocate with line-of-sight to opportunities that will help lead negotiations towards a positive outcome.

From a party's perspective, mediation is not about 'resolving' conflict, but about **4-091** getting results. This section addresses certain considerations about the negotiation process that takes place before, during, and perhaps even after the mediation, and that parties can use to obtain the best possible outcome for themselves.

A.   PROCEDURAL FLEXIBILITY OF MEDIATION

In an international mediation, namely one involving parties from different **4-092** countries, it is common for at least one of them to be less familiar (or perhaps even unfamiliar) with any concept of mediation. But because success in mediation is measured by the ability to reach agreement, the level of familiarity with it should not advantage or disadvantage any party. A competent mediator will ensure that each side remains comfortable with the process and will not feel disadvantaged by inexperience.

Parties to an international commercial dispute can fairly anticipate the 'procedural' **4-093** steps that will be taken in the course of organising a mediation and, to a certain degree, also how it will be conducted. In practice, most mediations will follow an established route. This will present the party's advocate with various opportunities to interact with the other side and favourably influence the negotiations. If the parties have successfully cooperated in selecting the mediator and setting up the mediation, they have already taken steps in the direction of establishing a useful degree of trust with each other.

Set out below are points of organisation and procedure that become relevant as the **4-094** date of mediation approaches and then gets underway. Each is discussed in more detail below.

Checklist 4c – Opportunities for the Mediation Advocate

• Pre-mediation preparation and advocacy: obtaining settlement authority and defining settlement objectives • Position papers and 'for mediator's eyes only' memos • Strategic use of opening offers and counteroffers • Advocacy at the plenary session • Effective advocacy during caucusing sessions • Establishing direct contact with the other side • Documenting the settlement (or the agreement in principle) • Keeping settlement negotiations alive 'after' the mediation

1.   Preparation and Advocacy before the Mediation Begins: Obtaining Settlement Authority and Defining Settlement Objectives

4-095 Once a date has been set for a mediation, the parties must turn their attention to the concrete goals they wish to achieve and their strategy to attain them. The most common mistake parties make is attending a mediation only to 'hear what the other side has to say', without a clearly defined view of what the party itself hopes to accomplish.

4-096 *Settlement authority.* In preparing for a mediation, the party will want to ensure that *both* sides will have sufficient authority to resolve the dispute, and that decision makers will be at the table. A mediator will usually enquire about the settlement authority of the party representatives who will attend the mediation. In the event the mediator fails to make this enquiry on his own (which occasionally happens), a party would be wise to request this. And while it is natural to be concerned about the attendance of the other side's decision makers, parties must make sure their own side will come to the table with sufficient authority to resolve the dispute.

Question:	In our view, the other side has asserted a grossly inflated claim. How much settlement authority should we obtain?
Answer:	As much as possible. The purpose of limiting the financial authority of employees in the first place is to prevent them from exceeding it. Even the CEOs of Fortune 50 companies must operate within constraints. Thus, the question of 'how much' authority is one for which there is no easy answer, and there may be significant gaps between an amount that a

> party's representatives perceive as being required to settle a
> case and what can be realistically granted.

Parties should attempt to address any constraints on their negotiating authority in **4-097**
advance of the mediation, such as upper management or board-level approval to
agree to a certain amount. As to the amount that should be authorised, our recommendation is to obtain as much authority as possible to settle and, if there is a risk of
this being insufficient to resolve the dispute, to ensure that there are senior employees at the table who can obtain authority on short notice by calling head office.

Defining settlement objectives. Consideration of the risks and costs of resolving the **4-098**
dispute can promote moderation and lead to settlement, even when each party is
relatively optimistic about the potential outcome. Not surprisingly, as the perception of risk and cost makes arbitration or litigation appear less attractive, the desire
to obtain a reasonable settlement should increase.

'Winning' defined as achieving commercial goals. Delivering a result that is just **4-099**
better than the worst-case scenario is not how businesses operate or measure
employee performance. Commercial parties will not expect to collect every
penny claimed, or defend every claim against them to the end. But they will be
unlikely to participate in a mediation enthusiastically (if at all) unless they expect
to improve on the outcome they are likely to achieve in the event they do not
resolve their conflict – in other words, unless they think that they can achieve a
settlement that is better than what they will get in arbitration or litigation. Thus,
while parties typically seek to establish their 'bottom lines' for settlement, that is,
the point at which they find continuing the dispute to be financially more attractive
than any of the available settlement options, they will want to establish settlement
objectives that are as high as can reasonably be obtained.

Mediation case study. To illustrate this point, let us consider a hypothetical dispute **4-100**
over a modest international sales contract that provides for arbitration of any
disputes. The dispute is seen initially from the seller's point of view, which
may be that the dispute, at least on its surface, appears difficult or impossible to
settle through negotiation.

The seller's view. The seller's claim arises shortly after the buyer terminated the **4-101**
contract, allegedly for breach, and refused to pay approximately USD 1 million that
was due at the time. The seller is about to initiate arbitration for the full claim even
though it recognises that, realistically, it should expect to recover no more than
USD 700,000 because the tribunal will expect reasonable steps to have been taken
to mitigate losses. To the seller's surprise the buyer rejected the offer to settle at
USD 700,000, arguing that the seller was in breach of the contract and that this
discharged the buyer's obligation to pay the balance due and also led to some
USD 500,000 in the buyer's own additional costs. The seller now learns that the
buyer intends to pursue the USD 500,000 counterclaim in the arbitration.

4-102 The contract contains a dispute resolution clause that provides for arbitration in Geneva before three arbitrators, and there do not appear to be any irregularities in the clause itself. The buyer has accepted to attempt settlement through mediation, because both sides recognise that the costs of the arbitration could easily be disproportionate to the overall amount in dispute.

4-103 In preparing for the mediation and setting its goals and expectations, the seller must consider the probable outcome in terms of quantum of the award, cost of the arbitration, and time (how long before an award will be issued). For the sake of simplicity, we assume the award will be paid in full when it is rendered, with no challenge and no enforcement proceedings needed. Thus, the seller first estimates that the cost of this particular arbitration will be approximately USD 240,000, consisting of USD 100,000 in arbitrators' fees, USD 100,000 in legal fees, and USD 40,000 in expert fees. Second, the seller evaluates in its estimate whether it can expect to recover a portion of these costs or be held to reimburse some portion of the amounts spent by the other side.[25] Third, on the assumption the seller has completed an Early Case Assessment (ECA), (section III, Chapter 3), it may anticipate something like the following range of potential outcomes:

- *Best case*: Award value of USD 820,000, assuming victory on all issues and award rendered within a year. Although the assessment of the best possible outcome reflects the most favourable determination of the legal and factual arguments, it is a 'reasonable' best case that must also be realistic about the time and resources that will be spent on the dispute. This value is arrived at as follows:
  - *Award*: The arbitration lasts one year and the tribunal finds that the seller's claim was well founded and that there is no reduction in damages for failure to mitigate the losses. The seller is awarded USD 1 million, with an order that the buyer reimburse two thirds of the seller's legal fees and arbitrators' fees, plus interest running from the date of the award.
  - *Valuation of award*: For the seller, the present value of USD 1 million in one year is approximately USD 900,000, assuming (again, best case) that the award is actually paid upon issuance of the award. Assuming the award is paid by the other side, and the unreimbursed legal, expert, and arbitrator fees are USD 80,000, then the 'net' value of the USD 1 million is USD 820,000, that is, the USD 900,000 present value less the USD 80,000 in unreimbursed costs.

---

25. In this example, we apply the general rule in international arbitration that the prevailing party is entitled to recover some or all of the costs of prosecuting or defending the claim. For the sake of simplicity, we have used the same amount of expenses for all three case scenarios, even though they are of varying duration. In reality, we would expect that the longer the arbitration lasts, the more legal fees are likely to be incurred. We also apply a flat 10% annual discount rate to reflect the 'time value' of money to be received in the future.

- *Worst case*: Negative USD 400,000. Like the best case, the seller should be realistic as to outcome, time, and cost and consider extreme results only if they are within the realm of reasonable possibility, and not ignore the consequences of cost:
  - *Award*: The arbitration lasts three years and the tribunal rejects the seller's claim, holding that termination was justified, but also rejects the buyer's counterclaim as being unsubstantiated. The tribunal further makes an assessment against the seller of two thirds of the buyer's legal fees and arbitration costs.
  - *Valuation of award*: Here, the seller must contend with its loss, its own costs, and some portion of the buyer's costs. Assuming the buyer has incurred costs similar to the seller's, the 'net' outcome is negative USD 400,000 (the USD 240,000 the seller spent on lawyers, arbitrators, and experts, plus USD 160,000 of the other side's costs.)
- *Most likely*: USD 380,000 net present value. After full consideration of the legal issues, available evidence, and all potential risks, the seller concludes that the most likely scenario is neither of the extremes:
  - *Award*: The arbitration lasts two years, and the tribunal finds that the seller was required to mitigate its losses and awards it USD 700,000. The tribunal rejects the buyer's counterclaim and orders the buyer to pay USD 100,000 of the seller's legal fees.
  - *Valuation of the award*: Applying the same reasoning, as with the best case, the USD 700,000 after two years would be given a present value of USD 520,000, less the USD 140,000 in unreimbursed legal costs. The seller's 'net' most likely case is therefore USD 380,000, as expressed in terms of present value.

As to the probability of the different 'case' scenarios being evaluated materialising, **4-104** each contains multiple factors, some of which are independent of the others (the duration of the arbitration and the likely outcome, for example, may be completely unrelated). The most likely case, however, is the one the party views as having at least a 50% chance of being achieved.

Based on a realistic assessment of probable outcomes and cost, obtaining less than **4-105** half of its USD 1 million claim in settlement could be considered a positive outcome for the seller, as any amount over USD 380,000 is in present terms better than what the seller should expect to obtain in arbitration under the 'most likely' scenario.

The same dispute as seen by the buyer. The negotiation gets more interesting if, like **4-106** a mediator, the seller could also see it from the buyer's point of view. Let us suppose the buyer has conducted a similar analysis but has reached a different conclusion about the likely outcome, which is often the case. The buyer believes the facts and law generally favour its position. Indeed, the buyer has concluded that the 'most likely' scenario is not an adverse decision of USD 700,000. In the buyer's view, USD 700,000 would be the *worst* case, as it believes the seller's claim is inflated and also ignores its obligation to mitigate losses. The buyer believes the most likely outcome to be that the seller will recover USD 250,000 after two years of arbitration.[26] Of course, the buyer, too, knows it will incur the costs of arbitration. It expects to spend USD 240,000 in arbitration and legal fees to defend the claim and does not expect to be able to recover these costs from the seller. In short, the buyer expects the financial impact of the litigation to be negative USD 490,000 (USD 250,000 in adverse determination plus USD 240,000 in litigation costs). That is less than half the USD 1 million claimed by the seller, and enough of a reason to persist with a strong defence to the USD 1 million claim.

4-107 *Overlapping versus non-overlapping settlement positions.* Despite opposing views held by the seller and buyer with respect to the merits of each side's case, they are already in what a negotiator would call a zone of possible agreement even without any major reassessment of relative strengths and weaknesses: the seller considers the net most likely outcome of arbitration to be a collection by it of USD 380,000, and the buyer considers the likely outcome to be a payment by it of USD 490,000. A negotiator might refer to this as a *positive* zone of possible agreement, with the only question being where within the range the parties will end up settling, or whether the capacities of their negotiators will succeed in narrowing or widening the range.

4-108 This can be contrasted with non-overlapping positions, that is, a negative zone of possible agreement. This is a case where the parties have assessed the probable outcomes and their willingness or desire to settle does not overlap. For example, the seller remains firmly of the view that it should accept nothing less than USD 700,000 and the buyer remains convinced that it should pay nothing. In such cases, the role of the advocates (with the assistance of a mediator) is to close the distance in each side's respective valuations of the case. All experienced litigators encounter cases that they believe should easily settle but do not. One possible reason for the failure of settlement in such cases is that, with each side insisting on its opening demand, they may have no way of knowing what the real distance between them is. Overcoming this gap in information is one of the things that makes mediation so attractive.

4-109 *Other risks, costs, and opportunities impacting on settlement valuations.* The hypothetical case above is an oversimplification of most disputes that arise out of international commercial transactions in which arbitration is the agreed method of binding dispute resolution. A good mediator will usually help the party advocates by bringing several other factors into consideration that will encourage parties to settle. These include additional costs and also potential opportunities.

4-110 *Considerations of award challenge and enforcement risk.* As we explain elsewhere in this book, obtaining an international arbitration award is only part

---

26. Although the same present value discounting analysis could be applied, we have chosen not to do so on the assumption that the seller will be required to set a reserve on its financial statements for the full amount of any liability that is deemed to be likely.

of the battle: awards can be challenged and, if not paid, must be enforced.[27] The possibility of both challenge and enforcement proceedings presents claimants with new rounds of risk, and additional cost for both the claimant and respondent. Parties to a potential international arbitration must consider these risks (and costs) as they calculate their settlement objectives, and there is some statistical support for the proposition that that is exactly what creditors of arbitration awards do. A survey of corporate counsel reported in 2008 that some 51% said that awards do not meet with voluntary compliance. Of those who brought enforcement actions, 56% reported they had recovered less than the full value of the award. Of those who negotiated a payment, 46% reported that they accepted less than half the amount of the award.[28] While these numbers may represent no more than the small sample group interviewed for this particular survey, the respondents consistently stated that they substantially devalued the amount of arbitration awards after they had been rendered.

Consideration of other costs of conflict. In most cases there will be other costs for **4-111** an ongoing business that go well beyond the straightforward evaluation of potential outcome and out-of-pocket expenditures. An international arbitration can make significant demands on a party's human resources, that is, the people who will be spending time in conference rooms with lawyers reviewing old documents instead of negotiating and implementing new contracts. Yet none of the cases presented above – best, worst, or most likely – can reasonably predict what these other costs will be: the lost time of employees, distraction for the business, or the lost opportunities from a soured relationship with the opposing party. Consideration of these factors may further narrow the true distance that separates the parties' formal positions.

Caution when proposing new commercial opportunities. While the possibility of **4-112** new contracts, projects, discounts, and so on may help parties close the gap between them, these should always be evaluated (and authorised, if necessary) before negotiations are underway. For example, if a party is considering whether it would accept a discount on new contracts in complete or partial payment of a settlement amount, how much of a discount would be acceptable, in what form, and would the discounts expire if not used within a fixed period of time? Answering these questions would require the party to spend some time considering its future purchasing needs, so that it could structure any concessions made in settlement to maximise any opportunities. Giving advance thought can also avoid any subsequent misunderstanding as to what the parties have agreed.

---

27. Chapter 6, *After the Arbitration.*
28. International Arbitration: Corporate Attitudes and Practices 2008, Executive Summary at 2.

Not that this ever really happens: consequences of failure to define key terms	The CEOs of the two companies had agreed to settle their dispute with a 'credit' of USD 5 million for goods and services, leaving their commercial teams to define what the credit was and how it would be used by the buyer in the future. Subsequently, the seller's commercial team proposed that the credit be in the form of a discount of 20% over list prices, as an enticement to purchase future goods and services. The buyer's team said they had understood the concept of a credit to apply differently, and that it would be for 100% of the cost of new purchases. No agreement about the details of the CEOs' agreement was reached, and the parties were soon back in arbitration.

4-113 *Applying future discounts as settlement value.* When parties are able to anticipate a future commercial relationship, there may be means of structuring a settlement so that it creates value for both sides simultaneously. For example, in a dispute between a seller and a buyer, the seller might decide to offer a 10% discount on future purchases up to a total purchased amount of USD 10 million. This would be, for the buyer, USD 1 million in total discount value. Assuming this value is genuine for the buyer, it would lead to a result that is not only better than the buyer's 'most likely' litigation or arbitration estimate, but actually beats its best-case estimate by a substantial margin. For the seller, it is possible that money may actually be made from this dispute, in addition to preserving or enhancing an important commercial relationship. If the seller's profit margin is over 10%, then it will earn money directly from its settlement 'payment' (and presumably more after that, having improved its commercial relationship with the buyer).

2.   Position Papers and 'For Mediator's Eyes Only' Memoranda

4-114 It is common practice in mediation for parties to exchange short position papers with each other and the mediator in advance of the mediation. From a party's perspective, it can be helpful to think of this as simply a starting point for negotiation. The position paper does exactly what the name implies: it sets out the party's position and, in broad terms, the reasons for which the position has been adopted.

4-115 *Position paper: length and contents.* With the caveat that the length of a position paper should be appropriate for each case, we use 'short' to mean genuinely short: three to five pages is common; rarely will a position paper need to run over twenty pages. Parties can also attach copies of any key documents, according to the mediator's preference or their own. The same documents can also be brought to the mediation if they would be helpful to explain and support a position.

If certain documents would assist the mediator in understanding the dispute, or in focusing the attention of the other party on something they may have previously overlooked, parties should also feel free to provide them.

'For mediator's eyes only' memoranda. Another way to bring a mediator quickly **4-116** up to speed on a dispute is to provide a private memo – for mediator's eyes only – that sets out the obstacles to resolution and any 'hot button' issues. This private information is sometimes sought by mediators prior to mediation, as it is a practice that can help a party think about its strategy and the difficulties it faces in reaching agreement with the other party. If the mediator does not request this document, a party can offer to provide it confidentially to the mediator.

Other presentation materials. In addition to position papers, parties may also want **4-117** to bring presentations that they will deliver at the start of the mediation, to focus immediate attention on any points that are likely to be key levers in causing the other side to reassess its risk in the dispute. To avoid surprise at the mediation, it is good practice for parties to inform the other side of their intention to make such a presentation. There is usually no requirement to provide presentation materials in advance of the mediation (but doing so may well be conducive to reaching a settlement).

3.   **Strategic Use of Opening Offers and Counteroffers**

Offers and counteroffers are an unavoidable part of any negotiation, and especially **4-118** a mediation. Parties will often ask themselves whether to be the first to open, how much of an offer to make, and when to make it. Parties should expect that the mediator will ask for an offer to be put on the table and that this could be early in the mediation. If a party comes to a negotiation with only two numbers in mind, they should be its ideal end point and where it intends to start:

Settlement goal:	**USD X**
Opening offer or counteroffer:	**USD Y**

For a successful party at a mediation, what falls between these two numbers is a strategy and a willingness to negotiate. In practical and somewhat more blunt terms, opening offers and counters are merely a means to start exploring what the other party's bottom line really is, and potentially lowering it further (or raising it, if payment is demanded).

Using and mitigating the anchoring effect. In the art of offers and counteroffers, **4-119** parties will often want to be the first to put money on the table in order to start discussions on their terms. All negotiations are susceptible to what psychologists term the 'anchoring effect', which we introduced earlier in this book and is the ability to shift the other side's expectations of potential outcomes by putting an initial offer on the table, usually one that is extremely favourable to the side making it. While unlikely to be accepted, an extreme opening offer can have the effect of causing the opposing party to redraw the line at which it believes a reasonable settlement can be achieved. It is particularly effective where both sides recognise a high degree of uncertainty as to the potential outcomes if they do not settle. Yet many parties fail to see the opening offer as an opportunity because they believe it is 'for the other side' to do so, generally without any regard for the potential tactical advantage being given away. Given the uncertainties inherent in most arbitrations and litigations, the common refrain of 'let's wait and see first what the other side puts on the table' will be the wrong approach in the majority of cases.

Not that this ever really happens: tradition or just a missed opportunity	The parties' dispute was in connection with a construction project, with dozens of claims and counterclaims creating, on their face, potential outcomes of USD 20 million to one side or the other (i.e., a USD 40 million negotiation range). The respondent's counsel advised its client that, 'it is traditional for the claimant to make the first offer'. While it is uncertain exactly which 'tradition' this could have been (perhaps in the counsel's law firm), it was not based on a consideration of effective negotiation strategy. A party would be unwise to surrender so easily a potentially strong negotiation advantage simply because one or another member of the team advances an argument that it is 'for the other side' to make the first offer.

4-120 *Countering the anchoring effect.* The antidote, or response, to an opening offer is not to compromise one's own strategy. Generally, a party will want to adhere to its overall objectives and counter in the range of what it had originally planned to make as its own initial opening offer.

4.   Advocacy at the Plenary Session

4-121 Parties inexperienced in mediation may be inclined to associate it with its cousin in private dispute resolution, arbitration. A common example of this is when a party's counsel sends the mediator the equivalent of an arbitration statement of claim or defence – a lengthy submission together with volumes of documentary attachments supporting its arguments. There is no downside for the party that does this, except that the additional effort does not add as much value as the party believes it will.

4-122 *Persuading the other side, not the mediator.* Parties (and particularly their counsel) will often attempt to persuade the mediator of the correctness of their position on a point of law or fact. For example, counsel may decide to summarise the party's arguments in a statement to the mediator. While this may be a consequence of deferring to the mediator as a figure of authority in the room, convincing the mediator may lead to the purest of Pyrrhic victories unless the same arguments also convince the other side.

Mediation is not arbitration, and presentations on key points are usually measured **4-123** in minutes (as in twenty or thirty minutes) rather than days, so a party should not expect to have the opportunity to fully brief its arguments and submit all evidence in support of its position. At the same time, however, the party should also not feel constrained about how it chooses to persuade the other side. Common approaches include the following:

- *PowerPoint presentations.* Although business leaders increasingly complain about overuse of PowerPoint, it remains a mode by which business managers communicate with each other. Often, a presentation given by one of the party's representatives can be an effective way of introducing one side's perspective to the other side's management team. In most cases, such presentations will be far more effective if the lawyers remain silent and allow the business people to communicate directly with the other side.
- *Key documents.* If a party believes that being able to focus on a small number of key documents would be an effective way of persuading the other party, then it should plan for this by bringing a sufficient number of copies to the mediation. In many cases, the mediator may ask for key documents to be provided in advance of the mediation.
- *Key witnesses.* Because mediation is not arbitration, there will be no need or expectation for witnesses to 'testify'. However, it can be helpful to have a particular witness at the mediation, whether to assist the party's other representatives to understand and respond to information learned from the other side, or to informally recount his version of events. There is generally no downside to having witnesses attend a mediation other than the cost of getting them there, although it is always a good idea to spend time with witnesses beforehand to fully understand what they will say and how they will express it. What is said in the course of a mediation is confidential and cannot be used by the opposing party in arbitration if the parties fail to settle.

Not that this ever really happens: strategic use of witnesses at mediation	In a dispute involving one of the authors, a potential key witness would have been the respondent's project director, who had left the respondent's employment under less than happy circumstances. Unfortunately for the claimant, while the project director expressed a willingness to help the parties settle, he did not want to be involved in an arbitration, and it was doubtful either party could have compelled him to testify. At the request of the claimant, however, he agreed to attend a settlement meeting with the parties, where he sat with the claimant's team. Although in private he had roundly criticised the

> management of his former employer, which he blamed as the cause of all project problems, he provided no such input at the meeting. Rather, his only comment was that 'perhaps both sides could have done a better job on this project'. Still, his presence and neutral comment was enough to provoke a settlement in which the respondent agreed to pay a substantial portion of the claim.

5. Effective Advocacy during Caucusing Sessions

4-124 *Borrowing the mediator's powers.* A common impediment to resolution in almost all dispute negotiations is the psychological concept, or heuristic, called 'reactive devaluation'. In simple terms, the concept is often expressed as, 'if the idea comes from you, then it must be bad'. This can lead parties to reject offers made by the other side that they would otherwise view as reasonable and even acceptable. A way to overcome this is to 'borrow the mediator's powers', to use the apt terminology of a leading US mediator, Dwight Golann.[29] If a party believes its offer is a genuinely reasonable one that could be accepted (rather than discounted as further party positioning), the party can ask the mediator to convey the offer to the other side as his own suggestion, or to ask the other side whether a settlement would be possible at the proposed number.

4-125 *Asking the mediator to provide an evaluation of legal or factual issues in dispute.* It is common for parties to have such starkly contrasting valuations of the dispute that settlement is not possible on the basis of negotiation alone, even when facilitated by a skilled mediator. To overcome this roadblock, many mediators will be willing to evaluate one or more key legal or factual issues in the dispute in an attempt to predict the likely arbitration outcome. (We have noted already that there is in fact an entire breed of mediators, called 'evaluative mediators', whose approach consists chiefly of helping parties settle by predicting the potential outcomes if they do not). A mediator should only do this, however, if both parties agree that it is appropriate. Before agreeing to an evaluation, parties would be wise to give consideration to the following issues:

- *Mediator's competence and credibility to evaluate the issue.* In an international business dispute it is entirely possible that the mediator will lack the credentials or confidence to issue even a non-binding advisory opinion on a disputed point.
- *Potential to delay the mediation.* Even when the mediator may be willing to provide, and capable of providing, an evaluation of the disputed issue, doing so may require additional time and briefing by the parties. This may delay

---

29. Prof. Golann explains this technique in his audio interview, 'How to Borrow a Mediator's Powers', which can be accessed as IDN 16 in the archives of the International Dispute Negotiation podcast at <www.cpradr.org>.

the mediation (and may not be practicable where parties and their counsel have arrived from different countries).
- *Information not conducive to settlement.* There is truth to the adage that a mediator should not 'tell parties at 9 am what they should learn at 5 pm'. Injecting an evaluative component too early in the mediation can easily leave one party delighted and the other unhappy with the prediction. Instead of bringing them closer together, an evaluation provided too early in the mediation can have the opposite effect, with one party becoming rooted in its (now supported) position and the other wanting to contest the evaluation as wrong. As described in an earlier example, one of the authors recalls a dispute in which an inexperienced mediator started the mediation by advising the parties that he had 'read the papers, understood the arguments, and this is how' he saw the dispute. By doing so, he instantly lost his appearance of neutrality with the 'losing' party, who subsequently disengaged from the mediation process and initiated an arbitration.
- *Risk of a murky or unclear evaluation.* When a mediator does undertake to provide an evaluation at an appropriate time, parties should brace themselves for a result that may not have the clarity they would expect from an arbitral tribunal or court. Mediators do not have the level of information about a dispute that the parties will make available to arbitrators over time. Hearing that the mediator sees the argument as 60/40 may be unsettling for the party that, for example, is operating under the belief that it is advancing a watertight claim or defence, such as a contractual clause limiting its total liability, and cannot imagine a 40% chance of losing.

6. Establishing Direct Contact with the Other Side

Once parties are immersed in a dispute, they will often have little opportunity **4-126** to communicate directly with each other, and any such communications will almost always be under the watchful eye of lawyers. Mediation provides an opportunity to bypass some of the formalities and facilitate candid discussion.

Informal one-on-one discussions. Discussion between the principals may encour- **4-127** age frank exchanges and a degree of reciprocal concession that may be more difficult to achieve when meeting in larger groups of people. Where informal one-on-one discussions would be beneficial, parties should feel free to seek out those opportunities. This can take place at coffee breaks, over lunch (there is no rule that says the principals must eat with their teams), or following an impromptu request for a one-on-one discussion. These meetings can be particularly effective when the negotiations have stalled and further progress appears difficult to achieve.

Not that this ever really happens: just go talk to them	The in-house course on informal dispute resolution taught by one of the authors presents teams of company employees the opportunity to practice their negotiation skills in a highly charged international project dispute. No matter where on the globe the course is taught, there almost always comes a moment when one of the negotiating teams will complain to the instructor that negotiations are deadlocked because the other team has taken extreme positions and/or is not negotiating in good faith. The instructor's response is, 'instead of discussing in teams, why don't you go meet with one of their managers one on one?' Although the advice is generally met with scepticism, the negotiators move past their deadlock and generate progress towards a settlement.

7.   Documenting the Settlement

4-128 Having spent months or even years contesting each factual and legal point in dispute, parties can be forgiven for showing surprise when, after nine or ten hours of mediation, they reach agreement on all major points of a settlement. The logical next step, of course, is to convert their agreement to a writing. But after a full day of mediation, they may not have the inclination to spend additional time reducing their deal points to specific written terms. The risk of leaving the written settlement to another day is that the parties may no longer have the momentum from their mediation and may drift apart again. But the problem with signing a full settlement at the mediation is that the parties may simply not have the time or energy necessary to do a capable job of drafting. The challenge is to strike the right balance, so as to leave the mediation with a writing that reflects what the parties actually agreed.

4-129 *Having a draft settlement at the mediation.* Some mediators recommend that parties come to the mediation with a draft settlement agreement in hand, leaving only the payment amount and terms to be completed. There is no doubt wisdom in this. Even if the document is never used, having prepared it will help the party focus on any particularly thorny issues that may need to be addressed during the negotiations.

4-130 *Points of agreement.* If the settlement complex, or if the parties simply do not have the inclination to spend time drafting or reviewing the terms, a simple term sheet of what has been agreed may be sufficient for the purpose of generating the full settlement document in short order. Many mediators will be careful to review each point of agreement together with the parties to ensure no doubts or ambiguities remain.

8.   **Concluding without Settlement**
                 but Leaving the Door Open

Question:	When does the mediation end?
Answer:	Theoretically, parties will expect the mediation to 'end' at some point at the time and place where it has been physically scheduled, whether at the point at which a settlement has been reached, at the end of the day when one of them must depart, or when the mediator declares the session concluded without success. It is probably more the rule than the exception that mediations scheduled to end at 5pm will instead continue beyond that point, into the evening and sometimes even the early morning hours. When the parties' parting positions are within reasonable distance of each other, a mediator may continue to work with the parties for days and even weeks after the scheduled mediation session itself has concluded.

In practical terms, a party should be willing to conclude a mediation when it has **4-131** reasonably decided that the potential benefits are not sufficient to justify the time and cost of continued participation. It is rare for this point to be reached during a scheduled mediation itself. Some mediations never formally 'end' at all, as a mediator who believes a settlement can still be achieved may continue the process of facilitating the parties' exchange of information and settlement efforts for weeks or months after the formal session has concluded. In our experience, parties welcome this approach and should generally keep communications open after a failed mediation session, including through the mediator.

Not that this ever really happens: brokering a settlement weeks after the mediation 'ended'	At the mediation, the claimant had finally lowered its demand from GBP 5 million to GBP 2.5 million, and the respondent had increased its offer from GBP 800,000 to GBP 1.5 million. Both parties informed the other that they were at their bottom line, that no further movement was possible, and the mediation concluded with a GBP 1 million difference in settlement positions. In private sessions with each party, however, the mediator had learned that each side remained willing to reduce or increase their offers if there was a guarantee of settlement. They were in reality GBP 550,000 apart instead of the GBP 1 million expressed by their formal offers. In the two weeks following the mediation, the mediator kept in contact with the parties and their counsel and eventually brokered a settlement at GBP 2.1 million.

B.   Common Pitfalls for Advocates in a Mediation

4-132 There are a number of tactical mistakes that an advocate in a mediation can make that, while not fatal in any sense from a procedural point of view, can result in a party failing to take advantage of the various negotiation opportunities that mediation presents. Below are common mistakes parties make in mediation, drawn from the points discussed above.

Checklist 4d – Common Advocacy Mistakes in an International Mediation

- Coming to the mediation to 'hear what the other side has to say' instead of to achieve a defined objective
- Treating the mediation as an arbitration hearing
- Attempting to persuade the mediator instead of the other side
- Overlooking potential advantages of being the first to make an offer, and making a counteroffer that is reactive rather than well-considered
- Failing to use the mediator effectively to convey offers

Chapter Five

The Conduct of the Arbitration

Introduction. In this chapter, we look at the different issues that arise and steps that **5-001** are taken in a typical international arbitration. One immediate obstacle is the difficulty in pinning down exactly what a typical arbitration is. We have described earlier how there is a growing practice of 'transnational', delocalised, and harmonised international arbitration, involving specialist arbitrators and arbitration lawyers. But even within that community it is not easy to generalise as to how an arbitration will proceed, as there are numerous variables – the parties, their lawyers, the institution, the arbitrators, the nature of the dispute – each of which will influence the conduct of the case. Alongside that group of 'truly international' arbitrations, there are as many or perhaps more 'local' international arbitrations, staffed by arbitrators and lawyers who are more familiar with national courts or domestic arbitration practice, and who therefore follow procedures that resemble the local practice more than any 'transnational' arbitration-specific procedures.

Movement towards 'transnational' procedures. We observe a movement towards **5-002** the transnational version of international arbitration and away from the local model. We believe this stems in part from a growing bar of international dispute resolution professionals familiar with transnational practices, and even more significantly from the expectations of international contracting parties: when they contract out of local court litigation by choosing arbitration, they don't expect to find themselves in a private proceeding that simply replicates what they would have experienced in the local court. Instead they have come to expect a method of dispute resolution that is not attached to any one legal system or culture, that reflects the international nature of the parties' relationship, and that is adapted to resolving disputes arising out of that international relationship. This chapter focuses on this transnational version of international arbitration, although we should emphasise once more that international arbitration can take on a very different, localised complexion.[1]

5-003 *Four phases of a typical international arbitration.* In this chapter, we divide a typical international arbitration into four phases: a preliminary phase, from the commencement of the case until the tribunal is constituted; a written phase, when parties put in their written evidence and submissions; a hearing phase, when the parties present the evidence of their witnesses and experts, and their own submissions, orally before the tribunal; and an award phase, when the arbitrators deliberate and then write and issue their award.

5-004 *Duration of a typical international arbitration.* How long will a typical arbitration last? This is not an easy question to answer; it will depend on a number of factors, and especially the extent to which the parties agree on a timeframe. If they do agree, and it is reasonable, the arbitrators will usually complete the arbitration within the allotted time. Other important factors influencing the duration of an arbitration include the number of arbitrators, their availability and that of the parties' lawyers, the size and complexity of the dispute, the institutional or other rules that apply, and most importantly the level of cooperation of the parties. In our experience, an international arbitration will usually take between one and two years from initial filing of the case to award. An ICC, ICDR or SIAC case before a sole arbitrator is more likely to be near or below the one-year mark than a case before three arbitrators before the same institutions. An ICSID arbitration, for a variety of reasons linked to the unique nature of investment disputes, can frequently take three or four years or more.

Question:	How long will the arbitration take?
Answer:	Although many institutions publish statistics on the average duration of their arbitrations, these can sometimes resemble the claims used by airline companies for their on-time arrivals: although the airline claims to deliver 99% of its passengers to their destinations on time, somehow your flight is always the one that gets delayed. In the case of international arbitration, the duration depends – first and foremost – on two factors: how cooperative the parties are, and who the arbitrators are. The duration can also be influenced by the complexity of the case, the lawyers involved, and the institution.

---

1. Whether the arbitration has a transnational or local complexion is often within the control of the disputing parties, through their choice of counsel and arbitrators. Whether or not a party should press for one variety of international arbitration or another in any given case will depend on the nature of the party's case, the identity of the opponent, and cost considerations, among other factors. *Introduction* and Ch. 3, *When the Dispute Arises.*

Example 5a – Time Line for a Typical ICC Arbitration

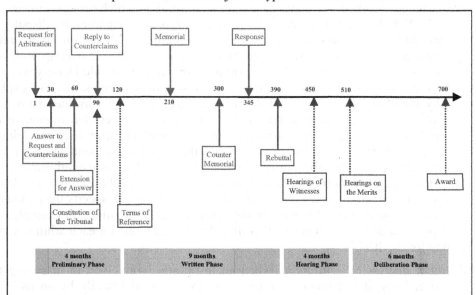

I.   THE PRELIMINARY PHASE

A.   COMMENCING THE ARBITRATION: THE REQUEST FOR ARBITRATION

Introduction. A party who wants to bring a claim to arbitration must submit (or 'file', **5-005** or even 'serve' in common law court parlance) a document requesting arbitration. This document is known as a 'Request for Arbitration' in, for example, ICC and LCIA arbitration, where the claimant must send the Request for Arbitration to the ICC in Paris or the LCIA in London, respectively. In SIAC arbitration and arbitration under the UNCITRAL Rules, the claimant submits a 'Notice of Arbitration', respectively to the SIAC in Singapore and directly to the other party.

Method of delivery of a request. Arbitration rules will specify how the request for **5-006** arbitration is to be delivered to the institution or the opposing party,[2] this is commonly by courier or hand delivery, against written acknowledgment of receipt, and with no need to follow the rules governing service of process in court litigation. That said, this is one area where it may be helpful to consider what will happen at the end of the arbitration. If the ability to enforce an award against the other party in a given country is important, then a party may want to check with counsel in that country whether the domestic litigation service procedures of that country need to be followed for an award to be enforceable.

---

2. See, e.g., Art. 4 of the LCIA Rules.

5-007 *Content of a request.* The arbitration rules will specify the nature and content of the document by which the claimant starts the arbitration, which for convenience we will call the Request. Usually the Request will introduce the parties, the dispute, the claimant's claims, and the relief it seeks. The claimant will base this on its initial investigation and preparation work which may consist of - or overlap with an - Earth Case Assessment (ECA).[3] Importantly, the Request should identify the arbitration agreement on the basis of which the arbitration has been started and explain why the claimant's claims fall within that agreement and why the claimant is entitled to raise its claims, against the opponents it has elected to sue, in the arbitration. Because arbitration requires the consent of all parties to it, the claimant can only bring to a given arbitration claims that it and the respondent have previously agreed (in their arbitration agreement) to refer to that form of arbitration. It is common practice for the Request to reproduce the full text of the arbitration clause, and to attach the entire contract as an exhibit.[4] The rules will specify the number of copies of the Request that must be delivered: in ICC arbitration, for example, one copy is needed for each party other than the claimant, one for each arbitrator, and one for the ICC.[5]

5-008 *Initial queries by institution.* When an institution is involved in managing the proceedings, it is common for questions to be raised (usually by an assigned case manager) in the initial correspondence with the parties regarding particular or unusual features of the dispute clause. So, for example, if the dispute clause requires the appointment of arbitrators within ten days of notification of the Request, but the institution's rules specify a period of twenty days, the institution may require the parties to comment on the significance of the different time periods.[6]

5-009 *Nomination of arbitrators in a request.* The Request will also address the constitution of the tribunal. This will probably mean, in the case of a three-member tribunal, that the claimant nominates an arbitrator in the Request.[7]

5-010 *Documentary evidence.* There is not usually a requirement that the claimant submit at this stage any documentary evidence in support of its case, although the claimant would be well advised to include a copy of the principal documents (including, as noted above, the contract containing the arbitration agreement on the basis of which it has commenced the arbitration). It may also be sensible, even if there is no specific requirement to this effect in the relevant rules or arbitration law, for

---

3. Chapter 3, *When the Dispute Arises.*
4. For a sample form of request in an ICC arbitration, see Appendix 7.
5. See Art. 3(1) of the ICC Rules.
6. As we note in Ch. 1, this can be avoided when drafting a dispute resolution clause simply by incorporating the institution's recommended language, which is always short and simple. The apparent advantages of creative drafting of procedures can often backfire by creating complications at the outset of a dispute.
7. See, e.g., Art. 4(3) of the ICC Rules.

the claimant to supply with the Request a power of attorney showing that its counsel or other representative is properly authorised to start the arbitration.

Advance on costs. There is, in institutional arbitration, invariably a requirement **5-011** that the claimant send with its Request an initial non-refundable advance payment of the costs of arbitration. There is no standard amount: in ICC arbitration at the time of writing, the initial deposit is USD 2,500 whereas in ICSID arbitration it is USD 25,000.

How comprehensive should a request be? In most international arbitrations the **5-012** Request is a relatively short, introductory document (sometimes no more than two pages, and usually less than twenty pages), containing relatively little argument or, as noted earlier, evidence. Its purpose is to start the arbitration, to ensure the opponent is notified that the arbitration has started, to explain why the claims are properly referred to arbitration, and to allow an appropriate tribunal to be constituted and a suitable procedural calendar (and terms of reference in ICC arbitration) to be drawn up. The Request is not intended as the claimant's opportunity to fully argue and prove its case in writing – the claimant will have that opportunity once the tribunal is constituted. The claimant may also wish to keep the Request short for tactical reasons: in order, for instance, to reduce its own preparation time and start the proceeding sooner. Or it may wish to avoid revealing too much of its case and its proof to the opponent at an early stage, thereby reducing the respondent's preparation time and perhaps getting it to commit to a position that is helpful for the claimant and to which it would not have committed had it previously seen the claimant's full case.

Benefits of a comprehensive request. There may also be advantages to more fully **5-013** articulating one's case at the inception of the proceeding. For example, the claimant may want to impress the tribunal or the opponent with a full, argued written pleading as its Request, accompanied by copious documentary evidence and legal authorities.

Disadvantages of a skeletal request. Conversely, the submission of a mere 'notice' **5-014** form of a request, with only a skeletal summary of the facts and no documentary support, may not put the tribunal or opposing party in a position to fully appreciate the seriousness of the claims. The risk is that by submitting a skeletal request, the claimant leaves the door open to the respondent to make a stronger impression through the submission of a comprehensive Answer and Counterclaim (discussed below).

Statement of claim submitted with notice of arbitration. The ICDR Rules require **5-015** the submission of the Statement of Claim with the Notice of Arbitration.[8] The UNCITRAL Rules and the SIAC Rules contemplate, but do not require, the

---

8. See Art. 2(3) of the ICDR Rules. Note though that the required content of the Statement of Claim in ICDR arbitration is similar to that of the Request for Arbitration in, e.g., ICC arbitration.

submission of the Statement of Claim (or Statement of Case) together with the Notice of Arbitration.[9] Submitting both the Notice of Arbitration and the Statement of Claim together at the outset of an arbitration can lead to time savings, as by having no separate submission of the Statement of Claim one of the more important procedural steps disappears. Combining Notice of Arbitration and Statement of Claim may also put the respondent under pressure, as it may have to file its defence sooner than would have been the case had the claimant submitted a separate Statement of Claim after the constitution of the tribunal.

5-016 *Consequences of a non-compliant request.* What if a Request does not comply with the different conditions imposed by the applicable rules? The rules and arbitration statutes do not deal with this question, but it seems that in practice there is effectively no penalty if the Request has actually been received by the institution; the institution will simply invite the claimant to rectify any non-compliance and will not reject the Request (which might cause the claimant significant prejudice if any contractual or legal time periods for submission of the Request have expired by that time).[10] In contrast, in ad hoc proceedings there is a risk the arbitration or the constitution of a tribunal may be delayed or even deemed a nullity if the formal requirements of the procedural law of the place of arbitration are not complied with. One example of this is the requirement of Italian procedural law that the Request specify the period of twenty days within which the respondent must nominate an arbitrator.[11] Failure to do so may provide a defaulting party with additional time to make their nomination.

5-017 *Determination of date of commencement.* The actual date of the commencement of the arbitration varies according to the agreement of the parties (which will usually incorporate arbitration rules directly addressing the issue). The ICC Rules, for example, stipulate that the arbitration is deemed to commence for all purposes on the date when the ICC Secretariat receives the Request for Arbitration.[12] In contrast, an ICSID arbitration is deemed to have been 'instituted' on the date of registration of the Request by ICSID's Secretariat.[13] This can be many months after ICSID's receipt of the Request.[14]

5-018 *Relevance of date of commencement.* The date of commencement of the arbitration may be important for a number of reasons, including because it is likely to stop (or 'toll') the running of contractual or legal time periods within which arbitration must be commenced. For example, a contract may stipulate that any arbitration

---

9. See Art. 3(4)(c), Art. 18 of the UNCITRAL Rules, Art. 3(2)(c) and Art. 16.3 of the SIAC Rules.
10. See, regarding ICC arbitration, Y. Derains & E.A. Schwartz, *A Guide to the ICC Rules of Arbitration*, 2nd edn (The Netherlands: Kluwer Law International, 2005), 51–53.
11. See Art. 1810 of the Italian Code of Civil Procedure provides a fixed time period for the respondent to appoint a co-arbitrator (twenty days), after which the claimant can request the relevant court to make the appointment.
12. See Art. 4(2) of the ICC Rules.
13. See ICSID Institution Rule 6(2).
14. Chapter 7, *ICSID and Investment Treaty Arbitration*.

must be brought within a given number of days from a specific start date, failing which the party loses its right to refer the matter to arbitration.[15] These sorts of provisions are likely to be valid, although the English Arbitration Act, for one, allows a court to extend such a time period on two grounds: (a) if the circumstances were outside the reasonable contemplation of the parties when they agreed to the provision in question, and that it would be just to extend the time; or (b) if the conduct of one party makes it unjust to hold the other party to the strict terms of the provision in question.[16] Courts tend to take a rather restrictive approach to applications made under this section.[17]

Statutes of limitation. Independently, statutes of limitation may require a party to **5-019** bring its claim to arbitration within a certain period, failing which the cause of action or at least the remedy will be extinguished. Statutes of limitation are likely to apply in arbitration in the same way as in the courts, with municipal law addressing questions such as the date when the period starts running and the actions a party must take to stop it. One difficult issue that can arise in international arbitration is the determination of which statute of limitation applies: is it that of the law applicable to the substance of the arbitration (the 'governing law' of the contract), that of the place of the arbitration, or that of some other law? Is it an issue of procedure or substance, and is that distinction relevant? The arbitrators will generally decide these and other choice-of-law questions as a preliminary issue. The determination of which statute of limitation applies is often an interesting intellectual exercise, but may also be of critical importance in practice as limitation periods vary widely from country to country: for example, the limitation period for contractual claims is six years under English law, while it is ten under Italian law and ten or thirty years under French law, depending on the type of contract.

Who should the claimant name as parties to the arbitration? One of the more **5-020** difficult issues confronting a claimant when preparing the Request is whom the claimant should name as the other parties to the arbitration. This is important because once the Request is submitted, it is not usually open to the claimant to amend it to change the parties. The identity of the opponent may seem obvious in a contract signed by two parties: one of them will be the claimant in the arbitration, and the other will be the respondent. But even here there may be nuances: what if the parties to the contract have changed, as the result of an assignment of the contract or a merger agreed by the original counterparty? The claimant may want, and be entitled, to sue both the original counterparty and the current counterparty.

---

15. Well-known examples of this include the FIDIC model contracts: see, e.g., <www.fidic.organd>; E.C. Corbett, *FIDIC 4th – A Practical Legal Guide* (London: Sweet & Maxwell, 1991), 441.
16. See s. 12(3) of the English Arbitration Act.
17. See *Harbour & General Works Ltd v. Environment Agency, Lloyd's Rep* 1 (2000): 65, for an explanation of the limited circumstances that would justify exercise of the court's powers under s. 12(3).

5-021 *Naming a non-signatory of the arbitration agreement as respondent.* Similar issues can arise if the contract was entered into by an agent on behalf of the principal, or if it was performed by someone other than its signatory, such as an affiliate company of the signatory. Where the claimant can show that the parties in fact intended a non-signatory to be bound by the agreement, the tribunal may accept that there has been an 'extension' of the arbitration agreement to the non-signatory.[18] In order for the claimant to preserve its right to argue that this extension exists, it must name the additional party in the Request. Claimants sometimes employ these sorts of theories to sue individual executives or owners of counterparty companies, often as a tactical move to apply pressure or, when there are concerns about the financial solvency of the counterparty, to obtain access to assets that will be necessary to satisfy an award.

5-022 *Where the claimant is a non-signatory of the arbitration agreement.* The same theories may operate in the reverse direction and allow, for instance, a successor in interest of the signatory, or an agent, or a non-signatory affiliate of the signatory to commence arbitration.

5-023 *Jurisdiction objections when non-signatories are involved.* Any party other than the 'current' signatory of the arbitration agreement (or the principal if an agent signed) who is sued in arbitration is likely to object to its inclusion in the arbitration. Likewise, any party to the arbitration agreement will also protest if it is sued by a claimant who is arguably not or no longer party to the arbitration agreement. The resolution of these jurisdiction objections will make the arbitration more complex, longer, and more expensive.

Not that this ever really happens: jurisdiction over individual who signed the contract	One of the authors was involved in an ICC arbitration in Spain, in which the claimant named two respondents: the company party to a construction contract and its owner, who the claimant argued had signed the contract in his personal capacity as well as on behalf of his company. The owner objected, and the ICC remanded the issue to the tribunal, which deemed it had jurisdiction over both the owner in his individual capacity and the company on whose behalf he had signed. An award was subsequently issued against both parties, and the owner challenged its enforcement in the Spanish courts. The Spanish courts upheld the tribunal's decision on jurisdiction.[19]

---

18. As discussed below, the tribunal will generally have jurisdiction to determine its own jurisdiction, including to hear disputes involving the consent to arbitration by any of the parties named in the Request. In the event the tribunal errs in this determination by improperly exercising jurisdiction over a non-signatory, the recourse available to that party will be an action to set aside the award in the courts of the place of arbitration.
19. Judgment 632/2004 of the Audiencia Provincial of Madrid (s. 9) dated 16 Nov. 2004 (Application for Annulment of Arbitral Award 407/2003).

Multiple parties. In cases where there are several parties to the contract, it may be **5-024**
that there will be more than one claimant: multiple claimants may group together to
sue one or more respondents. This is particularly common where two or more
affiliate companies, or a consortium of independent parties, have contracted
together with one or more counterparties. To secure the full range of remedies
available, all the affiliates or parties with similar interests may need to be party to
the arbitration; the lead or representative company may well be unable to sue on
behalf of the others. The claimant may also choose to sue multiple respondents, or
may pick and choose among the other parties to the contract and only sue some of
them. While it is rare in practice for a respondent to successfully request the joinder
of a third party to the arbitral proceedings, it is not without precedent. In particular,
recent cases suggest that the ICC Court may allow a third party to be joined in the
arbitration at the respondent's request, if the third party has signed the arbitration
agreement on the basis of which the request for arbitration has been filed and the
respondent has introduced claims against the new party. These requests must be
made before constitution of the tribunal unless all parties agree to the joinder.[20]

Not that this ever really happens: joinder of a third-party respondent without claimant's consent	One of the authors was involved in LCIA Case No. UN 2401, between a European contractor claimant and a Chinese owner respondent. The case was administered by the LCIA under the UNCITRAL Rules, with a seat in London and a distinguished international tribunal chaired by a prominent English arbitrator. The respondent requested that a third-party affiliate (also a signatory to the contract) be joined to bring claims against the claimant. The claimant objected. The tribunal directed in its award that the third party should be joined to the arbitration. The Partial Award noted that the UNCITRAL Rules did not contain a provision similar to Art. 22.1(h) of the LCIA Rules, which permitted joinder with the consent of the applicant and the third party. The tribunal also noted that section 35 of the English Arbitration Act provides that the tribunal has no power, without the agreement of the parties, to order consolidation with other arbitral proceedings. But it went on to find that since the third party's claims were identical to those of the respondent and arose under the same arbitration agreement, section 35 was not applicable. The tribunal relied on the judgment of Rix J in *Charles M Willie & Co (Shipping) Ltd v. Ocean Laser Shipping Ltd and others (The 'Smaro')* (1999) *Lloyds Rep.* 1, 225–248 (noting that the arbitration at issue in that case pre-dated the Arbitration Act), and emphasised the

---

20. A.M. Whitesell & E. Silva-Romero, *Multiparty and Multicontract Arbitration: Recent ICC Experience* (Complex Arbitrations – Special Supplement 2003 ICC International Court of Arbitration Bulletin), 10–11.

> considerable cost and delay that would result should the third
> party be required to commence a separate arbitration. It per-
> mitted the third party to be joined, and the claimant did not
> challenge the Partial Award.

5-025 *Differing interests of multiple parties.* In cases where there are multiple parties on
one or both sides, specific questions emerge. For example, should all claimants or
all respondents hire the same lawyers, or should they be separately represented?
Hiring the same lawyers will almost always save money and reduce cost, and will
usually be advisable if all the parties belong to the same corporate group, in which
case their interests are likely to be closely aligned in practice. In other circumstances – where the parties are fully independent of each other, or where they are
independent but are members of a consortium or joint venture – there may well be a
case for separate legal representation. Each party, although their interests may have
been aligned when the contract was entered into, may take differing or even
conflicting positions after a dispute arises. For example, one party may want to
settle at any cost, while another is determined to fight to the bitter end. Having
separate counsel in these cases is recommended, and may be unavoidable as ethical
duties may prevent counsel from representing two clients with actually or potentially conflicting interests.

The problems of consortia and joint ventures	Parties should not assume that an existing agreement that establishes the rights and obligations of the consortium parties among themselves translates into the same or even common interests in the arbitration. For example, Party A and Party B may enter into a railway construction contract either through a common enterprise (joint venture) or consortium agreement that gives 60% of a contract to Party A for the provision of locomotives and railway technology, while 40% goes to Party B for construction of the related track works and train stations. If the owner breaches the contract by cancelling that portion relating to the construction of stations, only Party B will be directly damaged. Party A may have an obligation to pursue the arbitration, but no interest in doing so. Party B's only option may be to insist that Party A authorise it to pursue arbitration against the defaulting party, without the participation of Party A (which will likely consent so as not to expose itself to a claim that it injured Party B's interests).

5-026 *Joint defence agreements.* In cases of separate representation of co-claimants or
co-respondents, the parties should enter into a joint defence or similar agreement to
coordinate the representation of the parties and, critically, to extend legal privilege

to communications between the co-claimants and co-respondents to which privilege might not otherwise attach.

Cost sharing among multiple claimants or respondents. Regardless of whether **5-027** representation is joint or separate, multiple parties on the same side should clearly establish by written agreement how the costs of the arbitration are to be distributed among them. For example, will one of them pay all costs and seek reimbursement from its co-party, or will each pay separately? (Separate invoices may not be advisable if there is risk that one of the parties will default.) An agreement on the allocation of costs should also contemplate the possibility of losing all or a portion of the arbitration and thus becoming liable for the opposing party's legal fees and other costs. A good rule of thumb is to specify that this liability should be allocated according to each party's proportionate responsibility for the claims or counterclaims adversely decided, and not according to an existing joint venture or consortium agreement, unless the parties' claims and defences are the same or identical.

Checklist 5a – Action Items for Request for Arbitration

- Investigate facts, gather and review evidence
- Ensure client has appropriate document preservation procedures in place
- Conduct client interviews and interviews of other potential witnesses
- Identify causes of action and possible counterparties
- Identify available remedies
- Identify possible counterclaims and defences
- Identify arbitration agreement and its scope (claims and parties). Parties may not be restricted to signatories
- Investigate statute of limitations and procedural issues such as contractual time limits
- Deliver letter before action or otherwise ensure claim is substantively ripe
- Ensure any contractual pre-arbitration requirements (e.g., good faith negotiations) have been complied with
- Consider court action for provisional measures such as attachments, injunctions
- Decide who to sue
- Decide which claims to bring
- Decide what relief to seek
- Select arbitrator if rules require
- Consider the need for expert witnesses and the benefits of retaining them early to prevent the respondent from retaining them, and to assist with developing the case strategy
- Draft request for arbitration, complying with pleading requirements in applicable rules, including: identification of parties, representation of

claimant, identification of arbitration agreement, description of dispute, and claims and description of relief sought
- Exhibit arbitration agreement and other key evidence
- Have client execute power of attorney and secure necessary corporate approvals
- Prepare and deliver initial advance payment
- Deliver the Request by means and in number of copies specified in rules

B.   OTHER INITIAL WRITTEN SUBMISSIONS: ANSWER AND REPLY

5-028 *Answer not required under all rules.* Under some arbitration rules, the respondent is required to submit its own initial pleading, known in ICC arbitration as the Answer and in LCIA and SIAC arbitration as the Response. There is no provision in the UNCITRAL Rules for an initial pleading by the respondent, although there is nothing to prevent the respondent from submitting an 'answer to the notice of arbitration', which can be useful in helping the tribunal organise the proceedings. For convenience here, we refer to this initial responsive document as the Answer.

5-029 *Content of the Answer.* The Answer generally mirrors the Request, in that it is usually an introductory document outlining the respondent's position on the claimant's claims and nominating an arbitrator if a three-member tribunal is called for. If a respondent has an objection to the tribunal's jurisdiction, it should raise it at this stage, as it is likely to be held to have waived any objection if it is silent now. At a minimum, the failure to mention in the Answer any objection to jurisdiction will undermine a later objection. If the respondent has counterclaims, it is expected to introduce them in the Answer. For a sample form of an Answer in ICC arbitration, see Appendix 8.

5-030 *In which proceeding to advance counterclaims.* In the same way that a claimant may only validly submit to arbitration claims that fall within the parties' arbitration agreement, a respondent is only entitled to raise counterclaims that fall within the same arbitration agreement. However, the respondent is not obliged to raise its own claims as counterclaims in the arbitration commenced against it. It may, for tactical reasons, prefer to start a fresh arbitration as claimant and to raise its claims in that proceeding. In some systems, such as ICC arbitration, this may lead to the consolidation of the arbitrations at the request of another party,[21] which will defeat the respondent's purpose. It may in any event be difficult for the respondent to justify commencing a second arbitration when the first tribunal would have jurisdiction over its claims, and when it would clearly be more efficient for one tribunal to hear the claims of both claimant and respondent.

---

21. See Art. 4(6) of the ICC Rules.

Submission of evidence with an answer. It is generally unnecessary to submit **5-031** documentary evidence with the Answer, although it is quite common for a respondent to submit a handful of key documents at this stage. As with the Request, it is either required or recommended that the party submit with its Answer a power of attorney or other evidence showing that its counsel is authorised to represent it.

Time for submission of an answer. The time given to a respondent by arbitration rules **5-032** for its Answer is often on the short side, especially where the claimant may have been preparing its Request for weeks or months and may not have notified the respondent that it was about to start arbitration. If the respondent intends to appoint counsel and has not done so already, this is one of the first tasks it should undertake when it receives the Request.[22] It is therefore routine for respondents in ICC arbitration, for example, to be given an extension of time to file the Answer. This extension is not usually more than thirty days (the initial period for filing the Answer is thirty days after receipt of the Request). In order to prevent delay, the ICC Court will only grant an extension if the respondent has taken a position on the constitution of the tribunal and, if applicable, has nominated an arbitrator.[23] This is why another of the respondent's priorities when it receives the Request is to select an arbitrator.

Claims by respondent against a third party. While it is rare in practice for a **5-033** respondent to successfully request the joinder of a third party to the arbitration, it is not without precedent. In particular, as noted above, recent cases suggest that the ICC Court may allow a third party to be joined in the arbitration at the respondent's request, if the third party has signed the arbitration agreement on the basis of which the request for arbitration has been filed and the respondent has introduced claims against the new party. A request for joinder must be made before constitution of the tribunal unless all parties agree to the joinder.

Checklist 5b – Action Items for Answer

- Determine deadline for responding to the Request and seek extension if possible and appropriate
- If respondent disputes the existence, validity, or scope of the arbitration agreement, submit any necessary applications to the institution (e.g., an application under Article 6(2) of the ICC Rules)
- Review claims and investigate facts and evidence
- Identify defences (including jurisdiction, statute of limitations, and procedural objections)
- Identify possible counterclaims and defences
- Consider court action, anti-suit injunctions
- Consider possible third-party joinder
- Decide which initial defences to raise

---

22. Chapter 3, *When the Dispute Arises.*
23. See Art. 5(2) of the ICC Rules.

- Decide which counterclaims to bring
- Decide what relief to seek
- Select arbitrator if rules require
- Draft answer, complying with pleading requirements in applicable rules, including: identification of parties, representation of respondent, any jurisdictional objection, description of defences and counterclaims, and description of relief sought
- Exhibit any key evidence
- Have client execute power of attorney and secure necessary corporate approvals
- Deliver the Answer by means and in number of copies specified in arbitration rules

5-034 *Reply to counterclaim.* If a respondent raises counterclaims in its Answer, some arbitration rules allow the claimant to file a further initial pleading – known in ICC arbitration as a Reply – in which it responds to the counterclaims. This is usually a shorter document than the Request or the Answer, as it will not address procedural or jurisdictional issues. It is not mandatory, in ICC arbitration at least, for a claimant to submit a Reply, and many elect not to do so, waiting instead to raise their defences to the counterclaim in a more comprehensive subsequent submission.

5-035 *Steps following initial pleadings.* Once the series of initial pleadings is complete, the focus will turn to the constitution of the tribunal, which we consider below.

5-036 *Special care with initial pleadings.* While the initial pleadings may be brief and serve a relatively limited role, they do need to be drafted with special care. They are often prepared before the parties and their lawyers have a full understanding of the case and the evidence, which means there is plenty of scope for making harmful admissions and prematurely committing oneself to a particular path. Certainly, when preparing later, more comprehensive submissions, parties may want to turn back to their own initial pleadings to ensure consistency, and to the opponent's initial pleadings to look for admissions, inconsistencies, and other areas to exploit.

C.   DEFAULT PROCEEDINGS: WHEN A PARTY DOES NOT PARTICIPATE IN THE ARBITRATION

5-037 *When is a party in default?* It may be that the respondent, or occasionally a claimant, will not participate at all or any longer in the arbitration. This is known as the party 'defaulting'. It can involve a respondent completely ignoring communications from the claimant, the institution, and the tribunal and failing to present a defence. Occasionally, a defaulting party will simply inform the institution or the tribunal that it will not be appearing, and it may add that it denies the claims or make some other substantive remarks. The defaulting party may also start litigation or arbitration against the other party, or perhaps even against the tribunal, in another forum.

Consequences of a claimant's default. The consequences of default in international **5-038** arbitration will depend on whether the defaulting party is the claimant or respondent and (when it is the claimant) whether the respondent has raised counter-claims. Unlike in some court systems, in most international arbitrations the con-sequence of default by a party with claims raised against it is not the automatic entry of judgment against the defaulting party when requested by the other party. So, when a claimant defaults and there is no counterclaim, the arbitration will not necessarily end automatically. The ICC Rules, for example, provide that the arbitration will proceed if 'any of the parties refuses or fails to take part'.[25] The UNCITRAL Rules require the tribunal to issue a termination order if the claimant does not communicate its claim after having submitted the Notice of Arbitration without showing cause,[26] as does the Model Law if the claimant does not submit its statement of claim, again without showing cause.[27] If a claimant defaults and is facing counterclaims, the respondent may continue to prosecute its counterclaims, and the consequences of the default will be the same as those described below in relation to a default by the respondent.

Consequences of a respondent's default. When a respondent defaults (which is the **5-039** more common scenario), the arbitration will proceed. Any arbitrator nomination in which the respondent was to participate will be performed in accordance with the arbitration rules or law on the issue – in practice, this will mean that the institution, court, or appointing authority will substitute for the respondent.[28] The claimant will still need to prosecute its case, which may involve submission of written pleadings and evidence and appearance at a hearing. The defaulting party must be given a full or at least adequate opportunity to participate in every stage of the arbitration, and all correspondence and submissions must continue to be addressed to it and records kept of those communications. If this is not done, the resulting award may be exposed to challenge or its enforcement refused for want of due process.[29]

Tribunal playing devil's advocate. While a default of the respondent should cause **5-040** the proceedings to move relatively quickly, the claimant should not assume that it will automatically receive a favourable award by virtue of the default, nor even that the tribunal will simply take its claims and evidence at face value. In order to show that due process was applied even in the absence of the respondent's participation, the tribunal will evaluate the claims and evidence, may suggest defences that

---

25. See Art. 6(3) of the ICC Rules.
26. See Art. 28.1 of the UNCITRAL Rules.
27. See Art. 25(a) of the Model Law.
28. For example, Art. 11 of the Model Law provides that where a party fails to appoint an arbitrator, upon the request of the non-defaulting party, the arbitrator shall be appointed by the court or authority designated in the relevant arbitration law.
29. See. e.g., Art. V.1(b) of the New York Convention.

would have been raised had the respondent appeared, and may even call a hearing and examine witnesses. If the tribunal has three members, the member nominated by or on behalf of the respondent may in practice take a more active role than the others in testing the claimant's arguments and evidence.

5-041 *Defaulting on grounds of cost.* Defaulting without good cause does not typically engender admiration within the tribunal for the defaulting party and is not likely to increase a party's chances of prevailing. We would therefore not counsel respondents or claimants facing a counterclaim to default, unless they really cannot afford to participate. But even if the cost of participating is a problem, there are different ways to go about a default: rather than maintaining 'radio silence' and ignoring the tribunal, a party may instead notify the tribunal that it is defaulting and why. Also, if the party is able to afford just one submission, even if very brief, stating its position and supplying key documents in support of its case, that may be a sound investment, as it could significantly improve the defaulting party's chances of success. It is important to appreciate that a defaulting party may still succeed in defeating the claims against it, or at least in ensuring that the amount awarded is significantly less than the amount claimed.

5-042 *Defaulting for reasons other than cost.* There is rarely, in our view, any good reason for a default other than cost. One might argue that where a party objects to jurisdiction, it considers by definition that it has not agreed to be party to the arbitration and is therefore not breaching its commitments by defaulting. That may be so, but a party objecting to jurisdiction will not be serving its cause by defaulting. Not appearing may lead the arbitrators to assume jurisdiction and decide the merits, resulting in an award against the defaulting party, without hearing what may be a perfectly valid objection. A more sensible strategy will be for the respondent to participate in the arbitration, object to jurisdiction before the tribunal (which is the judge of its own jurisdiction),[30] and make it clear that its appearance is for the purposes of objecting to jurisdiction and is without prejudice to that objection. The objecting party should not be considered by the courts (in most jurisdictions, at least) or the arbitrators to have waived its objection to arbitral jurisdiction by participating in the arbitration in this way. Importantly, any costs that the objecting party incurs in paying legal or arbitrators' fees may well be recoverable from the opponent if the objection to jurisdiction succeeds.

5-043 *Default by party who is 'judgment proof'.* The most frequent defaults are by parties who feel they have nothing to lose by not appearing because they are not at risk if an award is made against them. Most commonly this will be where the party considers the chances of an award being enforced against it to be very low. This may be because all its assets are in jurisdictions where the courts are reluctant to enforce arbitral awards (especially against nationals or companies from that country), or because the party has few assets to enforce against (which may be the result of deliberately transferring them to another party to avoid enforcement),

---

30. Chapter 1, *The Elements of an International Dispute Resolution Agreement.*

or for both reasons. The defaulting party may therefore feel that the expense and effort that the arbitration would demand of it are not justified.[31]

Little reason for claimant to default. There is little reason for a claimant facing no **5-044** counterclaims to default, in the sense of abruptly ignoring the tribunal. If a claimant no longer wishes to pursue the arbitration, it may ask to withdraw its claims and request the tribunal to terminate the proceedings. Reasons a claimant may no longer wish to pursue its claims include its inability or unwillingness to continue meeting the cost of doing so, a change in its assessment of the likelihood of recovery (if, for example, the opponent files for bankruptcy), the claimant's (often misguided) impression that withdrawing claims will promote settlement, or perhaps its dissatisfaction with the tribunal. The claimant in these situations would be well advised to secure the respondent's agreement to the withdrawal, without which the respondent may seek an order of costs and an order that the claims are withdrawn with prejudice (so that they cannot be raised again in another forum). For instance, Article 32 of the Model Law prevents the tribunal from issuing a termination order upon withdrawal of the claimants' claims if the respondent objects 'and the arbitral tribunal recognises a legitimate interest on its part in obtaining a final settlement of the dispute'. Similarly, the ICDR Rules provide that if a party fails to appear or to present its case at any stage of the proceedings without showing sufficient cause, the tribunal may proceed with the arbitration and consider the evidence before it.[32]

D. EARLY DISPOSAL FOR LACK OF JURISDICTION

Introduction. Under some arbitration rules, the institution has the power to termi- **5-045** nate the arbitration if it determines that a tribunal under its auspices will clearly have no jurisdiction. The goal of these sorts of rules is to weed out at an early stage cases brought on frivolous jurisdictional grounds. The best known example of this type of mechanism is Article 6(2) of the ICC Rules, which provides that if a party – either the respondent with respect to claims or the claimant with respect to counterclaims – challenges jurisdiction, the ICC Court must be 'prima facie satisfied' that an arbitration agreement under the ICC Rules 'may exist' in order for the arbitration to proceed. If it is not so satisfied, the parties will be notified that the arbitration cannot proceed. If the ICC Court is so satisfied, any decision as to the jurisdiction of the tribunal will be taken by the tribunal itself.[33]

Submissions by parties. Although the ICC rules do not call for submissions from **5-046** the parties on this issue, the parties will routinely provide their observations, which may or may not be contained in their initial pleadings.

---

31. Chapter 3, *When the Dispute Arises*; and Ch. 6, *After the Arbitration*.
32. See Art. 23 of the ICDR Rules. See also Art. 15.8 of the LCIA Rules and ICSID Rule 42(1).
33. Chapter 1, *The Elements of an International Dispute Resolution Agreement.*

5-047 *Practice in ICC arbitration.* In practice, it is rare for the ICC Court to find that the arbitration cannot proceed. More commonly it will refer the jurisdiction objection to the tribunal for resolution, and its decision will be without prejudice to the tribunal's later determination of the objection.[34] However, the Court may find that the arbitration cannot proceed if the party has neither signed the arbitration agreement nor participated in its negotiation, execution, performance, or termination. For example, in an ICC arbitration in which one of the authors was involved, the ICC Court refused to allow the arbitration to proceed with respect to three individual respondents – officers of the corporate respondent – who had signed the arbitration agreement on behalf of the corporate respondent, presumably on the basis that they clearly did not sign the agreement in their personal capacities, but as agents or representatives of the respondent. The ICC Court does not give reasons for its decisions under Article 6(2).[35]

5-048 *ICSID practice.* A similar mechanism exists in ICSID arbitration, where the institution is required to register any request for arbitration but can refuse to do so – preventing the case from proceeding – if it decides that the dispute is 'manifestly outside' its jurisdiction.[36] ICSID's review of a claimant's request for arbitration is long and thorough, and it may involve requests for further information and evidence from the claimant as to how it believes it satisfies ICSID's stringent jurisdictional conditions. ICSID does not give reasons for its decisions to register or refuse to register a case. There is no provision for a review of ICSID's decisions concerning registration, although a decision to register a case is without prejudice to any subsequent objection to jurisdiction by a party before the arbitral tribunal.

5-049 *ICSID Rule 41.* In addition, a recently introduced ICSID provision creates an expedited mechanism that allows parties to raise preliminary objections, within thirty days of the constitution of the tribunal, on the basis that the claim is 'manifestly without legal merit'. A party must 'specify as precisely as possible the basis for the objection', after which the other party is given the right to respond.[37]

Not that this really ever happens: putting jurisdiction	In institutional arbitrations systems other than the ICC and ICSID, the institution may in practice carry out a similar gate-keeper role to that found in the rules of the ICC and ICSID. This is not always welcome. For example, in an SIAC case in which one of the authors was involved, the claimant sued not only the

---

34. See Art. 6(2) of the ICC Rules.
35. As the decisions of the ICC Court are 'administrative in nature', they are not capable of appeal, and the ICC Court need not state the grounds on which they are based (Art. 7(4) of the ICC Rules). Where the ICC Court is not satisfied prima facie that an arbitration agreement under the ICC Rules may exist, and informs the parties that the arbitration cannot take place, each party retains the right to refer the case, if necessary, to a state court for a decision on whether or not there is a binding arbitration agreement between the parties. See, Schäfer, Verbist, & Imhoos, *ICC Arbitration in Practice* (The Netherlands: Kluwer Law International, 2005), 43.
36. See Art. 36(3) of the ICSID Convention.
37. See ICSID Rule 41.

issues to the tribunal despite the institution's contrary ruling	signatory of the arbitration agreement but also its non-signatory parent, on the basis that the parties intended the non-signatory to be bound by the arbitration agreement. The SIAC refused to 'accept' the claims against the parent company, on the grounds that the parent had not signed the arbitration agreement, despite vociferous protests by the claimant that this was a matter for the tribunal, not the institution. However, the claimant then ignored the institution's position and put its claims against the parent directly before the tribunal when it had been constituted. The tribunal permitted the claimant to assert its claims against the parent and ultimately dismissed the parent's ensuing objection to jurisdiction and went on to hear the merits of those claims against the parent.

E.   APPOINTMENT OF ARBITRATORS

Appointment of arbitrators in general. It is during the preliminary phase of the **5-050** arbitration that the arbitrators are appointed and the tribunal is thus formed (or 'constituted'). This process is critically important to the conduct and outcome of the arbitration, as it involves the parties, or the institution or appointing authority to which they have entrusted the matter, choosing the person or people who will decide the case. It follows that the parties, if they retain a say in the process, should exercise great diligence when nominating a co-arbitrator or agreeing with the other side upon the nomination of a sole arbitrator or chair of the tribunal.

Importance of a tribunal's composition. The composition of the tribunal is impor- **5-051** tant not simply because its member or members will eventually write the award that resolves the dispute. The arbitrators also are highly influential in determining how the case is to be conducted, or the 'style' of the arbitration. We have explained earlier that for every specialised, 'transnational' international arbitration, there is a 'local' international arbitration that mimics domestic court litigation – usually litigation in the court of the place of arbitration. We are not suggesting that one form of international arbitration is inherently 'better' than the other. However, we are suggesting that whether the parties' international arbitration is transnational or local is largely within the control of the parties, not least because they appoint the arbitrators in many cases, and the arbitrators shape the procedure. So, if a party is involved in an arbitration with a seat in London, and is keen for some reason to have it resemble proceedings in the English High Court, one way to achieve that may be to appoint as arbitrator an English Queen's Counsel with an active High Court practice, or a retired High Court judge. The chances are that an arbitrator with one of these profiles will be naturally disposed towards treating the arbitration as a 'London arbitration' rather than as a truly transnational arbitration. Conversely, if the party wants to put some distance between the High Court and its arbitration, appointing – for example – a continental European professor of law with an active practice in international arbitration would be a wiser course. The same principle goes for both the appointment of co-arbitrators and (where the parties have a say) the appointment of sole arbitrators or chairs. The difference between a 'London arbitration' and a more 'continental' affair can be significant, both in terms of what procedures are adopted and their cost.

5-052 The desired 'style' of the arbitration is just one of several important factors that a party appointing arbitrators should take into account. We will look at the other factors shortly.

5-053 *Procedures for appointment.* We do not propose to examine in depth the different methods of arbitrator nomination and appointment. Each set of arbitration rules, as well as virtually every arbitration law, lays down its own procedures and deadlines for arbitrator appointment, and the parties' arbitration agreement may add its own directions. What follows is the general picture.

5-054 *Number of arbitrators: one or three.* International arbitral tribunals hearing business disputes today consist of one or three arbitrators. If the parties have not specified this in their arbitration agreement, then the administering institution, or the arbitration law if there is no institution, will determine the number.[38]

5-055 *Various methods of appointment.* If the tribunal is to comprise one arbitrator, she will either be nominated by agreement of the parties, for confirmation by the institution (or court, in the absence of an institution), or appointed directly by the institution (or court or appointing authority, in the absence of an institution). If the tribunal is to comprise three arbitrators, each party will nominate one arbitrator – known as a 'co-arbitrator' or 'party-appointed arbitrator' – for confirmation by the institution or court. The third arbitrator will chair the tribunal and is referred to as the 'chair' (or the 'president' in ICSID arbitration). He will either be appointed by the institution, or by a court or appointing authority, or by agreement of the parties or the co-arbitrators. If party agreement or appointment is required, but is not forthcoming within the specified deadline, the institution, court, or appointing authority will make the appointment instead.

5-056 *Appointment involving multiple parties.* If there are multiple parties and a three-member tribunal is called for, the practice is that each side (or group of parties with aligned interests) will jointly nominate an arbitrator. But this runs into difficulties if a group of claimants or respondents cannot reach agreement on a joint nomination, which may happen where the arbitration is multi-sided, that is, where the interests of all the claimants or all the respondents are not the same, leading to three or more 'sides' to the arbitration (referred to by some as 'triagonal' or 'polygonal' proceedings). In this situation, the danger is that the parties will not all have equal rights in the appointment of the arbitrators, which may lead to a lack of due process and grounds for challenging or refusing to enforce the award. The way around this is for the institution or the courts to appoint all the arbitrators, although the major institutions do not offer clear rules or guidelines as to how they would handle

---

38. Chapter 1, *Elements of an International Dispute Resolution Agreement.*

requests to appoint arbitrators for multi-sided proceedings. Article 10(2) of the ICC Rules, for example, provides that where there are multiple parties but no joint nomination or agreement as to method of appointment of the arbitrators, the ICC Court will appoint the whole tribunal and will designate one of the three arbitrators as chair.

Institutional panels of arbitrators. Certain institutions maintain panels of arbitra- **5-057** tors, from which they may or must – depending on the institution and the circumstances – select arbitrators that they are required to appoint. This is the case of ICSID, the HKIAC, and the SIAC, for example. The ICC does not maintain a panel of arbitrators. Instead, it appoints sole arbitrators and chairs after seeking and receiving a proposal by an ICC National Committee of an appropriate candidate. The National Committees are autonomous organisations that each elect representatives to the ICC World Council, the ICC's supreme governing body.[39] For example, if the ICC Court decides that a Swiss chair would be suitable for the dispute at hand, it will invite a National Committee to propose a candidate. The Court is not obliged to accept the proposal, and if it does not, it may request another proposal from the same or another National Committee.[40] If necessary, the ICC may make appointments from a country where there is no National Committee if the parties do not object.[41]

List method of appointing arbitrators. By contrast, other arbitration rules, includ- **5-058** ing the UNCITRAL Rules, employ the 'list' method of selecting arbitrators, in which the parties receive lists of candidates for chair or sole arbitrator and are asked to rank them in order of preference.[42] This method is sometimes followed by party-appointed arbitrators appointing a chair in arbitrations conducted under the rules of other institutions or in ad hoc proceedings.

UNCITRAL Rules and the appointing authority. Under the UNCITRAL Rules, the **5-059** chair or sole arbitrator, if not agreed by the parties, will be appointed by the 'appointing authority' specified in the Rules. If the parties' arbitration agreement does not designate an institution to act as an appointing authority, the Permanent Court of Arbitration (PCA) in The Hague will do so.[43] This does not mean the PCA will appoint the chair or sole arbitrator; rather, it requires the parties to file a request for the designation of an appointing authority with the PCA, which, after considering the parties' place of origin and the circumstances of the dispute, will select the appointing authority. The designated authority may be one of the well-known international arbitration institutions. While the PCA can be expected to do a good job in the designation of appointing authorities, this is a step that parties can easily avoid either by agreeing on the appointing authority at the time of contracting or at the inception of the dispute.

---

39. Derains & Schwartz, 2.
40. See Art. 9(3) of the ICC Rules.
41. See Art. 9(4) of the ICC Rules; and Derains & Schwartz, 167, 170–171.
42. See Arts 6(3) and 7(3) of the UNCITRAL Rules; and Art. 14 of the NAI Rules.
43. See Art. 6 of UNCITRAL Rules.

Not all appointing authorities are created equal	International institutions such as the ICC, ICDR, and SIAC are relatively safe choices as appointing authorities given their experience with international arbitration. The same cannot be said of local institutions. For example, while the Law Society of England & Wales offers to serve as appointing authority, the organisation provides no rules or guidelines as to how such appointments are made in the event of a dispute between international parties. Presumably, the appointment will be an English lawyer of sufficiently high calibre, but without the guarantee of any knowledge or experience in truly international proceedings.

5-060 *Agreement among parties better than choice by institution?* While the panels of many institutions are strong, and it is difficult to quarrel with most appointments made by institutions and other appointing authorities, they do not always get it right. It therefore almost always makes sense to try and reach agreement with the opposing party on the nomination of a chair or sole arbitrator. In this way, you may not get the most desirable candidate, but you will by definition get an acceptable candidate. Most importantly, you will avoid unsatisfactory appointments by the third party, which, although rare, are certainly not unheard of.

5-061 *Nationality of appointees.* Under many arbitration rules, sole arbitrators and chairs cannot be of the same nationality as any of the parties, unless the parties agree. In our view, rules that do not contain this safeguard should be adapted by the parties adding a requirement that the sole arbitrator or chair must not be a national of a disputing party.[44]

A question of terminology?	In certain systems of international arbitration, there is substantial confusion between three terms employed in the constitution of the tribunal: nomination, confirmation, and appointment of arbitrators. We attempt below to clarify what each term means – and they each bear different meanings – by reference to Articles 7 to 9 of the ICC Rules. In practice, however, little distinction is made between nomination and appointment, which may lead to difficulties where contracts specify that deadlines, such as those for appointment of one arbitrator, run from the appointment of another arbitrator.

---

44. Examples of rules without this safeguard are those of the UNCITRAL, CIETAC and the ICDR.

Nomination	The proposal by a party or the parties of an arbitrator for confirmation by the institution or appointing authority
Confirmation	The acceptance by the institution or appointing authority of the proposal of the nomination of an arbitrator
Appointment	The selection by an institution or appointing authority of an arbitrator, without the involvement of the parties

Basic rule of independence and impartiality. One of the core principles of **5-062** international arbitration is that the arbitrators must be independent of the parties for the duration of the arbitration, and must also be impartial. This is expressed in different ways in the various arbitration rules and laws, but the thrust is the same. For example, the 'General Principle' of the IBA Guidelines on Conflicts – which are widely regarded as expressing best practice in this area – states that '[e]very arbitrator shall be impartial and independent of the parties at the time of accepting an appointment to serve and shall remain so during the entire arbitration proceeding'.[45]

Independence and impartiality distinguished. What is the difference between inde- **5-063** pendence and impartiality? Independence is measured by an arbitrator's relationship with the parties, and not his state of mind. It is therefore relatively easy for a third party to discern and evaluate. Independence goes to the absence of a relationship (past or present, direct or indirect, financial or otherwise) between an arbitrator and the parties that could affect, or be perceived to affect, the arbitrator's freedom of judgment. Impartiality is a more subjective notion and concerns an arbitrator's state of mind with respect to the parties and the issues in dispute. It is accordingly harder to identify and assess, which is why the ICC Rules, for example, refer to independence but not to impartiality.[46] We would define impartiality as the absence of bias towards one of the parties or in relation to the subject matter of the dispute.

IBA Guidelines on Conflicts. The IBA Guidelines on Conflicts set down a series of **5-064** general standards on arbitrator independence and impartiality, followed by examples of 'practical application' of the general standards. The IBA Guidelines are just that: guidelines and not rules or law. But they do reflect sound international practice, and while they may not coincide exactly with arbitration rules or laws, institutions and courts hearing challenges of arbitrators increasingly refer to the Guidelines.

The IBA Guidelines' main principles are that: **5-065**

- An arbitrator should decline or resign an appointment if he has doubts as to his ability to be or remain independent and impartial, or if facts exist that a reasonable third person with knowledge of the facts would consider

---

45. This is a mandatory rule, and parties cannot derogate from it by agreement.
46. See Derains & Schwartz, 116–134.

give rise to justifiable doubts as to the arbitrator's independence or impartiality.[47]

- If facts exist that may, in the eyes of the parties, give rise to doubts as to the arbitrator's independence or impartiality, the arbitrator is required to disclose them to the parties or the institution, on the understanding that the arbitrator still considers himself to be independent and impartial, otherwise he would have resigned.[48]
- If the parties do not object to the arbitrator within thirty days, they are deemed to have waived any potential conflict of interest.[49]

5-066 Some acute cases of conflicts of interest, which appear on the IBA Guidelines' 'Red List', cannot be waived. Other less severe examples – appearing on the 'Waivable Red List' – require an express waiver by the parties, not simply a failure to object. The 'Orange List' contains examples of situations that may give rise to justifiable doubts, in the eyes of the parties, as to an arbitrator's independence and impartiality and therefore should be disclosed by the arbitrator. Disclosure, again, does not constitute an admission of a lack of independence or impartiality – quite the reverse – but it is an acknowledgement that the parties may see things differently. Finally, the 'Green List' gives examples of situations where no disclosure is needed.

5-067 The following table provides examples of conflict situations within each list:

Example 5b – Conflict Situations within the IBA Guidelines' Lists

• **Non-waivable Red List:**   – The arbitrator regularly advises the appointing party or an affiliate of the appointing party, and the arbitrator or his/her firm derives a significant financial income therefrom.   • **Waivable Red List:**   – The arbitrator is a lawyer in the same law firm as the counsel to one of the parties.   – The arbitrator is a manager, director, or member of the supervisory board, or has a similar controlling influence, in an affiliate of one of the parties, if the affiliate is directly involved in the matters in dispute in the arbitration.   • **Orange List:**   – The arbitrator has within the past three years been appointed as arbitrator on two or more occasions by one of the parties or an affiliate of one of the parties.   – The arbitrator's law firm has within the past three years acted for one of the parties or an affiliate of one of the parties in an unrelated matter without the involvement of the arbitrator.

47. IBA Guidelines, General Standard 2(a), 2(b).
48. IBA Guidelines, General Standard 3(a), 3(b).
49. IBA Guidelines, General Standard 4(a).

- The arbitrator currently serves, or has served within the past three years, as arbitrator in another arbitration on a related issue involving one of the parties or an affiliate of one of the parties.
- The arbitrator has within the past three years received more than three appointments by the same counsel or law firm.
- **Green List:**
  - The arbitrator has previously published a general opinion (such as in a law review article or public lecture) concerning an issue that also arises in the arbitration (but this opinion is not focused on the case that is being arbitrated).
  - The arbitrator's law firm has acted against one of the parties or an affiliate of one of the parties in an unrelated matter without the involvement of the arbitrator.

Issue conflict. Apart from conflicts arising from an arbitrator's relationship with **5-068** the parties and their counsel, an arbitrator's relationship with the subject matter in dispute (such as prior statements made about an issue in dispute) may result in a conflict of interest known as an 'issue conflict'. In such cases, the Guidelines provide that a previously published general opinion concerning an issue that arises in the arbitration (but not focused on the particular case) does not require disclosure. On the other hand, a concurrent appointment as counsel and arbitrator in separate proceedings raising similar issues is likely to result in an issue conflict that should be disclosed.[50]

Role of a co-arbitrator. What the IBA Guidelines do not explain is what the role of **5-069** a co-arbitrator is, if it is not to serve as the appointing party's advocate within the tribunal. The view prevailing in practice is that the co-arbitrator's role is to ensure that the whole tribunal understands the arguments and the evidence presented by the party that appointed it. But this does not mean that a party-appointed arbitrator must blindly espouse the case of the appointing party, which would be infringing the arbitrator's duty of impartiality. In any event, doing so is unlikely to be fruitful, as the other members of the tribunal will rarely be fooled or impressed, and the arbitrator risks losing his most valuable asset on a tribunal: his credibility.[51]

> **Question:** Is it ever acceptable for a party or its lawyer to communicate with 'its' arbitrator concerning the dispute after his appointment?

---

50. See *Republic of Ghana v. Telekom Malaysia Berhad*, Case No. HA/RK 2004, 667, Decision of the District Court of The Hague dated 18 Oct. 2004; and *Republic of Ghana v. Telekom Malaysia Berhad*, Case No. HA/RK 2004, 788, Decision the District Court of The Hague dated 5 Nov. 2004), reproduced in *ASA Bulletin* 23, no. 1 (2005): 186 et seq.
51. See N. Blackaby & C. Partasides with A. Redfern & M. Hunter, *Redfern & Hunter on International Arbitration*, 5th edn (Oxford: Oxford University Press, 2009), para. 4–74.

> **Answer:** We think the only time that a party or its counsel and arbitrators should communicate regarding the arbitration is when they liaise about any appointment by agreement between the co-arbitrators of the chair. In that situation, it is understood in practice (although not affirmatively authorised by institutional rules or by law) that the co-arbitrator will consult with her appointing party on acceptable candidates for the chair. However, once the chair is appointed, there should be no further ex parte communication concerning the case until the award is released. It is fair to say that this rule is not universally complied with in international arbitration.

5-070 *Other attributes to look for in an arbitrator candidate.* All potential arbitrator candidates should, for the reasons just explained, be independent of the parties and impartial. There is little sense in a party nominating a candidate who, if appointed, is vulnerable to being challenged and removed for want of independence. Even if he remains in place, if it is apparent that he is not independent or impartial – and it generally will be apparent – his credibility with other members of the tribunal will be diminished. Appointing such a candidate is therefore likely to be counterproductive.

5-071 *Case-by-case approach.* Assuming only candidates who are independent and impartial are being considered for appointment, what other attributes should the appointing party look for? How should it distinguish between different candidates who come into view? We would make two general remarks at the outset. First, there is no satisfactory answer to these questions in the abstract. Much will depend on the profile of the particular dispute: relevant factors will include the subject matter of the dispute, its size, its complexity, the governing law, and the identity of the other party and of any arbitrator appointed by that party. The goals of the appointing party in relation to the particular dispute will be of equal importance: how significant is it, in financial, commercial, and other terms?

5-072 *Credibility: a key attribute of a co-arbitrator.* Our second general remark is that, whatever the profile of the dispute, and whatever the appointing party's specific goals, we think the overall objective of a party appointing a co-arbitrator should be to select someone who will have as positive an influence as possible on the tribunal, as a whole. In fact, the co-arbitrator's first task will be to identify candidates for the chair who may be acceptable both to the appointing party and the other side. Beyond that, we see the role of the party-appointed arbitrator, as discussed earlier, to be to ensure that his appointing party's case and evidence are considered and understood by the other arbitrators. An arbitrator will be best able to discharge these responsibilities if he has credibility with, and the respect of, the remainder of the tribunal.

5-073 *Anticipating the profile of the chair.* The problem is that when a party is considering the appointment of a co-arbitrator, it will not know who the chair is (except in the rare cases of the appointment of a replacement co-arbitrator in the course of the arbitration). It may not even know who the other co-arbitrator is. So how can a party know whether a candidate will be effective in appointing a chair who meets the party's expectations of fairness and efficiency, and who will command the respect of the other tribunal members? The answer is that it cannot know, but it can at least hazard a reasonable guess if the chair is to be appointed in the first instance by agreement of the parties or of the co-arbitrators (who will, in practice, consult on the issue with their appointing parties). Even if the parties have no control over the appointment of the chair, it should be possible to anticipate what sort of individual the institution or other appointing authority is likely to designate. In some cases, the arbitration agreement may set out conditions that the person must meet (as to profession, nationality, or language ability, for instance). More often, the arbitration rules will provide some indication of who the chair will be in the absence of agreement of the parties, especially if they require the institution to appoint from among the arbitrators on its panel. While there is no panel in ICC arbitration, the chair or sole arbitrator will not be of the same nationality of the parties[52] and, in practice, probably not of the same nationality as a co-arbitrator, if the two co-arbitrators are of different nationalities.[53] Although the Rules do not preclude the Court from appointing a chair of the same nationality as one of the co-arbitrators, and in some cases the Court has done so, the Court generally avoids forming a tribunal that may appear to favour one of the parties in this regard. The ICC will also look at the arbitrator's residence and availability.[54]

Criteria for appointment by institutions. The most important factors in any decision **5-074** by a competent institution or appointing authority are likely to be the experience and reputation of the candidates as international arbitrators, the law governing the dispute, and geographical proximity. Experienced, reputed arbitrators will garner most appointments, and institutions will usually try to appoint as chair or sole arbitrator an individual who resides close to the seat and who is familiar with the governing law, or at least with laws of the same tradition as the governing law. So, for example, arbitrators from Australia and New Zealand – countries whose laws are similar to English law – are often appointed to chair arbitrations where English law governs, but no Australian or New Zealand parties, respectively, are involved. This is especially true in Asia, which is relatively close to Australia and New Zealand in geographical terms. Likewise, arbitrators from civil law countries such as Belgium or Switzerland will often be appointed to chair arbitrations involving French parties, especially with a seat in Europe, where French law – another civil law system – governs, but no Belgian or Swiss parties, respectively, are involved.

---

52. See Art. 9(5) of the ICC Rules.
53. See Derains & Schwartz, 173.
54. See Art. 9(1) of the ICC Rules.

Checklist 5c – Attributes to Look for in Co-arbitrator Candidates

---

Here is a non-exhaustive list of the qualities to look for in a co-arbitrator candidate:

- *Familiarity with likely candidates for chair:* A co-arbitrator's first and most important task will be to assist in the formation of the tribunal, meaning the appointment of the chair. To accomplish this well, the co-arbitrator will need to be on sufficiently good terms (and have experience) with a variety of potential candidates for chair who would be acceptable to the appointing party.
- *Familiarity with languages relevant to the dispute:* An arbitrator who does not speak the language of the arbitration is a liability, so fluency in that language is essential. But fluency in other languages, especially the language of the evidence (if it is different from the language of the arbitration), can be valuable too.
- *Expectations as to remuneration:* The best qualified arbitrators are often the most expensive. So if a candidate expects remuneration at a level that is not compatible with the fees anticipated to be on offer in the arbitration (perhaps because the amount in dispute is low, or the institution's fee scale is not generous), he should not be considered.
- *Experience as arbitrator in similar arbitrations:* The candidate should have a track record as arbitrator (and preferably as co-arbitrator) that will enable him to behave appropriately and speak with authority.
- *Gravitas:* The candidate should have the somewhat indefinable trait of gravitas, which will help ensure that he commands the respect of the other tribunal members.
- *Reputation:* The candidate should have a strong reputation among peers as an arbitrator, which will also give assurance that he will command respect within the tribunal.
- *Availability:* Assuming the party wants a swift disposal of the case, the candidate must be available over the expected duration of the arbitration, and particularly when hearings and deliberations are slated to take place. However, some parties seeking to delay may deliberately appoint a busy arbitrator.
- *Procedural approach:* If a party would prefer a particular approach to the procedure – for example, a 'local' style of arbitration, rather than a transnational style – it should prefer a candidate who naturally favours that sort of procedure.
- *Relationship with counsel on each side:* While a candidate's independence is essential,[55] it is helpful if the appointing party's counsel is

---

55. The IBA Guidelines see no issue where the arbitrator has a relationship with counsel through membership in the same professional or social organisation, or where they have previously served together as arbitrators or as co-counsel (Green List 4.4). However, under the Guidelines the

familiar with the arbitrator, in order to be able to anticipate how he will react; it is certainly unhelpful if the two do not get on. Conversely, an appointing party may prefer a candidate who is not known to opposing counsel, or not known to have a strong relationship with that counsel.

- *Familiarity with governing law:* It is helpful if a candidate for a co-arbitrator berth is familiar with the law applicable to the merits of the dispute, especially in a case expected to turn on the law.
- *Familiarity with technical areas relevant to dispute:* If technical, non-legal matters (such as engineering or financial issues) will be of significant relevance to the outcome of the dispute, a candidate's mastery of them may be a significant benefit.
- *Residence:* It will be more convenient and cheaper to appoint a candidate who resides close to where the hearings will be held, and who is in the same time zone as the other arbitrators.

The process of appointing an arbitrator in practice. How should a party go about **5-075** identifying a potential arbitrator, either for nomination by it as co-arbitrator, or to propose to the opposing party for joint nomination as sole arbitrator or chair? Information about arbitrators that is relevant to appointment decisions and the formation of tribunals is notoriously difficult to obtain. What is in the public domain – mainly biographical data, scholarly writings, or participation in conferences – does not tell parties how someone will conduct himself on the tribunal. In the absence of better alternatives, parties must rely on sketchy and anecdotal information, frequently transmitted through multiple (and dubious) filters.

Suggested steps. The party should therefore draw up a shortlist of candidates on **5-076** the basis of information culled from publicly available sources, but mostly by word-of-mouth; approach the shortlisted candidates to see if they are free of conflicts and willing to serve; conduct further due diligence on the candidates, which may include reviewing their publications and publicly available awards, or even interviewing them; and then evaluate the different candidates before reaching a decision.

1. Drawing up a Shortlist: Obtaining Information about Arbitrator Performance

Word-of-mouth. While there are different projects underway to provide informa- **5-077** tion about arbitrator performance,[56] at present the *only* source of genuinely useful

---

arbitrator must disclose if they are in the same barristers' chambers, affiliated in the same arbitration within the past three years, have a close friendship, or if the arbitrator has received more than three appointments by the same counsel or law firm within the three previous years (Orange List 3.3).

56. See generally E. Eftekhari, 'The Development of a Template Form for Providing Party Feedback to Arbitrators', *Transnational Dispute Management* (9 Oct. 2007).

information about potential arbitrators is lawyers experienced in arbitration (whether in the party's in-house legal department, or in private practice). An experienced arbitration lawyer may well know suitable candidates personally and, best of all, may have appeared before them as counsel or sat with them as arbitrator. This will allow him to evaluate the candidates based on this relevant, first-hand experience. A party or its counsel can also take soundings via word-of-mouth from other members of the international arbitration community, or members of other circles in which appropriate candidates may move. The most relevant contribution is, again, likely to come from counsel who have themselves appeared before the candidates in arbitrations or sat with them as arbitrators and have therefore 'seen them in action'.

5-078 *Reliability of word-of-mouth information.* As noted, the main problem with this approach is that it is inherently unreliable. Information about people passed via word-of-mouth is charitably called hearsay, and less charitably gossip. In all instances the information may well be coloured by whether and how much the source ultimately liked the previous outcome. As an arbitrator who is properly doing his job will often leave one side unhappy, perceptions of counsel in particular are unlikely to be uniformly reliable.

5-079 *Publicly available sources of information.* If a party does not have access to lawyers experienced in international arbitration, as at least a starting point, there are a number of publicly available lists of arbitrators, which include the panels of arbitral institutions (such as the SIAC and ICSID) and directories of associations (such as the IAI and the Association Suisse de l'Arbitrage (ASA)).[57] Regrettably, inclusion on these panels or in these directories does not necessarily reflect an individual's aptitude to serve as an arbitrator, nor does it provide any indication of how the person is likely to conduct himself on the tribunal if appointed. Some legal publications (such as Chambers Global and Global Arbitration Review) compile rankings of arbitrators, but again their assessments are largely based on anecdotal information from parties that may have had little experience with the proposed arbitrator, and the accuracy of the information should not be taken for granted. An arbitrator's formal qualifications in the field of arbitration – such as those bestowed by the Chartered Institute of Arbitrators (CIArb) – may be some indication of an individual's capability as an arbitrator. Our impression, at any rate, is that many or most of the world's leading arbitrators have no formal training or qualifications as arbitrators. While that may one day change, it would be unwise for a party today – or an institution or appointing authority for that matter – to restrict its pool of arbitrator candidates to those with such formal training or qualifications.

---

57. See, e.g., <www.siac.org.sg>, <http://icsid.worldbank.org/ICSID>, <www.iaiparis.com>, and <www.arbitration-ch.org>.

A limited pool of qualified candidates?	We often hear about the international arbitration 'mafia' or, more generously, the international arbitration 'club'. (There is a joke that 'MAFIA' stands for Mutual Association For International Arbitration). Whatever the appellation, international arbitration is validly criticised for being too clubby, and for its high barriers to entry. In a discipline that prides itself on being transnational and designed for the resolution of cross-cultural disputes around the globe, is it acceptable that the vast majority of prominent international arbitrators are white, male lawyers or law professors over the age of 50?

The shortlist. Judicious use of these different resources will help a party to draw up **5-080** a shortlist of perhaps three to five arbitrator candidates although, again, the paucity of useful information about arbitrator candidates requires parties to be prudent when doing so.

2.   Approaching the Candidates

Calling each candidate. The next step in the arbitrator selection process should be **5-081** for the party, probably through its lawyer, to approach the shortlisted candidates to see if each is willing to serve and is free of conflicts of interest. This is best done on the telephone, with an e-mail or fax to follow up to ensure the candidate has properly noted the names of the parties for the purposes of checking conflicts.

Disclosure of details of the dispute to candidates. The party will need to disclose **5-082** some details of the dispute to the candidates, as well as the names of the disputing parties. These details will include the nature and size of the dispute and the expected duration of the arbitration, to give the candidate an idea of the time that he will need to commit and the remuneration that will be on offer. The party may also ask the candidate whether he satisfies the conditions laid down in the arbitration agreement, or other key criteria – such as fluency in the language of the arbitration or familiarity with the governing law – that may be important to the appointing party.

**3.   Interviewing Arbitrator Candidates and
        Further Due Diligence**

Propriety of interviewing arbitrator candidates. It is relatively common in the **5-083** United States for parties appointing an international arbitrator to interview candidates on the shortlist who are willing and available to serve, and who meet any of the party's other basic criteria for appointment. The practice is less common in Europe and Asia, where it has traditionally been regarded with suspicion by both arbitrators and counsel. However, it is now clearly becoming more popular in these regions too, and maybe even mainstream, as indicated by the promulgation in 2007 of 'Practice Guideline 16: The Interviewing of Prospective Arbitrators' by the CIArb.

5-084 *CIArb guidelines.* In the first instance, these guidelines provide that while co-arbitrators may be interviewed separately by a party, candidates for a sole arbitrator position 'should not be interviewed except by the parties jointly'. (Guidelines, Article 4.) Subject to the above restrictions, the Guidelines permit inquiry into the following areas during the interview in order to assess the candidate's 'expertise, experience, language proficiency, and conflict status':

- the names of the parties in dispute and any third parties involved or likely to be involved;
- the general nature of the dispute;
- sufficient detail, but no more than necessary, of the project to enable both interviewer and interviewee to assess the latter's suitability for the appointment;
- the expected timetable of the proceedings;
- the language, governing law, seat of and rules applicable to the proceedings if agreed, or the fact that some or all of these are not agreed; and
- the interviewee's experience, expertise, and availability.

5-085 As to the nature of the dispute, the Guidelines state what can and what cannot be discussed. In order to assess the candidate's 'experience and expertise', the Guidelines state that questions may be asked to test his knowledge and understanding of (1) the nature and type of project in question; (2) the particular area of law applicable to the dispute; and (3) arbitration law, practice, and procedure. 'Such questions should be general in nature and neutrally put in order to test the interviewee and should not be put in order to ascertain his/her views or opinions on matters which may form part of the case. Questions concerning the interviewee's publishing history (if any) may be put subject to the same proviso.' The Guidelines provide that, in all events, the following areas may not be discussed, 'either directly or indirectly', during the interview:

- the specific circumstances or facts giving rise to the dispute;
- the positions or arguments of the parties; and
- the merits of the case.

5-086 The CIArb Guidelines largely capture what was already viewed as acceptable practice in interviewing candidates for co-arbitrators, and extend this to the possibility of interviewing sole arbitrators and candidates for chair. Importantly, they are intended to provide safeguards against challenge by requiring that the interview be memorialised, and stipulating that an interview cannot be grounds for subsequent challenge.[58]

---

58. See generally D. Bishop & L. Reed, 'Practical Guidelines for Interviewing, Selecting and Challenging Party-appointed Arbitrators in International Commercial Arbitration', *Arbitration International* 14, no.4 (1998): 395–430; Redfern & Hunter, paras 4–69–4–71.

Additional research. An appointing party may wish to do further research, such as **5-087** gathering and reviewing publications and awards by the candidate, especially those in the relevant fields. An Internet search against the candidate will also be worthwhile, if it has not already been done. This sort of research may reveal pertinent information concerning the candidates, including any relationships with the parties and their lawyers, and how the candidates are likely to react to the substantive and procedural issues expected to arise in the case at hand. These are steps that a party should also take with respect to the other members of the tribunal.

4.   Evaluation and Decision

Once the party has completed its research and any interviews of candidates for the **5-088** co-arbitrator slot, it should be in a position to evaluate the candidates still in contention and make its decision. A party may wish to inform the unsuccessful candidates that they have not been selected, but as a practical matter should abstain from doing so until after the appointment has been confirmed. As we discuss below, it is by no means guaranteed that a nominated arbitrator will be confirmed, and the party will be well served by having other names ready in the event confirmation is not forth coming. Also, the party may wish to propose the candidates not chosen as co-arbitrator for the position of chair.

5.   Selection of Sole Arbitrator or Chair by
Agreement of Parties or Co-arbitrators

The parties' arbitration agreement or the applicable arbitration rules may require **5-089** the parties to attempt to agree on the joint nomination of a sole arbitrator or, in the case of a three-member tribunal, they may require the parties or the co-arbitrators to attempt to agree on the joint nomination of the chair. Also, as noted earlier, even if the selection of sole arbitrator or chair has been delegated to an institution or other appointing authority, it is usually worth approaching the opposing party to see if the two can agree upon an appointee acceptable to both of them.

Negotiating with the other party on arbitrator appointment. There are various ways **5-090** to go about this process of negotiation. The parties can begin with the steps described above, including asking shortlisted candidates if they are willing and available to serve, and possibly interviewing candidates together with the opposing party. The parties can then try to conclude the process through a simple and informal exchange – or, more likely, series of exchanges – of the names of acceptable candidates, in the hope of reaching agreement. The difficulty in practice may be that each party will be reluctant to accept a candidate proposed by the other side. So a more formal system may be preferred, such as the drawing up of a list of candidates, with each party allocating points to their preferred candidates (say, five points to a party's preferred candidate on a list of five, four points to the number two candidate, and so on). The parties exchange their lists with scores marked on them, or provide their lists to the co-arbitrators (perhaps without seeing the other side's rankings), and the candidate with the highest combined score (the maximum score being ten in this example) is selected. In the event of a tie, it is reasonable for the co-arbitrators to choose the chair from the two who have been listed. If a deadlock cannot be avoided, then there may be no alternative but the default of having the institution or appointing authority step in and make the appointment for the parties.[59]

5-091 *Involvement of co-arbitrators in the choice of chair by parties.* If the parties are to agree upon the appointment of a chair, as opposed to seeking agreement through the co-arbitrators, it makes sense for each party to ask the co-arbitrator whom it nominated for her views on the candidates being discussed. This is to ensure that the co-arbitrator and the chair get on: the better the relationship between the co-arbitrator and chair, the more effective the co-arbitrator is likely to be in discharging her role on the tribunal.

5-092 *Involvement of parties in the choice of chair by co-arbitrators.* Conversely, where the co-arbitrators are attempting to agree on the joint nomination of the chair, it is typical that they will consult with their nominating parties about suitable candidates. While the parties are not required to disclose to each other that they are consulting with the co-arbitrators in this way, they may also benefit from being candid with the opposing party about concerns raised or information gleaned during these discussions about potential candidates for chair. The co-arbitrators may ultimately have the most useful information about a candidate for chair. For example, they may know that the candidate has largely retired or become disengaged from the practice of arbitration, fails to read submissions or follow proceedings closely, or has a tendency to conduct proceedings in a way that both parties would prefer to avoid.

Common law versus civil law arbitrators: some differences in approach to conducting international arbitrations	Participants in international arbitration often suggest, when considering arbitrator appointments, that there are substantial differences between the approach to conducting an international arbitration taken by arbitrators from a common law background on the one hand, and from a civil law background on the other. In our view, these differences are losing their currency, as international arbitration increasingly becomes a sui generis practice which draws on both common and civil law traditions, and which is distinct from the courts of any one jurisdiction or tradition. But in very general and perhaps stereotypical terms, here are some thoughts as to how arbitrators from each tradition might approach cases before them.

---

59. For a form of this list procedure, see Art. 6(3) of the UNCITRAL Rules.

Common Law Arbitrators	**Civil Law Arbitrators**
1. Written Submissions	
More likely to provide for three rounds of submissions (e.g., Statement of Claim, Statement of Defence, Reply), giving the Claimant the 'last word' (usually on the basis that the Claimant bears the burden of proof)	More likely to provide for four rounds of submissions (e.g., Statement of Claim, Statement of Defence, Reply, Rejoinder), giving the Respondent the 'last word' (usually on the basis that each party should have an equal opportunity to present its case)
2. Document Production	
More permissive of document production requests (willing to construe 'relevance' and 'materiality' more broadly)	More limited or no document production
3. Hearing Length	
Open to longer hearings (more willing to hear extensive witness testimony; preference for oral submissions)	Preference for shorter hearing schedule (less interested in extensive cross-examination; preference for documentary evidence and written submissions)
4. Nature of Proceedings: Inquisitorial versus Adversarial	
More likely to leave witness examination to counsel	May take a more pro-active approach, examining witnesses directly or using witness conferencing
5. Rules of Evidence	
More likely to intervene to prevent overly leading questions of a party's witnesses	Less likely to police the style of questioning
May be more inclined to disallow or discount 'hearsay' testimony	More likely to accept 'hearsay' testimony
6. Tribunal-Appointed Experts	
Less inclined to propose tribunal-appointed experts	More inclined to propose tribunal-appointed experts
7. Witness Conferencing	
Less likely to propose witness conferencing and, if so, typically limited to expert witnesses	More likely to propose witness conferencing (for both fact and expert witnesses)
Where adopted, more likely that the parties will take the lead in questioning the witnesses	Where adopted, more likely that the tribunal will take the lead in questioning the witnesses

F.   CHALLENGE, REMOVAL, AND REPLACEMENT OF ARBITRATORS

5-093 *Introduction.* Once an arbitrator has been appointed, a party may challenge him and seek his removal from the tribunal. The grounds and procedures for doing so are set out in the applicable arbitration rules or, if there are none, in the arbitration law of the place of arbitration.

5-094 *Grounds for challenge.* Generally speaking, the grounds for challenge will be that the arbitrator is not independent or impartial. We have looked earlier at the circumstances in which, under the IBA Guidelines on Conflicts, an arbitrator will be considered not to be independent or impartial. These guidelines represent a distillation of worldwide practice and will often assist authorities hearing challenges. But in any individual case the standards applied by the authority deciding the challenge will be those found in the applicable rules and law, and therefore those standards – and the outcome of the challenge – may differ from the standards contained in the Guidelines. An arbitrator may in some circumstances be challenged on the basis that he 'does not possess qualifications agreed to by the parties', although, if the challenging party appointed the arbitrator or participated in his appointment, this is only possible for reasons that the challenging party becomes aware of *after* the appointment has been made.[60]

5-095 *Timing of challenge.* A party seeking to challenge an arbitrator must do so within a specified period of time after learning of the circumstances on which the challenge is based. The party will send the challenge, including its reasons for it, to the relevant authority: in institutional arbitration this is usually the institution, and in ad hoc arbitration it is either the courts of the place of arbitration or, under the UNCITRAL Rules, the appointing authority. The challenged arbitrator, any other tribunal members, and the other party are usually invited to comment on the challenge.

| **When an arbitrator is challenged: impact on the duration of the proceedings** | Proceedings can become unduly protracted, usually at the outset of a case, when one or more members of the arbitral tribunal are subject to challenge. When a party challenges an arbitrator, it may or may not cause the arbitration to be suspended, depending on the applicable arbitration rules or laws. Automatic suspension, as happens in ICSID arbitration and happened under the previous version of the SIAC rules, may encourage parties to raise spurious challenges at inopportune moments for tactical reasons. For example, on the eve of the final hearing in a recent arbitration under the previous SIAC rules, the respondent challenged the sole arbitrator on obviously far-fetched grounds. Although the SIAC soon dismissed the challenge, the automatic suspension meant the hearing due to start the following day had to be postponed for several |

---

60. See, e.g., Art. 12(2) of the Model Law.

months because of the busy schedules of the participants. Achieving this delay, which doubled the length of the arbitration, was no doubt the respondent's real objective. The SIAC, to its credit, has now changed its rules so that the Registrar may order the suspension of the arbitration when a challenge is received, but is not required to. This should help prevent abusive challenges such as that just described. Unfortunately, for proceedings yet to get underway, a challenge will necessarily stop the arbitration from going forward until the issue is resolved and the tribunal can be fully constituted. Institutions may not resolve such conflicts expeditiously and/or may give parties extended periods to nominate replacement candidates, with still further periods of time for the raising of new objections. It is not unusual for challenges to delay the commencement of the proceedings by three months or more.

Who decides the challenge? The administering institution, court, or appointing **5-096** authority will usually decide the challenge, although in ICSID arbitrations where one member of a three-member tribunal is challenged, it is the two other arbitrators who will decide (if they disagree, or if the challenge is of a sole arbitrator or a majority of a three-member tribunal, the Chair of ICSID's Administrative Council will decide).[61]

Reasons for challenges. The ICC court gives no reasons for its decision on chal- **5-097** lenges.[62] Challenge decisions by ICSID arbitrators usually contain reasons.[63] The LCIA Court does give reasons for its challenge decisions and has announced that it will publish challenge decisions.[64] This has met with widespread approval, including by arbitration users who rightly believe that they are entitled to understand the grounds for what is, by any measure, an important decision in the life of the arbitration. One interesting development is the recent agreement by the parties to an investment treaty arbitration under the UNCITRAL rules to refer the challenge of one of the arbitrators not to the PCA (the appointing authority) but to the LCIA, as the latter gives reasons for its decisions, whereas the former does not.[65]

---

61. See ICSID Rule 9.
62. See Art. 7(4) of the ICC Rules: 'The decisions of the Court as to the appointment, confirmation, challenge or replacement of an arbitrator shall be final and the reasons for such decisions shall not be communicated.'
63. See, for instance, *Compañia de Aguas del Aconquija S.A. & Vivendi Universal v. Argentine Republic* (ICSID Case No. ARB/97/3), Decision on the Challenge to the President of the ad hoc Committee, 3 Oct. 2001.
64. See 'LCIA to publish challenge decisions', *LCIA News Archive* (June 2006), at <www.lcia.org/NEWS_folder/news_archive3.htm#article1>.
65. *National Grid plc v. The Argentine Republic*, UNCITRAL (UK/Argentina BIT); 'Argentina and UK firm send arbitrator-challenge to venue where reasons are provided', *Investment Treaty News* (30 Oct. 2007), at <www.iisd.org/pdf/2007/itn_oct30_2007.pdf>. See also 'Argentine challenge to arbitrator in National Grid case is rejected in reasoned decision', *Investment Treaty News* (5 Feb. 2008), at <www.iisd.org/pdf/2008/itn_feb5_2008.pdf>.

5-098 *Consequences of a successful challenge.* An arbitrator who is successfully challenged will be replaced by the institution, court, or appointing authority.[66] The same will generally apply if an arbitrator dies, resigns, or is considered by the institution or appointing authority to be incapable of performing his functions. An arbitrator may also be removed by agreement of the parties.

5-099 *Recourse against challenge decisions.* The law of the arbitration will regulate the recourse available to parties following challenge decisions. For example, the Model Law allows an unsuccessful party in a challenge before an institution or appointing authority to continue its challenge in the courts.[67] If no separate avenue of recourse exists, a party who has unsuccessfully attempted to challenge the appointment of an arbitrator may have no choice but to seek to set aside the award rendered by the challenged arbitrator for lack of impartiality or independence. In such a case, the parties must put their objections on the record in short order to avoid being considered to have waived their rights.[68]

5-100 *Procedure for replacing an arbitrator.* When an arbitrator is to be replaced, the usual procedure is that the replacement arbitrator will be appointed in the same way as the initial appointee. In ICSID arbitration, where the remaining members of the tribunal have not accepted the resignation of a co-arbitrator, the resigning arbitrator will be replaced by the institution rather than by party nomination.[69] In ICC arbitration, the ICC Court will decide whether or not to follow the original nominating process.[70] These rules are intended to discourage untimely resignations by party-appointed arbitrators designed to frustrate the arbitration.

Not that this ever really happens: the 'new' co-arbitrator	Party A nominates an arbitrator, who is subsequently confirmed and involved in the appointment of the chair. Once proceedings are underway, the co-arbitrator resigns and Party A nominates as his replacement a new arbitrator who is known to be close to the chair, either professionally or socially, although not sufficiently close for either of them to be disqualified. This situation does happen from time to time and is difficult for institutions and appointing authorities to prevent.

Not that this ever really happens: the 'new' counsel	A more common variation on the situation above is when one party appoints new counsel after the tribunal has been constituted, with the new lawyer being someone who knows the chair, either socially or professionally. We have seen many instances of this. Two examples at the extremes are (1)

---

66. Chapter 1, *The Elements of an International Dispute Resolution Agreement.*
67. See Art. 13(3) of the Model Law.
68. See Lew, Mistelis & Kröll, 312–313.
69. See ICSID Rule 11.
70. See Art. 12(4) of the ICC Rules.

where a party hired as counsel a lawyer who had developed a professional friendship with the chair after having served on various arbitration committees together, and (2) where a party hired as counsel a lawyer who shared the same offices with the chair but kept his own letterhead. Both of these cases were ad hoc arbitrations, with the local courts as the eventual forum to hear any challenge. In the first of these examples, the chair immediately disclosed the existence of the friendship and past collaboration with the lawyer, and then took steps during the proceedings to avoid any appearance of doing his friend any favours. Indeed, the tactic did not appear to help the party, which subsequently lost the arbitration. In the second example (of shared offices), the affiliation was not disclosed to the parties by the chair or the counsel. Rather, the opposing party happened by chance to observe while transmitting its first submission to opposing counsel and the tribunal that the new lawyer and the chair shared the same fax number. When that party raised the matter at the subsequent hearing, the new lawyer picked up his papers and walked out of the hearing room in evident embarrassment. The chair nonchalantly insisted that the counsel's immediate resignation removed any impediment to his continuing as chair. The opposing party protested at the lack of prior candour, and the chair subsequently resigned rather than face the public embarrassment of a challenge proceeding in the local courts.[71]

Truncated tribunals. Similar concerns allow tribunals operating under most institutional arbitration rules to proceed with the arbitration in 'truncated' form – in other words, with just the two remaining members – when one arbitrator dies, resigns, or otherwise fails to participate in the arbitration at a late stage of the arbitration (usually close to or during the final hearing, or during the deliberations).[72] **5-101**

The successful operation of a truncated tribunal	A classic example of the successful operation of a truncated tribunal can be seen in the *Himpurna v. Indonesia* arbitration, which involved dramatic and exceptional circumstances
	20 September 1999: Two days before a deliberation session convened at The Hague, agents of the Republic of Indonesia intercepted one of the co-arbitrators, Professor Priyatna

---

71. For a similar example, in which the tribunal ruled that a barrister retained by a party late in the arbitration who was a member of the same chambers as the chair could not participate in the case, see *Hrvatska Elektroprivreda d.d. v. Republic of Slovenia* (ICSID Case No. ARB/05/24), Tribunal's Ruling dated 6 May 2008 regarding the participation of David Mildon QC in further stages of the proceedings, available at <http://ita.law.uvic.ca/chronological_list.htm>.
72. See, e.g., Art. 12(5) of the ICC Rules.

Abdurrasayid, at Schiphol airport in Amsterdam and prevailed upon him to return under escort to Jakarta. Professor Priyatna did not subsequently present himself at the appointed time for deliberations.

26 September 1999: The remaining two arbitrators signed the Interim Award with respect to matters decided and deliberated upon by all three members of the tribunal.

16 October 1999: The tribunal issued their Final Award, which explained that:

> Although the Republic of Indonesia's readiness to sabotage these proceedings gave rise to an extraordinary event, the Arbitral Tribunal has not found it necessary to innovate in order to ensure the fulfilment of its mandate under the Terms of Appointment. The weight of well-established international authority makes clear that an arbitral tribunal has not only the right, but the obligation, to proceed when, without valid excuse, one of its members fails to act, withdraws, or – although not the case here – even purports to resign. . . . The Republic of Indonesia should not benefit from Professor Priyatna's absence. Finding that there is no valid excuse for it, the Arbitral Tribunal proceeds to fulfil its mandate and render this Final Award.[73]

5-102 *Repeating the proceedings.* If a member of the tribunal is replaced during the arbitration, to what extent should the proceedings be repeated? This is a delicate question, with a balance to be struck between, on the one hand, the need for all the arbitrators to have an adequate opportunity to hear and test the evidence and, on the other, the need to avoid inconvenient repetition of steps taken in the arbitration. Most rules leave the matter to the discretion of the tribunal itself.[74] Typically there will be no need to repeat any steps if there have been no substantive hearings when the replacement arbitrator is appointed. If, however, by that time there has been a hearing of the evidence, it may be sufficient for the replacement arbitrator to read the transcript. Alternatively, if there is no transcript, or if the evidence of the witnesses could be critical to the outcome, the reconstituted tribunal may well prefer to hear again some or even all of the evidence previously presented at the hearing. In some cases, the newly constituted tribunal will ask the parties whether evidence should be repeated. Putting this issue to the parties obviously

---

73. *Himpurna California Energy Ltd v. Republic of Indonesia*, Final Award (16 Oct. 1999), paras 4–5, *Yearbook Commercial Arbitration*, vol. XXV (2000), 11 et seq. See also, 'Arbitrator's War Story – Indonesian Arbitrator Explains Why He Didn't Sit for Sessions', *Mealey's International Arbitration Report* 18, no. 6 (June 2003): 3–4.

74. See, e.g., Art. 12(4) of the ICC Rules.

gives rise to the risk that one of them will use this as an opportunity to delay the arbitration, or to recover for mistakes or gaps left in the evidence previously presented.

G.   APPOINTMENT OF A SECRETARY TO THE TRIBUNAL AND
       THE RISK OF A 'FOURTH ARBITRATOR'

Role of the secretary. In a large or complex arbitration, the chair or sole arbitrator **5-103** may wish to have administrative assistance in managing the arbitration. This is particularly true in ad hoc arbitration, where there will be no arbitral institution to carry out administrative tasks. The sole arbitrator or tribunal may therefore appoint a 'secretary' to the tribunal to perform this role. The role will generally encompass all administrative matters not otherwise performed by an institution, including arranging collection and distribution of the tribunal's fees in ad hoc arbitration. In his administrative capacity, he will also communicate with the parties on the tribunal's behalf. The secretary will usually organise and attend the hearings and the deliberations of the tribunal,[75] without playing a substantive role. For example, he takes no part in the questioning of counsel or witnesses at the hearing, and no part in the deliberations themselves; he is not a member of the tribunal and he does not take part in the determination of the dispute.

The 'fourth arbitrator'. The secretary may in fact exert a more substantive role in his **5-104** interaction with the tribunal, as he is generally charged with keeping track of all of the proceeding's official documentation, including all correspondence, submissions, and exhibits of the parties. The secretary may also be tasked with drafting documents for the tribunal, such as minutes of hearings or, in ad hoc proceedings, the tribunal's summary of the evidence and arguments presented (where no transcript will be taken). Not surprisingly, there is considerable risk in such cases that the secretary can become the proverbial sorcerer's apprentice, as a de facto 'fourth arbitrator' who, even unwittingly, may exert undue influence over the tribunal with his familiarity with the facts and opinions on the merits of the case.

Disclosure by secretary. Whenever a sole arbitrator or tribunal suggests the **5-105** appointment of a secretary, a party may properly request the same level of disclosure of possible conflicts as provided by the arbitrators.

Procedure for appointment of a secretary. Under most rules, the tribunal has no **5-106** automatic entitlement to a secretary, but if it wants one, it will propose the appointment to the parties, who will generally agree – often feeling they have no choice but to accept the tribunal's decision. The secretary is usually chosen by the tribunal and is often a junior lawyer from the law firm of one of the arbitrators (usually the chair

---

75. See Redfern & Hunter, paras 4–183 et seq. See also, generally, C. Partasides, 'The Fourth Arbitrator? The Role of Secretaries to Tribunals in International Arbitration', *Arbitration International* 18, no. 2 (2002): 147–163.

in a three-member tribunal). The parties usually agree to pay the fees and expenses of the secretary.

5-107 *ICC guidelines on secretaries.* The ICC issues guidelines[76] on the appointment of secretaries. Its main points are that (1) prior to appointing a secretary, the arbitral tribunal must advise the parties of the person whom it wishes to appoint after having verified that such person satisfies the same requirements of independence as are laid down in the Rules for the arbitrators; (2) the arbitral tribunal should inform the ICC Secretariat and the parties as early as possible of the estimated cost of the administrative secretary so that this may be taken into account when the Court fixes the advance on costs for the arbitration; and (3) the duties of the administrative secretary must be strictly limited to administrative tasks, and he must not influence in any manner whatsoever the decisions of the arbitral tribunal.[77]

5-108 *ICSID practice.* In ICSID arbitration, a counsel from ICSID's own Secretariat is appointed by operation of the ICSID rules to serve as secretary to the tribunal. In his role as secretary, he will conduct all communications with the parties and carry out all logistical arrangements for the tribunal. He will also attend the hearing, but not the deliberations unless the tribunal decides otherwise.[78] In some ICSID cases, the tribunal will appoint an assistant to serve alongside the secretary.

H.   ARBITRATORS' FEES AND EXPENSES

5-109 *Arbitrators' fees in institutional arbitration.* In institutional arbitration, the institution will generally fix the arbitrators' fees and expenses, collect payment from the parties, and distribute it to the arbitrators when appropriate. There are different methods and procedures for doing so across different institutions, as considered in our earlier look at the institutions.[79]

5-110 *Arbitrators' fees in ad hoc arbitration.* In ad hoc arbitration, where there is no institution to fix and administer costs, the situation is more complex. The parties will be required to negotiate fees and payment terms with the tribunal. Some tribunals will be guided by institutional fee scales, such as that of the ICC, while others will ask for payment of their usual hourly rates, which may also appear as daily rates for hearings. In some ad hoc proceedings, an unfortunate practice is for the tribunal to identify the highest hourly rate among its members and 'extend' it to the entire tribunal, purportedly to ensure parity in compensation. In addition to hourly fees, arbitrators may ask parties to pay cancellation or commitment fees, to compensate

---

76. 'Note Concerning the Appointment of Administrative Secretaries by Arbitral Tribunals' (1 Oct. 1995) in Derains & Schwartz, 421–422.

77. *Ibid.*

78. 'ICSID Administrative and Financial Regulation 25', available at <http://icsid.worldbank.org/ICSID/ICSID/RulesMain.jsp>; ICSID Rule 15; C.H. Schreuer et al., *The ICSID Convention – A Commentary*, 2nd edn (Cambridge: Cambridge University Press, 2009), 824, 1210.

79. Chapter 1, *The Elements of an International Dispute Resolution Agreement.*

the arbitrators if hearings are cancelled close to the hearing date because they will have been unable to take on other work during the hearing period. Cancellation fees have proved controversial in some circumstances.[80]

Basis for calculating arbitrators' fees. Arbitrators' fees may be based either on the **5-111** time spent at a rate agreed between the parties or may be dependent on the amount in dispute. In ad hoc arbitrations, the arbitrators' fees are usually negotiated when the full tribunal is constituted and before the proceedings start in earnest. If the agreed fees turn out to be insufficient during the arbitration, an increase may be sought, although all parties have to reach agreement in this regard. Whether an arbitrator who is replaced is entitled to fees for the services rendered will depend on the applicable arbitration rules or law and the circumstances surrounding his resignation or removal.[81]

Tribunal fixing its own fees. One practice that may seem odd to business people but **5-112** that is common in ad hoc proceedings is for the tribunal to fix its own fees and inform the parties of the decision. Little has been written about what options are available to parties if they find the tribunal's fees excessive (either in rate or amount of time devoted to the case), or how they can attempt to regulate the costs of a tribunal that is periodically assessing its own fees. We suspect that while some parties simply default on the tribunal's fees hoping that the other party will absorb these costs under its joint and several liability for them, few formally protest the reasonableness of them.

Question:	Why do less diligent co-arbitrators receive the same compensation as harder-working co-arbitrators?
Answer:	Generally, co-arbitrators receive the same compensation, regardless of the amount of work they have actually performed. In some institutional proceedings, co-arbitrator compensation is simply fixed at equal amounts. The ICC Court's general practice, for example, is to award 40% of the arbitrators' total fees to the chair and 30% to each of the co-arbitrators, unless the arbitrators agree otherwise. In other arbitration systems, however, less diligent co-arbitrators each receive the same level of compensation as their harder-working colleagues simply because there is no viable mechanism – and likely no desire of the other arbitrators – to single out the compensation of an individual member of the tribunal. It is unfortunate that co-arbitrators can play little or no role in the arbitration and yet still receive full compensation that is intended to remunerate work performed. But it may well be the case that word will

---

80. See, e.g., *ICT Pty Ltd v. Sea Containers Ltd* (2000) 17(3) Mealey's IAR B1; Lew, Mistelis & Kröll, 261.
81. Lew, Mistelis & Kröll, 284–286.

> spread about the energy levels of these arbitrators and they will,
> as a result, get fewer appointments in the future than their more
> diligent colleagues.

5-113 *Staged payments*. In institutional arbitration, the party commencing the arbitration will, when filing its initial submission, make an initial advance payment on the costs of the arbitration. The costs of the arbitration comprise the fees and expenses of the institution, which will be modest, and the fees and expenses of the arbitrators, which will be much more substantial. This initial deposit will be soon followed by a demand for a larger advance by both sides. Further advance payments may be payable during the course of the arbitration, although in ICC arbitration, to take just one example, all or most of the fees are payable in the early stages of the case (despite the tribunal performing most of its work at the end).[82]

5-114 *Separate advances on costs*. Although the ICC Rules provide initially for a single advance on costs covering all of the claims and counterclaims referred to arbitration, they also permit the Court to fix separate advances on costs when counterclaims are submitted in addition to the principal claims.[83] This provision was originally introduced to discourage the submission of exorbitant counterclaims by respondents seeking to increase the amount of the advance on costs that the claimant might be required to bear. In practice, the Court is unlikely to fix a separate advance in the absence of a request by one of the parties.[84]

5-115 *Party failing to pay arbitration costs*. What happens if one party fails to make its advance payment? The general rule is that, if the party has asserted claims, those claims will be deemed withdrawn without prejudice: so if the defaulting party is the claimant, and the respondent has not raised counterclaims, the claimant's failure to pay will lead the arbitration to end; if the defaulting party is the counterclaimant, the counterclaims will be considered withdrawn and only the claimant's claims will be heard.[85] But if a respondent that has not asserted counterclaims fails to make the advance payment, the claimant will be required to pay the full amount, including the respondent's share, in order for the arbitration to proceed and its claims to be heard. If a claimant facing counterclaims fails to make payment, the counterclaimant will have to pay the full amount if it wishes to pursue its counterclaims although, as discussed, the claimant's claims will be deemed withdrawn.[86]

5-116 *Reallocation by tribunal of arbitration costs*. Irrespective of who pays the costs of the arbitration up front, the tribunal in its award may reallocate the burden between the parties. This may follow the instructions of the parties in their arbitration

---

82. Chapter 1, *The Elements of an International Dispute Resolution Agreement*.
83. See Art. 30(2) of the ICC Rules.
84. See Derains & Schwartz, 341.
85. See, e.g., Art. 30(4) of the ICC Rules; Art. 24.4 of the LCIA Rules; Art. 26.5 of the SIAC Rules.
86. See Arts 30(3), 30(4) of the ICC Rules; Arts 24.3, 24.4 of the LCIA Rules; Arts 26.5, 26.7 of the SIAC Rules.

agreement or in the arbitration rules they have selected. Most often, neither gives specific direction and instead they leave the matter to the tribunal's discretion. The usual practice today in international arbitration – with the exception of ICSID arbitration, where costs are shared more often than not – is that the tribunal will order the loser, if one can be identified, to pay some or all of the arbitration costs, and frequently the legal fees, of the winner.[87]

Should a party ever decline to pay arbitration costs? Should a respondent who has **5-117** asserted no claims pay its share of the arbitration costs? Our advice is that if it can, it should, as it will have committed to do so when agreeing to arbitration. The failure to live up to that commitment may leave a poor impression with the tribunal at an early stage of the arbitration, unless there are good grounds for not making the payment. One situation where there may well be good grounds for not making payment is where the respondent contests, in good faith, the jurisdiction of the tribunal. In this situation, the respondent will argue that as it has not agreed to submit disputes to arbitration, it has not agreed to pay any arbitration costs, and it should not be required to do so.

Interim measures requiring a party to pay arbitration costs. If one party fails to pay **5-118** its share of the arbitration costs, it may make sense for the opposing party to seek an interim measure, usually from the arbitral tribunal and not a court, ordering the defaulting party to pay up.[88] If successful, this could reduce the financial burden of the moving party and, in any event, it may effectively highlight to the tribunal the bad faith or otherwise inappropriate conduct of the defaulting party. The trend is for tribunals to make such an order if one is sought, unless the defaulting party has objected in good faith to the tribunal's jurisdiction.[89] Whether the defaulting party will comply with the tribunal's order is another matter, and the sanction if it does not comply is unclear. From a practical enforcement perspective, arbitral tribunals generally lack the coercive powers of state courts to enforce their orders. Penalties for non-compliance are only possible if the parties have either agreed upon them or they are specifically allowed by the applicable law. In all other cases the intervention of the courts is necessary for these measures to be enforced.[90]

I.   Preliminary Steps Taken by the Tribunal When Constituted: Procedural Timetable and 'Terms of Reference'

Introduction. Once the arbitrators have all been appointed or confirmed by the **5-119** institution, court, or appointing authority, the tribunal will be constituted and it can

---

87. Chapter 3, *When the Dispute Arises.*
88. See below at M.
89. See Derains & Schwartz, 345–350. See also M. Secomb, 'Awards and Orders Dealing with the Advance on Costs in ICC Arbitration: Theoretical Questions and Practical Problems', *ICC Court Bulletin* 14, no. 1 (2003): 59–70.
90. See Lew, Mistelis & Kröll, 610.

proceed with the arbitration. If there is an institution involved, it will transfer the file to the constituted tribunal. The institution's role will become less prominent going forward, with the tribunal taking over the management of the case to a greater or lesser extent depending on the institution. However, the institution will continue to look after the arbitration costs and compliance with any applicable deadlines for issuance of the award. Usual practice is that all communications to and from the tribunal in the arbitration are sent in copy to the institution.

5-120 *Procedural timetable.* The initial step typically taken by the tribunal once it is formed will be to fix the timetable for the future conduct of the arbitration. This is often done at a preliminary hearing or meeting (sometimes held by conference call) convened by the tribunal. Before that takes place, the tribunal will usually solicit the parties' views, and the parties may reach agreement among themselves, subject to the tribunal's approval, on the procedure and deadlines.

5-121 *Typical steps on the timetable.* The typical items negotiated in this way, and which will end up on the procedural calendar, include:

– the dates for submission of the parties' written argument and the content of those submissions (and, notably, whether they include documentary evidence, witness statements, expert reports, and legal authorities);
– whether there are any preliminary issues the tribunal should decide at the outset of the arbitration, or whether the proceedings should be bifurcated to promote efficiency;
– the dates for submission of the parties' written evidence and authorities (if these are not submitted with the parties' written argument);
– the different steps in any discovery or document production process;
– the date of any pre-hearing conference;
– the dates of the hearing.

We provide an example of a procedural timetable in Appendix 10.

5-122 *Different procedural phases.* The position may be more complex if the arbitration is split into different phases. For example, and as discussed further below, objections to jurisdiction may be heard and decided before the merits, or issues of liability may be heard before quantum (the amount of damages, if any are due). If this is the case, each of the steps listed above may need to be scheduled for each phase.

5-123 *Other procedural directions.* At the same time as the tribunal establishes the procedural timetable, it may issue directions on different procedural issues, if these have not already been agreed upon by the parties. Examples include the need for translation of written evidence and the detailed procedures for presentation of argument and witness testimony at the hearing. UNCITRAL has published 'Notes on Organizing Arbitral Proceedings', which provide a helpful checklist and commentary on the procedural matters that a tribunal and the parties may want to consider at this stage, or later in the arbitration.[91]

---

91. Available at <www.uncitral.org/pdf/english/texts/arbitration/arb-notes/arb-notes-e.pdf>.

Terms of reference. The ICC Rules of Arbitration require the tribunal to draw up a **5-124** document called the 'terms of reference' within two months of receiving the arbitration file from the ICC. This document is something of an anachronism from a time when the procedural laws of many countries, most notably of France, did not allow parties to opt out of the jurisdiction of the courts in advance of a dispute actually arising. Dispute resolution clauses in contracts were therefore generally considered unenforceable. To overcome this and avoid having their disputes resolved by the courts, parties began summarising their existing dispute in a document that specifically referred it to arbitration. Since that time, most countries have gradually adopted procedural laws that uphold the validity of arbitration agreements contained in contracts, obviating the need for terms of reference as a means of ensuring that arbitrators have jurisdictions to hear the disputes before them. Yet the practice remains, most notably at the ICC.

Content of terms of reference. The purpose advanced today for the terms of **5-125** reference is to crystallise at an early stage of the arbitration the content and scope of the arbitration to be conducted. It will include a summary of the parties' claims and counterclaims, an indication of the amount in dispute (to allow the ICC to calculate the arbitrators' fees), and a list of the issues that the tribunal is to resolve, as well as confirmation of the place of arbitration, applicable procedural rules, and details of the parties and the arbitrators.[92] The ICC Rules require the parties and the arbitrators to sign the terms of reference, after which the tribunal will forward it to the ICC Court for approval. If a party declines to sign, the tribunal will still transmit the document to the ICC Court for approval. Once the Court approves, the arbitration can proceed. There are those who believe the terms of reference add value in the proceedings; others see it as a relatively meaningless procedural step which adds only cost. In practice, however, the document is most likely to be a cut-and-paste copy of the claims, defences and counterclaims from the parties' initial pleadings together with standard language imported from other arbitrations. So, even if it is a necessary procedural step that in itself adds little value to the overall proceedings, it is not a step that should require a large investment of time or cost.

Preparing the terms of reference. The tribunal usually prepares a draft of the terms **5-126** of reference and circulates it for input from the parties. The tribunal will often ask the parties to each draft a summary of its claims and the relief it seeks, for inclusion in the document. Each party has a free hand to include what it wants in this section, within reasonable space constraints: certainly, the other side should not be entitled to change the first party's summary, as it will be made clear that each party's summary reflects only that party's position and, by signing the terms, the opposing party is not making any admissions regarding the content of that summary.

---

92. See Art. 18(1) of the ICC Rules.

5-127 *New claims.* The simplest and most common practice in drafting the summaries is, as noted, to import the relevant text by cutting and pasting from the parties' initial pleadings (Request, Answer, and possibly Reply). However, it is open to the parties to effectively amend their initial pleadings at any time up to the signature of the terms of reference, and notably to raise in the terms of reference – and thus in the arbitration – new claims and counterclaims not mentioned in the initial pleadings. One of the important consequences of the terms of reference is that it in theory precludes the parties from making, after the terms have been signed, new claims or counterclaims outside the limits of the terms of reference, unless specifically authorised to do so by the tribunal.[93] However, the limits of the terms of reference may be unclear, especially if the arbitrators choose general language that may commit them to resolving all issues that emerge from the parties' submissions, whether or not raised before the terms of reference were signed. And in any event, arbitrators will often prefer to hear together all disputes that belong together, unless the party raising the claim or counterclaim is inexcusably dilatory in doing so.

5-128 *Other points to include in terms of reference.* The tribunal may include provisions on other matters in the terms of reference. For example, it is good practice for a tribunal to include a statement that the parties at that time have no objections, and no grounds for objection of which they are aware, regarding the conduct of the arbitration and the jurisdiction and constitution of the tribunal. If the parties then sign the document without reservation, they may well be held to have waived any right to challenge or resist enforcement of an award based on facts of which they were aware at that time. If a party wishes to object to the constitution or jurisdiction of the tribunal, it should not sign the terms of reference unless the document records the existence of the objection.

5-129 *Signature of terms of reference.* The terms of reference will ordinarily be finalised and signed by the parties at the preliminary hearing, if one is held, after which the parties and the tribunal will generally discuss and determine the procedural calendar (called the provisional timetable in ICC arbitration). If no hearing is held, the terms of reference will be circulated to the parties and each tribunal member for signature.

5-130 *Effect of terms of reference.* As well as possibly precluding new claims, the terms of reference will – if signed by the parties – form a new arbitration agreement, which may correct defects or ambiguities in the original arbitration agreement. It is also, arguably, binding on the arbitrators, who may not be able to depart from it or from any procedural decisions it contains without the agreement of the parties.[94] Still, the establishment of the provisional timetable is of more importance in practice, and the subject of more negotiation and disagreement, than the terms of reference.

---

93. See Art. 19 of the ICC Rules.
94. See Lew Mistelis & Kröll, 529–530.

Instruments similar to terms of reference. Among the other major arbitral institu- **5-131** tions, only the SIAC has an instrument similar to the ICC's terms of reference. Article 17, introduced in the 2007 edition of the SIAC Rules, requires the tribunal to draw up a 'memorandum of issues' for signature by the tribunal and the parties. As its name suggests, the document need only contain a list of issues to be resolved by the tribunal, not summaries of the parties' positions or other items. Interestingly, the memorandum is to be drawn up after the exchange of the parties' written submissions (and not before, as with the terms of reference in ICC arbitration). This should allow the tribunal to define with more precision what it is to decide in its award.

ICC terms of reference: missing an important opportunity?	Benign though it may be, the current practice in ICC arbitration of presenting parties with terms of reference that merely parrot the initial pleadings misses an important opportunity. The outset of the arbitration could be a time during which the parties and the tribunal together attempt to identify the most critical issues in dispute and the most appropriate methods of deciding them. In other words, the tribunal and the parties could negotiate in greater depth over the most efficient and satisfactory way to conduct the proceedings. Instead, the drawing up of the terms of reference has become a largely perfunctory exercise that tribunals and parties comply with only because the ICC requires it for the arbitration to proceed.

Preliminary hearing to finalise the timetable. Provided the amount in dispute is **5-132** enough to make the time and expense worthwhile, holding a preliminary hearing is helpful in any arbitration – whether or not there are terms of reference to sign. Not only does a hearing in person allow for live debate of the proposals for the procedural calendar, it enables each party to get a better feel for its judges and, more generally, for a proceeding that may be of great importance to it, and which is likely to consume substantial amounts of money, time, and manpower. The arbitrators will also benefit from meeting the parties and their representatives, and perhaps each other if they are not already acquainted. Holding the preliminary exchanges in person in this way, rather than by telephone or even in correspondence, clearly makes subsequent interaction between the tribunal and the parties easier.

Other reasons for holding a preliminary hearing. Having a hearing at this stage **5-133** may also allow the tribunal to hear in person any procedural or interlocutory applications that the parties may have, such as requests for interim measures. If a preliminary hearing is held, the venue will be the place of arbitration or another more convenient location. There is usually no call for a transcript of the hearing, although the tribunal will usually keep and issue minutes. The meeting will rarely last for more than half a day, unless there are significant applications to be heard.

Checklist 5d – Issues which may be Addressed at Preliminary Hearing[95]

- Location of bearings
- Administrative services for tribunal (e.g., appointment of an administrative secretary)
- Deposits in respect of costs
- Confidentiality of information
- Routing of written communications
- Means of sending documents
- Arrangements for the exchange of written submissions
- Method of submission, copies, numbering, references
- Defining points at issue; order of deciding issues
- Possible settlement negotiations
- Fixing the procedural calendar (including hearing dates)
- Addressing applications for bifurcation of the arbitration
- Documentary evidence
- Determining the scope of document production and the document production timetable
- Witnesses
- Experts and expert witnesses
- Hearing procedure
- Multi-party arbitration
- Interim measures

J.   TIME LIMITS FOR THE COMPLETION OF THE ARBITRATION

5-134 The parties' arbitration agreement or arbitration rules may specify a time limit within which the arbitration must be completed and an award rendered. One well-known example is the ICC Rules, which specify that the tribunal must render its final award within six months of the date of the last signature of the terms of reference.[96] In our experience, this deadline is almost always extended by the ICC Court, usually on its own initiative (as the Rules permit),[97] because in practice even a simple ICC arbitration is rarely completed in that six-month time frame. The

---

95. See the UNCITRAL Notes on Organizing Arbitral Proceedings (2006), available at <www.uncitral.org/pdf/english/texts/arbitration/arb-notes/arb-notes-e.pdf>. See also J. Van den Berg, 'Organizing an International Arbitration: Practice Pointers' in *The Leading Arbitrators' Guide to International Arbitration*, ed. L.W. Newman & R.D. Hill (United States: Juris, 2008), 156–158.
96. See Art. 24(1) of the ICC Rules.
97. See Art. 24(2) of the ICC Rules.

tribunal and parties to an ICC arbitration should therefore expect to periodically receive a standard letter informing them that the ICC Court has extended the period for rendering the award by some months. This does not mean that the ICC Court has actually taken a special interest in the case. Rather, the letter is sent by the assigned case manager to ensure that the award will not be unenforceable by virtue of having been rendered after the expiration of the time limitation stated in the ICC's own rules.

Intermediate time limits. The parties may agree in their arbitration agreement on **5-135** intermediate deadlines and time limits for various procedural steps. Some arbitration rules, such as those of the LCIA and the SIAC, set out specific deadlines for submission of written statements, although these can be overridden by party agreement or by decision of the tribunal. In ICC and ICSID arbitration, the arbitration rules give the tribunal the power to fix the deadlines not agreed by the parties. In all arbitration systems, the tribunal will generally set the timetable for submissions after consulting the parties – often before or at the preliminary hearing.

Determining the length of deadlines. How long these deadlines eventually are will **5-136** depend on a number of factors, including any direction or guidelines in the parties' agreement and the arbitration rules, the complexity of the case, the practice in a given arbitration system, the parties' respective positions, and the availability for the final hearing of the parties and the arbitrators. If the final hearing cannot be held for a year, it makes little sense to set deadlines for the submission of all written argument and evidence within six months.

Non-compliance with deadlines. Parties will often request and receive extensions **5-137** to the applicable time limits, although the tribunal will be keen to ensure that each party is treated equally, at least in rough terms. The tribunal is likely to be reluctant to grant an extension that would cause the final hearing to be postponed, or to significantly curtail time for preparation of the hearing after submission of all written argument and evidence. Generally speaking, arbitrators and opponents will tolerate the failure by a party to precisely comply with time limits for submissions of argument and evidence, unless harsher treatment has previously been ordered by the tribunal or agreed by the parties. Exactly how tolerant should the tribunal be, and what is the appropriate penalty where a party is substantially or persistently late in meeting deadlines? The tribunal has to weigh up, in the circumstances, considerations of fairness and equal treatment of the parties, such as the reasons for the delay and the prejudice that the penalty would cause to the delaying party as compared to the prejudice that the delay would cause to the compliant party.[98]

---

98. See Redfern & Hunter, para. 6–58; Lew, Mistelis & Kröll, 541.

K.   BIFURCATION (OR EARLY DISPOSAL OF DISCRETE
                     ISSUES BY THE TRIBUNAL)

5-138 *Issues suited to early disposal.* The default position in most international arbitrations is that all the issues will be briefed, evidenced, heard, and decided together. This has the benefit of simplicity, but it may also be extremely inefficient.[99] There are many situations where the early disposal of certain discrete issues, especially of a legal nature, could achieve substantial savings of time and money. We discuss several examples below.

5-139 *Preliminary decision of an objection to jurisdiction.* Probably the best example of an issue that is ripe for early adjudication is a party's objections to jurisdiction. It may well be that a successful objection to jurisdiction will bring the case to an end, as the tribunal will not have the power to proceed to hear the merits. This is why certain arbitration rules and laws contain a presumption or rule that jurisdiction objections should be heard as a preliminary issue.[100] Even if there is no such express presumption or rule, the powers to determine the procedure given to the tribunal by most arbitration rules will permit the arbitrators to hear and dispose of issues early. Also, of course, the parties may agree – either in their arbitration agreement or after the arbitration has begun – to have jurisdiction objections and similar issues resolved at the outset.

5-140 *Choice of law.* If the parties proceed to the merits with the governing law still in dispute, they may be required to argue their case under two or more different laws, with the attendant increase in time and cost. The choice of law will have to be argued and decided at some stage: common sense dictates that this should be at the outset, allowing the parties to present their case in the law that they are sure applies.

5-141 *Time bar defences.* Time bar and similar defences are often factually independent of the merits of the case and may, if successful, prevent the entire case going forward. Rather than have the parties expensively brief and prove the merits, it will often be more cost effective for a discrete defence such as this, which will have to be decided at some stage, to be resolved as a preliminary matter.

5-142 *Liability versus quantum.* Similarly, it may make sense to hear and decide issues of liability before questions of quantum, because a finding of no liability will dispense with the need to address and prove quantum – which is often an extremely laborious and expensive exercise.

5-143 *Issues not dispositive of the entire case, but which substantially narrow the scope of the dispute.* Many critical issues can usefully be decided upfront if they are independent of the rest of the case. For example, a common defence against a lost profits claim is reliance on a limitation of liability provision in the parties'

---

99. See, e.g., M. McIlwrath & R. Schroeder, 'The view from an International Arbitration Customer: In Dire Need of Early Resolution', *Arbitration* 74, no. 3 (2008).

100. See, e.g., Art. 21(4) of the UNCITRAL Rules; Art. 186(3) of the Swiss Private International Law Act.

contract, which, on its face, prevents recovery for lost profits. The lost profits claim may be significantly larger than any claim for actual loss, and an early decision that lost profits are not recoverable would therefore streamline the arbitration, saving time and cost, and could promote early settlement. Again, the effectiveness of the defence will have to be decided at some stage, so why not do so at the outset? In most cases there will be discrete legal or contractual issues of this sort that can be decided early and productively without the need for much or any factual discussion and, crucially, without significant document production and witness testimony.

Grounds for resisting bifurcation. Although the early resolution of potentially **5-144** dispositive issues often makes good sense, not all arbitrators are inclined to 'bifurcate' proceedings in this way, especially if one of the parties objects. Parties (usually claimants or counterclaimants) often do object, sometimes on tactical grounds as they fear the elimination or reduction of their settlement leverage. A frequent and occasionally valid objection to early disposal is that the potentially dispositive application and the merits of the case are so intertwined that the application cannot properly be heard and decided independently of the merits. Another valid objection may be that the time, cost, and inconvenience involved in briefing, hearing, and deciding a preliminary issue, and the delay caused if the preliminary issue is decided against the moving party, outweigh the savings achieved if the moving party is successful. Still, in many cases it will make sense for the parties and the tribunal to consider whether at least some issues should be decided at the outset.

Partial awards. Tribunals may render partial awards in relation to specific and **5-145** discrete issues appropriate for resolution at an early stage in the arbitration, for example, on jurisdiction or the applicable law. Partial awards are final, as they finally resolve the disputes they cover, but they only cover part of the dispute. This is in contrast with interim awards, which are provisional and not final (but which may cover part or all of the dispute). While the early resolution of specific preliminary issues may streamline the arbitration and be conducive to settlement, the risk with partial awards is that they will delay the arbitration even if they are not challenged in the courts of the seat of arbitration, and that if they are then challenged, the delay and disruption will be greater still.[101]

L. Fast-Track or Expedited Arbitration

No summary judgment in international arbitration. One of the perceived disad- **5-146** vantages of international arbitration is that there is no mechanism for the rapid disposal of straightforward claims. In most court systems, a claimant can move for

---

101. See Lew Mistelis & Kröll, 632.

summary judgment, which is a decision made on the basis of statements and evidence presented for the record without a trial. In international arbitration, summary judgment is not available under any of the major arbitration rules. The parties may agree in their contract to some form of summary judgment process, although this is seldom done in practice.

5-147 *Fast-track arbitration.* The parties may also agree, either in their contract or when a dispute arises, to a form of accelerated or 'fast-track' procedure, the goal of which is to have the dispute resolved by an award rendered in a period of months, weeks, or even days. It usually involves having a sole arbitrator, a reduced number of written pleadings and evidence, short deadlines (including for issuance of the award), and a short hearing (or no hearing at all). The difficulty where the parties have agreed to a fast-track procedure in their contract is that when a dispute later arises, one of the parties may be unwilling to go fast. Without the cooperation of both parties, it may be difficult in practice to achieve an award on an expedited basis, and any award obtained may be vulnerable to challenge for lack of due process. Imagine, for instance, that a claimant has been preparing its claim for months without notifying the opponent, and then suddenly demands fast-track arbitration and submits reams of pleadings and evidence. If the opponent, pursuant to the parties' agreement, has only days or weeks to respond, it may not be able to adequately present its case. Fast-track arbitration will therefore work better where the parties already have a dispute that both, at that stage, want resolved on an accelerated basis. But in that case it may still be challenging to find a suitable arbitrator or tribunal available and willing to meet the expedited deadlines laid down by the parties.[102]

5-148 *Procedural rules for expedited arbitrations.* Suggestions for the adoption of procedural rules to facilitate the speedy commencement of arbitration and resolution of the dispute might include an express provision for (1) appointment of a sole arbitrator; (2) electronic correspondence and telephone conferencing; (3) limits on the lengths of briefs; (4) time limits for exchange of pleadings and for the hearing; (5) truncated grounds of decision; and (6) the exclusion of appeal mechanisms.[103] At the time of this writing, for example, the HKIAC, the SCC, the German Arbitration Institute (DIS) and the International Institute for Conflict Prevention and Resolution (CPR) have issued special rules for arbitration proceedings on an accelerated timetable, which parties can adopt if they want proceedings concluded quickly and with a less burdensome procedural approach than might otherwise be adopted.

---

102. One example of a successful fast-track arbitration, where the institution (the ICC) and the parties cooperated, is described in Redfern & Hunter, paras 6–266-6–269.
103. See Redfern & Hunter, 6–273; 'Techniques for Controlling Time and Costs in Arbitration', *ICC Court Bulletin* 18, no.1 (2007): 23–42.

Article 9, LCIA rules. Article 9 of the LCIA Rules contemplates the expedited **5-149** formation of the tribunal where there is 'exceptional urgency'. It authorises the LCIA Court, in its complete discretion, to 'abridge or curtail' any time limit contained in the rules concerning the formation of the tribunal. Although this is not a true fast-track process, as it covers only the formation of the tribunal and not the balance of the arbitration, it can be highly effective in accelerating the arbitration as a whole. It shows that even within the framework of the existing rules of major institutions, it is possible to have the rapid disposal of claims without the specific agreement of the counterparty to an accelerated procedure (see panel). However, the requirement that the moving party show exceptional urgency is a high threshold. Still, Article 9 of the LCIA Rules is a valuable, distinguishing feature of LCIA arbitration.

Not that this really ever happens: arbitration in seven weeks without fast-track procedures	In an LCIA arbitration in London in which one of the authors was involved, the claimant requested arbitration on 12 January, seeking the expedited formation of the tribunal on the grounds that the respondent's only disclosed asset was its stake in a company that was in turmoil (which in turn made it uncertain that on issuance of the final award the shares would hold their then current value), and that the respondent was likely to dissipate its other assets to prevent effective enforcement of a final award; on 15 January the LCIA Court agreed that there was exceptional urgency; on 17 January the LCIA Court appointed the tribunal (the arbitration agreement called for a sole arbitrator, which made the Court's task easier); written pleadings and evidence were exchanged and two hearings were held, one on interim measures on 21 January and one on the merits on 1 March; and the arbitrator issued his award on 5 March, finding in favour of the claimant on the merits after previously granting interim measures. In other words, only seven weeks passed between request for arbitration and award, despite there being no formal fast-track procedure, and despite the respondent participating in the arbitration but not agreeing to the accelerated conduct of the case. There was no action to set aside and no attempt by the respondent to resist enforcement on the grounds of an absence of due process. It is fair to say that in this example the sole arbitrator and the institution were unusually flexible in moving things along, and that if the arbitration clause had called for three arbitrators, the case would have taken much longer.

Fast-track ad hoc arbitration. By contrast, it is virtually impossible to engage in a **5-150** fast-track ad hoc proceeding absent the consent of both parties. This is because the cooperation of each is needed to constitute the tribunal and get the arbitration underway.

M.   Urgent or Provisional Measures

5-151 *Types of urgent or provisional measures.* At any stage of the arbitration, and even before it starts, a party may apply to the tribunal, court, or other authority (such as an ICC pre-arbitral referee) for provisional measures relating to the arbitration. Applications for provisional measures (also referred to as conservatory, interim, or interlocutory measures) are most common at the outset of an arbitration. The situations where these measures are sought, and the nature of the measures themselves, are numerous and varied, and are seldom restricted by applicable laws or arbitration rules. Measures typically granted include injunctions to prevent harm caused by the opponent's ongoing conduct or to stop the opponent suing the applicant in another forum, orders to preserve evidence that may otherwise disappear, the attachment of assets to prevent their dissipation, or the provision of security for the moving party's claims or for its costs. What these applications usually have in common is that the claimant believes urgent relief is needed on a temporary basis pending the issuance of the award in order to prevent its suffering serious or perhaps irreparable harm.

5-152 *Concurrent jurisdiction of tribunal and court.* Provisional measures can be sought by a party to an arbitration (or by a party who is bound by an arbitration agreement) either from the arbitral tribunal or from a court with jurisdiction, unless the parties' agreement or applicable law provides otherwise. National law will govern whether a court has jurisdiction to hear the application – a court of the seat of the arbitration will often have jurisdiction. Some laws give priority to the arbitrators, requiring the parties to apply first to the tribunal if it is formed and has the power to act.[104] Others, such as Italian law or Chinese law, do not allow arbitrators to award any interim measures.[105] Where a court in an arbitration-friendly jurisdiction does hear an application for interim measures, it will generally do so with a view to supporting, rather than supplanting, the arbitral tribunal, and the court's decision will be subject to later review by the tribunal.[106]

5-153 *No waiver of arbitration agreement.* Applying to a court for provisional measures will not in itself be a waiver of a party's rights to insist that the merits of the case be resolved in arbitration under the arbitration agreement. The Model Law allows a

---

104. See, e.g., s. 44(5) of the English Arbitration Act; and Art. 183 of the Swiss Private International Law Act.

105. See Art. 818 of the Italian Code of Civil Procedure, which provides that 'The arbitrators may not grant attachments or other interim measures of protection, except if otherwise provided by the law.' See C. Giovannucci-Orlandi, 'La nouvelle réglementation italienne de l'arbitrage après la loi du 2 février 2006', *Revue de l'arbitrage* 1 (2008): 29. On Chinese law, see N. Darwazeh & M.J. Moser, 'Arbitration inside China', in *Managing Business Disputes in Today's China*, ed. M.J. Moser (The Netherlands: Kluwer Law International, 2007), 79–81.

106. E. Gaillard & J. Savage (eds), *Fouchard Gaillard Goldman on International Commercial Arbitration* (The Netherlands: Kluwer Law International, 1999), 1130; J. Lew, L. Mistelis & S. Kröll. Comparative International Commercial Arbitration (Kluwer Law International, 2003), para. 23–130.

party to go to court for interim measures, and a court to grant them, without that being 'incompatible with an arbitration agreement'.[107] Similarly, the ICC Rules provide that any application by a party to court for provisional measures, before and even after the constitution of the tribunal, 'shall not be deemed to be an infringement or waiver of the arbitration agreement'.[108] Being able to go to court for provisional measures without waiving rights to arbitration is important, as in many cases the urgent relief is needed before the arbitration has started, or in the period of three months or so after the arbitration has started but before the tribunal has been constituted. At that juncture there is no tribunal to which a party in need of urgent relief can apply; its only option will be to go to court. Applications to court after the tribunal is constituted will not lead to a waiver either, but are likely to be viewed with more of a critical eye by courts in arbitration-friendly jurisdictions, who will need persuading that the arbitrators are not in a position to order the relief.

Ex parte applications. Parties may apply to certain courts for interim measures on **5-154** an ex parte basis (without informing the opponent), but ex parte interim measures by arbitral tribunals are not currently permitted under any major system of international arbitration. A controversial provision on ex parte interim measures was incorporated in the 2006 version of the Model Law.[109] However, at the time of writing, only New Zealand had implemented this provision into its arbitration law (while Hong Kong and Singapore were considering it).

Standards for an award of provisional measures. International arbitrators hearing **5-155** applications for interim measures may, in practice, not look to standards for granting such measures found in any one legal system (such as the law of the place of arbitration or the law governing the substance of the dispute). They often prefer instead to apply standards that they consider to be more broadly accepted. These will invariably include a requirement that the claimant show at least an arguable prima facie case, urgency, and some level of risk of serious or irreparable harm. Whether the harm can be adequately compensated by a damages award will be another factor, as will the balance of convenience: whether granting the measure will cause the respondent more harm than the harm the claimant would suffer if the application were refused. The tribunal may also ask the claimant to post some form of undertaking or security to compensate the respondent, if the respondent were to prevail in the final award, for the harm has suffered as a result of the grant of the provisional measure.

Enforcement of interim measures. Interim measures ordered by a court may be **5-156** difficult to enforce outside the jurisdiction of that court, particularly if no treaty applies governing the enforcement of judgments. In practice, arbitral tribunals frequently decide on interim measures in the form of an 'order' rather than in

---

107. See Art. 9 of the Model Law.
108. See Art. 23(2) of the ICC Rules.
109. See Ch. 4, s. 2 of the Model Law as amended in 2006, available at <www.uncitral.org/uncitral/en/uncitral_texts/arbitration/1985Model_arbitration.html>.

an 'award'. Even if granted by tribunals in an 'interim award' or another instrument described as an 'award', interim measures may still be tricky to enforce as, by their nature, they do not finally decide any part of the dispute. Whatever label is applied, interim measures are therefore unlikely to qualify as awards for the purpose of enforcement. As a result, they are unlikely to be covered by the New York Convention or similar national enforcement legislation outside the jurisdiction where they are rendered. That said, a party that does not comply voluntarily with provisional measures ordered by a tribunal (or a court for that matter) is not likely to be improving its chances of success on the merits.

5-157 *ICC Pre-Arbitral Referee Procedure.* The parties may refer urgent matters for rapid, preliminary disposal under the ICC Rules for a Pre-Arbitral Referee Procedure.[110] An express agreement by the parties to do so is required.[111] Mere reference to arbitration under the ICC Arbitration Rules does not encompass the Pre-Arbitral Referee Procedure. Also, reference to the ICC Rules for a Pre-Arbitral Referee Procedure may be combined with arbitration under the auspices of an arbitral institution other than the ICC, or ad hoc arbitration. The Rules for a Pre-Arbitral Referee Procedure provide for the appointment of a referee by the ICC to hear and decide an application for certain provisional measures within thirty days of receiving the application. According to national court decisions to date, the referee's decision is provisional and is considered to be of a contractual nature, not an arbitral award. Although the pre-arbitral referee mechanism was not used for many years, recently it has been put to the test and has performed well[112] – and can be a valuable addition to an international arbitration agreement.[113] The ICDR Rules organise a similar process in their Article 37, which allows for the appointment of an emergency arbitrator to hear an application for urgent measures pending the constitution of the tribunal. This has the added merit of not requiring a specific reference in the arbitration clause: selection of the ICDR Rules will suffice.

5-158 *Provisional measures in ICSID arbitration.* Disputing parties in the ICSID arbitration system may only apply for provisional measures from the arbitral tribunal, and not from national courts, unless the parties agree otherwise in their arbitration agreement or applicable investment treaty. However, parties need not wait until the tribunal is constituted to make their application: they may apply for the measure as soon as the arbitration is registered by ICSID, and the ICSID Secretary General will fix a briefing schedule so that

---

110. See the ICC Rules for a Pre-Arbitral Referee Procedure, available at <www.iccwbo.org/court/ arbitration>.
111. The ICC Model Clause reads: 'Any party to this contract shall have the right to have recourse to and shall be bound by the pre-arbitral referee procedure of the ICC in accordance with its Rules for a Pre-arbitral Referee Procedure.'
112. See, e.g., E. Gaillard & P. Pinsolle, 'The ICC Pre-Arbitral Referee: First Practical Experiences', *Arbitration International* 20, no. 1 (2004): 1 et seq.; and E. Gaillard, 'ICC Pre-Arbitral Referee: A Procedure into Its Stride', *New York Law Journal* (5 Oct. 2006).
113. Chapter 1, *The Elements of an International Dispute Resolution Agreement.*

the application is ready for rapid disposal by the tribunal as soon as it is constituted.[114] ICSID tribunals only 'recommend' provisional measures,[115] rather than order them, although ICSID tribunals have held the provisional measures they recommend to be binding on the parties. The tribunal will recommend measures 'if it considers that the circumstances so require . . . to preserve the respective rights of either party'.[116]

Example 5c – Examples of Provisional Measures Ordered by Courts or Arbitral Tribunals

Measure Ordered	Name of Case	Ordering Court or Tribunal or Referee	Grounds for Order
Security for costs	ICC Case No. 1632/JJA[117]	Arbitral tribunal	Risk that award would not be carried out
Security for claim	LCIA Case No. 5620[118]	Arbitral tribunal	High risk of dissipation of assets by respondent
Anti-suit injunction	*SGS v. Pakistan*[119]	Arbitral tribunal	Protection of the claimant's right of access to international adjudication
Order preserving status quo (one party to continue performance of contract pending decision on the merits)	Procedure ICC No. 11904/DB[120]	Pre-Arbitral referee	Urgency and prevention of an irreparable loss

---

114. See ICSID Rule 39.
115. See Art. 47 of the ICSID Convention.
116. *Ibid.*
117. Interim Award (27 Jan. 1993), unpublished.
118. Interim Award (21 Jan. 2005), unpublished.
119. *Société Générale de Surveillance S.A. v. Islamic Republic of Pakistan* (ICSID Case No. ARB/01/13), Procedural Order No. 2 (16 Oct. 2002), available at <http://ita.law.uvic.ca>.
120. An English translation of the Referee's Order dated 6 Feb. 2002 is reproduced as Appendix 1 to E. Gaillard & P. Pinsolle, 'The ICC Pre-Arbitral Referee: First Practical Experiences', *Arbitration International* 20, no. 1 (2004): 24 et seq.

Attachment of assets in an amount of USD 300 million in support of ICC arbitration	*Exxon Mobil v. PDVSA*[121]	US Federal Court	Judge found it probable that Exxon would succeed on the merits in the arbitration Attachment to guarantee payment of award in case of victory[122]
Order requiring preservation of evidence	*Biwater Gauff v. Tanzania*[123]	Arbitral tribunal	Potential need for the evidence in question and urgency

II.   WRITTEN SUBMISSIONS AND EVIDENCE

5-159 *Second phase of the arbitration.* Once the tribunal is constituted and the timetable set, the arbitration moves into its second phase, which involves the parties submitting written argument on the issues in dispute and gathering and presenting written evidence to support their case.

5-160 *Possibility of bifurcation.* As discussed in the previous section, this phase of the arbitration may be a relatively simple affair, dealing with all the disputed issues together. Sometimes, however, it may be 'bifurcated', or split, so that certain issues – such as objections to jurisdiction or dispositive defences on the merits – are addressed before others. The discussion in this chapter should be relevant whichever approach is taken: whatever the contested issues, and whether they are heard alone or together with other issues, the chances are that for each of them there will be written submissions and the presentation of written evidence.

---

121. *Mobil Cerro Negro, Ltd v. PDVSA Cerro Negro S.A.*, United States District Court Southern District Court of New York, Civil Action No. 07 Civ. 11590 (DAB), 23 Feb. 2008, oral argument and Order Confirming Attachments dated 20 Feb. 2008. See also 'Venezuela fights freezing orders', *Global Arbitration Review*, News (15 Feb. 2008).
122. In the words of the judge as reported: 'to make sure there's something to pay at the end of the arbitration'. See 'Venezuela Fights Freezing Orders', *Global Arbitration Review*, News (15 Feb. 2008).
123. *Biwater Gauff (Tanzania) Ltd v. United Republic of Tanzania* (ICSID Case No. ARB/05/22), Procedural Order No. 1 (31 Mar. 2006), available at <http://ita.law.uvic.ca>.

A.   WRITTEN SUBMISSIONS

Purpose of submissions. The usual procedure in international arbitrations is that **5-161**
parties set out in written submissions (also called 'pleadings', 'briefs', 'statements', or 'memorials') the facts and contentions of law on which they rely',
and the relief they seek. The parties' submissions should be consistent with, but
more detailed than, their initial pleadings. The purpose of the submissions is to
present the parties' detailed arguments and evidence, and to persuade the tribunal
of their correctness. The advocacy contained in the submissions is likely to be at
least as important as that delivered orally in hearings, as it is increasingly common
for hearings to be taken up with the evidence (the examination of witnesses and
experts), with little opportunity for oral argument.[124]

Number of submissions. The number of submissions will be fixed by the tribunal **5-162**
if not agreed by the parties. The tribunal may simply follow the procedure laid
down in the arbitration rules: the rules of the LCIA and the SIAC, for example, as
well as the UNCITRAL rules, give specific direction as to which submissions
should be filed when, unless the parties agree or the tribunal determines
otherwise. The ICC rules, in contrast, give no instruction as to how or even
whether written submissions should be made, although Article 20(2) does appear
to assume the existence of written submissions, which is consistent with the
practice in ICC cases.

Different arrangements regarding timing of submissions. The variables here **5-163**
include whether to have written submissions at all, if so their number (and
which party files the last submission), their content, whether they should be
exchanged consecutively or simultaneously, and how much time the parties should
be given to submit them. The situation will be more complicated if counterclaims
have been raised, as these may need to be briefed on a different schedule to the
affirmative claims. Document production and other steps relating to the gathering
of evidence may also have an impact on this schedule. We do not propose to go
through all the different permutations here, but what we most frequently see in
practice is as follows: two consecutive exchanges of written submissions, called
(for example) 'statement of claim', 'statement of defence', 'statement of reply',
and 'statement of rejoinder'; between one and three months are ordinarily granted
for the preparation of each submission, and each submission will contain, in addition to the party's argument, all the written evidence and legal authorities (including documents, witness statements, and expert reports) on which the submitting
party relies. The parties' second submissions are intended to respond to the other
party's prior submission, and may contain additional evidence, including witness
statements, in response to arguments or evidence raised. If the respondent has
raised counterclaims, they may be addressed in separate submissions filed on

---

124. See below at III.

the same dates as the submissions on the affirmative claims (so, for example, when the claimant submits a statement of claim, the respondent will submit a statement of counterclaim) or in the same submissions as the affirmative claims (so the statement of counterclaim will accompany the statement of defence).

5-164 *New claims.* Under the ICC Rules, no party is permitted to make new claims or counterclaims that fall outside the limits of the terms of reference (discussed above) unless it has been authorised to do so by the arbitral tribunal.[125] This helps to ensure that the arbitration process is not unduly disrupted by the need to consider new matters. That said, the distinction between what falls within the 'limits' of the terms of reference may be subject to controversy; one such example is an increase in the amount claimed. Generally, however, the rule should not preclude new factual or legal arguments in support of claims already submitted.[126]

5-165 *Who has the last word?* In many international arbitrations each party will have the right to make the same number of written submissions, so the respondent will 'have the last word' and will therefore submit the last brief before the hearing. However, in jurisdictions or under arbitration rules that follow the tradition of English court litigation, the claimant may be given the last word. This can be seen in the default position under Article 15 of the LCIA Rules. Respondents may argue, with some force, that giving the claimant the last word (and thus two submissions whereas the respondent has just one) is unequal treatment and a violation of due process in jurisdictions which do not follow the English rule.

5-166 *Content of a written submission.* A submission in international arbitration will usually comprise an introduction or preliminary statement, a description of the relevant facts, analysis of the relevant rules of law, argument on the different issues in dispute (such as jurisdiction, liability, damages, interest, and costs), and a prayer for relief. The evidence (documents, witness statements, and expert reports) and legal authorities will often accompany the submission in an indexed 'bundle' (or file) of exhibits, each of which is stamped with a reference number. A persuasive submission will cite liberally to the exhibits in support of the allegations of fact and propositions of law advanced. Submissions may be prepared in electronic format, with hyperlinks to the exhibits to allow the arbitrators to more conveniently review the submission and its supporting documents together. Submissions may also contain photographs, charts and diagrams, and anything else that will clarify the facts and help the tribunal understand them. Below is an example of how photographs can be effectively used to rebut a contention.

---

125. See Art. 19 of the ICC Rules.
126. See Derains & Schwartz, 269.

Example 5d – Use of Photographs in Submissions

 The Claimant rejects the contention that the equipment should have been able to support the weight of workers walking on it, without damage being incurred. This would have been, charitably stated, an unusual requirement. The photo at left shows the height and steep incline workers would have been required to scale in  order to "step" on the equipment after it was installed. Before installation, any worker who needed to step on the equipment could have done so using boards, as shown at right, without causing damage.

Formal 'pleadings'. Formal written 'pleadings' in the peculiar style of the English **5-167** courts – where laconic, stylised paragraphs are advanced by the plaintiff and rebutted paragraph by paragraph by the defendant – are unusual in international arbitrations. They will generally be seen only when the arbitrators and lawyers are all more familiar with English court litigation than with the more transnational version of international arbitration. Instead, submissions in international arbitration will be expressed in relatively ordinary parlance and will 'tell the story' rather than comply with a menu of technical pleading requirements.

Preparation of submissions. The preparation and drafting of the written submissions, **5-168** and collection and presentation of the written evidence, is a time-consuming and expensive exercise. However, it is a crucial one, as the parties' case essentially resides in those submissions and accompanying exhibits. The parties will therefore conduct renewed factual investigation, based on their own additional document gathering and review, on the examination of documents provided by the opponent (either in document production or placed on the record by the opponent in support of its own position), and on interviews with witnesses, technical experts, and other people with knowledge of the relevant events and issues. There will also be more extensive legal research and analysis than earlier in the arbitration, sometimes with the assistance of an expert legal witness. All the pieces will then be brought together, the party's theory of the case refined, and the submission drafted and delivered. This task is made much easier if the respondent has already completed an Early Case Assessment (ECA),[127] which at this

---

127. Chapter 3, *When the Dispute Arises*.

stage will require updating in light of any new facts or evidence to emerge from the other side's submission.

5-169 *Length of submissions.* How long should a brief be? How long is a piece of string? The length of a submission should depend, in our view, on the number, size, and complexity of the claims being addressed: one of the authors fondly recalls submitting a 1,000 page statement of defence in a large and highly technical construction dispute, with over sixty individual claims and counterclaims. This was no doubt as challenging to read as it was to write, but in the circumstances – where each claim and counterclaim could have been the subject of its own fully-fledged arbitration – it was in fact a convenient and concise way to deal with all the claims advanced. That said, in many cases the parties' submissions are too long, and tribunals could usefully impose or recommend appropriate page limits more often than they do.

B.   WRITTEN EVIDENCE

5-170 *Introduction.* A party's written submissions contain its argument. That argument will be founded on allegations as to what the relevant facts are (e.g., the respondent failed to build a power plant by the date agreed in our contract, and this caused us loss), and contentions as to what the relevant rules of law say (e.g., a party who fails to build a power plant by an agreed date breaches the contract and is liable to compensate the counterparty for resulting loss). It is the tribunal's job to establish what the relevant facts are[128] and to identify the relevant rules of law and apply them to the facts. The parties, by presenting evidence as to facts, and authorities and opinions on the law, will assist the arbitrators in doing their job and deciding the case.

5-171 *Burden of proof.* The obligation of each party to prove the facts upon which it relies is often referred to as the 'burden of proof' – and it is a concept that applies in international arbitration as in the courts.

5-172 *Rules of evidence.* In most international arbitrations, technical rules of evidence (and particularly the complex rules of evidence found in common law systems) take a back seat in favour of a more pragmatic and discretionary approach. Few if any international arbitration rules or laws mandate the application, for example, of the law of evidence of the place of arbitration. On the contrary, many of them instead give the tribunal the discretion to determine as it sees fit the admissibility and relevance of any evidence.[129]

5-173 *IBA rules of evidence.* In practice, evidence in international arbitration today is frequently governed, or at least influenced, by the IBA Rules on the Taking of Evidence in International Commercial Arbitration (the IBA Rules). These rules, which were being revised by the IBA at the time of writing, were prepared by a

---

128. See, e.g., Art. 20(1) of the ICC Rules.
129. See, e.g., Art. 19(2) of the Model Law; Art. 9(1) of the IBA Rules.

Working Party comprising some of international arbitration's most respected practitioners from a broad array of jurisdictions. The Rules are intended to allow arbitrators and parties to conduct the evidentiary phase of international arbitrations in an efficient and economical manner.[130] They are designed to be used in conjunction with arbitration rules and reflect procedures in use in many different legal systems.[131] In the Working Party's view, the Rules 'may be particularly useful when the parties come from different legal cultures'.[132] In our experience, IBA Rules provide a reasonable and practical solution for a wide range of what otherwise – especially in transnational cases – can be extremely difficult issues. This is no small achievement, and is why the IBA Rules are widely regarded as a codification of best practice in international arbitration.

Four types of evidence addressed in IBA rules. The four types of evidence **5-174** addressed in the IBA Rules are contemporaneous documents, witnesses of fact, experts, and inspections. We look at each in turn below.

1. Contemporaneous Documents

Relevance of documentary evidence. In international arbitration, relevant **5-175** documents generated contemporaneously with the facts in dispute are probably the most persuasive form of evidence. This is especially true in cases that involve parties and arbitrators who are not from a common law litigation background (common law courts and lawyers often accord greater weight to oral testimony of witnesses).

Which documents to volunteer. The usual procedure in international arbitration is **5-176** that a party will offer with and in support of its submissions the contemporaneous documents on which it relies.[133] There is no real restriction on the form these documents can take. They may include correspondence – including letters, memoranda, and, importantly in practice, e-mails – among the disputing parties, among each party internally, and with and among third parties. The documents offered may also be publicly available, such as securities filings and press cuttings, as well as internal corporate documents, such as meeting minutes, board resolutions, financial statements, and so on. If the opposing party has already submitted the documents, there is generally no need to submit them again.[134]

Exhibit bundles. The documents furnished in this way will usually be contained in a **5-177** tabbed and indexed bundle (or file) of exhibits that is delivered to the tribunal and the opponent together with the parties' written submissions. For convenience, the exhibits should each be given a reference, which is stamped on the first page to

---

130. See IBA Rules, Foreword.
131. *Ibid.*
132. *Ibid.*
133. See, e.g., Art. 3(1) of the IBA Rules.
134. *Ibid.*

allow the document's provenance to be traced when it is removed from its bundles (at hearings, for example). Usually the reference will be a letter denoting the party who submitted the document (often 'C' for claimant and 'R' for respondent) followed by the number of the tab where the document is filed.

5-178 *Only copies of documents are needed.* A party in international arbitration needs to produce only its own copies of the documents it wishes to exhibit, not the originals or certified copies, unless there is an agreement or direction otherwise from the tribunal. If a party challenges the authenticity of a document, then a tribunal may require the parties to submit originals or certified copies and may be interested in having witnesses testify about the origin of the document.

5-179 *Translations of documents.* If the document is in a language other than the language of the arbitration, a translation may need to be supplied with the original document. This will depend on the instructions of the tribunal: it may be that no translation is required because the parties and arbitrators are sufficiently conversant with the language of the document. If a translation is required, it will not usually need to be certified or notarised, although this may be required if the unofficial translation is contested.

5-180 *Document production.* Except where a party opts, for tactical reasons, to be the first to disclose and explain potentially troublesome documents that it knows are in the possession of the other side, a party will generally provide with its submissions only those documents that are favourable to its case (or that are at least not unfavourable). This may mean that there will be documents within each disputing party's control that are favourable to the other party's case, but which the other party cannot immediately access. In the courts of common law jurisdictions (but not in many civil law courts) each party is entitled to ask the other to provide it with documents that the other party has not already placed on the record and that the first party believes will be relevant to its case. This practice is now common in international arbitration, although the degree to which it is followed usually depends on the background of the parties, their lawyers, and the arbitrators: as a rule of thumb, the greater the proportion of participants from civil law countries, the less probable it is that broad document production will be ordered or agreed.

5-181 *Terminology of document production.* The terminology here may vary, but ultimately it is not really material. Sometimes the word 'discovery' is used, but strictly speaking this is a US litigation term for a number of different evidence-gathering techniques, including the production of documents but also depositions and interrogatories (which we discuss below). English lawyers prefer to use the word 'disclosure' when referring to document production. The IBA Rules refer to the production of documents and do not employ the words 'discovery' or 'disclosure' in this context. We prefer and will use the terminology of the IBA Rules.

5-182 *Tribunal's discretion regarding document production.* As introduced earlier, there are few arbitration rules or laws that address with any specificity the production of documents or, indeed, other methods of gathering evidence. The matter is instead entrusted to the arbitral tribunal, which has the discretion to order whatever document production procedures it considers appropriate. Tribunals increasingly follow the IBA Rules in this area, either on their own initiative or following an agreement by the parties.

Document production under the IBA Rules. The IBA Rules find a sensible middle **5-183** ground between the expansive document production practices of most common law jurisdictions, and the reluctance in civil law systems to compel parties to produce documents. An interesting and perhaps counter-intuitive trend is that of civil law arbitrators using the IBA Rules to justify a greater amount of document disclosure than is afforded in civil law court practice, and common law practitioners using the IBA Rules to restrict disclosure. This suggests that the IBA Rules have indeed struck a proper balance between civil and common law practices.

Document production procedure under the IBA Rules. It is common for **5-184** the parties and the tribunal to agree that document production will be dealt with by the parties without involving the tribunal except where disputes arise. In the absence of such an agreement, the IBA Rules provide that a party may submit a request to produce to the tribunal, demanding that the other side produce certain documents. Regardless of whether a party submits its request to the other side directly or through the tribunal, the main principles of the IBA Rules that apply are as follows:

- the request may validly seek production of (1) individual documents, which must be described in a way sufficient to identify them; and (2) 'narrow and specific' categories of documents that are reasonably believed to exist and are described 'in sufficient detail (including subject matter)';
- the requesting party must describe how the documents requested are 'relevant and material to the outcome of the case';
- the requesting party must state that the documents requested are not in its possession, custody, or control;
- the requesting party must state the reason it assumes the documents requested are in the possession, custody, or control of the other party;
- the other party may object to the production of the requested documents on a number of grounds (such as lack of relevance or materiality, legal privilege, loss or destruction of the documents, confidentiality, or the unreasonable burden that production would impose);
- if the other party does not object to the requested production, the tribunal will order it to produce the documents to the requesting party;
- if the other party does object, the tribunal will decide the objection and will order the other party to produce in light of that decision.

The IBA Rules' principal criteria. The thrust of the IBA Rules is thus that a valid **5-185** request to produce must either be for documents that are individually identified or for narrow, specific categories of documents, and all those documents must be relevant and material to the outcome of the dispute. The existence of these two conditions, at least superficially, appears to create a streamlined and focused process, far removed from the much-criticised 'fishing expeditions' routinely associated with litigation in the US courts. In practice, however – and especially in large, complex disputes – requests to produce under the IBA Rules can be long and detailed. This, not surprisingly, generates long, detailed, and numerous objections, which the tribunal must determine.

5-186 *Document requests and objections.* A typical request to produce under the IBA Rules will set out generic instructions to the producing party, followed by a number of requests, which should include the statements (notably as to relevance) specified by the rules. We include an example of a form of request to produce at Appendix 11. Objections may be conveniently marked on a 'Redfern Schedule', a document named after a prominent arbitrator on which the parties and the tribunal collaborate: it lists in four columns (1) the documents requested; (2) the requesting party's justification for its request; (3) the producing party's objection; and (4) a column in which the tribunal inserts its decision on each request. For an example of a Redfern Schedule, see Appendix 13.

5-187 *Production.* Once the tribunal has decided which documents the parties are required to produce, it will give the party time to produce them. The producing party must ensure it has received all the possibly relevant documents from the different custodians within its organisation, review them for their responsiveness to the requests to produce (as determined by the tribunal), and then assess which of the otherwise responsive documents are covered by privilege and similar protections from production. There is usually no obligation to organise the documents to be produced, or to index or number them. In practice the parties may agree or the tribunal may order, at a minimum, that the documents be 'bates-stamped', that is, numbered sequentially on each page of the production, usually at its foot. The expectation is that the documents will be produced in copies that reflect exactly their original state (with all attachments and handwritten markings included), and in their original language (even if it is not the language of the arbitration). In most cases the documents are produced only to the requesting party, and not to the tribunal. It is then for the requesting party to review the documents and introduce them into the record in the arbitration if it considers appropriate, usually as exhibits to its written submissions (with any translations that are needed).

5-188 *Form of documents produced.* It is common today for documents to be delivered in electronic form, as files written to a digital disc or simply posted on a website set up for the task and accessible to the parties.

5-189 *Privilege log.* At the same time as the production, the producing party should deliver its privilege log, if one is called for. In this document the party will list the documents that are responsive to the request to produce but that the producing party believes are privileged and therefore protected from production. The privilege log will describe the document (giving its date, author, any recipients, what it is, what privilege the producing party asserts, and why). The requesting party may then argue that these documents are not in fact privileged, giving the tribunal a further issue to determine. For an example of a Redfern Schedule, see Appendix 12.

Other forms of discovery. While the IBA Rules of Evidence offer a relatively **5-190** comprehensive set of rules for the production of documents, they do not provide for other forms of discovery typically available in court litigation in the United States and other common law jurisdictions. The US Federal Rules of Civil Procedure provide for five discovery mechanisms in addition to compulsory document production, namely: (1) deposition of witnesses; (2) written interrogatories; (3) physical inspections of objects or property; (4) physical and mental examination of persons; and (5) requests for admissions.[135] We consider depositions and interrogatories next.

Depositions. Oral 'depositions' – the questioning of a party or witness, under **5-191** oath and with a verbatim transcript, typically well in advance of the hearing and without the presence of the judge (or tribunal) – are a common feature in US litigation. However, they are virtually unheard of in international arbitration. They are likely only to be used in cases where US counsel are involved, and where there is agreement among the parties (e.g., to reciprocal depositions of the parties' officers and relevant employees).[136] Still, depositions have been described as being 'potentially of great interest in international arbitration' as a means of 'presenting testimony outside hearings and thus limiting their length'.[137]

Interrogatories. Similarly, 'interrogatories' (written questions from one side **5-192** regarding factual or legal positions taken by the other side, requiring a written answer) and 'requests to admit' (written requests from one party that the other admit that a certain issue is true, requiring a written answer) are typically unavailable in international arbitration, unless both parties agree to these procedures.[138] However, parties will often engage in less formal methods of requesting information from the other side, such as correspondence between opposing counsel requesting pertinent information or clarifications.[139]

---

135. See Federal Rules of Civil Procedure, Rules 26–37. See also, G. Bernini, 'The Civil Law Approach to Discovery: A Comparative Overview of the Taking of Evidence in the Anglo-American and Continental Arbitration Systems', in *The Leading Arbitrators' Guide to International Arbitration*, 268–269.
136. See G.B. Born, *International Commercial Arbitration* (The Netherlands: Kluwer Law International, 2009), 1902; L. Craig, W. Park, & J. Paulsson, *International Chamber of Commerce Arbitration*, 3rd edn (New York: Oceana Publ,. 2000), 457–458.
137. Craig, Park, & Paulsson, 457.
138. P.D. Friedland, *Arbitration Clauses for International Contracts*, 2nd edn (United States: Juris, 2007), 32.
139. *Ibid.*, 33.

Question:	Which rules of legal privilege apply in international arbitration?
Answer:	This is a difficult question, because almost all international arbitrations will be between parties from different countries with different rules or laws of privilege. In common law systems, communications between lawyer and client, and communications generated in connection with or in contemplation of legal proceedings (such as arbitration), are protected from disclosure in litigation or arbitration. In other jurisdictions, the laws of privilege may be quite different; in some countries, such as China, there seems to be no independent concept of legal privilege. Does this mean that in an arbitration between a US party and a Chinese party, for example, the US party's communications with its lawyers are protected from disclosure, but the Chinese party's are not? An argument can certainly be made that the US party had a reasonable expectation that its correspondence with counsel, when written, would not be produced later in litigation, while the Chinese party could not rightly expect such protection. But there is something inherently unfair about affording the US party a protection against production of certain documents while denying it to the Chinese party. The problem is perhaps most acute in practice when it comes to communications from in-house lawyers to their clients. In common law countries, these are typically privileged, while they are not in many civil law countries.[140] There is no guidance on privilege in the IBA Rules (other than an acknowledgement that it operates as a valid objection to production) or in arbitration rules and laws. Fortunately, the flexibility of international arbitration procedures allows a tribunal to devise an appropriate solution when such issues arise. We suggest that to apply different privilege standards to different parties in the same case would be to treat them unfairly and unequally, and the better approach is that of the 'lowest common denominator', namely that whichever of the competing privilege rules is the most protective should apply to all parties.

---

140. But see the recent decision by the European Court of First Instance in Joined Cases T-125/03 and T-253/03, *Akzo Nobel Chemicals Ltd and Akcros Chemicals Ltd. v. Commission of the European Communities*, Judgment of the Court of Justice of the European Communities (Court of First Instance), 17 Sep. 2007, which held that in-house lawyers could not rely on the same legal privilege as external lawyers. However, this was in the narrow context of 'dawn raids' under European competition laws, and in any event was under appeal to the European Court of Justice at the time of writing.

Checklist 5e – Document Production Guided by IBA Rules

- Request for Production
  - General instructions for production (e.g., clarifying the definition of 'possession, custody, or control' to be applied or requiring an explanation to be provided for responsive documents that have been lost or destroyed)
  - Description of requested document sufficient to identify it
  - Description in sufficient detail of a narrow and specific requested category of documents that are reasonably believed to exist
  - Description of how the documents requested are relevant and material to the outcome of the case
  - Statement that the documents requested are not in the possession, custody, or control of the requesting party
  - Reason that party assumes the documents requested to be in the possession, custody, or control of the other party
- Grounds for Objection
  - Lack of sufficient relevance or materiality
  - Legal impediment or privilege under the legal or ethical rules determined by the arbitral tribunal to be applicable
  - Unreasonable burden to produce the requested evidence
  - Loss or destruction of the document that has been reasonably shown to have occurred
  - Commercial or technical confidentiality that the arbitral tribunal determines to be compelling
  - Special political or institutional sensitivity that the arbitral tribunal determines to be compelling
  - Considerations of fairness or equality of the parties that the arbitral tribunal determines to be compelling

How document production works in practice. The various steps involved in doc- **5-193** ument production in international arbitration combine, in practice, to create what can be a time-consuming and expensive exercise, especially in a large or complex dispute. This is true even where the applicable standards are considered restrictive (which is often how parties view the IBA Rules). Further, if parties are less than scrupulous in complying with directions to produce, the exercise may not be fruitful. Some parties from jurisdictions where court litigants are not routinely required to produce unfavourable documents are, not surprisingly, unwilling to do so in international arbitration. The consequence may be either reluctance to engage in the document production process or, more likely, a clearly selective production which excludes any potentially unfavourable material. Parties may also try to disguise their non-compliance by overwhelming the opponent with a massive production of documents of dubious relevance and responsiveness. One variation on this theme is for the non-compliant party to produce only documents passing between the parties. If the requesting party keeps its records well, it will already have all of these documents and will not need to receive them from the opponent.[141]

5-194 *Achieving compliance with document production obligations.* What action can the requesting party take if it believes that its opponent is not complying with its document production duties? The answer is, in practice, not very much. The requesting party can apply to have the tribunal order the party to comply, or to submit a witness statement or affidavit certifying that it has complied or, if it has not, why not. One of the drawbacks of international arbitration is that the tribunal itself has no power to compel the parties to comply with its directions. While Article 9(5) of the IBA Rules does permit the tribunal to draw adverse inferences (i.e., to 'infer that [the document not produced] would be adverse to the interests' of the producing party), this may not be a particularly satisfactory remedy where there is a blatant and inexcusable failure to produce a document that could be critical to the outcome of the arbitration. Tribunals in any event appear reluctant to draw adverse inferences in practice, although at least one international arbitrator is known to have issued an 'unless order': unless the producing party disclosed the document at issue, the tribunal would rule against it on the merits (how enforceable the resulting award would be is unclear). Other tribunals have ordered producing parties who fail to disclose documents to instead answer questions in writing from the requesting party about the documents requested and the issues they are believed to cover. Even in the United States, there is generally no right to any discovery in international arbitrations. In general, the courts will not interfere to expand any right of discovery ordered by the arbitral tribunal.[142]

5-195 *'E-discovery'.* Litigation procedures in the United States have given rise in recent years to an entire cottage industry providing support for so-called 'e-discovery', which refers to the process of collecting, preparing, reviewing, and producing electronically stored information in litigation or arbitration.[143] The extraction and production of such information – often embedded within digital networks – can be exceedingly time consuming and expensive for parties, and has been criticised for substantially increasing the costs of litigation without a reasonably proportionate corresponding benefit. Because it is peculiar to US litigation practice, e-discovery has not yet made major inroads into international arbitration. International arbitration may therefore offer US companies a means of

---

141. It is implicit in Art. 3(3)(c) of the IBA Rules that a requesting party may not request production of documents that it already has.
142. See Redfern & Hunter, para. 6-72.
143. The US Federal Rules of Civil Procedure were amended in 2006 to specifically address e-discovery issues. See, generally, R.H. Smit & T.B. Robinson, 'E-Disclosure in International Arbitration', *Arbitration International* 24, no. 1 (2008): 105–135.

contracting out of the costs of e-discovery associated with domestic US litigation and arbitration.[144]

Documents held by third parties. The IBA Rules allow limited production of **5-196** relevant and material documents from a person or organisation which is not a party to the arbitration.[145] However, if the tribunal's direction is not voluntarily complied with, the reality is that an arbitral tribunal does not have jurisdiction over those third parties. This problem of enforcement may be mitigated to some extent if the applicable laws provide for assistance from the national courts: it may be possible, for example, to apply to the courts in the United States or England to compel attendance of a witness at a hearing or to produce material documents.[146]

Document production and the level playing field.	One criticism levelled at the document production process in international arbitration is that it gives parties from common law jurisdictions an unfair advantage because they are accustomed to the process, as a result of the discovery or disclosure practices in their home courts. This will often mean that those parties have document management policies in place designed to ensure that important company documents, including those that might be useful in a litigation, are retained, and extraneous or unimportant documents regularly discarded. These policies may include generating fewer documents in the first place, routine destruction of internal documents (and especially e-mails) after a given period, careful retention of all external correspondence, erasure of metadata, and maximising the protection offered by legal privileges. Despite this, it is not always the case in our experience that English or American parties manage or retain their documents more diligently in practice than parties from civil law countries. A cynical view, in any case, would be that parties from civil law countries level the playing field in international arbitration by discharging their production obligations with less rigour than parties from common law countries.

---

144. However, the Chartered Institute of Arbitrators issued in October 2008 a 'Protocol for E-disclosure in Arbitration' available at <www.arbitrators.org/institute/CIArb_e-protocol_b.pdf> for cases 'where potentially disclosable documents are in electronic form and in which the time and cost for giving disclosure may be an issue'.
145. See Art. 3(8) of the IBA Rules.
146. See s. 43 of the English Arbitration Act; and s. 7 of the US Federal Arbitration Act 1925. See also discussion below regarding 28 U.S.C. § 1782.

2.   **Witnesses and Experts**

5-197 *Witnesses distinguished from experts.* International arbitration practice generally distinguishes 'witnesses' from 'experts'. The former, known as 'witnesses of fact', present 'witness evidence', that is, their personal knowledge of some or all of the aspects of the facts in dispute. Experts, by contrast, are people who did not experience the disputed events first-hand, but who have reviewed a critical aspect of the case and present 'expert evidence' in the form of a report. Both witnesses and experts generally present their evidence by testifying at an evidentiary hearing at which they can be subjected to examination by opposing counsel and by the tribunal.

a.   *Witnesses of Fact*

5-198 *Fact witnesses, generally.* Factual evidence in international arbitration may be found in contemporaneous documents, as considered above, or in the evidence of witnesses. Presentation of evidence through witnesses is more typical of litigation in common law courts than of litigation in civil law countries. As a result, witness testimony will generally play a more significant role in international arbitrations with a common law flavour than in those more influenced by civil law. However, in this area too, many international arbitrations resemble a simplified hybrid of common law and civil law litigation: witness testimony will generally be permitted or even expected, but in the majority of cases it is likely to be given less weight than the contemporaneous documents – or at least less weight than would be the case in a common law court.

5-199 *Laws and rules concerning witnesses.* Most arbitration laws and rules say little about witness evidence. They neither require it nor prohibit it, instead leaving it to the parties and the arbitrators to determine whether to permit and how to present witness evidence. If there is no specific party agreement – and there usually is none – the tribunal will be free to give directions as to whether and how witness evidence will be heard. For example, the Model Law says nothing directly about witnesses,[147] and the ICC Rules say only that 'the Arbitral Tribunal may decide to hear witnesses'.[148]

5-200 *Articles 4 and 8, IBA Rules.* The IBA Rules of Evidence address the presentation of witness evidence in some detail. As seen above in relation to document production, the IBA Rules (which are in the process of being revised at the time of writing) reflect standard, but not universal, practice on evidence in international arbitration today. Articles 4 and 8 of the IBA Rules set out procedures for the presentation of

---

147. However, Art. 20 (Place of arbitration) and Art. 26 (Expert appointed by arbitral tribunal) make passing mention of 'hearing witnesses' and 'expert witnesses'.
148. See Art. 20(3) of the ICC Rules.

witness evidence in writing and in person at hearings. We consider now the key points of Article 4:

- *Who may give evidence.* Any person may present evidence as a witness, including a party to the arbitration, or an officer or party of the employee.[149] This is important, as in some legal traditions parties and their officers are not accorded the same status as witnesses who are not affiliated with the parties.
- *Interviewing witnesses.* It is not improper for parties or their lawyers to interview its witnesses or potential witnesses (but see our panel below on the 'preparation' by counsel of witnesses).[150]
- *Witness statements.* The tribunal may order – and in practice normally does order – the parties to submit a written statement, known as a 'witness statement', by each witness upon whose testimony the party relies.[151] These statements should contain the details of the witness and their relationship with the parties, as well as a 'full and detailed description of the facts, and the source of the witness's information as to those facts'.[152] The witness should affirm the truth of and sign the statement and give its date and place of signature (see our panel on affirmations and oaths by witnesses).[153] In practice, some tribunals will direct the witnesses to begin their statement with an executive summary, and to append a photograph to allow the arbitrators to better recollect after the hearing which witness made which written statement.
- *Availability to be examined at hearing.* Witnesses who have submitted statements must appear at the hearing to give oral testimony.[154] If a witness fails to do so, the tribunal will disregard their testimony unless there are exceptional circumstances.[155]
- *Compelling witnesses to appear.* Any party may request the tribunal to take steps legally available to it to obtain the evidence of a person unwilling to give evidence.[156] In practice, this means the tribunal applying to the courts of the place of arbitration (and possibly the courts of other jurisdictions)[157] for an order compelling the witness to testify or bring documents.[158] It is also open in some countries for a party to apply directly to the courts for this sort of assistance in taking evidence,[159] although any party making an application directly

---

149. See Art. 4(2) of the IBA Rules.
150. See Art. 4(3) of the IBA Rules.
151. See Art. 4(4) of the IBA Rules.
152. See Art. 4(5)(a)–(b) of the IBA Rules.
153. See Art. 4(5)(c)–(d) of the IBA Rules.
154. See Art. 4(7) of the IBA Rules.
155. See Art. 4(8) of the IBA Rules.
156. See Art. 4(10) of the IBA Rules.
157. See, e.g., Art. 27 of the Model Law. See also, in the United States, 28 U.S.C. § 1782, and J. Fellas, 'Using Section 1782 in International Arbitration', *Arbitration International* 23, no.3 (2007): 379–404.
158. In England and the United States see, respectively, s. 43 of the English Arbitration Act and s. 7 of the US Federal Arbitration Act 1925.
159. See, e.g., 28 U.S.C. § 1782.

to a court will be well advised to have received the approval of the tribunal, or at least to have informed the tribunal of its application.

5-201 *Basics of witness statements.* There may be just one exchange of witness statements, or a second exchange to allow a witness whose evidence is challenged an opportunity to rebut that challenge in writing. Witness statements can vary in length from a summary document of one or two pages (often favoured by parties or counsel from civil law jurisdictions) to extremely comprehensive accounts running to dozens or even hundreds of pages. The tribunal often orders the parties to submit their witness statements at the same time as their written pleadings. Tribunals of a common law persuasion may direct that the statements be submitted by each side (either simultaneously or consecutively) after document production has been completed and the written pleadings submitted, potentially lengthening the proceedings by some months.

5-202 *Whether to offer witness evidence.* Should a party to an international arbitration always offer witness evidence? Where a case may turn on disputed facts, it would be unusual for a party not to offer witness testimony. However, witness evidence may not be needed in the rare arbitrations where the dispute is a purely legal matter. The availability and quality of potential witnesses are other important factors, as are the availability and quality of contemporaneous written evidence: if the facts are relevant and are in dispute, and the contemporaneous documents are not conclusive, witness testimony is likely to be desirable or essential.

5-203 *Selection of witnesses.* If a party wishes to present witness evidence, whom should it put forward as witnesses? The obvious candidates will be individuals with personal knowledge of the disputed facts, who are available and willing to prepare written statements and to be examined at the hearing and, ideally, who will present well under examination. Seniority in the relevant organisation should not be a relevant criterion. If the person with the most relevant knowledge is a top executive, arbitrators will nonetheless expect her to be presented as a witness rather than a subordinate who is less familiar with the disputed facts. Conversely, if the subordinate was directly involved in the events at issue and the executive was not, arbitrators would expect the former to be offered as a witness before the latter, and the evidence of the former will – because only he has direct knowledge of the relevant events – be given more weight by the tribunal.

5-204 *Number of witnesses.* The number of witnesses that a party will choose to present will depend on factors such as the relevance of the disputed facts to the outcome, the breadth of the knowledge of the potential witnesses, the strength of the contemporaneous documents, the amount in dispute, and the make-up of the tribunal. In a situation where the disputed facts are reasonably limited and one person is familiar with them all, it may well make sense for that witness to be the only one offered. But, in a large multifaceted dispute – typical of many construction arbitrations – knowledge of the facts is likely to be shared among many individuals, and having a dozen witnesses or more is not unheard of.

Use of witness statements in submissions and witness examination. If the witness **5-205**
statements are submitted with or before the parties' written pleadings, the parties
will use those statements (as well as contemporaneous documents) to support their
allegations and arguments in those pleadings. They will also use them in support of
oral submissions made in hearings, as well as a basis for examination of the witness
by counsel and the tribunal. We discuss the examination of witnesses in more detail
below in section III on hearings.

Oaths and affirmations	In international arbitration, written statements of witnesses may be submitted on oath in the form of sworn, or sometimes notarised, affidavits. More commonly, they will simply be signed with an affirmation by the author of the truth of the statement. In either case, if the witness is called to give evidence in person, it is likely that the tribunal will ask him to make some from of oath or formal declaration as to the truth of his written and oral evidence. The laws of the place of the hearing may contain requirements in this regard.[160]

b.   Expert Witnesses

Expert witnesses, generally. In many international arbitrations, especially those of **5-206**
a technical nature, the parties present 'expert' evidence. The expert will be
appointed and paid by the party presenting the evidence, but will generally be
independent of the party, in the sense that she is not affiliated with the party
and was not involved in the disputed events (the IBA Rules describe these experts
as 'party-appointed', not as independent). The tribunal may also appoint its own
expert, and in some jurisdictions (such as France) the courts may appoint an expert
as an interim measure in support of the arbitration.[161]

When expert evidence is needed. The evidence given by experts is in the form of **5-207**
their opinion rather than evidence of fact (which is the domain of witnesses of fact).
There are many areas in which expert opinions may be valuable, as the issues in
dispute may be so complex that a tribunal will only be able to properly comprehend
them with explanation and guidance from experts in the relevant field or fields. For
example, delay claims on large construction projects are rarely made or defended
without the assistance of experts. Without expert support, it can be impossible for
parties or a tribunal to unravel and present the causes of the delay when dozens or

---

160. See, e.g., s. 38(5) English Arbitration Act; s. 12(2) of the Singapore International Arbitration
     Act; Art. 1041(1) of the Netherlands Code of Civil Procedure. In England, e.g., 'it is perjury for
     a person lawfully sworn as a witness or interpreter in an arbitration to make a statement,
     material in the proceedings, which he knows to be false or does not believe to be true',
     D. St. John Sutton, J. Gill, & M. Gearing, *Russell on Arbitration*, 23rd edn (London: Sweet
     & Maxwell, 2007), 247 (citing the English Perjury Act 1911, ss 1(1)–(2)).
161. See, e.g., Derains & Schwartz, 301–302.

hundreds of activities were undertaken simultaneously on a project. Similarly, complex damages claims often require expert input, notably where a party contends it would have earned profits but for the conduct of the opponent complained of. Another example is where a dispute turns on whether a party's conduct met specified standards arbitrators may have difficulty identifying these standards where they are of a technical nature (such as 'good engineering practices'), and whether they have been met, without the benefit of expert evidence.

5-208 *Arbitration laws and rules concerning experts.* Most arbitration laws and rules allow the parties to present the evidence of experts, or are silent on the point and therefore do not prevent the parties from presenting expert evidence. For example, the Model Law does not directly address the subject of party-appointed experts, and the ICC Rules state only that the tribunal 'may decide to hear ... experts appointed by the parties'.[162]

5-209 *Article 5, IBA Rules.* The IBA Rules, as may be expected, give more guidance, and again reflect standard practice in international arbitration. Article 5 permits parties to adduce the evidence of party-appointed experts, and then prescribes the content of expert reports, namely:

- the expert's details, including a description of his relationship with the parties and his qualifications;
- a statement of the facts on which he is basing his opinion and conclusions;
- his opinion and conclusions, including a description of the method, evidence, and information used in reaching his conclusions;
- an affirmation of the truth of the content of the report; and
- the expert's signature.[163]

5-210 *Failure by an expert to testify in person.* In most other respects, the IBA Rules on expert evidence are similar to those governing the evidence of witnesses of fact. In particular, the expert must agree to examination by the parties and the tribunal, failing which (unless the expert has a valid reason or there are exceptional circumstances) the tribunal will disregard the expert's evidence.[164]

5-211 *Experts conferring in advance of and at hearings.* The IBA Rules also make provision for the tribunal to order the experts to meet before giving oral evidence and to confer on the areas of difference between them.[165] The aim is for the experts to identify what is and is not in dispute. In practice, we think this can be beneficial, substantially streamlining what is a time-consuming and tedious part of many a hearing. The confrontation and/or conferencing of party-appointed experts at the hearing can be similarly useful, as we discuss in section III below.

---

162. See Art. 20(3) of the ICC Rules.
163. See Art. 5(2) of the IBA Rules.
164. See Arts 5(4), 5(5) of the Rules.
165. See Art. 5(3) of the IBA Rules.

Need for legal experts. It is common for parties to adduce expert evidence on **5-212** legal issues, especially where the arbitrators and/or the parties' counsel are not familiar with the governing law. However, arbitrators who are lawyers are often less receptive to legal expert testimony than to the evidence of technical experts, as the arbitrators believe that even if they are not familiar with the governing law, with the assistance of counsel and with access to the relevant legal source documents, they will be able to make the necessary determinations of law without the involvement of legal experts. Even where the parties present legal experts, tribunals frequently seek to limit or dispense altogether with their oral testimony,[166] preferring instead to devote more time to the hearing of fact witnesses. Much of the value in submitting expert reports on the applicable law will be in providing a concise summary of and opinion on the key legal issues in dispute, to which reference can be made in the parties' written and oral submissions.

Selection of legal experts. Typically, parties will select leading professors, or **5-213** renowned legal professionals, to act as legal experts. While position, experience, reputation, and significant publications are all important when selecting a legal expert, parties should also assess a potential legal expert's availability to attend the hearing, opinions expressed in his legal writings, his ability to effectively (and concisely) explain key legal concepts in the language of the arbitration (both orally and in writing), and his willingness to take the time to understand the parties' positions and the key factual aspects of the case.

Expert legal opinions. In addition to complying with the requirements of rel- **5-214** evant procedural rules (such as Article 5 of the IBA Rules), an expert legal opinion should set out (1) the expert's educational and professional background; (2) the assumed facts on which the legal opinion is based; (3) the specific legal questions or issues the expert has been asked to address; (4) a summary of the conclusions drawn; and (5) an analysis of the legal source material that leads to those conclusions. As a matter of style, a legal expert should provide an explanation of the relevant law without assuming the role of the tribunal and giving her view on how the issues in dispute should be decided. Where the relevant source materials are in the language of the arbitration, these can be produced in a separate bundle. However, where these are in another language, unless the arbitration rules or the tribunal's procedural directions require that they be produced, it may be advisable for the expert to indicate that these materials are available in their original language and can be translated for the tribunal's reference, if required. As many tribunals may be content to rely on the expert's written and oral testimony, this approach may save significant translation costs.

---

166. See B. Hanotiau, 'The Conduct of Hearings', in *The Leading Arbitrators' Guide to International Arbitration*, 376.

5-215 *Qualities to look for in experts.* Whatever her provenance, and whatever the subject matter of her expertise, the qualities a party will look for in an expert will be her credibility, her competence, her availability, and her ability to communicate her opinions and conclusions to the party appointing her and to the tribunal. Her credibility comes from her qualifications and experience in the given field, as well as her independence from the events in dispute and from the party presenting her evidence – in the sense that she is not blindly leaning towards the case of the party presenting her evidence, even if she is retained and paid by them.

5-216 *Expert's obligations.* As a general rule, the primary obligation owed by a party-appointed expert is to assist the arbitral tribunal and, as mentioned, not to uncritically endorse the position of the party that retained her. This duty of honesty and candour is reflected in a protocol issued by the CIArb, which states that 'an expert's opinion shall be independent, objective, unbiased, and uninfluenced by the pressures of the dispute resolution process or by any party'.[167] In addition, the Protocol expressly provides that '[a]ll instructions to, and any terms of appointment of, an expert shall not be privileged against disclosure in the Arbitration', although such disclosure is not ordinarily envisaged without good cause.[168] These guidelines may be consistent with and supported by English case law,[169] but they are not widely followed in international arbitration.

5-217 *At which stage to hire an expert.* Parties in cases where technical issues are at the heart of the dispute will be well advised to engage experts early. This will improve the preparation of the party's case. But it will also ensure that the party has a bigger pool from which to choose its expert. In certain fields, and in certain parts of the world, strong experts are few and far between, and the first mover will therefore have a meaningful advantage. It is not unheard of in large cases for parties to engage multiple experts, sometimes with no intention of using them all, to create conflicts of interest that prevent the experts from assisting the adversary.

5-218 *Timing of submission of expert reports.* There is no fixed rule as to when expert reports must be submitted, although the parties will generally submit them at the same time as the statements of witnesses of fact; this can be at the same time as the parties' submissions, or in later (or possibly earlier) exchanges. Alternatively, the parties or the arbitrators may prefer to have expert reports submitted after the witness statements, to allow the experts to take account in their reports of the witnesses' written testimony. In either case, each expert will usually be given the opportunity to respond in writing to the report submitted by the opposing expert.

---

167. CIArb Protocol for the Use of Party-Appointed Expert Witnesses in International Arbitration, Art. 4(4).
168. *Ibid.*, Art. 5(1).
169. See, e.g., *Whitehouse v. Jordan*, WLR 1 (1981): 246; *National Justice Compania Naviera SA v. Prudential Assurance Co, The Ikarian Reefer*, Lloyd's Rep 1 (1955): 455.

Use of expert reports in submissions and witness examination. If expert reports are **5-219** submitted with or before the parties' written pleadings, the parties will refer to those reports in those pleadings to support their position. Otherwise they will use them in support of oral submissions made at the hearing, as well as a basis for examination of the expert by counsel and the tribunal. We discuss the examination of experts in more detail below in our section III on hearings.

Preparation of witnesses and experts	To what extent is it permissible for a party, or its counsel, to prepare fact or expert witnesses whose testimony they intend to present to the arbitral tribunal? Subject to the applicable national laws and rules of professional conduct, the practice of 'interviewing' witnesses in international arbitration is expressly permitted by the LCIA Rules (Article 20.6) and the IBA Rules on the Taking of Evidence (Article 4(3)). However, there are clearly limits on the extent of 'preparation' of witnesses. For example, it would be unethical by any standard for a lawyer to deceive the tribunal by woodshedding a fact witness to present a version of facts that is untrue. The other extreme is often encountered in English practice where lawyers, and particularly barristers, may not (or at least do not) prepare witnesses before trial. Although the proper role of counsel is to assist witnesses to testify truthfully based upon the witnesses' own knowledge or recollection of the facts, the preparation of witnesses is one of the most important components of successful lawyering in international arbitration. This demanding and often unglamorous process might include: requesting the witness to review the case independently, reviewing and explaining the strategy of each party to the witness, reviewing the evidence in detail with the witness, and preparing for questioning by opposing counsel or the tribunal. This may extend to the conduct of a mock cross-examination, which may be filmed and later analysed by counsel and witness together.[170]

c.   *Tribunal-Appointed Experts*

Tribunal-appointed experts, generally. The tribunal may also appoint one or more **5-220** experts to assist it in reaching its decision, whether or not the parties appoint their own experts. The tribunal's power to do so is usually specifically set out in the relevant arbitration laws and rules: for example, Article 26 of the Model Law entitles a tribunal to appoint an expert unless otherwise agreed by the parties.

---

170. See D. Roney, 'Effective Witness Preparation for International Commercial Arbitration: A Practical Guide for Counsel', *Journal of International Arbitration* 20, no. 5 (2003): 429–435.

The expert's role is to submit a report on 'specific issues to be determined by the arbitral tribunal', and the parties have the right to require the expert to attend a hearing and be examined by the parties on his report. Article 20(4) of the ICC Rules similarly allows the tribunal to appoint one or more experts, and the parties to examine them in a hearing.

5-221 *Tribunal-appointed experts and the IBA Rules.* Article 6 of the IBA Rules deals with tribunal-appointed experts. It provides a reasonably detailed procedure for the appointment of the expert and the performance of his role. The tribunal is required to consult with the parties before appointing an expert, and before fixing his terms of reference. The expert must submit a statement of independence, which the parties may challenge, with the tribunal deciding any challenge. The expert has the same powers as the tribunal to request documents, goods, or a site for inspection. The expert's report is submitted to the parties for their responses, and they are entitled to review all documents examined by the expert and all correspondence between the tribunal and the expert. They may also put questions to the expert at a hearing. Recent case law suggests that the confidentiality of communications between a tribunal-appointed expert and the tribunal will be respected unless the terms of engagement provide that all communications are to be disclosed to the parties.[171]

5-222 *Profile of tribunal-appointed experts.* Experts appointed by tribunals tend to be similar in profile to those appointed by the parties, although independence from the parties is critical in the case of a tribunal-appointed expert,[172] not simply desirable as in the case of party-appointed experts. Whether a tribunal will choose to appoint an expert will depend on a variety of factors: the technical complexity of the dispute, the existence of relevant expertise within the tribunal, the assistance provided by the parties' experts (if any are appointed), and the amount at stake. A tribunal that counts lawyers among its members will be unlikely to appoint an expert to assist it on issues of law.

5-223 *Role of tribunal-appointed experts.* The role of a tribunal-appointed expert is not to decide the dispute for the arbitrators. Instead, as the provisions considered above suggest, the expert assists the tribunal by reporting on specific issues that the tribunal itself must decide. In practice, however, where the tribunal does feel the need to appoint an expert, it is likely to give substantial weight to the expert's contribution. The parties should therefore pay special attention to convincing the expert of the correctness of positions on the issues within the expert's remit. The expert may also help the arbitrators identify and request relevant documents from the parties.

5-224 *Remuneration of tribunal-appointed experts.* A tribunal-appointed expert will be paid for his work by the parties, usually on the basis of an hourly rate. The CIArb

---

171. See *Luzon Hydro Corporation v. Transfield Philippines*, SLR 4 (2004): 705, para. 19.
172. See, e.g., Art. 6(2) of the IBA Rules.

Protocol recommends that the expert disclose the basis of remuneration in his opinion.[173]

d.   *Court-Appointed Experts*

The French example. In France at least, prior to the constitution of the arbitral **5-225** tribunal, a party may apply to the court for the appointment of an expert as a provisional measure.[174] This procedure is commonly used in French litigation, and is also available in international arbitration where the seat is in France, in cases where immediate investigation would be beneficial (e.g., to establish the cause of a construction defect). The expert is 'not to act as a substitute for those who will later have the task of deciding the case, but simply to provide clarification and detail on points linked to the actual or potential subject matter of the dispute'.[175] However, as a practical matter, the factual findings of a court-appointed expert may have a significant impact on the outcome of the dispute.

3.   Inspection of Goods or a Site

Inspections, generally. The evidence – such as the site of a project or goods of **5-226** disputed quality – may be capable of inspection by the arbitrators. In some cases, it can be productive for the arbitrators to conduct such an inspection, and they will usually have the power to do so.[176] In practice, however, site inspections are rare in international arbitrations for logistical reasons: arranging for the arbitrators, parties, counsel, and perhaps witnesses and experts – who are often from different parts of the world – to visit a site will be an expensive and time-consuming process, and it may in any event be no more effective than evidence provided through photographs, models, or video.

III.   THE HEARING PHASE

Introduction. The hearing phase marks, for the parties and counsel at least, the **5-227** ultimate and most intense period of an international arbitration. This phase will comprise one or (occasionally) more hearings, as well as the submission by the parties in most cases of written post-hearing briefs. Multiple hearings, while still popular in countries such as India, are increasingly rare in most international arbitrations, as they lead to significant additional expense and delay in the many cases

---

173. See Art. 4(5)(c) of the CIArb Protocol for the Use of Party-Appointed Expert Witnesses in International Arbitration.
174. See Derains & Schwartz, 301–302; J. Hauteclocque, 'French Judicial Expertise Procedure and International Arbitration', *Journal of International Arbitration* 4, no. 2 (1987): 77–102.
175. Hauteclocque, 78–79.
176. See, e.g., Art. 7 of the IBA Rules.

where the participants are based around the world. The discussion below therefore focuses on international arbitrations where only one hearing is held.

A.   THE HEARING

5-228 *Hearing is mandatory on party request.* Although many international arbitration laws and rules allow arbitrators to issue an award 'on the documents' – without holding a hearing – this is usually subject to the parties' agreement. In other words, if one or both parties request a hearing, the arbitrators must hold one.[177]

5-229 *Organisation of the hearing.* The conduct of hearings is left to the agreement of the parties and the discretion of the tribunal.[178] The tribunal will typically invite the parties to agree on a proposed hearing timetable, and will convene a telephone conference in the weeks preceding the hearing in order to finalise the schedule and the procedure at the hearing.

5-230 *Pre-hearing submissions.* In some arbitrations, particularly where the arbitrators are from a common law background, the tribunal will ask the parties to provide it before the hearing with written documents such as a skeleton argument (a summary of the party's case), a chronology of key events, a dramatis personae (identifying the key players in the dispute), and a glossary.

5-231 *Location of the hearing.* The hearing will usually be held at the place of arbitration, although in some cases practical considerations will mean it is held elsewhere.[179] It will take place in a large conference room, most commonly in a hotel or an arbitral institution, but it can also take place in the offices of one of the arbitrators or, less frequently, of one of the law firms representing the parties. In addition to the main hearing room, each party and the tribunal generally requires a 'break-out' room where they can convene privately before and after the hearing hours and during the breaks.

5-232 *Hearings in camera.* Hearings are, unless the parties agree otherwise, not open to the public. However, in investment treaty arbitration there is a movement towards allowing public attendance at hearings, because of the public interest aspect of investment treaty disputes. The presence and participation of persons at ICSID hearings is regulated by ICSID Arbitration Rule 32(2), which provides that, unless either party objects, the tribunal may allow other persons (besides the parties, their agents, counsel, witnesses and experts during their testimony, and officers of the tribunal) to attend or observe all or part of the hearings, subject to appropriate logistical arrangements. Public hearings took place in the *Methanex v. United States of America* and *UPS v. Canada* cases (which were North American Free

---

177. See, e.g., Art. 24(1) of the Model Law; Art. 20(6) of the ICC Rules.
178. See, e.g., Art. 14 of the LCIA Rules; Art. 15 of the SIAC Rules.
179. Chapter 1, *The Elements of an International Dispute Resolution Agreement.*

Trade Agreement (NAFTA) cases held at ICSID under the UNCITRAL Rules). In each case, the parties specifically consented to the public attending the hearings.

Participants in hearings. The participants at hearings will be the arbitrators, any **5-233** secretary appointed by the tribunal, the parties' representatives (this may be individuals who are parties, officers, or employees of corporate parties and, in each case, their counsel), witnesses, experts, interpreters, and stenographers or technicians recording the proceedings. Typically the arbitrators (and secretary and stenographer) will sit at the end of a large 'U' shaped table, with the representatives of each party sitting along each side of the table, facing each other. The witnesses and experts will give their evidence seated in the middle of the 'U', facing the tribunal.

Transcripts of hearings. Hearings in most international arbitrations are recorded by **5-234** a transcription service, which will generate a transcript of the hearing for the parties to use when preparing any post-hearing briefs, and for the tribunal to use when preparing its award. The transcript may be made available to the tribunal and the parties in real time on computer screens. Alternatively it may be supplied overnight or some time after the hearing. Having a real-time transcript is a powerful tool, as it allows for more precise witness examination, and enables the parties and their counsel to analyse witness responses immediately. It is also more expensive than the alternatives, and may not be worthwhile if the amount in dispute is small or if there are few or no witnesses or experts.

Emphasis on evidence, not argument. Hearings in international arbitrations generally **5-235** focus on the evidence of the witnesses and experts, as opposed to oral argument. Most international arbitrators have little appetite for lengthy opening statements and closing submissions, delivered by counsel, in the English court tradition. In fact, many tribunals will attempt to dispense with oral argument altogether, assuring the parties that there is no need for it because the arbitrators have carefully read all the submissions and documents, and that the purpose of the hearing should instead be to test the evidence of the witnesses and experts. The most common arrangement in current international arbitration practice seems to be for the tribunal to begin the hearing by reviewing with the parties how the examinations will be conducted, in what order, and any outstanding procedural issues; counsel will then deliver short opening statements (each lasting one hour or so), followed by the examination of witnesses and experts; short closing submissions may then conclude the hearing, although there is a tendency for arbitrators to require closing argument in written post-hearing briefs instead of (or sometime in addition to) oral closings; the tribunal may also hold a question and answer session with counsel at the end of the hearing, as well as asking questions at other times during the hearing.

Opening statements. If an opening statement is delivered, it will usually be an **5-236** overview of the party's case and an introduction to the witnesses that the party is about to present, and their evidence. Counsel typically aim to accomplish three goals in the opening statement: (1) provide a road map of the case so the tribunal will understand the issues and what evidence and witnesses will be forthcoming; (2) provide important background information necessary to understand the case (e.g., definitions of technical terms, discussion of the key terms of the relevant contract); and (3) persuade the tribunal that the party has a meritorious case by telling a compelling story that puts the evidence into an overall structure, and by pointing to the best evidence.[180] The use of a slide-show presentation showcasing key evidence can be an effective tool to support the opening statement. An opening statement can be especially important as it gives the arbitrators the crucial first impression of the party, its counsel and its case.

5-237 *Closing submissions.* If permitted, a closing submission will usually be shorter than the opening statement. It will focus on the key evidence emerging from the witnesses at the hearing and will ask the tribunal to draw certain conclusions from that evidence. Unless there are post-hearing written briefs (which are increasingly common and are considered below), oral closing submissions may offer the last chance for a party to explain its position to the arbitrators.[181]

5-238 *Witness examination.* The emphasis placed on witness testimony, and the length of time devoted to hearing it can vary substantially depending on the background of the arbitrators and counsel. The examination of witnesses or experts may, depending on their number, last several days or, in the biggest cases, weeks. Arbitration laws and rules do not regulate the conduct of the examination, leaving that instead to the agreement of the parties and the discretion of the arbitrators. However, the IBA Rules of Evidence do address the presentation of evidence at hearings, and once again they reflect something close to standard practice today in international arbitration. They are notable for the controlling role they give to the arbitrators. Article 8 of the IBA Rules provides in short that:

- The tribunal has 'complete control' over the hearing of evidence and may limit or exclude a question to a witness (which includes an expert), an answer, or the appearance of a witness, if it considers the question, answer, or appearance irrelevant, immaterial, burdensome, duplicative, or covered by another of the objections set forth in Article 9(2) of the IBA Rules (such as privilege or confidentiality).
- 'Unreasonably leading' questions (leading questions are those that suggest the answer) are not permitted on direct or re-direct examination (where the witness is questioned by a representative of the party presenting him).
- The claimant will usually present its witnesses first, followed by the respondent's witnesses, and then by the claimant's rebuttal witnesses (rebuttal witnesses being rare in practice). Direct examination (by the party presenting the witness) is followed by cross-examination by representatives of the other parties, with an opportunity for re-direct by the presenting party. The tribunal can vary this procedure as it sees fit, including through

---

180. See R.D. Bishop, 'Advocacy in International Commercial Arbitration: United States', in *The Art of Advocacy in International Arbitration*, ed. R.D. Bishop (United States: Juris, 2004) 343–344; See also, M. Baker, 'Advocacy in International Arbitration', in *The Leading Arbitrators' Guide to International Arbitration*, 398–399.
181. See Baker, 399.

the confrontation or conferencing of witnesses (discussed below) or, in practice, by allowing the parties not presenting the witness an opportunity for 're-cross' examination, that is, further questions put to the witness on subjects raised during the re-direct.

– The tribunal is entitled to ask questions of the witnesses at any time.

– Each witness will affirm 'in a manner determined appropriate by the Arbitral Tribunal' that he is telling the truth, and will 'confirm' any witness statement or expert report submitted in the arbitration.

– The parties may agree or the tribunal may order that the witness statement or expert report will serve as direct testimony (or 'evidence-in-chief'). This frequently happens in practice. Even where it does not, direct testimony will usually be limited in duration as arbitrators find little assistance in what is often the dry repetition by the witness of a written statement that the arbitrators will already have read. Direct examination may be useful in some instances, however, such as to highlight the key points of the witness' evidence, especially if there is a risk that the cross-examining counsel will not ask questions on those points, thus preventing any examination on them at all.

– The tribunal may also call and examine a witness not called or presented by the parties. If it does so, the parties will be able to question the witness.

Party agreement on procedure for examination. The parties will attempt to reach **5-239** agreement on the nature, sequence, and duration of witness examination. If they do not agree, these issues are likely to be the major topic of discussion during the pre-hearing conference with the tribunal, and the tribunal will give the necessary directions. The tribunal will need to reconcile its concern that each party benefits from equal treatment and an adequate or full opportunity to present its case (as may be required by the applicable arbitration law or rules),[182] and its desire to conduct the arbitration in as efficient a manner as possible.[183]

Time allotted to examination of witnesses. One frequent point of contention is how **5-240** much time each party should have to examine the witnesses. The simplest approach is probably to give each party an equal amount of time: say, a total of twelve hours each for all their questions to witnesses, and they are free to use that time as they see fit. However, this system breaks down where one party presents significantly more witnesses than another. If the claimant presents five witnesses, and the respondent just one, the respondent is likely to want more than twelve hours in which to question the claimant's five witnesses, whereas twelve hours of

---

182. See, e.g., Art. 18 of the Model Law ('The parties shall be treated with equality and each party shall be given a full opportunity of presenting its case.'); s. 33(1)(a) of the English Arbitration Act ('The tribunal shall act fairly and impartially as between the parties, giving each party a reasonable opportunity of putting his case and dealing with that of his opponent.').

183. See Lew, Mistelis & Kröll, 526–527 ('In practice it is not always necessary to grant absolute equality in quantitative terms to both parties. Often one party needs less time and less evidence to prove its case or rebut the case against it.').

questioning of the respondent's one witness will probably be excessive. The solution is pragmatism and flexibility on the part of the parties and the tribunal in light of the number of the witnesses presented by each side and the relevance of their testimony.

5-241 *'Chess-clock' arrangements.* Tribunals vary in their attitudes to ensuring that parties stick to their allotted time at hearings. Some are relatively flexible and relaxed, while others favour a 'chess-clock' system, with strict enforcement of each party's allowance using a chess clock. Parties and their counsel will be well advised to be familiar with the approach that their tribunal is likely to take towards timing, as some prominent arbitrators are well known for taking a hard line and cutting lawyers off in the middle of their examination or submissions.

5-242 *Arbitrators' tolerance of cross-examination.* While lawyers from common law jurisdictions are generally keen to test a witness' evidence through cross-examination, lawyers from civil law countries will be less familiar with cross-examination. Likewise, common law arbitrators will generally be more tolerant of lengthy cross-examination than their civil law brethren.[184]

5-243 *Witness conferencing.* A relatively new development in evidentiary hearings is the introduction of 'witness conferencing'. This is a technique similar to the confrontation of witnesses, involving two or more witnesses who testify on the same subject examined side by side, rather than in sequence. As there are no applicable rules or guidelines, the actual procedure employed varies from case to case. If civil law traditions dominate, the tribunal may lead, asking both questions of its own choosing and questions proposed by the parties (either by agreement or separately), with counsel playing a secondary role. If the common law tradition prevails, counsel are likely to assume their traditional role of examiner, with the novelty being that they may pose the questions to either witness, or both (which may mean asking the second witness – usually the one presented by the questioning party – to comment on the answer given by the first witness).

5-244 *Conferencing of fact witnesses or experts only.* Witness conferencing is used more often in practice for expert witnesses than for witnesses of fact, although there is no reason in principle why fact witnesses cannot be examined in conference too. Perhaps the feeling is that testifying live is already such an ordeal for lay witnesses that there is no need to compound it through the conferencing process. Or arbitrators may feel that witnesses should not be present during the presentation of another witness's testimony, in order to prevent their own testimony from being influenced by what they hear. In any event, we think conferencing of experts saves

---

184. Redfern & Hunter suggest civil law arbitrators see cross-examination as 'embarrassing (if not barbaric)'. Redfern & Hunter, para. 6–208. This is perhaps less true today than it was, although common law counsel cross-examining witnesses before civil law arbitrators will still be well advised to keep their examinations briefer and more to the point than they would before a common law tribunal or court, and to focus more on the substance of the evidence and less on attempting to impeach credibility.

time as compared to their examination in sequence, and the quality of each expert's evidence is enhanced by the presence of the 'adverse' expert on the stand: areas of disagreement, and the reasons for them, can much more readily be identified and evaluated by the tribunal. Of course, the exercise may turn into a free-for-all if not kept on a tight rein, and the tribunal will therefore need to be vigilant. Effective witness conferencing also requires that the tribunal be well prepared and have a full command of the file. With these caveats, we believe the conferencing of experts has much to recommend it.[185]

Hearing 'bundles'. Although the main goal of the hearing is to see and hear the **5-245** witnesses in person, the documentary record will also receive considerable scrutiny at the hearing, both during the oral submissions by counsel and during the examination of witnesses. For this reason, the parties will prepare compilations of various sorts of the documents on the record, sometimes referred to as 'bundles'. So, for example, the parties may prepare a 'joint' or 'common' bundle of documents (actually a series of binders) that are on the record and to which they will refer during the hearing. If this is not possible, each party may prepare its own bundle of documents to which it will refer. In document-intensive cases, there may be a separate bundle of documents for each witness. If compiled, referenced, and indexed competently, these bundles should make the tribunal's job easier at the hearing and during deliberations, and should also be convenient for the parties and the witnesses.

Introducing new documents at hearing. A vexed question is whether parties should **5-246** be permitted to introduce new documents at hearings. It is not unheard of, for example, for parties to attempt to surprise witnesses on the stand by putting before them documents that are not part of the record and that the witness may not, as a result, have discussed with representatives of the party presenting him. The tribunal may issue directions on this in advance, or may decide on a case-by-case basis whether to admit the document if a party objects. Generally speaking, factual documents – especially if not in the public domain or not authored by the witness – are unlikely to be admitted at the hearing where a party objects, unless there is a good reason to introduce the document at that late stage. A good reason may be that the document was only generated or came into the possession of the party then, and not as a result of its earlier lack of diligence. The more a party appears to be seeking the element of surprise (e.g., by not warning the adverse party beforehand of its intention to introduce the document), the more likely a tribunal is to refuse admission of the document.

Introducing new legal authorities at hearing. As for the legal authorities on which **5-247** the parties wish to rely – statute, judicial decisions, arbitral awards, commentary,

---

185. See W. Peter, 'Witness "Conferencing"', *Arbitration International* 18, no. 1 (2002): 47–58; and W. Peter, 'Witness Conferencing Revisited', in Arbitral Procedure at the Dawn of the New Millennium, Reports of the International Colloquium of CEPANI, (Brussels: Bruylant, 2005), 155 et seq.

and so on – one school of thought is that they may be introduced at any time, even at or after the hearing, as the tribunal and the parties are deemed to have notice of the law. We think this is not always warranted, and there may be circumstances in which a tribunal would rightly reject the late admission of legal authorities. Certainly, where at least some of the parties and the arbitrators hail from countries other than that of the governing law, there is less reason to attribute knowledge of the governing law to the parties and the arbitrators – and therefore less reason to allow the late submission of authorities. On the other hand, issues of law may emerge only late in the proceedings when the evidence is heard, and therefore may need to be addressed at that stage with the support of newly introduced authorities.

5-248 *Opportunity to present rebuttal documents or authorities.* In cases where a tribunal does allow a party to introduce a new factual document or a legal authority at the hearing, good practice would be to allow the other party a reasonable time to review the document and comment on it, in order to ensure equal treatment of the parties.

5-249 *Use of technology.* We have already touched on the use of real-time transcription services at hearings. There are other uses of technology at hearings, ranging from the run-of-the-mill PowerPoint presentation to the use of sophisticated trial software, which organises exhibits, statements, and case presentations for more effective delivery during the hearing. Witnesses unable to attend the hearing may give their evidence and be cross-examined by videoconference, although this will often be a poor substitute for live testimony.

B.   POST-HEARING SUBMISSIONS

5-250 *Steps taken by the parties after the hearing.* At the close of the hearing, or shortly afterwards, the tribunal will consult with the parties and give directions as to the steps that it wishes them to take during the period between the hearing and the issuance of the award. There may be no further steps needed, but more commonly the tribunal will ask the parties to review and correct the transcript and to make submissions regarding the costs of the arbitration. As noted earlier, the tribunal may also direct the parties to submit post-hearing briefs and further evidence.

5-251 *Correcting the transcript.* When the transcript is prepared, errors will inevitably creep in. The tribunal will therefore invite the parties to attempt to agree among themselves on an errata list, for communication to the transcription service, which will then issue a finalised transcript. If the parties cannot agree, the tribunal will usually ask them to submit their proposed corrections, which the tribunal will take into account when reviewing the transcript itself. Alternatively, the tribunal may decide itself which corrections proposed by the parties should stand.

Costs submissions. As explained earlier, that current practice in international arbi- **5-252**
tration, in the absence of party agreement otherwise, is that the tribunal will order
the loser to pay some or all of the costs incurred by the victorious party in the
arbitration. These costs will include the arbitrators' fees and expenses, as well as
those of any administering institution and, importantly, those of the party's
counsel, witnesses, and experts.

Tribunal's decision on costs. The tribunal will usually wish to address costs in its **5-253**
award, although some tribunals may follow the English court tradition of issuing
the award first and then deciding on costs through a process described as 'taxation'
of costs.[186] In order to address costs in its award, the tribunal will ask the parties to
provide a statement of the costs that it has incurred and its submissions on whether
and why the opponent should be ordered to pay them. The form and content of the
statement of costs is left to the discretion of the tribunal: they may range from a
single page with little detail and no evidence supplied, to a comprehensive break-
down of all the expenses incurred, together with copies of the relevant invoices or
other evidence, and/or contemporaneous records of the work performed by
counsel. The tribunal may also ask the parties or their counsel to provide an
affidavit as to the veracity of their costs statements. The tribunal will generally
ask for costs statements to be exchanged a week or two after the hearing (if there
are no post-hearing briefs scheduled), or after the submission of post-hearing
briefs. Each party will then be given the opportunity to comment on the costs
statement of the other.

Post-hearing briefs. The tribunal may also direct the parties to submit further **5-254**
written pleadings after the hearing. Again, the format and content of these
'post-hearing briefs' will be left to the discretion of the tribunal. The purpose of
the pleadings is usually to replace or flesh out oral closing submissions with a
written review of the evidence that emerged at the hearing, and the conclusions that
each party draws from that evidence. In some cases, the tribunal may direct the
parties to address certain specific issues or questions, and may also lay down a page
limit and other restrictions designed to ensure the briefs provide the tribunal with
the assistance it requires without delaying the proceeding. Post-hearing briefs are
commonly submitted by the parties simultaneously, four to eight weeks after the
hearing, without the opportunity to address the arguments raised in the other
party's post-hearing brief. Sometimes the submissions are sequenced so that the
respondent is allowed the last word.

Request by tribunal for further evidence and information. The tribunal may also **5-255**
request the parties to provide additional evidence after the hearing where, for
example, testimony or argument has focused on a document that is not in the

---

186. See, e.g., Singapore International Arbitration Act (Cap 143A), s. 21 ('Any costs directed by an
    award to be paid shall, unless the award otherwise directs, be taxable by the Registrar of the
    Singapore International Arbitration Centre.').

record and therefore not available to the tribunal. The tribunal may also put specific questions to the parties (usually in writing) outside the framework of post-hearing briefs.

5-256 *Importance of post-hearing briefs.* Given that at the post-hearing stage the tribunal will be focusing carefully on the dispute and on the elements that it will need in order to write its award, post-hearing briefs need to be prepared with special attention. This is particularly true where the tribunal has given specific direction as to questions it wants answered, or issues it wants clarified. Although tribunals will commonly preface these sorts of questions with cautionary words to the effect that it has not made up its mind and its questions are entirely without prejudice to its forthcoming decision, it goes without saying that in most cases a tribunal will ask for answers or clarification primarily on those matters that it considers relevant and material to the outcome.

5-257 *Close of proceedings.* Once the parties have accomplished the steps required of them after the hearing, the tribunal may declare the proceedings closed. This means that the parties have completed the presentation of their case and are not entitled to submit further argument or evidence without the tribunal's authorisation.[187] This step is mandatory in ICC arbitration[188] and ICSID arbitration,[189] for example, and in the latter case the closure of the proceedings triggers the running of the applicable deadlines for the rendering of the award.[190]

IV.   THE AWARD PHASE

5-258 Once the parties have made their final submissions, be it at the final hearing, in post-hearing briefs, or in response to the tribunal's subsequent written questions, the arbitration enters its ultimate chapter: the award phase. This comprises two or three separate stages, at least where the tribunal consists of three arbitrators. These stages are the tribunal's deliberations, the writing of the award itself, and post-award procedures within the arbitration, such as the correction or interpretation of the award.

A.   DELIBERATIONS

5-259 *Majority decision required?* If the tribunal consists of three members, they will deliberate among themselves in order to reach a decision on the conflicting claims

---

187. Many arbitrators will not permit submission of argument or evidence outside the specific timetable established for that purpose at the outset of the arbitration, unless the tribunal gives its prior approval.
188. See Art. 22 of the ICC Rules.
189. See ICSID Rule 38.
190. See ICSID Rule 46.

and defences before them. Ideally, the decision will be unanimous. However, if unanimity is not achievable, the award will be rendered by a majority, with a dissenting opinion usually offered by the minority arbitrator. In rare situations, it may not even be possible to achieve a majority. In these cases, most arbitration rules and statutes provide that the chair will issue the award alone.[191] However, neither the Model Law nor the UNCITRAL Rules address the situation where there is no majority within the tribunal. The same is true in ICSID arbitration, leaving the tribunal in these cases with no option but to work harder towards a majority decision.

Procedure for deliberations. There is no specific procedure to be followed in a **5-260** tribunal's deliberations. What happens in practice is that arbitrators will hold one or more meetings together, often beginning with a meeting on the day following the end of the hearing, to understand the position of each tribunal member and to develop a process for arriving at an award. Additional discussions may be held by telephone or by exchanges of correspondence. In the later stages of deliberations, the debate will focus on a draft of the award. The whole draft may be prepared by one of the arbitrators, usually the chair, for discussion among the tribunal. Alternatively, each arbitrator may be responsible for drafting a different portion of the award, with each submitting her portion for comments by her co-arbitrators.[192]

Place of deliberations. There is no requirement that the deliberations be held at the **5-261** seat of arbitration or in any other place. In any one case, they are often held in different places around the world, reflecting the provenance and mobility of most international arbitrators.

Confidentiality of deliberations. Deliberations are confidential.[193] This of course **5-262** means that arbitrators may not reveal the content of deliberations to the parties before the award is rendered. This rule is not universally respected in practice, with occasional leaks from arbitrators aimed at persuading the party appointing her that it may be wise to settle the case before the award is issued, or at eliciting information from the party to be used to convince the other tribunal members. The confidentiality of deliberations also means that the arbitrators cannot disclose, after the award is rendered, the content of their discussions. This leads to difficult questions regarding the extent to which arbitrators who issue a dissenting opinion may refer to the deliberations, and whether arbitrators may give evidence in court regarding the deliberations during actions to set the award aside or to resist its enforcement.[194]

Deliberations by a sole arbitrator. Where the tribunal consists of a sole arbitrator, **5-263** there is evidently no need for formal deliberations, in the sense of discussions with

---

191. See, e.g., Art. 25(1) of the ICC Rules; and Art. 27.4 of the SIAC Rules.
192. See, for further discussion, Redfern & Hunter, para. 9–153 et seq; Craig, Park, & Paulsson, 368–370; L.Y. Fortier CC QC, 'The Tribunal's Deliberations', in *The Leading Arbitrators' Guide to International Arbitration*, 477–482.
193. See Craig, Park, & Paulsson, 369; Lew, Mistelis & Kröll, 638; Gaillard & Savage, 750–751.
194. See, e.g., Gaillard & Savage, 765; M.T. Reilly, 'The Court's Power to Invade the Arbitrators' Deliberation Chamber', *Journal of International Arbitration* 9, no. 3 (1992): 27–38.

others. But before writing the award, the sole arbitrator will need to undertake the same process as a tribunal of three would do: carefully considering the evidence, the law, and the submissions to decide which of the parties' claims and defences should prevail, and to what extent.

B.   THE AWARD

5-264 *Definition of 'award'.* There is no accepted definition of an award, but, it is generally understood that is a decision that finally disposes of the substantive disputed issues that it addresses. It should have the legal effect of res judicata as regards those issues. Awards are distinct from 'orders' issued by the tribunal, in that orders are decisions that do not finally resolve substantive issues disputed by the parties, whereas awards do – irrespective of whether the decision is entitled 'order' or 'award'.[195]

5-265 *Enforceability of award.* The arbitrators' duty in rendering their award is to decide the dispute in accordance with the applicable rules of law and procedure, and in view of the evidence before them, but also, in the words of Article 35 of the ICC Rules to 'make every effort to make sure that the Award is enforceable at law'.[196] Arbitrators must therefore be conscious – or be made conscious by the parties, especially the claimant[197] – of the grounds on which enforcement of an award can be resisted in the countries where it is likely to be enforced, and of the grounds for setting it aside at the place of arbitration.

5-266 *Requirements of form.* The award should therefore comply with applicable requirements concerning its form (including language or languages) and content. These requirements may be found in the parties' arbitration agreement, in the terms of reference or other agreements reached by the parties, in orders made by the tribunal during the arbitration, in the applicable arbitration rules, and in the arbitration law of the place of arbitration and the enforcement law of the place of the arbitration (which, in most jurisdictions, will be the New York Convention).[198] For example, Article 31 of the Model Law requires that the award shall:

– be in writing;
– be signed by the arbitrators (or the majority of the arbitrators, with reasons given for the absence of the signature of any arbitrator);

195. See *Publicis Communications and Publicis S.A. v. True North Communications Inc.* (7th Cir. 2000), *Yearbook of Commercial Arbitration*, vol. XXV (2000), 1152–1157; See also 'Arbitrators' Order "Was Final"', 7th Circuit Rules', *Mealey's IAR* 15, no. 4 (2000): 4.
196. See also Art. 32.2 of the LCIA Rules; G.J. Horvath, 'The Duty of the Tribunal to Render an Enforceable Award', *Journal of International Arbitration* 18, no. 2 (2001): 135–158.
197. See Redfern & Hunter, para. 9–13.
198. Chapter 6, *After the Arbitration.*

- state the reasons upon which it is based, unless the parties agree that no reasons are to be given; and
- state its date and the place of arbitration.[199]

Substantive grounds for refusing enforcement. The New York Convention sets out **5-267** grounds on which enforcement of an award may be refused, and which a tribunal may wish to take into account when rendering its award:[200]

- the arbitration agreement must have been validly entered into (and, notably, the parties to it must not have been under any incapacity);
- the parties to the arbitration must have been able to present their case;
- the award must deal with all the matters submitted to the tribunal and not with any matters not submitted to it;
- the tribunal must have been constituted and the arbitral procedure conducted in accordance with the agreement of the parties or, in the absence of an agreement, in accordance with the law of the place of arbitration;
- the subject matter of the award must be arbitrable (i.e., capable of settlement by arbitration) under the law of the country of enforcement; and
- the award must not be contrary to the public policy of the place of enforcement.

Statements of no objection. In order to bolster the enforceability of the award, **5-268** arbitral tribunals may wish to seek the parties' confirmation on the record, at different stages of the proceedings (notably in the terms of reference and at the close of the final hearing), that they have no objection to the composition of the tribunal or to the tribunal's conduct of the arbitration. If a party gives that confirmation, it will have more difficulty later seeking to set aside the award, or resist enforcement, on grounds known to it at the time it gave its confirmation.[201]

Structure of awards. In practice, most awards in international arbitrations will **5-269** begin with an account of the procedure, as well as the arbitration agreement and constitution of the tribunal, and will record that the parties had at least an adequate opportunity to present their cases. The award will then set forth the parties' respective claims and defences, and the relief they seek, before listing the issues that the tribunal must resolve. The arbitrators will go on to address each of the disputed issues, including liability, relief, interest, and (in most cases) costs, often stating in turn each party's position before giving its own findings and the reasons for reaching them. The tribunal may also need to decide its own jurisdiction or other disputed issues of a preliminary nature, such as the governing rules of law. The award will conclude with its operative part, in which the tribunal will set out its decision in terms similar to those used in the prayers for relief with which parties conclude

---

199. See also the much longer list of mandatory contents of ICSID awards set forth in ICSID Rule 47.
200. Chapter 6, *After the Arbitration.*
201. *Ibid.*

their submissions. The date of the award, the place of arbitration, and the signatures of the arbitrators will follow.[202]

5-270 *Remedies awarded.* Remedies that may be the subject of an arbitration award include: (1) payment of money; (2) punitive damages; (3) specific performance; (4) injunctive relief; (5) declaratory relief; (6) restitution; (7) rectification; (8) gap filling and contract adaptation; (9) interest; and (10) costs.[203] The tribunal will determine the availability of a remedy in a given case by reference to the law governing the merits of the case and, possibly, the laws of the place of arbitration and place of enforcement.

5-271 *Payment of money.* An order that a party pay a sum of money to another is regarded as the 'natural' remedy in international arbitration and is the remedy most commonly awarded. The amount may be a sum owed under a contract (a debt) or compensation (damages) for loss suffered, or both.[204]

5-272 *Punitive damages.* Punitive damages have been awarded by arbitral tribunals, particularly in the United States, where either the law governing the arbitration or the applicable law provided for multiple or punitive damages. However many jurisdictions do not recognise punitive damages, and some (such as Germany) consider them to be contrary to public policy.[205] Accordingly, while an arbitral tribunal may have the power to award punitive damages, there is a danger that the resulting award may not be enforced for violation of public policy under Article V(2)(b) of the New York Convention.[206]

5-273 *Specific performance.* An arbitral tribunal may be authorised by the parties or by the applicable law (either the substantive law or the law of the place of arbitration) to order specific performance of a contract. Although they have the power to award specific performance, in practice arbitral tribunals are reluctant to do so, especially where such an award will be difficult to enforce.[207]

5-274 *Injunctive relief.* Injunctions may be available in arbitration, and the tribunal's power to issue injunctions is expressly provided for in some arbitration laws.[208]

---

202. See, e.g., the awards published on ICSID's website <www.worldbank.org/icsid>. See also the bibliography at Appendix 14.
203. See Lew, Mistelis & Kröll, 650; see also Redfern & Hunter, para. 9–39.
204. See Lew, Mistelis & Kröll, 651.
205. See Redfern & Hunter, paras 8–13 and 9–49 (citing Bundesgerichtshof, Neue Juristische Wochenschrift 1992, 3096 et seq.); Supreme Court Tokyo, 11 Jul. 1997, reported in T. Tateishi, 'Recent Japanese Case Law in Relation to International Arbitration', *Journal of International Arbitration* 17, no. 4 (2000): 71–72.
206. See Lew, Mistelis & Kröll, 651–652; see also Redfern & Hunter, para. 9–49.
207. See Lew, Mistelis & Kröll, 650–651; see Redfern & Hunter, para. 9–52. See also T.E. Elder, 'The Case against Arbitral Awards of Specific Performance in Transnational Disputes', *Arbitration International* 3, no. 1 (1997): 1–32.
208. See, e.g., s. 48(5)(a) of the English Arbitration Act.

Declaratory relief. Declaratory relief is often expressly provided for in arbitration **5-275** laws[209] and will determine the legal position between the parties. Parties will often combine requests for monetary damages with requests for a declaration that a contract has been breached. Declaratory relief can also be a useful remedy where the parties wish to resolve a dispute without damaging an ongoing relationship by requesting monetary damages.[210]

Gap filling and contract adaptation. Some arbitration laws allow tribunals to fill **5-276** gaps in contracts or otherwise amend them to address situations where the parties have failed in their contract to provide for a particular contingency that arises. Most tribunals are reluctant to change the terms of a contract unless the arbitration agreement contains an express power authorising them to do so. A tribunal's ability to adapt a contract may also derive from the law applicable to the substance of the dispute, which may allow the amendment of contracts under doctrines of changed circumstances or hardship.[211]

Interest. There is no consensus on the method of awarding interest in international **5-277** arbitration. Where monetary compensation is awarded, and interest is sought, arbitrators generally add interest, pre-award and/or post-award, to the underlying amount awarded. In deciding a request for an award of interest, the tribunal will need to determine: (a) whether the award debtor is liable to pay interest; (b) the rate of interest to apply; (c) the start and end dates for the running of interest (e.g., from the date of default until the award, in the case of pre-award interest, and from the date of the award until its satisfaction for post-award interest); and (d) whether interest should be compounded and, if so, how frequently.[212]

Laws and rules concerning interest. As most arbitration rules do not contain **5-278** express provisions concerning the award of interest, the right to it will typically derive from the parties' underlying contract or the applicable law. Some laws leave the question of interest to the tribunal's discretion.[213] Others may specify a statutory rate of interest.[214] Islamic countries with legal systems based on Shari'a do not allow interest as part of an award. If a tribunal expects the award to be enforced in a country where interest is not lawful, it may decide to make a separate award on interest, which can be enforced separately in other countries where the debtor may have assets, without tarnishing the whole award on the merits.[215]

Costs. As considered above, in international arbitration, the tribunal usually has the **5-279** power to require the losing party to pay or contribute towards the legal costs of the

---

209. See, e.g., s. 48(3) of the English Arbitration Act.
210. See Redfern & Hunter, para. 9–63.
211. See Redfern & Hunter, paras 9–66 et seq.
212. See Lew, Mistelis & Kröll, 656.
213. See, e.g., s. 49(3) of the English Arbitration Act; ss 25(1), 26 of the Australian International Arbitration Act; ss 2GH, 2GI of the Hong Kong Arbitration Ordinance; s. 12(5)(b), 20 of the Singapore International Arbitration Act.
214. See Redfern & Hunter, para. 9–76.
215. See Lew, Mistelis & Kröll, 656–657.

winning party.[216] The general practice is that the tribunal will exercise that power and order the loser to pay most or all of the winner's costs (costs of the arbitration and its own costs), if the winner and loser can be clearly identified, if the winner's costs are reasonable and if there are no exceptional or mitigating circumstances. This may be in the final award itself or, less commonly, in a separate later award.

5-280 *The need for a tribunal's reasons.* The reasons for the tribunal's decision are at the core of any international arbitral award, except in the rare cases where the parties agree that the tribunal need give no reasons. This is in contrast to some domestic arbitration systems, where an arbitral award need not give reasons: a simple statement of the tribunal's decision will suffice.[217] The parties, and especially the losing party, will generally want to know why the tribunal has reached its decision. There is also an argument that a tribunal will only be able to reach the correct decision by properly articulating its reasons.[218]

5-281 *Sufficiency of reasons.* The parties' agreement, or the applicable arbitration rules or law, will stipulate whether reasons need be given. The more controversial question relates to the sufficiency of reasons, and how specific and detailed they ought to be. In ICSID arbitration, the failure of the tribunal to give reasons for its award is one of the five specific and exhaustive grounds on which an award may be annulled.[219] This has led to extensive debate in ICSID cases and commentary as to what is meant by a failure to state reasons, with the current position being that the reader must be able to follow the tribunal's reasoning from start to finish, but the reasons do not have to be correct or convincing.[220]

5-282 *Dissenting or concurring opinions.* Where the tribunal comprises three arbitrators, the chair will generally strive to achieve unanimity, although the award does not need to be unanimous. Sometimes one of the arbitrators, usually a party-appointed arbitrator, may not agree with the decision or the reasoning of the majority or (where there is no majority) with the chair. In that case, it is open to him to issue a dissenting opinion, which explains why he disagrees. Where he disagrees with the reasons but not with the result, he may issue a separate or concurring opinion.

5-283 *Appropriateness of dissenting opinions.* Dissenting opinions, when they respect the confidentiality of the deliberations and are put in suitably measured terms, are an appropriate and effective way for an arbitrator to express his genuine disagreement

---

216. The most commonly used arbitration rules generally leave the question of costs to the tribunal to decide in its discretion. See, e.g., Art. 40 of the UNCITRAL Rules, Art. 31 of the ICC Rules, and Art. 28 of the LCIA Rules.
217. See, e.g., Art. R-42 of the AAA Commercial Arbitration Rules.
218. See Lord Justice Bingham, 'Reasons and Reasons for Reasons: Differences between a Court Judgment and an Arbitral Award', *Arb Int* 4, no. 2, 141 (1988): 145.
219. See Art. 52(1)(e) of the ICSID Convention.
220. See C. Schreuer, 'Three Generations of ICSID Annulment Proceedings' in *Annulment of ICSID Awards*, ed. E. Gaillard & Y. Banifatemi (United States: Juris, 2004), 33–38. Chapter 7, *ICSID and Investment Treaty Arbitration.*

with the decision of the majority or (where there is no majority) with the chair.[221] However, dissents are on occasion a vehicle for a less-than-impartial arbitrator to show support for the party that appointed him, notably by undermining the award in the eyes of an enforcement court.

The threat of a dissent. Because the chair will desire unanimity, the 'threat' of a **5-284** dissenting opinion can also be used by a co-arbitrator during deliberations to achieve a compromise – an award that comes closer to the outcome that the co-arbitrator believes is correct than the position taken by the majority. For example, a tribunal may issue a unanimous award finding in favour of a party on all or a substantial portion of the claims, but deny the recovery of costs (legal fees) as a concession to the losing party. We do not argue that these are necessarily accept-able practices; we merely note that parties should be aware that in practice the dynamics of a three-arbitrator tribunal and the desire for unanimity may lead to a more nuanced award than a sole arbitrator might hand down in the same circumstances.

Scrutiny by arbitral institutions. The applicable rules of arbitration may require the **5-285** tribunal to submit a draft award to the administering institution for scrutiny. This is the case of the ICC (Article 27, providing for scrutiny by the ICC Court) and the SIAC (Article 27.1, providing for submission of the award to the Registrar). The goal of this procedure, as explained earlier, is to provide a level of quality control designed to ensure an award of an appropriate standard.[222] In each case, the involvement of the institution is, in theory at least, to 'lay down modifications as to the form of the Award', and the tribunal may not render the award until the institution has approved it.[223] The institution 'without affecting the Arbitral Tribunal's liberty of decision, may also draw its attention to points of sub-stance'.[224] In practice, the institutions will not hesitate to suggest that arbitrators amend points of substance in their draft award, although they cannot and will not insist on the arbitrators doing so. It is another matter whether the institutions will, in subsequent cases, appoint arbitrators who have declined their invitations to amend the substance of their awards.

Delay caused by scrutiny. The scrutiny procedure may add one or more months to **5-286** the time taken to issue the award. The extent of the delay will depend on the number of changes requested by the institution, and the tribunal's receptiveness to them, as well as on the availability of the institution. The ICC Court, for example, has traditionally taken longer to scrutinise an award during the holiday months of August and December than at other times. After the tribunal makes the

---

221. For a prominent example, see the dissenting opinion of Bernardo Cremades in *Fraport AG Frankfurt Airport Services Worldwide v. Philippines* (ICSID Case No. ARB/03/25), Award 16 Aug. 2007.
222. Chapter 1, *The Elements of an International Dispute Resolution Agreement.*
223. See Art. 27 of the ICC Rules (Art. 27.1 of the SIAC Rules is virtually identical).
224. *Ibid.*

agreed changes, it will sign the award, which the institution (or the tribunal, if there is no institution) will then deliver to the parties.

5-287 *Time limit for rendering the award.* The parties' arbitration agreement or chosen arbitration rules may specify a time limit for rendering the award. Careful attention should be paid to these time limits, especially if they are capable of being extended only with the agreement of all parties. An overly short and mandatory deadline may allow a delinquent party to delay the arbitration to the point where the award cannot be issued within the time frame, or where any award that is issued within the time frame is rushed and not compliant with the principles of due process. In either case, the award will be exposed to challenge or a court's refusal to enforce.[225]

5-288 *Examples of time limits for rendering awards.* The ICC is well known for its rule, at Article 24, that the award is to be rendered within six months of the signature of the terms of reference. This rule is rarely observed, and is instead extended by the ICC Court, usually on its own initiative, to give the arbitrators a longer period in which to render the award.[226] The time limit for rendering the award may instead run from the close of proceedings – this is the case of ICSID arbitration, in which the arbitrators have up to 180 days from the close of proceedings in which to complete their award.[227] In practice, the close of proceedings is announced once the award is close to finalisation, to ensure compliance with the deadline.

5-289 *Confidentiality of the award.* The tribunal, the institution, and the parties will bear at least some form of obligation of confidentiality with respect to the arbitration as a whole, unless the parties agree otherwise.[228] This extends to the award in particular. However, some institutions will publish awards, edited to remove the names of parties and other identifying details, or excerpts of the award's legal reasoning.[229] In investment treaty arbitration it is common for awards to be published in full, either with the agreement of both parties or, less frequently, through unilateral disclosure by one or other party.[230] Leaking an award, or publishing it without the consent of all parties, does not generally lead to adverse consequences for the disclosing party, although in one well-known arbitration the disclosure of the award by lawyers for the victorious party led the award to be successfully challenged in the courts of Sweden, the place of arbitration. This decision was later reversed on appeal.[231]

5-290 *Disclosure of awards in challenge and enforcement actions.* The award may also be disclosed in setting aside or enforcement actions in national courts, although

---

225. Chapter 1, *The Elements of an International Dispute Resolution Agreement*.
226. See Art. 24.2 of the ICC Rules, and discussion above.
227. See ICSID Rule 46.
228. Chapter 1, *The Elements of an International Dispute Resolution Agreement*.
229. See, e.g., Art. 27.8 of the ICDR Rules, and ICSID Rule 48(4).
230. See the bibliography at Appendix 14.
231. See *Bulgarian Foreign Trade Bank Limited v. AI Trade Finance Inc.*, *Yearbook Commercial Arbitration*, vol. XXIVa (1999), 321–328; *Yearbook Commercial Arbitration* XXVI (2001), 291–298.

some courts may restrict disclosure of the award and submissions from the arbitration in order to preserve their confidentiality.[232]

C. CORRECTION, INTERPRETATION OR REVISION OF THE AWARD

Post-award steps in the arbitration. There is the possibility of further proceedings **5-291** in the arbitration within a short period of time after the issuance of the final award. Most arbitration rules allow the award to be corrected, either at the initiative of the tribunal or on application by either party, if it contains a clerical or computational error.[233] The parties may also apply to the tribunal for an interpretation of the award.[234] The purpose of interpretation is to obtain clarification of the meaning or scope of an award. It cannot be used as a means for deciding new points that go beyond the limits of the award.[235] In ICC arbitration, the application for correction or interpretation of the award must be made within thirty days of the date of the award, and will be performed by the tribunal issuing an addendum to it.[236] The correction or interpretation of awards is a part of the original arbitration and is the task of the original tribunal.[237] Correction or interpretation are distinct from setting aside and enforcement actions taken out before national courts, which we explore in the following chapter.

D. EFFECTS OF THE AWARD

Functus officio. The effect of the award (after any correction or interpretation has **5-292** been performed or the deadline for such measures has expired) is that the arbitration is at an end, and the tribunal's service is complete. The tribunal is 'functus officio', which is loosely translated from the Latin as 'having performed its office'.

Res judicata. In addition, the dispute between the parties that is submitted to **5-293** the tribunal is finally resolved, assuming there is no action to set the award

---

232. See, e.g., ss 2D, 2E of the Hong Kong Arbitration Ordinance. See also J. Paulsson & N. Rawding, 'The Trouble with Confidentiality', *Arbitration International* 11, no. 3 (1995): 305, 311–313.
233. See, e.g., Art. 29 of the ICC Rules.
234. *Ibid.*
235. See, e.g., Derains & Schwartz, 322–326.
236. *Ibid.*
237. But see the specific procedures that apply to interpretation and revision of ICSID awards, under ICSID Rules 50 and 51. For a published example of the interpretation of an ICSID award, see *Wena Hotels Ltd v. Arab Republic of Egypt* (ICSID Case No. ARB/98/4), Decision on Application for Interpretation of the Award (31 Oct. 2005), before a new tribunal composed of Dr Klaus Sachs, Prof. Ibrahim Fadlallah, and Mr Carl F. Salans. A new tribunal was required as one member of the original tribunal had passed away in the period between the issuance of the award and the commencement of the interpretation proceeding.

aside. The award therefore has res judicata effect between the disputing parties with respect to that dispute. This means that the same dispute between the same parties cannot be submitted to another court or tribunal for resolution.

5-294 Finally, and perhaps most importantly, the award may give the victorious party a title to enforce against its opponent, allowing it to secure effective relief. This is the subject of the next chapter.

Chapter Six

After the Arbitration: Challenge, Recognition and Enforcement of the Award

Getting a favourable award in an arbitration is sometimes the easy part of the **6-001** dispute resolution process. Where the successful party – the award creditor – has been awarded money damages and the debtor resists payment, the creditor will need to take further steps in order to actually be paid, with each step presenting another opportunity for the award debtor to resist or just delay payment. This chapter examines (1) the process of challenging an award at the place of arbitration; and (2) the process of having an award recognised and enforced against the debtor, with attention to some of the pitfalls that can occur (and be avoided).

Voluntary compliance. The award creditor will ask the award debtor to comply **6-002** voluntarily with the award, which it may do, especially if it sees no grounds for challenging the award or resisting enforcement and it has assets in a jurisdiction where enforcement through the courts is likely to be straightforward. But if the debtor chooses not to pay, the creditor will need to enforce the award through the courts of the place or places where the debtor's assets are located.

Preliminary question before attempting to enforce: does the debtor have assets in a **6-003** *place where an arbitration award can be enforced?* In many countries, especially in the developing world, enforcement of arbitral awards is difficult or impossible in practice if the award debtor resists enforcement in the local courts. This is true whether or not the state in question is party to the New York Convention, and is because local courts may lack the impartiality to impose enforcement or the efficiency to achieve it on a reasonable time scale. This is the Achilles heel of international arbitration although, as discussed in earlier chapters, it will still be easier to enforce an international arbitration award in most parts of the world than a judgment of a foreign court.[1] Fortunately, these countries are more the exception than the rule, which must be the case in order for commerce to exist on any scale. And the number of exceptions is diminishing with time, as states improve their court systems and their courts become more familiar with international arbitration. But an award creditor will think twice before beginning enforcement proceedings in countries. This chapter looks, in section II below, at the situation where local courts will give some degree of support to an enforcement action against a debtor.

6-004 *Preliminary question before attempting to enforce: can or will the award be challenged?* There is, even before arriving at enforcement proceedings, a threshold opportunity for the award debtor to prevent the award creditor securing the awarded remedy: by challenging the award, usually in an 'action to set aside', before the courts of the place of arbitration. This procedure, examined in section I, can lead to the annulment of the award so that, at least within the jurisdiction of that court, it is no longer capable of being enforced.

I.   CHALLENGING INTERNATIONAL
                     ARBITRAL AWARDS

6-005 *Effect of successful challenge: annulment.* Many arbitration agreements and most arbitration rules stipulate that the arbitral awards that result from arbitration under those agreements or rules are 'final' and/or 'binding'.[2] Yet there is almost always the possibility for a party to challenge the award, whether or not the parties have agreed (directly in their contract or indirectly in the applicable arbitration rules) that the award is final and/or binding. A successful challenge will usually result in the award being 'set aside', 'vacated', or 'annulled', and therefore ceasing to exist, at least within the jurisdiction of the court setting it aside. This effectively means the clock goes back to before the arbitration began.

6-006 *Anticipating and proactively managing the risk of a challenge during the arbitration.* Experienced international arbitrators will generally be aware of the applicable grounds for challenge and will take them into account in the way they manage the proceedings. The difficulty is that some arbitrators may be too willing to sacrifice efficiency in order to avoid any risk of annulment. Therefore, parties to international arbitrations should be aware of the availability of a challenge at the place of arbitration and of the grounds on which it may succeed. This will enable them to help ensure the arbitrators conduct the proceedings maintaining a

---

1. *Introduction*; and Ch. 2, *Negotiating an International Dispute Resolution Agreement.*
2. See, e.g., the ICC Model Clause, which provides that '[a]ll disputes arising out of or in connection with the present contract shall be finally settled under the Rules of Arbitration of the ICC...'; Art. 28(6) of the ICC Rules, which provides that '[e]very Award shall be binding on the parties'; and Art. 26.9 of the LCIA Rules, which provides that '[a]ll awards shall be final and binding on the parties'.

degree of efficiency while mitigating the risk of a successful challenge. In fact, the parties themselves, and especially the claimant, should bring any unusual grounds for challenge to the arbitrators' attention. And if a possible reason for annulment does arise in the arbitration, the parties (or, again, at least the claimant) may wish to propose action to reduce or eliminate the risk.

The dilemma with extensions	As each deadline falls due, the respondent writes to the tribunal asking for more time. The claimant must weigh its frustration at the delay against the risk that a court may subsequently rule that the tribunal did not give the respondent an adequate opportunity to present its case. Obviously, the claimant will want to be reasonable (and appear to be acting reasonably) and will generally be able to accommodate a limited number of modest extensions, as they will not greatly delay the proceedings overall. Repeated requests for extensions of time, however, can have the effect of substantially lengthening the proceedings, and there is a risk that the tribunal will be willing to grant such requests long after the claimant's patience has been exhausted.

Reducing the risk of both challenge and delay: start at the beginning	Parties can reduce the risk of successful challenges by suggesting to the tribunal, at the start of the arbitration, that it secure the parties' agreement on issues which might otherwise give rise to a challenge. For example, the tribunal may include a provision in the initial procedural order, terms of reference, or equivalent document, recording that the parties do not object to the constitution of the tribunal, the tribunal's authority to conduct the proceedings expeditiously, or the conduct of the arbitration to date. If both parties sign that document without qualification, a subsequent reviewing court may find they have waived a later challenge of the award based on those grounds. Given the reduced risk of challenge, a tribunal may feel less inclined to tolerate, for example, one side's dilatory tactics during the proceedings.

A.   Types of Challenge

Action to set aside versus appeal. The grounds on which an award may be chal- **6-007** lenged under modern international arbitration laws are narrowly drawn and, in particular, do not allow a review of the merits. But in countries with less progressive legislation or traditions of court intervention in arbitration, the laws may – in addition to the usual action to set aside discussed below – allow parties to appeal the award before the courts. For example, section 69 of the English Arbitration Act 1996 provides for an appeal to the English courts on a point of law in certain circumstances.[3] A widely held view is that this sort of appeal has no place in a modern transnational environment where the parties' objective in agreeing to arbitration is usually to get away from the courts of whatever country and entrust the resolution of their disputes – and especially of the merits of their disputes – to international arbitrators.[4]

6-008 *Special review procedures.* There are, however, certain instances in which parties should legitimately expect some review of the merits by another instance to occur.

6-009 *Review of the merits permitted by arbitration rules.* There may be a mechanism allowing a review of the award within the system of arbitration to which the parties have referred their disputes. Perhaps the best-known example of something approaching an 'internal' appeal procedure is in ICSID arbitration, where a party's only recourse against an award is before an ad hoc committee established by ICSID itself under Article 52 of the ICISD Convention. We consider this specific mechanism, and the extent to which it allows a review of the merits of an award, in Chapter 7 on investment treaty arbitration. Also, in GAFTA arbitrations – which resolve certain commodities disputes – a party has a right to appeal to a Board of Appeal within thirty days of an award.[5] The appeal involves a new hearing and the Board of Appeal may confirm, amend, or set aside the initial award.

6-010 *Review of the merits permitted by party agreement.* Alternatively, the parties may themselves agree that an award issued by a first arbitral tribunal can be reviewed by a second arbitral tribunal, through a particular set of rules of an arbitral institution or a bespoke 'appeal' mechanism drafted by the parties. For example, the CPR Institute Arbitration Appeal Procedure provides an 'opt in' procedure[6] that applies only if the parties include it in their arbitration clause, or in a submission agreement at the time the dispute arises, and provides for a second tribunal to review the award rendered by the first. It is not clear whether this sort of two-tier arbitration is valid under all arbitration laws. Certainly, an arbitral award or confirmation rendered on top of another award increases the potential grounds for challenge. In any event, such provisions are rare, and rules providing for appeal are not popular in the international context. Because appeal by agreement is rarely encountered in international practice, we will not consider it further here.[7]

---

3. This is examined in more detail later in this section.
4. Proponents of a right to appeal might argue, e.g., in England, that the right is of limited effect as the parties are permitted to waive or 'contract out' of it. We would suggest that the better position would be, if there is to be provision for an appeal at all, to allow international parties to opt in to it, rather than having the right to an appeal being the default position and requiring parties (who may be unfamiliar with English arbitration law) to opt out in their contracts.
5. See, Grain and Feed Trade Association (GAFTA) Arbitration Rules 10:1 and 12:4.
6. Available at <www.cpradr.org>.
7. On a related point, parties generally cannot agree to a broader standard of review of an award than that provided by law. See, e.g., *Hall Street Associates, L.L.C. v. Mattel Inc.*, 552 U.S. 1 (2008).

Actions to set aside. By far the most important type of challenge of an arbitral **6-011** award is an action to set aside conducted before a court of the place of arbitration. The local arbitration law will invariably allow an action to set the award aside (also referred to as 'recourse' against or 'review' of the award, or as an action to 'vacate' or 'annul' the award). For example, Chapter VII of the Model Law is entitled 'Recourse against the Award' and contains just one article, Article 34, entitled 'Application for setting aside as exclusive recourse against arbitral award.' It allows a party to apply to a court to have an award set aside, as the exclusive means of recourse against the award, providing the court is of the place of arbitration.[8]

Waiving the right of challenge. An action to set aside is therefore quite different **6-012** from an appeal: it is designed to ensure that a state, through its courts, exercises a minimum level of control over the procedural and jurisdictional integrity of international arbitration taking place on its territory. But some countries regard even this low level of control as unnecessary and are content to leave matters within the hands of the arbitrators; for instance, Belgium, Sweden and Switzerland permit parties to waive in their arbitration agreement their right to seek to set an award aside, provided that the parties are not nationals of or incorporated in the country in question.[9] These international arbitrations are therefore substantially 'delocalised', as the parties sever one of the key links with the place of arbitration by validly removing the award from the control of the courts of that jurisdiction.[10] While we do not encourage it, as the exercise of limited control by the courts of these three countries is no bad thing, parties may waive an action to set aside by putting language in their dispute resolution clause along the following lines:

Example 6a – Waiving the Right of Challenge in a Dispute Resolution Clause

> The award will not be subject to any right of appeal, challenge, or action to set aside, which the parties hereby irrevocably waive.

---

8. See Art. 1(2) of the Model Law regarding the Law's scope of application.
9. Article 1717.4 of the Belgian Code Judiciaire allows a waiver 'where none of the parties is either an individual of Belgian nationality or residing in Belgium, or a legal person having its head office or a branch there'; s. 51 of the Swedish Arbitration Act allows a waiver '[w]here none of the parties is domiciled or has its place of business in Sweden'; and Art. 192 of the Swiss Private International Law Act allows a waiver of an action to set aside '[i]f none of the parties have their domicile, their habitual residence, or a business establishment in Switzerland'. Belgium previously experimented with a law that removed entirely the parties' right to recourse against the award (rather than making it subject to the agreement of the parties) where none of the parties was a national of or incorporated in Belgium.
10. The courts of the place or places of enforcement will retain a role if a party seeks to enforce the award. However, enforcement courts rule on whether or not the award should be recognised and enforced within their jurisdiction, not on whether the award itself should subsist or be annulled.

B.   PROCEDURE FOR AN ACTION TO SET ASIDE

6-013 Most or all modern arbitration laws, including those inspired by the Model Law, contain provisions on setting aside international awards that are similar to those of the Model Law: a dissatisfied party may challenge the award, but only in an action to set aside, only on limited grounds that preclude a review of the merits, and only in the courts of the place of arbitration. The procedure for an action to set aside will vary from jurisdiction to jurisdiction, and we summarise the main points here.

6-014 *Time limitations.* In most countries there is a short time limit within which the action must be brought. For example, Article 34.3 of the Model Law requires an action to set aside to be brought within three months of the date on which the party making the application received the award (or from the date any application in the arbitration for correction or interpretation was disposed of by the tribunal).[11] In Switzerland, the deadline is shorter: the application to set the award aside must be made within thirty days of notification of the award.[12] In England, an action to set aside or appeal must be brought within twenty-eight days of the date of the award or of the date of notification to the applicant of the outcome of any arbitral process of appeal or review.[13] Not all countries provide such a short time for lodging a challenge. In Italy, the period is ninety days from the date the party received notification of the award, and an absolute cut-off of one year from the date of the signing of the award.[14]

Not that this ever really happens: one day too late	Deadlines in arbitration-related court proceedings, such as actions to set aside, are likely to be more strictly enforced than deadlines in arbitrations. In one case in which one of the authors was involved, the respondent in an UNCITRAL arbitration in Geneva was on the wrong end of an award of several hundred million dollars. There were at least reasonable grounds on which to challenge the award, and the party geared up to do so. However, it failed to make payment of the required court filing fee by the specified deadline (it was one day late) and, as a result, its action to set aside was held by the court to be out of time.

---

11. Note that, under Art. 16(3) of the Model Law, an application to the court regarding a tribunal's preliminary ruling retaining jurisdiction must be made within thirty days of receipt of notice of the ruling.
12. See Art. 100 of the Swiss Federal Statute of the Swiss Federal Supreme Court, dated 17 Jun. 2005.
13. See s. 70(3) of the English Arbitration Act 1996.
14. See Art. 828 of the Italian Civil Procedure Code (Recourse for nullity): A recourse for nullity may be filed with the court of appeal covering the city in which the arbitration has its seat, within ninety days after the notification of the award. No recourse may be filed after one year from the date of the last signature.

Court in which action should be filed. As we have noted elsewhere, only the courts **6-015**
of the place of arbitration should have jurisdiction to hear any challenge of an
award or action to set aside. The relevant national law will specify which precise
court will hear the action, and the detailed procedures for doing so. Taking
Switzerland as an example again, the country's arbitration statute stipulates that
all actions to set aside must be brought before the Federal Tribunal, the country's
highest court,[15] and the Swiss Federal Statute governing proceedings before the
Federal Tribunal lays down the procedure to be followed.[16] In France and Italy, the
court of appeals covering the city named as the place of arbitration hears any
actions to set aside, and the court's decision in that regard is subject to review
by the country's supreme court (the court of cassation).[17] The Model Law provides
in Article 6 that actions to set aside are to be heard by the court or courts identified
in that provision by each country when enacting the law: in Singapore, for
example, the court identified in Article 6 is the High Court.[18] In some countries,
such as the United States, actions to set aside are not submitted to one central court
as they are in Switzerland or Singapore, which may diminish the quality and
consistency of the case law of that country concerning international arbitration.

In a few instances, courts other than those of the place of arbitration have purported **6-016**
to set aside an international arbitral award, although these cases have tended to be
in countries that lack a reputation for robust judicial independence or support for
international arbitration. For example, in the *Pertamina v. Karaha Bodas* case,[19] an
Indonesian court 'set aside' an award where the place of arbitration was in
Switzerland, despite there being no indication that the parties had agreed on the
law of the arbitration being other than that of the Swiss seat. The court went on to
issue an anti-suit injunction prohibiting the award creditor from enforcing the
award abroad. When the award creditor attempted to enforce the award against
Pertamina's assets in the United States, the US Court of Appeals for the Fifth
Circuit disregarded the Indonesian courts' decision and injunction, holding that
under the New York Convention it had discretion to recognise and enforce the
award.[20] More recently, in the *Venture v. Satyam* case, India's Supreme Court
allowed the challenge of an award rendered in London in an LCIA arbitration.[21]

---

15. See Art. 191 of the Swiss Private International Law Act.
16. See Art. 77 of the Swiss Federal Statute of the Swiss Federal Supreme Court, dated 17 Jun. 2005.
17. See Art. 828 of the Italian Code of Civil Procedure.
18. See Art. 8 of the Singapore International Arbitration Act.
19. See District Court, Central Jakarta, *Perusahaan Pertambangan Minyak Dan Gas Bumi Negara v. Karaha Bodas Company, LLC*, reproduced in *Mealey's International Law Reports* (2003) and discussed in E. Gaillard, '"*KBC v. Pertamina*": Landmark Decision on Anti-Suit Injunctions', *New York Law Journal* (2 Oct. 2003); and G. Petrochilos, *Procedural Law in International Arbitration* (Oxford: Oxford University Press, 2004), 76 et seq.
20. *Ibid.*
21. See *Venture Global Engineering v. Satyam Computer Services Limited*, Supreme Court of India, 10 Jan. 2008.

Not that this ever really happens: failure to appreciate the ability to enforce abroad	One of the authors was involved in an arbitration involving an Eastern European country as the respondent, with the place of arbitration in a major Western European country. During settlement negotiations, the country's external counsel admitted certain weaknesses in the respondent's defences but stated that the respondent had no fear of an adverse outcome because the courts of the respondent's country would never enforce the foreign award. The counsel was obviously referring to certain domestic procedures for enforcing a judgment or arbitration award in the respondent's country, without appreciating the enforceability of an award in other countries. Perhaps on account of having received bad advice on enforceability, the respondent refused to settle, lost the arbitration, and only then understood the risk that the claimant could garnish its assets around the world, without ever having stepped foot in the respondent's country.

6-017 *Appeal of court's decision on the challenge.* Whether the designated court's decision on the action to set aside can be appealed is a matter for the law of that jurisdiction. There is nothing on this point in the Model Law, although Article 16(3) does provide that when a tribunal decides to retain jurisdiction as a preliminary matter, the court identified in Article 6 will, on request of any party, decide the issue of jurisdiction with no possibility of further appeal. In Swiss law, there is no appeal from or reconsideration of the decisions of the Federal Tribunal on actions to set aside. In Singapore, an appeal to the Court of Appeal (the highest court) is possible from a decision of the High Court made under Article 16(3) of the Model Law, but only with the leave of the High Court, and there is no appeal against a refusal by the High Court to grant leave.[22]

A word of warning: obtaining timely advice	Because of the short time limit and the specific procedures that will apply in different countries, it is essential that parties considering an action to set aside seek advice as soon as possible after receiving the award (if they have not done so before) from litigation lawyers active in the courts of the place of arbitration.

---

22. See s. 10 of the Singapore International Arbitration Act.

C.   GROUNDS FOR AN ACTION TO SET ASIDE

The law in theory versus its application by local courts. As already indicated, in **6-018** most jurisdictions the grounds on which the law permits a court to set an award aside are limited and, in most cases, exclude the review by the court of the merits of the award. That said, while arbitration laws around the world – and especially those based on the Model Law – are increasingly similar occasionally there are material differences when it comes to the grounds for annulling an award.

In fact, it is probably not sufficient just to look at the relevant arbitration law in **6-019** theory, as the application in practice by the courts of that law may not be what a party from outside the jurisdiction will expect. For example, most laws (including the Model Law) allow a court to set aside an award if it infringes public policy. Yet the concept of 'public policy' is interpreted very differently by courts around the world, as discussed below.

Setting aside: Model Law jurisdictions versus other jurisdictions. The Model Law **6-020** is a modern, high-quality international arbitration statute that is the inspiration for dozens of arbitration laws around the world. Therefore, rather than survey the many different arbitration laws, we discuss first the grounds for setting aside found under the Model Law, and then consider a handful of arbitration statutes in major jurisdictions that differ materially in this area, the most prominent of which is the English Arbitration Act.

Model Law: grounds for setting aside. Article 34 of the Model Law lists six **6-021** grounds on which a court may set an award aside. Five of these are of what might loosely be called a jurisdictional or procedural nature, with the sixth, public policy, touching on the merits of the dispute. The grounds are virtually identical to the six grounds on which Article V of the New York Convention allows enforcement of an award to be refused (the remaining Convention ground – which is that the award has been set aside – is necessarily absent from the grounds for setting an award aside). The list of six grounds is exhaustive.[23]

Article 34 splits the six grounds into a group of four (the first four below, which **6-022** appear in Article 34.2(a)), which must be raised and proved by the applicant, and a second group of two grounds (the fifth and sixth ground below, which appear in Article 34.2(b)), which a court may raise on its own initiative. The six grounds are (i) the incapacity of a party or invalidity of the arbitration agreement; (ii) a failure to notify an arbitrator appointment or initiation of proceedings; (iii) the award was beyond the scope of the arbitration agreement; (iv) invalid constitution of the arbitral tribunal; (v) the subject matter was not arbitrable (not capable of resolution by arbitration); and (vi) violation of public policy.

---

23. See Art. 34(1) of the Model Law. See also the title of Art. 34, 'Application for setting aside as exclusive recourse against arbitral award.'

6-023 *Procedural violations as grounds for challenge.* Below are the first five Model Law grounds for setting aside an award, followed by a short discussion of each:

Article 34(2)(a)(i): incapacity invalidity	A party to the arbitration agreement was under some incapacity, or the arbitration agreement was not valid under the law to which the parties subjected it or, if there is none, under the law of the place of arbitration.

- Here there are really two separate grounds: *incapacity*, which is rarely encountered, and the much broader category of the *invalidity* of the arbitration agreement.
- A party may be under some incapacity if, for example, he is a natural person and not of the age required to enter into a binding contract or, if it is a juridical person (such as a company), its representatives acted ultra vires when entering into the arbitration agreement. Capacity issues may also arise where a state or a state entity agrees to arbitrate, although it is widely acknowledged that a state may not rely on its own law to escape from its agreement to arbitrate.[24]
- The arbitration agreement may be invalid for whatever reasons are specified in the applicable law. A common example is if it does not comply with the formalities of the applicable law – if, for example, it is not in writing, as required by Article 7(2) of the Model Law.

Article 34(2)(a)(ii): due process	Where the applicant was not given proper notice of the appointment of an arbitrator or of the arbitral proceedings or was otherwise unable to present its case.

- This ground is based on the principles of natural justice or due process, and is found in most jurisdictions. The difficulty lies in establishing exactly when a party is unable to present its case. The standards here vary from country to country, but it is probably sufficient if the tribunal gives the parties a fair hearing by allowing each of them a reasonable and roughly equal opportunity at every stage of the arbitration to present its case.

Article 34(2)(a)(iii): beyond scope	Where the award deals with a dispute or matters outside of the terms or the scope of the submission to arbitration.

---

24. See, e.g., the Resolution of Institute of International Law on Arbitration between States, State Enterprises and State Entities, Session of Santiago de Compostela, 1989, which provides at Art. 5 that: '[a] State, a state enterprise, or a state entity cannot invoke incapacity to arbitrate in order to resist arbitration to which it has agreed'.

- This covers awards where the tribunal addresses issues that were not submitted to it by the parties for decision; this will include, arguably, claims that are outside the jurisdiction of the tribunal. If the issues outside the scope of the parties' agreement can be separated from those within the scope of the agreement, the court will only set aside the part of the award that was outside that scope.

Article 34(2)(a)(iv): procedure violates agreement or law	Where the composition of the tribunal or the arbitral procedure was not in accordance with the parties' agreement (unless that agreement is in conflict with a mandatory provision of the law) or with the law of the place of arbitration, in the absence of party agreement on a given point.

- If the arbitrators do not possess the attributes specified in the parties' agreement, the award may be set aside. The rendering of an award by a truncated tribunal (a tribunal that does not comprise the full complement of arbitrators agreed by the parties) may also be a ground for setting an award aside.[25]

Article 34(2)(b)(i): arbitrability	If the subject matter of the dispute is not capable of settlement by arbitration under the law of the place of arbitration.

- This ground concerns the arbitrability of the claims raised in the arbitration. As noted earlier, the words 'arbitrability' and 'arbitrable' are used in some parts of the world, notably the United States, to refer to claims within the jurisdiction of the tribunal. We use the terms to refer instead to claims that are capable of resolution by arbitration. The group of disputes not capable of settlement by arbitration will vary from national law to national law, but will typically include matrimonial and family disputes, criminal matters, certain intellectual property disputes, and certain bankruptcy-related disputes.

Public policy violations as grounds for challenge. Most or all arbitration laws **6-024** allow the challenge of an award on the grounds that it violates public policy.

---

25. For a decision from a jurisdiction where the Model Law is not in force, *Agence Transcongolaise des Communications – Chemin de fer Congo Océan (ATC-CFCO) v. Compagnie Minière de l'Ogooue – Comilog S.A.*, Paris Court of Appeal, 1 Jul. 1997, *Yearbook Commercial Arbitration XXIV* (1999): 281 et seq., in which the Paris Court of Appeal annulled an award rendered by a truncated tribunal, holding that the composition of the tribunal was no longer in accordance with the parties' agreement.

It is the most troublesome of the six grounds listed in the Model Law, in that there is no accepted definition of public policy:

Article 34(2)(b)(ii): public policy	If the award is in conflict with the public policy of the place of arbitration.

- Courts hearing an action to set aside may construe the public policy of their jurisdiction so broadly that it becomes virtually indistinguishable from the laws of that jurisdiction, so that any conflict of the award with the law of the place of the arbitration will lead the court to set the award aside. This broad view of public policy is prevalent in certain developing nations, and courts frequently employ it to justify the review of the merits of the award. A well-known example is the *Saw Pipes* case in which the Supreme Court of India put forward a broad interpretation of the concept of 'public policy', which consisted in the fundamental policy of Indian law, the interests of India, justice, or morality, as well as patent illegality, thereby opening the door to a review of the merits of the award.[26]
- At the other end of the spectrum, the courts of many countries with developed arbitration laws and practice will construe public policy more narrowly, deeming it to mean 'international public policy' (a concept under which public policy applicable to foreign awards is less broad than that applicable to domestic awards). While it is difficult to define 'international public policy', it is generally understood to be limited to a state's most basic notions of morality and justice.[27]

6-025 *Jurisdiction of the arbitrators as grounds for challenge.* Article 34 of the Model Law does not contain a specific ground allowing the annulment of an award where the tribunal lacks jurisdiction.[28] However, Article 16(3) provides that where a tribunal retains jurisdiction over a claim as a preliminary matter, the ruling can be referred to the courts for a final decision within thirty days.[29] Instead of making

---

26. See *Oil and Natural Gas Corporation v. SAW Pipes Ltd* (2003) 5 SCC 705. This decision applied only to domestic arbitral awards, but was subsequently extended to the international arena in *Venture Global Engineering v. Satyam Computer Services Ltd*, Supreme Court of India, 10 Jan. 2008.
27. See the International Law Association – Committee on International Commercial Arbitration, Interim Report on Public Policy as a Bar to Enforcement of International Arbitral Awards, London Conference (2000), and Final Report on Public Policy as a Bar to Enforcement of International Arbitral Awards, New Delhi Conference (2002). See also Gaillard & Savage, 953 et seq.
28. This is in contrast with the position in French law (see Art. 1484(3) of the French New Code of Civil Procedure), Swiss law (see Art. 190(2) of the Swiss Private International Law Act) and English law (see s. 67 of the England Arbitration Act).
29. While it is commonly accepted that courts can review positive findings of jurisdiction under Art. 16(3) of the Model Law, arbitration laws differ when it comes to the issue of whether a

an interlocutory appeal to the courts (where available), parties can also object to jurisdiction before the arbitral tribunal, which may decide to hear the claim on the merits before determining whether it has jurisdiction over it. Where an objection to jurisdiction is heard with the merits and not therefore caught by Article 16(3), an action to set aside founded on the absence of jurisdiction will be available under Article 34(2)(a)(iii), on the basis that the award deals with a dispute not contemplated by or falling within the terms of the submission to arbitration, and also perhaps under Article 34(2)(a)(i), on the basis that the arbitration agreement is invalid.[30]

Interestingly, Article 34(4) of the Model Law allows a court, where requested by a **6-026** party, to suspend the setting aside proceedings and to give the arbitral tribunal the opportunity to resume the arbitration or take other action needed to eliminate the grounds for setting aside.

Grounds for setting aside outside the Model Law. The Model Law grounds for **6-027** setting aside awards considered above are similar or identical to those found in many national laws, including of course laws inspired by the Model Law but also those that predate or are otherwise not influenced by it. In certain major jurisdictions, however, there are grounds for setting aside that are materially different from those on the Model Law's list.

England: appeal on point of law. One prominent example of a ground for challenge **6-028** (although not strictly an action to set aside) that departs substantially from the Model Law is the availability in England of an appeal on a point of law, discussed earlier.[31] Section 69 of the English Arbitration Act 1996 allows a party to appeal an award to the English courts on a question of law, and the court may confirm, vary, or set aside the award as a result, or remit it to the arbitral tribunal for reconsideration. This appeal is confined to points of English law, and to cases where the place of arbitration is England,[32] and is only available with the permission of the court.[33] The court will grant permission only if 'the decision of the tribunal on the question is obviously wrong, or the question is one of general public importance and the decision of the tribunal is at least open to serious doubt, and [if], despite the agreement of the parties to resolve the matter by arbitration, it is just and proper in all the circumstances for the court to determine the question'.[34]

---

finding of no jurisdiction by a tribunal can be reviewed by a court. For example, Courts in Switzerland, England, and France allow a review while those in Singapore, Hong Kong, and Germany do not.

30. See, e.g., Redfern & Hunter, para. 10–39.
31. Chapter 1, *The Elements of an International Dispute Resolution Agreement.*
32. See s. 82(1) of the English Arbitration Act. See also, D. St John Sutton, J. Gill, & M. Gearing, *Russell on Arbitration*, 23rd edn (London: Sweet & Maxwell, 2007), 508.
33. See s. 69(2) of the English Arbitration Act.
34. See s. 69(3) of the English Arbitration Act.

6-029 Importantly, the English statute allows parties to waive, or 'contract out' of, their right to appeal on a point of law. The courts have held that the incorporation by the parties of arbitration rules, such as those of the ICC and the LCIA,[35] which state that the parties are deemed to have waived all recourse to the extent permitted by law, constitute an effective waiver of the right to an appeal on a point of law.[36]

6-030 The availability of an appeal on a point of law in England is a trap for unwary parties who might expect a recent English arbitration statute to be consistent with recent arbitration laws elsewhere in the world (and especially with the Model Law), and not therefore permit an appeal of the merits of an award. This is one reason parties may prefer to have the place of their international arbitration outside England. If they locate their arbitration in England, they should apply institutional rules such as those of the ICC or the LCIA and, unless they truly wish to subject their arbitration award to the possibility of review on points of law by the courts, expressly state in their arbitration clause that they waive their right to an appeal under section 69 of the English Arbitration Act.[37]

6-031 Other examples of grounds for setting aside not listed in the Model Law include, in Italy, non-compliance by the tribunal with a deadline agreed by the parties for the issuance of the award[38] and, in Belgium, the award containing conflicting 'provisions'.[39]

6-032 To conclude on the grounds for setting awards aside, all arbitration laws are different, and some laws give an award debtor more of an opportunity than others to set awards aside. But more important still is the difference in practice between the interpretation and application by the courts around the world of the same or similar grounds for setting awards aside. This difference is especially marked with respect to the public policy ground. For these reasons it pays to investigate the law *and* practice of the place of arbitration regarding actions to set aside *before* agreeing to situate one's arbitration in that country.[40] It also pays to keep that law and practice in mind as any arbitration progresses, in order to minimise the risk of exposing a later award to annulment.

---

35. See Art. 28(6) of the ICC Rules; Art. 29.2 of the LCIA Rules.
36. See Russell, 506–507. But see, for a recent decision holding that the UNCITRAL Rules do not contain such a waiver, *Shell Egypt Manzala GmbH & Others v. Dana Gas Egypt Limited (formerly Centurion Petroleum Corporation)*, [2009] EWHC 2097 (Comm).
37. Chapter 1, The *Elements of an International Dispute Resolution. Agreement.*
38. See Art. 829(4) of the Italian Code of Civil Procedure.
39. See Art. 1704(1)(j) of the Belgian Judicial Code.
40. Chapter 1, The *Elements of an International Dispute Resolution Agreement.*

D.   EFFECTS OF THE SETTING ASIDE OF AN AWARD

Setting aside in part or entirely. Awards may be set aside in part or entirely.[41] If the **6-033**
award is affirmed in part and vacated in part, the consequence is essentially a
modified award. Partial nullity is possible only when the defect affects a part of
the award that is separable from the others. The rest of the award remains valid.

Setting aside in part	One well-known example of an award set aside in part only was in *Metalclad v. Mexico*, a NAFTA award brought by Mexico before the Supreme Court of British Columbia. The court found that the NAFTA tribunal, in its conclusions on the existence of a concept of transparency, had decided upon matters beyond the scope of the submission to arbitration under NAFTA Chapter Eleven.[42] The court therefore struck down this portion of the award, but upheld the remainder of it.

Entire award. If the entire award is set aside, the effect is, in theory anyway, that it **6-034**
ceases to exist and cannot be enforced. This is certainly the effect in practice within
the jurisdiction of the court that set the award aside. However as discussed below in
section II with respect to enforcement, there is continuing debate as to whether it
is possible to enforce, in jurisdictions other than the place of arbitration, an award
that has been set aside at the place of arbitration. Suffice to say for present purposes
that courts in certain countries have enforced awards that were set aside in other
countries, but the more common position is that an award that has been set aside
cannot be enforced anywhere.

Effect of annulment on arbitration agreement and subsequent proceedings. **6-035**
Depending on the grounds given, the setting aside of the award may not affect the
arbitration agreement. If it does not, it will not prevent a party from bringing a fresh
arbitration against the same opponent on the basis of the original arbitration agreement. So, for example, where the award is set aside for procedural reasons – such as a
lack of due process or a failure to comply with the parties' arbitration agreement – the
arbitration can effectively be repeated, tiresome and expensive though that will be.

If, however, the court holds the arbitration agreement to be invalid, a fresh arbi- **6-036**
tration will not be possible, at least on the basis of that same arbitration agreement.
The court may also hold the claim to be outside the scope of the arbitration
agreement, which should likewise prevent a party from bringing the same claim
against the same party on the basis of that arbitration agreement. In these cases, in
the absence of another arbitration agreement covering the same disputes as the

---

41. See, e.g., s. 67(3) of the English Arbitration Act; see also Art. 830 of the Italian Code of Civil
    Procedure.
42. See *The United Mexican States v. Metalclad Corporation*, Judgment of the Supreme Court of
    British Columbia, dated 2 May 2001.

original, the party seeking resolution of the dispute will need to pursue its claim before the appropriate courts, as if the parties' contract had never contained an arbitration clause.

6-037 *Most challenges fail in arbitration-friendly countries.* The multiple grounds on which a court can set aside an award should not mislead parties into believing that there is a high probability that courts will do so. Where the place of arbitration is friendly to arbitration, this friendliness should translate into a general reluctance of the courts to allow challenges to succeed in the absence of clear and unambiguous grounds. In practice, the burden of establishing grounds for challenge will not be easy for a party to discharge in these jurisdictions, and applications to set aside international arbitral awards will rarely prosper.

II.   RECOGNITION AND ENFORCEMENT OF INTERNATIONAL ARBITRAL AWARDS

6-038 When an award comes down and a party is dissatisfied with it, its thoughts will usually turn to challenging it. Possible challenges have been considered in the previous section. If, on the other hand, a party is satisfied, it will want to enforce the award if that is necessary to receive the benefit of it. There are circumstances where there is no need for enforcement: for example, if a party is the respondent in the arbitration and the tribunal dismisses all claims (but does not award it costs), there is nothing to enforce.[43] And if the award debtor complies voluntarily with the award, there is no need to enforce the award through the courts. There are also situations where it may not be worth the expense and aggravation to pursue enforcement because, for example, the award debtor is insolvent or its assets are located in a jurisdiction where enforcement of international awards against local parties is difficult or impossible in practice.

6-039 We discuss below the essential steps a party will need to take to enforce – or resist enforcement of – an award that provides for the payment of sums to the prevailing party. The associated costs of enforcing, and the risk of not succeeding in efforts to collect, may be considerable. We therefore preface this with a discussion of the common practice of attempting to negotiate a settlement to avoid enforcement of the award. This is followed by a look at the laws applicable to enforcement of a foreign award, administrative procedures that may be necessary at the place of arbitration to convert the award into a right to collect at the place of enforcement, and the court procedures to be followed at the place of enforcement. We have been careful to note the potential costs of seeking to enforce an award at each stage of the process.

---

43. Recognition of the award may still be desirable, to enhance the ability of the successful party to use the award to resist the same claims brought in another forum.

This section largely presumes, as suggested in Chapter 3, *When a Dispute Arises,* **6-040** that before obtaining an award the creditor will have engaged in some amount of planning for the event of obtaining a favourable arbitration award, and will already have some idea of whether the debtor has any assets, where they are located, and therefore the country or countries in which enforcement should take place.

A.   NEGOTIATION AND SETTLEMENT OF INTERNATIONAL
       ARBITRAL AWARDS

Where the tribunal has granted the award creditor a remedy in the form of payment **6-041** of a monetary amount (such as damages or costs), the award creditor will need to take certain steps to collect the amount awarded. The first step will be to request the debtor to comply voluntarily. This is usually done by a formal written demand that by a certain deadline the debtor pay the sums due into the creditor's bank account, or perform the other actions ordered in the award. As noted earlier, the debtor may agree to comply, especially if not to do so would increase its exposure to interest on the award and collection costs that it will eventually be held to pay (which presumes the debtor has assets in jurisdictions where enforcement of international awards in the courts is straightforward and effective) or would harm its reputation (which is often a concern of blue-chip companies or states).

Negotiation leverage. A 2008 survey of corporate counsel reported rather discoura- **6-042** ging statistics: it found that 51% of awards rendered do not meet with voluntary compliance, and of those companies that negotiated a payment with the award debtor, 46% reported that they agreed to accept payment of less than half the amount of the award. Apparently, they gave up most of what they won for good reason, as 56% of those surveyed reported that they recovered less than the full value of awards through enforcement proceedings. Thus, a negotiation between the disputing parties after the award of a monetary remedy will turn on the time, cost, and predictability of enforcement measures, as well as the financial ability of the debtor to satisfy the amount awarded.[44] While the reliability of such statistics as a fair reflection of corporate experiences worldwide may be questionable,[45] there is little doubt that perceptions matter, and a creditor's negotiation leverage will be directly proportional to how concerned the debtor is about the consequences of refusing to comply with the award.

Seizing assets to increase leverage. There are steps that can be taken to bring an **6-043** award debtor to the table that can be described as both creative and effective. Parties should not overlook the negotiation leverage offered by the enforceability

---

44. See International Arbitration: Corporate Attitudes and Practices 2008, Executive Summary, at 2.
45. For a critique of the same survey, see M. McIlwrath, 'Ignoring the Elephant in the Room: International Arbitration: Corporate Attitudes and Practices 2008', in *74 Arbitration 424* (November 2008), reprinted in *2 World Arbitration & Mediation Review (WAMR)* 111–125 (JurisNet 2008).

of an international arbitration award in multiple jurisdictions. The creditor may have more than one bite at the apple, and different ways of biting, if the debtor has assets in more than one jurisdiction, and these assets can be attached or seized in order to satisfy an award. Sometimes, the threat alone of seizing a debtor's foreign assets – even if they are less than the value of the award – may lead the debtor to comply. For example, if the award is rendered against a debtor whose main assets are in a jurisdiction known to be unfriendly to arbitration, the creditor may still have a negotiation advantage if it is able to locate even a small asset in an arbitration-friendly country. Although insufficient to satisfy the entire amount of the award, enforcement proceedings against the asset may encourage the debtor to pay the award in full in order to avoid impact on its reputation, credit rating, and its relations with any domestic or foreign partners, or to avoid further enforcement actions against other small assets located elsewhere.

Not that this ever really happens: threatening enforcement against museum exhibits	One of the authors was once involved in an arbitration in which the respondent was a state that had organised a large and valuable exhibition of its historical artefacts hosted by a leading museum in a major European capital. The claimant obtained an award of damages and asked the respondent to comply with it, failing which it would attempt to seize the exhibition. The respondent, aware of the poor publicity that would ensue as well as the claimant's at least reasonable chances of success, agreed to pay the awarded amounts in full.

6-044 *Settlement discounts.* As part of the negotiation process, it is not uncommon for an award debtor to offer an immediate payment with an 'enforcement discount'. Under this arrangement, the debtor will comply promptly with the award if the creditor agrees to discount the amount of money to be paid. This allows the creditor to collect at least a portion of the amount awarded and to avoid the cost, effort, and uncertainty associated with actions to challenge and enforce the award. Whether this makes sense for the award creditor will depend on circumstances, including the urgency of the creditor's need for the money, the likelihood of the debtor being able to resist enforcement in the courts, the time and cost that an enforcement action would demand, and whether the enforcement court will order the debtor to pay the creditor's costs if the creditor prevails.

A word of warning: the dangers of 'settling' an award	Any agreement reached to settle an arbitration award in return for immediate payment should be carefully crafted so as not to supersede or weaken the creditor's right to enforce the award if payment is not received. All rights provided in the award should be preserved until the specified payment is received. One of the authors once experienced a situation in which an overzealous manager, eager to obtain payment of an

international arbitration award against a vendor, entered into a 'settlement agreement' by which the vendor-debtor was given a discount from the amount of the award in return for immediate payment. Unfortunately, the manager viewed a payment negotiation as a simple matter that did not require the advice of counsel. He decided to make the agreement binding, did not provide that the award remained effective pending receipt of payment, and included an arbitration clause borrowed from his division's recommended standard terms and conditions for purchasing contracts. When the debtor did not pay, and the creditor threatened enforcement proceedings in the courts, the debtor objected on the grounds that the dispute arose under a new agreement that contemplated arbitration, not court enforcement. The mistake was an expensive one that ultimately cost the creditor over EUR 300,000 in an *additional* settlement discount in return for immediate payment, and cost the manager his job.

B. RECOGNITION VERSUS ENFORCEMENT OF FOREIGN ARBITRAL AWARDS

If the award debtor does not voluntarily comply with the award, the creditor will **6-045** need to take out enforcement proceedings in the relevant courts if it wishes to secure the remedies awarded. In the remainder of this section we look at this enforcement process.

Significance of national law. It is important to bear in mind that the enforcement of **6-046** international arbitral awards is governed by the national laws and procedures of the country of enforcement. These may vary significantly from country to country – or at least the procedures and practice will vary – even if most countries today are party to the New York Convention and therefore follow at a minimum, at least in theory, the enforcement rules laid down in that treaty. We look first at the general legal framework for enforcement with reference to the New York Convention and the Model Law,[46] and then consider the particular requirements imposed in selected countries before a party may proceed to enforce an award.

Recognition versus enforcement. Generally speaking, parties refer to the 'enforce- **6-047** ment' of international awards, rather than to their 'recognition and enforcement'. But these are in fact two distinct concepts. The full title of the New York Convention is 'The New York Convention on the Recognition and Enforcement of Foreign Arbitral Awards', and the Convention itself deals with both concepts. Similarly, the title of the Model Law's Chapter VIII is 'Recognition and

---

46. We look at the enforcement of ICSID awards, which is largely governed by the ICSID Convention, in Ch. 7, *ICSID and Investment Treaty Arbitration*.

Enforcement of Awards', and the provisions of that chapter deal with both recognition and enforcement.

6-048 *Recognition defensive, enforcement offensive.* The distinction between recognition and enforcement is, in short, that recognition on its own is defensive, while enforcement is an offensive or affirmative step. Recognition allows the applying party to rely on the binding force of the award in the jurisdiction at issue, and thereby to defend against actions over the claims resolved in the award. As the New York Convention mandates, the state 'shall recognise arbitral awards as binding'.[47] Similarly, the Model Law provides that arbitral awards 'shall be recognised as binding'.[48] Enforcement allows the applicant to go one step further than recognition and to seek an affirmative remedy in the enforcement jurisdiction (such as the payment of a monetary sum). In some countries, an applicant may need to secure the recognition of an award before it can be enforced. One example is France.[49]

C.   THE LEGAL FRAMEWORK FOR RECOGNITION AND ENFORCEMENT OF INTERNATIONAL ARBITRAL AWARDS

6-049 Recognition and enforcement of international arbitral awards takes place under rules established (1) by treaties, most often the New York Convention, and (2) by national laws.

1.   Treaties Concerning Enforcement of International Arbitral Awards

6-050 *New York Convention.* As noted in Chapter 2, one of the attractions of international arbitration is that the arbitral awards are easier to enforce around the world than judgments of national courts. This is due in large part to the New York Convention.[50] This treaty now counts over 140 member countries, including all countries of economic significance on the world stage. The Convention's principal achievement is to create a standardised and simplified regime in all of its member countries, at least in theory, for the enforcement of international arbitral awards.[51] The grounds for refusing or adjourning recognition and enforcement, which form

---

47. See Art. III of the New York Convention.
48. See Art. 35(1) of the Model Law.
49. See Art. 1498 NCPC ('Arbitral awards shall be recognised in France where their existence has been established by the one claiming a right under it and where recognition of the same would not manifestly be contrary to public international order. Under the same conditions, they shall be rendered enforceable in France by the judge for enforcement.').
50. New York Convention on the Recognition and Enforcement of Foreign Arbitral Awards dated 10 Jun. 1958.
51. The Convention also deals, in its Art. II, with the enforcement of international arbitration agreements.

an exhaustive list, are contained in Articles V and VI of the Convention and are examined further below.

Scope of the Convention. The New York Convention applies to the recognition and **6-051** enforcement of 'foreign' arbitral awards – or, more precisely, to the recognition and enforcement (1) of arbitral awards made in a state other than where recognition or enforcement is sought, and (2) of arbitral awards made within the state of enforcement that are not considered by its laws to be domestic awards.[52]

Reservations. When becoming a party to the New York Convention, a state may **6-052** restrict its application by making two permitted reservations: the reciprocity reservation and the commercial reservation.[53]

Reciprocity reservation. A state that makes the reciprocity reservation agrees to **6-053** apply the Convention only to awards made in the territory of another Convention state. Given the large number of states now party to the Convention, this is not as meaningful a restriction as it once was.

Commercial reservation. A state that makes the commercial reservation agrees to **6-054** apply the Convention only to differences arising out of legal relationships considered as 'commercial' under that state's national law. This is perhaps the more significant of the two reservations today, especially as the law of the state of enforcement will dictate whether or not the relationship at issue is commercial, and there is no uniformity in national law on this point. Examples of refusal by national courts to apply the New York Convention because of the commercial reservation have been seen in India – although the Supreme Court has since reversed the restrictive approach taken by the lower courts – and in Tunisia.

Other enforcement treaties. There are other conventions on the recognition and **6-055** enforcement of arbitral awards, but they are of more limited geographical scope than the New York Convention, and we therefore only briefly mention them here. The 1975 Inter-American Convention on International Commercial Arbitration, to which sixteen South-American states and the United States are party, sets out grounds for refusal of recognition and enforcement that are broadly the same as those of the New York Convention.[54] The 1987 (Amman) Arab Convention on Commercial Arbitration, to which over ten Arab states are party,[55] provides that the courts of the contracting states may only refuse enforcement of awards made

---

52. See Art. I.1 of the New York Convention.
53. See Art. I.3 of the New York Convention.
54. The text of the Inter-American Convention on International Commercial Arbitration is available at <www.jus.uio.no/lm/inter-american.international.commercial.arbitration.convention. panama.1975/doc.html>.
55. The text (in French) of the Amman Convention is available at <www.jus.uio.no/lm/arab.l_arbitrage.commercial.convention.1987/doc>. It was signed by: Algeria, Djibouti, Iraq, Jordan, Lebanon, Libya, Mauritania, Morocco, Palestine, Sudan, Syria, Tunisia and Yemen.

under the auspices of the Arab Centre for Commercial Arbitration where the award violates public policy.[56]

2.   National Laws on Enforcement of Arbitral Awards

6-056 *National law versus New York Convention.* In many countries, the New York Convention is effectively the country's law on the recognition and enforcement of international arbitral awards.[57] But a state may also have, alongside the New York Convention and any other relevant treaties to which it is party, its own municipal laws governing the enforcement of international arbitral awards. These too may play a significant role in the enforcement process where they are more favourable to enforcement than the Convention.

6-057 *Enforcement provisions of the Model Law.* In the Model Law, Articles 35 and 36 reproduce the essence of the New York Convention (its Articles III, IV, V, and VI) but make certain important changes to promote enforcement: for example, Article 35(1) provides that the state enacting the Model Law will apply the provisions of Articles 35 and 36 to *all* arbitral awards, irrespective of where they are made. So, unlike the Convention, the Model Law contains no optional condition of reciprocity. Also, the Model Law does not contain the Convention's rather vague reference to recognition being binding and enforcement being mandatory 'in accordance with the rules of procedure' of the state of enforcement. Article 35(1) instead mandates that arbitral awards '*shall be recognised as binding and, upon application in writing to the competent court, shall be enforced*' subject to the provisions of Articles 35 and 36.

6-058 *National laws favourable to enforcement.* The arbitration laws of certain jurisdictions may be more favourable still towards enforcement of awards. For example, French law on the enforcement of international awards – found in Article 1502 of the New Code of Civil Procedure – does not contain or reflect the Convention's provision allowing the suspension of the enforcement proceedings pending an action to set the award aside. Nor does it allow a court to refuse enforcement on the ground that the award has been set aside elsewhere.

6-059 *Convention allows reliance on national law.* When a party seeks to enforce an award in a given state, Article VII of the Convention is often construed as allowing the party to rely on both the Convention and national law (as well as other enforcement treaties). Any party looking to enforce an award should not therefore limit its options to the New York Convention, especially in the situation discussed below of the enforcement of awards set aside in another jurisdiction.

---

56. See Art. 35 of the Amman Convention. Note that the Amman Convention imposes Arabic as the language of arbitrations (Art. 23) under the auspices of the Arab Centre for Commercial Arbitration, which limits its worldwide relevance in practice.

57. For examples of national statutes providing that recognition and enforcement of foreign awards will be governed by the New York Convention, see Art. 194 of the Swiss Private International Law Act; and s. 1061 of the German ZPO.

D.   ADMINISTRATIVE STEPS BEFORE ENFORCEMENT PROCEEDINGS

Where the debtor's assets are in different countries – the need for coordination **6-060**
across jurisdictions. Even with the benefit of the New York Convention, it may be
necessary – at the initial stage of enforcement at least – to consider the laws of more
than one jurisdiction: the country in which the award originated (place of arbitration), and the country (or countries) in which the debtor has assets against which
the party is seeking to enforce its right of payment. A party in all likelihood will
need to have lawyers in each location who can coordinate with each other in order
to ensure that procedures are followed, as the terminology, form, substance, and
associated costs of each step may vary from one country to another. As noted in
Chapter 3, a claimant should be aware before starting arbitration proceedings of the
administrative steps necessary for enforcement which may impose significant post-
arbitration costs.

Multi-jurisdictional coordination among counsel	*Counsel in England (place of arbitration):* What will you need from us in order to have the award transmitted to you in compliance with your country's procedures for enforcing foreign arbitral awards?
	Counsel in Turkey (place of debtor's assets and enforcement): We will need you to provide an affirmation that the period for challenging the award under English law has expired and that the award has not been successfully challenged, a certification from the English courts that the award is validly rendered under English procedural law, and then you must provide us with the award itself, duly apostilled by the Turkish consulate in London, together with the original signed copy either of the arbitration agreement or the contract containing the arbitration clause.
	Counsel in England: We will do this. What are the procedures that you will then be required to follow for purposes of enforcement?
	Counsel in Turkey: We will have the award translated and certified by a legal translator. In addition, the client will need to pay both a notarial registration fee of 5.4% and a stamp duty (tax) amounting to 1.5% of the amount of the arbitration award.
	Counsel in both England and Turkey: We should advise the client that these are the minimum expenditures, and are based on the assumption that the debtor will not challenge the award or oppose enforcement. The client should understand that the costs of collecting anything on its award will increase substantially if the debtor elects to put up resistance in either or both countries.

6-061 The civil procedure rules of many countries require that, before an award rendered in a foreign country is enforced, it must first be subjected to procedures at the place of arbitration that assure its compliance with the enforcing country's principles of due process and fairness. Some of these procedures, such as the requirement that an enforcing party produce an original signed contract on which the award is based, are important to know before the party commences arbitration. For example, where an original of the contract cannot be found, it is important to understand the risk of an eventual award being unenforceable.

6-062 Fortunately, the New York Convention provides a standard framework within which signatory states are allowed to impose procedures for recognising and enforcing awards. The Convention requires contracting states to recognise awards as binding, and to enforce them in accordance with the rules of procedure of the enforcing state and under the conditions laid down in the Convention. The conditions laid down in the Convention consist in affirmative formal requirements for recognition and enforcement, and grounds on which a state is entitled to refuse or adjourn recognition and enforcement.

6-063 *Affirmative steps at the place of arbitration.* Article IV of the New York Convention lays down certain affirmative formal requirements that an applicant for recognition or enforcement must fulfil: it must supply an authenticated original or a certified copy of the award and of the arbitration agreement, with a certified translation into the language where recognition and enforcement are sought.[58] While these requirements should not impose impossible burdens on the enforcing party, they are not necessarily straightforward and demand careful attention.

6-064 *Authentication and certification.* The terms 'authentication and certification' mean different things but both address concerns about the genuineness of documents on which enforcement proceedings will be based. Authentication is the process designed to confirm that the original signed document is genuine, by having someone of sufficient authority attest to the authenticity of the original. Certification is similar, but is designed to confirm that a copy faithfully reflects the existence and content of the original.

6-065 *Arbitration award and arbitration agreement – authenticated or certified.* The arbitral tribunal or the officiating institution will in all likelihood provide each party with a copy or copies of the award signed in original by the sole arbitrator or all three members of the tribunal. This is the document that the parties have paid the tribunal to provide. But in order to have the award 'authenticated' or 'certified', the party may be required to take steps that include, for example, having a court at the place of arbitration provide an attestation or seal that the award was rendered there. Similarly, the arbitration agreement – usually the main contract – may be required to be produced in original or certified copy, together with attestations of its authenticity.

---

58. See Art. IV of the New York Convention.

Not that this ever really happens: failure to locate the original signed contract	The claimant, a French company, agreed to license certain of its technology to an Italian-based company in the 1980s. Almost two decades later, long after the agreement had expired, the French company commenced arbitration in Geneva under the parties' contract, alleging that the Italian company was continuing to use its technology, in violation of the contract. After obtaining a hard-fought award of damages, the claimant encountered a serious obstacle that prevented it from commencing enforcement proceedings against the debtor's assets in Italy: it could not locate the original signed agreement. It goes without saying that parties to international transactions should exercise diligence with respect to retaining original signed contracts in a secure place, to avoid reaching the end of an arbitration only to realise they have only photocopies, none of which are sufficient for the purposes of enforcement.

In England, for example, the court will provide an award creditor with a package **6-066** for it to apply for certification of a foreign award. In order to obtain certification, counsel for the award creditor must provide a witness statement to the court, confirming that the award has not been subject to an appeal or any application to remit it or set it aside, that the time for any such appeal or application has expired, and that the award is final and binding on the parties under section 58 of the English Arbitration Act. This is submitted together with a nominal filing fee, and the court takes approximately a week to return the certificate. This can then be provided to counsel at the place of enforcement (see below) for further steps.

Apostille. The award creditor may also be required to have the relevant documents, **6-067** together with any attestation of courts or authorities at the place of arbitration, certified by the consular authorities of the country of enforcement located in the country of the place of arbitration. This is known as an apostille.

Administrative steps at the place of enforcement. Once all necessary steps are **6-068** completed at the place of arbitration, the party will likely be required to fulfil still further administrative steps in the country of enforcement as a prerequisite to commencing the enforcement proceeding itself. These steps may include the following:

- *Translation, and legalisation of the translation.* Depending on the jurisdiction, the court may require the enforcing party to translate the award and even the contract containing the arbitration agreement and, further, to have the translation 'legalised' by a judicial authority attesting to its accuracy.
- *Notarisation.* In lieu of or in addition to legalisation, the civil procedure rules at the place of enforcement may require the creditor to pay a notary to attest that the documents are all properly assembled and in order.

    – *Court/filing fees and taxes.* Finally, in some places, the filing of an award will be conditioned on the creditor's payment upfront of a substantial court fee or tax. For example, in Turkey the award creditor will be required to pay, in addition to official translation and notarisation fees, a 'stamp duty' of 5.4% of the amount of the award ('fifty-four per thousand').[59] An award rendered in Italy is subject to a similar 'registration' tax of 3% of the amount awarded, before a party can begin proceedings to enforce it in Italy.[60] The award creditor will sometimes be able to include all or part of these amounts in the recovery it seeks from the debtor.[61] Even so, they can impose a substantial additional burden on a creditor when it may be uncertain whether the debtor has sufficient assets even to pay the award itself.

6-069 *Costs of administrative steps prior to enforcement.* All of this indicates that an award creditor can begin to incur rather substantial administrative costs even before commencing the enforcement proceedings. Although some of these costs may be proportionate to the amount of the award, others may represent fixed costs and can consume a material portion of the value of an award of modest size. Some costs may be recoverable, depending on the jurisdiction, but rarely will the creditor get them all back. The amount of these costs and the likelihood of their recovery will be factors that the award creditor will need to put in the mix when considering whether an enforcement action is worth the candle.

6-070 *Tax consequences of an award at the creditor's place of residence.* As if the above fees, charges, and duties were not enough, the award creditor may be subject to income tax on an award rendered in its favour, even though the creditor has not yet collected a penny from the debtor, and indeed may never do so.

This could really happen: tax on awards before collection	The claimant commenced arbitration in Milan and obtained an award of EUR 10 million against the respondent. Because the respondent had defaulted on the fees of the arbitration institution and the tribunal, the claimant had spent EUR 2 million in pursuing the arbitration by the time the award was rendered (most of these costs were, however, included within the EUR 10 million awarded). Before initiating enforcement proceedings against the debtor's assets in Italy, however, the claimant had to pay Italy's 3% tax on arbitration awards

---

59. See Law on Charges (Law 492).
60. This is a function of Italian tax law ('imposta di registro'), not civil procedure, and payment is a condition of the ability to enforce an award in Italy.
61. In both examples provided above, Turkey and Italy, recovery of costs from the debtor is possible, at least with respect to the fees for having the award recognised. Fees subsequently payable to enforce against assets may be subject to different rules that may or may not allow recovery from the debtor.

(EUR 300,000) in order to 'register' it for purposes of enforcement. In addition, the creditor discovered it would also be required by its own domestic income tax law to treat the award as income, a gain within the year, even though it had yet to collect a penny and, in fact, might never collect. To reduce its tax liability within the year and avoid further costs, the creditor considered settling with the debtor for EUR 1.5 million, an amount less than what it spent obtaining the award, as its taxation would be based on the lower (but paid) settlement amount rather than the unfulfilled award.

E.   PROCEDURE FOR ENFORCEMENT AND RESISTING ENFORCEMENT

Assuming that the award creditor has decided to proceed with enforcement against **6-071** the debtor, has paid all the required fees, and has complied with the various administrative steps necessary to start enforcement procedures, the parties will turn their attention to the court proceedings proper, and the grounds on which enforcement should take place or be resisted. In the remainder of this section, for convenience, the word 'enforcement' is used to refer to both recognition and enforcement, except where specifically referring to recognition or where the context demands otherwise.

Attention to local variation. The procedures for enforcing an international award, **6-072** and for resisting its enforcement, will vary from jurisdiction to jurisdiction, and may vary from court to court within that jurisdiction. This is why a party seeking to enforce an award should obtain appropriate advice from a lawyer active before the courts of each potential place of enforcement.

Enforcement deadlines. Particular care needs to be given to the deadline within **6-073** which enforcement proceedings must be begun. For example, in the United States, the time limit for commencing enforcement proceedings regarding an award under the New York Convention is three years from the date of the award,[62] whereas under French law there is no specific time limit.[63]

Provisional enforcement. In certain countries it may be possible to enforce the **6-074** award on a provisional basis when an action to set aside is pending or may still be launched. This will be of substantial value where the action to set aside is likely to last a long time, and may incentivise the award debtor to accelerate any setting aside proceedings or not to bring an action to set aside at all. For instance, in France, the enforcement court may order the provisional enforcement of an

---

62. See Title 9 of the US Code, at § 207.
63. See, e.g., J. Paulsson (ed.), *International Handbook on Commercial Arbitration*, Suppl. 26 (February 1998), 45.

award rendered in France, on condition that the award itself specifies that it may be provisionally enforced.[64]

6-075 *Notification to award debtors of enforcement action and ex parte orders.* In some countries, there is no need to notify the debtor of the commencement of the enforcement proceedings until after an enforcement order has been issued. This may be advantageous for a party concerned that the debtor will hide or remove assets from the jurisdiction. In France, for instance, the practice has been for enforcement applications to be examined by the enforcement court in an ex parte proceeding, and for the court to render an ex parte order granting or refusing enforcement after a prima facie review of the award. Under French law, orders granting enforcement need not state reasons, although orders refusing enforcement must do so. An appeal against the order of the court of first instance granting or refusing enforcement is possible before the Court of Appeal in inter partes proceedings.[65]

F.   GROUNDS FOR RESISTING ENFORCEMENT

6-076 The beauty of the New York Convention and legislation that it has inspired resides, in theory at least, in the limitations placed on the grounds for resisting enforcement. There are only seven such grounds, listed in Article V of the Convention and, for example, in Article 36 of the Model Law. The listed grounds are exhaustive.

6-077 The grounds for resisting enforcement under the Convention and the Model Law are virtually identical to the six grounds on which the Model Law permits a court to set an award aside, all of which are discussed in section I above. The seventh ground – found in the enforcement context but necessarily absent from the setting aside context – is at Article V.1(e) of the Convention and Article 36(1)(a)(v) of the Model Law. This provides that enforcement may be refused if the award has not yet become binding on the parties or has been set aside by the courts of the place of the country in which, or under the law of which, the award was made.

6-078 The seven grounds are listed below. The first five must be raised and proved by the applicant, whereas the last two may be raised by a court on its own initiative:

- Incapacity of a party, or invalidity of the arbitration agreement.
- No notification of the arbitration or appointment of an arbitrator, or absence of due process.
- The award deals with disputes or issues outside the terms or the scope of the parties' submission to arbitration.

---

64. See Art. 1479 of the French New Code of Civil Procedure. Note that the party who has applied to have the award set aside may petition the First President of the Court of Appeal to obtain the suspension of the provisional enforcement. See also Art. 45 of the Spanish Arbitration Act 60/2003.
65. See Gaillard & Savage, 894 et seq.

- The composition of the tribunal or the arbitral procedure was not in accordance with the parties' agreement or applicable law.
- The award is not yet binding on the parties or has been set aside.
- The subject matter of the dispute is not arbitrable (i.e., not capable of settlement by arbitration).
- The recognition or enforcement of the award would be contrary to the public policy of the enforcing state.

The problem of public policy (again). As with actions to set aside under the Model **6-079** Law, which are discussed in section I of this chapter, much of the difficulty in the enforcement context surrounds the definition of 'public policy', because the meaning and boundaries of the concept vary substantially around the world. The result – in general terms – is that the law of pro-arbitration countries will take a narrower view of what is meant by public policy, with the result that courts rarely refuse enforcement on this ground; in contrast, courts in countries that are less friendly to arbitration, may favour a broader interpretation, leading them more frequently to refuse enforcement on public policy grounds.

Court discretion in refusing to enforce. A great deal of attention has been paid to **6-080** the use of the word 'may' in Article V of the Convention and Article 36 of the Model Law: these provisions stipulate that enforcement 'may be refused' only if one of the seven grounds is satisfied, not that it 'must be refused'. This has been interpreted as leaving it open to the enforcement court to enforce the award even if one of the seven grounds for refusing enforcement is satisfied. One instance in which a court might consider it appropriate to exercise its discretion in this way would be where the party invoking the ground for refusal of enforcement is estopped from doing so.[66] A further and controversial illustration arises in the context of the enforcement of awards that have been set aside by the courts of the seat of the arbitration.

G.   ENFORCEMENT OF AWARDS SET ASIDE AT THE
       SEAT OF ARBITRATION

Awards set aside can still be enforced. In certain circumstances, awards that are set **6-081** aside at the place of arbitration may still be enforced in another jurisdiction. This is the subject of one of international arbitration's more interesting debates, and it is not merely a theoretical matter: there have been several cases where awards set aside in one jurisdiction have been enforced elsewhere – counter-intuitive though

---

66. See J. van den Berg, *The New York Convention of 1958 – Towards a Uniform Judicial Interpretation* (The Netherlands: Kluwer Law International, 1981), 265. See also, for a practical illustration, *China Nanhai Oil Joint Service Corporation Shenzen Branch v. Gee Tai Holdings Co. Ltd*, Supreme Court of Hong Kong, 13 Jul. 1994, published in *Yearbook Commercial Arbitration XX* (1995): 671 et seq.

that might sound. The issue is of substantial importance in practice: the possibility of enforcing an award that has been set aside is especially attractive to parties who, in a not infrequent scenario, consider that they did not receive a fair hearing from the court deciding the action to set aside.

6-082 *Legal framework for enforcing an award set aside in another country.* Courts enforcing awards set aside elsewhere rely primarily on Article VII of the New York Convention, which, as seen above, is construed as allowing parties to rely on the enforcement provisions of local law if they are more favourable than the rights granted under the Convention. Certain laws, and notably French law, are more favourable than the Convention as they allow the enforcement of an award made elsewhere even if it has been set aside (or, put another way, French law does not include the setting aside of the award as a ground for refusing enforcement). So, under this approach, if none of the other grounds for refusing enforcement under local law are available to the award debtor, enforcement of an award set aside elsewhere should be permitted.

6-083 The underlying rationale for this approach is that the court of the place of the arbitration should not be the judge of the validity or enforceability of the award outside its own borders, and that an international arbitral award is not anchored in the legal system of the state where the place of arbitration is located, so that it does not cease to exist when it is annulled by the courts of that state. The seat of the arbitration is often chosen by chance, or is deliberately chosen as a neutral place where the arbitration can be held without the intervention of the local courts. The courts of the place of arbitration, so the argument goes, should not therefore have the power to undermine the enforceability of the award in other jurisdictions – especially where they set the award aside based on local standards of annulment that are not shared by other countries. Instead, it should be for each enforcement court to evaluate whether under its own laws the award should be admitted into the legal order of that jurisdiction and enforced there.[67]

6-084 There are some difficulties with this justification. Notably, parties expect some degree of predictability when entering into a contract and may base their enforcement expectations on the standards applied at the place of arbitration. If courts in other jurisdictions are to enforce awards even after they have been set aside at a place agreed by the parties to represent the legal seat of the arbitration, and to generate its procedural framework for, then it might be said that the courts of the enforcement state have in a material way ignored the parties' expectations at the time of entering into their contract.

---

67. See, e.g., J. Paulsson, 'Enforcing Arbitral Awards Notwithstanding a Local Standard Annulment', *ICC Bulletin* (May 1995): 14 et seq.; P. Fouchard, 'La portée internationale de l'annulation de la sentence arbitrale dans son pays d'origine', *Revue de l'arbitrage* (1997): 329 et seq.; E. Gaillard, 'L'execution des sentences annulées dans leur pays d'origine', *Journal du Droit International* 3 (1998): 645 et seq.

Examples of enforcement of awards set aside elsewhere. Decisions allowing the **6-085**
enforcement of awards set aside elsewhere have been made by the French courts,[68]
the Belgian courts,[69] and the US courts.[70] In the United States, the District Court
for the District of Columbia allowed enforcement of an award set aside by a Cairo
court in an arbitration with its seat in Egypt. The Cairo court's grounds for setting
aside the award were that the arbitral tribunal had failed to apply the governing law,
which is not a ground for validly resisting enforcement under the US Federal
Arbitration Act. The US court based its decision on the discretion of the enforcement court under Article V(1)(e) of the Convention to refuse enforcement, or to
allow it where one of the grounds for refusal is present, as well as on the US public
policy in favour of final and binding arbitration.

But in more recent case law, US courts have taken the opposite stance and refused **6-086**
to enforce an award on grounds that it was set aside by the courts at the seat of the
arbitration.[71]

Conflicting trends. So, to summarise, most jurisdictions around the world are likely **6-087**
to refuse enforcement of an award that has been set aside in another country.
However, this is not the universal position: courts in certain countries have
been receptive in the past to enforcing awards set aside elsewhere based on
local annulment standards, and this trend may grow as international arbitration
around the world becomes more transnational in character and less deferential
towards the place of arbitration. It is also possible we will instead see, as in the

---

68. See *Société Ticaret Limited c/ Norsolor*, Cass, 1ère, 9 Oct. 1984, *Revue de l'arbitrage* (1985):
431 et seq.; *Société Hilmarton Ltd v. Omnium de traitement et de valorisation*, Cass. 1ère civ.,
23 Mar. 1994, *Revue de l'arbitrage* (1994): 327 et seq.; *The Arab Republic of Egypt v. Chromalloy Aeroservices, Inc.*, Paris Court of Appeal, 14 Jan. 1997, *Revue de l'arbitrage* (1997): 395
et seq.; *Société Bargues Agro Industries v. Société Yong Pecan Company*, Paris Court of Appeal,
10 Jun. 2004, *Revue de l'arbitrage* (2006): 733 et seq.; *Directorate General of Civil Aviation of
the Emirates of Dubai v. International Bechtel Co. Ltd*, Paris Court of Appeal, 29 Sep. 2005,
Revue de l'arbitrage (2006): 695 et seq.; and *Société PT Putrabali Adyamulia c/ Rena Holding
et Société Moguntia Est Epices*, Cass. 1 ère civ., 29 Jun. 2007, *Revue de l'arbitrage* (2007): 507
et seq. See also, for a commentary, E. Gaillard, 'Souveraineté et autonomie: réflexions sur les
représentations de l'arbitrage international', *Journal du Droit International* (2007): 1163 et seq.
69. See *Sonatrach v. Ford, Bacon and Davis*, Brussels Court of First Instance, 6 Dec. 1988, *Yearbook Commercial Arbitration* XV 1990): 370 et seq.
70. See *Chromalloy Aeroservices Inc. v. Arab Republic of Egypt*, 939 F. Supp. 907 (D.D.C. 1996).
71. See *TermoRio SA ESP et al. v. Electrificadora del Atlantico*, US District Court, District of
Columbia, 17 Mar. 2006, 421 F Supp. 2d 87; and *TermoRio SA ESP et al. v. Electranta SP et al.*,
US Court of Appeals for the District of Columbia, 17 May 2007, *Revue de l'arbitrage* (2007):
559 et seq. The US Court of Appeals held in this case that the award that had been set aside did
not have any legal existence and, for this reason, could not be enforced. For criticism, see
F. Mantilla-Serrano, 'Case Note: TermoRio S.A. E.S.P. et al v. Electranta S.P. et al', *Journal
of International Arbitration* 25, no. 3 (2008): 397 et seq; J. Paulsson, 'Note – 25 mai 2007 –
Etats-Unis US. Court of Appeal, District of Columbia', *Revue de l'arbitrage* (2007): 559 et seq.
See generally, D. Freyer, 'The Enforcement of Awards Affected by Judicial Orders of Annul-
ment at the Place of Arbitration', in *Enforcement of Arbitration Agreements and International
Arbitral Awards: The New York Convention in Practice*, ed. E. Gaillard & D. Di Pietro (United
Kingdom: Cameron May, 2008), 757 et seq.

United States, more deference by enforcing courts to actions to set aside at the place of arbitration.

6-088 An unsuccessful attempt to set aside an award at the place of arbitration may harm the award debtor's chances of resisting enforcement in other jurisdictions. Whether the debtor should instead bypass that stage and resist enforcement wherever it is attempted will of course depend on the nature of the grounds for setting aside the award and a comparative analysis of the record of the courts of the place of arbitration and the courts of the places of enforcement. In all events, and for the time being, a party whose award has been set aside should look with particular care for assets belonging to the award debtor that are situated in jurisdictions, such as France, where courts have a record of enforcing awards set aside elsewhere.

Not that this ever really happens: public policy objection at place of enforcement only	The dispute was over a licensing agreement between competitors based in two different countries of the European Union. The claimant alleged that the respondent breached the agreement by selling into certain EU countries that were prohibited under the agreement. The respondent's defence was that under EU competition law this prohibition was an impermissible restriction of competition and, as such, was void. The parties' contract provided for arbitration in Geneva. The arbitral tribunal found that the respondent had breached the restriction on distribution of products, but ignored the defence that the restriction itself was invalid. The respondent obtained an opinion from EU competition counsel that the award contradicted fundamental principles of EU competition law. There seemed to be a basis, therefore, to challenge the award on the grounds that it violated public policy. Before initiating a challenge proceeding, however, the respondent also obtained an opinion from counsel in Geneva, who advised that Swiss courts would not regard EU competition law as a matter of public policy, as Switzerland is not a member state of the European Union. Thus, the respondent elected to bypass its opportunity to challenge the award at the place of arbitration (Geneva), since it had no assets there and instead asserted its public policy objection for the first time when the claimant sought to enforce it in the European Union. As of this writing, the issue has yet to be finally determined by the enforcement courts.[72]

---

72. See *Schlumberger S.A. v. Nuovo Pignone S. A.*, 'Decision of the Corte di Appello, Florence, 17 May 2005', *Yearbook Commercial Arbitration* XXXII (2007): 403.

H.   SOVEREIGN IMMUNITY AS A DEFENCE TO ENFORCEMENT

As noted in Chapter 1, *The Elements of an International Dispute Resolution* **6-089**
Agreement, parties contracting with states or state entities are well advised to
include in their arbitration clauses a comprehensive waiver of sovereign immunity.
This is chiefly to prevent the state party later relying on its sovereign immunity to
resist enforcement of an arbitral award against it.[73]

General non-waiver of immunity from execution. The law of immunities is com- **6-090**
plex and varies from jurisdiction to jurisdiction, and therefore generalisation is of
limited utility. In many western countries, a state entering into an arbitration
agreement will be considered as waiving its immunity from jurisdiction – its
immunity is not therefore a defence to an arbitration brought against it.
However, an arbitration agreement is not usually held to be a waiver of a state's
immunity from execution.

Scope of immunity from execution. In many countries, there is a restrictive doctrine **6-091**
of immunity from execution, under which only the property of the state used for
sovereign purposes (acta iure imperii) will be immune. Property of the state used
for commercial purposes (acta jure gestionis) especially where those purposes are
connected with arbitration – are less likely to be immune.[74]

Express and implied waivers. Courts in France have allowed parties to circumvent **6-092**
a state's immunity from execution by construing an arbitration agreement as a
waiver of immunity where it incorporates arbitration rules – such as those of the
ICC – that contain an undertaking by the parties to carry out the award.[75] Still,
without an express waiver, a state will be in a far stronger position to resist
enforcement of an award against it.

---

73. On sovereign immunities generally, see I. Pingel-Lenuzza, *Les immunités des états en droit International* (Bruxelles: Bruylant, 1997); A. Dickinson, R. Lindsay & J.P. Loonam, *State immunity: Selected Materials and Commentary* (Oxford: Oxford University Press, 2004); H. Fox, *The Law of State Immunity* (Oxford: Oxford University Press, 2008).

74. In the United States, for instance, property of a foreign state used for commercial activities may be attached to satisfy a judgment given against it provided such property is or was used for the commercial activity upon which the claim was based. In the United Kingdom, property in use or intended use for commercial purposes (i.e., transactions or activities in relation to a sale of goods or a supply of services, a transaction for provision of finance, or a commercial, industrial, professional, or industrial activity) is similarly subject to attachment. In France, the state's immunity from execution may be set aside if the property seized is connected to a private law economic or commercial activity that is the subject matter of the proceedings before the court. See generally, H. Fox, *The Law of State Immunity* (Oxford: Oxford University Press, 2008), 606–609.

75. See *Creighton Limited (Caiman Islands) v. Minister of Finance and Minister of Internal Affairs and Agriculture of the Government of the State of Qatar*, Decision of the French Court of Cassation, 6 Jul. 2000, *Yearbook Commercial Arbitration XXV* (2000): 458–460. The parties in this case had agreed to refer disputes in ICC arbitration, and Art. 24 of the ICC Rules at the time provided that 'the parties shall be deemed to have undertaken to carry out the resulting award without delay'.

I.   Effects of a Refusal to Enforce or Recognise an Award

6-093 *Effect confined to one jurisdiction.* The effect of a final refusal by the courts of a given jurisdiction to enforce an award is that, in the jurisdiction of that court, the award cannot be enforced. However, this does not mean that the award cannot be enforced in other jurisdictions: the award itself is unaffected by the decision not to enforce it – rather, the award cannot enter the legal order of the enforcement jurisdiction and be enforced against assets there. The decision of an enforcement court in one jurisdiction, while it may be put before the enforcement court of another jurisdiction, will not bind courts in any other country.

6-094 *Multiple simultaneous enforcement actions.* The award creditor can therefore attempt to enforce the award in any other jurisdiction where the award debtor has assets. If the award is substantial and the debtor has assets in multiple countries, there should be no restriction on the creditor's ability to have more than one enforcement action pending on the same award in different jurisdictions. As a practical matter, however, the costs of initiating enforcement actions in different countries, discussed above, may limit a creditor's appetite to pursue enforcement on multiple fronts at the same time.

6-095 *Investment arbitration as a fallback enforcement option.* In practice, the option of taking action in other jurisdictions may not be open, because the debtor has assets only in the jurisdiction where enforcement has been refused. One of the options that has recently been proposed in this situation is for the creditor to commence arbitration under any applicable investment treaty against the state where enforcement has been refused, if it appears that the refusal to enforce is without basis. A creditor taking such action will claim that the refusal of the court (which is an organ of the state) to enforce the award violates the state's obligations to protect and promote the creditor's investment in the state. Two cases on these lines have been commenced before ICSID: one was settled,[76] and in the second, *Saipem v. Bangladesh*, the tribunal held that the Bangladeshi courts' interference in the arbitration resulted in an expropriation of Saipem's investment.[77]

6-096 *Sale of the award.* Rather than incur the cost and risks of enforcement, an award creditor may find it possible to sell the award at a discount to a company specialised in purchasing litigation claims and judgments. Some companies will purchase arbitration awards, while others will act as brokers, earning a commission by matching clients (award creditors) with capital providers.

6-097 *Debt-collection assistance.* Another possibility, and one that may yield a higher return for the award creditor, is to retain the services of a company specialised in the identification of assets in foreign jurisdictions. These companies may be better

---

76. See *Western NIS Enterprise Fund v. Ukraine* (ICSID Case No. ARB/04/02).
77. See *Saipem S.p.A. v. People's Republic of Bangladesh* (ICSID Case No. ARB/05/07), Award (30 Jun. 2009). On investment treaty arbitration more generally, see Ch. 7, *ICSID and Investment Treaty Arbitration*.

equipped to identify foreign assets – if any exist – and achieve enforcement than the award creditor. They do not necessarily invest in the litigation, but provide active support through asset tracing and intelligence about the jurisdictions in which to initiate enforcement. They may also have specialised expertise with respect to cross-border enforcement and collections against states and state-owned entities.

Example 6b – A Proposal to Purchase an Arbitration Award or Partner in Identifying and Collecting Against a Debtor's Assets

---

A dispute led to an ICC arbitration award of USD 20 million in damages against a party known to have assets in multiple countries but also a reputation for resisting enforcement. A company that specialises in collection of international arbitration awards proposed the following options to the creditor:

(i) It would purchase the award in its entirety at an 80% discount, with immediate payment to the creditor of 20% of the face value awarded.
(ii) It would broker the sale of the award to other investors, providing the award creditor with an estimated 35% of the value of the amount awarded (65% discount) but not immediately.
(iii) It would 'partner' with the creditor on a risk-sharing basis in which the company would identify assets in multiple jurisdictions and enforce against them, assuming the costs of collection and providing the creditor with approximately 70% of the amounts collected.

J.   ENFORCEMENT IN PRACTICE

As highlighted throughout this book, one of the chief attractions of international **6-098** arbitration is that the resulting awards are better currency abroad than judgments of state courts, thanks in large part to the New York Convention, with its broad membership and limited grounds for refusal of enforcement. However, the ease of enforcement of international arbitral awards is relative – being easier to enforce than court judgments does not necessarily mean being easy to enforce. In practice, there may be a number of obstacles to actual collection on an award. Some hurdles are not specific to international arbitration, such as debtors dissipating their assets before the creditor can enforce against them. It can be challenging for creditors to detect, prevent, or unravel this sort of conduct in developed jurisdictions. It will be more problematic still in less developed parts of the world.

More specific to international arbitration and equally common are situations **6-099** where, in practice, the courts of the enforcement jurisdiction do not follow the New York Convention or other enforcement legislation in force in that jurisdiction.

This may be because the treaty has not been properly integrated into the national law, or because the courts are simply unfamiliar with how the treaty or its implementing law work. It may also be because the courts are biased in favour of the debtor: after all, in many cases, the scenario will be one of a foreign party seeking to enforce an award in the debtor's home courts. Those courts may have more sympathy for the local debtor than for the foreign party. In other cases the courts may be corrupt or, as in the case of India in particular, inefficient by any standards, as in the example below.

Example 6c – Extreme Delay due to Court Inefficiency

Excerpt from *Global Arbitration Review, 8 April 2008*
(reproduced with permission):

Indian award enforcement delayed twelve years

Two Canadian companies that have been trying to enforce an arbitration award in India for over a decade are pinning their hopes on a hearing this summer, after a scheduled January date was adjourned.

The award, dating back to 1996, entitles General Electric Canada and MIL Group Inc to about USD 700,000 damages each from India's state-run hydroelectric body, NHPCL (National Hydroelectric Power Company Ltd) – for breaches of a hydroelectric supply contract. But before enforcement can take place, Delhi High Court must recognise the award and pass an enforcement decree, after hearing any objections raised by NHPCL. The requirements exist under India's old arbitration legislation, introduced in 1940. The court has said the old law applies because the arbitral proceedings took place before the present law was adopted in January 1996. Under the same outdated legislation, NHPCL has been able to obtain an injunction from the court, preventing enforcement of the award anywhere but in India.

A lawyer in India who is familiar with the case says the January adjournment – for reasons that have not been disclosed – was the latest in a long list of delays – both party created and systemic. For four years, the lawyer says, the parties argued about whether the award was governed by the Arbitration Act 1940, or the 1996 act based on the UNCITRAL model.

The court's decision that the old law prevailed – as argued by NHPCL – meant that General Electric had to fulfil time-consuming statutory requirements to obtain the enforcement decree, including filing records of the entire arbitral proceedings with the court. It also meant NHPCL was able to challenge the award in domestic courts – which is no longer possible under the new law.

'Obtaining the arbitration records, in particular, has been a lengthy ordeal', the source says. 'The ICC would initially disclose only partial records, in accordance with its rules. But the 1940 arbitration law requires full records – including pleadings, evidence, and procedural orders.'

> The two Canadian companies have also battled the court's reluctance to schedule a lengthy hearing on the validity of the award and alleged 'delay tactics' by the state-run body. General Electric declined to comment on the pending litigation.

How has the New York Convention performed over the past five decades? **6-100**
A review of reported enforcement decisions reveals that in approximately 10% of these cases enforcement of the award was refused. Many of the decisions refusing enforcement resulted from a mistake of one kind or another – parties drafting inadequate arbitration clauses, arbitral tribunals or arbitral institutions not paying sufficient attention to the conduct of the proceedings, or courts misunderstanding the meaning of the Convention.[78]

Yet it remains difficult to speak with any authority on the environment for enforce- **6-101**
ment of international arbitral awards in individual countries, as there is rarely reliable data – even in more developed nations – from which to draw meaningful conclusions. Instead, much of the available information is anecdotal.[79] What is clear is that there are numerous difficulties that an enforcing party might face, ranging from complicated recognition and enforcement procedures, laws substantively unfavourable to enforcement, high costs, lengthy delays, right through to the corruption of judges and administrative personnel of the local courts.

Enforcement in Asia. It is fair to say that the enforcement record of most countries **6-102**
in Asia, with the exceptions of Hong Kong, Japan, Korea, and Singapore, has plenty of room for improvement. Enforcement in India is hampered, in particular, by the inefficiency of the courts. China's enforcement record appears to be improving, with structural measures implemented in an effort to prevent local courts from wrongly refusing enforcement. These include, at least in theory, the requirement that the Supreme People's Court (the country's highest court) give its approval before a lower court refuses to enforce an international award.[80] However, the record of successful enforcement in China is still significantly poorer than that of, say, Hong Kong or Singapore. Bangladesh and Indonesia are other Asian jurisdictions where enforcement, especially against a local debtor, is likely to be extremely difficult – largely because of the weaknesses of the local court systems.

---

78. See A.J. van den Berg, 'New York Convention of 1958: Refusals of Enforcement', *ICC International Court of Arbitration Bulletin* 18, no. 2 (2007).
79. *Ibid.*
80. To minimise inaction and delays, Chinese courts accepting an application for the enforcement of foreign awards (including New York Convention awards) must deal with the application on an expedited basis. The court must issue its ruling within two months from the date on which the application is accepted. If the court decides not to enforce the award, it is required to report its refusal to the Supreme People's Court within two months of accepting the application. See *Provisions of the Supreme People's Court on the Charges and Examination Period for the Recognition and Enforcement of Foreign Arbitral Awards*, promulgated on 21 Oct. 1998 and effective as of 21 Nov. 1998.

6-103 *Enforcement in Western Europe.* The countries of Western Europe are generally characterised by strong enforcement traditions, with no serious outliers. As discussed earlier, French law is more favourable to the recognition and enforcement of awards than the New York Convention, as the setting aside of an award at a foreign seat of arbitration is not a ground under French law to refuse enforcement. The practice – and costs – of both challenging and enforcing an arbitration award may vary substantially from one state to another.

6-104 *Enforcement in Eastern Europe, Russia, and CIS countries.* While there is anecdotal evidence of a strong enforcement record in Hungary, enforcement in other Eastern European countries tends to be more problematic. Reports from Russia, for example, suggest there has been a tendency amongst certain judges to assert the primacy of the national court system over international commercial arbitration and to narrow the scope of what may be submitted to arbitration.[81] In Ukraine, statistics on the number of international awards actually enforced are not encouraging. Practical problems arising include (1) confusion by the courts of arbitral awards with foreign court judgments; (2) a lack of priority accorded to the New York Convention, and application of bilateral treaties on mutual legal assistance instead; (3) unusually strict adherence to formalities; (4) motion practice lasting years; and (5) a wide conception of public policy.[82]

6-105 *Enforcement in Africa and the Middle East.* Enforcement proceedings in the African and Middle Eastern regions are often unreliable, with the enforcement by foreign parties of international arbitration awards being the exception rather than the rule. In the United Arab Emirates (UAE), the courts have appeared to place a heavy evidential burden on applicants seeking the enforcement of foreign awards. In this, however, international arbitration may simply offer the same result as, or at least one that is no worse than, local justice: one of the authors has even had trouble getting a local court decision enforced against a refinery in the UAE. At the time of writing, the case is still pending in the enforcement phase some six years after all appeals on the merits were exhausted.

6-106 At the time of writing, there had been no reported case of enforcement in the UAE under the New York Convention (we note, though, that the UAE's accession dates back only to 2006) and no record of a foreign arbitration award being enforced in Saudi Arabia.[83]

6-107 *Enforcement in Central and South America.* Enforcement proceedings in Central and South America are usually characterised by significant delay, despite recent efforts to improve the arbitration regime.

6-108 However, arbitration in Brazil has undergone a dramatic change over the past decade. A new arbitration-friendly legal framework has been implemented,

---

81. See H. Oda, 'Enforcement of International Commercial Arbitration Awards in Russia', *ICC International Court of Arbitration Bulletin* 16, no. 2 (Fall 2005).
82. See *The European & Middle Eastern Arbitration Review* 2009, Ukraine Overview.
83. *Ibid.*, Middle East Overview.

followed by an increasing body of case law that is in line with the interpretation of modern arbitration laws in the most arbitration-friendly countries. Yet, there remains room for improvement, particularly within the courts of first instance across the country.[84] Another source of concern is the possible conflict between the multiple international conventions that apply, for example, the New York Convention, the Panama Convention of 1975, the Montevideo Convention of 1978, and the Mercosur of 1998.[85]

Enforcement in North America. The enforcement environment in North America is generally in line with the standards prevailing in Western Europe. However, recent studies suggest that US courts deny enforcement of New York Convention awards in 26% of cases. By way of comparison, the average rate of reported cases worldwide in which courts deny enforcement of ICC awards is 10%.[86] **6-109**

Healthy scepticism regarding statistics. When considering the enforcement records of different countries, it is important to distinguish between awards that have been enforced in part and those enforced in full. Some countries or institutions may claim that a large percentage of international awards have been enforced by their courts, but may not disclose that by 'enforcement', they mean collection by the creditor of 10 or 20 cents on each dollar awarded. China has certainly taken this approach in the past when publicising its 'enforcement' record. **6-110**

In short, parties contracting with counterparties with assets located principally or exclusively in other countries with poor – or not demonstrably good – records of actually enforcing international arbitral awards should always place those poor enforcement records high among the risks involved in the transaction. Likewise, any party considering launching arbitration in order to obtain a monetary remedy should take a cold look beforehand at the enforcement environment *in practice* in the places where the opponent has assets, before committing to the substantial effort and expense that go with arbitration. **6-111**

Not that this ever really happens: when the other side are crooks	International arbitration may often be the most effective form of dispute resolution for international business transactions, but it is by no means a panacea for the problems that may arise after signing the contract, particularly where the other parties are crooks. In a case in which one of the authors was involved, the claimant was from Asia and the counterparty was a company incorporated in the British Virgin Islands (BVI),

---

84. See C.C. Roos & R.S. Grion, 'Arbitration in Brazil: Law and Practice from an ICC Perspective', *ICC International Court of Arbitration Bulletin* 17, no. 2 (2006).
85. See F. Mantilla-Serrano, 'Le traitement législatif de l'arbitrage en Amerique Latine', *Revue de l'arbitrage* 3 (2005).
86. See C. Amirfar, '2009 Status and Trends of Enforcement of Arbitral Awards in US Courts', Fourth Annual ICC New York Conference, 14 Sep. 2009; and A.J. van den Berg, 'New York Convention of 1958: Refusals of Enforcement', *ICC International Court of Arbitration Bulletin* 18, no. 2 (2007).

and owned by European 'businessmen'. The claimant had in good faith and perhaps naively contracted with the BVI company without obtaining any security for payment or guarantees. When the BVI company failed to make payment, the claimant called in arbitration lawyers and they turned to debt-collection companies to identify and evaluate the adversary's assets. These were discovered to have all been quietly dissipated by the company, although the shareholders continued to own castles in their home countries and drive luxury cars. The lawyers advised that, although the case on the merits was very strong, the chances of collecting on any award were slim. The claimant decided to proceed with the arbitration nonetheless and obtained an order of provisional security for its claim and a subsequent award for all the damages that it sought. However, because the shareholders had looted the company, the claimant has only been able to recover a small amount on the award, and pending proceedings to reach the shareholders (as well as criminal proceedings against them) have yet to yield any fruit.

Chapter Seven
ICSID and Investment Treaty Arbitration

Introduction. Even though international arbitration is often less confidential than **7-001** parties may suppose,[1] the fact is that little is publicly known about how most international arbitrations are conducted. Investment treaty arbitrations and ICSID arbitrations are exceptions to this rule, and in recent years they have become perhaps the main window through which outsiders can observe the practice of international arbitration. These arbitrations determine claims by private investors against the states hosting their investment. Because they necessarily involve states and therefore the interests of the taxpayer, investment treaty arbitrations (many but not all of which are ICSID arbitrations) are often in the public domain; ICSID arbitrations (most but not all of which are investment treaty arbitrations) are always in the public domain if only because ICSID publishes details of its cases on its website.[2] Many of these disputes also bring up novel legal issues and address questions of public interest beyond the simple impact that a successful claim or defence will have on state coffers. For these reasons too, these cases grab more headlines than 'ordinary' international arbitrations, with parties and lawyers, as well as authors, journalists, and non-governmental organisations (NGOs) keen and able to talk and write profusely about them. So much so that one would be forgiven for concluding, from arbitration publications in particular, that the number of investment treaty arbitrations substantially outweighs the number of ordinary international arbitrations.

---

1. Chapter 2, *Negotiating an International Dispute Resolution Agreement.*
2. See the ICSID website at <http://www.icsid.worldbank.org/ICSID/Index.jsp>. The existence of the arbitration and the procedural details are published on ICSID website, as well as the award if both parties consent. Absent the parties' consent, only excerpts of the legal reasoning contained in the award are published. See ICSID Rule 48.

7-002 *Investment treaty arbitrations are few in number.* It is easy to overstate the significance of investment treaty arbitration and ICSID arbitration in the broader context of international arbitration. The truth is that investment treaty arbitrations and ICSID arbitrations represent only a small fraction of all international arbitrations. There have only ever been 200 or so ICSID investment treaty arbitrations (including ICSID Additional Facility cases), and maybe 300 or so investment treaty arbitrations in total.[3] These numbers have grown enormously in percentage terms in recent years, but that growth appears to be flattening out.[4] This compares with a total of over 15,000 ICC arbitrations, with a total of 600 or so new cases each year just for this one institution (few or none of the ICC's cases are investment treaty arbitrations).

7-003 *Relative significance of investment treaty arbitration.* Investment treaty disputes thus occupy a small, specialised place in the arbitration universe, and most users of arbitration and many arbitration lawyers will never encounter them. Ordinary commercial disputes between companies remain the bread and butter of international arbitration.

7-004 *Differences between investment treaty arbitration and other arbitrations.* Although ICSID and investment treaty arbitrations are relatively rare, we have devoted this separate chapter to them because there are a number of important differences between those forms of arbitration and ordinary international arbitrations. These differences are not so much in the way the proceedings are conducted, but more in the legal regime governing the arbitrations: the conventions, rules, and substantive law applicable in investment treaty and ICSID cases are typically quite different from those found ordinarily in international arbitration.

Question:	Does investment treaty arbitration involve only certain types of special investments in a foreign country, such as the exploitation of natural resources?
Answer:	No, disputes under investment treaties arise out of virtually any type of business activity that takes place in a host country, and where it is alleged that state involvement (or the failure of the state to act or provide required protections) negatively affects those activities.

7-005 *Low awareness of investment treaties.* Another reason for giving investment arbitration special attention is that awareness of investment treaties, and of the protections they provide, is still low – despite the publicity given to them in the arbitration

---

3. See United Conference on Trade and Development, IIA Monitor No. 1 (2009), International Investment Agreements – Latest Developments in Investor-State Dispute Settlement, UNCTAD/WEB/DIAE/IA/2009/6, available at <www.unctad.org/en/docs/webdiaeia20096_en.pdf>.
4. *Ibid.*

press – whether among investors, lawyers, or even some of the states that conclude the treaties. The relatively low level of awareness prevents investors from securing the full benefit of the protections and deprives the states of the additional investment that greater investor awareness would presumably generate.[5] This may be partly due to a misunderstanding that 'investment' treaties and investment treaty arbitration operate only with respect to a narrow range of business activities, when, in fact, they can cover all types of business activities in a foreign country in which state involvement (or lack of it) negatively impacts the financial returns from those activities.

Question:	What is the difference between an investment treaty arbitration and ICSID arbitration?
Answer:	The phrase 'investment treaty arbitration' is a reference to the nature of the arbitration agreement between the investor and the state. It is based on an offer of arbitration found in an investment treaty between that state and one or more other states. 'ICSID arbitration' refers to the arbitral institution – it is arbitration conducted under the auspices of ICSID, which is the arbitral institution affiliated with the World Bank. Many investment treaty arbitrations (probably the majority) are also ICSID arbitrations, as they are administered by ICSID; some investment treaty arbitrations are not ICSID arbitrations, as they are administered by other institutions or are ad hoc arbitrations (not administered by any institution). The vast majority of ICSID arbitrations are investment treaty arbitrations, but not all: for example, a state and an investor can agree in a contract to ICSID arbitration, even though no investment treaty covers their relationship.[6]

---

5. States entering into investment treaties usually say, in each treaty's recitals, that the instrument is intended to promote and protect investment by investors of the other state. However, the jury is still out on the extent to which investment treaties actually have any impact on the amount of foreign investment into a given state. See, e.g., J.W. Salacuse & N.P. Sullivan, 'Do BITs Really Work? An Evaluation of BITs and their Grand Bargain', *Harvard International Law Journal* 46, no. 1 (Winter, 2005): 67 et seq; K.P. Sauvant & L.E. Sachs, *The Effect of Treaties on Foreign Direct Investment* (Oxford: Oxford University Press, 2009); and International Institute for Sustainable Development, 'Do Bilateral Investment Treaties Lead to More Foreign Investment?' (30 Apr. 2009), available at <www.investmenttreatynews.org/cms/news/archive/2009/04/30/do-bilateral-investment-treaties-lead-to-more-foreign-investment.aspx>.
6. A small number of ICSID arbitrations are brought under the host state's investment laws. These are very similar to arbitrations under investment treaties and we treat them as identical unless stated otherwise.

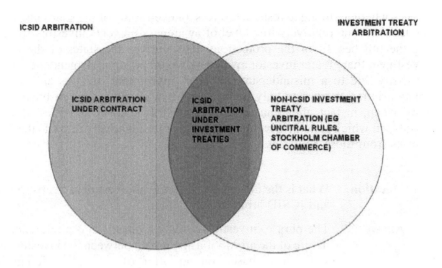

7-006 This chapter continues with a look first at investment treaty arbitration, before considering in more detail some of the specificities of ICSID.

I.   INVESTMENT TREATY ARBITRATION

7-007 *Broad meaning of 'investment'.* As already introduced, a common misunderstanding is that only a vaguely defined class of international commercial transactions fall under the rubric of 'investments' which benefit from treaty protections. In fact, the term 'investment' is misleading, in that there are a large number of international commercial projects and even transactions that could easily fall within the ambit of the protections provided by an investment treaty. Thus, it is important for parties transacting international business to understand the protections that may be available to them, both when negotiating their project or transaction, so that they enhance their ability to benefit from those protections, and in the event that the benefit of their investment is somehow harmed by action or inaction by the host state.

In what ways is investment treaty arbitration different from 'ordinary' international arbitration?	The key difference is that the arbitration agreement in investment treaty arbitration is found in the acceptance by the investor of the state's offer of arbitration in the investment treaty, while the arbitration agreement in other forms of arbitration is found in a more traditional contract. But there are other differences in practice. For example, investment treaty arbitration: • always involves a state on one side and a private investor on the other;

- usually involves application of international law to procedural and substantive issues;
- raises frequent and complex jurisdiction issues, especially in ICSID cases;
- is staffed by a pool of arbitrators and counsel who are often specialised in these sorts of arbitrations and in international law;
- tends to take more time than other arbitration, mainly because states move slowly and because of the frequent and complex jurisdiction objections that must be decided at the outset of the arbitration; and
- involves greater transparency of proceedings through publicity, NGO interventions as amicus curiae, and so on.

Still, in many ways the arbitral proceedings themselves are quite similar to ordinary international arbitrations. For example, the same (UNCITRAL) or similar (ICSID) arbitration rules are used.

What is an investment treaty? Investment treaties are agreements between two or **7-008** more states in which each state party undertakes to protect 'investments' in its territory made by investors (who we refer to for convenience as 'qualifying investors') of other states that are party to the treaty. As part of the protections offered in most investment treaties, each state agrees that qualifying investors may sue it in neutral offshore arbitration, without the need for a pre-existing arbitration agreement with the particular investor.

Types of investment treaties. There are two types of investment treaties: bilateral **7-009** investment treaties (BITs), entered into by two states, and multilateral investment treaties, entered into by three or more states. There are over 2,500 BITs worldwide, most of which are concluded by at least one developing country.[7] Certain free trade agreements (FTAs) contain chapters protecting investments, and for present purposes these can be assimilated with investment treaties.

Multilateral investment treaties. There are a handful of multilateral investment **7-010** treaties that cover certain regions or industry sectors. The best known multilateral investment treaties are:

- the North American Free Trade Agreement (NAFTA), to which Canada, Mexico, and the United States are party, or more precisely, Chapter 11 of NAFTA, which is the treaty's investment chapter;[8]

---

7. The text of many investment treaties is available on the website of the United Nations Conference on Trade and Development (UNCTAD) at <www.unctadxi.org/templates/DocSearch____779. aspx>.
8. Available at <www.naftaclaims.com>.

- the Agreement among ASEAN Governments for the Promotion and Protection of Investments, to which the ten ASEAN countries are party;[9]
- the United Agreement for the Investment of Arab Capital in Arab States, to which around twenty Arab states are party;[10] and
- the Energy Charter Treaty, which covers the energy sector, and to which over forty-five countries worldwide are party.[11]

7-011 *A BIT in diagram form.* A bilateral investment treaty (one between only two states) is represented diagrammatically as follows:

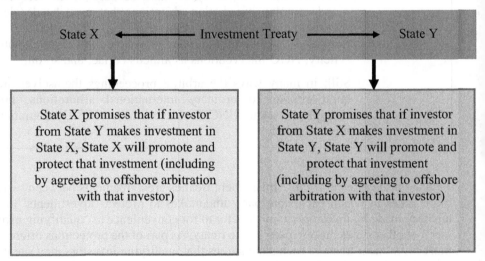

State X ◄──────── Investment Treaty ────────► State Y

| State X promises that if investor from State Y makes investment in State X, State X will promote and protect that investment (including by agreeing to offshore arbitration with that investor) | State Y promises that if investor from State X makes investment in State Y, State Y will promote and protect that investment (including by agreeing to offshore arbitration with that investor) |

7-012 *International treaty network of investment protection.* It is important to understand that the worldwide investment treaty network is extensive but far from comprehensive. Some countries have concluded relatively few investment treaties: Japan, for example, had concluded at the time of writing fewer than twenty investment treaties, but has been increasingly entering into FTAs with investment chapters. Other countries have entered into a large number of treaties, but the protection provided by those treaties may be less effective than the norm. For example, China has more than 100 treaties, but many of these provide for only limited access to neutral offshore arbitration. Because the investment treaty network is not comprehensive and does not provide a universal standard of protection, it would be a mistake to assume that *every* foreign investment is covered by an effective

---

9. ASEAN is the Association of Southeast Asian Nations. The 1987 ASEAN investment agreement is due to be replaced before the end of 2009 by the ASEAN Comprehensive Investment Agreement, which was signed by ASEAN Member States in February 2009. ASEAN investment agreements are available at <www.aseansec.org/6462.htm>.
10. Available at <www.unctad.org/Templates/webflyer.asp?docid=1592&intItemID=2323&lang=1&mode=toc>.
11. Available at <www.encharter.org>.

investment treaty. This is why investors – especially those who intend to do business in developing countries – should exercise particular care if they want to secure investment treaty protection (this is discussed further below).

Model investment treaties. The following sections introduce some of the important **7-013** provisions common to most investment treaties. Two model treaties are attached in Appendices 15 and 16, one of which (the Dutch Model) is a traditional, older treaty, and the second of which (the US Model) is a more contemporary instrument. Many bilateral and multilateral investment treaties adopt a similar structure and contain broadly similar provisions. However, investment treaties are almost never identical. There are often apparently minor differences between corresponding provisions in treaties that can result in significant disparity in the level of protection provided.

A.   WHICH INVESTORS AND INVESTMENTS ARE
            PROTECTED BY INVESTMENT TREATIES?

Investors and investments. States agree in investment treaties to protect only **7-014** certain 'qualifying' investors who make certain 'qualifying' investments. This will mean, among other things, that only these investors are entitled to bring disputes to arbitration against a state under the treaty. The definitions of investor and investment are usually found in the initial provisions of the investment treaty.

1.   Investors

Protected investors. Investment treaties protect a limited group of investors, usu- **7-015** ally nationals or companies of each state party to the treaty. Companies are usually considered to be 'of' a state if they are incorporated there or organised under its laws.[12] Some treaties may limit the group of qualifying investors further, by adding conditions: for example, the treaty may require that a company, in order to fall within the definition of investor and qualify for coverage by the treaty, be owned by nationals of the state in which it is incorporated, or conduct business in the state in which it is incorporated, or both.[13]

---

12. See, e.g., Art. 1(b)(ii) of the Dutch Model BIT, at Appendix 15 and Art. 1 of the US Model BIT, at Appendix 16.
13. See, e.g., Art. 1 of the US Model BIT, at Appedix 16. See also Art. 72 of the Agreement between Japan and the Republic of Singapore for a New-Age Economic Partnership Agreement: '(e) the term "investor of the other Party" means any natural person of the other Party or any enterprise of the other Party; ... (h) the term "enterprise of the other Party" means any enterprise duly constituted or otherwise organised under applicable law of the other Party, except an enterprise owned or controlled by persons of non-Parties and not engaging in substantive business operations in the territory of the other Party'.

7-016 *Foreign-owned investors incorporated in host state.* Certain treaties also provide that companies incorporated in one state party to the treaty (or even in a third state depending on how expansive the language of the treaty is) but owned or controlled by nationals of the other state party will be regarded as nationals of that other state party for the purpose of the treaty. This sort of language is commonly found in Netherlands BITs. As an illustration, Article 1.2 of the Kuwait-Netherlands BIT defines 'investors' as follows: 'The term 'investors' shall comprise with regard to a Contracting Party: (a) natural persons having the nationality of either Contracting Party; (b) legal persons constituted under the law of either Contracting Party; (c) the Government of either Contracting Party or its institutions; (d) *legal persons not constituted under the law of either Contracting Party but owned or controlled, directly or indirectly, by natural or legal persons referred to in (a), (b), or (c) above*' (emphasis added). So, where a company X is incorporated in Kuwait, or in a third state, but is owned or controlled by nationals of the Netherlands, then that company X may be entitled to investment protection under the investment treaty between Kuwait and the Netherlands. This is important in practice, because much foreign investment is made through companies incorporated in the host state or a third state.

7-017 *Acquiring foreign status under Article 25(2)(b) of ICSID Convention.* This type of provision in an investment treaty will be regarded as the agreement of the parties for the purposes of Article 25(2)(b) of the ICSID Convention to treat a company that has the nationality of the contracting state to the dispute as a national of another contracting state because of its foreign control. Again, this is of great importance in practice, given the amount of foreign investment made through local companies. So, in our example, a company incorporated in Kuwait but controlled by Dutch investors will qualify as a 'national of another contracting state' for the purposes of the ICSID Convention, and will be entitled to initiate ICSID arbitration, provided that all other jurisdictional conditions are also met.

7-018 *Multiple levels of indirect ownership of an investment implicate multiple treaty options.* Many foreign investors use a complex investment structure in which there may be several levels of ownership in place between the business activity conducted in the host state and its ultimate owner. The ultimate owner will generally be entitled to protection under an investment treaty between its home state and the host state in respect of this indirectly owned investment, as will the intermediate owners under treaties applicable to them. A minority or non-controlling shareholder in an investment will, absent wording to the contrary, be entitled to protection under an investment treaty between that shareholder's home state and the host state of the investment.[14]

---

14. See, e.g., S.A. Alexandrov, 'The "Baby Boom" of Treaty-Based Arbitrations and the Jurisdiction of ICSID Tribunals – Shareholders as "Investors" under Investment Treaties', *Journal of World Investment & Trade* 6, no. 3 (June 2005): 387 et seq. See for an illustration, *CMS Gas Transmission Company v. The Republic of Argentina* (ICSID Case No. ARB/01/8) Decision of the Tribunal on Objections to Jurisdiction (17 Jul. 2003), available at <http://ita.law.uvic.ca>.

2.   Investments

'Investments' broadly defined. Because of the attention given to large resource and **7-019**
infrastructure projects, one could be forgiven for assuming that treaties protect only
large-scale, complex contracts and projects involving billions of dollars, made
directly with the host state. In fact, most treaties protect a broad range of business
activities and assets in the host state, of any size, both tangible and intangible. Most
investment treaties thus define the 'investments' falling within their ambit very
broadly to include 'every kind of asset'. They then go on to give illustrations of
what falls within this broad group, which typically include:

- movable and immovable property;
- shares and interests in companies;
- claims to money or to any performance under contract having financial
  value;
- intellectual property rights, including goodwill and know-how; and
- business concessions conferred by law or under contract (e.g., to explore,
  extract and exploit natural resources).

Are contracts investments? It would be a mistake, therefore, to rely on a lay **7-020**
definition of investment when a potential investor or a host state is examining
whether a treaty may provide protection for business activities in the host state. In
particular, the third illustrative set of investments listed above – claims to money or
contractual performance having financial value – may effectively mean that most
contracts, including service contracts, qualify for the protection of investment
treaties.[15] Arbitrators certainly hold construction contracts to be qualifying investments, with the result that they generally find claims by construction contractors
against states relating to those contracts (but brought on the basis of investment
treaties) to be within their jurisdiction.[16] Unless there is a specific restriction in the
particular treaty, contracts that may qualify as an 'investment' are not limited to
contracts between the investor and the host state. If the contract was entered into
directly between the investor and the host state, it may enjoy more protection under
an investment treaty than contracts between the investor and third parties. For
example, the protection offered by the so-called 'umbrella clause' may, according
to recent decisions, be applied only to contracts entered into directly between the
investor and the host state.[17]

---

15. See for an illustration, *SGS Société Générale de Surveillance S.A. v. Republic of the Philippines*
    (ICSID Case No. ARB/02/6), Decision of the Tribunal on Objections to Jurisdiction (29 Jan.
    2004), available at <http://ita.law.uvic.ca>.
16. See for an illustration, *Salini Costruttori S.P.A. and Italstrade S.P.A. v. Kingdom of Morocco*
    (ICSID Case No. ARB/00/4), Decision on Jurisdiction (16 Jul. 2003); and *Bayindir Insaat
    Turizm Ticaret Ve Sanayi A.S. v. Islamic Republic of Pakistan* (ICSID Case No. ARB/03/
    29), Decision on Jurisdiction (14 Nov. 2005), available at <http://ita.law.uvic.ca>.
17. See, e.g., *CMS Gas Transmission Company v. Argentine Republic* (ICSID Case No. ARB/01/8),
    (Annulment Proceeding), Decision of the ad hoc Committee on the Application for Annulment of
    the Argentine Republic (25 Sep. 2007), available at <http://ita.law.uvic.ca>.

7-021 *Limitations on what qualifies as an investment.* Some treaties restrict the category of assets or activities qualifying as investments by adding conditions to the typical definition of investment described above. Examples include the requirement that the investment be authorised under national law, or that the investment be made in compliance with laws. As an illustration, in *Yaung Chi Oo v. Myanmar*, an arbitral tribunal in an investment treaty case between a Singaporean investor and Myanmar under the ASEAN Investment Agreement declined jurisdiction over claims by an investor that had not obtained the necessary approval for its investment – a brewery joint venture – from the Myanmar government.[18] In another case, the tribunal declined jurisdiction because it found that the investment in dispute – shares of a company developing an airport terminal in the Philippines – had been made in violation of Philippine investment laws, and was not an 'investment' for the purpose of the relevant treaty, which conditioned coverage on compliance with the host State's law.[19]

B.   WHAT PROTECTIONS ARE OFFERED TO INVESTMENTS
            COVERED BY INVESTMENT TREATIES?

7-022 *Investment treaty protections generally.* Most treaties require states to provide foreign investments with broadly similar standards of treatment, which we describe below in general terms.[20] However, the wording of the provisions varies from treaty to treaty, and parties need to look carefully at each treaty provision to determine the exact scope of the protections it offers. In addition, the precise meaning of certain of the standards is still uncertain and is the subject of much debate in arbitration decisions and commentary. In a nutshell, an investment treaty will generally require the host state to treat the investment fairly and equitably, to treat the investment no less favourably than it treats investments by its own nationals or nationals of any third state, and not to expropriate the investment without payment of compensation. In addition, a number of investment treaties oblige the host state to observe commitments it has undertaken with respect to investments. This is often considered to place a duty on the state under international law to observe obligations under contracts that it has entered into in relation to the investment.

---

18. See *Yaung Chi Oo Trading Pte. Ltd v. Government of the Union of Myanmar*, ASEAN I.D. Case No. ARB/01/1, Award (31 Mar. 2003), available at <http://ita.law.uvic.ca>.

19. See *Fraport AG Frankfurt Airport Services Worldwide v. Republic of the Philippines* (ICSID Case No. ARB/03/25), Award (16 Aug. 2007), available at <http://ita.law.uvic.ca>. An annulment proceeding against the Award commenced by Fraport was pending at the time of writing.

20. See generally, C. McLachlan, L. Shore & M. Weiniger, *International Investment Law* (Oxford: Oxford University Press, 2007); R. Dolzer & C. Schreuer, *Principles of International Investment Law* (Oxford: Oxford University Press, 2008); C.F. Dugan, D. Wallace, N.D. Rubins & B. Sabahi, *Investor-State Arbitration, Oxford University Press* (Oxford: Oxford University Press, 2008); and A. Newcombe & L. Paradell. Law and Practice of Investment Treaties: Standards of Treatment (The Netherlands: Kluwer Law International, 2009); and P. Muchlinski, F. Ortino & C. Schreuer (eds), *The Oxford Handbook of International Investment Law* (Oxford: Oxford University Press, 2008).

Fair and equitable treatment. Most investment treaties require the host state to **7-023** treat qualifying investments fairly and equitably. This fair and equitable treatment provision is a key feature of the protection offered by investment treaties and is often relied upon by foreign investors as a 'catch-all' duty imposed on states. The scope of the obligation to treat the investment fairly and equitably will depend on the specific wording of the treaty. In particular, some treaties link the standard to the customary international law minimum standard of treatment of aliens. This approach provides the foreign investor with less protection than the arguably autonomous standard found in other treaties.[21]

Case-by-case definition of fair and equitable treatment. Still, what the words 'fair **7-024** and equitable treatment' actually mean is hard to pin down: cases and commentary have difficulty coming up with a definition that is accepted without reservation. Instead, tribunals tend to make their own definitions on a case-by-case basis, paying a varying degree of attention to the ordinary meaning of the words 'fair and equitable' and to other recognised rules of treaty interpretation. By way of illustration, the types of conduct by host states that have been held by arbitrators to breach the fair and equitable treatment standard in investment treaties include:

- *Lack of stability of a host state's investment framework (its laws and regulations governing investments).* The tribunal in the *CMS v. Argentina* case found that Argentina's alteration of the legal and business environment under which the investment was made, through the adoption of emergency laws and regulations in response to a financial crisis, and where guarantees had been given by Argentina with respect to the legal framework, gave rise to a breach of the fair and equitable treatment provision contained in the Argentina-United States BIT.[22]
- *Failure by the host state to act consistently and transparently.* In the *Occidental v. Ecuador* case, the tribunal found that a change in Ecuador's tax law that lacked clarity gave rise to a breach by Ecuador of the fair and equitable treatment provision contained in the Ecuador-United States BIT.[23]
- *Frustration of the foreign investor's legitimate expectations.* In the *CMS v. Argentina* case considered above, the tribunal found that Argentina's

---

21. On fair and equitable treatment, see, e.g., OECD, Fair and Equitable Treatment Standard in International Investment Law, Working Papers on International Investment Number 2004/3 (September 2004); and C.H. Schreuer, 'Fair and Equitable Treatment in Arbitral Practice', *Journal of World Investment & Trade* 6, no. 3 (June 2005): 357 et seq. For an illustration of the different interpretations encountered in case law, see, e.g., *Mondev International Ltd v. United States of America* (ICSID Case No. ARB(AF)/99/2), Final Award (11 Oct. 2002); and *Compañiá de Aguas del Aconquija S.A. and Vivendi Universal v. Argentine Republic* (ICSID Case No. ARB/97/3), Award (20 Aug. 2007), available at <http://ita.law.uvic.ca>.
22. See *CMS Gas Transmission Company v. Argentine Republic* (ICSID Case No. ARB/01/8), Award (12 May 2005), available at <http://ita.law.uvic.ca>.
23. See *Occidental Exploration and Production Company v. The Republic of Ecuador* (LCIA Case No. UN3467), Final Award (1 Jul. 2004), available at <http://ita.law.uvic.ca>.

conduct, which frustrated the investor's legitimate expectations created by Argentina, gave rise to a breach of the fair and equitable provision contained in the Argentina-United States BIT.[24]

– *Harassment of the investment and the lack of due process.* In the *Middle East Cement v. Egypt* case, in which the tribunal found that Egypt's seizure and auction of the investor's ship, without proper notification of the auction to the investor, gave rise to a breach of the fair and equitable treatment provision contained in the Egypt-Greece BIT.[25]

7-025 *National treatment.* Many treaties require host states to treat investments by investors of the other contracting state no less favourably than investments by its own nationals. This is known as the 'national treatment' standard.

7-026 *'Importing' protections through most favoured nation clauses.* Most treaties also contain a most-favoured-nation (MFN) clause that requires the host state to treat investments by investors of the other contracting state no less favourably than investments by investors from other countries. As a result, an MFN clause will generally allow a qualifying investor to 'import' into the investment treaty that covers its investment the more favourable treatment offered by the same host state to investors of third countries in treaties entered into between the host state and those third countries. This is a far-reaching mechanism that allows the foreign investor to enhance significantly the protection it is owed by the host state. As an illustration, in the *MTD v. Chile* case, the investor was able to rely on the MFN provision contained in the Chile-Malaysia BIT to avail itself of the more favourable protection offered by Chile BITs with Denmark and with Croatia (notably regarding the host state's obligation to grant the necessary permits for an investment it had authorised).[26]

7-027 *MFN and dispute resolution.* The real controversy surrounding MFN clauses is not whether they can be used to enhance an investor's substantive protection – for example, to import from another treaty entered into by the host state a more favourable fair and equitable treatment clause. That consequence is now widely accepted. Instead, the debate centres on whether the MFN clause applies also to procedural matters, and especially whether it applies to enhance (or even create) an investor's access to a dispute resolution forum. In other words, can an investor invoke an MFN clause to import into its treaty a more favourable dispute resolution clause (say, an ICSID arbitration clause rather than ad hoc arbitration clause) from another treaty to which the host state is party? It can be argued with some conviction that the state's agreement to arbitration of disputes relating to an investment is 'treatment' of that investment, and unless the treaty excludes dispute resolution

---

24. See *CMS Gas Transmission Company v. Argentine Republic* (ICSID Case No. ARB/01/8), Award (12 May 2005), available at <http://ita.law.uvic.ca>.
25. See *Middle East Cement Shipping and Handling Co. S.A. v. Arab Republic of Egypt* (ICSID Case No. ARB/99/6), Award (12 Apr. 2002), available at <http://ita.law.uvic.ca>.
26. See *MTD Equity Sdn. Bhd. and MTD Chile S.A. v. Republic of Chile* (ICSID Case No. ARB/01/7), Award (25 May 2004), available at <http://ita.law.uvic.ca>.

from the scope of the MFN provision, the investor should be entitled to the benefit of more favourable dispute resolution 'treatment' made available by the state to investors in other treaties.[27]

Full protection and security. Most investment treaties provide that the host state **7-028** should ensure the full protection and security in its territory of investments made by investors of the other contracting state. This 'full protection and security' standard is thought to place on the host state an obligation of vigilance and due diligence.[28] In other words, the host state is required to take all reasonable measures to ensure the protection and security of the investment in its territory. Arbitral tribunals remain divided as to whether the standard is limited to ensuring the physical security of the investment or extends to the protection and security of the investor's intangible rights to own, control, and enjoy the benefits of its investment.[29] As an illustration, in the *Wena v. Egypt* case, the tribunal found that Egypt's failure to take action to prevent or remedy the seizure of the investment (two hotels) by employees of a state entity gave rise to a breach of the full protection and security provision contained in the Egypt-United Kingdom BIT.[30]

'Umbrella clause'. The phrase 'umbrella clause' refers to a treaty provision that **7-029** typically stipulates that the host state shall observe obligations it has entered into with respect to investments of an investor of the other contracting party. While contrary views exist, this clause is understood by most as applying to contracts entered into directly with the host state. The majority thinking is that an umbrella clause converts or elevates a breach by the host state of its contractual obligations into a violation of the treaty, for which compensation may be sought under the dispute resolution mechanism provided for in the treaty. However, the wording of umbrella clauses varies significantly from one treaty to another, and not all of them

---

27. On MFN clauses and dispute resolution, see, e.g., E. Gaillard, 'Establishing Jurisdiction through a Most-Favored-Nation Clause', *New York Law Journal* (2 Jun. 2005); and OECD, 'Most-Favored-Nation Treatment in International Investment Law', Working Papers on International Investment Law, No. 2004/2 (September 2004). For a selection of cases, see, e.g., *Emilio Agustín Maffezini v. The Kingdom of Spain* (ICSID Case No. ARB/97/7), Decision of the Tribunal on Objections to Jurisdiction (25 Jan. 2000); *Plama Consortium Limited v. Republic of Bulgaria* (ICSID Case No. ARB/03/24), Decision on Jurisdiction (8 Feb. 2005); and *RosInvestCo UK Ltd v. The Russian Federation*, SCC Case No. Arb. V079/2005, Award on Jurisdiction (October 2007), available at <http://ita.law.uvic.ca>.
28. See, e.g., *Wena Hotels Ltd v. Arab Republic of Egypt* (ICSID Case No. ARB/98/4), Award (8 Dec. 2000), available at <http://ita.law.uvic.ca>.
29. See, e.g., for an illustration of the more restrictive approach, *Saluka Investments BV v. The Czech Republic* (UNCITRAL), Partial Award (17 Mar. 2006); and for an illustration of the broader approach, *Compañiá de Aguas del Aconquija S.A. and Vivendi Universal v. Argentine Republic* (ICSID Case No. ARB/97/3), Award (20 Aug. 2007), available at <http://ita.law.uvic.ca>.
30. See *Wena Hotels Ltd v. Arab Republic of Egypt* (ICSID Case No. ARB/98/4), Award (8 Dec. 2000), available at <http://ita.law.uvic.ca>.

will be interpreted as resulting in the elevation of a breach of a contractual obligation into a treaty violation.[31]

7-030 *Transfer of funds out of host state.* The foreign investor's right to freely transfer funds (capital and returns) out of the host state is usually guaranteed by investment treaties.

7-031 *Compensation for expropriation.* Most investment treaties provide that states may not expropriate qualifying investments except for a public purpose. When they do so, it must be in a non-discriminatory manner, under due process of law, and accompanied by payment of compensation. The expropriation may be direct (an outright seizure or nationalisation of the investment) or indirect, where the foreign investor retains nominal ownership but is effectively deprived of the economic use, enjoyment, or benefits of its investment. Indirect expropriation may occur through a single measure or through a 'creeping expropriation', which consists of a series of measures over time that have the aggregate effect of an expropriation.[32] As an illustration, measures that have been found by arbitral tribunals to give rise to 'indirect' expropriations include: regulatory action and unilateral amendment of a concession agreement (a contract to operate a public service, such as a road, railway or post) that left the investor with no choice but to terminate the concession agreement;[33] the transfer of a company's management to host-state-appointed management;[34] the denial of a construction permit;[35] the refusal to renew an operating permit;[36] the issuance of an ecological decree barring the operation of

---

31. On umbrella clauses, see, e.g., C.H. Schreuer, 'Travelling the BIT Route – Of Waiting Periods, Umbrella Clauses and Forks in the Road', *The Journal of World Investment & Trade* 5, no. 2 (April 2004): 231 et seq.; OECD, The Interpretation of the Umbrella Clause in Investment Agreements, Working Papers on International Investment, No. 2006/3 (October 2006). For an illustration of the conflicting views in case law, see, e.g., *SGS Société de Surveillance S.A. v. Islamic Republic of Pakistan* (ICSID Case No. ARB/01/13), Decision of the Tribunal on Objections to Jurisdiction (6 Aug. 2003); and *Eureko B.V v. Republic of Poland*, Partial Award (19 Aug. 2005), available at <http://ita.law.uvic.ca>.

32. On expropriation generally, see, e.g., W.M. Reisman & R.D. Sloane, 'Indirect Expropriation and its Valuation in the BIT Generation', *British Yearbook of International Law* 74 (2004): 115 et seq.; J. Paulsson & Z. Douglas, 'Indirect Expropriations in Investment Treaty Arbitrations', in *Arbitrating Foreign Investment Disputes*, ed. N. Horn (The Netherlands: Kluwer Law International, 2004).

33. See *Compañiá de Aguas del Aconquija S.A. and Vivendi Universal v. Argentine Republic* (ICSID Case No. ARB/97/3), Award (20 Aug. 2007), available at <http://ita.law.uvic.ca>.

34. See *Tippetts et al. v. TAMS-AFFA Consulting Engineers of Iran* et al., Award No. 141-7-2 (22 Jun. 1984), Iran-United States Claims Tribunal Reports 6, 219 et seq.

35. See *Metalclad Corporation v. Mexico* (ICSID Case No. ARB(AF)/97/1) (NAFTA), Award (30 Aug. 2000), available at <http://ita.law.uvic.ca>.

36. See *Técnicas Medioambientales Tecmed, S.A. v. United Mexican States* (ICSID Case No. ARB(AF)/00/2), Award (29 May 2003), available at <http://ita.law.uvic.ca>.

the investment;[37] and the prohibition of the import of material critical to the investment's activity.[38]

'Regulatory expropriation'. One of the most difficult issues in international **7-032** investment law is the extent to which a host state's exercise of its right or duty to issue laws and regulations in the public interest can constitute an expropriation requiring payment of compensation. For example, will an environmental regulation restricting or prohibiting the use of certain potentially harmful products, or financial regulations adopted in response to an economic crisis, give rise to an expropriation for which compensation is owed to the investor by the host state? Opinions are divided, but the trend in arbitrations conducted under investment treaties appears to be against requiring payment of compensation to foreign investors unless the regulation at issue is discriminatory or contravenes specific assurances given to the foreign investor, or where the effect of the measure is disproportionate to the objective sought to be achieved. Similar difficulties arise when considering whether a regulation infringes a state's obligations of fair and equitable treatment and full protection and security.[39]

C. THE AVAILABILITY OF ARBITRATION TO ENFORCE TREATY PROTECTIONS

Treaty arbitration available without specific arbitration agreement. Almost all **7-033** investment treaties contain a dispute settlement provision offering the foreign investor a right to claim directly against the host state, usually in neutral, offshore international arbitration. No other pre-existing arbitration agreement with the foreign investor is needed for it to be able to sue the host state in arbitration under the treaty. Coverage by the treaty will suffice, as the state's offer of arbitration in the treaty is accepted by the investor when it starts arbitration. The investor's acceptance perfects the parties' consent to arbitration.

Different arbitration options provided by treaties. Investment treaties usually **7-034** provide several alternative arbitration options for the foreign investor. These commonly include ICSID arbitration (discussed below in section II) and ad hoc arbitration under the UNCITRAL Rules. Other options may include arbitration under the rules of major arbitration institutions such as the ICC. ICSID arbitration

---

37. See *Metalclad Corporation v. Mexico* (ICSID Case No. ARB(AF)/97/1), Award (30 Aug. 2000), available at <http://ita.law.uvic.ca>.
38. See *Middle East Cement Shipping and Handling Co. S.A. v. Arab Republic of Egypt* (ICSID Case No. ARB/99/6), Award (12 Apr. 2002), available at <http://ita.law.uvic.ca>.
39. On expropriation and the right of the host state to regulate, see, e.g., OECD, '"Indirect Expropriation" and the "Right to Regulate" in International Investment Law', Working Paper on International Investment Number 2004/4 (September 2004); A. Newcombe, 'The Boundaries of Regulatory Expropriation in International Law', *ICSID Review – Foreign Investment Law Journal* 20, no. 1 (2005): 1 et seq.

is an attractive option for some investors, as it is specialised in investment disputes between foreign investors and host states, and also because ICSID awards cannot be set aside in local courts and are directly enforceable in the roughly 140 ICSID Member States in the same way as local court judgments.

7-035 *Election of dispute remedies.* Some dispute resolution clauses in investment treaties contain a so-called 'fork in the road' provision, offering investors a choice between litigation before state courts and arbitration. A foreign investor who initiates litigation proceedings before state courts may lose its right to submit the same dispute to arbitration, and vice versa. As an illustration of a 'fork in the road' clause, Article 9(2) of the 2003 Chinese Model BIT reads as follows: 'If the dispute cannot be settled through negotiations . . . , it shall be submitted by the choice of the investor: (a) to the competent court of the Contracting Party that is a party to the dispute; (b) to [ICSID]. . . . Once the investor has submitted the dispute to the competent court of the Contracting Party concerned or to ICSID, the choice of one of the two procedures shall be final.'

Checklist 7a – Parties with Grievances Against Host States

A party is likely to be able to submit a claim under an investment treaty if it can answer yes to all the following questions	• Do you have a dispute with a state other than your 'home' state, or an organ of that other state? • Is there a bilateral or multilateral investment treaty in force between that state and your 'home' state? • Does that treaty contain an offer by the host state of resolution by arbitration of investment disputes with investors of your 'home' state? • Do you qualify as an investor as defined by the treaty? • Does your dispute concern a business activity or asset that qualifies as an investment as defined by the treaty? • Does your dispute comply with all other conditions contained in the treaty's dispute resolution provision, particularly any that concern prior recourse to local courts?

D.   Types of Conduct for which Parties have sought
                Redress in Arbitration under Investment Treaties

7-036 The selection of cases below is digested to illustrate the different sorts of claims addressed by investment treaty arbitrators (in most or all of the cases, the monetary awards cited were paid voluntarily by the respondent states, or the parties settled for payment of a lower amount).

Denial of necessary permit by government authority	**Case Name:** *Metalclad v. Mexico*[40] **Held:** unfair/inequitable treatment and expropriation without compensation – USD 16 million awarded. **Dates:** Arbitration initiated in January 1997. Award in August 2000. Mexico's challenge of the award rejected in large part by the Supreme Court of British Columbia in May/August 2001.
Refusal to renew operating permit	**Case Name:** *Tecmed v. Mexico*[41] **Held:** unfair/inequitable treatment and expropriation without compensation – USD 5.5 million awarded. **Dates:** Arbitration initiated in August 2000. Award in May 2003.
Governmental decree prohibiting import of a certain product	**Case Name:** *Middle East Cement Shipping and Handling Co. v. Egypt*[42] **Held:** expropriation without compensation – USD 3.75 million awarded. **Dates:** Arbitration initiated in November 1999. Award in April 2002.
Discreditable domestic court proceedings	**Case Name:** *Loewen v. United States*[43] **Held:** unfair/inequitable treatment, but claims dismissed for failure to exhaust local remedies. **Dates:** Arbitration initiated in November 1998. Decision on jurisdiction in January 2001. Final Award in June 2003. Decision on respondent's request for a supplementary decision in September 2004. Motion to vacate the award dismissed by US court in October 2005.
Failure to enforce contractual arbitration awards and agreements – claims of unfair/ inequitable treatment	**Case Name:** *Western NIS Fund v. Ukraine* **Held:** settlement agreed by the parties. **Dates:** Arbitration initiated in January 2004. Settlement agreed by the parties and proceedings discontinued in June 2006.

---

40. *Metalclad Corporation v. The United Mexican States* (ICSID Case No. ARB(AF)/97/1), Award (30 Aug. 2000), available at <http://ita.law.uvic.ca>.
41. *Técnicas Medioambientales Tecmed, S.A. v. United Mexican States* (ICSID Case No. ARB(AF)/ 00/2), Award (29 May 2003), available at <http://ita.law.uvic.ca>.
42. *Middle East Cement Shipping and Handling Co. S.A. v. Arab Republic of Egypt* (ICSID Case No. ARB/99/6), Award (12 Apr. 2002), available at <http://ita.law.uvic.ca>.
43. *Loewen v. United States* (ICSID Case No. ARB(AF)/98/3), Final Award (26 Jun. 2003), available at <http://ita.law.uvic.ca>.

Failure to enforce contractual arbitration awards and agreements	**Case Name:** *Saipem SpA v. Bangladesh* **Held:** expropriation. USD 6 million awarded. **Dates:** Arbitration initiated in April 2005. Decision on jurisdiction and recommendation on provisional measures in March 2007. Award in June 2009.
Arbitrary change of tax policy	**Case Name:** *Occidental v. Ecuador*[44] **Held:** unfair/inequitable treatment, breach of national treatment standard – award: compensation of over USD 70 million. **Dates:** Arbitration initiated in November 2002. Final award in July 2004. Ecuador's application to challenge the award dismissed by English Court of Appeals in July 2007.
Denial of financial assistance offered to local competitors by host state	**Case Name:** *Saluka v. Czech Republic*[45] **Held:** unfair/inequitable treatment – award: USD 236 million. **Dates:** Arbitration initiated in June 2001. Partial award rendered in March 2006 finding that the Czech Republic had breached several provisions of the Netherlands-Czech Republic BIT. Tribunal ordered Czech Republic to pay Saluka USD 236 million.
Breach of contractual obligations by host state	**Case Name:** *Eureko v. Poland*[46] **Held:** unfair/inequitable treatment, violation of 'umbrella clause' – determination of compensation pending. **Dates:** Arbitration initiated in February 2003. Partial award in August 2005, finding that Poland had breached several provisions of the Netherlands-Poland BIT. Compensation phase pending.

---

44. *Occidental Exploration and Production Company v. The Republic of Ecuador* (LCIA Case No. UN3467), Final Award (1 Jul. 2004), available at <http://ita.law.uvic.ca>. Note that a number of Latin American countries – Bolivia, Cuba, Ecuador, Nicaragua, and Venezuela – formed the Alternativa Bolivariana para Las Américas y El Caribe and have been recently taking steps adverse to ICSID arbitration: Bolivia denounced the ICSID Convention as from November 2007; Ecuador notified ICSID in December 2007 of a class of disputes that it would not consent to submit to ICSID (namely, disputes relating to the exploitation of natural resources), and, in June 2009, it denounced the ICSID Convention. See, E. Gaillard, 'Anti-Arbitration Trends in Latin America', *New York Law Journal* (5 Jun. 2008).
45. *Saluka Investments BV v. The Czech Republic* (UNCITRAL), Partial Award (17 Mar. 2006), available at <http://ita.law.uvic.ca>.
46. *Eureko B.V v. Republic of Poland*, Partial Award (19 Aug. 2005), available at <http://ita.law.uvic.ca>.

Emergency measures in response to a financial crisis	**Case Name:** *Sempra v. Argentina*[47] **Held:** unfair/inequitable treatment, breach of 'umbrella clause' – award: USD 128 million. **Dates:** Arbitration initiated in December 2002. Jurisdiction decision in May 2005. Award in September 2007. ICSID annulment proceeding pending.
Seizure of investment by state-owned company	**Case Name:** *Wena Hotels v. Egypt*[48] **Held:** unfair/inequitable treatment, expropriation without compensation, failure to protect and secure investment – award: over USD 20 million. **Dates:** Arbitration initiated in July 1998. Jurisdiction decision in June 1999. Award in December 2000. Decision rejecting Egypt's application for annulment of the award in February 2002. Decision on Wena's application for interpretation of the award in October 2005.

E.   ENHANCING INVESTMENT TREATY PROTECTION WHEN PLANNING
       FOREIGN BUSINESS ACTIVITIES

We have seen that investment treaties offer businesses powerful protection, includ-   **7-037**
ing the right to have disputes with host states resolved in offshore arbitration.
Parties looking to engage in business abroad, and particularly in developing
countries where state interference with private business may be more likely, should
therefore examine carefully whether their planned activities will benefit from the
protection of one or more investment treaties. It will often be possible for businesses to structure their transactions in a manner that enhances that protection.[49]

Treaty shopping. 'Treaty shopping' is the convenient but slightly controversial   **7-038**
phrase for the process where a party planning to engage in business with or in a
foreign country examines all investment treaties of the host state, including treaties
with the party's home state and those with other countries, to see which offers the
most protection, and structures its transaction or business activities in the light of
that analysis. This is not as difficult or complicated as it may sound. A foreign
investor may notably 'shop' for favourable treaty protection simply by structuring

---

47. *Sempra Energy International v. The Argentine Republic* (ICSID Case No. ARB/02/16), Award
    (28 Sep. 2007), available at <http://ita.law.uvic.ca>.
48. *Wena Hotels Ltd v. Arab Republic of Egypt* (ICSID Case No. ARB/98/4 (ICSID)), Award
    (8 Dec. 2000), available at <http://ita.law.uvic.ca>. See also, the Decision for the Interpretation
    of the Arbitral Award dated 8 Dec. 2000 (31 Oct. 2005), available at <http://ita.law.uvic.ca>.
49. On 'treaty shopping', see, e.g., J. Savage, 'Ch. 17 – Investment Treaty Arbitration', in *Asian
    Leading Arbitrators' Guide to International Arbitration*, ed. M. Pryles & M.J. Moser (United
    States: Juris, 2007).

its foreign business activity through a special purpose vehicle set up in a third country that has a favourable treaty with the host state on the assumption that the foreign investor's home state does not have a favourable investment treaty with the host state, or any treaty at all with it.

7-039 *Criticism of treaty shopping.* This 'treaty shopping' exercise is not without its critics, but has been validated by arbitral tribunals called upon to address it to date, provided that the treaty under consideration does not contain any express language excluding from its ambit forms of business through which treaty shopping can occur. Some treaties exclude 'special purpose vehicles' from their scope by requiring, through their definition of 'investor', that the foreign party engage in *substantive* business operations in the territory of the home state, and/or that it be owned by companies or nationals of the state in which it is incorporated. The thinking here, is presumably that the host state is only agreeing to provide advantages to investors of the other contracting state, which treats investors of the host state in similar fashion, and is not agreeing to provide advantages to investors from third states that may not have made reciprocal commitments to the host state's investors.

7-040 *Cases of abuse.* Arbitral tribunals have also suggested that such 'treaty shopping' will be invalidated in cases of abuse. One example might be if the investor creates the special purpose vehicle after the dispute has arisen (which would in any event raise other issues of jurisdiction) for the purpose of gaining access to arbitration under the investment treaty.[50]

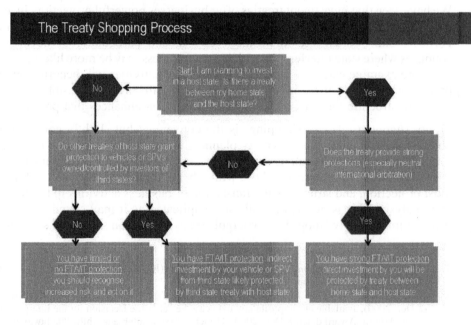

The Treaty Shopping Process

---

50. See, e.g, *Tokios Tokelés v. Ukraine* (ICSID Case No. ARB/02/18), Decision on Jurisdiction (29 Apr. 2004), para. 56 available at <http://ita.law.uvic.ca>.

II.   ICSID ARBITRATION

Introduction. In the previous section we considered investment treaties and arbi- **7-041**
trations brought by investors against states under those treaties. Many investment
treaty arbitrations are conducted at ICSID, a specialised arbitral institution that
exclusively administers investment disputes. ICSID stands for 'International
Centre for Settlement of Investment Disputes.'[51] What is meant by 'investment
disputes' is disputes between states hosting foreign business activities or assets
and the foreign parties conducting the activities or owning the assets. These days,
investment disputes are mostly, but not exclusively, investment treaty disputes,
and for this reason – as discussed in the previous section – the large majority of
ICSID cases consist of investment treaty arbitrations. There is still, however, the
odd ICSID case brought on the basis of an arbitration agreement in a contract
between a private foreign party and a state,[52] or on the basis of the acceptance by
the foreign party of an offer to arbitrate made by the state in its investment
legislation.[53]

Growth in ICSID caseload. The recent rise of investment treaty arbitration has **7-042**
fuelled enormous growth in ICSID's caseload in the past five to ten years, although
the number of cases it administers is still modest when compared with the gener-
alist international arbitral institutions such as the ICC, ICDR, LCIA and SIAC.[54]
However, because they are in the public domain and often involve novel and
important questions of legal and public interest, ICSID arbitrations are typically
more prominent and more closely followed than arbitrations under the auspices of
other institutions.[55]

Framework of ICSID arbitration. ICSID operates within its own specialised frame- **7-043**
work, which distinguishes it starkly from other arbitral institutions and systems
of arbitration. ICSID was established by the 1965 ICSID Convention (also
referred to as the 'ICSID Convention') as an arm of the World Bank, and it operates
in accordance with that Convention. This means that the New York Convention on

---

51. See, C.H. Schreuer et al., *The ICSID Convention – A Commentary*, 2nd edn (Cambridge:
    Cambridge University Press, 2009); L. Reed, J. Paulsson & N. Blackaby, *Guide to ICSID
    Arbitration* (The Netherlands: Kluwer Law International, 2004).
52. See, for a recent example, *Noble Energy Inc and MachalaPower Cia Ltda v. Ecuador and
    Consejo Nacional de Electricidad* (ICSID Case No. ARB/05/12), Decision on Jurisdiction
    (5 Mar. 2008), available at <http://ita.law.uvic.ca>.
53. See *Tradex Hellas S.A. v. Republic of Albania* (ICSID Case No. ARB/94/2), Decision on
    Jurisdiction (24 Dec. 1996), available at <http://ita.law.uvic.ca>.
54. Chapter 1, *The Elements of an International Dispute Resolution Agreement.*
55. Aside from arbitration, ICSID also offers conciliation. See Ch. III of the ICSID Convention, and
    ICSID Rules of Procedure for Conciliation Proceedings, available at <http://icsid.worldbank.
    org>. Dispute resolution clauses in some (but not most) investment treaties give the investor the
    option to resort to conciliation under the auspices of ICSID. However, in practice, ICSID
    conciliation is little used: there have been only four ICSID conciliation proceedings since
    the creation of ICSID, and none was pending at the time of writing.

the enforcement of foreign arbitral awards[56] and national arbitration statutes do not apply to ICSID arbitrations (and probably not to ICSID awards),[57] which instead are governed by the norms laid down in the ICSID Convention and the accompanying ICSID Rules of Procedure for Arbitration Proceedings (Arbitration Rules).[58]

7-044 *Limited ICSID jurisdiction.* ICSID arbitration is designed specifically and exclusively for the resolution of disputes between states and foreign investors concerning investments by those investors. As a result, access to ICSID jurisdiction is strictly limited by Article 25(1) of the ICSID Convention. A dispute must satisfy four conditions before it falls within ICSID's jurisdiction:

- *The dispute must be a 'legal dispute'.* This is apparently intended to prevent political disputes or mere conflict of interests being submitted. To our knowledge, no party has successfully objected to jurisdiction on this ground.
- *The dispute must be between a Member State (or one of its agencies or subdivisions) and a national of another Member State.* This is one of the fundamental characteristics of ICSID arbitration: a national of one state will be on one side of the case, and a state (other than that of the first party) will be on the other side. The only exception will be where the home state and the host state have agreed to treat a company from the host state as a foreign investor for the purpose of the ICSID Convention because of its foreign control.[59] The ICSID Convention counts roughly 140 member states. However, unlike the New York Convention, there are a number of major powers that are not party to the ICSID Convention, and therefore neither those states nor their nationals can be party to an ICSID arbitration. At the time of writing these states included Brazil, India, Mexico and Poland. A number of states have signed but not yet ratified the Convention. These include Canada, Ethiopia, Russia and Thailand. In addition, certain states have notified the Centre of classes of disputes that they would not consider submitting to the jurisdiction of the Centre;[60] these include China and Turkey.[61]

---

56. Chapter 6, *After the Arbitration.*
57. An exception to this will be arbitration conducted under ICSID's Additional Facility Rules. These Rules apply to disputes between a state and a national of another state, where the parties agree to ICSID arbitration but where the dispute does not fall within the scope of the ICSID Convention (notably where the State party is not a member of the ICSID Convention or the other party is not a national of a State which is a member of the ICSID Convention). See the ICSID Additional Facility Rules, available at <http://icsid.worldbank.org>.
58. See Arts. 53 and 54 of the ICSID Convention. See also, Schreuer, 1100 et seq.; and Dolzer & Schreuer, 287 et seq.
59. See Art. 25(2)(b) of the ICSID Convention.
60. See Art. 25(4) of the ICSID Convention.
61. China's notification under Art. 25(4) of the ICSID Convention reads as follows: '[P]ursuant to Article 25(4) of the Convention, the Chinese Government would only consider submitting to the

– *The dispute must arise directly out of an investment.* The difficulty here is that the ICSID Convention does not define what is meant by an investment; this is in contrast with investment treaties which, as seen, define in detail what is meant by an investment. This condition in the Convention, and the uncertainty resulting from the lack of a definition, have led to frequent objections to jurisdiction, and the position as to what is meant by 'investment' and 'arise directly out of' remains unsettled. It is important to note that the 'investment' test for jurisdiction under the ICSID Convention is independent of the similar test one finds in investment treaties, so that an investor in an ICSID investment treaty arbitration will have to satisfy two separate 'investment' tests for an ICSID tribunal to have jurisdiction. Although the two tests are distinct, if the investor satisfies the test in the investment treaty, it is likely to meet the test in the ICSID Convention too.
– *The parties must consent to submit the dispute to ICSID arbitration.* As observed already, this consent usually consists today in the acceptance by a party of a state's offer of ICSID arbitration found in an investment treaty. But it can also be found in a contract or in the acceptance by the party of an offer of ICSID arbitration in a host state's investment law.[62]

Frequency of jurisdiction objections. In practice, the four conditions found in **7-045** Article 25(1) of the ICSID Convention routinely lead to objections to jurisdiction by the host state before the arbitral tribunal, and those objections are successful in a significant minority of cases. These regular jurisdiction objections and the additional expense and time they involve are, in practice, among the most important of ICSID arbitration's defining characteristics.

Preliminary review of jurisdiction. The Convention's jurisdiction conditions also **7-046** lead ICSID, the institution, to itself examine – sometimes at great length – whether the dispute is 'manifestly outside the jurisdiction of the Centre'.[63] ICSID conducts

---

jurisdiction of the ICSID disputes over compensation resulting from expropriation and nationalisation.' States' notifications under Art. 25(4) of the ICSID Convention are available at <http://icsid.worldbank.org>.

62. This condition will, in investment treaty cases, lead to a two-stage test: the determination of whether there is consent given through the investment treaty – in other words, whether all the conditions for application of the dispute resolution terms of the investment treaty are satisfied; *and* a determination of whether the other conditions set out in the ICSID Convention are fulfilled.

63. See Art. 36(3) of the ICSID Convention. Cases where ICSID is understood to have refused registration include a dispute where an investor, who was claiming under an investment treaty between its home state and the host state in which it had invested, asserted jurisdiction based on the consent of the host state to ICSID arbitration found not in the host state's treaty with the investor's home state, but in a treaty with another state; the claimant argued that the most-favoured-nation (MFN) provision in the treaty with its home state led the 'more favourable' consent in the treaty with the third state to be incorporated into the treaty with the home state, allowing the investor to sue on the basis of the latter treaty with consent to ICSID arbitration incorporated into it. ICSID refused to register the request, despite the MFN provision being successfully used in other cases to import provisions from another treaty concerning dispute resolution.

this exercise prior to registering the dispute, and from time to time the process does result in the refusal by ICSID of registration – which means the case cannot be submitted to an ICSID arbitral tribunal. There is no recourse within the ICSID system against a decision to refuse registration. ICSID's Arbitration Rules were recently amended to allow a party to make a preliminary objection before the arbitral tribunal that a claim is 'manifestly without legal merit'.[64] This new procedure is essentially an expedited mechanism for resolving, and ultimately deterring, frivolous claims. However, it means that an investor will have to address and prevail on the issue of jurisdiction on up to three occasions before an ICSID tribunal reaches the merits of its case: first, during the registration process; second, during the preliminary objection process; and third, when resisting fully-fledged objections to jurisdiction before the tribunal.

7-047 *Limited jurisdiction reduces appeal of ICSID for investors.* As access to ICSID arbitration is strictly limited by the Convention and an investor may have to argue issues of jurisdiction on up to three successive occasions, any claimant opting to have its dispute resolved by ICSID arbitration is likely to get embroiled in a long, expensive, and perhaps unsuccessful battle over jurisdiction. This is an important factor for an investor to weigh against the advantages of ICSID arbitration when offered a choice of another system of arbitration – a choice which many investment treaties do offer.

7-048 *Appointment of arbitrators.* The appointment and challenge of arbitrators in ICSID arbitrations do not differ greatly from the same processes in other arbitration systems: the general principle is that each party appoints one arbitrator and the institution appoints the third, who serves as chair. The ICSID Rules allow the parties to agree on the president of the tribunal or to agree that the co-arbitrators will choose the president.[65] If the parties or the co-arbitrators fail to agree within the time limit, the Chair of the ICSID Administrative Council will make the appointment.[66] Sole arbitrators are appointed only with the agreement of the parties. One difference from other arbitration systems is that appointments by ICSID must be made from one of its panels of arbitrators. ICSID's panels of arbitrators and conciliators comprise designees of the ICSID Contracting States on the one hand, and designees of the Chair of the ICSID Administrative Council.

7-049 *Typical profile of ICSID arbitrators.* Given the nature of ICSID arbitrations and the applicability of international law to the disputes, many arbitrators in ICSID arbitrations – especially those designated by ICSID itself – are more grounded in the world of public international law than arbitrators serving in most international

---

64. See ICSID Rule 41(5). See, for the first decision interpreting ICSID Arbitration Rule 41(5), *Trans-Global Petroleum, Inc. v. Jordan* (ICSID Case No. ARB/07/25), Decision on the Respondent's Objection under Rule 41(5) of the ICSID Arbitration Rules (12 May 2008), available at <http://ita.law.uvic.ca>.
65. See ICSID Rule 3.
66. See ICSID Rule 4.

commercial arbitrations. For example, former and serving judges of the International Court of Justice, and professors of public international law, are frequently appointed to ICSID tribunals.

Challenge of arbitrators. Another specificity of ICSID arbitration is that the **7-050** challenge of one member of the tribunal is decided by the other arbitrators. If they cannot agree, the Chair of ICSID's Administrative Council will decide, as will be the case if more than one arbitrator is challenged.[67]

Greater transparency of proceedings. Another defining feature of ICSID arbitra- **7-051** tion is that the proceedings are more transparent than ordinary international commercial arbitration. This means that information about the dispute (i.e., its existence, the names of the parties and of the members of the tribunal, as well as the status of the proceedings) is more available to the public, through ICSID's website. It also means that parties other than those to the dispute may participate in the case as amici curiae (friends of the court) in certain circumstances, that the public may attend the hearings under certain conditions (which include the agreement of the parties), and that ICSID awards (or sanitised extracts) are published.[68] Parties considering whether to start ICSID arbitration need to take full account of these departures from the traditional confidentiality of arbitration. In some cases, claimants may perceive the additional public scrutiny of the dispute to be a good thing – as a way of putting pressure on the government to settle the dispute, for example. On the other hand, certain claimants may not want to have their dispute publicly aired, and the involvement of third parties, such as NGOs, will often mean a longer, more expensive and more arduous arbitration, especially for claimants.[69]

Governing laws routinely include international law. Article 42(1) of the ICSID **7-052** Convention provides that international law will govern ICSID arbitrations, along with the law of the state party to the dispute, unless the governing law has been chosen by the parties. In practice, the parties to ICSID arbitrations – especially investment treaty cases – only infrequently agree upon a governing law, and therefore the default provision applies in most cases. Nothing in the ICSID Convention or Arbitration Rules clarifies the interrelationship between international law and the law of the host state in this more common, default situation. Arbitrators have held that the law applicable to the dispute in such a case is primarily the investment treaty.[70] This means that the disputing parties will need to base their claims and

---

67. See ICSID Rule 9.
68. See ICSID Rules 37(2), 38(2), and 48(4).
69. In the investment treaty cases where friends of the court have intervened, they have generally opposed the claimants' position, particularly where the dispute involves matters perceived to be of public interest. Examples include *Suez, Sociedad General de Aguas de Barcelona, S.A. and Vivendi Universal, S.A. v. Argentine Republic* (ICSID Case No. ARB/03/19), available at <http://ita.law.uvic.ca> which involved a dispute in relation to a water concession in Buenos Aires. In this case, the tribunal allowed a number of NGOs to make amicus curiae submissions.
70. See *Wena Hotels Ltd v. Arab Republic of Egypt* (ICSID Case No. ARB/98/4), (Annulment Proceeding), Decision rendered by the ad hoc Committee (18 Jan. 2002), available at <http://ita.law.uvic.ca>.

defences more on the vaguer norms of international law (including the nascent body of investment treaty law) than on any one municipal law.

7-053 *No legal seat of arbitration or supervision by courts.* In ICSID arbitration, there is no procedural seat in the traditional sense of a chosen place of arbitration which brings with it certain legal consequences (usually resulting from the arbitration law of the jurisdiction of the seat). None of the laws and regulations of a municipal jurisdiction apply to the arbitration, which remains governed by its own, self-contained set of norms contained in the ICSID Convention and the ICSID Arbitration Rules. This is unlike ordinary international arbitration, where the courts of the seat retain a supervisory role before and during the arbitration.

7-054 *Place of hearings.* As with ordinary arbitration, the place where hearings take place in ICSID arbitration is of no legal consequence (except, in very limited circumstances, where both parties agree).[71] ICSID hearings are held in Washington, DC,[72] unless the parties otherwise agree.[73] In practice, the parties do agree to hold ICSID hearings outside Washington, DC, including in London, Paris, The Hague, and Singapore.

7-055 *Annulment of awards within the ICSID system, not before national courts.* In the same way as national courts play no role during an ICSID arbitration, they cannot hear a challenge of (or action to set aside) an ICSID arbitral award. Instead, the challenge of ICSID awards is governed by the ICSID Convention, which allows a party dissatisfied with the award to challenge it in a bespoke process of 'annulment' before an 'ad hoc' committee of three members appointed by ICSID from its panels.[74] The grounds for annulment are somewhat different to those on which ordinary international awards may be set aside, although it is probably fair to say that the principles underlying both procedures are similar: neither challenge is an appeal, where the merits of the award are reviewed; instead, the integrity of the process is tested.

7-056 *Grounds for annulment.* The five, exhaustive grounds for annulment of an ICSID award are as follows:

- that the tribunal was not properly constituted;
- that the tribunal manifestly exceeded its powers;
- that there was corruption on the part of a member of the tribunal;
- that there was a serious departure from a fundamental rule of procedure; or
- that the award failed to state the reasons on which it is based.[75]

7-057 *Annulment in practice.* The ICSID annulment process has proved controversial in the past. Initial applications for annulment were successful, with ad hoc

---

71. See Art. 62 of the ICSID Convention.
72. See Art. 63 of the ICSID Convention.
73. See ICSID Rule 39(6) (Provisional Measures).
74. See Art. 52 of the ICSID Convention.
75. *Ibid.*

committees appearing to take a broad view of the scope of annulment. This approach attracted criticism, and some later ad hoc committees have taken a narrower view of the annulment process – some might say too narrow.[76] This being said, a number of ICSID awards have been annulled in recent years, and the ratio of ICSID annulments to annulment applications is still much higher than that of successful challenges before national courts of non-ICSID awards.[77] The fact remains that a participant in ICSID arbitration must come to terms with the absence of court control of the award, and the presence instead of an annulment process, the boundaries of which are not yet fully settled in practice.

Direct enforcement of ICSID awards as final judgments of highest local court. The **7-058** ICSID Convention governs the enforcement of ICSID awards in its Contracting States, and removes them, at least in theory, from the scope of review by national courts. Whereas the New York Convention allows the award debtor to resist enforcement in the courts of the jurisdiction of enforcement, the ICSID Convention requires all Member States to enforce ICSID awards directly, as if they were final judgments of the highest local court.[78] This clearly places an ICSID award creditor in a stronger position than a creditor of many ordinary international arbitration awards. However, an ICSID award creditor will still have to rely on the machinery of the courts and agencies of the enforcement jurisdiction in order to actually receive the awarded remedy – assuming the award debtor does not voluntarily comply with the award. More importantly (given that debtors of ICSID awards are generally states), the ICSID Convention explicitly stipulates that states party to an ICSID arbitration do not waive their immunity from execution by participating in the arbitration. Sovereign immunity, to the extent enjoyed by the debtor under the law of the enforcement jurisdiction, can therefore be an effective defence to the enforcement of an ICSID award. That defence will be heard by the courts of the enforcement jurisdiction.[79]

Are ICSID awards more enforceable? An ICSID award, because of the powerful **7-059** enforcement provisions of the ICSID Convention, is a significantly more enforceable title worldwide than an award rendered in an ordinary international commercial arbitration. This is borne out, perhaps, in the strong record of ICSID award debtors, which are mainly states, complying voluntarily with ICSID awards. One reason for this is surely that they evaluate their chances of successfully resisting enforcement to be low; another reason may be that they do

---

76. See, for instance, *CMS Gas Transmission Company v. Argentine Republic* (ICSID Case No. ARB/01/8), (Annulment Proceeding), Decision of the ad hoc Committee on the Application for Annulment of the Argentine Republic (25 Sep. 2007), available at <http://ita.law.uvic.ca>.
77. See, for a recent illustration, *Malaysian Historical Salvors, SDN, BHD v. Malaysia* (ICSID Case No. ARB/05/10), Decision on the Application for Annulment (16 Apr. 2009), available at <http://ita.law.uvic.ca>. See also, G. Verhoosel, 'Annulment and Enforcement Review of Treaty Awards: to ICSID or not ICSID?', ICCA Conference Book (2008).
78. See Art. 54 of the ICSID Convention.
79. Chapter 6, *After the Arbitration.*

not wish to be seen by the international community and the World Bank as having failed to comply with an award with a World Bank imprimatur.

7-060 *Predictability of outcomes in ICSID arbitration.* It is important for parties to remember that investment treaty arbitration is less predictable than ordinary international arbitration: it is really only in its infancy and has been developing rapidly and unevenly over the past ten years or so. There is no rule of binding precedent nor any appeals mechanism, with the consequence that the case law is unsettled, to say the least, on a number of key substantive and procedural questions (such as the meaning of 'fair and equitable treatment', the effect of 'umbrella clauses', and the use of an MFN clause with respect to dispute resolution).

Pros and cons of ICSID arbitration	**Pros:** • ICSID specialises in investment disputes between states and foreign investors. • Self-contained dispute resolution mechanism: local courts cannot interfere with the arbitration. • ICSID awards are directly binding in over 140 Contracting States and may be enforced as if final judgments of the local court of the state where enforcement is sought. • From the standpoint of the investor: higher profile of the claims and under the auspices of the World Bank, perhaps meaning more pressure on the host state. • Transparency of process, with proceedings subject to public scrutiny. **Cons:** • Slow (minimum two to three years). • High profile, not confidential (if discretion is of value). • Likely to be more expensive than commercial arbitration. • Limited predictability: developing area, with inconsistent case law.

Table of Appendices

Appendix 1

Glossary of International Arbitration Terms and Abbreviations

AAA	American Arbitration Association, a domestic US and international arbitration institution.
Ad hoc arbitration	Arbitration that is not administered by an arbitration institution. Contrast with institutional arbitration.
Ad hoc committee	The panel of three members which is appointed in ICSID arbitrations, on a case by case basis, to hear an action by one of the parties seeking to annul an award.
Action to set aside (an arbitral award)	A proceeding in which a party to an arbitration applies to a state court, usually located at the place of arbitration, to have an award rendered in that arbitration annulled, or set aside, generally on narrow grounds of a jurisdictional or procedural nature. Also referred to as the challenge of an award, or an action to annul an award. Contrast with an appeal and with enforcement proceedings.
Advance on costs	An advance payment made by a party, usually to an arbitration institution, to cover the costs of the arbitration. The costs of the arbitration for these purposes generally comprise the fees and expenses of the arbitrators and the administrative expenses of the arbitration institution (if one is involved).
Annulment (of an arbitral award)	Action to set aside (an arbitral award).

Answer	The respondent's written reply to the request for arbitration, which may also contain an objection to jurisdiction and a counterclaim.
Appeal	A judicial remedy which allows a state court to re-examine one or more aspects of a dispute, and notably the merits of a dispute, decided by a lower court or an arbitral tribunal. Contrast with action to set aside in the context of international arbitration.
Appointing authority	The arbitration institution or other entity designated, by the parties, a state court or another body, to appoint one or more arbitrators in a given arbitration.
Arbitral award (or 'award')	The final decision of the arbitrators on all or part of the dispute submitted to them. It may be a partial award, an interim award, a final award, a consent award, a declaratory award or a default award.
Arbitration institution	The body that administers the arbitration, performing tasks such as the appointment of arbitrators, handling their payment and scrutinising draft awards. Institutions usually also issue arbitration rules and model arbitration clauses.
Arbitral tribunal	The arbitrator or arbitrators appointed to resolve a given dispute.
Arbitration	Binding resolution of dispute by an arbitral tribunal.
Arbitration agreement	An agreement by which two or more parties agree that present or future disputes are to be resolved by arbitration.
Arbitration clause	An arbitration agreement which is included in a broader contract (which is often referred to as the main contract).
Arbitration rules	A set of rules which govern the procedure followed in an arbitration. Often issued by an arbitration institution.
Arbitrator	A person appointed to an arbitral tribunal directly or indirectly by the parties.
BAC	Beijing Arbitration Commission, an arbitration institution in china.
CEDR	Center for Effective Dispute Resolution, a mediation institution.
CIETAC	China International Economic and Trade Arbitration Commission, an arbitration institution in china.

CIArb	Chartered Institute of Arbitrators.
Chair	The arbitrator who chairs the arbitral tribunal (known as the President in ICSID arbitration).
Claimant	The party who initiates the arbitration by issuing a request for arbitration or similar document.
Closing of proceedings	The cut-off date declared by the arbitral tribunal beyond which no new document or evidence can be submitted unless requested or authorised by the arbitral tribunal.
Closing submissions	Oral presentation by a party's representative at the end of a hearing which summarises the party's case and its evidence (especially that emerging at the hearing).
CMAP	Paris Arbitration and Mediation Center, an arbitration and mediation institution.
Competence-Competence	Doctrine under which an arbitral tribunal is the first instance with jurisdiction to decide its own jurisdiction over a dispute.
Consent award	A settlement reached by the parties which is recorded by the arbitral tribunal in the form of an award.
Counterclaim	A claim by the respondent against the claimant. Usually filed with the respondent's answer.
CPR	The International Institute for Conflict Prevention and Resolution, a US arbitration institution.
CRCICA	Cairo Regional Center for International Commercial Arbitration, an arbitration institution.
Cross-examination	First round of oral questioning of a witness or expert by the party which did not present the witness or expert. Follows direct examination and usually followed by re-direct examination.
DIAC	Dubai International Arbitration Centre, an arbitration institution.
DIFC-LCIA	Dubai International Financial Centre, which created an arbitration institution in partnership with the LCIA.
Direct examination	First round of oral questioning of a witness or expert by the party which presented the witness or expert. Precedes cross-examination.
Directions	Procedural instructions issued by the arbitral tribunal.

DIS	German Arbitration Institute, an arbitration institution.
Early Case Assessment	An internal process undertaken by a party at the outset of a dispute to assess possible outcomes and strategies. Commonly referred to as an ECA.
ECA	See Early Case Assessment.
Expert	A person with special skills, technical knowledge or professional qualifications called upon by the parties to give evidence or by the tribunal to assist it in reaching its award. Sometimes described as an expert witness.
Expert report	The evidence given by an expert in writing. Also referred to as an expert opinion.
Final award	Generally used to refer to the award on the last aspect of the dispute in question.
Hearing	Appearance of parties, usually represented by counsel, before an arbitral tribunal. Final hearing sometimes referred to, using litigation parlance, as a trial.
HKIAC	Hong Kong International Arbitration Centre, an arbitration institution.
IBA	The International Bar Association, a grouping of lawyers which, in the field of international arbitration, has issued rules on the taking of evidence in international arbitration, and guidelines on conflicts of interest in international arbitration.
IBA Guidelines (on Conflicts)	The IBA Guidelines on Conflicts of Interest in International Arbitration, adopted by the IBA on 22 May 2004, which address the impartiality, independence and duty of disclosure of arbitrators.
IBA Rules (of Evidence)	The IBA Rules on the Taking of Evidence in International Commercial Arbitration, adopted by the IBA on 1 June 1999, and widely used today as rules or guidelines in international arbitration.
ICC	International Chamber of Commerce, an international arbitration institution.
ICDR	International Centre for Dispute Resolution, the international arm of the AAA.
IMI	International Mediation Institute, a Netherlands based institute promoting international mediation standards and providing an international database of experienced mediators.

ICSID	International Centre for Settlement of Investment Disputes, an arm of the World Bank and an arbitration institution, specialised in the resolution of investment disputes between foreign investors and states.
Institutional arbitration	Arbitration that is administered by an arbitral arbitration institution. Contrast with ad hoc arbitration.
Insurance notification	Notification by a party against which a claim is made to its insurers informing the insurers of the claim.
Interim award	An 'award' of interim relief. Sometimes used to mean a partial award, i.e. an award finally disposing of part of the dispute.
JAMS	Judicial Arbitration and Mediation Services Inc., a US arbitration and mediation institution.
JAMS International ADR Center	The International arm of JAMS
JCCA	Japanese Commercial Arbitration Association, an arbitration institution.
KCAB	Korean Commercial Arbitration Board, an arbitration institution.
KLRCA	Kuala Lumpur Regional Centre for Arbitration, an arbitration institution.
LCIA	London Court of International Arbitration, an international arbitration institution.
Language of arbitration	The language in which the arbitration is conducted. There may be more than one language of an arbitration.
Lex arbitri	The law of the place of the arbitration, usually considered to be the law governing the arbitration and, at least in literal translation, the law of the arbitration. Contrast with the law governing the contract or the merits of an arbitration.
Lex mercatoria	Transnational rules which are created by and for the participants in international trade and which may be chosen by the parties or the arbitral tribunal to govern the merits of an arbitration.
Memorandum of Issues	A document signed by the parties and the tribunal in a SIAC arbitration, which defines the issues to be determined by the arbitral tribunal.

Memorials	The principal written statements by the parties of their respective cases. Sometimes referred to as briefs or submissions. Different memorials may be described as statement of claim (or statement of case, or simply memorial), statement of defence (or counter-memorial), reply and rejoinder.
Milan Court of Arbitration	A regional arbitration institution affiliated with the Milan Chamber of Commerce in Italy
Model Law	A model arbitration statute adopted by UNCITRAL in 1985 (amended in 2006) and enacted, usually in modified form, by many countries around the world.
Multi-party arbitration	Arbitration between more than two parties.
NAI	Netherlands Arbitration Institute, an arbitration institution.
New York Convention	The New York Convention on the Recognition and Enforcement of Foreign Arbitral Awards, signed on 10 June 1958, which facilitates the worldwide enforcement of arbitration agreements and the worldwide recognition and enforcement of arbitral awards.
Notice of Arbitration	Initial pleading in some forms of arbitration, similar to request for arbitration.
Opening statement	Oral presentation by a party representative immediately before the hearing of witnesses that summarises the salient points of the party's case and may introduce the witnesses.
Order	A decision issued by the arbitral tribunal, usually on matters of procedure.
Partial award	An award which deals with some, but not all, aspects of a dispute.
Party-appointed arbitrator	An arbitrator nominated, or appointed, to the arbitral tribunal by one of the parties. Sometimes referred to as 'wingman'.
Party representative	A person acting for, or speaking on behalf of, a party to the arbitration. Usually a lawyer.
Place of arbitration	The city to which the arbitration is attached in a legal sense. Will be selected by the parties, the arbitration institution or the arbitral tribunal. Also known as the seat of arbitration.

Post-hearing submission	Written submission by a party after a hearing, which usually addresses evidence emerging at the hearing and specific questions raised by the tribunal. It may also summarise each party's case.
Pre-hearing/pre-trial conference	A conference held in the weeks before the main hearing, and often conducted by telephone, attended by the parties (usually through their representatives) and the arbitral tribunal, at which the conduct of the hearing is organised.
Provisional measures	Measures that are granted by a court or arbitral tribunal to support the arbitration, or preserve a party's rights during the pendency of the arbitration, or to preserve evidence. Sometimes referred to as interim or interlocutory or conservatory measures.
Provisional timetable	A timetable drawn up by the arbitral tribunal in ICC arbitrations in consultation with the parties, setting out the provisional schedule for the conduct of the remainder of the arbitration.
Reply	The claimant's initial submission, in ICC arbitration, in which it addresses any counterclaims filed by the respondent. Also used to describe a claimant's second memorial.
Request for arbitration	The claimant's written submission which commences the arbitration and outlines the claimant's claims, the relief it seeks, and its desire to have the claims resolved in arbitration. Notice of arbitration is similar.
Request to produce	A written request by one party to the other or to the arbitral tribunal seeking the production of documents by the other party.
Respondent	The party to the arbitration against whom the claim or claims are made.
Seat of arbitration	The place of arbitration.
SCC	Arbitration Institute of the Stockholm Chamber of Commerce, an international arbitration institution.
SIAC	Singapore International Arbitration Centre, an international arbitration institution.
Skeleton argument	An outline of a party's position on the facts and the law which is usually presented at or shortly before a hearing on those issues. A creature of English court practice. Pleading notes are the civil law equivalent.

Stay of proceedings	Suspension of a judicial action. In an arbitration context, often refers to the suspension of a court action while the claim brought before the court is resolved in arbitration.
Submissions	Oral or written argument by a party in an arbitration.
TAB	Arbitration Tribunal of Barcelona, a domestic arbitration institution in Spain.
Terms of reference	A document signed by the parties and the tribunal in an ICC arbitration, that is issued at an early stage of an ICC arbitration, and determines the parties' claims and counterclaims, as well as the main procedural rules applicable in the arbitration.
Transnational rules	See lex mercatoria.
UNCITRAL	United Nations Commission on International Trade Law, a commission of the United Nations which has promulgated arbitration rules (the UNCITRAL Arbitration Rules) for parties to adopt for ad hoc arbitration proceedings and the Model Law for states to adopt as their domestic civil procedure law governing arbitral proceedings.
Witness	Individual who gives evidence of fact in an arbitration, at the request of a party or, occasionally, the arbitral tribunal.
Witness statement	The written statement of a witness setting out the evidence of that witness.

Appendix 2

Caseload of Selected Arbitral Institutions*

Arbitration Institution	Number of Cases Filed								
	2000	2001	2002	2003	2004	2005	2006	2007	2008
American Arbitration Association (AAA)	510	649	672	646	614	580	586	621	703
China International Economic and Trade Arbitration Association (CIETAC)	543	562	468	422	461	427	442	429	548
Hong Kong International Arbitration Centre (HKIAC)	298	307	320	287	280	281	394	448	602
International Chamber of Commerce (ICC)	541	566	593	580	561	521	593	599	663
International Centre for Settlement of Investment Disputes (ICSID) (including cases under the ICSID Additional Facility Rules)	12	12	16	30	27	26	24	35	31

* For reasons explained in Chapter 1, we have reservations about the accuracy of certain of these figures, or at least about whether the 'number of international cases administered' is understood in the same way by all institutions. These figures were obtained from the websites of the respective institutions, with the following exceptions: the AAA statistics were obtained from the SIAC and HKIAC websites; the statistics for 2000 and 2001 for CIETAC, LCIA and SCC were obtained from the SIAC website.

Arbitration Institution	Number of Cases Filed								
	2000	2001	2002	2003	2004	2005	2006	2007	2008
London Court of International Arbitration (LCIA)	87	71	88	104	87	118	133	137	221
Singapore International Arbitration Centre (SIAC)	41	44	38	35	48	45	65	70	71
Arbitration Institute of the Stockholm Chamber of Commerce (SCC)	66	68	55	82	50	56	74	87	85

Appendix 3

List of Selected International Arbitration and Mediation Institutions, Rules, Laws, Conventions and Other Instruments

I.   INTERNATIONAL ARBITRATION AND MEDIATION INSTITUTIONS AND RULES

Arbitration Institution	Arbitration Rules	Weblink
American Arbitration Association (AAA)/ International Centre for Dispute Resolution (ICDR)	International Dispute Resolution Procedures (including Mediation and Arbitration Rules) (Effective 1 September 2007)	http://www.adr.org/commercial_arbitration
China International Economic and Trade Arbitration Association (CIETAC)	CIETAC Arbitration Rules (Effective 1 May 2005)	http://www.cietac.org.cn/

Arbitration Institution	Arbitration Rules	Weblink
Hong Kong International Arbitration Centre (HKIAC)	Administered Arbitration Rules (Effective 1 September 2008) Mediation Rules (Effective 1 August 1999)	http://www.hkiac.org/show_content.php?article_id=34 http://www.hkiac.org/documents/en_mediation.pdf
International Chamber of Commerce (ICC)	Rules of Arbitration (Effective 1 January 1998; cost scales effective 1 January 2008) ADR Rules (in force as of 1 July 2001)	http://www.iccwbo.org/uploadedFiles/Court/Arbitration/other/rules_arb_english.pdf http://www.iccwbo.org/uploadedFiles/Court/Arbitration/other/adr_rules.pdf
International Centre for Settlement of Investment Disputes (ICSID)	Rules of Procedure for Arbitration Proceedings (Arbitration Rules) (Effective 10 April 2006) Rules of Procedure for Conciliation Proceedings (Conciliation Rules) (Effective 10 April 2006)	http://icsid.worldbank.org/ICSID/ICSID/RulesMain.jsp
London Court of International Arbitration (LCIA)	LCIA Arbitration Rules (Effective 1 January 1998) LCIA Mediation Procedure (Effective 1 October 1999)	http://www.lcia.org/ARB_folder/arb_english_main.htm http://www.lcia.org
Singapore International Arbitration Centre (SIAC)	Arbitration Rules of the SIAC (Effective 1 July 2007)	http://www.siac.org.sg/rules-siac.htm
Arbitration Institute of the Stockholm Chamber of Commerce (SCC)	Arbitration Rules of the Arbitration Institute of the SCC (Effective 1 January 2007) Rules of the Mediation Institute of the SCC (Effective 1 April 1999)	http://www.sccinstitute.com/skiljeforfarande-2.aspx http://www.sccinstitute.com/?id=23721

Swiss Arbitration Association (ASA)	Swiss Rules of International Arbitration (Effective 1 January 2004)	http://www.sccam.org/sa/en/ rules.php
N/A	United Nations Commission on International Trade Law, a commission of the United Nations (UNCITRAL) Arbitration Rules	http://www.uncitral.org/pdf/ english/texts/arbitration/ arb-rules/arb-rules.pdf
	UNCITRAL Conciliation Rules	http://www.uncitral.org/

II. LEGISLATION

Country	Title of Law	Weblink
China	Arbitration Law of the People's Republic of China (1994)	http://www.cietac.org.cn/
England	Arbitration Act 1996	http://www.opsi.gov.uk/ ACTS/acts1996/ 1996023.htm
France	New Code of Civil Procedure, Articles 1442 to 1507	http://www.legifrance.gouv.fr/ initRechCodeArticle. do (French) http://www.legifrance. gouv.fr/html/codes_traduits/ somncpca.htm (English translation)
Germany	Code of Civil Procedure, Chapter 10	http://www.dis-arb.de/ materialien/ schiedsverfahrensrecht98- e.html
Hong Kong	Arbitration Ordinance (Amended in 1996 and 2000)	http://www.legislation.gov.hk/ eng/home.htm
Singapore	International Arbitration Act 1994 – Chapter 143A	http://statutes.agc.gov.sg
Sweden	The Swedish Arbitration Act of 1999 (SFS 1999:116)	http://www.sccinstitute.com/ the-swedish-arbitration-act- sfs-1999121.aspx

Country	Title of Law	Weblink
Switzerland	Federal Statute of Private International Law 1987, Chapter 12 on International Arbitration (Articles 176 to 194)	http://www.admin.ch/ch/f/rs/ 291/index.html (French) https://www.sccam.org/sa/ download/ IPRG_english.pdf (English translation)
USA	The Federal Arbitration Act	http://www.adr.org/ sp.asp?id=29568
UNCITRAL	UNCITRAL Model Law on International Commercial Arbitration 1985 (With amendments adopted in 2006)	http://www.uncitral.org/pdf/ english/texts/arbitration/ ml-arb/07-86998_Ebook.pdf

III.   CONVENTIONS

Short Title	Full Title	Weblink
Energy Charter Treaty	Energy Charter Treaty (1994)	http://www.encharter.org/ index.php?id=28&L=0
European Convention	European Convention on International Commercial Arbitration (1961)	http://www.jurisint.org/en/ins/ 153.html
ICSID Convention	Convention on the Settlement of Investment Disputes Between States and Nationals of Other States (1965)	http://www.worldbank.org/ icsid/basicdoc/partA.htm
Inter-American Convention	Inter-American Convention on International Commercial Arbitration (1975)	http://www.oas.org/juridico/ English/treaties/b-35.html
NAFTA	North American Free Trade Agreement (1992)	http://www.nafta-sec-alena.org
New York Convention	Convention on the Recognition and Enforcement of Foreign Arbitral Awards (1958)	http://www.uncitral.org/ uncitral/en/uncitral_texts/ arbitration/NYConvention. html

IV.   OTHER INTERNATIONAL INSTRUMENTS

Short Title	Full Title	Weblink
Chartered Institute of Arbitrators' Practice Guidelines and Protocols on Arbitration and Mediation		http://www.ciarb.org/ information-and-resources/ practice-guidelines- and-protocols/
IBA Guidelines (on Conflicts)	IBA Guidelines on Conflicts of Interest in International Arbitration, adopted by the IBA on 22 May 2004	http://www.ibanet.org/ Publications/publications_ IBA_guides_and_free_ materials.aspx
IBA Rules (of Evidence)	IBA Rules on the Taking of Evidence in International Commercial Arbitration, adopted by the IBA on 1 June 1999	http://www.ibanet.org/ Publications/publications_ IBA_guides_and_free_ materials.aspx
ICC – Small Claims Guidelines	Guidelines for Arbitrating Small Claims under the ICC Rules of Arbitration	http://www.iccwbo.org/court/ arbitration/id4095/ index.html
ICC – Techniques for Controlling and Costs	Techniques for Controlling Time and Costs in Arbitration – Report from the ICC Commission on Arbitration	http://www.iccwbo.org/ uploadedFiles/ TimeCost_E.pdf
UNCITRAL Notes	UNCITRAL Notes on Organizing Arbitral Proceedings	http://www.uncitral.org/pdf/ english/texts/arbitration/ arb-notes/arb-notes-e.pdf

Appendix 4

Model Clauses for Institutional Arbitration

Model Clause for Institutional Arbitration

All disputes arising out of or in connection with the present contract shall be finally settled by arbitration under the auspices of [*insert name of arbitration institution*] in accordance with [*insert name of rules of arbitration, preferably rules promulgated by that institution*].

The number of arbitrators shall be [*select and insert* 'one' *or* 'three'].

The seat of arbitration shall be [*insert name of city and country*].

The language of the arbitration shall be [*specify the language*].

Model Clause for Mediation Followed by Institutional Arbitration

ATTEMPT AT SETTLEMENT. In the event of a dispute, controversy, or claim arising out of or relating to this agreement, including any question regarding its existence, validity, breach, or termination, the parties shall first seek settlement of that dispute by mediation in accordance with the rules of mediation of [*insert name of institution providing mediation services and its mediation rules*].

ARBITRATION. If the dispute is not settled by mediation within [*insert number*] days of the first referral of the dispute to mediation by either party, or such further period as the parties shall agree in writing, the dispute shall be referred to and finally resolved by arbitration under the auspices of [*insert name of arbitration institution*] in accordance with [*insert name of rules of arbitration, preferably rules promulgated by that institution*].

The number of arbitrators shall be [*select and insert* 'one' *or* 'three'].

The seat of arbitration shall be [*insert name of city and country*].

The language of the arbitration shall be [*specify the language*].

Appendix 5
Model Clause for Ad Hoc Arbitration

All disputes arising out of or in connection with the present contract shall be finally settled by arbitration in accordance with the UNCITRAL Arbitration Rules.

The appointing authority shall be [*insert name of institution or person selected as appointing authority*]. Pursuant to Article 6 of the UNCITRAL Arbitration Rules, the functions referred to in articles 11(3), 11(4), 13(3), 14, 16(3) and 34(2) shall be performed by [*name of appointing authority*].

The number of arbitrators shall be [*select and insert* 'one' *or* 'three'].

The seat of arbitration shall be [*insert name of city and country*].

The language of the arbitration shall be [*specify the language*].

Appendix 6

Model Early Case Assessment (ECA) Template

Parties and counsel (if any):

Place of dispute resolution (country/city):

Court/arbitral body:

Applicable law(s):

Judge/arbitrators (if appointed):

Summary of case and claims:

Current status (claim filed/arbitration notified):

Assessment of judge/arbitrator(s)/Opposing counsel:

Key legal issues:

Key factual issues:

Key witnesses:

Amount of claims:

Amount of counterclaims:

Estimated costs of dispute resolution through conclusion:

Current assessment of range of exposure, and likely outcome if case is not settled:

Factors (legal or factual issues) that could materially impact range of potential outcomes:

Assessment of settlement potential:

Recommendation of settlement methods (negotiation, mediation, etc.):

Strategy if no settlement:

Appendix 7

Suggested Model Request for Arbitration for ICC Arbitration[1]

INTERNATIONAL CHAMBER OF COMMERCE

INTERNATIONAL COURT OF ARBITRATION

[INSERT NAME OF CLAIMANT]

Claimant

v.

[INSERT NAME OF RESPONDENT]

Respondent

REQUEST FOR ARBITRATION

[Insert name and address of the Claimant's counsel]
Counsel for the Claimant

[Insert Date]

---

1. Note: this and all suggested submissions and instruments appearing in these appendices are prepared by the authors without the involvement or approval of the ICC.

[*NAME OF THE CLAIMANT*]

v.

[*NAME OF THE RESPONDENT*]

REQUEST FOR ARBITRATION

TABLE OF CONTENTS

I.   INTRODUCTION

1.   [*Insert name of Claimant*] (the '**Claimant**'), hereby requests arbitration against [*insert name of Respondent*] (the '**Respondent**') under the Rules of Arbitration of the International Chamber of Commerce (the '**ICC Rules**') in connection with [*briefly describe the transaction and/or contract under which the dispute arises*].

2.   [*Optional: include brief (one or two paragraph) and argumentative summary of the Claimant's case*]

3.   Pursuant to Article 4(3) of the ICC Rules, the Claimant sets out below: (II) the particulars of the parties; (III) a description of the nature and circumstances of the dispute giving rise to the claims against the Respondent; (IV) a statement of the relief sought; (V) details of the arbitration agreement; (VI) relevant particulars concerning arbitrators; and (VII) comments relating to certain aspects of the arbitral procedure.

4.   The Claimant submits with this Request for Arbitration [*state total number of exhibits*] exhibits, numbered from C-1 to C-[*state number of last exhibit*]. [*Note: as a Request for Arbitration is generally a brief and summary document, the number of exhibits will likely be small*] The letter C indicates that the exhibit in question was produced by the Claimant. [*Note: we would advise referring in footnotes or in the body of the submission to exhibits and other support for a party's submissions*]

II.   THE PARTIES

A.   THE CLAIMANT

5. [*Provide full name, type of entity, country of incorporation/principal place of business and description of business of the Claimant (Article 4(3) of the ICC Rules). Attaching certificate of incorporation or good standing may be advisable if the Claimant is not well known. Attaching the Claimant's latest annual report and/or referring to its website is often sensible*]

6. The contact details for the Claimant are as follows:

[*Insert contact details of the Claimant*]

7. In this arbitration, the Claimant is represented by its duly authorised counsel:

[*Insert full name, address and contact details (including telephone, fax and e-mail) of the Claimant's counsel*]

A power of attorney executed by [*name*], a duly authorised representative of the Claimant, on behalf of the Claimant and in favour of [*name of counsel*] is attached at **Exhibit C-1**. All communications for the attention of the Claimant in connection with this arbitration should be directed to [*insert name of Claimant's counsel*].

B.   THE RESPONDENT

8. [*Provide full name, type of entity, country of incorporation/principal place of business and description of business of the Respondent (Article 4(3) of the ICC Rules)*]

9. The Respondent's contact details are as follows:

[*Insert contact details of the Respondent*]

III.   NATURE AND CIRCUMSTANCES OF THE DISPUTE

10. [*Insert a description of the nature and circumstances of the dispute giving rise to the claim, the basis of the Claimant's argument(s) and details of the agreement(s) under which the dispute arises. Attach these agreement(s) as exhibits to the Request for Arbitration (see Article 4(3) of the ICC Rules)*]

IV.   RELIEF SOUGHT BY THE CLAIMANT

11. For the reasons set forth in this Request for Arbitration and in subsequent submissions, the Claimant requests that the Tribunal to be constituted in this arbitration issue an award: [*state the relief that the Claimant is seeking including, to the extent possible, an indication of any amount(s) claimed (see Rule 4(3) of the ICC Rules). This will usually include some, or all, of the following requests to the Arbitral Tribunal in addition to the principal relief sought (such as damages or specific performance)*]

(a) ...;
(b) ...;
(c) ordering the payment by the Respondent of interest to the Claimant on the sums awarded to the Claimant, such interest to be at [*state appropriate rate or rates, whether simple or compounded, and if compounded, how frequently*] payable from [*appropriate date from which interest is to run*] until final payment of the awarded sums is received by the Claimant;
(d) ordering the reimbursement to the Claimant by the Respondent of all costs and expenses incurred by the Claimant in pursuing the arbitration, including without limitation all fees and expenses of the arbitrators, the ICC, legal counsel, experts, consultants, witnesses and the Claimant's own officers and employees;
(e) ordering that the award shall be immediately enforceable, notwithstanding the pendency of any action to set it aside; and
(f) granting all further or other relief which the Tribunal deems appropriate.

V.   THE ARBITRATION AGREEMENT

12.   The arbitration agreement pursuant to which the Claimant is now requesting arbitration is found at [*insert relevant clause reference and the name of the agreement containing the arbitration agreement*]. The arbitration provides as follows:

[*Set out in full the text of this provision (see Article 4(3) of the ICC Rules)*]

VI.   RELEVANT PARTICULARS CONCERNING ARBITRATORS

13.   [*Refer to the provision of the arbitration agreement which specifies the number of arbitrators to be appointed and how they are nominated and appointed (see Article 4(3) of the ICC Rules). If this is not stated in the arbitration agreement, the Claimant should suggest the number of arbitrators (one or three) and ask the Respondent to agree and/or the ICC Court of Arbitration to so decide*]

14.   [*If the arbitration agreement and the ICC Rules permit the Claimant to nominate an arbitrator*] The Claimant nominates as arbitrator for confirmation by the ICC Court, [*give name of nominee, and his/her contact details (address, telephone number, fax number and e-mail address) (Article 4(3) of the ICC Rules)*]

15.   [*If the arbitration agreement and the ICC Rules do not permit the Claimant to nominate an arbitrator, insert a paragraph which is appropriate in light of the* *arbitration agreement and the ICC Rules: e.g. requesting the ICC Court to appoint a sole arbitrator, or all the arbitrators, or requesting the Respondent to contact the Claimant to select a sole arbitrator candidate, or proposing a sole arbitrator candidate for the Respondent's consideration]*

16.   The Claimant confirms that, to the best of its knowledge, *[name of nominated or proposed arbitrator]* is willing to serve as arbitrator in this arbitration and is independent of the Parties.

VII.   COMMENTS AS TO PROCEDURE

17.   *[Identify the provisions of the applicable agreements(s) which state (a) the place of the arbitration; (b) the language of the arbitration; and (c) the governing law, and specify what each of these is]*

18.   *[In some cases, the Claimant may request the ICC Court or the Arbitral Tribunal to take certain specific measures, such as expediting the arbitration, because of particular circumstances or because the parties' arbitration clause provides for it. If so, reasons should be given to support this request]*

19.   The Claimant reserves its right to amend and amplify its claims, and the relief that it seeks, during the course of the arbitration.

20.   In accordance with Article 3(1) of the ICC Rules, this Request for Arbitration, together with all accompanying documents, is submitted in *[number]* copies.

[Note: Article 3(1) of the ICC Rules requires the Claimant to submit one copy for each party plus one for each arbitrator and one for the Secretariat of the International Court of Arbitration. So, for example, if there are two parties and three arbitrators, the Request should be submitted in six copies]

21.   In accordance with Article 4(4) of the ICC Rules, a cheque of USD 2,500 accompanies this Request, in payment of the advance on costs prescribed in Appendix III, Article 1(1) of the ICC Rules.

[Alternatively, the Claimant may prefer to make a wire transfer to the ICC using bank details found on its website at http://www.iccwbo.org/court/arbitration/. If so, we would recommend that this be done before the Request is filed and evidence of the transfer exhibited with the Request]

[insert date]

Respectfully submitted on behalf of the Claimant,
[Insert name of the Claimant]

By: *[Claimant's counsel to sign]*

[Insert names of Claimant's counsel and firm]

Exhibits to Request for Arbitration	
C-1	[*insert description of exhibit, including nature of document, date, author and addressee as appropriate*]
C-2	[*as above, and the same again for all exhibits provided*]

Appendix 8

Model Answer to Request for Arbitration [and Counterclaim] for ICC Arbitration[1]

INTERNATIONAL CHAMBER OF COMMERCE

INTERNATIONAL COURT OF ARBITRATION

ICC Case No. [*insert case number*]

[*INSERT NAME OF CLAIMANT*]

Claimant

v.

[*INSERT NAME OF RESPONDENT*]

Respondent

_____

**ANSWER TO REQUEST FOR ARBITRATION
[AND COUNTERCLAIM]**

_____

[*Insert name and address of Respondent's counsel*]

[*Insert Date*]   Counsel for the Respondent

_____

1. Note: this and all suggested submissions and instruments appearing in these appendices are prepared by the authors without the involvement or approval of the ICC.

[*NAME OF CLAIMANT*]

v.

[*NAME OF RESPONDENT*]

ANSWER TO REQUEST FOR ARBITRATION [AND COUNTERCLAIM]

TABLE OF CONTENTS

I.   INTRODUCTION

1. [*Insert name of Respondent*] (the '**Respondent**') [*Note: if a counterclaim is raised, the Respondent may wish to define itself as 'Respondent and Counterclaimant'*] submits this Answer [and Counterclaim] [*Note: all references to counterclaim should be included if the Respondent is advancing a counterclaim*] (the '**Answer**'), in response to the Request for Arbitration (the '**Request**') submitted by the Claimant [*insert name of Claimant*] (the '**Claimant**') dated [*insert date of Request*].

2. Save where expressly admitted herein, the Respondent denies all allegations made by the Claimant in the Request. [*Set out any further reservations, such as that the Respondent is challenging jurisdiction and is therefore participating in this arbitration and making this submission without prejudice to that objection to jurisdiction*]

3. [*Optional: include brief (one or two paragraph) and argumentative summary of the Respondent's case*]

4. In accordance with Article 5.1 of the ICC Rules of Arbitration, the Respondent sets out below: (II) its name, description and address; (III) its comments as to the nature and circumstances of the dispute giving rise to the claims; (IV) the relief it seeks; (V) its comments concerning the nomination of arbitrators, and (VI) its comments concerning the place of arbitration, the applicable rules of law and the language of the arbitration. [*if the Respondent objects to jurisdiction and/or raises a counterclaim, include sections on the objection and the nature and circumstances of counterclaim*]

5. The Respondent submits with this Answer [*state total number of exhibits*] exhibits, numbered from R-1 to R-[*state number of last exhibit*]. [*As an Answer is generally a brief and summary document, the number of exhibits will generally be small*] The letter R indicates that the exhibit in question was produced by the Respondent. [*Note: we would advise referring in footnotes or in the body of the submission to exhibits and other support for a party's submissions*]

II.   THE RESPONDENT'S NAME IN FULL, DESCRIPTION AND ADDRESS

6. [*Provide full name, address, type of entity, country of incorporation/principal place of business and description of business of the Respondent (Article 5(1) of the ICC Rules). Attaching certificate of incorporation or good standing may be advisable if the Respondent is not well known. Attaching the Respondent's latest annual report and/or referring to its website is often sensible*]

7. The contact details of the Respondent are as follows:

[*Insert contact details of the Respondent*]

8. In this arbitration, the Respondent is represented by:

[*Insert full name, address and contact details (including telephone, fax and e-mail) of the Respondent's counsel*]

A power of attorney executed by [*duly authorised representative of the Respondent*] on behalf of the Respondent and in favour of [*name of counsel*] is attached at **Exhibit R-1**. All communications for the attention of the Respondent in connection with this arbitration should be directed to [*insert name of Respondent's counsel*].

III.   THE RESPONDENT'S COMMENTS AS TO THE NATURE AND CIRCUMSTANCES OF THE DISPUTE GIVING RISE TO THE CLAIMS

9. [*State again whether the Respondent denies all claims and allegations made by the Claimant in the Request*]

10. [*If the Respondent denies any/all claims and allegations made by the Claimant, it should briefly comment on each denied claim and allegation and provide its summary arguments in support of its case. All documents to which the Respondent refers in the Answer which are not attached as exhibits to the Request for Arbitration should be attached as exhibits to the Answer.*]

IV.   RELIEF SOUGHT

11. [*State the Respondent's response to the relief sought by the Claimant, and the relief which it seeks itself. If the Respondent simply denies all the claims made by the Claimant, its response regarding the relief sought will usually be along the following lines*]

12. For the reasons set out in this Answer and to be developed in future submissions, the Claimant is entitled to none of the relief which it seeks in the Request. For the same reasons, the Respondent requests that the Tribunal issue a final award:

  (a) dismissing with prejudice all claims advanced by the Claimant; [*Note: if the Respondent objects to jurisdiction, the relief first requested should be a declaration that the Tribunal lacks jurisdiction over the claims advanced and their dismissal on that basis, with the subsequent request for a dismissal on the merits being made in the alternative*];
  (b) [*If the Respondent has submitted a counterclaim as part of its Answer, include the relief it seeks in respect of the counterclaim, including, to the extent possible, an indication of any amounts counterclaimed (Article 5(5) of ICC Rules). Include a request for interest and immediate enforcement, as per model Request for Arbitration*];
  (c) ordering the reimbursement to the respondent by the claimant of all costs and expenses incurred by the Respondent in pursuing the arbitration, including without limitation all fees and expenses of the arbitrators, the ICC, legal counsel, experts, consultants, witnesses and the Respondent's own officers and employees; and
  (d) granting all further or other relief which the Tribunal deems appropriate.

V.   COMMENTS CONCERNING NOMINATION
                 OF ARBITRATORS

13. [*State the Respondent's position concerning the number of arbitrators and the method of their selection in light of the Claimant's position on these points set forth in the Request*]

14. [*If the arbitration agreement and the ICC Rules permit the Respondent to nominate an arbitrator*] The Respondent nominates as arbitrator for confirmation by the ICC Court [*give name of nominee, and his/her contact details (address, telephone number, fax number and e-mail address) (Article 4(3) of the ICC Rules)*].

15. [*If the arbitration agreement and the ICC Rules do not permit the Respondent to nominate an arbitrator, insert a paragraph which is appropriate in light of the arbitration agreement, the ICC Rules, and the position taken by the Claimant on these issues in the request, e.g., stating or agreeing with the Claimant that the ICC Court should appoint a sole arbitrator, or all the arbitrators, or agreeing with the*

Claimant's proposed sole arbitrator candidate, or proposing a candidate for sole arbitrator for the Claimant's consideration]

16. The Respondent confirms that, to the best of its knowledge, [*name of nominated or proposed arbitrator*] is willing to serve as arbitrator in this arbitration and is independent of the Parties.

VI.   COMMENTS CONCERNING PLACE OF ARBITRATION, APPLICABLE RULES OF LAW AND LANGUAGE OF ARBITRATION

17. [*State the Respondent's position on: (a) the place of the arbitration; (b) the applicable rules of law; and (c) the language of the arbitration, together with references to the relevant provisions of the applicable agreement(s)*]

18. The Respondent reserves its right to amend and amplify its defence [and its counterclaim], as well as the relief that it seeks, during the course of the arbitration.

19. In accordance with Article 3(1) of the ICC Rules, this Answer, together with all accompanying documents, is submitted in [*state number*] copies.

[*Article 3(1) of the ICC Rules requires that there should be enough copies submitted for each party plus one for each arbitrator and one for the Secretariat of the International Court of Arbitration. So, for example, if there are two parties and three arbitrators, the Request should be submitted in six copies*]

[*insert date*]

Respectfully submitted on behalf of the Respondent,
[*insert name of Respondent*]

By: [*Respondent's counsel to sign*]

[*Insert names of Respondent's counsel and firm*]

Exhibits to the Answer	
R-1	[*insert description of exhibit, including nature of document, date, author and addressee as appropriate*]
R-2	[*as above, and the same again for all exhibits provided*]

Appendix 9

Suggested Model Terms of Reference for ICC Arbitration[1]

INTERNATIONAL CHAMBER OF COMMERCE

INTERNATIONAL COURT OF ARBITRATION

ICC Case No. [*insert case number*]

[*INSERT NAME OF CLAIMANT*]

Claimant

and

[*INSERT NAME OF RESPONDENT*]

Respondent

_____

TERMS OF REFERENCE

_____

[*Insert Date*]

---

1. Note: this and all suggested submissions and instruments produced in appendices are prepared by the authors without the involvement or approval of the ICC.

[*NAME OF CLAIMANT*]

v.

[*NAME OF RESPONDENT*]

TERMS OF REFERENCE

TABLE OF CONTENTS

I.   NAMES AND DESCRIPTIONS OF THE PARTIES

1. The Claimant:

[*Provide full name, type of entity, country of incorporation/principal place of business and the address of the Claimant*], herein referred to as the 'Claimant'.

The Claimant is represented in this arbitration by its duly authorised counsel:

[*Insert full name, address and contact details (including telephone, fax and e-mail) of the Claimant's counsel*]

2. The Respondent:

[*Provide full name, type of entity, country of incorporation/principal place of business and the address of the Respondent*], herein referred to as the 'Respondent' and, together with the Claimant, as the 'Parties'.

The Respondent is represented in this arbitration by its duly authorised counsel:

[*Insert full name, address and contact details (including telephone, fax and e-mail) of the Respondent's counsel*]

3. Any change of name, description, address, telephone, fax number or e-mail address of the Parties shall be immediately notified to the party representatives, the Arbitral Tribunal and the ICC Secretariat, in the same manner as any other submissions. Prior to receipt of any such notification, all communications sent to the last known address shall have been validly served.

II.   NOTIFICATIONS AND COMMUNICATIONS

Notifications to the Arbitral Tribunal

4. Notifications to and communications with the Arbitral Tribunal shall be sent to the [arbitrators/the Sole Arbitrator] by [*state agreed methods of communication, e.g. express courier service, fax, e-mail*], at the address[es] for each set out in Section V below.

Notifications to the Parties

5. Written submissions and communications together with enclosures shall be sent in one copy to the listed representatives of the Parties at the same time as to the Arbitral Tribunal and by the same means.

Notifications to the ICC

6. Copies of all notifications or communications to or from the Parties shall also be sent to the Secretariat of the ICC International Arbitration Court (the '**Court**') in accordance with Article 3 of the ICC Rules.

III.   SUMMARY OF THE PARTIES' CLAIMS AND RELIEF SOUGHT

7. The purpose of the following summary is to satisfy the requirements of Article 18(1)(c) of the ICC Rules, without prejudice to any other or further allegations, arguments and contentions contained in the pleadings or submissions already filed and in such submissions as will be made in the course of this arbitration. Accordingly, the Arbitral Tribunal shall be entitled, subject to Articles 15 and 19 of the ICC Rules and other applicable procedural requirements such as, *inter alia*, procedural time limits, to take into consideration further allegations, arguments, contentions and oral or written submissions. By signing these Terms of Reference, neither party subscribes to, or acquiesces in, the summary of the other party's claims and relief sought set out below.

A.   THE CLAIMANT

Summary of the Claimant's Claims

8. [*Insert the background to, and insert a summary of, the Claimant's claims, based on the Request for Arbitration. State when the Request for Arbitration* *and any Reply to Counterclaim was filed. State the Claimant's position on any counterclaims*]

The Claimant's Request for Relief

9. [*Set out the relief that is sought by the Claimant, including the dismissal of any counterclaim (if applicable). Indicate, to the extent possible, the amounts claimed*]

B.   THE RESPONDENT

Summary of the Respondent's Defences to the Claimant's Claims [and Respondent's Counterclaim]

10. [*State when the Respondent filed its Answer to the Request for Arbitration. Set out the background to, and a summary of, the Respondent's defences and any counterclaims*]

Respondent's Request for Relief

11. [*Set out the relief that is sought by the Respondent, including in respect of any counterclaim. Indicate, to the extent possible, the amounts counterclaimed*]

IV.   ISSUES TO BE DETERMINED BY THE
                ARBITRAL TRIBUNAL

12. Without prejudice to the provisions of Article 19 of the ICC Rules, the issues to be determined by the Arbitral Tribunal shall be those questions of law and fact appearing from the Parties' previous and future submissions, statements and pleadings, including any issues of their admissibility, validity and effectiveness raised by the parties, and, in addition, any further questions of fact or law which the Arbitral Tribunal, in its own discretion, may deem necessary to decide upon for the purpose of rendering any arbitral award in this arbitration.

[*Consider, in the alternative, inserting a list of specific issues to be determined*]

V.   THE ARBITRAL TRIBUNAL

13. The jurisdiction of the Arbitral Tribunal is founded on [*insert clause reference and name of agreement in which the arbitration agreement appears*]:

[*Set out in full the text of this provision*]

14. [*Set out how arbitrator(s) were appointed. The following paragraphs apply in the common case where a three member tribunal where the co-arbitrators were* *nominated by the parties and the chair nominated by the co-arbitrators*] On [*state date*], the Secretary General of the Court, in accordance with Article 9(2) of the ICC Rules, confirmed as co-arbitrator upon the nomination of the Claimant:

[*Insert full name, address and contact details (including telephone, fax and e-mail) of the arbitrator nominated by the Claimant*]

15. On [*state date*], the Secretary General of the Court, in accordance with Article 9(2) of the ICC Rules, confirmed as co-arbitrator upon the nomination of the Respondent:

[*Insert full name, address and contact details (including telephone, fax and e-mail) of the arbitrator nominated by the Respondent*]

16. On [*state date*], the Court appointed as Chair of the Arbitral Tribunal, upon proposal of the co-arbitrators:

[*Insert full name, address and contact details (including telephone, fax and e-mail) of the arbitrator nominated by the Court*]

17. The Court forwarded the file to the Arbitral Tribunal on [*state date*].

18. By signing these Terms of Reference, the Parties confirm that at the time of signing, they know of no reason or basis to challenge any of the arbitrators and have no reservations or objections to express with regard to the constitution of the Arbitral Tribunal.

VI.   PLACE OF ARBITRATION

19. [*Refer to the provision of the relevant agreement which identify the place of the arbitration and state what that place is*]

20. In accordance with Article 14(2) of the ICC Rules, the Arbitral Tribunal may, after consultation with the Parties, conduct hearings and meetings at any location it considers appropriate unless otherwise agreed by the Parties.

21. In accordance with Article 14(3) of the ICC Rules, the Arbitral Tribunal may deliberate at any location it considers appropriate.

22. The Arbitral Tribunal is also free, at its discretion, to conduct telephone conference or video conference calls to determine procedural and other issues with the legal representatives of the Parties if considered appropriate for the orderly progress of the arbitration.

VII.   APPLICABLE LAW

23. [*Refer to the provision of the relevant agreement that identifies the governing law, and state what the governing law is*]

VIII.   APPLICABLE PROCEDURAL RULES AND MISCELLANEOUS MATTERS

Procedure

24. Subject to any applicable mandatory rules of law of the place of arbitration, proceedings before the Arbitral Tribunal shall be governed by the ICC Rules of Arbitration (in force as from 1 January 1998).

Language

25. [*Refer to the provision of the relevant agreement that identifies the language of the arbitration and state what that language is*]

Miscellaneous

26. [*The Parties may wish to refer to other miscellaneous matters in this section, e.g. rules for the taking of evidence; whether, for convenience, the Chair can decide procedural matters on his own, or can issue directions on procedural matters on his own after consulting and deciding with his co-arbitrators; if the Arbitral Tribunal is free to decide any issue by way of an order, a partial or interim award, or by its final award; confidentiality, etc.*]

Signed in [*state number*] original copies on [*state date*].

For and on behalf of [*insert name of Claimant*]

For and on behalf of [*insert name of Respondent*]

By:

By:

_____
[*Insert name of signatory*]

_____
[*Insert name of signatory*]

For the Arbitral Tribunal: [*note: this assumes a three member tribunal*]

Co-arbitrator:

Co-arbitrator:

By:

By:

_____
[*Insert name of Co-arbitrator*]

_____
[*Insert name of Co-arbitrator*]

Chair:

By:

_____
[*Insert name of Chair*]

Appendix 10

Suggested Model Provisional Timetable for ICC Arbitration[1]

INTERNATIONAL CHAMBER OF COMMERCE

INTERNATIONAL COURT OF ARBITRATION

ICC Case No. [*insert case number*]

[*INSERT NAME OF CLAIMANT*]

Claimant

v.

[*INSERT NAME OF RESPONDENT*]

Respondent

PROVISIONAL TIMETABLE

[*Insert Date*]

PROVISIONAL TIMETABLE

Event	Party Responsible	Deadline
[State the events for which deadlines are set, e.g. submission of memorials, production of evidence, hearings. Set out below are some examples of events that may be included in the provisional timetable, in a sequence where document production occurs before exchange of memorials, there is a counterclaim, and there is only one exchange of memorials prior to hearing]	*[State party who is to provide the deliverables]*	*[Insert date by when the deliverables are to be provided. Examples of possible dates are set out below]*
Terms of Reference	Arbitral Tribunal, Claimant, Respondent	[●] *[note: often the same day as provisional timetable]*
Parties exchange Requests to Produce	Claimant, Respondent	*[1 week later]*
Parties raise any objections to Request to Produce	Claimant, Respondent	*[1 week later]*
Tribunal determines any objections to Request to Produce	Claimant, Respondent	*[2 weeks later]*
Production of documents	Claimant, Respondent	*[2 weeks later]*
Full Statement of Claim with exhibits, witness statements and all other supporting materials	Claimant	*[4 weeks later]*
Full Statement of Defence and Counterclaim with exhibits, witness statements and all other supporting materials	Respondent	*[6 weeks later]*
Full Statement of Defence to Counterclaim with exhibits, witness statements and all other supporting materials	Claimant	*[4 weeks later]*
Pre-hearing conference call	Arbitral Tribunal, Claimant, Respondent	*[4 weeks later]*

Event	Party Responsible	Deadline
Hearing	Arbitral Tribunal, Claimant, Respondent	[*4 weeks later*]
Post-Hearing Briefs	Claimant, Respondent	[*4 weeks later*]
Award	Arbitral Tribunal	[*3 to 6 months later*]

Date: [*insert date*]

Signed by the Arbitral Tribunal:

Co-arbitrator: Co-arbitrator:

By: By:

———————————————   ———————————————

   [*Insert name of Co-arbitrator*]   [*Insert name of Co-arbitrator*]

Chair:

By:

———————————————

[*Insert name of Chair*]

Appendix 11

Suggested Model Request to Produce Documents for ICC Arbitration[1]

INTERNATIONAL CHAMBER OF COMMERCE

INTERNATIONAL COURT OF ARBITRATION
ICC Case No. [*state case number*]

[*INSERT NAME OF CLAIMANT*]

Claimant

v.

[*INSERT NAME OF RESPONDENT*]

Respondent

[INSERT NAME OF CLAIMANT/RESPONDENT]'S
REQUEST TO PRODUCE

[*Insert Date*]

[*Insert name and address of requesting party's counsel*]
Counsel for the [Claimant/Respondent]

---

1. Note: this and all suggested submissions and instruments appearing in the appendices are prepared by the authors without the involvement or approval of the ICC.

1. The [Claimant/Respondent] requests the [Respondent/Claimant] to produce the documents identified below in accordance with the instructions set forth below.

2. In this Request to Produce, further to the definition of 'document' contained in the IBA Rules on the Taking of Evidence in International Commercial Arbitration (the 'IBA Rules'), the term 'document' shall include without limitation any agreements, corporate registration or application forms or papers, internal and external correspondence (including e-mail), drafts, presentations, memoranda, minutes of shareholder, board, committee or other meetings (typed or in manuscript), reports, studies, analyses, records (financial or other), personal notes (including diaries and calendars), in whichever form, oral or written. This Request extends to the production of documents that are either in paper form or stored on electronic or magnetic media.

3. The [Respondent/Claimant] is requested to produce documents responsive to these Requests in accordance with the following instructions:

(1) Documents to be produced should be grouped according to each numbered Request.

(2) For production in response to each numbered Request, wherever possible, documents should be arranged in chronological order.

(3) The [Respondent/Claimant]'s document production should be accompanied with a master index of the documents produced, addressing each numbered Request.

(4) If any portion of any document is responsive to any Request, the entire document should be produced.

(5) If any of these Requests cannot be satisfied in full or in part, the [Respondent/Claimant] should produce documents to the extent possible, specifying the reason for its inability to produce further documents.

(6) Pursuant to the IBA Rules, where the [Respondent/Claimant] objects to a specific Request below on the ground that the discovery sought lacks sufficient relevance or materiality, the [Respondent/Claimant] should specify its objections in writing with reasons for such objection. The reasons for the objections shall be as set forth in Article 9(2) of the IBA Rules.

(7) Where the [Respondent/Claimant] objects to a specific Request below on the ground that the discovery sought involves an unreasonable burden to produce the requested evidence, the [Respondent/Claimant] should identify whether and why responding to the Request involves such an unreasonable burden and identify an accessible source for obtaining the requested discovery which is more convenient, less burdensome, or less expensive.

(8) [Sections of documents that are subject to confidentiality rules may be redacted to the extent necessary to comply with applicable legal obligations and the [Respondent/Claimant] may redact irrelevant information of a sensitive or confidential nature, as well as privileged information; provided, however, that, to the extent possible, the [Respondent/Claimant] shall not redact information which permits a reader to identify the author,

recipient, document type and date of the document. In the event such information is redacted, the [Respondent/Claimant] shall provide such information to the [Claimant/Respondent] so that the basis of the redaction can be appropriately reviewed.]

(9) [In respect of each document withheld or redacted on the ground of privilege, the [Respondent/Claimant] is required to produce a 'privilege log' identifying the author, recipient, document type and date of the document and containing (i) a brief description of the subject matter of the document, without disclosing any possible privileged content and (ii) a brief description of why the [Respondent/Claimant] believes that the document is privileged.]

(10) Where the [Respondent/Claimant] objects to a specific Request on the ground the documents requested were, but are no longer, in the possession, custody or control of the [Respondent/Claimant], the [Respondent/Claimant] should (i) describe in detail the nature of the documents and their contents; (ii) specify the date on which the documents were prepared; (iii) identify the persons who authored the documents; (iv) identify the persons to whom the documents were transmitted and the date of such transmissions; (v) state whether the documents are missing, lost, have been destroyed or have otherwise been disposed of and specify the date on which the foregoing has occurred or was discovered; (vi) if destroyed, specify the reasons for such destruction and the persons requesting and performing the destruction; and (vii) identify the persons having knowledge of the contents of the documents.

(11) Where the [Respondent/Claimant] objects to a specific Request on the ground the document requested has already been provided to the [Claimant/Respondent], the [Respondent/Claimant] should clearly identify where and when the document or documents which the [Respondent/Claimant] claims respond to the specific Request were provided.

(12) Where, at any time following their production of documents requested herein or other response to this Request to Produce, [Respondent/Claimant] learns that its production or response was incomplete or incorrect, it should immediately supplement or correct that production or response.

(13) The terms '[Respondent/Claimant]' used herein shall include all directors, officers, employees, agents and representatives of [Respondent/Claimant].

(14) [*Insert any specific instructions regarding the production of documents set out in any Provisional Orders, e.g., if sections of the documents may be redacted for confidentiality reasons*]

REQUESTS

Request 1

Identification of Document(s) to be Produced

[*Identify the first document or category of documents production of which is requested*]

Relevance and Materiality

[*Explain why the requested documents are relevant and material to the outcome of the dispute*]

Possession, Custody or Control

[*State why the requesting party believes that the requested documents (to the extent they exist) would be within the other party's possession, custody or control*]

[*State why the requested documents are not within its possession, custody or control of the requesting party*]

[Subsequent Requests]

[*Follow same format as for Request 1 above*]

[*Insert Date*]   Respectfully submitted on behalf of the [*Claimant/Respondent*]

By: [*Requesting Party's counsel to sign*]

[*Insert names of Requesting Party's counsel and the firm*]

Appendix 12

Suggested Model Privilege Log for ICC Arbitration[1]

INTERNATIONAL CHAMBER OF COMMERCE

INTERNATIONAL COURT OF ARBITRATION
ICC Case No. [*state case number*]

[*INSERT NAME OF CLAIMANT*]

Claimant

v.

[*INSERT NAME OF RESPONDENT*]

Respondent

PRIVILEGE LOG ACCOMPANYING [*INSERT NAME OF CLAIMANT/RESPONDENT (AS APPLICABLE)*]'S DOCUMENT PRODUCTION IN RESPONSE TO [*INSERT NAME OF RESPONDENT/CLAIMANT (AS APPLICABLE)*]'S REQUEST TO PRODUCE DATED [*STATE DATE*]

---

1. Note: This and all suggested submissions and instruments appearing in the appendices are prepared by the authors without the involvement or approval of the ICC.

[Claimant/ Respondent] Request No.	Document No.	Document Date	Document Type	Author	Addressee	Description	Basis of Privilege
[Insert reference to request to produce privileged document]	[Insert any reference number for document withheld]	[Insert date of document]	[State type of document, e.g. e-mail, fax, letter]	[Insert name of author]	[Insert names of all addressees]	[Describe the document and state subject matter and any other features relevant to privilege, e.g. identify if author or addressee are lawyers and whether the document contains or requests legal advice]	[State the basis of the privilege, e.g. legal advice privilege or litigation privilege]

Appendix 13

Suggested Model 'Redfern Schedule' for ICC Arbitration[1]

INTERNATIONAL CHAMBER OF COMMERCE

INTERNATIONAL COURT OF ARBITRATION
ICC Case No. [*state case number*]

[*INSERT NAME OF CLAIMANT*]

Claimant

v.

[*INSERT NAME OF RESPONDENT*]

Respondent

'REDFERN SCHEDULE' TO [*INSERT NAME OF CLAIMANT/RESPONDENT (AS APPLICABLE)*]'S REQUEST TO PRODUCE DATED [*STATE DATE*]

---

1. Note: this and all suggested submissions and instruments appearing in the appendices are prepared by the authors without the involvement or approval of the ICC.

Request No.	Description of Requested Documents	[Claimant's/ Respondent's] Justification for the Request	[Respondent's/ Claimant's] Response	Arbitral Tribunal's Decision
1.	*[Provide description of requested documents from the Request to Produce. List each request separately]*	*[State justification for the request, based on relevance and materiality and possession, custody or control, as set out in the Request to Produce]*	*[State whether the other party agrees or not to produce the requested documents. If it objects, provide reasons why it objects]*	*[Arbitral Tribunal to insert decision on whether the requested documents should be produced or not]*

Appendix 14
Bibliography

A.   SELECTED TREATISES ON INTERNATIONAL
       ARBITRATION

1. K.P. Berger. *Private Dispute Resolution in International Business: Negotiation, Mediation, Arbitration.* Kluwer Law International, 2006.
2. G.B. Born. *International Commercial Arbitration.* 3rd edn. Kluwer Law International, 2009.
3. E. Gaillard. *Aspects philosophiques de l'arbitrage international.* Académie de Droit International de La Haye. Martinus Nijhoff Publishers, 2008.
4. E. Gaillard & J. Savage (eds). *Fouchard, Gaillard, Goldman on International Commercial Arbitration.* Kluwer Law International, 1999.
5. D. St John Sutton, J. Gill & M. Gearing. *Russell on Arbitration.* 23rd edn. Sweet & Maxwell, 2007.
6. J. Lew, L. Mistelis & S. Kröll. *Comparative International Commercial Arbitration.* Kluwer Law International, 2003.
7. M.J. Mustill & S.C. Boyd. *Commercial Arbitration.* 2nd edn. LexisNexis: Butterworths, 1989 and 2001 Companion Volume.
8. J. Paulsson. *The Idea of Arbitration.* Oxford University Press, publication forthcoming.
9. J.F. Poudret & S. Besson. *Comparative Law of International Arbitration.* 2nd edn. Sweet & Maxwell, 2007.
10. N. Blackaby & C. Partasides, with A. *Redfern & M. Hunter, Redfern & Hunter on International Arbitration.* 5th edn. Oxford Univeristy Press, 2009.
11. M. Rubino-Sammartano. *International Arbitration Law and Practice.* 2nd edn. Kluwer Law International, 2001.

B.   SELECTED MATERIALS ON ARBITRATION
                     INSTITUTIONS AND UNCITRAL

i.   ICC

12. M.W. Bühler & T.H. Webster. *Handbook of ICC Arbitration –
    Commentary, Precedents, Materials.* 2nd edn. Sweet & Maxwell, 2008.
13. L. Craig, W. Park & J. Paulsson. *International Chamber of Commerce
    Arbitration.* 3rd edn. Oceana Publications, 2000.
14. Y. Derains & E.A. Schwartz. *A Guide to the ICC Rules of Arbitration.* 2nd
    edn. Kluwer Law International, 2005.
15. E. Schäefer, H. Verbist & C. Imhoos. *ICC Arbitration in Practice.* Kluwer
    Law International, 2004.
16. Collection of ICC Arbitral Awards, 1974–1985, Vol. I, ICC Publication
    No. 433 (1990).
17. Collection of ICC Arbitral Awards, 1986–1990, Vol. II, ICC Publication
    No. 514 (1994).
18. Collection of ICC Arbitral Awards 1991–1995, Vol. III, ICC Publication
    No. 553 (1997).
19. Collection of ICC Arbitral Awards 1996–2000, Vol. IV, ICC Publication
    No. 647 (2003).
20. Collection of ICC Arbitral Award 2001–2007, Vol. V, ICC Publication
    No. 699 (2009).
21. Collection of ICC Procedural Decisions 1993–1996, ICC Publication
    No. 567 (1997).

ii.   LCIA

22. P. Turner & R. Mohtashami. *A Guide to the LCIA Arbitration Rules.*
    Oxford University Press, 2009.

iii.   ICSID

23. E. Gaillard. *La Jurisprudence du CIRDI.* Pedone, 2004.
24. E. Gaillard & Y. Banifatemi (eds). *Annulment of ICSID Awards, IAI Series
    on International Arbitration No. 1.* Juris Publishing, 2004.
25. L. Reed, J. Paulsson & N. Blackaby. *Guide To ICSID Arbitration.* Kluwer
    Law International, 2004.
26. C.H. Schreuer et al. *The ICSID Convention – A Commentary.* 2nd edn.
    Cambridge University Press, 2009.
27. Reports of Cases Decided Under the Convention on the Settlement of
    Investment Disputes between States and Nationals of Other States
    (ICSID Reports), vol. 1 to 14, Cambridge University Press.

iv.   SCC

28. F. Madsen. *Commercial Arbitration in Sweden: A Commentary on the Arbitration Act and the Rules of the Arbitration Institute of the Stockholm Chamber of Commerce.* 3rd edn. Oxford University Press, 2007.
29. S. Jarvin & A. Magnusson (eds). *SCC Arbitral Awards – 1999–2003.* Juris Publishing, 2006.

v.   UNCITRAL

30. H.C. Alvarez, C. Henri, N. Kaplan & D.W. Rivkin. *Model Law Decisions: Cases Applying the UNCITRAL Model Law on International Commercial Arbitration (1985–2001).* Kluwer Law International, 2003.
31. P. Binder. *International Commercial Arbitration and Conciliation in UNCITRAL Model Law Jurisdictions.* 3rd edn. Sweet & Maxwell, 2009.
32. D.D. Caron, M. Pellonpää & L.M. Caplan. *The UNICTRAL Arbitration Rules – A Commentary.* Oxford University Press, 2006.
33. M. Holtzmann & J.E. Neuhaus. *A Guide To The UNCITRAL Model Law On International Commercial Arbitration – Legislative History and Commentary.* Kluwer Law and Taxation Publishers, 1989.
34. P. Sanders. *The Work of UNCITRAL on Arbitration and Conciliation.* 2nd edn. Kluwer Law International, 2004.

C.   SELECTED TREATISES ON SPECIFIC
            REGIONS/COUNTRIES

35. E. Al Tamini. *The Practioner's Guide to Arbitration in the Middle East and North Africa.* Juris Publishing, 2009.
36. A.A. Asouzu. *International Commercial Arbitration and African States – Practice, Participation and Institutional Development, Cambridge Studies in International and Comparative Law (No. 18).* Cambridge University Press, 2001.
37. L.E. Barin & P. Little. *The Osler Guide to Commercial Arbitration in Canada – A Practical Introduction to Domestic and International Commercial Arbitration.* Kluwer Law International, 2006.
38. K. P. Berger & C. Kessedjian. *Forum Internationale: The New German Arbitration Law in International Perspective.* Kluwer Law International, 2000.
39. N. Blackaby, D. Lindsey & A. Spinillo. *International Arbitration in Latin America.* Kluwer Law International, 2003.
40. E. Bergsten. *International Commercial Arbitration Pacific Rim.* Oxford University Press, 2008.

41. S.V. Berti, H. Honsell, N. Peter Vogt & A. K. Schnyder. *International Arbitration in Switzerland – An Introduction and Commentary on Articles 176–194 of the Swiss Private International Law Statute.* Kluwer Law International, 2000.
42. K. Böckstiegel, S. Kröll & P. Nacimiento. *Arbitration in Germany: The Model Law in Practice.* Kluwer Law International, 2008.
43. G.B. Born. *International Commercial Arbitration: Commentary and Materials.* 2nd edn. Transnational Publishers, 2001.
44. A. Bucher & T. Tschanz. *International Arbitration in Switzerland.* Helbing & Lichtenhahn 1989.
45. T.E. Carbonneau. *The Law and Practice of Arbitration.* 3rd edn. Juris Publishing, 2009.
46. T.E Carbonneau & M.H. Mourra. *Latin American Investment Treaty Arbitration – The Controversies and Conflicts.* Kluwer Law International, 2008.
47. J.B. Casey. *Arbitration Law of Canada: Practice and Procedure.* Juris Publishing, 2005.
48. L. Devolvé, J. Rouche & G. Pointon. *French Arbitration Law and Practice: A Dynamic Civil Law Approach to International Arbitration.* 2nd edn. Kluwer Law International, 2009.
49. L. Flannery & R. Merkin. *Arbitration Act 1996.* 4th edn. Informa Law, 2008.
50. P. Habegger, T. Zuberbühler & K. Müller (eds). *Swiss Rules of International Arbitration: Commentary.* Kluwer Law International, 2005.
51. A. Hamid El-Ahdab. *Arbitration with the Arab Countries.* 2nd edn. Kluwer Law International, 1998.
52. B. Harris, R. Planterose & J. Tecks. *The Arbitration Act 1996: A Commentary.* 4th edn. Blackwell Publishing, 2007.
53. L. Heuman. *Arbitration Law of Sweden: Practice and Procedure.* Juris Publishing, 2003.
54. L. Heuman & S. Jarvin (eds). *The Swedish Arbitration Act of 1999, Five Years On: A Critical Review of Strengths and Weaknesses.* Juris Publishing, 2006.
55. M.H. Hunter & T. Landau. *The English Arbitration Act 1996: Text & Notes.* Kluwer Law International, 1998.
56. G. Kaufmann-Kohler & B. Stucki (eds). *International Arbitration in Switzerland: A Handbook for Practitioners.* Kluwer Law International, 2004.
57. J. Kleinheisterhamp. *International Commercial Arbitration in Latin America – Regulations and Practices in MERCOSUR and the associated countries.* Oceana Publications, 2005.
58. P. Lalive, J.-F. Poudret & C. Reymond. *Le droit de l'arbitrage interne et international en Suisse.* Payot, 1989.
59. C. Liebscher. *The Austrian Arbitration Act 2006: Text and Notes.* Kluwer Law International, 2006.
60. C. Liebscher (ed.). *Arbitration Law and Practice in Central and Eastern Europe.* Juris Publishing, 2006.

61. F. Madsen. *Commercial Arbitration in Sweden: A Commentary on the Arbitration Act and the Rules of the Arbitration Institute of the Stockholm Chamber of Commerce.* 3rd edn. Oxford University Press, 2007.
62. M.J. Moser (ed.). *Arbitration in Asia.* 2nd edn. Juris Publishing, 2008.
63. M.J. Moser (ed.). *Managing Business Disputes in Today's China: Dueling with Dragons.* Kluwer Law International, 2007.
64. M.J. Moser & Y.W. Cheng (eds). *Arbitration in Hong Kong: A User's Guide.* Kluwer Law International, 2004.
65. J.T. de Paiva Muniz & A. Tereza Palhares Basilio. *Arbitration Law of Brazil: Practice and Procedure.* Juris Publishing, 2006.
66. M. Pryles (ed.). *Dispute Resolution in Asia.* 3rd edn. Kluwer Law International, 2006.
67. J. Tao. *Arbitration Law and Practice in China.* 2nd edn. Kluwer Law International, 2008.
68. M.B. Trevor. *Arbitration and Mediation in the Southern Mediterranean Countries.* Kluwer Law International, 2007.

D.   SELECTED TREATISES ON INVESTMENT
                TREATY ARBITRATION

69. R.D. Bishop, J. Crawford & W.M. Reisman. *Foreign Investment Disputes: Cases, Materials and Commentary.* Kluwer Law International, 2005.
70. A. Bjorklund, J.F.G. Hannaford & M. Kinnear. *Investment Disputes under NAFTA. An Annotated Guide to NAFTA Chapter 11.* Kluwer Law International, 2006.
71. C. Binder, U. Kriebaum, A. Reinisch & S. Wittich (eds). *International Investment Law for the 21st Century – Essays in Honour of Christoph Schreuer.* Oxford University Press, 2009.
72. G. Coop & C. Ribeiro (eds). *Investment Protection and The Energy Charter Treaty.* Juris Publishing, 2008.
73. R. Dolzer & M. Stevens. *Bilateral Investment Treaties.* Martinus Nijhoff Publishers, 1994.
74. R. Dolzer & C. Schreuer. *Principles of Investment Law.* Oxford University Press, 2008.
75. Z. Douglas. *The International Law of Investment Claims.* Cambridge University Press, 2009.
76. C. Dugan, N. Rubins & D. Wallace. *Investor-State Arbitration.* Oxford University Press, 2008.
77. T.J. Grierson Weiler (ed.). *International Investment Law: Leading Cases from the ICSID, NAFTA, Bilateral Treaties and Customary International Law.* Cameron May Ltd., 2005.

78. T.J. Grierson Weiler (ed.). Investment Treaty Arbitration and International Law. Vol. 1. JurisNet, 2008.

79. T.J. Grierson Weiler & I. Laird (eds.). Investment Treaty Arbitration and International Law. Vol. 2. JurisNet 2009.

80. C. McLachlan, L. Shore & M. Weiniger. *International Investment Arbitration – Substantive Principles.* Oxford University Press, 2007.

81. P. Muchlinski, F. Ortino & C. Schreuer (eds). *The Oxford Handbook of International Investment Law.* Oxford University Press 2008.

82. A. Newcombe & L. Paradell. *Law and Practice of Investment Treaties: Standards of Treatment.* Kluwer Law International, 2009.

83. A. Reinisch. *Standards of Investment Protection.* Oxford University Press, 2008.

84. C. Ribeiro (ed.). *Investment Arbitration and the Energy Charter Treaty.* Juris Publishing, 2006.

85. S. Ripinsky & K. Williams. *Damages in International Investment Law.* British Institute of International and Comparative Law, 2008.

86. M. Sornarajah. *The International Law on Foreign Investment.* 2nd edn. Cambridge University Press, 2004.

87. M. Sornarajah. *The Settlement of Foreign Investment Disputes.* Kluwer Law International, 2001.

E.   SELECTED TREATISES ON SPECIFIC ARBITRATION TOPICS

88. A. Berkeley & K. Karsten (eds). *Arbitration: Corruption, Money Laundering and Fraud.* Kluwer Law International, 2006.

89. R.D. Bishop. *The Art of Advocacy in International Arbitration.* Juris Publishing, 2004.

90. R.D. Bishop (ed.). *Enforcement of Arbitral Awards against Sovereigns.* Juris Publishing, 2009.

91. G.B. Born. *International Arbitration and Forum Selection Agreements: Drafting and Enforcing.* 2nd edn. Kluwer Law International, 2006.

92. T.E. Carbonneau, H. Smit & L. Mistelis (eds). *The Roster of International Arbitrators.* 2nd edn. Juris Publishing (updated quarterly).

93. B. Cremades (ed.). Parallel State and Arbitral Procedures in International Arbitration, ICC Publication No. 692 (2005).

94. Y. Derains, Yves & R. Kreindler (eds). Evaluation of Damages in International Arbitration, ICC Publication No. 668 (2006).

95. P.D. Friedland. *Arbitration Clauses for International Contracts.* 2nd edn. Juris Publishing, 2007.

96. E. Gaillard (ed.). *Anti-Suit Injunctions in International Arbitration, IAI Series on International Arbitration No. 2.* Juris Publishing, 2005.

97. E. Gaillard, P. Pinsolle, A.V. Schlaepfer & L. Degos (eds). *Toward a Uniform International Arbitration Law? IAI Series on International Arbitration No. 3.* Juris Publishing, 2005.

98. E. Gaillard (ed.). *States Entities in International Arbitration, IAI Series on International Arbitration No. 4.* Juris Publishing, 2008.

99. E. Gaillard & Y. Banifatemi (eds). *Precedent in International Arbitration, IAI Series on International Arbitration No. 5.* Juris Publishing, 2008.

100. E. Gaillard & D. Di Pietro (eds). *Enforcement of Arbitration Agreements and International Arbitral Awards: The New York Convention 1958 in Practice.* Cameron May Ltd., 2008.

101. E. Gaillard (ed.). *The Review of International Arbitral Awards, IAI Series on International Arbitration No. 6.* Juris Publishing, 2009.

102. B. Hanotiau. *Complex Arbitrations: Multiparty, Multicontract, Multi-Issue and Class Actions.* Kluwer Law International, 2005.

103. R.D. Hill & L.W. Newman (eds). *The Leading Arbitrators' Guide to International Arbitration.* 1st edn. JurisNet, 2004.

104. R.D. Hill & L.W. Newman (eds). *The Leading Arbitrators' Guide to International Arbitration.* 2nd edn. Juris Publishing, 2008.

105. J. Jenkins & S. Stebbings. *International Construction Arbitration Law.* Kluwer Law International, 2006.

106. D. Joseph. *Jurisdiction and Arbitration Agreements and their Enforcement.* Sweet & Maxwell, 2005.

107. M. Kantor. *Valuation for Arbitration – Compensation Standards, Valuation Methods and Expert Evidence.* Kluwer Law International, 2008.

108. L. Lévy & V. V. Veeder (eds). Arbitration and Oral Evidence, ICC Publication No. 689 (2004).

109. J.D.M. Lew & L.A. Mistelis (eds). *Pervasive Problems in International Arbitration.* Kluwer Law International, 2006.

110. M.J. Moser & M. Pryles (eds). *The Asian Leading Arbitrators' Guide to International Arbitration.* Juris Publishing, 2007.

111. J. Paulsson, E.A. Schwartz, N. Rawding & L. Reed. *The Freshfields Guide to Arbitration and Alternative Dispute Resolution: Clauses in International Contracts.* Kluwer Law International, 1999.

112. G. Petrochilos. *Procedural Law in International Arbitration.* Oxford: Oxford University Press 2004.

113. P. Sheridan. *Construction and Engineering Arbitration.* Sweet & Maxwell, 1999.

114. A.J. van den Berg. *The New York Arbitration Convention of 1958.* Kluwer Law and Taxation Publishers, 1981.

115. A. Yesilirmak. *Provisional Measures in International Commercial Arbitration.* Kluwer Law International, 2005.

F.   SELECTED ARBITRATION JOURNALS

116. The American Review of International Arbitration
117. Arbitration: The Journal of the Chartered Institute of Arbitrators
118. Arbitration International
119. Arbitration Law Monthly
120. ASA Bulletin
121. Asian International Arbitration Journal
122. Contemporary Asia Arbitration Journal
123. DIAC Journal – Arbitration in the Middle East
124. Dispute Resolution Journal
125. Global Arbitration Review
126. ICCA Congress Series
127. ICCA Yearbook Commercial Arbitration
128. ICC International Court of Arbitration Bulletin
129. ICSID Review – Foreign Investment Law Journal
130. International Arbitration Law Review
131. International Legal Materials
132. Journal du droit international
133. Journal of International Arbitration
134. Journal of World Trade & Investment
135. Lebanese Review of Arab and International Arbitration
136. Lloyd's Arbitration Reports
137. Model Arbitration Law Quarterly Reports
138. Mealey's International Arbitration Report
139. Mealey's International Arbitration Quarterly Law Review
140. Revue de l'arbitrage
141. Stockholm International Arbitration Review
142. The Swiss International Arbitration Law Reports
143. Transnational Dispute Management
144. World Arbitration and Mediation Review
145. World Trade and Arbitration Materials

G.   SELECTED TREATISES ON MEDIATION

146. H.I. Abramson. Mediation Representation: Advocating in a Problem-Solving Process. National Institute for Trial Advocacy, 2004.
147. J. Beer & E. Steif. The Mediator's Handbook. 3rd edn. New Society Publishers, 1998.
148. H. Brown & A. Marriott. ADR: Principles and Practice. 2nd edn. Thomson Professional Pub., 1999.
149. E. Carroll, Lord Hurd & K. Mackie. International Mediation: The Art of Business Diplomacy. 2nd edn. Kluwer Law International, 2006.

150. K. Cloke. Mediating Dangerously – The Frontiers of Conflict Resolution. Jossey-Bass, 2001.
151. J.W. Cooley. Mediation Advocacy. 2nd edn. National Institute for Trial Advocacy, 2002.
152. S. Erickson & M. McKnight. A Practitioner's Guide to Mediation: A Client Centred Approach. John Wiley & Sons, 2001.
153. J. Folberg & D. Golann. Mediation: The Roles of Advocate and Neutral. Aspen Publishers, 2006.
154. R. Hasson & K. Slaikeu. Controlling the Costs of Conflict: How to Design a System for your Organization. Jossey-Bass, 1998.
155. K.J. Mackie (ed.). A Handbook of Dispute Resolution: ADR in Action. Taylor & Francis, 2007.
156. K. Mackie, W. Marsh & D. Miles. The ADR Practice Guide. 2nd edn. LexisNexis, 2000.
157. B. Mayer. Staying with Conflict: A Strategic Approach to Ongoing Disputes. Jossey-Bass, 2009.
158. C. Menkel-Meadow, L. Porter Love & A.K. Schneider. Mediation: Practice, Policy and Ethics. Aspen Publishers, 2006.
159. C. Menkel-Meadow & M. Wheeler (eds). What's Fair – Ethics for Negotiators. Jossey-Bass, 2004.
160. M.V.B. Partridge. Alternative Dispute Resolution – An Essential Competency for Lawyers. Oxford University Press, 2009.
161. B.G. Picker. Mediation Practice Guide: A Handbook for Resolving Business Disputes. 2nd edn. ABA, 2004.
162. D. Richbell. Mediation of Construction Disputes. Blackwells, 2008.
163. M. Schonewille. Toolkit – Generating Outcomes. M&SD, undated.
164. M. Schonewille. Toolkit – Mediation Advocacy. M&SD, 2008.

H.   WEBSITES AND OTHER ONLINE RESOURCES
      ON ARBITRATION

Name of Website/Online Resource	*Weblink*
American Arbitration Association (AAA)/International Centre for Dispute Resolution (ICDR)	http://www.adr.org
American Society of International Law – Guide to Electronic Resources for International Law: International Commercial Arbitration	http://www.asil.org/arb1.cfm
Arbitration Institute of the Stockholm Chamber of Commerce (SCC)	http://www.sccinstitute.com
Asia Pacific Regional Arbitration Group (APRAG)	http://www.aprag.org
Australian Centre for International Commercial Arbitration	http://www.acica.org.au

Name of Website/Online Resource	*Weblink*
Beijing Arbitration Commission (BAC)	http://www.bjac.org.cn/en/index.asp
Cairo Regional Centre for International Commercial Arbitration	http://www.crcica.org.eg
Chartered Institute of Arbitrators (CiArb)	http://www.arbitrators.org
China International Economic and Trade Arbitration Commission (CIETAC)	http://www.cietac.org
Corte de Arbitraje Internacional para el MERCOSUR	http://www.arbitraje.com.uy
DIS (German Institution of Arbitration)	http://www.dis-arb.de
Dubai International Arbitration Centre (DIAC)	http://www.diac.ae
Global Arbitration Review	http://www.globalarbitrationreview.com
Hong Kong International Arbitration Centre (HKIAC)	http://www.hkiac.com
International Centre for Settlement of Investment Disputes (ICSID)	http://icsid.worldbank.org
International Court of Arbitration of the International Chamber of Commerce (ICC)	http://www.iccwbo.org/policy/ arbitration/id2882/index.html
International Arbitration Institute	http://www.iaiparis.com
Investment Arbitration Reporter	http://www.iareporter.com
International Bar Association (IBA)	http://www.ibanet.org
International Council for Commercial Arbitration (ICCA)	http://www.arbitration-icca.org
International Dispute Negotiation Podcast Series	http://www.cpradr.org/TrainingEvents/ Podcasts/tabid/261/Default.aspx Also available on iTunes (search 'arbitration podcast')
International Institute for Conflict Prevention & Resolution (CPR)	http://www.cpradr.org
International Law in Brief Newsletter	http://www.asil.org/ilibmenu.cfm
Investment Claims	www.investmentclaims.com
Investment Treaty Arbitration	http://ita.law.uvic.ca
Investment Treaty News	http://www.investmenttreatynews.org
JAMS	http://www.jamsadr.com
London Court of International Arbitration (LCIA)	http://www.lcia.org

Name of Website/Online Resource	Weblink
Kluwer Arbitration	http://www.kluwerarbitration.com/ arbitration
Kuala Lumpur Regional Centre for Arbitration (KLRCA)	http://www.rcakl.org.my
Lex Mercatoria – International Commercial Arbitration	http://www.jus.uio.no/lm/arbitration/ toc
Maxwell Chambers (Singapore)	http://www.maxwell-chambers.com
NAFTA Claims	http://www.naftaclaims.com
New York Convention on the Recognition and Enforcement of Foreign Arbitral Awards	http://www.uncitral.org/uncitral/en/ uncitral_texts/arbitration/ NYConvention.html
Peace Palace Library	http://www.ppl.nl
The Permanent Court of Arbitration (PCA)	http://www.pca-cpa.org
Singapore International Arbitration Centre (SIAC)	http://www.siac.org.sg
Swiss Arbitration Association	http://www.arbitration-ch.org
Transnational Dispute Management	http://www.transnational-dispute- management.com
UNCITRAL	www.uncitral.org
UNCTAD (Bilateral Investment Treaties online)	http://www.unctadxi.org/templates/ DocSearch____779.aspx
United Nations Reports of International Arbitral Awards/ Recueil des sentences arbitrales	http://www.un.org/law/riaa
World Intellectual Property Organization (WIPO) Arbitration and Mediation Center	http://www.wipo.int/amc

I.   WEBSITES AND OTHER ONLINE RESOURCES
        ON MEDIATION

Name of Website/Online Resource	Weblink
ACB Group B.V.	http://www.acb-group.com
ACCTM	http://www.acctm.org
ADR Blogs – World Directory	http://adrblogs.com
ADR-Blog by Marcus Brinkmann (Germany)	http://www.adr-blog.de
ADR Chambers Canada	http://www.adrchambers.ca
ADR Group	http://www.adrgroup.co.uk
ADR Institute of Canada	http://www.adrcanada.ca
ADR Services Inc	http://www.adrservices.org

Name of Website/Online Resource	Weblink
Africa Centre for Dispute Settlement (ACDS)	http://www.usb.ac.za/ disputesettlement
Arbitration and Conciliation Center of the Bogota Chamber of Commerce (CACCCB)	http://www.cacccb.org.co
Arbitrators' and Mediators' Institute of New Zealand (AMINZ)	http://www.aminz.org.nz
Association of Dispute Resolvers (LEADR)	http://www.leadr.com.au http://www.leadr.co.nz
Brains On Purpose blog, by Stephanie West Allen (US)	http://westallen.typepad.com/ brains_on_purpose
Brussels Business and Mediation Center (BBMC)	http://www.bbmc-mediation.be
Business Conflict Blog by F. Peter Phillips(US)	http://businessconflictmanagement. com/blog
California Academy of Distinguished Neutrals (CADN)	http://www.californianeutrals.org
CEDR Solve Direct	http://www.cedr.com
Centre de médiation et d'arbitrage de la Chambre de commerce et d'industrie de Paris (CMAP)	http://www.cmap.fr
Centrul de Mediere Craiva (MCC)	http://www.mediere.ro
CONCILIA	http://www.concilia.it
Conflict Zen blog by Tammy Lenski (US)	http://conflictzen.com
Core Mediation	http://www.core-mediation.com
CPR Institute	http://www.cpradr.org
Deutschen Gesellschaft für Mediation in der Wirtschaft (DGMW)	http://www.dgmw.de
Dominique.Lopez-Eychenie Blog (France)	http://www.avocats.fr/space/ dominique.lopez-eychenie/blog
Engaging Conflicts blog, by Gini Nelson (US)	http://www.engagingconflicts.com
Florida Circuit-Civil Mediator Society (FCCMS)	http://www.floridamediators.org
Georgia Academy of Mediators & Arbitrators (GAMA)	http://www.georgiamediators.org
Independent Mediators	http://www.independentmediators.co.uk
Indian Institute of Arbitration & Mediation (IIAM)	http://www.arbitrationindia.org

Name of Website/Online Resource	Weblink
In Place of Strife, The Mediation Chambers	http://www.mediate.co.uk
Institut de médiation et d'arbitrage du Québec (IMAQ)	http://www.IMAQ.org
International Academy of Mediators (IAM)	http://www.iamed.org
International Mediation Institute (IMI) searchable database of competent mediators worldwide	www.IMImediation.org
International Trademark Association (INTA)	http://www.inta.org
JAMS ADR Center	http://www.adrcenter.it
Malaysian Mediation blog by Chan Kheng Hoe (Malaysia)	http:// malaysianmediation.blogspot.com
Mediator Blah Blah blog by Geoff Sharp (NZ)	http://mediatorblahblah.blogspot.com
Mediation Channel blog by Diane Levin (US)	http://mediationchannel.com
Mediators' Institute of Ireland (MII)	http://www.themii.ie
The Mediator Magazine	http://www.themediatormagazine. co.uk
The Mediation Times blog by Amanda Bucklow (UK)	http://blog.amandabucklow.co.uk
National Conflict Resolution Center (NCRC)	http://www.ncrconline.com
Negotiation & Conflict Management Group (NCMG)	http://www.ncmggroup.org
Netherlands Mediation Institute (NMI)	http://www.nmi-mediation.nl
North Carolina Academy of Superior Court Mediators (NCASCM)	http://www.ncmediators.org
Réseau Mediation blog by Dominique Foucart (Belgium)	http://interactes.wordpress.com
ResoLex	http://www.resolex.com
Secretos del Mediador Exitoso blog (Argentina)	http://www.mediadorexitoso.blogspot. com
Settle It Now: Negotiation Law blog (US) by Victoria Pynchon	http://www.negotiationlawblog.com
Schweizerische Kammer für Wirtschaftsmediation (SKWM-CSMC)	http://www.skwm.ch

Name of Website/Online Resource	Weblink
Singapore Mediation Centre (SMC)	http://www.mediation.com.sg
Tokiso Dispute Settlement	http://www.tokiso.com
Washington Arbitration & Mediation Service (WAMS)	http://www.usamwa.com
World Intellectual Property Organization (WIPO) Arbitration and Mediation Center	http://www.wipo.int/amc

Appendix 15

Netherlands Model Bilateral Investment Treaty

Standard text March 2004.[1]

Agreement on encouragement and reciprocal protection of investments between

_____

and the Kingdom of the Netherlands

The_____

and

the Kingdom of the Netherlands,

hereinafter referred to as the Contracting Parties,

Desiring to strengthen their traditional ties of friendship and to extend and intensify the economic relations between them, particularly with respect to investments by the nationals of one Contracting Party in the territory of the other Contracting Party,

Recognising that agreement upon the treatment to be accorded to such investments will stimulate the flow of capital and technology and the economic development of the Contracting Parties and that fair and equitable treatment of investments is desirable,

Recognising that the development of economic and business ties will promote internationally accepted labour standards,

Considering that these objectives can be achieved without compromising health, safety and environmental measures of general application,

_____

1. Reproduced with the kind permission of the Ministry of Economic Affairs of the Netherlands.

Have agreed as follows:

Article 1

For the purposes of this Agreement:

(a) the term 'investments' means every kind of asset and more particularly, though not exclusively:

- (i) movable and immovable property as well as any other rights in rem in respect of every kind of asset;
- (ii) rights derived from shares, bonds and other kinds of interests in companies and joint ventures;
- (iii) claims to money, to other assets or to any performance having an economic value;
- (iv) rights in the field of intellectual property, technical processes, goodwill and know-how;
- (v) rights granted under public law or under contract, including rights to prospect, explore, extract and win natural resources.

(b) the term 'nationals' shall comprise with regard to either Contracting Party:

- (i) natural persons having the nationality of that Contracting Party;
- (ii) legal persons constituted under the law of that Contracting Party;
- (iii) legal persons not constituted under the law of that Contracting Party but controlled, directly or indirectly, by natural persons as defined in (i) or by legal persons as defined in (ii).

(c) the term 'territory' means:

the territory of the Contracting Party concerned and any area adjacent to the territorial sea which, under the laws applicable in the Contracting Party concerned, and in accordance with international law, is the exclusive economic zone or continental shelf of the Contracting Party concerned, in which that Contracting Party exercises jurisdiction or sovereign rights.

Article 2

Either Contracting Party shall, within the framework of its laws and regulations, promote economic cooperation through the protection in its territory of investments of nationals of the other Contracting Party. Subject to its right to exercise powers conferred by its laws or regulations, each Contracting Party shall admit such investments.

Article 3

1) Each Contracting Party shall ensure fair and equitable treatment of the investments of nationals of the other Contracting Party and shall not

impair, by unreasonable or discriminatory measures, the operation, management, maintenance, use, enjoyment or disposal thereof by those nationals. Each Contracting Party shall accord to such investments full physical security and protection.

2) More particularly, each Contracting Party shall accord to such investments treatment which in any case shall not be less favourable than that accorded either to investments of its own nationals or to investments of nationals of any third State, whichever is more favourable to the national concerned.

3) If a Contracting Party has accorded special advantages to nationals of any third State by virtue of agreements establishing customs unions, economic unions, monetary unions or similar institutions, or on the basis of interim agreements leading to such unions or institutions, that Contracting Party shall not be obliged to accord such advantages to nationals of the other Contracting Party.

4) Each Contracting Party shall observe any obligation it may have entered into with regard to investments of nationals of the other Contracting Party.

5) If the provisions of law of either Contracting Party or obligations under international law existing at present or established hereafter between the Contracting Parties in addition to the present Agreement contain a regulation, whether general or specific, entitling investments by nationals of the other Contracting Party to a treatment more favourable than is provided for by the present Agreement, such regulation shall, to the extent that it is more favourable, prevail over the present Agreement.

Article 4

With respect to taxes, fees, charges and to fiscal deductions and exemptions, each Contracting Party shall accord to nationals of the other Contracting Party who are engaged in any economic activity in its territory, treatment not less favourable than that accorded to its own nationals or to those of any third State who are in the same circumstances, whichever is more favourable to the nationals concerned. For this purpose, however, any special fiscal advantages accorded by that Party, shall not be taken into account:

a) under an agreement for the avoidance of double taxation;
b) by virtue of its participation in a customs union, economic union or similar institution; or
c) on the basis of reciprocity with a third State.

Article 5

The Contracting Parties shall guarantee that payments relating to an investment may be transferred. The transfers shall be made in a freely convertible currency, without restriction or delay. Such transfers include in particular though not exclusively:

a) profits, interests, dividends and other current income;
b) funds necessary
   (i) for the acquisition of raw or auxiliary materials, semi-fabricated or finished products,
      or
   (ii) to replace capital assets in order to safeguard the continuity of an investment;
c) additional funds necessary for the development of an investment;
d) funds in repayment of loans;
e) royalties or fees;
f) earnings of natural persons;
g) the proceeds of sale or liquidation of the investment;
h) payments arising under Article 7.

Article 6

Neither Contracting Party shall take any measures depriving, directly or indirectly, nationals of the other Contracting Party of their investments unless the following conditions are complied with:

a) the measures are taken in the public interest and under due process of law;
b) the measures are not discriminatory or contrary to any undertaking which the Contracting Party which takes such measures may have given;
c) the measures are taken against just compensation. Such compensation shall represent the genuine value of the investments affected, shall include interest at a normal commercial rate until the date of payment and shall, in order to be effective for the claimants, be paid and made transferable, without delay, to the country designated by the claimants concerned and in the currency of the country of which the claimants are nationals or in any freely convertible currency accepted by the claimants.

Article 7

Nationals of the one Contracting Party who suffer losses in respect of their investments in the territory of the other Contracting Party owing to war or other armed conflict, revolution, a state of national emergency, revolt, insurrection or riot shall be accorded by the latter Contracting Party treatment, as regards restitution, indemnification, compensation or other settlement, no less favourable than that which that Contracting Party accords to its own nationals or to nationals of any third State, whichever is more favourable to the nationals concerned.

Article 8

If the investments of a national of the one Contracting Party are insured against non-commercial risks or otherwise give rise to payment of indemnification in respect of such investments under a system established by law, regulation or government contract, any subrogation of the insurer or re-insurer or Agency designated by the one Contracting Party to the rights of the said national pursuant to the terms of such insurance or under any other indemnity given shall be recognised by the other Contracting Party.

Article 9

Each Contracting Party hereby consents to submit any legal dispute arising between that Contracting Party and a national of the other Contracting Party concerning an investment of that national in the territory of the former Contracting Party to the International Centre for Settlement of Investment Disputes for settlement by conciliation or arbitration under the Convention on the Settlement of Investment Disputes between States and Nationals of other States, opened for signature at Washington on 18 March 1965. A legal person which is a national of one Contracting Party and which before such a dispute arises is controlled by nationals of the other Contracting Party shall, in accordance with Article 25 (2) (b) of the Convention, for the purpose of the Convention be treated as a national of the other Contracting Party.

Article 10

The provisions of this Agreement shall, from the date of entry into force thereof, also apply to investments, which have been made before that date.

Article 11

Either Contracting Party may propose to the other Party that consultations be held on any matter concerning the interpretation or application of the Agreement. The other Party shall accord sympathetic consideration to the proposal and shall afford adequate opportunity for such consultations.

Article 12

1) Any dispute between the Contracting Parties concerning the interpretation or application of the present Agreement, which cannot be settled within a reasonable lapse of time by means of diplomatic negotiations, shall, unless the Parties have otherwise agreed, be submitted, at the request of either Party, to an arbitral tribunal, composed of three members. Each Party shall appoint one arbitrator and the two arbitrators thus appointed shall

together appoint a third arbitrator as their chair who is not a national of either Party.

2) If one of the Parties fails to appoint its arbitrator and has not proceeded to do so within two months after an invitation from the other Party to make such appointment, the latter Party may invite the President of the International Court of Justice to make the necessary appointment.

3) If the two arbitrators are unable to reach agreement, in the two months following their appointment, on the choice of the third arbitrator, either Party may invite the President of the International Court of Justice to make the necessary appointment.

4) If, in the cases provided for in the paragraphs (2) and (3) of this Article, the President of the International Court of Justice is prevented from discharging the said function or is a national of either Contracting Party, the Vice-President shall be invited to make the necessary appointments. If the Vice-President is prevented from discharging the said function or is a national of either Party the most senior member of the Court available who is not a national of either Party shall be invited to make the necessary appointments.

5) The tribunal shall decide on the basis of respect for the law. Before the tribunal decides, it may at any stage of the proceedings propose to the Parties that the dispute be settled amicably. The foregoing provisions shall not prejudice settlement of the dispute ex aequo et bono if the Parties so agree.

6) Unless the Parties decide otherwise, the tribunal shall determine its own procedure.

7) The tribunal shall reach its decision by a majority of votes. Such decision shall be final and binding on the Parties.

Article 13

As regards the Kingdom of the Netherlands, the present Agreement shall apply to the part of the Kingdom in Europe, to the Netherlands Antilles and to Aruba, unless the notification provided for in Article 14, paragraph (1) provides otherwise.

Article 14

1) The present Agreement shall enter into force on the first day of the second month following the date on which the Contracting Parties have notified each other in writing that their constitutionally required procedures have been complied with, and shall remain in force for a period of fifteen years.

2) Unless notice of termination has been given by either Contracting Party at least six months before the date of the expiry of its validity, the present Agreement shall be extended tacitly for periods of ten years, whereby each Contracting Party reserves the right to terminate the Agreement upon

notice of at least six months before the date of expiry of the current period of validity.

3) In respect of investments made before the date of the termination of the present Agreement, the foregoing Articles shall continue to be effective for a further period of fifteen years from that date.

4) Subject to the period mentioned in paragraph (2) of this Article, the Kingdom of the Netherlands shall be entitled to terminate the application of the present Agreement separately in respect of any of the parts of the Kingdom.

IN WITNESS WHEREOF, the undersigned representatives, duly authorised thereto, have signed the present Agreement.

DONE in two originals at ...., on..., in the ...., Netherlands and English languages, the three texts being authentic. In case of difference of interpretation the English text will prevail.

For .... :   For the Kingdom of the Netherlands:

Appendix 16

US Model BIT*

The Government of the United States of America and the Government of [Country] (hereinafter the 'Parties');

Desiring to promote greater economic cooperation between them with respect to investment by nationals and enterprises of one Party in the territory of the other Party;

Recognizing that agreement on the treatment to be accorded such investment will stimulate the flow of private capital and the economic development of the Parties;

Agreeing that a stable framework for investment will maximize effective utilization of economic resources and improve living standards;

Recognizing the importance of providing effective means of asserting claims and enforcing rights with respect to investment under national law as well as through international arbitration;

Desiring to achieve these objectives in a manner consistent with the protection of health, safety, and the environment, and the promotion of internationally recognized labor rights;

Having resolved to conclude a Treaty concerning the encouragement and reciprocal protection of investment;

---

* http://www.ustr.gov/sites/default/files/U.S.%20model%20BIT.pdf

Have agreed as follows:

SECTION A

Article 1: Definitions

For purposes of this Treaty:

'**central level of government**' means:

  (a) for the United States, the federal level of government; and
  (b) for [Country], [____].

'**Centre**' means the International Centre for Settlement of Investment Disputes ('ICSID') established by the ICSID Convention.

'**claimant**' means an investor of a Party that is a party to an investment dispute with the other Party.

'**covered investment**' means, with respect to a Party, an investment in its territory of an investor of the other Party in existence as of the date of entry into force of this Treaty or established, acquired, or expanded thereafter.

'**disputing parties**' means the claimant and the respondent.

'**disputing party**' means either the claimant or the respondent.

'**enterprise**' means any entity constituted or organized under applicable law, whether or not for profit, and whether privately or governmentally owned or controlled, including a corporation, trust, partnership, sole proprietorship, joint venture, association, or similar organization; and a branch of an enterprise.

'**enterprise of a Party**' means an enterprise constituted or organized under the law of a Party, and a branch located in the territory of a Party and carrying out business activities there.

'**existing**' means in effect on the date of entry into force of this Treaty.

'**freely usable currency**' means 'freely usable currency' as determined by the International Monetary Fund under its *Articles of Agreement*.

'**GATS**' means the *General Agreement on Trade in Services*, contained in Annex 1B to the WTO Agreement.

'**government procurement**' means the process by which a government obtains the use of or acquires goods or services, or any combination thereof, for governmental purposes and not with a view to commercial sale or resale, or use in the production or supply of goods or services for commercial sale or resale.

'**ICSID Additional Facility Rules**' means the *Rules Governing the Additional Facility for the Administration of Proceedings by the Secretariat of the International Centre for Settlement of Investment Disputes.*

'**ICSID Convention**' means the *Convention on the Settlement of Investment Disputes between States and Nationals of Other States*, done at Washington, March 18, 1965.

['**Inter-American Convention**' means the *Inter-American Convention on International Commercial Arbitration*, done at Panama, January 30, 1975.]

'**investment**' means every asset that an investor owns or controls, directly or indirectly, that has the characteristics of an investment, including such characteristics as the commitment of capital or other resources, the expectation of gain or profit, or the assumption of risk. Forms that an investment may take include:

(a) an enterprise;
(b) shares, stock, and other forms of equity participation in an enterprise;
(c) bonds, debentures, other debt instruments, and loans;[1]
(d) futures, options, and other derivatives;
(e) turnkey, construction, management, production, concession, revenue-sharing, and other similar contracts;
(f) intellectual property rights;
(g) licenses, authorizations, permits, and similar rights conferred pursuant to domestic law;[2,3] and
(h) other tangible or intangible, movable or immovable property, and related property rights, such as leases, mortgages, liens, and pledges.

'**investment agreement**' means a written agreement[4] between a national authority[5] of a Party and a covered investment or an investor of the other Party, on which the covered investment or the investor relies in establishing or acquiring a covered

---

1. Some forms of debt, such as bonds, debentures, and long-term notes, are more likely to have the characteristics of an investment, while other forms of debt, such as claims to payment that are immediately due and result from the sale of goods or services, are less likely to have such characteristics.
2. Whether a particular type of license, authorization, permit, or similar instrument (including a concession, to the extent that it has the nature of such an instrument) has the characteristics of an investment depends on such factors as the nature and extent of the rights that the holder has under the law of the Party. Among the licenses, authorizations, permits, and similar instruments that do not have the characteristics of an investment are those that do not create any rights protected under domestic law. For greater certainty, the foregoing is without prejudice to whether any asset associated with the license, authorization, permit, or similar instrument has the characteristics of an investment.
3. The term 'investment' does not include an order or judgment entered in a judicial or administrative action.
4. 'Written agreement' refers to an agreement in writing, executed by both parties, whether in a single instrument or in multiple instruments, that creates an exchange of rights and obligations, binding on both parties under the law applicable under Art. 30[Governing Law](2). For greater certainty, (a) a unilateral act of an administrative or judicial authority, such as a permit, license, or authorization issued by a Party solely in its regulatory capacity, or a decree, order, or judgment, standing alone; and (b) an administrative or judicial consent decree or order, shall not be considered a written agreement.
5. For purposes of this definition, 'national authority' means (a) for the United States, an authority at the central level of government; and (b) for [Country], [ ].

investment other than the written agreement itself, that grants rights to the covered investment or investor:

(a)   with respect to natural resources that a national authority controls, such as for their exploration, extraction, refining, transportation, distribution, or sale;

(b)   to supply services to the public on behalf of the Party, such as power generation or distribution, water treatment or distribution, or telecommunications; or

(c)   to undertake infrastructure projects, such as the construction of roads, bridges, canals, dams, or pipelines, that are not for the exclusive or predominant use and benefit of the government.

'**investment authorization**'[6] means an authorization that the foreign investment authority of a Party grants to a covered investment or an investor of the other Party.

'**investor of a non-Party**' means, with respect to a Party, an investor that attempts to make, is making, or has made an investment in the territory of that Party, that is not an investor of either Party.

'**investor of a Party**' means a Party or state enterprise thereof, or a national or an enterprise of a Party, that attempts to make, is making, or has made an investment in the territory of the other Party; provided, however, that a natural person who is a dual national shall be deemed to be exclusively a national of the State of his/her dominant and effective nationality.

'**measure**' includes any law, regulation, procedure, requirement, or practice.

'**national**' means:

(a)   for the United States, a natural person who is a national of the United States as defined in Title III of the Immigration and Nationality Act; and

(b)   for [Country], [____].

'**New York Convention**' means the *United Nations Convention on the Recognition and Enforcement of Foreign Arbitral Awards*, done at New York, June 10, 1958.

'**non-disputing Party**' means the Party that is not a party to an investment dispute.

'**person**' means a natural person or an enterprise.

'**person of a Party**' means a national or an enterprise of a Party.

'**protected information**' means confidential business information or information that is privileged or otherwise protected from disclosure under a Party's law.

---

6.   For greater certainty, actions taken by a Party to enforce laws of general application, such as competition laws, are not encompassed within this definition.

'**regional level of government**' means:

    (a) for the United States, a state of the United States, the District of Columbia, or Puerto Rico; and

    (b) for [Country], [_____].

'**respondent**' means the Party that is a party to an investment dispute.

'**Secretary-General**' means the Secretary-General of ICSID.

'**state enterprise**' means an enterprise owned, or controlled through ownership interests, by a Party.

'**territory**' means:

    (a) with respect to the United States, [_____].

    (b) with respect to [Country,] [_____].

'**TRIPS Agreement**' means *the Agreement on Trade-Related Aspects of Intellectual Property Rights*, contained in Annex 1C to the WTO Agreement.[7]

'**UNCITRAL Arbitration Rules**' means the arbitration rules of the United Nations Commission on International Trade Law.

'**WTO Agreement**' means the *Marrakesh Agreement Establishing the World Trade Organization*, done on April 15, 1994.

Article 2: Scope and Coverage

1. This Treaty applies to measures adopted or maintained by a Party relating to:

    (a) investors of the other Party;

    (b) covered investments; and

    (c) with respect to Articles 8 [Performance Requirements], 12 [Investment and Environment], and 13 [Investment and Labor], all investments in the territory of the Party.

2. A Party's obligations under Section A shall apply:

    (a) to a state enterprise or other person when it exercises any regulatory, administrative, or other governmental authority delegated to it by that Party; and

    (b) to the political subdivisions of that Party.

3. For greater certainty, this Treaty does not bind either Party in relation to any act or fact that took place or any situation that ceased to exist before the date of entry into force of this Treaty.

---

7. For greater certainty, 'TRIPS Agreement' includes any waiver in force between the Parties of any provision of the TRIPS Agreement granted by WTO Members in accordance with the WTO Agreement.

Article 3: National Treatment

1. Each Party shall accord to investors of the other Party treatment no less favorable than that it accords, in like circumstances, to its own investors with respect to the establishment, acquisition, expansion, management, conduct, operation, and sale or other disposition of investments in its territory.

2. Each Party shall accord to covered investments treatment no less favorable than that it accords, in like circumstances, to investments in its territory of its own investors with respect to the establishment, acquisition, expansion, management, conduct, operation, and sale or other disposition of investments.

3. The treatment to be accorded by a Party under paragraphs 1 and 2 means, with respect to a regional level of government, treatment no less favorable than the treatment accorded, in like circumstances, by that regional level of government to natural persons resident in and enterprises constituted under the laws of other regional levels of government of the Party of which it forms a part, and to their respective investments.

Article 4: Most-Favored-Nation Treatment

1. Each Party shall accord to investors of the other Party treatment no less favorable than that it accords, in like circumstances, to investors of any non-Party with respect to the establishment, acquisition, expansion, management, conduct, operation, and sale or other disposition of investments in its territory.

2. Each Party shall accord to covered investments treatment no less favorable than that it accords, in like circumstances, to investments in its territory of investors of any non-Party with respect to the establishment, acquisition, expansion, management, conduct, operation, and sale or other disposition of investments.

Article 5: Minimum Standard of Treatment[8]

1. Each Party shall accord to covered investments treatment in accordance with customary international law, including fair and equitable treatment and full protection and security.

2. For greater certainty, paragraph 1 prescribes the customary international law minimum standard of treatment of aliens as the minimum standard of treatment to be afforded to covered investments. The concepts of 'fair and equitable treatment' and 'full protection and security' do not require treatment in addition to or beyond that which is required by that standard, and do not create additional substantive rights. The obligation in paragraph 1 to provide:

---

8. Article 5 [Minimum Standard of Treatment] shall be interpreted in accordance with Annex A.

(a) 'fair and equitable treatment' includes the obligation not to deny justice in criminal, civil, or administrative adjudicatory proceedings in accordance with the principle of due process embodied in the principal legal systems of the world; and

(b) 'full protection and security' requires each Party to provide the level of police protection required under customary international law.

3. A determination that there has been a breach of another provision of this Treaty, or of a separate international agreement, does not establish that there has been a breach of this Article.

4. Notwithstanding Article 14 [Non-Conforming Measures](5)(b) [subsidies and grants], each Party shall accord to investors of the other Party, and to covered investments, non-discriminatory treatment with respect to measures it adopts or maintains relating to losses suffered by investments in its territory owing to armed conflict or civil strife.

5. Notwithstanding paragraph 4, if an investor of a Party, in the situations referred to in paragraph 4, suffers a loss in the territory of the other Party resulting from:

(a) requisitioning of its covered investment or part thereof by the latter's forces or authorities; or

(b) destruction of its covered investment or part thereof by the latter's forces or authorities, which was not required by the necessity of the situation,

the latter Party shall provide the investor restitution, compensation, or both, as appropriate, for such loss. Any compensation shall be prompt, adequate, and effective in accordance with Article 6 [Expropriation and Compensation] (2) through (4), *mutatis mutandis.*

6. Paragraph 4 does not apply to existing measures relating to subsidies or grants that would be inconsistent with Article 3 [National Treatment] but for Article 14 [Non-Conforming Measures](5)(b) [subsidies and grants].

Article 6: Expropriation and Compensation[9]

1. Neither Party may expropriate or nationalize a covered investment either directly or indirectly through measures equivalent to expropriation or nationalization ('expropriation'), except:

(a) for a public purpose;

(b) in a non-discriminatory manner;

(c) on payment of prompt, adequate, and effective compensation; and

(d) in accordance with due process of law and Article 5 [Minimum Standard of Treatment](1) through (3).

---

9. Article 6 [Expropriation] shall be interpreted in accordance with Annexes A and B.

2. The compensation referred to in paragraph 1(c) shall:

    (a) be paid without delay;

    (b) be equivalent to the fair market value of the expropriated investment immediately before the expropriation took place ('the date of expropriation');

    (c) not reflect any change in value occurring because the intended expropriation had become known earlier; and

    (d) be fully realizable and freely transferable.

3. If the fair market value is denominated in a freely usable currency, the compensation referred to in paragraph 1(c) shall be no less than the fair market value on the date of expropriation, plus interest at a commercially reasonable rate for that currency, accrued from the date of expropriation until the date of payment.

4. If the fair market value is denominated in a currency that is not freely usable, the compensation referred to in paragraph 1(c) – converted into the currency of payment at the market rate of exchange prevailing on the date of payment – shall be no less than:

    (a) the fair market value on the date of expropriation, converted into a freely usable currency at the market rate of exchange prevailing on that date, plus

    (b) interest, at a commercially reasonable rate for that freely usable currency, accrued from the date of expropriation until the date of payment.

5. This Article does not apply to the issuance of compulsory licenses granted in relation to intellectual property rights in accordance with the TRIPS Agreement, or to the revocation, limitation, or creation of intellectual property rights, to the extent that such issuance, revocation, limitation, or creation is consistent with the TRIPS Agreement.

Article 7: Transfers

1. Each Party shall permit all transfers relating to a covered investment to be made freely and without delay into and out of its territory. Such transfers include:

    (a) contributions to capital;

    (b) profits, dividends, capital gains, and proceeds from the sale of all or any part of the covered investment or from the partial or complete liquidation of the covered investment;

    (c) interest, royalty payments, management fees, and technical assistance and other fees;

    (d) payments made under a contract, including a loan agreement;

    (e) payments made pursuant to Article 5 [Minimum Standard of Treatment] (4) and (5) and Article 6 [Expropriation and Compensation]; and

    (f) payments arising out of a dispute.

2. Each Party shall permit transfers relating to a covered investment to be made in a freely usable currency at the market rate of exchange prevailing at the time of transfer.

3. Each Party shall permit returns in kind relating to a covered investment to be made as authorized or specified in a written agreement between the Party and a covered investment or an investor of the other Party.

4. Notwithstanding paragraphs 1 through 3, a Party may prevent a transfer through the equitable, non-discriminatory, and good faith application of its laws relating to:

(a) bankruptcy, insolvency, or the protection of the rights of creditors;
(b) issuing, trading, or dealing in securities, futures, options, or derivatives;
(c) criminal or penal offenses;
(d) financial reporting or record keeping of transfers when necessary to assist law enforcement or financial regulatory authorities; or
(e) ensuring compliance with orders or judgments in judicial or administrative proceedings.

Article 8: Performance Requirements

1. Neither Party may, in connection with the establishment, acquisition, expansion, management, conduct, operation, or sale or other disposition of an investment of an investor of a Party or of a non-Party in its territory, impose or enforce any requirement or enforce any commitment or undertaking:[10]

(a) to export a given level or percentage of goods or services;
(b) to achieve a given level or percentage of domestic content;
(c) to purchase, use, or accord a preference to goods produced in its territory, or to purchase goods from persons in its territory;
(d) to relate in any way the volume or value of imports to the volume or value of exports or to the amount of foreign exchange inflows associated with such investment;
(e) to restrict sales of goods or services in its territory that such investment produces or supplies by relating such sales in any way to the volume or value of its exports or foreign exchange earnings;
(f) to transfer a particular technology, a production process, or other proprietary knowledge to a person in its territory; or
(g) to supply exclusively from the territory of the Party the goods that such investment produces or the services that it supplies to a specific regional market or to the world market.

2. Neither Party may condition the receipt or continued receipt of an advantage, in connection with the establishment, acquisition, expansion, management, conduct,

---

10. For greater certainty, a condition for the receipt or continued receipt of an advantage referred to in para. 2 does not constitute a 'commitment or undertaking' for the purposes of para. 1.

operation, or sale or other disposition of an investment in its territory of an investor of a Party or of a non-Party, on compliance with any requirement:

(a) to achieve a given level or percentage of domestic content;
(b) to purchase, use, or accord a preference to goods produced in its territory, or to purchase goods from persons in its territory;
(c) to relate in any way the volume or value of imports to the volume or value of exports or to the amount of foreign exchange inflows associated with such investment; or
(d) to restrict sales of goods or services in its territory that such investment produces or supplies by relating such sales in any way to the volume or value of its exports or foreign exchange earnings.

3. (a) Nothing in paragraph 2 shall be construed to prevent a Party from conditioning the receipt or continued receipt of an advantage, in connection with an investment in its territory of an investor of a Party or of a non-Party, on compliance with a requirement to locate production, supply a service, train or employ workers, construct or expand particular facilities, or carry out research and development, in its territory.

(b) Paragraph 1(f) does not apply:
(i) when a Party authorizes use of an intellectual property right in accordance with Article 31 of the TRIPS Agreement, or to measures requiring the disclosure of proprietary information that fall within the scope of, and are consistent with, Article 39 of the TRIPS Agreement; or
(ii) when the requirement is imposed or the commitment or undertaking is enforced by a court, administrative tribunal, or competition authority to remedy a practice determined after judicial or administrative process to be anticompetitive under the Party's competition laws.[11]
(c) Provided that such measures are not applied in an arbitrary or unjustifiable manner, and provided that such measures do not constitute a disguised restriction on international trade or investment, paragraphs 1(b), (c), and (f), and 2(a) and (b), shall not be construed to prevent a Party from adopting or maintaining measures, including environmental measures:
(i) necessary to secure compliance with laws and regulations that are not inconsistent with this Treaty;
(ii) necessary to protect human, animal, or plant life or health; or
(iii) related to the conservation of living or non-living exhaustible natural resources.
(d) Paragraphs 1(a), (b), and (c), and 2(a) and (b), do not apply to qualification requirements for goods or services with respect to export promotion and foreign aid programs.
(e) Paragraphs 1(b), (c), (f), and (g), and 2(a) and (b), do not apply to government procurement.

---

11. The Parties recognize that a patent does not necessarily confer market power.

(f) Paragraphs 2(a) and (b) do not apply to requirements imposed by an importing Party relating to the content of goods necessary to qualify for preferential tariffs or preferential quotas.

4. For greater certainty, paragraphs 1 and 2 do not apply to any commitment, undertaking, or requirement other than those set out in those paragraphs.

5. This Article does not preclude enforcement of any commitment, undertaking, or requirement between private parties, where a Party did not impose or require the commitment, undertaking, or requirement.

Article 9: Senior Management and Boards of Directors

1. Neither Party may require that an enterprise of that Party that is a covered investment appoint to senior management positions natural persons of any particular nationality.

2. A Party may require that a majority of the board of directors, or any committee thereof, of an enterprise of that Party that is a covered investment, be of a particular nationality, or resident in the territory of the Party, provided that the requirement does not materially impair the ability of the investor to exercise control over its investment.

Article 10: Publication of Laws and Decisions Respecting Investment

1. Each Party shall ensure that its:

(a) laws, regulations, procedures, and administrative rulings of general application; and
(b) adjudicatory decisions

respecting any matter covered by this Treaty are promptly published or otherwise made publicly available.

2. For purposes of this Article, 'administrative ruling of general application' means an administrative ruling or interpretation that applies to all persons and fact situations that fall generally within its ambit and that establishes a norm of conduct but does not include:

(a) a determination or ruling made in an administrative or quasi-judicial proceeding that applies to a particular covered investment or investor of the other Party in a specific case; or
(b) a ruling that adjudicates with respect to a particular act or practice.

Article 11: Transparency

1. Contact Points

(a) Each Party shall designate a contact point or points to facilitate communications between the Parties on any matter covered by this Treaty.

(b) On the request of the other Party, the contact point(s) shall identify the office or official responsible for the matter and assist, as necessary, in facilitating communication with the requesting Party.

2. Publication

To the extent possible, each Party shall:

(a) publish in advance any measure referred to in Article 10(1)(a) that it proposes to adopt; and

(b) provide interested persons and the other Party a reasonable opportunity to comment on such proposed measures.

3. Provision of Information

(a) On request of the other Party, a Party shall promptly provide information and respond to questions pertaining to any actual or proposed measure that the requesting Party considers might materially affect the operation of this Treaty or otherwise substantially affect its interests under this Treaty.

(b) Any request or information under this paragraph shall be provided to the other Party through the relevant contact points.

(c) Any information provided under this paragraph shall be without prejudice as to whether the measure is consistent with this Treaty.

4. Administrative Proceedings

With a view to administering in a consistent, impartial, and reasonable manner all measures referred to in Article 10(1)(a), each Party shall ensure that in its administrative proceedings applying such measures to particular covered investments or investors of the other Party in specific cases:

(a) wherever possible, covered investments or investors of the other Party that are directly affected by a proceeding are provided reasonable notice, in accordance with domestic procedures, when a proceeding is initiated, including a description of the nature of the proceeding, a statement of the legal authority under which the proceeding is initiated, and a general description of any issues in controversy;

(b) such persons are afforded a reasonable opportunity to present facts and arguments in support of their positions prior to any final administrative action, when time, the nature of the proceeding, and the public interest permit; and

(c) its procedures are in accordance with domestic law.

5. Review and Appeal

(a) Each Party shall establish or maintain judicial, quasi-judicial, or administrative tribunals or procedures for the purpose of the prompt review and, where warranted, correction of final administrative actions regarding matters covered by this Treaty. Such tribunals shall be impartial and independent of the office or authority entrusted with administrative

enforcement and shall not have any substantial interest in the outcome of
the matter.

(b) Each Party shall ensure that, in any such tribunals or procedures, the
parties to the proceeding are provided with the right to:
  (i) a reasonable opportunity to support or defend their respective posi-
      tions; and
  (ii) a decision based on the evidence and submissions of record or, where
       required by domestic law, the record compiled by the administrative
       authority.

(c) Each Party shall ensure, subject to appeal or further review as provided in
its domestic law, that such decisions shall be implemented by, and shall
govern the practice of, the offices or authorities with respect to the administrative action at issue.

Article 12: Investment and Environment

1. The Parties recognize that it is inappropriate to encourage investment by weak-
ening or reducing the protections afforded in domestic environmental laws.[12]
Accordingly, each Party shall strive to ensure that it does not waive or otherwise
derogate from, or offer to waive or otherwise derogate from, such laws in a manner
that weakens or reduces the protections afforded in those laws as an encouragement
for the establishment, acquisition, expansion, or retention of an investment in its
territory. If a Party considers that the other Party has offered such an encouragement, it may request consultations with the other Party and the two Parties shall
consult with a view to avoiding any such encouragement.

2. Nothing in this Treaty shall be construed to prevent a Party from adopting,
maintaining, or enforcing any measure otherwise consistent with this Treaty
that it considers appropriate to ensure that investment activity in its territory is
undertaken in a manner sensitive to environmental concerns.

Article 13: Investment and Labor

1. The Parties recognize that it is inappropriate to encourage investment by weak-
ening or reducing the protections afforded in domestic labor laws. Accordingly,
each Party shall strive to ensure that it does not waive or otherwise derogate from,
or offer to waive or otherwise derogate from, such laws in a manner that weakens or
reduces adherence to the internationally recognized labor rights referred to in
paragraph 2 as an encouragement for the establishment, acquisition, expansion,
or retention of an investment in its territory. If a Party considers that the other Party
has offered such an encouragement, it may request consultations with the other

---

12. For the United States, 'laws' for purposes of this Article means an act of the United States
    Congress or regulations promulgated pursuant to an act of the United States Congress that is
    enforceable by action of the central level of government.

Party and the two Parties shall consult with a view to avoiding any such encouragement.

2. For purposes of this Article, 'labor laws' means each Party's statutes or regulations,[13] or provisions thereof, that are directly related to the following internationally recognized labor rights:

    (a) the right of association;

    (b) the right to organize and bargain collectively;

    (c) a prohibition on the use of any form of forced or compulsory labor;

    (d) labor protections for children and young people, including a minimum age for the employment of children and the prohibition and elimination of the worst forms of child labor; and

    (e) acceptable conditions of work with respect to minimum wages, hours of work, and occupational safety and health.

Article 14: Non-Conforming Measures

1. Articles 3 [National Treatment], 4 [Most-Favored-Nation Treatment], 8 [Performance Requirements], and 9 [Senior Management and Boards of Directors] do not apply to:

    (a) any existing non-conforming measure that is maintained by a Party at:

        (i) the central level of government, as set out by that Party in its Schedule to Annex I or Annex III,

        (ii) a regional level of government, as set out by that Party in its Schedule to Annex I or Annex III, or

        (iii) a local level of government;

    (b) the continuation or prompt renewal of any non-conforming measure referred to in subparagraph (a); or

    (c) an amendment to any non-conforming measure referred to in subparagraph (a) to the extent that the amendment does not decrease the conformity of the measure, as it existed immediately before the amendment, with Article 3 [National Treatment], 4 [Most-Favored-Nation Treatment], 8 [Performance Requirements], or 9 [Senior Management and Boards of Directors].

2. Articles 3 [National Treatment], 4 [Most-Favored-Nation Treatment], 8 [Performance Requirements], and 9 [Senior Management and Boards of Directors] do not apply to any measure that a Party adopts or maintains with respect to sectors, subsectors, or activities, as set out in its Schedule to Annex II.

3. Neither Party may, under any measure adopted after the date of entry into force of this Treaty and covered by its Schedule to Annex II, require an investor of the

---

13. For the United States, 'statutes or regulations' for purposes of this Article means an act of the United States Congress or regulations promulgated pursuant to an act of the United States Congress that is enforceable by action of the central level of government.

other Party, by reason of its nationality, to sell or otherwise dispose of an investment existing at the time the measure becomes effective.

4. Articles 3 [National Treatment] and 4 [Most-Favored-Nation Treatment] do not apply to any measure covered by an exception to, or derogation from, the obligations under Article 3 or 4 of the TRIPS Agreement, as specifically provided in those Articles and in Article 5 of the TRIPS Agreement.

5. Articles 3 [National Treatment], 4 [Most-Favored-Nation Treatment], and 9 [Senior Management and Boards of Directors] do not apply to:

(a) government procurement; or
(b) subsidies or grants provided by a Party, including government-supported loans, guarantees, and insurance.

Article 15: Special Formalities and Information Requirements

1. Nothing in Article 3 [National Treatment] shall be construed to prevent a Party from adopting or maintaining a measure that prescribes special formalities in connection with covered investments, such as a requirement that investors be residents of the Party or that covered investments be legally constituted under the laws or regulations of the Party, provided that such formalities do not materially impair the protections afforded by a Party to investors of the other Party and covered investments pursuant to this Treaty.

2. Notwithstanding Articles 3 [National Treatment] and 4 [Most-Favored-Nation Treatment], a Party may require an investor of the other Party or its covered investment to provide information concerning that investment solely for informational or statistical purposes. The Party shall protect any confidential business information from any disclosure that would prejudice the competitive position of the investor or the covered investment. Nothing in this paragraph shall be construed to prevent a Party from otherwise obtaining or disclosing information in connection with the equitable and good faith application of its law.

Article 16: Non-Derogation

This Treaty shall not derogate from any of the following that entitle an investor of a Party or a covered investment to treatment more favorable than that accorded by this Treaty:

1. laws or regulations, administrative practices or procedures, or administrative or adjudicatory decisions of a Party;

2. international legal obligations of a Party; or

3. obligations assumed by a Party, including those contained in an investment authorization or an investment agreement.

Article 17: Denial of Benefits

1. A Party may deny the benefits of this Treaty to an investor of the other Party that is an enterprise of such other Party and to investments of that investor if persons of a non-Party own or control the enterprise and the denying Party:

- (a) does not maintain diplomatic relations with the non-Party; or
- (b) adopts or maintains measures with respect to the non-Party or a person of the non-Party that prohibit transactions with the enterprise or that would be violated or circumvented if the benefits of this Treaty were accorded to the enterprise or to its investments.

2. A Party may deny the benefits of this Treaty to an investor of the other Party that is an enterprise of such other Party and to investments of that investor if the enterprise has no substantial business activities in the territory of the other Party and persons of a non-Party, or of the denying Party, own or control the enterprise.

Article 18: Essential Security

Nothing in this Treaty shall be construed:

1. to require a Party to furnish or allow access to any information the disclosure of which it determines to be contrary to its essential security interests; or

2. to preclude a Party from applying measures that it considers necessary for the fulfillment of its obligations with respect to the maintenance or restoration of international peace or security, or the protection of its own essential security interests.

Article 19: Disclosure of Information

Nothing in this Treaty shall be construed to require a Party to furnish or allow access to confidential information the disclosure of which would impede law enforcement or otherwise be contrary to the public interest, or which would prejudice the legitimate commercial interests of particular enterprises, public or private.

Article 20: Financial Services

1. Notwithstanding any other provision of this Treaty, a Party shall not be prevented from adopting or maintaining measures relating to financial services for prudential reasons, including for the protection of investors, depositors, policy holders, or persons to whom a fiduciary duty is owed by a financial services supplier, or to ensure the integrity and stability of the financial system.[14] Where such measures do

---

14. It is understood that the term 'prudential reasons' includes the maintenance of the safety, soundness, integrity, or financial responsibility of individual financial institutions.

not conform with the provisions of this Treaty, they shall not be used as a means of avoiding the Party's commitments or obligations under this Treaty.

2.   (a) Nothing in this Treaty applies to non-discriminatory measures of general application taken by any public entity in pursuit of monetary and related credit policies or exchange rate policies. This paragraph shall not affect a Party's obligations under Article 7 [Transfers] or Article 8 [Performance Requirements].[15]

     (b) For purposes of this paragraph, 'public entity' means a central bank or monetary authority of a Party.

3. Where a claimant submits a claim to arbitration under Section B [Investor-State Dispute Settlement], and the respondent invokes paragraph 1 or 2 as a defense, the following provisions shall apply:

     (a) The respondent shall, within 120 days of the date the claim is submitted to arbitration under Section B, submit in writing to the competent financial authorities[16] of both Parties a request for a joint determination on the issue of whether and to what extent paragraph 1 or 2 is a valid defense to the claim. The respondent shall promptly provide the tribunal, if constituted, a copy of such request. The arbitration may proceed with respect to the claim only as provided in subparagraph (d).

     (b) The competent financial authorities of both Parties shall make themselves available for consultations with each other and shall attempt in good faith to make a determination as described in subparagraph (a). Any such determination shall be transmitted promptly to the disputing parties and, if constituted, to the tribunal. The determination shall be binding on the tribunal.

     (c) If the competent financial authorities of both Parties, within 120 days of the date by which they have both received the respondent's written request for a joint determination under subparagraph (a), have not made a determination as described in that subparagraph, the tribunal shall decide the issue left unresolved by the competent financial authorities. The provisions of Section B shall apply, except as modified by this subparagraph.

        (i) In the appointment of all arbitrators not yet appointed to the tribunal, each disputing party shall take appropriate steps to ensure that the tribunal has expertise or experience in financial services law or

---

15. For greater certainty, measures of general application taken in pursuit of monetary and related credit policies or exchange rate policies do not include measures that expressly nullify or amend contractual provisions that specify the currency of denomination or the rate of exchange of currencies.

16. For purposes of this Article, 'competent financial authorities' means, for the United States, the Department of the Treasury for banking and other financial services, and the Office of the United States Trade Representative, in coordination with the Department of Commerce and other agencies, for insurance; and for [Country], [_____].

practice. The expertise of particular candidates with respect to financial services shall be taken into account in the appointment of the presiding arbitrator.

(ii) If, before the respondent submits the request for a joint determination in conformance with subparagraph (a), the presiding arbitrator has been appointed pursuant to Article 27(3), such arbitrator shall be replaced on the request of either disputing party and the tribunal shall be reconstituted consistent with subparagraph (c)(i). If, within 30 days of the date the arbitration proceedings are resumed under subparagraph (d), the disputing parties have not agreed on the appointment of a new presiding arbitrator, the Secretary-General, on the request of a disputing party, shall appoint the presiding arbitrator consistent with subparagraph (c)(i).

(iii) The non-disputing Party may make oral and written submissions to the tribunal regarding the issue of whether and to what extent paragraph 1 or 2 is a valid defense to the claim. Unless it makes such a submission, the non-disputing Party shall be presumed, for purposes of the arbitration, to take a position on paragraph 1 or 2 not inconsistent with that of the respondent.

(d) The arbitration referred to in subparagraph (a) may proceed with respect to the claim:

(i) 10 days after the date the competent financial authorities' joint determination has been received by both the disputing parties and, if constituted, the tribunal; or

(ii) 10 days after the expiration of the 120-day period provided to the competent financial authorities in subparagraph (c).

4. Where a dispute arises under Section C and the competent financial authorities of one Party provide written notice to the competent financial authorities of the other Party that the dispute involves financial services, Section C shall apply except as modified by this paragraph and paragraph 5.

(a) The competent financial authorities of both Parties shall make themselves available for consultations with each other regarding the dispute, and shall have 180 days from the date such notice is received to transmit a report on their consultations to the Parties. A Party may submit the dispute to arbitration under Section C only after the expiration of that 180-day period.

(b) Either Party may make any such report available to a tribunal constituted under Section C to decide the dispute referred to in this paragraph or a similar dispute, or to a tribunal constituted under Section B to decide a claim arising out of the same events or circumstances that gave rise to the dispute under Section C.

5. Where a Party submits a dispute involving financial services to arbitration under Section C in conformance with paragraph 4, and on the request of either Party within 30 days of the date the dispute is submitted to arbitration, each Party shall, in the appointment of all arbitrators not yet appointed, take appropriate steps to ensure that the tribunal has expertise or experience in financial services law or practice. The expertise of particular candidates with respect to financial services shall be taken into account in the appointment of the presiding arbitrator.

6. Notwithstanding Article 11(2) [Transparency – Publication], each Party shall, to the extent practicable,

(a) publish in advance any regulations of general application relating to financial services that it proposes to adopt;
(b) provide interested persons and the other Party a reasonable opportunity to comment on such proposed regulations.

7. The terms 'financial service' or 'financial services' shall have the same meaning as in subparagraph 5(a) of the Annex on Financial Services of the GATS.

Article 21: Taxation

1. Except as provided in this Article, nothing in Section A shall impose obligations with respect to taxation measures.

2. Article 6 [Expropriation] shall apply to all taxation measures, except that a claimant that asserts that a taxation measure involves an expropriation may submit a claim to arbitration under Section B only if:

(a) the claimant has first referred to the competent tax authorities[17] of both Parties in writing the issue of whether that taxation measure involves an expropriation; and
(b) within 180 days after the date of such referral, the competent tax authorities of both Parties fail to agree that the taxation measure is not an expropriation.

3. Subject to paragraph 4, Article 8 [Performance Requirements] (2) through (4) shall apply to all taxation measures.

4. Nothing in this Treaty shall affect the rights and obligations of either Party under any tax convention. In the event of any inconsistency between this Treaty and any such convention, that convention shall prevail to the extent of the inconsistency. In the case of a tax convention between the Parties, the competent authorities under that convention shall have sole responsibility for determining whether any inconsistency exists between this Treaty and that convention.

---

17. For the purposes of this Article, the 'competent tax authorities' means:

(a) for the United States, the Assistant Secretary of the Treasury (Tax Policy), Department of the Treasury; and
(b) for [Country], [_____].

Article 22: Entry into Force, Duration, and Termination

1. This Treaty shall enter into force thirty days after the date the Parties exchange instruments of ratification. It shall remain in force for a period of ten years and shall continue in force thereafter unless terminated in accordance with paragraph 2.

2. A Party may terminate this Treaty at the end of the initial ten-year period or at any time thereafter by giving one year's written notice to the other Party.

3. For ten years from the date of termination, all other Articles shall continue to apply to covered investments established or acquired prior to the date of termination, except insofar as those Articles extend to the establishment or acquisition of covered investments.

SECTION B

Article 23: Consultation and Negotiation

In the event of an investment dispute, the claimant and the respondent should initially seek to resolve the dispute through consultation and negotiation, which may include the use of non-binding, third-party procedures.

Article 24: Submission of a Claim to Arbitration

1. In the event that a disputing party considers that an investment dispute cannot be settled by consultation and negotiation:

    (a) the claimant, on its own behalf, may submit to arbitration under this Section a claim

        (i) that the respondent has breached

            (A) an obligation under Articles 3 through 10,

            (B) an investment authorization, or

            (C) an investment agreement;

      and

        (ii) that the claimant has incurred loss or damage by reason of, or arising out of, that breach; and

    (b) the claimant, on behalf of an enterprise of the respondent that is a juridical person that the claimant owns or controls directly or indirectly, may submit to arbitration under this Section a claim

        (i) that the respondent has breached

            (A) an obligation under Articles 3 through 10,

            (B) an investment authorization, or

            (C) an investment agreement;

      and

        (ii) that the enterprise has incurred loss or damage by reason of, or arising out of, that breach, provided that a claimant may submit pursuant to subparagraph (a)(i)(C) or (b)(i)(C) a claim for breach of an investment agreement only if the subject matter of the claim and the claimed damages directly relate to the covered investment that was established or acquired, or sought to be established or acquired, in reliance on the relevant investment agreement.

2. At least 90 days before submitting any claim to arbitration under this Section, a claimant shall deliver to the respondent a written notice of its intention to submit the claim to arbitration ('notice of intent'). The notice shall specify:

  (a) the name and address of the claimant and, where a claim is submitted on behalf of an enterprise, the name, address, and place of incorporation of the enterprise;
  (b) for each claim, the provision of this Treaty, investment authorization, or investment agreement alleged to have been breached and any other relevant provisions;
  (c) the legal and factual basis for each claim; and
  (d) the relief sought and the approximate amount of damages claimed.

3. Provided that six months have elapsed since the events giving rise to the claim, a claimant may submit a claim referred to in paragraph 1:

  (a) under the ICSID Convention and the ICSID Rules of Procedure for Arbitration Proceedings, provided that both the respondent and the non-disputing Party are parties to the ICSID Convention;
  (b) under the ICSID Additional Facility Rules, provided that either the respondent or the non-disputing Party is a party to the ICSID Convention;
  (c) under the UNCITRAL Arbitration Rules; or
  (d) if the claimant and respondent agree, to any other arbitration institution or under any other arbitration rules.

4. A claim shall be deemed submitted to arbitration under this Section when the claimant's notice of or request for arbitration ('notice of arbitration'):

  (a) referred to in paragraph 1 of Article 36 of the ICSID Convention is received by the Secretary-General;
  (b) referred to in Article 2 of Schedule C of the ICSID Additional Facility Rules is received by the Secretary-General;
  (c) referred to in Article 3 of the UNCITRAL Arbitration Rules, together with the statement of claim referred to in Article 18 of the UNCITRAL Arbitration Rules, are received by the respondent; or
  (d) referred to under any arbitration institution or arbitral rules selected under paragraph 3(d) is received by the respondent.

A claim asserted by the claimant for the first time after such notice of arbitration is submitted shall be deemed submitted to arbitration under this Section on the date of its receipt under the applicable arbitral rules.

5. The arbitration rules applicable under paragraph 3, and in effect on the date the claim or claims were submitted to arbitration under this Section, shall govern the arbitration except to the extent modified by this Treaty.

6. The claimant shall provide with the notice of arbitration:

    (a) the name of the arbitrator that the claimant appoints; or

    (b) the claimant's written consent for the Secretary-General to appoint that arbitrator.

Article 25: Consent of Each Party to Arbitration

1. Each Party consents to the submission of a claim to arbitration under this Section in accordance with this Treaty.

2. The consent under paragraph 1 and the submission of a claim to arbitration under this Section shall satisfy the requirements of:

    (a) Chapter II of the ICSID Convention (Jurisdiction of the Centre) and the ICSID Additional Facility Rules for written consent of the parties to the dispute; [and]

    (b) Article II of the New York Convention for an 'agreement in writing[.'] [;' and

    (c) Article I of the Inter-American Convention for an 'agreement.']

Article 26: Conditions and Limitations on Consent of Each Party

1. No claim may be submitted to arbitration under this Section if more than three years have elapsed from the date on which the claimant first acquired, or should have first acquired, knowledge of the breach alleged under Article 24(1) and knowledge that the claimant (for claims brought under Article 24(1)(a)) or the enterprise (for claims brought under Article 24(1)(b)) has incurred loss or damage.

2. No claim may be submitted to arbitration under this Section unless:

    (a) the claimant consents in writing to arbitration in accordance with the procedures set out in this Treaty; and

    (b) the notice of arbitration is accompanied,

        (i) for claims submitted to arbitration under Article 24(1)(a), by the claimant's written waiver, and

        (ii) for claims submitted to arbitration under Article 24(1)(b), by the claimant's and the enterprise's written waivers

    of any right to initiate or continue before any administrative tribunal or court under the law of either Party, or other dispute settlement procedures, any proceeding with respect to any measure alleged to constitute a breach referred to in Article 24.

3. Notwithstanding paragraph 2(b), the claimant (for claims brought under Article 24(1)(a)) and the claimant or the enterprise (for claims brought under Article 24(1)(b)) may initiate or continue an action that seeks interim injunctive relief and does not involve the payment of monetary damages before a judicial or administrative tribunal of the respondent, provided that the action is brought for the sole purpose of preserving the claimant's or the enterprise's rights and interests during the pendency of the arbitration.

Article 27: Selection of Arbitrators

1. Unless the disputing parties otherwise agree, the tribunal shall comprise three arbitrators, one arbitrator appointed by each of the disputing parties and the third, who shall be the presiding arbitrator, appointed by agreement of the disputing parties.

2. The Secretary-General shall serve as appointing authority for an arbitration under this Section.

3. Subject to Article 20(3), if a tribunal has not been constituted within 75 days from the date that a claim is submitted to arbitration under this Section, the Secretary-General, on the request of a disputing party, shall appoint, in his/her discretion, the arbitrator or arbitrators not yet appointed.

4. For purposes of Article 39 of the ICSID Convention and Article 7 of Schedule C to the ICSID Additional Facility Rules, and without prejudice to an objection to an arbitrator on a ground other than nationality:

    (a) the respondent agrees to the appointment of each individual member of a tribunal established under the ICSID Convention or the ICSID Additional Facility Rules;

    (b) a claimant referred to in Article 24(1)(a) may submit a claim to arbitration under this Section, or continue a claim, under the ICSID Convention or the ICSID Additional Facility Rules, only on condition that the claimant agrees in writing to the appointment of each individual member of the tribunal; and

    (c) a claimant referred to in Article 24(1)(b) may submit a claim to arbitration under this Section, or continue a claim, under the ICSID Convention or the ICSID Additional Facility Rules, only on condition that the claimant and the enterprise agree in writing to the appointment of each individual member of the tribunal.

Article 28: Conduct of the Arbitration

1. The disputing parties may agree on the legal place of any arbitration under the arbitral rules applicable under Article 24(3). If the disputing parties fail to reach agreement, the tribunal shall determine the place in accordance with the applicable arbitral rules, provided that the place shall be in the territory of a State that is a party to the New York Convention.

2. The non-disputing Party may make oral and written submissions to the tribunal regarding the interpretation of this Treaty.

3. The tribunal shall have the authority to accept and consider *amicus curiae* submissions from a person or entity that is not a disputing party.

4. Without prejudice to a tribunal's authority to address other objections as a preliminary question, a tribunal shall address and decide as a preliminary question any objection by the respondent that, as a matter of law, a claim submitted is not a claim for which an award in favor of the claimant may be made under Article 34.

    (a) Such objection shall be submitted to the tribunal as soon as possible after the tribunal is constituted, and in no event later than the date the tribunal fixes for the respondent to submit its counter-memorial (or, in the case of an amendment to the notice of arbitration, the date the tribunal fixes for the respondent to submit its response to the amendment).

    (b) On receipt of an objection under this paragraph, the tribunal shall suspend any proceedings on the merits, establish a schedule for considering the objection consistent with any schedule it has established for considering any other preliminary question, and issue a decision or award on the objection, stating the grounds therefor.

    (c) In deciding an objection under this paragraph, the tribunal shall assume to be true claimant's factual allegations in support of any claim in the notice of arbitration (or any amendment thereof) and, in disputes brought under the UNCITRAL Arbitration Rules, the statement of claim referred to in Article 18 of the UNCITRAL Arbitration Rules. The tribunal may also consider any relevant facts not in dispute.

    (d) The respondent does not waive any objection as to competence or any argument on the merits merely because the respondent did or did not raise an objection under this paragraph or make use of the expedited procedure set out in paragraph 5.

5. In the event that the respondent so requests within 45 days after the tribunal is constituted, the tribunal shall decide on an expedited basis an objection under paragraph 4 and any objection that the dispute is not within the tribunal's competence. The tribunal shall suspend any proceedings on the merits and issue a decision or award on the objection(s), stating the grounds therefor, no later than 150 days after the date of the request. However, if a disputing party requests a hearing, the tribunal may take an additional 30 days to issue the decision or award. Regardless of whether a hearing is requested, a tribunal may, on a showing of extraordinary cause, delay issuing its decision or award by an additional brief period, which may not exceed 30 days.

6. When it decides a respondent's objection under paragraph 4 or 5, the tribunal may, if warranted, award to the prevailing disputing party reasonable costs and attorney's fees incurred in submitting or opposing the objection. In determining whether such an award is warranted, the tribunal shall consider whether either the claimant's claim or the respondent's objection was frivolous, and shall provide the disputing parties a reasonable opportunity to comment.

7. A respondent may not assert as a defense, counterclaim, right of set-off, or for any other reason that the claimant has received or will receive indemnification or other compensation for all or part of the alleged damages pursuant to an insurance or guarantee contract.

8. A tribunal may order an interim measure of protection to preserve the rights of a disputing party, or to ensure that the tribunal's jurisdiction is made fully effective, including an order to preserve evidence in the possession or control of a disputing party or to protect the tribunal's jurisdiction. A tribunal may not order attachment or enjoin the application of a measure alleged to constitute a breach referred to in Article 24. For purposes of this paragraph, an order includes a recommendation.

9.   (a) In any arbitration conducted under this Section, at the request of a disputing party, a tribunal shall, before issuing a decision or award on liability, transmit its proposed decision or award to the disputing parties and to the non-disputing Party. Within 60 days after the tribunal transmits its proposed decision or award, the disputing parties may submit written comments to the tribunal concerning any aspect of its proposed decision or award. The tribunal shall consider any such comments and issue its decision or award not later than 45 days after the expiration of the 60-day comment period.

   (b) Subparagraph (a) shall not apply in any arbitration conducted pursuant to this Section for which an appeal has been made available pursuant to paragraph 10 or Annex D.

10. If a separate, multilateral agreement enters into force between the Parties that establishes an appellate body for purposes of reviewing awards rendered by tribunals constituted pursuant to international trade or investment arrangements to hear investment disputes, the Parties shall strive to reach an agreement that would have such appellate body review awards rendered under Article 34 in arbitrations commenced after the multilateral agreement enters into force between the Parties.

Article 29: Transparency of Arbitral Proceedings

1. Subject to paragraphs 2 and 4, the respondent shall, after receiving the following documents, promptly transmit them to the non-disputing Party and make them available to the public:

   (a) the notice of intent;
   (b) the notice of arbitration;
   (c) pleadings, memorials, and briefs submitted to the tribunal by a disputing party and any written submissions submitted pursuant to Article 28(2)

[Non-Disputing Party submissions] and (3) [*Amicus* Submissions] and Article 33 [Consolidation];

(d) minutes or transcripts of hearings of the tribunal, where available; and

(e) orders, awards, and decisions of the tribunal.

2. The tribunal shall conduct hearings open to the public and shall determine, in consultation with the disputing parties, the appropriate logistical arrangements. However, any disputing party that intends to use information designated as protected information in a hearing shall so advise the tribunal. The tribunal shall make appropriate arrangements to protect the information from disclosure.

3. Nothing in this Section requires a respondent to disclose protected information or to furnish or allow access to information that it may withhold in accordance with Article 18 [Essential Security Article] or Article 19 [Disclosure of Information Article].

4. Any protected information that is submitted to the tribunal shall be protected from disclosure in accordance with the following procedures:

(a) Subject to subparagraph (d), neither the disputing parties nor the tribunal shall disclose to the non-disputing Party or to the public any protected information where the disputing party that provided the information clearly designates it in accordance with subparagraph (b);

(b) Any disputing party claiming that certain information constitutes protected information shall clearly designate the information at the time it is submitted to the tribunal;

(c) A disputing party shall, at the time it submits a document containing information claimed to be protected information, submit a redacted version of the document that does not contain the information. Only the redacted version shall be provided to the non-disputing Party and made public in accordance with paragraph 1; and

(d) The tribunal shall decide any objection regarding the designation of information claimed to be protected information. If the tribunal determines that such information was not properly designated, the disputing party that submitted the information may (i) withdraw all or part of its submission containing such information, or (ii) agree to resubmit complete and redacted documents with corrected designations in accordance with the tribunal's determination and subparagraph (c). In either case, the other disputing party shall, whenever necessary, resubmit complete and redacted documents which either remove the information withdrawn under (i) by the disputing party that first submitted the information or redesignate the information consistent with the designation under (ii) of the disputing party that first submitted the information.

5. Nothing in this Section requires a respondent to withhold from the public information required to be disclosed by its laws.

Article 30: Governing Law

1. Subject to paragraph 3, when a claim is submitted under Article 24(1)(a)(i)(A) or Article 24(1)(b)(i)(A), the tribunal shall decide the issues in dispute in accordance with this Treaty and applicable rules of international law.

2. Subject to paragraph 3 and the other terms of this Section, when a claim is submitted under Article 24(1)(a)(i)(B) or (C), or Article 24(1)(b)(i)(B) or (C), the tribunal shall apply:

(a) the rules of law specified in the pertinent investment authorization or investment agreement, or as the disputing parties may otherwise agree; or
(b) if the rules of law have not been specified or otherwise agreed:
  (i) the law of the respondent, including its rules on the conflict of laws;[18] and
  (ii) such rules of international law as may be applicable.

3. A joint decision of the Parties, each acting through its representative designated for purposes of this Article, declaring their interpretation of a provision of this Treaty shall be binding on a tribunal, and any decision or award issued by a tribunal must be consistent with that joint decision.

Article 31: Interpretation of Annexes

1. Where a respondent asserts as a defense that the measure alleged to be a breach is within the scope of an entry set out in Annex I, II, or III, the tribunal shall, on request of the respondent, request the interpretation of the Parties on the issue. The Parties shall submit in writing any joint decision declaring their interpretation to the tribunal within 60 days of delivery of the request.

2. A joint decision issued under paragraph 1 by the Parties, each acting through its representative designated for purposes of this Article, shall be binding on the tribunal, and any decision or award issued by the tribunal must be consistent with that joint decision. If the Parties fail to issue such a decision within 60 days, the tribunal shall decide the issue.

Article 32: Expert Reports

Without prejudice to the appointment of other kinds of experts where authorized by the applicable arbitration rules, a tribunal, at the request of a disputing party or, unless the disputing parties disapprove, on its own initiative, may appoint one or more experts to report to it in writing on any factual issue concerning environmental, health, safety, or other scientific matters raised by a disputing party in a

---

18. The 'law of the respondent' means the law that a domestic court or tribunal of proper jurisdiction would apply in the same case.

proceeding, subject to such terms and conditions as the disputing parties may agree.

Article 33: Consolidation

1. Where two or more claims have been submitted separately to arbitration under Article 24(1) and the claims have a question of law or fact in common and arise out of the same events or circumstances, any disputing party may seek a consolidation order in accordance with the agreement of all the disputing parties sought to be covered by the order or the terms of paragraphs 2 through 10.

2. A disputing party that seeks a consolidation order under this Article shall deliver, in writing, a request to the Secretary-General and to all the disputing parties sought to be covered by the order and shall specify in the request:

> (a) the names and addresses of all the disputing parties sought to be covered by the order;
> (b) the nature of the order sought; and
> (c) the grounds on which the order is sought.

3. Unless the Secretary-General finds within 30 days after receiving a request under paragraph 2 that the request is manifestly unfounded, a tribunal shall be established under this Article.

4. Unless all the disputing parties sought to be covered by the order otherwise agree, a tribunal established under this Article shall comprise three arbitrators:

> (a) one arbitrator appointed by agreement of the claimants;
> (b) one arbitrator appointed by the respondent; and
> (c) the presiding arbitrator appointed by the Secretary-General, provided, however, that the presiding arbitrator shall not be a national of either Party.

5. If, within 60 days after the Secretary-General receives a request made under paragraph 2, the respondent fails or the claimants fail to appoint an arbitrator in accordance with paragraph 4, the Secretary-General, on the request of any disputing party sought to be covered by the order, shall appoint the arbitrator or arbitrators not yet appointed. If the respondent fails to appoint an arbitrator, the Secretary-General shall appoint a national of the disputing Party, and if the claimants fail to appoint an arbitrator, the Secretary-General shall appoint a national of the non-disputing Party.

6. Where a tribunal established under this Article is satisfied that two or more claims that have been submitted to arbitration under Article 24(1) have a question of law or fact in common, and arise out of the same events or circumstances, the tribunal may, in the interest of fair and efficient resolution of the claims, and after hearing the disputing parties, by order:

(a) assume jurisdiction over, and hear and determine together, all or part of the claims;

(b) assume jurisdiction over, and hear and determine one or more of the claims, the determination of which it believes would assist in the resolution of the others; or

(c) instruct a tribunal previously established under Article 27 [Selection of Arbitrators] to assume jurisdiction over, and hear and determine together, all or part of the claims, provided that

    (i) that tribunal, at the request of any claimant not previously a disputing party before that tribunal, shall be reconstituted with its original members, except that the arbitrator for the claimants shall be appointed pursuant to paragraphs 4(a) and 5; and

    (ii) that tribunal shall decide whether any prior hearing shall be repeated.

7. Where a tribunal has been established under this Article, a claimant that has submitted a claim to arbitration under Article 24(1) and that has not been named in a request made under paragraph 2 may make a written request to the tribunal that it be included in any order made under paragraph 6, and shall specify in the request:

(a) the name and address of the claimant;

(b) the nature of the order sought; and

(c) the grounds on which the order is sought.

The claimant shall deliver a copy of its request to the Secretary-General.

8. A tribunal established under this Article shall conduct its proceedings in accordance with the UNCITRAL Arbitration Rules, except as modified by this Section.

9. A tribunal established under Article 27 [Selection of Arbitrators] shall not have jurisdiction to decide a claim, or a part of a claim, over which a tribunal established or instructed under this Article has assumed jurisdiction.

10. On application of a disputing party, a tribunal established under this Article, pending its decision under paragraph 6, may order that the proceedings of a tribunal established under Article 27 [Selection of Arbitrators] be stayed, unless the latter tribunal has already adjourned its proceedings.

Article 34: Awards

1. Where a tribunal makes a final award against a respondent, the tribunal may award, separately or in combination, only:

(a) monetary damages and any applicable interest; and

(b) restitution of property, in which case the award shall provide that the respondent may pay monetary damages and any applicable interest in lieu of restitution.

A tribunal may also award costs and attorney's fees in accordance with this Treaty and the applicable arbitration rules.

2. Subject to paragraph 1, where a claim is submitted to arbitration under Article 24(1)(b):

- (a) an award of restitution of property shall provide that restitution be made to the enterprise;
- (b) an award of monetary damages and any applicable interest shall provide that the sum be paid to the enterprise; and
- (c) the award shall provide that it is made without prejudice to any right that any person may have in the relief under applicable domestic law.

3. A tribunal may not award punitive damages.

4. An award made by a tribunal shall have no binding force except between the disputing parties and in respect of the particular case.

5. Subject to paragraph 6 and the applicable review procedure for an interim award, a disputing party shall abide by and comply with an award without delay.

6. A disputing party may not seek enforcement of a final award until:

- (a) in the case of a final award made under the ICSID Convention,
    - (i) 120 days have elapsed from the date the award was rendered and no disputing party has requested revision or annulment of the award; or
    - (ii) revision or annulment proceedings have been completed; and
- (b) in the case of a final award under the ICSID Additional Facility Rules, the UNCITRAL Arbitration Rules, or the rules selected pursuant to Article 24(3)(d),
    - (i) 90 days have elapsed from the date the award was rendered and no disputing party has commenced a proceeding to revise, set aside, or annul the award; or
    - (ii) a court has dismissed or allowed an application to revise, set aside, or annul the award and there is no further appeal.

7. Each Party shall provide for the enforcement of an award in its territory.

8. If the respondent fails to abide by or comply with a final award, on delivery of a request by the non-disputing Party, a tribunal shall be established under Article 37 [State-State Dispute Settlement]. Without prejudice to other remedies available under applicable rules of international law, the requesting Party may seek in such proceedings:

- (a) a determination that the failure to abide by or comply with the final award is inconsistent with the obligations of this Treaty; and
- (b) a recommendation that the respondent abide by or comply with the final award.

9. A disputing party may seek enforcement of an arbitration award under the ICSID Convention or the New York Convention [or the Inter-American Convention] regardless of whether proceedings have been taken under paragraph 8.

10. A claim that is submitted to arbitration under this Section shall be considered to arise out of a commercial relationship or transaction for purposes of Article I of the New York Convention [and Article I of the Inter-American Convention].

Article 35: Annexes and Footnotes

The Annexes and footnotes shall form an integral part of this Treaty.

Article 36: Service of Documents

Delivery of notice and other documents on a Party shall be made to the place named for that Party in Annex C.

Section C

Article 37: State-State Dispute Settlement

1. Subject to paragraph 5, any dispute between the Parties concerning the interpretation or application of this Treaty, that is not resolved through consultations or other diplomatic channels, shall be submitted on the request of either Party to arbitration for a binding decision or award by a tribunal in accordance with applicable rules of international law. In the absence of an agreement by the Parties to the contrary, the UNCITRAL Arbitration Rules shall govern, except as modified by the Parties or this Treaty.

2. Unless the Parties otherwise agree, the tribunal shall comprise three arbitrators, one arbitrator appointed by each Party and the third, who shall be the presiding arbitrator, appointed by agreement of the Parties. If a tribunal has not been constituted within 75 days from the date that a claim is submitted to arbitration under this Section, the Secretary-General, on the request of either Party, shall appoint, in his/her discretion, the arbitrator or arbitrators not yet appointed.

3. Expenses incurred by the arbitrators, and other costs of the proceedings, shall be paid for equally by the Parties. However, the tribunal may, in its discretion, direct that a higher proportion of the costs be paid by one of the Parties.

4. Articles 28(3) [*Amicus Curiae* Submissions], 29 [Investor-State Transparency], 30(1) and (3) [Governing Law], and 31 [Interpretation of Annexes] shall apply *mutatis mutandis* to arbitrations under this Article.

5. Paragraphs 1 through 4 shall not apply to a matter arising under Article 12 or Article 13.

IN WITNESS WHEREOF, the respective plenipotentiaries have signed this Treaty.

DONE in duplicate at [city] this [number] day of [month, year], in the English and [foreign] languages, each text being equally authentic.

FOR THE GOVERNMENT OF   FOR THE GOVERNMENT OF
THE UNITED STATES OF AMERICA: [Country]:

Annex A

Customary International Law

The Parties confirm their shared understanding that 'customary international law' generally and as specifically referenced in Article 5 [Minimum Standard of Treatment] and Annex B [Expropriation] results from a general and consistent practice of States that they follow from a sense of legal obligation. With regard to Article 5 [Minimum Standard of Treatment], the customary international law minimum standard of treatment of aliens refers to all customary international law principles that protect the economic rights and interests of aliens.

Annex B

Expropriation

The Parties confirm their shared understanding that:

1. Article 6 [Expropriation and Compensation](1) is intended to reflect customary international law concerning the obligation of States with respect to expropriation.

2. An action or a series of actions by a Party cannot constitute an expropriation unless it interferes with a tangible or intangible property right or property interest in an investment.

3. Article 6 [Expropriation and Compensation](1) addresses two situations. The first is direct expropriation, where an investment is nationalized or otherwise directly expropriated through formal transfer of title or outright seizure.

4. The second situation addressed by Article 6 [Expropriation and Compensation](1) is indirect expropriation, where an action or series of actions by a Party has an effect equivalent to direct expropriation without formal transfer of title or outright seizure.

  (a) The determination of whether an action or series of actions by a Party, in a specific fact situation, constitutes an indirect expropriation, requires a case-by-case, fact-based inquiry that considers, among other factors:
    (i)   the economic impact of the government action, although the fact that an action or series of actions by a Party has an adverse effect on the economic value of an investment, standing alone, does not establish that an indirect expropriation has occurred;
    (ii) the extent to which the government action interferes with distinct, reasonable investment-backed expectations; and
    (iii) the character of the government action.
  (b) Except in rare circumstances, non-discriminatory regulatory actions by a Party that are designed and applied to protect legitimate public welfare objectives, such as public health, safety, and the environment, do not constitute indirect expropriations.

Annex C

Service of Documents on a Party

United States

Notices and other documents shall be served on the United States by delivery to:

Executive Director (L/EX)
Office of the Legal Adviser
Department of State
Washington, D.C. 20520
United States of America

[Country]

Notices and other documents shall be served on [Country] by delivery to:

[insert place of delivery of notices and other documents for [Country]]

Annex D

Possibility of a Bilateral Appellate Mechanism

Within three years after the date of entry into force of this Treaty, the Parties shall consider whether to establish a bilateral appellate body or similar mechanism to review awards rendered under Article 34 in arbitrations commenced after they establish the appellate body or similar mechanism.

Index